The
UNRELEASED
BEATLES

The UNRELEASED BEATLES

BEATLES

Music & Film

Richie Unterberger

Backbeat
Books
San Francisco

Published by Backbeat Books
600 Harrison Street,
San Francisco, CA 94107
www.backbeatbooks.com
email: books@musicplayer.com

An imprint of the Music Player Network
Publishers of *Guitar Player*, *Bass Player*, *Keyboard*, *EQ*, and other magazines
United Entertainment Media, Inc.
A CMP Information company

CMP
United Business Media

Distributed to the book trade in the US and Canada by
Publishers Group West, 1700 Fourth Street, Berkeley, CA 94710

Distributed to the music trade in the US and Canada by
Hal Leonard Publishing, P.O. Box 13819, Milwaukee, WI 53213

Text Design by Leigh McLellan Design
Composition by Leigh McLellan Design
Cover Design by Richard Leeds-BigWigDesign.com
Cover Photographs: Harrison: Barrie Wentzell/Star File; Lennon and Martin: Camera Press/Frank Hermann/Retna Ltd. USA; Full Band: London Features International

Library of Congress Cataloging-in-Publication Data

Unterberger, Richie, 1962-
  The unreleased Beatles : music & film / Richie Unterberger.
    p. cm.
  Includes bibliographical references (p. 379) and index.
  ISBN-13: 978-0-87930-892-6 (alk. paper)
  ISBN-10: 0-87930-892-3 (alk. paper)
  1. Beatles--Discography. 2. Beatles--Film catalogs. I. Title.

ML156.7.B4U57 2006
782.42166092'2--dc22
                      2006027479

Printed in China
06 07 08 09 10   5 4 3 2

Contents

Introduction

The first album I ever bought was *Meet the Beatles*. The *second* album I ever bought was a Beatles album that hadn't even been released. Impossible? Not in April 1970, when the Beatles had just broken up and my lifelong passion for the group had just begun.

Eight years of age at the time, I'd only just begun to buy singles, the first of *those* being the Beatles' "Hey Jude"/"Revolution," still readily available in Woolworth's more than a year after its release. Now came the big step up to LPs, of which I could get not just *one*, but *two*, as part of the first holiday gifts I was allowed to choose for myself. There was no question as to whose records I wanted to buy, but less certainty as to which to select. Even if it was already considered old-fashioned, I really did want their 1964 LP *Meet the Beatles*, ancient six-year-old relic that it was. I loved "I Want to Hold Your Hand" and I'd only heard the other songs once (on an older brother's reel-to-reel, played as a special treat), but I knew it would be great. But what to get as the second album? Older brothers already had the two most obvious choices, *Abbey Road* and *Sgt. Pepper's Lonely Hearts Club Band*. *The White Album* was the most logical next option, but as a double LP, that might have been considered exorbitant, and anyway that would soon come into the house via another brother. At any rate, the small record shop on Bala Avenue in the Philadelphia suburbs where we went to pick out the album was only carrying a few Beatles LPs, not all of them.

Whether she sniffed an easy, deceitful sale or was just trying to be genuinely helpful, the one clerk on duty pointed out, "We have the *new* Beatles album." New Beatles album? That was news to me. *Let It Be* wasn't out yet, *Abbey Road* had been out for about six months, and the Beatles had just broken up anyway, though no one seemed to know if that was permanent or temporary. Nor did the LP *look* like a Beatles album, or any album I'd seen before, for that matter. No "Beatles" name anywhere, no picture of the Beatles, in fact nothing but a plain white sleeve. And even then, I was hip enough to know it *wasn't The White Album. This* was the new Beatles album?

I got the record anyway. When I played it at home, I wouldn't say I was disappointed, but I was certainly baffled. A few of the songs were familiar from singles I'd heard on the radio ("Get Back," "Let It Be," "Don't Let Me Down"), but these certainly were *not* the same versions. Nor did the center label—you really noticed those things when you were eight years old and putting them onto a small portable phonograph— look remotely like any of the Capitol or Apple labels with which I was already familiar, without any of those songwriting credits and song times I'd already come to expect. The LP's title, *Kum Back*, was downright weird, its naughtier implications wholly sailing over my eight-year-old head. The fidelity, though not quite rotten and certainly listenable, sure wasn't up to the standards I took for granted on other vinyl. Nor were the false starts and muffled between-track chatter exactly standard fare on any of the other records in the house. And what *were* all those songs, with unfamiliar titles like "On Your Way Home," "Don't Keep Me Waiting," "Who Knows," "Sweet & Lovely," "Teddy Don't Worry," and "Can He Walk"? *I* certainly hadn't heard them before, and they weren't getting played on any radio station I was listening to—an impossibility for a "new" Beatles album in the spring of 1970.

An older brother explained that I had a "bootleg," which confused me even more. When you're eight years old, "bootlegs" are things you put into a boot when it snows, not contraband product. Nor was the record *shaped* like a bootleg, which was a physical impossibility in any case. Whatever—I was still thrilled, convinced I was one of the few people in the world who had access to this somehow unavailable Beatles music, which had somehow made its way into, of all places, that hole-in-the-wall record shop on Bala Avenue. Just a few weeks later, of course, the jig was up: the *Let It Be* LP came out, including most of those songs I had on *Kum Back,* for all the world to hear.

Still, even then, I could tell that syrupy version of "The Long and Winding Road" blanketing the AM airwaves was *not* the same as the stringless track identified as "Don't Keep Me Waiting" on my *Kum Back* bootleg. The same song? Sure, but even then, I thought the *Kum Back* version immeasurably superior to the "official" one on the chart-topping single. (Paul McCartney would have been proud!) The whole thing seemed fishy to me, right down to the new song titles on the *Let It Be* LP (to this day, I *still* think "On Our Way Home" makes a much better title than "Two of Us"). And why wasn't "Teddy Don't Worry" on *Let It Be* in *any* form?

I didn't even bother buying *Let It Be* back then (though I'd break down and get it a few years later). I already had most of the songs, and there were a bunch of other official Beatles albums with tracks I hadn't yet heard at all. I didn't look for any more "bootleg" (or "new") Beatles

The inner label for the Kum Back *LP, the first widely distributed Beatles bootleg, still bearing the handwritten name of the author of this book and the estimated song times he scrawled as an eight-year-old Beatles fan.*

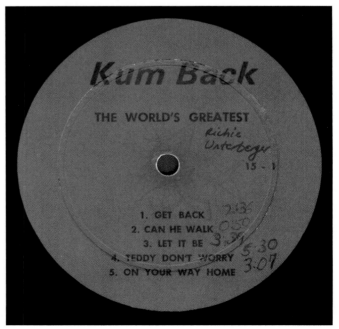

albums anymore, either. There weren't going to be any new Beatles albums, now that their spring 1970 split was sticking for good. As for that shop on Bala Avenue, it was soon gone too. I can't remember its name, if I even ever knew it.

What I didn't realize—what *no one* realized, even the Beatles—was that there was more of the same material where *Kum Back* had come from. *Much* more of the same kind of material, not just from the January 1969 sessions at which *Kum Back* was recorded, but from the group's entire career. So much, in fact, that it's still coming out.

● ● ●

When the three two-CD sets of the *Anthology* series came out in the mid-'90s (preceded by a two-CD *Live at the BBC* compilation in 1994), it marked most general listeners' first realization of just how much unreleased Beatles material lay in the vaults. Literally millions of others, however, knew better. For a quarter century they'd been avidly collecting all they could, however they could, of anything the greatest group of all time had recorded, whether it had come out on official releases or not. Studio outtakes, live concerts, BBC recordings, home tapes, television broadcasts, rehearsals, demos—all were fair game. Dozens of hours piled up, then hundreds. For all their extensive length, the *Anthology* and *Live at the BBC* volumes contain just a small fraction of what's known to exist.

It would be a while before I got my next Beatles bootleg, not because of any lack of interest in hearing this stuff, but because of sheer ignorance as to where to find it. What little I heard eked out on FM radio weekend-long Beatles specials, and I captured some of it here and there on tape if I was lucky enough to have access to a recorder at the moment. I still remember, indeed, the highlights of what I was able to catch on my crummy-quality cassettes, or failing that, at least hear, once, on the radio: their ultra-catchy 1963 BBC track "Don't Ever Change" (in transistor-radio-level fidelity, and which I thought for many years was actually titled "Please Don't Ever Change"); their funny-as-hell 1969 rip through "Besame Mucho"; their mid-'60s Hollywood Bowl tapes, misidentified by the DJ as their Shea Stadium concert and issued on "Pine Tree Records"; and the mysterious "September in the Rain," from their failed January 1962 audition for Decca Records.

In 1979, now a high school senior, I finally got my *second* vinyl Beatles bootleg, a mishmash of Decca demos (including "September in the Rain"), more tinny BBC tapes, a muffled but enormously galvanizing 1962 live Cavern performance of "Some Other Guy," and that legendary 1962 studio outtake of "How Do You Do It" that I'd read about way back in 1970. Then, just a year and a half later, came an unexpected Holy Grail of sorts: *The Beatles Broadcasts,* offering not just a bunch of BBC tapes I'd never heard before (some of them songs I'd never heard the Beatles do on *any* record), but also sound quality virtually on par with official releases. Having completed my "official" Beatles collection back in 1973 as an 11-year-old kid, I was hooked, and I've kept on looking for more "new" (if not newly recorded) Beatles music ever since, even as my tastes have expanded to encompass collecting hundreds and then literally thousands of other artists.

Through all those years, the relative lack of reliable information about this unreleased material was a considerable source of frustration. You certainly (with rare exceptions) couldn't hear it on the radio, and (again with rare exceptions), you couldn't preview it at record stores or friends' houses either. Like almost everyone else, I usually had to

take chances on sounds unheard. And for all the hundreds of hours I accumulated, when I decided to do a book about the whole deal, there was yet more to track down to make sure no stone had been left unturned. Anyone who thought there wasn't nearly enough material to write a book on the subject should have their suspicions quelled by the sheer size of the tome you now hold in your hands.

There have been other books largely devoted to, or with sizable sections about, the music the Beatles did not release. You'll find plenty of coverage, in books and other sources, as to what unreleased music the Beatles recorded, where it's come out, and even how long the tracks are and how mixes differ from source to source. That's not to belittle the efforts of numerous expert researchers who've concentrated on the basic facts, several of whom are cited throughout this book and in the bibliography. Yet what frustrated me—as someone who's a listener first, a critic/historian second, and a collector (a perhaps distant) third—is how unconcerned much of this literature seemed to be with how the music actually sounds. With a group so compellingly human and utterly enjoyable as the Beatles, that always seemed to me the first, and primary, side of their art. That is what this volume emphasizes, along with placing the music in a historical and critical context, I hope, that will enable fans to maximize their enjoyment and appreciation of this wonderful body of work—not just find out what was done when.

Is the unreleased music of the Beatles worth such serious scrutiny, particularly when they issued such a staggering wealth of great rock on their official releases? Yes, on several counts. First, there's simply a lot of good-to-great music that the group never put out during their lifetime, easy to enjoy whether or not you care about when it was recorded or why it didn't come out. Their ferocious 1962 Cavern performances of "Some Other Guy" (yes, there was more than one version); all those BBC performances of "Hippy Hippy Shake" (there were *five* versions); John Lennon and Paul McCartney cracking each other up during live performances of "If I Fell" during their wild summer 1964 North American tour; John's acoustic solo tapes of "Strawberry Fields Forever," before the Beatles ever worked on it in the studio; the acoustic versions of "Revolution" and "Back in the U.S.S.R." from their home demos of *White Album* material—all are hugely fun, listenable recordings on their own terms, even if they're not quite as hi-fi as the tracks you'll find on Beatles CDs in the chain stores.

More subtly, when you're talking about the greatest music act of all time, this material is not only immensely fascinating from a historical standpoint, but essential for a full appreciation of the group's evolution, influences, and creative process. Want to hear how they sounded when drummer Pete Best was in the lineup? There's their Decca audition tape, which also demonstrates just how vastly they improved by the time they did their first LP a little more than a year later. Want to hear them as stumbling teenagers, with Stuart Sutcliffe on bass? Turn to their 1960 rehearsal tapes (in fact, it could be argued, there's *too* much on those 1960 tapes). Want to hear just how good they were as a live band, even during the wildest Beatlemania days? There are plenty of live mid-'60s concert tapes of decent quality that the Beatles never put out during the lifetime of the group, easy to enjoy. What were their formative influences? There are not only those BBC tapes, but also their marathon January 1969 *Get Back* sessions, where they covered hundreds of songs. How did they write their songs? Listen to George Harrison work out "Something" during those *Get Back* sessions, or John Lennon compose "If I Fell" on a home tape. How much did they argue during those *Get*

Back sessions? The evidence, sometimes sadly, was often captured on tape. The list goes on.

Many of the Beatles' unreleased recordings, contrary to some stereotypes, have good-to-excellent fidelity. However, you'll also come across quite a few that are poor-to-awful, as well as some *performances* that are poor to awful (and, sadly, some that are both poor-sounding and poorly performed). Even these, however, have their place for sheer historical value. Nothing reflects the disorganization of the Beatles in early 1969 more than their interminable half-baked jams on oldies covers during the *Get Back* sessions; those 1960 rehearsal tapes show just how ordinary the Beatles were before they *became* the Beatles; the 1965 outtakes of "That Means a Lot" show just how much that song resisted being molded into a satisfactory Beatles track, despite multiple efforts. Even the many false starts, bum notes, and whispered chatter have their charm, both as illustrations of their human foibles and as evidence of their great humor and teamwork. The witty banter in that between-song chatter, in fact, epitomizes the endearing qualities of the group—as people, not just musicians—which have made tens of millions of listeners who've never met them feel almost as though John, Paul, George, and Ringo are unofficial brothers of sorts, both among themselves and to us.

This book does not pretend to argue that the Beatles' unreleased work is *better* than their official discography. It isn't, and in fact it isn't as good as their standard catalog, by any measure. Nor could you reasonably argue, as you could with artists such as Bob Dylan, Neil Young, and the Grateful Dead, that much of their unissued studio and live work is on par with what they've authorized for release (and for some artists like those, even *better* than what they've decided to release at some points). But these are the *Beatles* here. Their unreleased recordings are not just far superior to the official discographies of most artists, but also lend themselves, like so many facets of their history, to almost inexhaustible (and pleasurable) analysis. In their own way, these recordings not only reflect the Beatles' artistic evolution almost as much as their official output; they also give us considerable (and surprising) insights into how the Beatles worked together, how they composed, and what they kept and discarded in their relentless quest for excellence.

● ● ●

While the format of this book should be self-explanatory, a few notes are in order. First, unlike many volumes detailing unreleased music by rock artists, this is not a bootleg guide, or a collection of bootleg listings and reviews. There are likely thousands of Beatles bootlegs, and unholy repetition of material between them—hundreds, if not actual thousands, of bootlegs overlap to some degree in the tracks they present. Constructing the coverage in such a fashion would not only have made it hard to fit into a single book, but also not made for a very entertaining read, considering how much space would have been solely devoted to rote figures. In addition, such material would have quickly gone out of date, as new bootlegs are appearing (and older ones disappearing) all the time. Instead, the main section of the book discusses all the unreleased Beatles *recordings* known to have circulated in some fashion, in chronological order. It doesn't cover *every* unreleased Beatles tape—some undoubtedly remain in private hands, and many of their studio outtakes remain in EMI's vaults—but I've done my best to include every one that's escaped into public scrutiny. (Please note that the author and publisher are not able to engage in correspondence as to where and how these recordings can be obtained.)

You'll also see that, while the great majority of recordings covered here have not been officially released in any fashion, some of them *have* gained authorized issue on compilations released after the Beatles' final album (*Let It Be*) came out in 1970. Specifically, these are the 1977 live LPs *The Beatles at the Hollywood Bowl* and *The Beatles Live! At the Star-Club in Hamburg, Germany; 1962;* the 1994 collection *Live at the BBC;* the three *Anthology* volumes (*Anthology 1, Anthology 2, Anthology 3*); and *Let It Be . . . Naked,* the 2003 makeover of *Let It Be.* As that's actually a fair amount of material taken all together, some might wonder whether it should be included in this volume at all, particularly as it's all easily available.

However, after beginning this project, I quickly realized that in many (and maybe all) instances, the unreleased material the group recorded at or around the same time as the sessions/performances covered here could not be clearly and properly discussed without referring to what *was* released as well. It seemed to make much more sense, for instance, to cover the 1964–1965 Hollywood Bowl recordings as a whole, rather than only the ones that didn't appear on *The Beatles at the Hollywood Bowl;* to cover everything from individual BBC sessions, rather than only the cuts that weren't plucked for *Live at the BBC;* all 15 tracks from their Decca audition, rather than only the ones that never came out with official blessings; and so forth. Laying it out this way also seems to make it far clearer, to novices to the field and even some veteran collectors, exactly what's come out on EMI/Apple and what hasn't. In any case, much of the material from the albums listed in the preceding paragraph has never received much critical discussion, and certainly not been gifted with nearly as much in-depth analysis as the material on conventional Beatles releases.

So think of this book as one that covers *all* music that, for one reason or another, the Beatles did not release before 1971, rather than solely the sounds that have never been made officially available. At the same time, it will be assumed that readers interested in this topic will have a good knowledge of the LPs, singles, and EPs the group put out between 1962 and 1970, so discographical details won't be given for those. All 1962–1970 releases referred to here are the British versions (except when specifically noted), as those are, with just a few exceptions, the versions on which the tracks first appeared and (in the case of albums) the format in which they are currently packaged on compact disc.

Finally, *The Unreleased Beatles: Music and Film* does not cover material of this nature that the four members recorded after the group broke up. I made an exception, however, for unissued tracks that John Lennon, Paul McCartney, George Harrison, and Ringo Starr cut as solo artists between the time of the official split (April 10, 1970) and the end of 1970 (when Paul sued the other three in an effort to end the group's legal partnership). At least some of this material had been written while the Beatles were together, and looking at what they were doing, even beyond the official record, in the immediate aftermath of their breakup sheds some light on just why that breakup occurred (or, perhaps, was even necessary). As a bonus, some of that early unissued solo work is quite interesting, to boot. You'll also notice that unreleased solo recordings that each member made while the Beatles were still active are also detailed, as they're both quite intriguing and essential to gaining a full picture of what the musicians were doing, both in and out of the public eye.

The main section of this book covers the Beatles' unreleased music audio recordings (not including spoken-word interview material and some off-the-cuff, brief hums, riffs, plucks, a cappella snatches, and such from interview tapes that were obviously not seriously intended as music performances) from 1957 to 1970, divided into chapters for each year (excepting 1957–1961, which is covered in just one chapter). There's also a section on rare and unreleased Beatles film that, while not as exhaustively comprehensive as the music chapters, details the major, most significant music footage of the band that's not available through standard mainstream channels. Also included are smaller sections on topics intimately related to unreleased Beatles music, including Beatles compositions given away to other artists; Beatles compositions that were never properly recorded by anyone; a brief overview of Beatles bootlegs; and the Beatles' own attitudes toward their unreleased music, from both marketing and aesthetic viewpoints.

It's a lot of material to sift through, as I found out while reintroducing myself to it over the course of the year or so it took to write this book. Yet for all the many years I've listened to the Beatles, it still came as a surprise not only to realize how *much* of this stuff was out there but how rewarding much of it remains. Friends, even fellow Beatles enthusiasts, kept asking me, not unreasonably, "Aren't you tired of listening to the Beatles yet? How can you stand it, listening to so much of them, all the time, month after month?" Yet, in what was something of a shock even to myself, all that listening had exactly the opposite effect. After so many years of listening—sometimes out of professional obligation—to so many different artists, many of them frankly mediocre or worse, it was a sheer delight to wake up most mornings knowing I was going to be listening to the *best* music there ever was. Not only that, I knew that every day the music would nonetheless always be different, and always be changing, just as the Beatles themselves had.

All along the way, there were unsuspected surprises, hidden connections to be made, and small-to-significant revelations as to what made this remarkable group tick behind the scenes. It got to the point where I felt like I sometimes caught just a faint trace of how thrilling it must have been to experience the Beatles' music while it was happening, always wondering what was next, always getting taken aback at the sharp turns they made, always marveling at their mastery of continuing to evolve while maintaining the identifiable qualities that had made them so appealing at the outset of Beatlemania. There was also a sadness at the end of the project, as exhausting as it was, that was something akin to the disappointment the world felt when the Beatles broke up. For I was hoping this kind of endless discovery, this waking up every morning to look forward to another day of ever-changing fun, could go on forever. Even though it was 2005, I sometimes felt like I was rooting for the Beatles to somehow stay together. But unlike the Beatles fans of the 1960s—and even the Beatles themselves, for a time—I knew that they wouldn't, and knew exactly how (and how unhappily, in many respects) the story would end. Now that the writing of my book has come to its end, I feel some regret, knowing I'll probably never again have such an extended magical mystery tour of part of the Beatles' world.

At the same time, there's also elation, in the hope that this book will spread appreciation of some of the least appreciated corners of their work. Having now finally heard *everything* they've done that's made the rounds, it never fails to amaze me just how *much* territory the Beatles covered. Eventually, it seemed, they absorbed *everything* good about music, not just from rock 'n' roll, but from blues, soul, country, classical, gospel, the avant-garde, vaudeville, electronic experimentation, mainstream pop, theatrical comedy, and beyond. Are the Beatles, like love (as they sang in a 1967 single), all you need, at least in music? No, not quite. But they came closer than anyone to both exploring everything, and putting everything together with magnificent brilliance.

Richie Unterberger
Oakland, California
August 2006

PART 1

The Unreleased Beatles Music

Paul McCartney and John Lennon performing at the Casbah in Liverpool in late 1959, shortly before the Quarrymen evolved into the Beatles. Just to the right of John is his future wife Cynthia.

1957 1961

From the Quarrymen to the Beatles

The Early Era in Review

Few people outside of their Liverpool and Hamburg fan bases had heard the Beatles before their first single, "Love Me Do"/ "P.S. I Love You," was released on October 5, 1962. And even today, few people realize that this official debut was preceded by more than five years' worth of recordings by the band, dating back to the exact date on which John Lennon met Paul McCartney—at which time McCartney wasn't even in the group, which wasn't even known yet as the Beatles.

The Beatles would not enter a professional recording studio until they backed Tony Sheridan on some tracks in June 1961, during one of their lengthy trips to Hamburg, Germany. Yet they had in fact been taped, in informal settings in a variety of hit-and-miss circumstances, almost from the time they started. These performances were never intended for release, though some of the material, oddly enough, would end up on a best-selling album. They were primarily done almost as exercises, to take some of the first opportunities they had to hear themselves on tape, to preserve a few souvenirs for posterity, and to work, albeit mighty haphazardly, on some primitive songwriting and instrumental ideas.

When these artifacts first came to light, it was a surprise to some to find that such early performances even existed. Teenagers of the Beatles' backgrounds had relatively little access to even rudimentary tape recorders in the late '50s and early '60s, particularly compared to today, when basic recording equipment is within the reach of almost anyone growing up in the Western world. But it was hardly unknown or even that rare for young British bands to document themselves in that manner at the time. A few similarly raw efforts by other Merseybeat groups were excavated in 2003–2005 on three *Unearthed Merseybeat* CD compilations, which included previously unissued 1961 recordings by the Beatles' biggest local rivals, Gerry & the Pacemakers. Volume one of that series also had a 1958 track by Kingsize Taylor & the Dominoes, whose leader would eventually be largely responsible for taping the Beatles onstage in Hamburg in late December 1962, that material finding official release 15 years later.

Even the Beatles' ultimate arch-rivals, the Rolling Stones, made their first known recording—with Mick Jagger and Keith Richards the only members who would still be in the lineup when they released their first single—in a bedroom in late 1961 on the reel-to-reel recorder of the parents of a schoolfriend. As that anonymous friend told *Record Collector* in May 1995, he taped some of the Stones' home rehearsals simply because "they wanted to know what they sounded like, so they could get better." That tape, like similar Beatles items, would eventually be sold for a grand price (£55,000, to Mick Jagger himself) at a major auction house (Christie's), and partially bootlegged for all the world to hear if listeners looked in the right place.

Despite the astronomical prices these embryonic Beatles relics have fetched—often, ironically, from the Beatles themselves or close associates of the group—listeners should be warned to approach these items with fairly low expectations. The fidelity is low and often awful, the performances amateurish, and the similarities to the music the Beatles became famous for during their official recording career slight. They are primarily of scholarly interest, as archeological evidence of what the musicians sounded like in their formative years. In truth, they didn't sound too different from countless other teenage bands stumbling to even master the rudiments of playing their own instruments (and playing in time). It was, however, a place from which to start—and proof that for all their amazing subsequent achievements, the Beatles did indeed begin as quite human, fairly ordinary lads.

1957

● July 6, 1957

Live Performance
Saint Peter's Church, Liverpool

Puttin' on the Style (fragment)

July 6, 1957, is now widely known as the day on which John Lennon met Paul McCartney, igniting the musical partnership that fueled the Beatles' brilliance. For a long time, many of the details surrounding this meeting remained obscure. The year was mistakenly reported as, variously, 1955 and 1956, with even Hunter Davies's 1968 authorized biography, *The Beatles,* reporting the date as June 15, 1956. The date was correctly pinned down about a decade later, and more detailed recollections emerged from various sources; there was even an entire book, *The Day John Met Paul,* dedicated to the event. Given that so much of what transpired was open to conjecture and poetic license, the yet more belated discovery of actual recordings of the Quarrymen (sometimes spelled Quarry Men)—the band John Lennon cofounded, which eventually evolved into the Beatles—playing on the evening in question must then have seemed like one of the ultimate Holy Grails of Beatles research. Right?

Not exactly. Like many such amazing finds, it plays better in the head than on tape. Not that many people have heard it yet, as it only

came to light when retired policeman Bob Molyneux offered it for sale via auction through Sotheby's of London in 1994. Molyneux, it turned out, had used a portable Grundig TK 8 tape recorder to make a few reel-to-reel tapes of the entertainment at Saint Peter's Church garden fete in Woolton that evening. Aside from tapes of the act with whom the Quarrymen shared the bill (the George Edwards Band), there were also four minutes of music from John Lennon's group—at this point including Lennon (on vocals and guitar), Eric Griffiths (guitar), Rod Davis (banjo), Colin Hanton (drums), Len Garry (tea chest bass), and Pete Shotton (washboard). Paul McCartney was not onstage. He had only just met John properly for the first time earlier that evening, and would not be invited to join the Quarrymen until a couple of weeks or so later. Molyneux had actually offered the tape to John Lennon through Ringo Starr in 1963, but Lennon didn't respond, and Molyneux put it into a vault until offering it to Sotheby's in mid-1994.

So what does it sound like? For the most part, it's unknown, as the tape was sold to EMI for £78,500 (an amount actually well below the $155,000–$230,000 Sotheby's expected) and has yet to be heard in full by the public. However, thirty seconds of one of the two Quarrymen songs, a cover of Lonnie Donegan's "Puttin' on the Style" (then residing at No. 1 on the British hit parade), have escaped onto bootleg as a result of being included on cassettes used to promote the auction sale of the tape. Given the primitive circumstances under which the recording was made, it's no surprise that it's something akin to listening to a voice trying to fight its way out of a wind tunnel. Some even suspect that echo was added on purpose, presumably to make it less bootleg-friendly (as if subpar fidelity has stopped many bootleggers in the past). But that voice *is* John Lennon's, singing with obvious exuberance, though barely any instruments (or lyrics) can be made out over the din.

As Stephen Maycock, the expert in charge of rock music–related sales for Sotheby's, told *The New York Times* in July 1994, "It sounds rough. It was recorded with a hand-held microphone in the worst venue you could want, a church hall with a high ceiling and probably a hard floor. Despite that, it has been stored carefully, and the sound has probably not deteriorated from what it was in 1957. And I've heard a copy that has been cleaned up using modern technology and the improvement was 100 percent. Still, we're not selling a high-quality recording, we're selling a recording made on a historic day."

Like many lo-fi, unissued Beatles recordings, this very first one is perhaps more interesting for what it might tell us about their music than for the music itself. It's still hard for many to fathom how the Beatles really did start as a skiffle band, particularly in the United States, where skiffle never took off as a fad and its biggest British proponent, Lonnie Donegan, had just a couple of hits. But here's the proof that Lonnie Donegan was very much a part of their early repertoire. (Further verification was supplied by a 1999 Sotheby's auction of Lennon memorabilia that revealed the teenaged Beatle's collection to include 78s of Donegan's "Lost John," "Don't You Rock Me Daddy-O," and "Cumberland Gap.")

An article about the event in the *South Liverpool Weekly News* does list a few of the other songs they performed that day, all of them traditional numbers familiar to the skiffle repertoire: "Maggie Mae" (which the Beatles would redo, albeit in a brief joke version, on the *Let It Be* album), "Railroad Bill," and the above-mentioned "Cumberland Gap." However, hardcore rock 'n' roll was also at the Beatles' foundation, and the other, as-yet-unheard song on the tape was a cover of

Elvis Presley's version of "Baby Let's Play House." Presley's influence would turn out to be far more enduring than Donegan's, and not just in a conceptual sense—Lennon pinched a line from the song for the Beatles' own "Run for Your Life" on the *Rubber Soul* album more than eight years later. John also sang Gene Vincent's "Be-Bop-A-Lula" at this performance, and McCartney has also recalled that another song in their set that day was a cover of the smash "Come Go with Me" by the American doo wop group the Dell-Vikings, Lennon improvising different lyrics, as he couldn't remember many of the words.

Will we ever hear these Quarrymen tapes in full? It seems doubtful, particularly as nothing from them was even used in the Beatles' own *Anthology* video and CD projects. *Anthology* producer Bob Smeaton told *Record Collector* in 1995, "If you listen to [the tape], it sounds OK on a cassette machine, but it wasn't really up to scratch to include in the TV program. I would have, but it wasn't my decision. Yoko owns it, and I think she wants to use it in the future on one of her John Lennon projects. The longer you hold on to something, the greater its value becomes." Truthfully, given the sound quality, it may be better heard as a recording in a museum than on a record, even a bootleg one. Confusingly, its current ownership has been variously attributed to Paul McCartney or Yoko Ono—which may be a moot point as far as the public's concerned, as both have been pretty selective about what ancient material they're willing to sanction for official release.

1958

● Circa Mid-1958

Studio Outtakes
Percy F. Phillips Studio, Liverpool

---

*That'll Be the Day

*In Spite of All the Danger

  appears on Anthology 1

The Quarrymen had little disposable income in mid-1958, and hadn't a prayer of either getting signed to a record label or raising enough cash to rent a proper recording studio. Yet even in the provincial backwaters of Liverpool, there was a small facility where local musicians could make recordings, albeit pretty much for their own pleasure rather than for any prospect of professional gain. The Quarrymen scraped together the seventeen shillings and six pence—a little less than a pound—to record a couple of songs in the studio at the back of Percy F. Phillips's electrical shop. And it really was an expense for teenagers of their limited means; as they only had fifteen shillings, Phillips held onto the shellac demo disc produced from the session until they came back with the rest of the fee. The tape used to make the disc, Phillips recalled in a 1977 interview with the *Liverpool Echo*, was erased, as he customarily did in order to save costs.

At this stage, the Quarrymen were the quintet of John Lennon, Paul McCartney, and George Harrison on guitars; John "Duff" Lowe on piano; and Colin Hanton on drums. The skiffle that had been such a big part of the Quarrymen's repertoire back in July 1957 was receding

from prominence, and these two recordings are far better indications of their rock 'n' roll roots. They also survived in far better sound quality than that July 1957 performance at Saint Peter's Church—even though the disc is scratchy and the sonics muffled, you really can hear the band playing, and detect some real similarities to the music they'd be playing in the 1960s as the Beatles.

Buddy Holly was a huge influence on the Beatles, and it's not a surprise that they covered his first hit (he recorded it as leader of the Crickets), "That'll Be the Day," which had soared to No. 1 in Britain in late 1957. While the Quarrymen's version is nothing special—just a straight recreation of the original arrangement—it doesn't sound at all bad for musicians still in their mid-teens. The playing's competent and the vocals are engagingly forceful. Most interestingly, they've clearly taken the time to work out some call-and-response between Lennon's lead vocal and the backup harmonies in a way that's a little different, and a little more active, than the backup vocals heard on the Holly/Crickets classic. These were very much the sort of solo-harmony vocal tradeoffs that contributed so much to the public's perception of the Beatles being very much a *group,* not just a band dominated by one or two particular singers and/or instrumentalists.

Not as musically enjoyable, yet just as interesting from a historical perspective, is the second number recorded by the Quarrymen this day. "In Spite of All the Danger" is a band original, testifying to just how much importance they placed on writing their own material right from the start. Certainly one supposes that few other British groups of the late '50s, given the very limited time and space to record a precious vanity disc, would devote one of the two allotted songs to one of their own tunes (not that many such groups would have even had one original composition available). The song, alas, isn't that much, being a very routine doo wop–like early rock 'n' roll ballad, of the sort that their idol Elvis Presley would do on occasion. Actually the resemblance isn't so much to Presley (though it's been speculated that the group was trying to emulate the early Elvis side "Trying to Get to You") as to some of the rather ersatz Elvis ballads to make the hit parade in the late '50s, like the Crescendos' "Oh, Julie." It's been reported that the version released on *Anthology 1* is edited, removing 42 seconds (a repeated verse and chorus) near the end.

What's most intriguing, however, is that this is a Paul McCartney–George Harrison composition—the only such writing collaboration the group ever recorded. Toss in John Lennon doing the lead vocals (on a Beatles song he didn't write), and it illustrates that the roles the Beatles assumed by the time they started their official recording career were by no means set at this point. (Incidentally, it would not be the only time George co-penned a Beatles song rather than writing on his own; "Cry for a Shadow," the instrumental the Beatles recorded during their sessions as Tony Sheridan's backup group in 1961, was authored by Harrison and Lennon.) Perhaps the decision Lennon and McCartney made to write together pretty much exclusively wasn't set in stone at this point, though Paul would recall for the *Anthology* book, "It was an option to include George in the songwriting team. John and I had really talked about it. I remember walking up past Woolton Church with John one morning and going over the question: 'Without wanting to be too mean to George, should three of us write or would it be better to keep it simple?' We decided we'd just keep to two of us."

The reality of the songwriting credit, however, could be more prosaic. "It says on the [demo] label that it was me and George," said

One of the first albums to feature 1960 Beatles rehearsal tapes shows the group (bassist Stu Sutcliffe on far left) as they appeared on May 10, 1960, when they auditioned in Liverpool for the position of backing band on a tour by early British rock 'n' roll singer Billy Fury.

McCartney when interviewed for Mark Lewisohn's 1988 *The Beatles Recording Sessions* book, "but I think it was actually written by me and George played the guitar solo!" Whatever the case, McCartney and Harrison would never write together for the Beatles again, excepting the cases of Lennon-McCartney-Harrison-Starkey credits for a few group jams. Paul did talk up the possibility of writing with George in the late '80s, but nothing came of it.

According to pianist Lowe, "In Spite of All the Danger" was the only original number in the Quarrymen's repertoire at the time. "I can well remember even at the rehearsal at his house in Forthlin Road, Paul was quite specific about how he wanted it played and what he wanted the piano to do," he told author Steve Turner in *A Hard Day's Write: The Stories Behind Every Beatles' Song*. "There was no question of improvising. We were told what we had to play. There was a lot of arranging going on even back then." For what it's worth, Lowe has also contended the songs were cut straight to disc, not to tape as Phillips remembered, which took away their chance to correct a couple of mistakes in Lennon's vocal.

The disc was passed among the members of the group, giving them the first thrill of hearing themselves on an actual record, however lo-fi and undistributed it was. It eventually passed into the hands of Lowe, who kept it at the bottom of a linen drawer(!) for years, selling it to Paul McCartney himself in 1981 for undisclosed terms (though it's known that Lowe turned down McCartney's initial £5,000 offer). That cleared the way for the eventual official release of both sides on *Anthology 1*, though McCartney played excerpts of "That'll Be the Day" back in 1985 on a documentary of Buddy Holly that unsurprisingly immediately found their way onto bootlegs. The original shellac demo, according to

the December 1998 issue of *Record Collector,* remains the most rare and valuable British record of all, its value estimated (at the time) to be at least £12,000. Drummer Colin Hanton, incidentally—who, like Lowe, left the band not long after the recording—didn't make quite as much belated money from the rarity as the pianist, but he did settle with Apple for a one-time royalty payment of £1,500 (up from the original offer of £500) for the use of the material on *Anthology 1*. As for Paul McCartney, he hasn't forgotten about this crude early songwriting effort—he was playing "In Spite of All the Danger" on his US concert tour in late 2005.

1960

● Circa Spring 1960

Private Tapes
Liverpool

*Hallelujah, I Love Her So (complete)
*Cayenne
*You'll Be Mine
I'll Follow the Sun
Hallelujah, I Love Her So (fragment)
One After 909 (complete)
One After 909 (incomplete)
Matchbox
Movin' and Groovin'
Ramrod
Wild Cat (complete)
Wild Cat (incomplete)
I'll Always Be in Love with You
That's When Your Heartaches Begin
Hello Little Girl
The World Is Waiting for the Sunrise
Some Days
Well, Darling
You Must Write Every Day
. . . plus about 50 minutes of untitled instrumentals and improvisations
appears on Anthology 1

Sometime around the time the Quarrymen were turning into the Beatles, they recorded quite a few informal home tapes, with three of the songs ("Hallelujah, I Love Her So," "You'll Be Mine," and "Cayenne") turning up on *Anthology 1* about 35 years later. These were, to many ears, the most lackluster items unearthed for the whole *Anthology* series. Yet the existence of more than an hour of additional material from the same source (or similar sources)—by far the largest chunk of unreleased Beatles predating 1962, and the only recordings on which bassist Stuart Sutcliffe plays—couldn't help but pique the curiosity of even some casual Beatles admirers.

Unfortunately, though the tapes do exist and most circulate on bootleg, they could be the most disappointing corner of the entire unreleased Beatles oeuvre. That's being too kind, perhaps. Not only are the performances among the very least enjoyable bootlegged Beatles recordings; objectively speaking, the worst half of them are among the most excruciatingly unpleasant unreleased music unearthed of any major rock artist.

The unpleasantness starts, in fact, with the head-hurting task of trying to get one's head around the mere establishment of when, where, and why this stuff was done in the first place. More confusion surrounds the tapes' murky origin than virtually anything else the Beatles recorded. It has been variously theorized that the tapes were recorded at the Art College of Liverpool, where Lennon and Sutcliffe were students at the time; at the Jacaranda club run by their first manager of sorts, Allan Williams; somewhere in Hamburg; or the apartments of John Lennon or Stuart Sutcliffe (who joined the band on bass in early 1960). Estimates for the dates of recording have varied between late 1959 and late 1960. Paul McCartney told Peter Hodgson, who sold him a tape with some of the material in 1995, that it was made in the bathroom of his home (which might at least partially explain the mounds of reverb) during a school vacation in April 1960.

That remains the best guess of date and location, though here's the first place in this volume to note that the Beatles' own memories of such details can't be taken as gospel, not when McCartney was mixing up the order of *Rubber Soul* and *Revolver* in a 1999 *MOJO* magazine interview, to give one example. It's pretty certain that the musicians on these crudities are Lennon, McCartney, Harrison, and Sutcliffe. Despite the presence of occasional erratic percussive beats, there's no real drummer involved; according, again, to McCartney, that's Paul's younger brother Mike, who never was an official member of the band. If you were listening to the Beatles for the first time on these tapes, you might assume that Paul was the undisputed leader, as it's his singing that's heard by far the most often.

It's most interesting, perhaps, to speculate on why—if the Beatles obviously went to some effort to do a good deal of recording, and if such opportunities were not common for them—they chose to do the material they did. Many of these efforts are not properly structured songs, but fragments, unfinished pieces that haven't coalesced into a whole, and loose, plodding jams. And, it must be emphasized, *lots* of loose, plodding jams, including several improvisations—some with off-the-cuff singing, some entirely instrumental—that add up to about 50 minutes of the available material. These, as well as three elementary vocal numbers with more (relatively speaking) standard structure, bear little relation to any known songs, Beatles-written or otherwise. Never officially named, whatever titles these pieces get depends on what bootleg you pick up, adding to the general agony of trying to make heads and tails out of the mess. The fidelity throughout is poor, the words often hard to distinguish, the instruments and voices bleeding all over each other. And Sutcliffe—who'd only been familiarizing himself with the bass for a few months—plays with an artless thump that does more to distract from the proceedings than fill out the sound, though at any rate it's often faint and hard to make out. It's also been mooted that echo and reverb have been added to the original tapes, though if so, it hardly seems likely that these constituted an improvement.

The low audio standards are perhaps forgivable considering the era and circumstances under which this was preserved. Worst of all, however, the Beatles themselves are often playing out of tune, out of time, and making a generally cacophonous racket. (Granted that's also true of the worst of the marathon *Get Back* sessions they'd undertake in 1969, yet at least those were much better recorded.) Unbelievably,

there are few performances here that are even up to the level of the demo disc of "That'll Be the Day" they'd cut almost two years or so earlier. As Peter Doggett wryly observed in *Record Collector,* the 1960 tapes, in contrast, "suggested the Beatles were running their career in reverse . . . they offered no hint that by the end of the year their creators would be unquestionably the best rock 'n' roll band on Merseyside."

Having braced yourself for the worst, it can be thankfully noted that there *are* a mere handful of tracks here that not only contain some definite seeds of Beatledom, but actually aren't all that unpleasant on the ear. Most notably, there are a couple of genuine Lennon-McCartney songs that the group would actually record for release years later, even if they're pretty ragged in these early stages. The better of these is "I'll Follow the Sun," the verses pretty much the same as the ones heard on their folky, acoustic-flavored recording of the song in late 1964 on their *Beatles for Sale* album. While the bridge is similar to the one the predominant composer of the song, Paul McCartney, would eventually polish off, it's clearly some ways off from taking final form, Paul singing something along the lines of "well don't leave me alone my dear, I'll hurry and call me my sweet." The real sticking point in this performance is George's guitar work, throwing in almost non sequitur roving up-and-down riffs to kick off the songs (and between the bridge and verse) that just don't fit. You can at least hear him starting to master Carl Perkins–style riffs, albeit in a stumbling fashion, in the brief instrumental break, and Paul's vocal sounds frankly much more assured than the instrumental backing does.

There are two versions of "One After 909"—one of them shorter than the other—which the Beatles would self-consciously revisit in January 1969 in their back-to-rock-'n'-roll-roots *Get Back* sessions, putting a live performance on their *Let It Be* album. Its presence here is a testament to just how far back the song was written (it's now known by most Beatles fans, of course, that the group also recorded a studio version in March 1963, an outtake from that session surfacing on *Anthology 1*). Here, more than anywhere else on these tapes, you can hear something approximating the actual early Beatles sound, particularly in the enthusiastic rhythmic drive and the close, uplifting unison lead harmony vocals of Lennon and McCartney. You can even hear spontaneous exclamations of "woo" in each version, which would became a trademark of the early Beatles' songs. Perhaps they had put more work into this than any of the other tunes, as the performances are pretty focused and together, lacking the laboriousness of most of the other tracks. Even George's solo has some sparkle, though it suffers from a little aimlessness. Most Beatles experts first became aware that the group had recorded the song on these tapes when Philip Norman referred to it in his 1981 book *Shout! The Beatles in Their Generation,* in which he aptly wrote, "The beat lifts; their voices coalesce, and for a moment they are recognizable as what they were to become."

The only other original song on this set to be revisited by the Beatles in the studio was "Hello Little Girl," which they'd record (in a performance now available on *Anthology 1*) in January 1962 at their Decca Records audition, and which the Fourmost would cover in 1963 for a British hit. Although the version here isn't nearly as together and developed as the one on the Decca tapes, it nonetheless has a clear Buddy Holly pattern to the guitar licks, while John and Paul harmonize nicely on the verses. There's some real sweetness to the tenuous performance, though the song obviously went through much reworking in the next year and a half. Only the beginnings of the verses are the same as the

Decca version. Thereafter they meander into some lines with a melody and half-mumbled, uncertain lyrics, which would both eventually be discarded for a tighter passage that put more accent on call-and-response between the lead and backup vocals, as well as a much more confident transition back to the main verse. Put simply, it would be made over from a near–Buddy Holly imitation into something far more identifiably Lennon-McCartneyized.

By comparison, the other original numbers on the tapes are primitive, almost generic early rock 'n' roll, lacking nearly any of the melodic finesse—or, for that matter, cheerfulness—so typical of the Beatles' later compositions. Starting with the two tracks that found their way onto *Anthology 1*, Lennon-McCartney's "You'll Be Mine" is a silly doo wop satire of sorts in which the Fabs' much-vaunted sense of humor fails them. They were still in their teens, after all, and it's a juvenile send-up with a dirge rhythm, a surprisingly stentorian lead vocal from Paul, jokingly effeminate high backup harmonies, and a spoken middle from John in which he seems to be trying to both imitate and take the piss out of the poker-faced romanticism of so many recitations by '50s black vocal groups. There is, however, his odd reference to his loved one's "National Health eyeball"—an early signifier of his arty wordplay, not to be truly unveiled to the public until his *In His Own Write* book in 1964, and not to find its way into Beatles songs for some time after that.

"Cayenne," a dark, minor-keyed instrumental with a slight Latin flavor, is a bit similar to the early-'60s work of the Shadows—the biggest group by far in Britain at the time—and early surf combos, although actual surf music wouldn't develop in the United States for another year or so. It's interesting that the song is credited to McCartney alone, a clue that although the Lennon-McCartney partnership is often characterized as not falling into nearly wholly separate songwriting endeavors until the second half of the '60s, the pair weren't necessarily writing together even in their pre-recording days.

The other three original songs with more or less conventional structures on these tapes are nonetheless so slipshod, and so unlike any other known existing Beatles songs, that it's even a matter of arbitrary taste as to what titles they're given. The one that's often dubbed "Some Days" has a passing resemblance to some of Eddie Cochran's songs with its rapid sequence of chords, periodic manic staccato Harrison riffs, and brisk McCartney vocal, though there's not much of a melody to hang it on. "You Must Write Every Day" is a yet more tossed-off standard three-chord workout without much drive or riffage, while Paul's lead vocal is rambling enough, and the lyrics so dully simplistic, to make one suspect the song is at least partly improvised. "Well, Darling," even relative to its surroundings, is a real bringdown, right from the doofus-like doom-clouded opening bass notes. It's a repetitious 12-bar dirge, though at least the fellows are putting a lot of effort into harmonizing the over-and-over again chorus (of "well, darling," natch). Some absolutely heinous Harrison guitar solos on this one, as well. The point has sometimes been made that Lennon and McCartney got most of their cruddy learn-by-doing songs out of the way before they began to record their own compositions for real, George Harrison observing in the *Anthology* book that "they'd written most of their bad songs before we'd even got into the recording studio." Well, here *are* some of the cruddy ones, as proof.

As the eventual release of 30 songs the Beatles recorded in concert in Hamburg in late 1962 demonstrated, their live set would remain almost totally devoted to cover versions for some time. Perhaps that's why so much of these tapes is comprised of original compositions, or attempts at same. They might have been wanting to concentrate on their own material, away from the pressures of an audience expecting familiar songs (and better ones than most of what the Beatles were writing at the time). However, there *were* a few covers on the 1960 tapes, most of which the group would never record again in any other setting. "Hallelujah, I Love Her So"—still in the Beatles' set on the December 1962 *Star-Club* tapes—was the one chosen for *Anthology 1*, and it is, again comparatively speaking, one of the tightest performances, lead singer Paul again showing his natural knack for forceful early rock 'n' roll. Incidentally, though Ray Charles is the song's original composer and performer, the Beatles' arrangement is clearly based on Eddie Cochran's cover version. If this was indeed recorded in April 1960, it was just the month after Cochran played (with fellow rockabilly great Gene Vincent) in Liverpool on his ill-fated British tour, at the end of which he died in a car crash. As it happens, the Beatles also cover a Vincent song, the rather obscure "Wild Cat," with Paul yet again on lead vocal, and the performance would be fairly acceptable if not for yet more utterly annoyingly ham-handed Sutcliffe bass.

While George's lead guitar work is often far from nimble on these tapes, he does provide at least a hint that he'd develop into a superior player on the instrumental medley of two Duane Eddy covers, "Movin' 'n' Groovin'" and "Ramrod." Harrison was heavily influenced by Eddy—the low, growling guitar lines of "I Want to Hold Your Hand" being one example—and he attacks "Movin' 'n' Groovin'" (known best to Americans as the source for the opening riff of the Beach Boys' "Surfin' U.S.A.") with real relish, peeling off frenzied riffs rather in the style of Chuck Berry's classic "Brown Eyed Handsome Man." (Note that the much shorter "Ramrod" seems to be just a fragment of the full performance.) Another big influence on George—perhaps the *biggest* influence, when it came to his guitar work—was Carl Perkins, and we also hear an early Beatles version of Perkins's "Matchbox," the only cover song on this set that the Beatles would eventually record for official release. He's some way toward getting the Perkins style of heavily country-soaked rockabilly picking down here, though it's folkier and not nearly as developed as the version the Beatles would record in 1964 (and, for that matter, less than a minute long, the group abruptly stopping mid-song). Ringo Starr would take lead vocals on the record, but of course he's not singing (or present in any way) here. It sounds like it's George himself singing on this arrangement, though it would actually be drummer Pete Best (and then John Lennon) who'd sing it onstage before the duties were handed to Ringo.

In a slower vein, "I'll Always Be in Love with You" is another nod to their early love for the kinds of ballads Elvis Presley did, although this is considerably more melodically rudimentary and unmemorable than those Elvis croon-alongs. It's a formative influence the Beatles seemed to have largely shaken off within a year or two—for the better, as their skills really didn't lie in that area, though John at least does a credible (if upper-register) Presley-styled vocal. (It must also be added that Sutcliffe's ineptness on bass becomes particularly irritating on this particular cut.) In *The Complete Beatles Chronicle*, Mark Lewisohn speculates the Beatles learned the song from Fats Domino's version, though it's worth noting that this popular standard had been recorded by many other jazz and blues musicians.

Speaking of Elvis, one of the few Beatles Presley covers to survive on tape in any way is another cut on this collection, "That's When Your Heartaches Begin" (a 1957 Presley B-side, though it had been done earlier by the black pop vocal group the Ink Spots). It seems like Paul's

QUARRYMEN REHEARSE
WITH STU SUTCLIFF
SPRING 1960

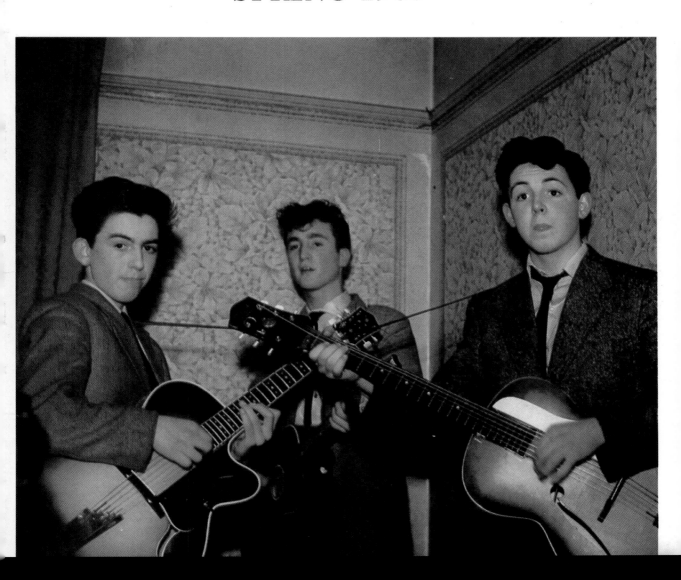

deliberately mocking Elvis's tendency to melodramatically drag out syllables here, though there's no questioning the Beatles' idolization of the King; indeed, it would be a couple of years or so before Paul himself eased the specifically imitative Elvis-like qualities out of his own voice. And speaking of corny, there's also a cover of "The World Is Waiting for the Sunrise," one of the fairly numerous pre-rock pop standards the Beatles put into their early repertoire, and which they had heard as done by Les Paul and Mary Ford in 1953. The Elvis vocal influence is again obvious here, the syllables so over-drawn-out that the effect is unintentionally comic.

In addition to a maybe-not-worth-noting nine-second fragment of an unknown song, that leaves almost an hour of additional recordings on the tapes—Beatles recordings through which, perhaps more than any other, even Beatlemaniacs dread to sift. Five of them are instrumentals that are virtually devoid of structure or tune; three others are seemingly improvised jams with just as apparently off-the-top-of-the-head vocals. They are untitled, bluesy, and beyond amateurish. Quite what the group had in mind in actually recording these numbers—which aren't even serviceable pre-rehearsal warm-ups—is rather unfathomable. Certainly no live audience would have withstood this kind of torture, and there aren't even germs of any workable songs to develop. It's even been speculated that these were recorded at an entirely different time and place than the song-oriented material on the tapes, though if so, it still certainly sounds as if the tracks were done in the same era.

Perhaps the Beatles were trying to master the rudiments of a more blues-oriented approach, as these "songs" often follow something like a standard 12-bar blues structure. As time would prove, their true forte did not lie in the realm of blues purism, and these relics could perhaps have had their (limited) value as a way of getting any such passing notions out of their system. The Beatles did occasionally visit standard blues progressions to good effect (as in "Yer Blues"), but if you're thinking there might be a buried hint of the likes of "For You Blue" here, think again. The tempo lumbers along with all the deftness of a waltzing rhinoceros, Sutcliffe plunk-plunks his bass like Charlie Brown attempting to duet with Schroeder, and George's leads are so pinched and hesitant you can almost see him sweating with frustration as he tries to will his fingers through the paces. Paul does attempt to inject some life into the grimness with some ad-libbed stereotypical blues lyrics, and occasional scat singing—things he seldom did at length on actual Beatles recordings—bolstering his image as the team player who did his best to lift flagging spirits when the group was getting bogged down (as he would do during similarly hellish moments in the *Get Back* sessions of January 1969).

The most interesting sections of the tapes, unfortunately, may be ones that have been reported to exist, but have not made it onto any bootlegs. Supposedly there are early versions of "When I'm Sixty-Four" (more than half a dozen years before it was reworked for *Sgt. Pepper's Lonely Hearts Club Band*!); the early Lennon-McCartney instrumental "Winston's Walk" (though considering how often the instrumental jams on the tapes have been misidentified by bootleggers as known unreleased early Len-Mac compositions, that might be a fiction); and "Ask Me Why," later done as the B-side of the Beatles' second single. (Also noted have been some unreleased fragments of just a few seconds each, though these are likely of little consequence.) It would be fascinating to hear "Ask Me Why" and particularly "When I'm Sixty-Four" in such early stages, though it's doubtful that they, in common with

any other selections on the tapes, would be top-notch performances in and of themselves.

Although the existence of these tapes wasn't generally known until the early 1980s, in fact a portion of "I'll Follow the Sun" had been played on German TV back on January 6, 1967, and the recordings had certainly been circulating among at least a few Beatles associates before escaping into the wider world. German television had used a copy belonging to Hans-Walter Braun, a Hamburg friend of the group who recalled being given a tape with the material by Paul McCartney in 1961. Other copies of material from the tapes ended up with Paul's brother Mike McCartney, and with Stuart Sutcliffe's fiancée (and early Beatles photographer) Astrid Kirchherr. It was eventually determined as likely that at least some of the tapes had been made on a Grundig TK 12 reel-to-reel recorder belonging to a neighbor of the McCartneys, Charles Hodgson (though Beatles biographer Hunter Davies had once written that the material from Kirchherr's copy was done on a recorder which John persuaded the Art College of Liverpool to buy for his own personal use). His nephew, Peter Hodgson, sold a tape with this material to Paul McCartney after it was discovered in Hodgson's grandfather's attic in 1994—which, in turn, might have cleared the path for the release of three of the tracks on *Anthology 1* in 1995.

The tapes were hardly of a standard, either in fidelity or quality of performance, that a group should seem eager to copy as samples of their work. That, however, is how they seem to have initially circulated, at least in Hamburg, though presumably by the time the Beatles had gathered a following in Hamburg they were far better in every respect than they'd been when they'd recorded the material back in Liverpool. The only plausible explanation seems that these recordings must have been the only available such tapes for curious parties at the time.

What's far stranger is that there was apparently interest from actual record companies in acquiring and releasing the music, though it seems like no amount of production tinkering could make it acceptable commercial product. Braun said he was offered 10,000 Deutschmarks for his copy after the 1967 German TV broadcast; Frank Dostal (of the German band the Rattles), who also had a tape with material from these "sessions," said he was offered 200,000 DM by EMI Germany in 1977, and that the same company had made a relatively paltry 50,000 DM offer to Kirchherr for her tape at around the same time. In the introduction to the 1985 edition of Davies's *The Beatles*, Astrid Kirchherr revealed, "One record company offered me 30,000 marks for it, and I said no. Then they said 50,000. I said no, not for 100,000 or any money. They just wanted to put the name Beatles on it and make a lot of money. But it wouldn't have done them any good. They were just having a laugh, playing around." It's been reported that Kirchherr—never one to financially exploit her close relationship with the Beatles in a distasteful manner—gave her copy back to her lifelong friend George Harrison in 1994.

Most of the available bootlegged material from the tapes began circulating in the late '80s, and it seems likely to remain far from official release schedules for the foreseeable future. Its ultimate value might, ironically, lie in its very ordinariness, even its unprofessionalism. For it's something that gives heart to every struggling teenage band the world over, and every parent cajoling a reluctant child to practice, as an illustration that even the very best group in the world sounded like rank amateurs at one point—even if only one such band of ragamuffins rose to truly conquer the world.

Another package of the 1960 rehearsal tapes, with eccentric cover art that manages to put Stu Sutcliffe's image on Mount Rushmore.

1957–1961 Noncirculating Recordings, Known and Rumored

Although the period between the live Quarrymen recording of July 6, 1957, and the Beatles' audition for Decca Records on January 1, 1962, takes in four-and-a-half years, there are large gaps in which no audio documents survive, or at least none that have circulated. There's nothing from mid-1958 through the circa-spring 1960 tapes, unless some of those 1960 tapes were actually done earlier. That's not wholly unexpected, as the group really wasn't very active during that time, with few documented gigs other than their Saturday night residency at the Casbah Coffee Club for about six weeks in the late summer and early fall of 1959.

More disappointing is the absence of anything between the 1960 tapes and the end of 1961. This year and a half or so was absolutely crucial to the Beatles' ascendance from near-bush-league status to acknowledgment as the top band in Liverpool, also taking in two separate lengthy stints in Hamburg that were enormously important in transforming them into a powerhouse rock 'n' roll band. True, they did most of their recordings with Tony Sheridan in Hamburg in June 1961, giving them the opportunity to record for the first time in a seriously professional studio environment, overseen by an internationally recognized musician-producer. Yet these weren't really representative of what the Beatles sounded like at the time. On all but two of those tracks,

they were merely functioning as the backing group to Sheridan, who—for all his importance in helping to mentor the band in their Hamburg days—was an unexceptional Elvis Presley–styled singer. And of the two songs they played on their own, one was an instrumental, the other a cover of a pre–World War II pop standard—not material that was too typical of their approach, even in 1961.

The group's apparent lack of anything better than the primitive 1960 tapes to offer their Hamburg friends as samples of their work seems to verify that there really were no such other endeavors lying around in the cupboard. A few scattered recordings are nonetheless known to exist or are at least rumored to, though none of them seem like artifacts that would have shown the infant Beatles to their best advantage, or even been representative of their early sound.

● 1957–1958

Private Tapes
4 Heyscroft Road, Liverpool

The Quarrymen sometimes practiced at the home of drummer Colin Hanton, and some of these rehearsals were recorded by his next-door neighbors. Alas, when Quarrymen banjo player Rod Davis borrowed the tapes in 1993, he found that the rehearsals had been taped over with other material.

● 1958–1959

Private Tape
The Liverpool Institute, Liverpool

Pick a Bale of Cotton

Paul McCartney recorded the folk song "Pick a Bale of Cotton," popularized by Leadbelly, with Neil Harding and two others in a classroom during a school lunch break. The tape cannot be found, and even if it is, it can probably be assumed that it's only of the most marginal interest.

● Early–Mid-1960

Private Tapes
Liverpool

As noted earlier in this chapter, there's material on the Beatles' 1960 home tapes that hasn't circulated, including early versions of "When I'm Sixty-Four" and "Ask Me Why," the early Lennon-McCartney instrumental "Winston's Walk," and unreleased fragments of just a few seconds each.

● June 1960

Private Tapes
Jacaranda Club, Liverpool

Allan Williams, who was beginning a bumbling career of sorts as an agent/manager for several Liverpool groups, gathered a bunch of them—including the Beatles—to record a tape he could take to Hamburg in hope of securing engagements there for the artists. Rather foolishly, instead of supervising the taping himself, he left for an appointment with his accountant, and, for that matter, didn't listen to the resulting tapes before heading off to Germany. There he played the tapes to Bruno Koschmider, who would end up giving the Beatles their first German club residency, at the Kaiserkeller. But as Williams recalled in his autobiography *The Man Who Gave the Beatles Away* (co-written with William Marshall), "What came out of the recorder was not music. It was an absolute cacophony. A sound track for a very poor horror movie."

Obviously the tape had somehow been technically fouled up and rendered useless. Which means that—even in the extremely unlikely event it should be found—it would be equally useless to Beatles scholars.

● October 15, 1960

Studio Outtakes
Akustik Studio, Hamburg

Fever
Summertime
September Song

On the face of it, this sounds tremendously interesting: a Hamburg recording on which John Lennon, Paul McCartney, George Harrison, and Ringo Starr all play, predating Ringo's actual entry into the Beatles by nearly two years. However, while such a recording was made, it's not exactly a Beatles performance per se. For in reality, the foursome were serving as a backing group of sorts for Lu Walters, singer and bassist in Starr's band of the time, Rory Storm & the Hurricanes. It was Walters who sang on this "session," recording not in a top-grade studio but in a facility more meant for do-it-yourself recordings, rather like the Liverpool one where the Quarrymen had done a couple of songs in 1958.

In common with other pre-1962 Beatles recordings, there's much confusion over what was done and why. It seems certain that "Fever," the classic early Little Willie John R&B-pop number (made into a bigger hit for the general pop market by Peggy Lee), was recorded. It seems likely, though not as certain, that George Gershwin's "Summertime" was also done. Some reports have it that another standard, "September Song," was also cut. There seems to be general agreement that Stuart Sutcliffe and Pete Best did not play on the tracks, and there's been speculation that "Summertime" and "September Song" feature only Walters, Starr, and two other Hurricanes (guitarists Johnny Byrne and Ty Brian), and also that Brian plays on all of the numbers. Ringo was used, apparently, because he was familiar with the songs from playing them with Walters—though why John, Paul, and George should be more familiar with the material than Pete has not been explained, fueling suspicion that the Beatles' plans to dump Best for Starr dates all the way back to this session. Although at least some acetates were made, it's unfortunately been impossible to verify what they include or what they sound like, as none have surfaced to date.

But even if they do, would it really be much of a musical revelation? It's not the Beatles; it's more like a Lu Walters recording with a combination of musicians from the Beatles and Hurricanes. The songs aren't all that typical of the rock 'n' roll the Beatles were playing in Hamburg clubs, even if they did always throw in some standards for variety (and McCartney at least had a definite affection for "Summertime," putting it on his all-covers 1988 Soviet-market album *CHOBA B CCCP*). And the sound quality would most likely be crappy, not only due to the age of the acetates (which typically degrade quickly when played, in any case), but also to the basic recording setup.

The instigator of this session was Allan Williams, who proclaimed in his autobiography that Walters "had a fantastic vocal range and the Beatles were fascinated by him. As a trained singer myself, I recognized Wally as having interesting potential. Perhaps with the Beatles' backing we would have a new sound." He further described "Fever" as "great. All except for Ringo on the drums. Because he had not been in a separate cubicle, his drums came over sounding like two coconuts being clapped together—or like the sort of gadget they use in radio plays to simulate horses' hoofbeats." The B-sides of however many acetates were made, incidentally, contained spoken-word commercials for leather goods, as the performances were recorded on discs with a side still open on which to put the music.

According to Williams, the Beatles then wanted to record a disc on their own, offering to pay the ten-pound fee themselves. Fearing retribution from Bruno Koschmider if the Beatles were late for their gig that night, however, Williams shunted them off to the Kaiserkeller club. But he did play the record they'd done with Walters for the Grade Organisation in London, with no positive results. In a more typical instance of the haphazard way he conducted his affairs, Williams lost his own copy at a London party years later, on his way to give it to Ringo so Starr could have one made for himself. Oddly, a photo of the record appears in Williams's autobiography; even odder, a December 1963 *Mersey Beat* article claimed, "The discs are still available in Liverpool and being played regularly." Should one finally turn up, it might break the record now held by the surviving 1958 Quarrymen "That'll Be the Day"/"In Spite of All the Danger" demo as the most valuable British disc.

● June 22–23, 1961

Studio Outtakes
Friedrich Ebert Halle, Hamburg

In June 1961, top German producer Bert Kaempfert—also an internationally popular orchestra leader whose instrumental "Wonderland By Night" had topped the American charts for three weeks just five months previously—took Tony Sheridan and the Beatles into the studio in Hamburg to record about an album's worth of material. Stuart Sutcliffe having recently left the band, it was the quartet of John Lennon, Paul McCartney, George Harrison, and Pete Best who played on these sides, primarily as a backing group for Sheridan. As noted earlier, there was little opportu-

nity to show what they were capable of, as it was Sheridan who took the lead vocals on all but two numbers, the pop standard "Ain't She Sweet" (with Lennon on lead vocal) and the instrumental "Cry for a Shadow" (a Lennon-Harrison composition).

However, when asked about the sessions nearly 15 years later in the September 6, 1975, issue of *New Musical Express (NME)*, Sheridan commented, "I seem to remember that we also recorded 'Kansas City,' and a couple of Chuck Berry songs. . . . I think John sang 'Rock and Roll Music' and 'Some Other Guy.' But as you can appreciate, it was quite some time ago." Before you whoop, "Now we're talkin'!" however, it seems nearly certain that those tracks do not exist. The vaults holding the Sheridan/Beatles recordings—issued, mostly after the Beatles rose to fame, by large labels all over the world—have been thoroughly combed for every possible commercial exploitation. The 38 cuts on the most thorough and well-documented package—the two-CD *Beatles Bop—Hamburg Days: Once Upon a Time in Germany*—has every mono version, stereo version, and alternate or overdubbed take known to man. None of those additional songs Sheridan brought up to *NME* as possibilities are on there, and if they weren't found for that 2001 compilation, they probably aren't anywhere.

If those songs were performed by Sheridan and/or the Beatles in the studio, it seems most likely they might have been done without the tape running, or (in a far less likely scenario) lost or erased. At least we do have great official 1964 Beatles covers of "Kansas City" and "Rock and Roll Music" on *Beatles for Sale,* and several excellent BBC versions of "Some Other Guy" (for that matter, "Kansas City" and "Rock and

The Beatles and Tony Sheridan on the same stage. Sheridan remembered the group recording outtakes with John Lennon on vocals during the early-'60s sessions in Germany when the Beatles served as his backing group, but none have been discovered.

The Missing Beatles

Had a Beatles live set been taped during that "gap" between mid-1960 and the end of 1961 from which no unreleased Beatles material circulates, what would it have sounded like? It's impossible to say, but we can at least speculate on what songs it may have included. Most likely, they wouldn't have differed much from the tunes heard on their December 1962 Hamburg *Star-Club* tapes: heavy on the classic rock 'n' roll covers, as the group actually did a relatively light percentage of their own compositions onstage prior to 1963. Of course, there would not have been some of the more recent rock 'n' roll and soul songs heard on the *Star-Club* recordings, à la their covers of the Isley Brothers' "Twist and Shout" and Tommy Roe's "Sheila," both of which were not hits until 1962. There would have been a lot of overlap, however, and thus a lot of songs that do not exist as pre-1962 Beatles recordings of any sort.

Some clues are provided by the earliest surviving Beatles setlist. It probably dates from around mid-1960, as the most recent song is the Everly Brothers' "Cathy's Clown," which wasn't a hit until spring of that year; the Beatles were always quick to learn songs they liked, and probably would have been playing some numbers of later vintage had the setlist originated from a later era. We do know, from a large all-caps-underlined scribble "GROSVENOR," that it was probably from a performance at the Grosvenor Ballroom in Wallasey, near Liverpool. (It should be made clear that the group probably didn't perform all 28 songs at the actual gig, as ten were noted as "ones which aren't done every week" and five bracketed as "possibles.") The list follows, with the original performers of the records on which the Beatles' versions were modeled noted in parentheses:

"Hallelujah, I Love Her So" (Eddie Cochran)
"That's All Right (Mama)" (Elvis Presley)
"Stuck on You" (Elvis Presley)
"Tutti Frutti" (Little Richard)
"Long Tall Sally" (Little Richard)
"What'd I Say?" (Ray Charles)
"Red Sails in the Sunset" (Joe Turner or Emile Ford and the Checkmates)
"Whole Lotta Shakin' Goin' On" (Jerry Lee Lewis)
"Mean Woman Blues" (Jerry Lee Lewis or Elvis Presley)
"I Don't Care If the Sun Don't Shine" (Elvis Presley)
"Honey Don't" (Carl Perkins)
"Clarabella" (the Jodimars)
"Rip It Up" (Little Richard)
"Fabulous" (Charlie Gracie)

"Lotta Lovin'" (Gene Vincent)
"Kansas City/Hey! Hey! Hey! Hey!" (Little Richard)
"Jenny, Jenny" (Little Richard)
"Little Queenie" (Chuck Berry)
"Ooh! My Soul" (Little Richard)
"Lucille" (Little Richard)
"Lawdy Miss Clawdy" (Elvis Presley)
"Cathy's Clown" (the Everly Brothers)
"One After 909" (Lennon-McCartney Beatles original)
"Words of Love" (Buddy Holly)
"I'll Never Let You Go" (Elvis Presley)
"I Wonder If I Care As Much" (the Everly Brothers)
"Sure to Fall" (Carl Perkins)
"You Win Again" (Jerry Lee Lewis)

A few notes of interest:
- Five of the songs ("Long Tall Sally," "Honey Don't," "One After 909," "Words of Love," "Kansas City") would eventually be recorded by the Beatles for official release.
- Five others ("That's All Right (Mama)," "Clarabella," "Ooh! My Soul," "Lucille," "Sure to Fall"), though never recorded by the Beatles for official release, were performed by the band on the BBC in 1963–1964, with tapes of each number fortunately surviving.
- Two others ("Little Queenie" and "Red Sails in the Sunset") eventually found release as part of the *Star-Club* tapes.
- One ("Sure to Fall") was done by the Beatles at their oft-bootlegged January 1962 Decca Records audition, though subsequent and superior versions were done for the BBC.
- Almost all of the 1950s greats of early rock 'n' roll are represented, with a lower percentage of songs by more obscure performers than would be typical of the Beatles' set over the next few years.
- There are about a half-dozen Elvis Presley covers, though—perhaps consciously—the group would never cover an Elvis song for official release, and would not do many Presley numbers on surviving live and BBC recordings.

If a tape of a 1960-1961 gig with a setlist similar to this should miraculously emerge, it would be an amazing document of the Beatles as they mastered the rock 'n' roll essentials. However, it's likely to remain something we'll be able to hear only in our heads.

Roll Music" were done for the BBC too—more on that later). Granting the extremely slim possibility that the Beatles recorded the songs during the Sheridan sessions, note that, in turn, it would be possible they were done when the Beatles recorded some backing tracks and background vocals for Sheridan recordings with pianist Roy Young in Hamburg on May 24, 1962. As Sheridan did not participate in those recordings, however, it seems unlikely those would have been the sessions he was recalling.

● November–December 1961

Live Performance
Cavern Club, Liverpool

In another tale which likely sounds far better on paper than on disc, Beatles press officer Tony Barrow has recalled on several occasions that he was given an acetate of the group performing live at the Cavern Club in Liverpool by Brian Epstein in late 1961. This was shortly after Epstein had first started to work with the band, taking his first baby steps toward getting his clients a recording contract. Barrow at that time was writing a record review column for the *Liverpool Echo* under the pseudonym Disker, though he was actually living in London, where he was writing sleeve notes for Decca Records (a task he would also undertake for the first Beatles LPs). After Barrow told Epstein he couldn't write about the Beatles until they had a record out, Brian brought him the acetate, perhaps thinking that would qualify as a "record."

A recording of the Beatles performing live at their favored local venue seems too good to be true, but as Barrow remembered in the early '70s in Peter McCabe and Robert D. Schonfeld's *Apple to the Core,* "it was cluttered with background noise and didn't sound too good." To Barrow's recollection, Epstein claimed it was from the soundtrack of an upcoming TV documentary about the Cavern—a claim that was almost certainly false, though the Beatles *were* filmed at the Cavern for real in August 1962. Barrow has also said he thinks it was in fact an acetate made from a recording Epstein had made himself of the Beatles at the club. Hopes that the relic, if retrieved, might still contain some interesting music were dashed by the more elaborate description he gave Baltimore radio broadcaster Dr. Bob Hieronimus in preparation for an interview in 2001. "Barrow remembers hearing the obvious enthusiasm of the crowd for the performers, but said otherwise all you could hear was a beat in the background," reported Hieronimus on the Internet (on the BeatleLinks Fab Forum) on May 23, 2001. "It was impossible to distinguish any music or the vocalist." In other words, it was of possibly even poorer fidelity than the 1957 Quarrymen tape of "Puttin' on the Style," on which you can at least readily identify John Lennon as the lead singer.

The acetate has never surfaced, and it seems that if it does, it will be of limited musical value. That's most unfortunate, as aside from the few minutes of material recorded by Granada TV when they filmed the Beatles in the late summer of 1962, there are no recordings of the group playing live in the Cavern—the club where, more than any other, the Beatles honed their sound and built their following. Again, like other poor and/or lo-fi Beatles artifacts, it's likely more interesting for what it tells us about their history than the music it might contain. For it's obvious that, for all his deserved success as a Beatles manager, Epstein must have been pretty green when he started, if he thought an acetate where "it was impossible to distinguish any music or the vocalist" was a ticket to getting newspaper publicity and a record deal.

Or maybe not. For one positive outcome of the meeting was that Barrow, again speaking in *Apple to the Core,* "agreed to try and get him an audition for them [the Beatles] on the strength of the acetate," indicating that perhaps the acetate wasn't quite so terrible as he made it out to be in 2001. It was easier to cut through the red tape of the record industry in those days, and Barrow remembered phoning the marketing department of his employer, Decca Records, which in turn led to an audition with Decca A&R man Mike Smith. Perhaps it wasn't quite so simple, as Smith did first check out the Beatles live at Liverpool on December 13, 1961. Whether that was the first part of the "audition" or not, a proper studio audition was indeed then set up for January 1, 1962—an audition which, although unsuccessful and largely unreleased to this day, *would* produce the first truly enjoyable and representative studio-standard recordings of the Beatles, and the first truly significant chapter in the story of their unreleased music.

The Beatles as they looked around the time of their January 1, 1962, Decca Records audition, with Pete Best still in the lineup on drums.

1962

Hello EMI, Good-Bye Star-Club

The Year in Review

While the Beatles released only one single in 1962, it was a year that was as busy and crucial to their evolution as any in their career. At its beginning, they were still unknown outside of Liverpool and Hamburg; still hoping for a record contract; still getting used to being handled by their new manager, Brian Epstein, who'd only met the band a couple of months before; and still using Pete Best as their drummer. By year's end, they'd have not only that record contract, but their first (albeit small) British hit single; a new, improved lineup with the replacement of Best by Ringo Starr; a talented and sympathetic producer, George Martin, who more than any other figure could lay claim to the title of "Fifth Beatle"; a chart-topping single in the can, awaiting release; and a slowly growing national profile via not only the success of "Love Me Do," but also increasingly regular appearances on BBC radio. There were some failures, even tempests, along the way: their rejection by several major record companies in the winter, the unexpected death in April of ex-bassist Stuart Sutcliffe, and the controversial sacking of the popular Best in mid-August. Not least, there was also a breathtakingly accelerating evolution of their music, as they became tighter and more polished, and as John Lennon and Paul McCartney's songwriting grew from embryonic promise to prolific brilliance.

Amazingly, although the group only officially issued two tracks that year (their October 1962 debut Parlophone single "Love Me Do"/ "P.S. I Love You"), we *are* able to trace their musical growth in quite a lot of detail. Indeed, there are about three or four albums' worth of material that survives. That's a pittance, admittedly, compared to the volumes of issued and unreleased work that circulates from every year of the Beatles' lifespan from 1963 onward. It's also too bad that there aren't yet more live and studio tapes to plug in gaps of our understanding of how they transformed, with such speed, from an outfit that couldn't pass their first major label audition to one on the verge of conquering the British pop scene. Yet what was preserved really does pretty much cover the most important bases, including the entirety of their fifteen-song audition for Decca Records on January 1, 1962; their first pair of BBC appearances, with Pete Best still on drums; material from their EMI audition and the sessions for their first Parlophone single; and even their first television appearance and a private rehearsal tape. It's all brought full circle, in a way, by the wealth of live recordings from their final stint in Hamburg in late December 1962, which serve almost as a farewell to their roots as a club band steeped in American rock 'n' roll.

Much of this material eventually saw official release, particularly via the late-'70s packages of the Hamburg tapes and the *Anthology 1* compilation of rarities from their early career. Yet much of it didn't, and even what did has seldom been scrutinized as heavily as the far more widely known Beatles sides that did see release during the 1960s. That's unfortunate, as it really is necessary to put these odds and ends into full context to gain an appreciation of how the Beatles' music and originality crystallized. For all the legal and artistic criticism that bootleggers have weathered, had it not been for their efforts in miraculously discovering as much as they did, this vital chapter in the group's musical history would have remained largely vacant.

Serious Beatles fans and researchers appreciate this. Yet for all this stuff's scholarly value, the most important point of all should not be overlooked. For this is the precise point at which unreleased Beatles music becomes not just *interesting*, but *good*. Listening becomes not a tough academic exercise, but *fun*—and, not infrequently, a joy, even if the nonstudio recordings are still of pretty rough fidelity. There are numerous moments to treasure here, starting with the nervous but sometimes endearing tone of the Decca audition (in full studio quality). There are early Lennon-McCartney originals, some very obscure, as their songwriting changed from passable to something more. There's the excitement of their first pair of BBC sessions, never issued officially, with Pete Best still in the drum chair. There's the chance to hear for yourself whether Best was as good or bad as various pundits claim. There's also the opportunity to hear numerous covers unavailable in any other form, as well as earlier, noticeably different versions of numbers the Beatles would later record for official release.

The surge in not just artistry, but in the musicians' own excitement in their growing popularity, is palpable. Neither they nor anyone else fully realized it, but all of the seeds of what made the band untoppable are to be heard in the wealth of unreleased Beatles music caught on tape in 1962. Their relentlessly inventive vocal harmonies, their infectious enthusiasm, their creative melodicism, the freshness which they gave to American rock 'n' roll oldies—it's all here. If only in hindsight, it's a nearly full map of the ways they would rearrange American rock 'n' roll into something entirely new—even if it took until 1963 for most of Britain to hear it, and 1964 to cross over to the United States.

● January 1

Studio Outtakes
Audition for Decca Records
Decca Studios, London

Love of the Loved
*Like Dreamers Do
*Hello Little Girl
*Three Cool Cats
September in the Rain
*Searchin'
*The Sheik of Araby
Take Good Care of My Baby
Besame Mucho
Memphis, Tennessee

To Know Her Is to Love Her
Sure to Fall (in Love with You)
Crying, Waiting, Hoping
Till There Was You
Money

appears on Anthology 1

Here is where the story of the Beatles' unreleased recordings—and, it could even be said, of the Beatles' work in professional studios as a whole—really begins. From the day John Lennon met Paul McCartney in July 1957 through the end of 1961, there had been sporadic amateur recordings of the band. None of them showed the group to great advantage; all of them would be utterly forgotten today, had the boys not unexpectedly developed in ways no one, even the musicians themselves, could have possibly foreseen. True, they had recorded in 1961 in a professional studio with a top German producer who was an international hit recording artist in his own right. But most of those tracks had been as a backing group to a journeyman rock 'n' roll singer, affording the Beatles little opportunity for any of their own personality or originality to emerge. Their January 1, 1962, audition for Decca Records—yielding 15 songs, known for decades among collectors simply as "the Decca tapes"—was the first audio document of any kind to capture a truly high-fidelity, professionally recorded performance of a group that had already been working for five years. As a fairly well-rounded sampling of their repertoire just half a year or so before they finally clinched that much-longed-for recording contract, it's of enormous historical significance. For it not only reveals what the band sounded like, more or less, just before they first established themselves as recording artists—it also illustrates just how far they had to go before they cut their first chart single eight months later. It's also by far the most comprehensive snapshot of how they sounded when Pete Best was still in the drummer's chair, his ousting in favor of Ringo Starr still seven-and-a-half months down the road.

The story behind how the Beatles came to be auditioning for one of Britain's largest record labels on New Year's Day 1962 is a long and winding tale in itself. Though it had been less than a month since Brian Epstein offered his services as manager, he'd swung into action immediately after their first meeting, even before the first contract had been signed to formalize the agreement. As an entry in the previous chapter stated, he'd played an acetate of the Beatles performing live at the Cavern for Tony Barrow that helped lead him to Decca A&R man Mike Smith. Taking full advantage of his leverage as the manager of NEMS, one of the biggest record stores in Northern England, Epstein had gotten Smith up from London to watch the Beatles play live at the Cavern on December 13, 1961. Decca was not just one of the two biggest record labels in the United Kingdom (EMI being the other), and one with a high international profile; it also knew full well the value of keeping the administrator of one of their most important retail outlets happy. Smith later even admitted that the label pretty much had to send someone to check out the group, so important was the NEMS account to the sales department.

Still, Smith seems to have been genuinely impressed by what he saw of the band onstage—albeit in front of a Liverpool audience, at the Beatles' chief stomping ground, that was guaranteed to give them an enthusiastic reception. "The Beatles were tremendous," he said about 40 years later when interviewed for the Pete Best DVD documentary *Best of the Beatles*. "Not so much my own reaction, but the crowd's reaction, was incredible." Such was the speed at which things could move even at major labels in those days that he arranged an audition in Decca's London studios for just a few weeks later.

It was a big break, so they thought, and no doubt the Beatles were both excited about the opportunity and impressed that their new manager had set something up so quickly. However, the audition would not take place under optimum circumstances. There was the matter of the date scheduled, to begin with. It's long puzzled some fans (particularly outside of the UK) why an audition would be scheduled for New Year's Day (on a Monday morning, no less), but in the early 1960s it wasn't yet a national holiday in Britain. It wasn't a holiday week for the Beatles either, who had just played the Cavern on Friday and Saturday nights, and spent most of Sunday in a van with their equipment on a ten-hour drive through snowstorms to London. Driver and roadie Neil Aspinall even got lost at one point, and as if the journey weren't enough to set them on edge, upon arrival a couple of seedy guys on the London streets tried to connive their way into using the van as a safe haven for smoking pot—still a highly exotic substance in 1961 and then, as now, illegal.

So Paul McCartney, John Lennon, George Harrison, and Pete Best probably weren't in the best of humor, or as well rested as they might have been, when they arrived at Decca Studios in West Hempstead in North London at around 11:00 a.m. the following morning. Brian Epstein (who'd traveled down separately by train) was there too, and all were nervous and slightly annoyed when Smith showed up late, having spent much of the previous night celebrating the New Year. Then Smith insisted that the Beatles use Decca's amplifiers, rather than the ones they'd gone to so much trouble to schlep down from Liverpool—not without some justification, as the amps, not top-of-the-line to start with, had seen much wear and tear over the course of several hundred gigs or so. (As a side note, this particular problem wouldn't even be fixed by the time of their ultimately successful audition for George Martin and EMI five months later, where some actual soldering had to be done before McCartney had a bass amp that was deemed up to scratch. It really wasn't until after that EMI audition that they, with the help of funds from Brian Epstein, started to give their equipment serious upgrades, as documented in Backbeat Books' *Beatles Gear.*)

Despite their experience recording in the studio as Tony Sheridan's backup unit in 1961, the Beatles were probably (if understandably) jumpy. Their anxiety was magnified by the studio's red light, customary in many such facilities to keep people from entering while sessions were in progress, but a new and intimidating feature to the inexperienced musicians. "They were pretty frightened," Neil Aspinall remembered about five or six years later in Hunter Davies's *The Beatles: The Authorized Biography.* "Paul couldn't sing one song. He was too nervous and his voice started cracking up. They were all worried about the red light on. I asked if it could be put off, but we were told people might come in if it was off. You what? we said. We didn't know what all that meant."

In spite of their jitters, the Beatles managed to lay down 15 songs, on two-track mono tape with no overdubbing, in the relatively small time allotted to them. (They remembered doing at least one more, "What'd I Say," in Billy Shepherd's obscure 1964 Beatles biography *The True Story of the Beatles,* but if they played it at Decca, it probably wasn't taped.) How long this took is still a matter of some conjecture. Some sources say the session lasted a mere hour, from around 11:00 a.m. to noon—which seems like undue haste even by the standards of the early '60s, and even considering that the 15 tracks altogether last only a little less than 35 minutes. In his autobiography, Pete Best would recall the recording kicking off around midday and going well into the afternoon. Whatever the clock really said, it may well have been a somewhat brisker audition than usual, as Smith had another group, Brian Poole and the Tremeloes, to audition later that same day. Since the tapes weren't being laid down with the intention of release, it's also likely that most or all of the songs were done in a single take. That was another contributing factor, possibly, to the nervousness that's often audible in the performances, though in fairness to Decca, the audition process undergone by the Beatles was probably fairly typical for its era.

And how did the Beatles do, the ultimate verdict (more on that a bit later) notwithstanding? Frankly, the group sounded ragged and tentative, at times with a sloppiness that verged on the unprofessional. The tempos sometimes wavered and the lead vocals quavered, particularly on some notes when McCartney reached into the upper register. George Harrison's guitar lines sometimes fumbled, as is most embarrassingly evident when comparing this early take of "Till There Was You" with the version they'd release at EMI nearly two years later, which featured a memorably beautiful and smoothly executed jazz-flamenco-tinged solo. Pete Best's drumming was thinly textured and rather unimaginative, occasionally to the point of monotony.

Their inexperience with studio vocal mikes was at times obvious, some tics, clicks, and pops getting picked up here and there, as when Paul landed on the last word of a line ("and when I look") in "Love of the Loved" with a "k" as hard as if he's biting into a cracker. The harmonies suffered from some disorganization and faintness, though the latter quality might be as attributable to whatever recording setup was used (and it certainly seems like it was on the basic, perfunctory side) as to any deficiencies in the group's vocals. McCartney's singing was still highly derivative of Elvis Presley in spots, as was particularly noticeable on parts of "Searchin'," "Like Dreamers Do," and "September in the Rain," as well as the closing lines of "Love of the Loved." A great role model to be sure, but it would take some time—not very much time at all, as it turned out—for Paul to find his own, more comfortable, yet equally distinctive and virtuosic voice.

For most of the rest of their career, the Beatles would perform exceedingly well, under superhuman pressure, time after time—whether playing in front of huge crowds and TV audiences on their world tours, writing brilliant material under strict deadlines, or managing to match or top themselves commercially and artistically with every new succeeding album and single. The Decca audition, to the contrary, is about the last time we hear the Beatles actually coming off as nervous and not wholly sure of themselves. While several songs end with almost improvised-sounding bits where the Beatles playfully scat, sing a super-brief operatic note or two, or laugh nonchalantly, there's more sense that they're whistling in the dark to relieve the tension, rather than genuinely feeling at ease in their surroundings.

Yet, particularly with the benefit of hindsight, the recordings were in some respects quite promising, and not without appeal. What's more, though no one in their right mind would put them on the same level as their subsequent official EMI-recorded material, they're fairly enjoyable in their own right. Although the arrangements are primitive and hollow—almost to the point of ghostliness—there are strong hints of the fresh enthusiasm and vigor that would be so key to the Beatles' approach, even on their covers of American rock 'n' roll songs, which comprised the majority of songs at the Decca audition. It's more present in the vocals than anything else, even if their vocal harmonies aren't nearly as fully worked out as we're accustomed to hearing. Still, there's energy and exuberance, albeit in a muted form, as if they hadn't quite yet found the courage to go for the jugular. Too, despite Best's limitations as a drummer, there's a youthful impatience to the arrangements that would be such a strong characteristic of the Merseybeat sound that would dominate 1963 and be exploited with greater skill by the Beatles than any other Liverpool act.

To be sure, the most striking of the 15 tracks are the three Lennon-McCartney originals, none of which the Beatles would release while they were active, although they were covered for British hits of varying size by other artists in 1963 and 1964. Indeed, those unfamiliar with the music of the pre-EMI Beatles might be first struck by the paucity of original material. Most of the songs the Beatles would cut at EMI, after all, were written by the band. More than anything else, perhaps, it's the quality of those songs that has made the Beatles' music so timeless (and commercially successful). It must be remembered, however, that at the beginning of 1962, Lennon and McCartney's songwriting talents were still in a formative stage (and Harrison wasn't writing at all, essentially, despite having co-authored the instrumental they recorded at the Tony Sheridan sessions, "Cry for a Shadow"). The three songs they presented to Decca, as meager as they were in comparison even to their only slightly later work, were probably about the best they had to offer at the time. Like the Decca tapes as a whole, these too were more promise than genius, though at the same time not at all bad on their own terms.

Of those three Lennon-McCartney-penned tracks, perhaps the most interesting is "Love of the Loved," as it's the only one of the threesome that hasn't found eventual official release (the other two, "Hello Little Girl" and "Like Dreamers Do," appearing on *Anthology 1* in 1995). Even at this early stage in the Lennon-McCartney partnership, it was already the case that much or all of the writing on some of the songs bearing their byline was in reality largely or wholly attributable to either John or Paul alone. "Love of the Loved" is definitely a Paul-dominated effort, and while it might sound a tad awkward and unpolished judged next to the songs the Beatles were coming up with by 1963, it has definite hallmarks of what would often characterize the group's compositions.

There are those unexpected, almost off-the-wall chord changes, almost to the extent that you feel this might have been one of the first times McCartney set out to deliberately explore unconventional structures; a blend of major and minor moods; the commanding glide from the bridge back to the main verse; and, as a quality prevalent in Paul's writing in particular, an almost pervasive, haunting eeriness. A strange, skittering guitar line recurs throughout this uneasily mid-tempo arrangement, and Paul feels a little more comfortably settled into his lead vocal than he does on some other cuts, despite the aforementioned leaps into some Elvis Presley–isms. You can also hear some almost subliminally soft (and, for the Beatles, not at all typical) vocal harmonies in the background when Paul shifts into a more uplifting bridge. These indicate that there might have actually been some deliberate effort on Smith's and/or the group's part to give the vocal arrangement a certain idiosyncratic flavor; it certainly doesn't sound like the backup singers are closely miked. Best's drumming is among his better work on this session, pushing the song along with a steady insistence.

In another foreshadowing of a device the Beatles often used later, the very end of the song takes off in a surprising melodic direction, McCartney drawing out the syllables of the last line before suddenly ascending into a near-falsetto as the guitars play a brief sequence not heard anywhere else in (yet similar to the rest of) the song. You don't need to get into technical analysis to enjoy "Love of the Loved," however, despite its somewhat over-serious romantic lyrics and the slightly forced pun of the title phrase. Cilla Black would have a small British hit with the tune when she put it on her first single in mid-1963, but the Beatles' version is far superior, as Black's used a wholly inappropriate uptempo brassy arrangement and belting vocal. As to why it didn't appear on *Anthology 1*, that's anyone's guess; perhaps McCartney, even three decades later, was dissatisfied or embarrassed about some aspect of the song or the Decca performance. It's too bad, as it's certainly deserving of release, and far better than some of the other pre-EMI tracks included on that collection.

McCartney is also to the fore on the Lennon-McCartney number "Like Dreamers Do," which *did* find release on *Anthology 1*. It's another case of a composer and singer finding his feet, with corny sentimental lyrics that are something of a throwback to the pre-rock Tin Pan Alley era. But there are some pretty unusual things going on too, especially the lurching introduction, whose chords go up the scale until there's almost nothing left. They don't form a conventional progression by any means, as most nonprofessional guitarists would find if they tried to play it by ear. Still, it's got that Beatlesque Merseybeat catchiness, if only as a bud not yet in blossom. Paul's nervousness does seem to betray him more in this cut than in some others, however, particularly when he almost breathlessly strains for some really high notes at the end of the bridge. There's almost a tangible sense of relief when he gets back into the more mid-range verse; the lads might have done well to knock down the tune a key or two. The way he stretches out "I-yi-yi-yi" in the bridge, too, smacks of lingering hokey 1950s rock 'n' roll and doo wop influences that would be ironed out within the year. It's not all Paul's show, with Best throwing in more drum rolls (though they're not always called for) than usual, and Harrison's guitar going into a nice speckly line near the end, with a dated reverb that—whether due to Decca's setup or not—would never reappear in his work on the Beatles' EMI sessions. The Applejacks took an even jauntier, less guitar-oriented arrangement of the song into the British Top 20 in 1964. But the Beatles' version, for all its imperfections, is far more satisfying and dare we say gutsier, even for such a relatively trivial Lennon-McCartney tune.

The final Lennon-McCartney song from the Decca date, "Hello Little Girl," had been worked up by the group for some time, as its appearance on one of their 1960 home tapes verifies. By January 1962, it had been tightened and refined quite a lot, the bridge bearing an almost entirely different melody. More John's song than Paul's, it points the way forward to the Beatles of 1963 more than anything else recorded at the Decca audition. For while many of the songs from the Decca tape have few or no backup vocals, here the Beatles sound like a real *group*, John and Paul singing the verse in unison, Lennon engaging in some nice call-and-response backup harmonies in the bridge with Paul and George. Though a slight and simple song on the whole, it's got a rough charm (and a rather skeletal and jagged guitar solo), and more than almost anything else the group cut, it puts their debt to Buddy Holly front and center. The Fourmost took the song into the British Top Ten in late 1963, and like the Applejacks took an approach so light and sing-songy as to make the Decca take, as innocuous as the tune was, downright earthy in comparison.

The remaining dozen songs on the tape are all covers, and while they're not as fascinating as the Lennon-McCartney-composed items, all of them are of some interest, even in the cases where the Beatles would later record far superior versions for EMI releases or the BBC. They also testify to the broad range of the Beatles' tastes and the versatility of their repertoire, encompassing '50s rock 'n' roll, early soul, rockabilly, and even some teen idol pop and pre-1950s Tin Pan Alley. Three of the tracks would be included on *Anthology 1,* and seven of the remaining nine tunes would emerge in a different, later version on either a real Beatles album or the *Live at the BBC* collection, leaving just two cover songs from the Decca tapes that were never included on an official Beatles release in any form.

One of those two covers is the pop standard "September in the Rain," based on the arrangement used by pop-jazz singer Dinah Washington. It's not what comes to mind when most people think of the Beatles' early influences, but for what it's worth, Paul McCartney really does sound like he's enjoying himself on this track, scatting with an almost ironic playfulness to kick things off. Perhaps this was one of the later cuts laid down in the session; on this and a few other songs, the group seems to have noticeably loosened up. Popular standards were a part of the Beatles' early repertoire, usually at the instigation of Paul, though only "A Taste of Honey" and "Till There Was You" serve as evidence in their official studio catalog. As they did with those two songs (on their first and second albums, respectively), the Beatles effectively adapt "September in the Rain" to a rock guitar setting, though without nearly as much imagination.

The other, almost equally unlikely song never revisited by the Beatles in either a recording studio or a BBC session was "Take Good Care of My Baby," which had just gone to No. 1 for American teen idol Bobby Vee in both the US and UK. This was precisely the kind of artist, and song, that the group usually avoided in their cover choices. Teen idol music personified the mild and soft sounds the early Beatles were counteracting, and doing a current chart-topping smash would be considered way too obvious for a band trying to be as original as the Beatles were, even at this early stage in their musical development. Perhaps this was one of the songs performed specifically at the suggestion of Brian Epstein, who as a record retailer kept a keen eye on what was popular on the charts, though it's been reported that it was George Harrison's idea, Best claiming in Spencer Leigh's *Drummed Out! The Sacking of Pete Best* that George, "more than the others, thought we should do one or two from the Top 20." Nonetheless, the fellows do a reasonable if somewhat perfunctory job on the song, which was, after all, written by one of Lennon and McCartney's favorite American songwriting teams, Gerry Goffin and Carole King. George—who did more lead singing than many fans realize in the days when the Beatles were playing mostly covers—takes the lead vocal. Paul's harmonies are a wee bit strained and vibrato-laden, and the arrangement's a little on the rushed and tiptoeing side. In all, it's not too much of a surprise that it didn't make the cut for *Anthology 1.*

The Coasters were big favorites of the Beatles, and at Decca they covered two of the great American vocal group's songs, as well as basing their arrangement of the Latin pop standard "Besame Mucho" on the one the Coasters had used in covering the same tune. That made three Coasters covers, essentially, the most familiar of which was "Searchin'," which eventually showed up on *Anthology 1* (where, annoyingly and for no apparent reason, the opening instrumental bars of the song were cut off). There's no doubt they and lead singer Paul McCartney loved the song; Paul, in fact, chose it as one of his "desert island discs" in 1982. But the Beatles' version is kind of forced and stilted, particularly when Paul launches into a dramatic falsetto without much of the comic flair for which the Coasters were famous.

Far cooler is "Three Cool Cats" (also on *Anthology 1*), George Harrison taking the lead vocal for a catchy minor-key, hangin'-on-the-street-corner vignette. (Incidentally, this song, originally used on a 1959 Coasters B-side, might not have been as obscure as many assume; early British rock singers Cliff Richard, Marty Wilde, and Dickie Pride sang it live on a May 1959 episode of the UK television program *Oh Boy!* and it's quite possible that one or more of the Beatles saw that exact broadcast.) George, John, and Paul attack the harmonies on the chorus with real relish, though it's a bit of a shock to hear Lennon attempt some not-too-accomplished mimicry of Caribbean-like accents in some brief (and not terribly funny) spoken comic interjections. Still, overall it's one of the best Decca cuts, as is "Besame Mucho," which didn't make it onto *Anthology 1,* probably because a different version (recorded five months later at their EMI audition) was used. Surprisingly, the Decca version has a big edge on the considerably tamer EMI one, on which for some reason the group decided to omit the backup harmonies and infectiously silly ensemble end-of-verse "cha-cha boom!" chants that help make the Decca take so fun. Again, maybe it's not the kind of song you expect to hear from the Beatles, but it really does rock pretty hard, and maybe it's another one from a point in the session where they'd gotten a little less inhibited than they were at its outset.

The weirdest relic of all from the Decca tape (eventually released on *Anthology 1*) is the cover of the relatively ancient theatrical standard "The Sheik of Araby" (which had actually been heard in the 1940 Hollywood movie *Tin Pan Alley*). Sung by Harrison as though he's trying to clip off the ends of each word, it's played by the Beatles with the absurd speed of men who'll miss their train if they don't force the song under the 90-second mark (which they don't quite manage, failing by just a few seconds). Even more bizarre were the nasal howls at the end of some verses, expelled with such overbearing volume that many would guess that some wise-ass bootlegger overdubbed them years later. But no, they were part of the original recording, though the levity they were no doubt intended to add was pretty contrived. The song's inclusion in the session wasn't as off-the-wall as it might appear; early British rock 'n' roll star Joe Brown had cut a rock version of the tune in 1961, and George was a Brown fan, taking lead vocals five months later on the Beatles' BBC cover of Joe's 1962 hit "A Picture of You." (What's more, Brown would become a close friend of George's in Harrison's later years; Harrison would even be best man at Brown's wedding in 2000.) As Best told Spencer Leigh in *Drummed Out! The Sacking of Pete Best,* "'The Sheik of Araby' was a very popular number and we nearly did it on the BBC shows because of the demand. George loved those kind of numbers."

There's not as much to say about the remaining half-dozen songs, as all of them are inferior to subsequent versions the Beatles would record by a wide margin. "Money," for instance, was one of the group's greatest covers and a highlight of their second album, *With the Beatles.* Next to that savage performance, the Decca version is kind of anemic, with the rushed tempo that afflicted much of the session and a far less assertive instrumental attack. *With the Beatles* included another cover first cut at Decca, "Till There Was You," most familiar to American audiences from the hit musical *The Music Man*, although the Beatles learned it from Peggy Lee's recording of the song. Here the gap in quality is yet wider, as both the rhythm and Paul McCartney's vocal are more hesitant than anywhere else in the session, his singing almost faltering into prissiness with apparent nerves. It's interesting, however, to hear them do an arrangement here with not one but two guitar solos, though as noted earlier, George's playing on this particular number would improve quite a bit by the time they recut it for EMI a year and a half later.

While the remaining four songs weren't redone for any of their EMI releases, the Beatles did record all of them for the BBC. In fact, in the case of "Sure to Fall" and "Memphis, Tennessee," they did them four and five times, respectively, for the BBC, though the other pair ("Crying, Waiting, Hoping" and "To Know Her Is to Love Her") were done on radio just once each. Carl Perkins's "Sure to Fall" suffers most in its Decca incarnation. Though Paul excelled at this kind of rockabilly material, his voice here is as shaky as it ever was at any time on any tape, and the song is taken a shade too fast, lacking the break into double-time in the bridge that distinguished the most imaginative version they did on the BBC. Chuck Berry's "Memphis, Tennessee" is a great song, but somehow this particular attempt, sung by John Lennon, plods a little more than it bounces, with a weird wobbling guitar chord bringing it to a finish.

Harrison takes lead vocals on Buddy Holly's "Crying, Waiting, Hoping," which isn't bad at all, with well-placed responsive backup harmonies. But the BBC version is much smoother, and Pete Best, like he does throughout most of the Decca session, just pushes the beat a little too fast for comfort. "To Know Her Is to Love Her," a No. 1 hit ballad in 1958 under the title "To Know Him Is to Love Him" for the Teddy Bears (whose lineup included Phil Spector, who wrote the song), is sung by John with major backup support from Paul and George. It's nice to hear Lennon's gentler side in evidence so early on, but again this pales next to the more accomplished BBC take; John's vocal is far less confident, and there are some lingering, lugubrious doo wop inflections to the harmonies that would be scrubbed out by the time it was redone for radio in mid-1963. (Incidentally, although Hunter Davies's book mentions that Paul sang another pop standard at the session, "Red Sails in the Sunset," this appears to be in error. At the very least, no tape of it from the Decca audition has surfaced, though it was certainly part of their live repertoire, as proven by its inclusion on *Live! At the Hamburg Star-Club* recorded almost exactly a year later, and on their earliest surviving handwritten setlist, probably from mid-1960.)

Of course, there was likely little such intense analysis of the tapes at the time, by either the Beatles or Decca. The main objective of the Beatles was to get that record deal; the main objective of Decca was to determine whether the Beatles were worth recording for real. At first, Epstein and the group thought they'd done well. Mike Smith had, according to Best, said the tapes were "terrific"; they even celebrated with a dinner in London that night. They were expecting a contract to be offered soon, went back to Liverpool to resume their gig schedule, and waited. The wait turned to weeks, and at the beginning of February 1962, Decca officially turned the Beatles down. The band was devastated, and although Epstein did meet with Decca A&R man Dick Rowe and sales manager Sidney Arthur Beecher-Stevens in London to attempt to persuade them to reconsider, he was squarely

rejected. Decca told him that groups were on the way out, a ridiculous rationale, as, in fact, "beat groups" would overrun the industry just a year later, the Beatles themselves leading the charge.

Much later, the Beatles were honest in assessing the merits of their performance that New Year's Day. "We were all excited, you know, Decca and all that," Lennon remembered in the 1970s (as quoted in Keith Badman's *Beatles Off the Record*), about ten years after the big disappointment. "So we went down, and we met this Mike Smith guy, and we did all these numbers and we were terrified and nervous. You can hear it on the bootlegs. It starts off terrifying and gradually settles down. We were still together musically. You can hear it's primitive, you know, and it isn't recorded that well, but the power's there. It was the tracks that we were doing onstage in the dance halls. We then went back to Liverpool and waited and waited and then we found out that we hadn't been accepted. We really thought that was it. We thought that was the end." In the same volume, McCartney admitted, "We couldn't get the numbers right, and we couldn't get in tune." (It should be noted that it's not 100 percent clear whether Lennon was remembering the Decca tapes accurately in his comment; he and Yoko Ono had sent Paul and Linda McCartney an acetate of what they thought were the Decca tapes as a Christmas gift in 1971, but it actually contained some of the tracks they'd recorded for the BBC!)

His enthusiasm at the time to the contrary, Mike Smith later claimed (as quoted in *The Beatles Off the Record*) that the Beatles "weren't very good in the studio. I took the tape to Decca House and I was told that they sounded like the Shadows. I had recorded two bands and I was told that I could take one and not the other. I went with Brian Poole & the Tremeloes because they had been the better band in the studio." In *Best of the Beatles* he added, "With hindsight, it's unfortunate that that excitement [of the Cavern show he'd witnessed] couldn't have been carried into the actual audition, which I have to say I think was very much a disappointment. It transpired later that they had written some wonderful songs that didn't appear that day, and so sadly, I said no. I certainly didn't envision them turning into the phenomenon that they were, which I regretted bitterly over the years. In terms of how they were as musicians . . . certainly the one that played the most bum notes was McCartney. I was very unimpressed with what was happening with the bassline. [In McCartney's defense, he'd only been playing bass for less than a year, having taken over the bass position when Stuart Sutcliffe left the band for good sometime in 1961.] But . . . we're talking about four young men in a very strange environment, probably a very overpowering environment. And as much as we tried to be friendly, it was a foreign area for them to be in."

Poole & the Tremeloes were a London band, which also seems to have been a factor in the decision, it being felt it would be easier to work with a local act than one that would need to travel down from Liverpool to Decca's studios. And, in fact, Brian Poole & the Tremeloes would come up with four British Top Ten hits and several smaller UK chart singles between 1963 and 1965, though of course they enjoyed nowhere near the ultimate success of the Beatles. This hasn't prevented a hailstorm of derision directed toward Decca over the last few decades for their apparent misjudgment, even though many qualified observers (and the Beatles themselves) were willing to admit that no one could have predicted how great the band would quickly become on the basis of what they played at their audition. The promise was there, but not everyone could hear it, though some certainly could detect it in hindsight. Asked by this author in 1985 whether he would have turned down the Beatles, for instance, American producer Shel Talmy—who was hired by Decca shortly after the Beatles' audition and (as an independent producer) went on to oversee hits by the Kinks, the Who, and others—replied, "I don't think I would have, because I've always been very song-oriented. Although they were not a wonderful band musically, the songs were outstanding, even then. And I'm sure I wouldn't have turned them down."

One also wonders whether one little-documented incident sealed Decca's reservations about working with this unknown provincial act. According to Pete Best's autobiography, at one point in the audition Epstein had the temerity to criticize something about Lennon's singing or guitar playing, upon which the Beatle burst into a brief tantrum, raging at his manager, "You've got nothing to do with the music! You go back and count your money, you Jewish git!" In retrospect, it seems rather unlikely that either Epstein would say something so bold to the volatile Lennon on such an important and tense occasion, or that Lennon—who for all his volatility was fully aware of what was hanging in the balance—would have jeopardized the Beatles' chances with such an outburst. But then again, Pete Best was there, and we weren't. (As a bizarre footnote, incidentally, Best would actually end up recording for Decca—with Mike Smith producing—as part of his subsequent group, Lee Curtis & the All Stars, and as part of the Pete Best Four on their June 1964 single "I'm Gonna Knock on Your Door"/"Why Did I Fall in Love With You?" long after the Beatles had started their run of hit records for EMI.)

For all the bitter disappointment of the Decca failure, the one thing the Beatles gained from the association—the actual audition tapes—proved in some ways quite useful, and would ironically in one small way help lead the band to a recording contract soon enough. For Epstein got to keep the two reel-to-reel audition tapes, which he took to play when he tried to shop the group around to other labels in early February. The manager of the HMV record store on London's main shopping strip, Oxford Street, suggested to Brian that it would be better to press the tapes onto discs rather than hauling around the less instantly playable reel-to-reels. Epstein took up the suggestion immediately, going right into a studio above the store where demos could be pressed.

As engineer Jim Foy was making the discs, he told Epstein that the Beatles sounded good. Epstein told him that three of the songs were group originals, and Foy got Sid Coleman, who ran a music publishing subsidiary of EMI (Ardmore & Beechwood) on the store's top floor, to give them a listen. Coleman liked those rudimentary Lennon-McCartney songs enough to talk about a publishing deal with Epstein there and then. Brian didn't take him up on that at the moment, as getting a recording contract was his most urgent mission. To help him out in that regard, Coleman called George Martin, the head of A&R at Parlophone, a subsidiary of EMI. That led to a meeting between Epstein and Martin, who in turn was interested enough in what he heard on the discs to—after another tangled sequence of events beyond the scope of this book—offer the Beatles a recording contract later in 1962. His decision wasn't based wholly on the Decca tapes; he auditioned the band at EMI himself in June 1962. Discussing the Decca tapes in a 1971 *Melody Maker* interview, he even clarified, "I wasn't knocked out at all, in defense of all those people who turned it down it was a pretty lousy tape, recorded in a back room, very badly balanced, not very good songs, and a rather raw group. But . . . I thought they were interesting enough to bring down for a test." So those tapes had indirectly led Epstein and the Beatles to Martin, the producer of almost everything the band recorded in the studio.

When the EMI deal was sealed, there seemed to be no more use for the Decca tapes. But although there was virtually no interest in or market for bootlegs of unreleased rock music at the time, it seems that the material almost immediately began to circulate outside the hands of Epstein or the labels with whom he'd been dealing. According to Hans Olof Gottfriddson's *The Beatles from Cavern to Star-Club*, in the spring of 1962 the group gave a tape of eight of the tracks to their close friend Astrid Kirchherr, who gave it to a friend of hers a year later. It still seems unlikely many people heard any of this material beyond a very select few before 1977, when—according to Clinton Heylin's *Bootleg: The Secret History of the Other Recording Industry*—the complete tape was acquired for $5,000 by a couple of New Yorkers. Immediately they began to leak it out on bootleg, though the way the songs were spread out over several releases (including a series of colored vinyl 45 picture sleeve singles) frustrated those who just wanted to hear all 15 tracks in one go. Indeed, it didn't take long for some of the tracks to actually get broadcast on commercial radio; the author remembers hearing a few on a Beatles "A–Z" weekend on an FM station in Philadelphia in the late '70s, for instance.

It also didn't take long for everything to get assembled on a single bootleg LP, *The Decca Tapes*, complete with extensive liner notes comprised of a fanciful piece of historical fiction by one "Grid Leek." The no doubt pseudonymous Mr. Leek wrote about the songs as if ten of them had been released on five 1962 Decca singles preceding their deal with Parlophone, and four of the others on two post-Parlophone-signing Decca 45s that were soon withdrawn from the market, with "Take Good Care of My Baby" an outtake "which was only recently retrieved from the Decca vaults." As tongue-in-cheek as it was, the packaging—complete with an excellent picture of the leather-clad Pete Best lineup on the cover—was vastly better than the remarkably shabby treatment much of the material got when it was issued by Phoenix Records in the US on the semi-official LPs *The Silver Beatles Vols. 1 & 2* in September 1982. As if the ugly nondescript sleeve graphics weren't bad enough, several of the tracks were mastered at the wrong speed, and half of them were lengthened artificially by editing and splicing. In 1988, the surviving Beatles finally sued the companies responsible for issuing this material in the US and UK, forcing them to take it off the market.

The Silver Beatles Vols. 1 & 2 had actually contained all of the songs (albeit sometimes in butchered form) from the Decca tapes except "Love of the Loved," "Like Dreamers Do," and "Hello Little Girl," perhaps because these gray-market labels didn't want to deal with any complications ensuing from issuing songs with Lennon-McCartney copyrights. They were so poorly distributed (and packaged), however, that the vast majority of listeners from the general public still had not heard any of the Decca tapes before five of the tracks were included on *Anthology 1*. Most Beatles fans still have yet to hear any of the other ten tracks, although they're perennials on uncounted bootlegs to the present day. Anyone willing to look just a little bit further than conventional record stores can find all 15 cuts, to be frank. But as one of the very most important groups of unreleased Beatles recordings, as well as a crucial document of the early days of the best band there ever was, the Decca audition deserves official release, with the kind of historically minded packaging it merits.

There are a couple of semimyths surrounding the Decca tapes, oft-repeated in books and articles about the Beatles, that bear serious reinvestigation and reassessment. One is the claim that Brian Epstein sabotaged the group's chances by selecting the songs they were to play at the audition, weighting them too heavily toward lightweight pop material that was neither suited for their strengths nor typical of what they liked or played onstage. It's probable that Epstein did have significant input into the song list, and it also seems likely that he was the force who pushed for the most pop-oriented tune, "September in the Rain"; he'd cited Dinah Washington's version as one of ten favorite records of 1961 in *Mersey Beat*. As a result of Epstein's blunder, the speculation goes, not only did Decca turn the band down, but the Beatles insisted that he never have anything to do with their musical policy again. Boyhood Beatles friend (and future longtime personal assistant to the group) Tony Bramwell writes in his recent memoir *Magical Mystery Tours: My Life with the Beatles* (co-written with Rosemary Kingsland), for instance, that "Paul did 'Besame Mucho' at Brian's insistence. He muttered that it was a silly ballad. 'We should have just done our own stuff,' he said."

Remarked Mike Smith on the *Best of the Beatles* DVD, "Some of the songs, they were really strange choices. The ones that I remembered had to be 'Sheik of Araby' and 'Three Cool Cats.' It may well be that I remember them because they were just sort of totally foreign to everything that they did afterwards. I may have interpreted it wrongly, but my take on auditions at that time was, you let the people do what they want to do. Because that's what they think represents them in the best possible light. And as it transpired, it wasn't the case. They weren't playing the songs that they thought portrayed themselves in their best light. They were probably very pissed off at having to do—well, I certainly would have been—at some of the stuff that they had to do."

In actual fact, however, the 15 songs performed for Decca are a fairly well-rounded sample of the material the Beatles were doing at the end of 1961, and on the whole pretty accurately reflect their tastes and eclecticism. There seems little question that the group, and particularly Lennon and McCartney, would be eager to present the best of their original material. They didn't play more original songs, most likely, because their live set was still almost wholly devoted to covers, and because they didn't have a whole lot of songs that would have impressed major label A&R men, with even most of the compositions they cut for EMI in 1962 and 1963 having yet to be written. As for the covers, it's simply absurd to suggest that any of them, aside from perhaps "September in the Rain," were done under duress. Not only did the Beatles actually record "Money" and "Till There Was You" again in 1963 for their second album, but they also later did "To Know Her Is to Love Her," "Memphis, Tennessee," "Sure to Fall," "Crying Waiting, Hoping," "Besame Mucho," and "Three Cool Cats" for the BBC (though their January 1963 and July 1963 BBC versions of "Three Cool Cats" weren't broadcast and, sadly, no tapes of those versions survive). They also did "Besame Mucho" and "To Know Her Is to Love Her" on their December 1962 Hamburg tapes. Certainly they wouldn't have revisited them if they had any dislike for the material.

What's more, they did one of the less rock-oriented songs, "Besame Mucho," again at their EMI audition for George Martin in June 1962, indicating that either Epstein was still pushing for them to play standards or (far more likely) that the Beatles really enjoyed doing the number. If the group was truly resolved not to let Epstein pressure them into playing prewar pop standards like "September in the Rain" at future auditions, it's odd indeed that the list of songs Brian sent to Martin shortly before their EMI session (as suggestions for what he should hear) included not just "Besame Mucho," but also numbers like "Over the Rainbow" and Fats Waller's "Your Feet's Too Big" (both to be sung by Paul), and—again—"September in the Rain," "Sheik of Araby," and "Take Good Care of My

Baby." In fact, this list (numbering 33 tunes in all) contained no less than ten of the same songs that had already been auditioned at Decca, with "Three Cool Cats," "Till There Was You," "To Know Her Is to Love Her," "Memphis, Tennessee," and all three Lennon-McCartney songs also reappearing. It wasn't a substantially different setlist than what had been played at Decca, though it was much longer. Either there was some major miscommunication going on between Epstein and the band, or, as seems evident, the more pop-inclined material was genuinely a part of their repertoire and influences, though just one part.

In truth, the majority of the Decca audition was devoted to the pure and hard American rock 'n' roll the Beatles loved most, from both the black and white spectrums. There was early Motown ("Money"), the black vocal group sound of the Coasters, rockabilly (Carl Perkins and Buddy Holly), Chuck Berry, and even Phil Spectorized doo wop ("To Know Her Is to Love Her"). Plus there were a few of their own compositions, a privilege that many of the managers of the time would have denied their clients of playing at an audition for one of the biggest record labels in the country. Decca did not turn down the Beatles because the material it heard was misleading or unrepresentative of the band. The company turned them down, rightly or wrongly, because it didn't like how they played it.

There's also the matter of whether it was really that big a disaster, for either Decca or the Beatles, that they didn't pass the audition. Ironically, Decca would sign the second biggest British '60s rock band the following year, after a chance spring 1963 meeting between George Harrison and Dick Rowe when they were judges at a talent competition in Liverpool. Harrison, according to Rowe, admitted that Decca was right to have turned the Beatles down, and that they hadn't played that well at the audition. (Of course, Harrison no doubt felt better about it now that the Beatles had already started to sell massive amounts of singles and albums for EMI.) George told the A&R man that he should check out a new London band that Harrison had just seen, the Rolling Stones—whom Decca quickly signed. Decca continued to sell loads of records throughout the 1960s, often by the very sort of rock groups they'd prophesized were on their way out when they turned down the Beatles. There's even been some speculation that the label overcompensated for its missed opportunity to nab the Beatles by signing as many bands as it could, many of whom wouldn't pan out or make the slightest impression on the charts (though Decca still managed to turn down Manfred Mann and the Yardbirds shortly after the Beatles rose to stardom).

As for the Beatles, as heartbroken as they must have been when the word came down from Decca in February 1962, was it really that bad a thing in the long run? Had they done the deal, they'd have been recording with drummer Pete Best, unless Decca, like George Martin a bit later, planned to replace him on recording dates with a session man. That would not only have been a musical liability, but it might have been harder to replace Best with the more talented and personally compatible Ringo Starr if the band had already started to release records. Plus the group wouldn't have had as much original material ready for release, and what material they had wouldn't have been nearly as good as what they were coming up with within a year. It's also often overlooked that the Beatles really weren't as good in January 1962 as they were even six months later, and certainly a year later. There's truly an enormous distance between the Decca tapes and their first album, *Please Please Me,* which, like the Decca audition, was (with the exception of four songs) recorded in a single day, in February 1963. Simply put, they were writing, singing, and playing a lot better (and with the right drummer) by the time they made their first big hit records, and benefited enormously from the wait, as brief and enforced as it was.

And, most importantly, they would not have been working with George Martin—probably the best producer imaginable for the Beatles, not only in 1962, but from 1962 until the band split up in 1970. Had they been on Decca, it's easy to imagine that they might have been paired with an unsympathetic or unimaginative production team that could have forced them to record inappropriate material, not allowed them to record their own songs, or simply not gotten the best out of them in the studio. For all the regret he subsequently expressed over rejecting the group, Mike Smith was probably not the man to be in charge, given that he actually told the Beatles fan magazine *The Beatles Book* that Pete Best "was a better drummer than Ringo." (This in turn illustrated his assertion in *Drummed Out! The Sacking of Pete Best* that "I don't think I could have worked with them the way that George Martin did—I would have got involved in their bad parts and not encouraged the good ones.") Had any or all of this been the case, it's easy to imagine the Beatles failing to make much of a commercial impact with Decca, and to even envision the band breaking up in discouragement before their art had truly been allowed to bloom.

When the Beatles were rejected by Decca they must have felt it was the worst thing that could have possibly happened to them. But time proved that it was one of the *best* breaks they ever got.

● March 7

BBC Session

Teenager's Turn (Here We Go) program
(broadcast March 8, 1962)
Playhouse Theatre, Manchester

Memphis, Tennessee
Dream Baby (How Long Must I Dream)
Please Mr. Postman

Although the failure to get a Decca contract had been a big setback, in fact the Beatles did continue to make some progress in advancing their prospects in the next few months, even in the absence of a label deal. Just six weeks or so after the Decca audition, Epstein arranged for them to audition for BBC radio in Manchester. They passed their February 12 audition, swiftly getting booked for the *Teenager's Turn* program, recorded live in Manchester on March 7 and broadcast the following day. Certainly it was no small deal for the Beatles themselves. Not only did they make their first stage appearance in suits on this date, but Pete Best recalled (in *The Beatles: The True Beginnings*) that he and some of the other lads in the group whooped it up to the max when they heard themselves on the radio, for the first time, the following day.

The importance of BBC radio performances in the early- to mid-'60s both for rock 'n' roll musicians and rock 'n' roll fans, cannot be overstated. Airplay for music in general, and rock 'n' roll in particular, was surprisingly scarce in Britain. American teenagers, even then, were accustomed to being able to hear rock 'n' roll on the radio pretty much around-the-clock, usually on more than one station. The UK, by contrast, had just three national BBC stations handling *all* radio program-

ming, not just music. Pop music was parceled out in small doses on just one of those networks, the Light Programme. There were just a few hours of rock 'n' roll records to be heard on the BBC each week, leading many British teenagers to brave the static-clouded nighttime signal of Radio Luxembourg to find more of what they wanted on the airwaves.

Fortunately, the BBC *did* program some live music, even by unsigned acts such as the Beatles. It's a measure of just how bureaucratic this government institution was that Epstein had to fill out a three-page application for the audition, upon which producer Peter Pilbeam wrote his comments after hearing the group. The four songs they played at the audition, as it happened, had all been done for Decca back on January 1 as well: "Like Dreamers Do," "Hello Little Girl," "Memphis, Tennessee," and "Till There Was You." Pilbeam, oddly, gave Paul McCartney's vocals a "no" and John Lennon's a "yes" in his terse evaluation, adding, "an unusual group, not as 'Rocky' as most, more C&W with a tendency to play music." Remembered Pilbeam on the 1982 *Beatles at the Beeb* ("the Beeb" is a colloquialism for the BBC in Britain) radio special, "That was in those days high praise indeed, because there was a hell of a lot of noise came out of most of the three guitars and drum group(s). There was a load of rubbish, masses of rubbish. They [the Beatles] impressed me at the time."

The inclusion of "Like Dreamers Do" and "Hello Little Girl" at the audition indicated that even then, the Beatles were turning their focus and priorities to developing and exposing their own material. However, the three songs that did make it onto their maiden BBC broadcast were all covers, two of which they'd never put on their official releases, and one of which is the only surviving version by the group. Unfortunately, the tape of this broadcast is of low, though not unlistenable, quality. Like quite a few tapes of their subsequent BBC spots in 1962 and 1963, it was almost certainly made off the radio, not by taping directly from the stereo signal as we do these days, but by putting a portable reel-to-reel next to a radio speaker.

That's probably why nothing from the session appears on the two-CD *Live at the BBC* compilation. That's a shame, as the set was not only an historic occasion, but also pretty musically enjoyable. Performing before a live audience, the Beatles sound considerably more confident and at ease than they did a couple of months previously at Decca. Pete Best's drums also are in better fettle, though they still have more of a thud and less imagination than Ringo's. Too, there's such a swell of approval from the crowd (particularly at the beginning of "Dream Baby") that it's hard to believe the group had yet to release a record.

Certainly the most interesting of the three songs is the only one unavailable in any other Beatles version, Roy Orbison's "Dream Baby (How Long Must I Dream)," sung by McCartney. Here again Paul's overt debt to Elvis Presley's style in his early vocals is perhaps overevident. But the arrangement's got a nice swing, and good backup harmonies that differ from the Orbison original, as well as the kind of dramatic guitar flourish at the end that George Harrison would employ on other covers (like Carl Perkins's "Everybody's Trying to Be My Baby," on *Beatles for Sale*). It's also evidence, incidentally, of how quick the Beatles could be to pick up on great new records and incorporate them into their repertoire; Orbison's single, which was on its way to No. 2 in the UK, had only been released in February. The Beatles would get their chance to see Roy himself do the song up-close-and-personal sooner than they expected, when they shared the bill with Orbison on their third British tour in the spring of 1963.

The Beatles at the BBC

Between March 1962 and May 1965, the Beatles recorded an incredible 53 radio programs for the BBC. As in so many aspects of the group's career, the sheer numbers in and of themselves are staggering. There were 275 recordings broadcast of 88 different songs, 36 of which the group never put on their official releases (though all but one of those 36 were covers, not originals). The exposure was particularly intense in 1963, which yielded an astonishing 40 sessions, the bulk of the band's BBC output. Especially considering the aforementioned scarce airtime for pop music on British radio, it's no exaggeration to note that their 1963 broadcasts in particular were absolutely crucial to solidifying their enormous popularity on home soil. Overwhelmed by other commitments and priorities as Beatlemania became global, however, they cut back and then ceased their BBC sessions, though they did manage to fit in a few more before their final spot on May 26, 1965.

Yet the Beatles recordings for the Beeb are ultimately most significant for supplying the most valuable and pleasurable portion of their unreleased body of work. The most interest, of course, has focused on those 36 songs they did not release while active, and for those alone, their BBC material would be essential. The covers testify to their masterful assimilation of such early rock 'n' roll giants as Little Richard, Elvis Presley, Chuck Berry, and Buddy Holly; the newly emergent early-'60s soul of Motown; the Brill Building pop of the great girl groups; and, on the most obscure selections, their nose for finding underappreciated rarities such as Chan Romero's "The Hippy Hippy Shake," Mario Marini's "The Honeymoon Song," and the Jodimars' "Clarabella." Every cover they released through mid-1965 was done on the BBC once or more, too, with the exception of "Bad Boy" and "Act Naturally." There were also BBC versions of many Lennon-McCartney originals—*all* of the originals from their first album and both sides of their first eight singles, in fact, as well as highlights from their other albums through *Help!*, although the post–*Please Please Me* LP-only originals are rather lightly represented. Unfortunately they did *not* take the opportunity to play any Lennon-McCartney songs that the group never officially released, with the one notable exception of their quite nice April 1963 BBC rendition of "I'll Be on My Way," which they'd already "given away" to Billy J. Kramer & the Dakotas, who put it on a 1963 B-side.

The BBC tapes also provide a chance to hear the Beatles working in a live, or at least live-in-the-studio, environment with far greater sound quality than could be attained with most recordings of actual Beatlemania-era concerts. Much of their ingratiating personality also comes over in the between-song banter, which though sometimes corny does contain its share of funny (and occasionally riotous) humor. The abundance of multiple versions—16 alone, for instance, of "From Me to You"—can tax the patience of non-Beatlemaniacs. Still, the radio renditions of even extremely familiar early Beatles songs often contain notable differences in the arrangements, as well as exhibiting a spontaneity not possible in a conventional recording studio setting.

The technological conditions under which the sessions were recorded were in some respects markedly inferior to the ones the Beatles enjoyed when recording for EMI at Abbey Road. The limited time available for taping meant that there was not nearly as much of an opportunity for multiple retakes (and, of course, *no* such opportunity for the several broadcasts transmitted live) and sound balancing. No multitracking was possible, the group essentially getting captured live-in-the-studio in mono. Even when the band was able to take advantage of overdubbing on their latter sessions only primitive embellishments could be made, BBC producer Bernie Andrews explaining in Kevin Howlett's *The Beatles at the BBC,* "We'd record one complete track including the whole band with one vocal and then we'd play the tape again, and, as we were recording onto another mono tape machine, we'd add another vocal." Yet the fidelity was basically clear and up to studio standards. And despite—and perhaps to a certain degree because—of these restrictions, there are certain features of the early Beatles' sound that come across particularly well on the sessions, sometimes more fully revealing idiosyncrasies not often heard on the official EMI recordings.

For example, Paul McCartney was able to showcase his dirtiest, rowdiest high rock 'n' roll vocals to a greater degree than he did on Beatles releases, not only on early versions of "Long Tall Sally" and "Kansas City," but also on a number of songs never committed to record by the group ("Clarabella," "The Hippy Hippy Shake," "Lucille," and "Ooh! My Soul" especially). McCartney's powerful, imaginative basslines are, unbelievably enough, sometimes better appreciated on the BBC recordings than the EMI counterparts. That's particularly the case on Beeb cuts where his instrument gets placed high in the mix (listen to the June 24, 1963, version of "Roll Over Beethoven" for one example).

George Harrison's contributions to the BBC sessions are particularly intriguing, in part because he didn't get to sing lead too much on the early Beatles records, particularly as Lennon and McCartney were singing and writing almost all of the original material. George had taken a higher percentage of the vocal chores onstage in the Cavern days, and got a little more exposure in that role on the radio, taking lead on more than a half dozen tunes that were not cut for EMI. The strongly Carl Perkins–informed rockabilly base of his guitar style also gets a greater airing, in part because the BBC repertoire drew more heavily from outside material than the band's official releases did. On the covers, and often even on Lennon-McCartney tunes, his playing is usually rawer, not only deviating from the solos on the "official" versions, but also often differing from version to version of the same song. Sometimes that leads to sloppiness, but often it also yields exhilarating jagged edges that can even verge on angry semidissonance that will surprise many listeners more accustomed to his slicker studio work. Finally, Ringo Starr doesn't get to sing much, but his underrated drumming is truly thrilling on the BBC tracks. He generates the great splash of sound that did much to give the band its unstoppable thrust, punctuated by inventive fills and a brilliant sense of altering his attack to just what each specific song needs.

The BBC saw so little in the future historical value of these programs that, amazingly, just five songs from their February 28, 1964, session and six from their November 26, 1964, session were actually kept in the main BBC Sound Archive. Had there not been transcription discs of some shows sent out to other radio outlets for broadcast, some of the other sessions might not have survived in good fidelity in any form. And, had there not been—even in 1962 and 1963—some fans making both lo-fi and (relatively) hi-fi recordings off the radio, some of the sessions would not survive in any form whatsoever. (Nor would the official *Live at the BBC* compilation, most of which was taken from privately recorded broadcasts, even exist.) Even so, no tapes whatsoever of four early sessions have been found, and various fragments of numerous others remain unrepresented even on bootleg. Fortunately, the substantial majority of the Beatles' BBC performances have been preserved, by some means or another, in good-to-excellent fidelity. Almost *all* of the Beatles' BBC broadcasts survive in some form, albeit sometimes (especially in the earlier broadcasts) via the crude "portable tape recorder next to a radio speaker" method.

It wasn't until rock music bootlegging took off in the early '70s, however, that most fans (particularly in America, where the sessions were never broadcast and knowledge of their very existence was uncommon) got the chance to hear any of the tracks. For all its tinny quality—probably taken from off-line recordings with machines pressed up to the radio speaker—the first of these, *Yellow Matter Custard,* was manna from heaven for Beatle lovers looking for previously unsuspected material when it came out in August 1971. Entirely comprised of covers from 1963 sessions, none of the 14 songs save one had also been recorded for EMI. Information surrounding the BBC recordings was so scarce that for years it was mistakenly reported—probably, in part, because the sound and material seemed so rooted in the Beatles' early rock 'n' roll influences—that the tracks dated from 1962. For that matter, knowledge of the original versions was so scarce that *Yellow Matter Custard* amusingly mistitled many of the songs, "The Honeymoon Song" becoming "Bound By Love"; "So How Come (No One Loves Me)" changed to "Everyone Wants Someone"; and "Crying, Waiting, Hoping" mutating to "Trying, Waiting, Hoping."

Only dribs and drabs of other BBC bits leaked out over the next few years. But the sudden appearance of an 18-track compilation with fabulous sound quality in 1980, *The Beatles Broadcasts,* raised hopes that more precious hi-fi material existed than had ever been realized, especially as it had such then-exotic gems as "Carol," "Soldier of Love," "Lend Me Your Comb," "Clarabella," "The Hippy Hippy Shake," and "I Got a Woman." The BBC itself fueled hunger for the airshots with its 1982 radio special *The Beatles at the Beeb.* Broadcast throughout the UK and US, it featured some of the best and most unusual material from the sessions, along with commentary from BBC producers and radio announcers who'd worked on the actual recordings.

No official BBC compilation was forthcoming, however, and between late 1986 and late 1988, the floodgates really burst open with the 13-volume vinyl bootleg series *The Beatles at the Beeb.* Not only did it contain numerous previously unbootlegged tracks, but it also presented numerous previously circulating recordings in much improved fidelity. There were even thorough and informed (if a bit overenthusiastic) liner notes, plus handsome sleeves with top-grade vintage pictures of the group, some of them paying witty homages to designs used on actual Beatles LP releases. As the CD era ramped up shortly afterward, the ball was picked up by several companies that produced ever-bigger, ever-more-thorough multidisc *Beatles at the Beeb* box sets that aimed to collate every track, every multiple version, all the chatter—every little thing, as the Beatles themselves once sang. The eventual official release of the cream of the crop was almost certainly due, at least in part, to the fairly ready availability of so much of it on so many bootlegs, which did more than anything else to keep knowledge of the BBC sessions alive.

The 1994 two-CD Apple compilation *Live at the BBC* finally made some of the material officially available (along with some of the between-

song banter), and did concentrate on the most desirable existing recordings, particularly those songs that hadn't previously made it onto official releases. (One such song, "Lend Me Your Comb," was inexplicably omitted, but did appear in 1995 on *Anthology 1.*) Some intense Beatles fans, by the way, feel that Apple's sonic restoration job on some of the material left something to be desired, and insist that the best existing circulating bootleg versions of some of the tracks are superior, though the average listener will not notice much or any difference. Some fans, too, did not appreciate the nonchronological sequencing, and as Allan Kozinn pointed out in *The New York Times,* "a third disc—hardly unheard of for this kind of release—would have allowed the inclusion of one version of every song the band played on the BBC."

The remainder of the BBC sessions—and there are many of them—have still not come out. Those include, most notably, five of the cover songs that did not appear on their official releases: Roy Orbison's "Dream Baby (How Long Must I Dream)," Joe Brown's "A Picture of You," Chuck Berry's "I'm Talking About You," and the standards "Besame Mucho" and "Beautiful Dreamer." (These particular five, perhaps understandably, have not been issued primarily because the fidelity on the best surviving tapes is somewhat-to-very substandard.) Yet they also include numerous full-fidelity versions of songs that have appeared as EMI studio recordings, along with additional versions of some of the non-EMI songs done for the radio network. There's enough, when all existing BBC sessions (released or not) are combined, to fill up a ten-CD box set. Admittedly this is way too much for the average fan to bear, but if you're reading this, you're probably not the average fan. Hearing them grouped together in such a box set, in sequence, does give you a good idea of how their BBC music evolved, as well as reflecting to some degree their greater overall evolution between 1962 and 1965. Whether you collect all or some of them, however, the Beatles' BBC sessions—whether they've been issued or

The inner label of the Beatles Broadcasts *LP, like many bootlegs of the group's BBC sessions, was printed to look as if it were an official BBC transcription disc.*

not—are essential listening for serious fans of the group, hiccups in sound quality and repetition of numerous songs notwithstanding.

Songs Performed by the Beatles on the BBC, 1962–1965

Covers never issued by the Beatles on their official 1960s releases

(Parentheses contain the number of versions performed by the Beatles on the BBC, and the performers of the versions upon which they were modeled.)

***

*** "Beautiful Dreamer" (one version; model for Beatles cover unknown)

*** "Besame Mucho" (one version; the Coasters)

* "Carol" (one version; Chuck Berry)

* "Clarabella" (one version; the Jodimars)

* "Crying, Waiting, Hoping" (one version; Buddy Holly)

* "Don't Ever Change" (one version; the Crickets)

*** "Dream Baby" (How Long Must I Dream) (one version; Roy Orbison)

* "Glad All Over" (two versions; Carl Perkins)

* "The Hippy Hippy Shake" (five versions; Chan Romero)

* "I Forgot to Remember to Forget" (one version; Elvis Presley)

* "I Got a Woman" (two versions; Elvis Presley)

* "I Got to Find My Baby" (two versions; Chuck Berry)

* "I Just Don't Understand" (one version; Ann-Margret)

* "I'm Gonna Sit Right Down and Cry" (Over You) (one version; Elvis Presley)

*** "I'm Talking about You" (one version; Chuck Berry)

* "Johnny B. Goode" (one version; Chuck Berry)

* "Keep Your Hands Off My Baby" (one version; Little Eva)

** "Lend Me Your Comb (one version; Carl Perkins)

* "Lonesome Tears in My Eyes" (one version; the Johnny Burnette Trio)

* "Lucille" (two versions; Little Richard)

* "Memphis, Tennessee" (five versions; Chuck Berry)

* "Nothin' Shakin'" (one version; Eddie Fontaine)

* "Ooh! My Soul" (one version; Little Richard)

*** "A Picture of You" (one version; Joe Brown)

* "A Shot of Rhythm and Blues" (three versions; Arthur Alexander)

* "So How Come" (No One Loves Me) (one version; the Everly Brothers)

* "Soldier of Love" (one version; Arthur Alexander)

* "Some Other Guy" (three versions; Richie Barrett)

* "Sure to Fall (in Love with You)" (four versions; Carl Perkins)

* "Sweet Little Sixteen" (one version; Chuck Berry)

* "That's All Right (Mama)" (one version; Elvis Presley)

* "To Know Her Is to Love Her" (one version; the Teddy Bears)

* "Too Much Monkey Business" (four versions; Chuck Berry)

* "Young Blood" (one version; the Coasters)

> *one BBC version officially issued in 1994 on* Live at the BBC
>
> **one BBC version officially issued in 1995 on* Anthology 1
>
> ***no BBC version ever officially issued*

Covers also issued by the Beatles on their official 1960s releases

(Parentheses contain the number of versions performed by the Beatles on the BBC, and the performers of the versions upon which they were modeled.)

***

*** "Anna (Go to Him)" (two versions; Arthur Alexander)

* "Baby It's You" (two versions; the Shirelles)

** "Boys" (seven versions; the Shirelles)

*** "Chains" (four versions; the Cookies)

** "Devil in Her Heart" (two versions; the Donays)

* "Dizzy Miss Lizzy" (one version; Larry Williams)

* "Everybody's Trying to Be My Baby" (four versions; Carl Perkins)

* "Honey Don't" (four versions; Carl Perkins)

* "Kansas City/Hey! Hey! Hey! Hey!" (three versions; Little Richard)

* "Long Tall Sally" (seven versions; Little Richard)

* "Matchbox" (two versions; Carl Perkins)

*** "Money" (That's What I Want) (six versions; Barrett Strong)

*** "Please Mister Postman" (three versions; the Marvelettes)

* "Rock and Roll Music" (one version; Chuck Berry)

* "Roll Over Beethoven" (seven versions; Chuck Berry)

* "Slow Down" (one version; Larry Williams)

* "A Taste of Honey" (seven versions; Lenny Welch)

* "Till There Was You" (eight versions; Peggy Lee)

*** "Twist and Shout" (ten versions; the Isley Brothers)

*** "Words of Love" (one version; Buddy Holly)

* "You Really Got a Hold on Me" (four versions; the Miracles)

> *one BBC version officially issued in 1994 on* Live at the BBC
>
> **one BBC version officially issued in 1995 on the* Baby It's You *CD-EP*
>
> ***no BBC version ever officially issued*

Lennon-McCartney originals:

(Parentheses contain the number of versions performed by the Beatles on the BBC.)

***

* "All My Loving" (four versions)

*** "And I Love Her" (one version)

*** "Ask Me Why" (four versions)

* "Can't Buy Me Love" (three versions)

*** "Do You Want to Know a Secret" (six versions)

*** "From Me to You" (16 versions)

* "A Hard Day's Night" (two versions)

*** "I Call Your Name" (one version)

* "I Feel Fine" (one version)

* "I Saw Her Standing There" (11 versions)

*** "I Should Have Known Better" (two versions)

* "I Wanna Be Your Man" (two versions)

*** "I Want to Hold Your Hand" (three versions)

*+ "I'll Be on My Way" (one version)

** "I'll Follow the Sun" (one version)

*** "I'll Get You" (five versions)

* "I'm a Loser" (two versions)

***v"I'm Happy Just to Dance with You" (one version)

*** "If I Fell" (two versions)

* "Love Me Do" (nine versions)

*** "Misery" (seven versions)

*** "The Night Before" (one before)

*** "Please Please Me" (12 versions)

*** "P.S. I Love You" (three versions)

*** "She Loves You" (ten versions)

* "She's a Woman" (two versions)

* "Thank You Girl" (three versions)

*** "There's a Place" (three versions)

* "Things We Said Today" (two versions)

*** "This Boy" (two versions)

* "Ticket to Ride" (one version)

*** "You Can't Do That" (four versions)

    *one BBC version officially issued in 1994 on Live at the BBC

    **one BBC version officially issued in 1995 on the Baby It's You CD-EP

    ***no BBC version ever officially issued

    +only Lennon-McCartney original performed on the BBC not released by the Beatles in the 1960s

Miscellaneous Jingles/Oddities

** "Beatles Crimble Medley" (half-minute medley of the A-sides of the Beatles' first five singles, done to the tune of Duane Eddy's "Shazam")

* "From Us to You" (five versions, one instrumental; "From Me to You" altered for use as theme song for special BBC programs featuring the Beatles)

** "Happy Birthday Saturday Club" (half-minute "Happy Birthday" jingle, lyrics changed to refer to BBC's *Saturday Club* program)

** "Pop Go the Beatles" (minute-long instrumental theme of the Beatles' 1963 BBC radio series *Pop Go the Beatles*, done to tune of "Pop Goes the Weasel")

** "Side by Side" (two versions; theme song of BBC radio series *Side by Side*, performed by the Karl Denver Trio with harmony vocals by the Beatles)

** "Tie Me Kangaroo Down, Sport" (performed by Rolf Harris, with backup vocals by the Beatles on the choruses)

** "Whit Monday to You" (sung a cappella to tune of "Happy Birthday")

    *one BBC version officially issued in 1994 on *Live at the BBC*

    **no BBC version ever officially issued

Finally, of the occasional songs recorded for programs but not broadcast, two were covers never done by the Beatles for EMI: "Sheila," originally by Tommy Roe, and "Three Cool Cats" (recorded for the BBC *twice* without being transmitted), originally by the Coasters.

Less interesting, but still worthwhile, was their cover of the Marvelettes' "Please Mr. Postman," which had come out just a few months earlier (and, unbelievably, was not a hit in Britain, though it went to No. 1 in America). The Beatles would record it for their second album more than a year later, and this first surviving version isn't much different in its arrangement, save for Best's less subtle drums and a "cold" (unfaded) ending which they wrap up with a burst of doo wop harmonies not heard on the *With the Beatles* track. There's also "Memphis, Tennessee," never the best of the group's Chuck Berry covers, where Best's beat is really heavy, though it's a more assured pass through the tune than the Decca take. (The Rolling Stones, for what it's worth, did a considerably snazzier job with the song when they did it for the BBC in February 1964, though like the Beatles they never put it on a studio release.)

Yet this session might be most significant as the inauguration of a lengthy association between the Beatles and the BBC over the next three years. Not only did it considerably boost the listenership of both the group and the radio network, but it also yielded an incredible wealth of unreleased material—recordings that, arguably, are more enjoyable than anything else in the whole of the unreleased Beatles canon.

● June 6

Studio Outtakes

Studio Two, Abbey Road, London

---

*Besame Mucho

*Love Me Do

    *appears on Anthology 1

For many years, the standard historical record of the Beatles' audition for EMI was straightforward: George Martin heard demos of the group, scheduled an audition, the Beatles showed up, the Beatles passed, the Beatles were signed, and the Beatles came back to record their first single a few months later. About a quarter-century down the line, however,

the discovery of a recording contract dated June 4, 1962, began to cast doubts as to whether it all happened that smoothly. It might have been an audition; it might have been a recording test; it might even have been a genuine recording session, for a possible first single. There's even confusion about whether George Martin really did schedule the audition promptly after Brian Epstein played him some demos; while the first Martin-Epstein meeting was first thought to have taken place in May 1962, Beatles authority Mark Lewisohn determined (in *The Complete Beatles Chronicle*) that this initial meeting had actually been in February.

It's unsurprising that there's also some confusion as to what the Beatles played and what they recorded at the audition, with Pete Best still in the drum seat. Lewisohn has reported that four numbers were taped: "Besame Mucho" and the Lennon-McCartney originals "Love Me Do," "P.S. I Love You," and "Ask Me Why." It's also been claimed more than once that they at least played Fats Waller's "Your Feet's Too Big," whether or not it was recorded. That might be dismissed as an unlikely rumor but for the comment of George Harrison himself, in *The Beatles Anthology,* that "we did 'Love Me Do,' 'P.S. I Love You,' 'Ask Me Why,' 'Besame Mucho,' and 'Your Feet's Too Big,' among others." But it's certainly probable that the Beatles played some material at the session that wasn't actually recorded, particularly if it was an audition. Brian Epstein, as previously noted, had, after all, suggested a whopping 33 songs (including, as it happens, "Your Feet's Too Big") for consideration on the list he sent George Martin (for the full list, see sidebar). Martin certainly wouldn't have wanted to hear all 33 of them, and in fact he wasn't even present for much of the session, which was largely delegated to fellow Parlophone producer Ron Richards. But at least a few other songs were probably played, with or without the tape recorder running. (The Beatles did, incidentally, manage to lay down a version of "Your Feet's Too Big" for posterity six months later, as part of the tapes of their live Hamburg performances in late December.)

Assuming that just the four numbers were taped, none of them were issued at the time, though later in 1962 the Beatles would cut "Love Me Do" and "P.S. I Love You" as the A- and B-sides, respectively, of their first single, and "Ask Me Why" as the flip side of their second 45.

The June 1962 EMI Audition

As noted in the main text, the Beatles almost certainly did not perform the entire list of 33 songs that Brian Epstein had suggested George Martin lend an ear to at their June 1962 EMI audition. The list makes for fascinating insight, however, into not only the material the Beatles were playing at the time, but also the material that Epstein thought might impress Martin and EMI the most. He also divided it into separate song lists for Lennon, McCartney, and Harrison's lead vocals, complete with an "opening medley" that would give all three a chance to sing. The list follows, with the performers of the versions on which the covers were modeled noted in parentheses.

John Lennon song list:
"Ask Me Why" (Lennon-McCartney original)
"Hello Little Girl" (Lennon-McCartney original)
"Baby It's You" (the Shirelles)
"Please Mister Postman" (the Marvelettes)
"To Know Her Is to Love Her" (the Teddy Bears)
"You Don't Understand" (probably "I Just Don't Understand," Ann-Margret)
"Memphis, Tennessee" (Chuck Berry)
"Show [sic] of Rhythm 'n' Blues" (aka "A Shot of Rhythm and Blues," Arthur Alexander)
"Shimmy Like My Sister Kate" (based on the arrangement of this standard by the Olympics, who retitled it "Shimmy Like Kate")
"Lonesome Tears in My Eyes" (the Johnny Burnette Trio)

Paul McCartney song list:
"P.S. I Love You" (Lennon-McCartney original)
"Love Me Do" (Lennon-McCartney original)
"Like Dreamers Do" (Lennon-McCartney original)
"Love of the Loved" (Lennon-McCartney original)
"Pinwheel Twist" (Lennon-McCartney original)
"If You've Gotta Make a Fool of Somebody" (James Ray)
"Till There Was You" (Peggy Lee)
"Over the Rainbow" (Gene Vincent)
"Your Feet's Too Big" (Fats Waller)
"Hey! Baby" (Bruce Channel)
"Dream Baby (How Long Must I Dream)" (Roy Orbison)
"September in the Rain" (Dinah Washington)
"The Honeymoon Song" (Marino Marini)

George Harrison song list:
"A Picture of You" (Joe Brown)
"The Sheik of Araby" (Joe Brown)
"What a Crazy World We Live In" (aka "What a Crazy World We're Livin' In," Joe Brown)
"Three Cool Cats" (the Coasters)
"Dream" (Cliff Richard)
"Take Good Care of My Baby" (Bobby Vee)

Opening medley:
"Besame Mucho" (the Coasters, sung by Paul)
"Will You Love Me Tomorrow" (the Shirelles, sung by John)
"Open (Your Lovin' Arms)" (Buddy Knox, sung by George)

Some notes of interest:
• George is obviously considered the least crucial of the three Beatles' lead singers, with substantially less songs on which he features than either John or Paul.
• Just six of the songs ("Love Me Do," "P.S. I Love You," "Ask Me Why," "Baby It's You," "Please Mr. Postman," and "Till There Was You") would be placed on the Beatles' official EMI releases.
• Just seven of the songs are Lennon-McCartney originals, four of which the Beatles would not officially release, indicating that they were not as skilled or prolific composers at this point as they would blossom into by 1963.
• Ten of the songs were on their Decca audition tape, which as noted earlier indicates that the Brian Epstein–forced choice of material for that audition only is something of a semimyth.
• The only circulating versions of the Beatles performing six of the other songs ("A Shot of Rhythm and Blues," "I Just Don't Understand," "Lonesome Tears in My Eyes," "The Honeymoon Song," "Dream Baby (How Long Must I Dream)," and "A Picture of You") are found on BBC recordings.
• The only circulating versions of the Beatles performing two of the songs ("I Wish I Could Shimmy Like My Sister Kate" and "Your Feet's Too Big") are on their December 1962 Hamburg live tapes.
• This leaves just eight songs ("Over the Rainbow," "If You've Gotta Make a Fool of Somebody," "Pinwheel Twist," "Hey! Baby," "Dream," "What a Crazy World We're Livin' In," "Open (Your Lovin' Arms)," and "Will You Love Me Tomorrow") that don't circulate as by the Beatles in any form.
• One of the Lennon-McCartney songs, "Pinwheel Twist," has still never been heard on any circulating Beatles recording (further details on page 357).
• Although the Beatles rarely performed covers of songs by early British rock 'n' rollers, George is listed as doing four here, one by Cliff Richard, and three by Joe Brown—confirming that Brown was the most influential British performer for the Beatles, and Harrison specifically, by far.
• Here's more confirmation that the Beatles were quick to pick up on records they liked, as "Baby It's You," "Hey! Baby," and "What a Crazy World We're Livin' In" had only been out a few months, and "A Picture of You" had only entered the charts in mid-May 1962.

As a whole, the list is a pretty well-rounded indication of the Beatles' stylistic roots and influences, though perhaps, like the Decca tapes, it's a little more tilted toward pop than they would have liked. It is, however, just a list, and not an existing tape that we'll ever get to hear, unless someone's sitting on the secret of the century.

These early versions of "P.S. I Love You" and "Ask Me Why" have never circulated, although they (like all four of the tracks) were pressed onto 78rpm acetate discs. Yet "Besame Mucho" had escaped onto bootleg by the mid-1980s, and "Love Me Do" was discovered in time for inclusion on *Anthology 1*. If "P.S. I Love You" and "Ask Me Why" do ever surface, they'd make for fascinating contrast with the official versions done later in 1962, but at least "Besame Mucho" and "Love Me Do" are both now easily available on *Anthology 1*.

It's a meager slice to evaluate, but those two tracks do seem to indicate that the Beatles still weren't at all comfortable in a studio environment. Paul's vocal sounds downright nervous on "Love Me Do," where the tempo speeds up so much in the latter part of the song that it's hard to tell whether Pete Best is rushing the beat or it might even have *been* the original arrangement. Best acquits himself pretty poorly on that track, especially at the juncture when the song almost comes to a dead stop after the instrumental break, giving ammunition to George Martin's verdict that Pete wouldn't be good enough to play on recordings—which, in turn, helped speed Best's exit from the group as a whole. "Besame Mucho," oddly, is the least spirited of any of the Beatles' versions of the song, mostly due to their strange decision to excise the backup harmonies (and backup "cha-cha-boom!"s) that make the other renditions pretty fun.

Martin subsequently commented, on numerous occasions, that the Beatles were signed not so much for their music as for the strong positive impressions they had made with their personalities, humor, and charm. (George Harrison's oft-quoted crack "I don't like your tie!" in response to Martin's question as to whether there was anything the group didn't like, came from this session.) If they were able (Best excepted) to converse with and entertain at length the EMI honchos in charge of determining their future, that does indicate they were most likely less jumpy than they had been at their Decca audition five months earlier. What survives of the tapes also justifies Martin's initial, somewhat lukewarm reaction to their music. But he did have the wisdom to sign them nonetheless, and the music they made together at EMI would quickly become pretty darned special.

The Best Year

The Complete Recording of Pete Best and the Betles June 1961 to June 1962

Every released and unreleased track the Beatles recorded with Pete Best on drums is on this unusual compilation.

● June 11

BBC Session

Teenager's Turn (Here We Go) *program (broadcast June 15, 1962)*
Playhouse Theatre, Manchester

Ask Me Why
Besame Mucho
A Picture of You

Just five days after their EMI (probably) audition, the Beatles consolidated their gains on another front by making their second BBC appearance. Like the first, this was for the *Teenager's Turn (Here We Go)* program in Manchester; like the first, it was primitively recorded off the radio; and like the first, it's never been officially issued. Lo-fi as it is, it would be their last recording of any sort to feature Pete Best, who'd be replaced by Ringo Starr two months later.

Again, the Beatles sound more relaxed than they had at either the Decca or EMI auditions, no doubt buoyed by the presence of a coachload of Liverpool supporters that the group's fan club bused in especially for the occasion. They also had the chance to present one of their own compositions, "Ask Me Why," the first Lennon-McCartney song to be heard on the radio, performed here five months before it would be recorded for EMI. The arrangement for the tune—one of the most obscure Beatles B-sides—is pretty close to the studio version, with the notable exception of the use of Bigsby vibrato guitar, which has the unusual wavering quality associated with records by instrumental combos such as the Ventures and the Shadows.

As for the two covers, this is the third version of "Besame Mucho," and although it's just five days after they taped the song at EMI, the infectiously silly backup vocals are back in place on a quite respectably powerful charge through the tune. To beat a dead horse, though "Besame Mucho" is sometimes singled out as one of the songs the Beatles were performing under protest at their Decca audition, the inclusion of it in their second BBC session (not to mention the gusto with which they play it) seems to signify that it was a genuine staple of their repertoire.

The most exotic item from this show—and one of the most exotic from their entire cache of BBC recordings—is "A Picture of You," a wistful country-influenced number that had entered the UK charts for Joe Brown just a month before. It's particularly unusual for American listeners, as chances are they've never heard of either the song (which went to No. 2 in Britain) or Joe Brown, who never made the slightest commercial impression across the water. The group follows Brown's arrangement pretty closely, but adds something of their own personality with their typically well-executed backup harmonies, which are an improvement on the slightly corny female ones heard on Brown's hit single. George takes lead vocal for the first time on a Beatles BBC performance, and his rockabilly guitar lines are about as country-fried here as they'd ever get.

Perhaps the band had made sure to stock the front rows with their fan club, as a busload of fans had come to the theater from Liverpool in a trip arranged by the young Beatles Fan Club. The crowd reception for each number here is quite loud and ebullient, and Pete Best has also recalled that early Beatlemania-type mob scenes greeted the boys at each of the BBC dates he played with the group. Without underselling their

frustration and anxiety as they waited for word on their EMI audition, it's difficult to imagine that a group sounding this good on BBC radio, and exciting such audible fan adulation even at this stage, could have remained without a recording contract for too long, even if they had never come to the attention of George Martin. Even British television would soon take its first notice of the group, though by that time, the Beatles had a new drummer. . . .

● August 22

Live Performance

Cavern Club, Liverpool

Some Other Guy

Now with an EMI contract finally secured, a new drummer in place, and the recording session for their first single only two weeks away, late August was an exciting and tumultuous time for the Beatles. August 22 was especially so, as Granada Television filmed the group performing live in their most hallowed stomping ground, Liverpool's Cavern Club. It was only Ringo Starr's fourth performance as a member of the band, and there's been speculation that Pete Best was dismissed (on August 16) to ensure that the Beatles' first TV appearance was with the Ringo-backed lineup that would be recording discs. On top of all this, it was the day before John Lennon's wedding to his first wife, the newly pregnant Cynthia Powell—not that many people other than Paul McCartney, George Harrison, and Brian Epstein knew this (even Ringo was still in the dark).

It's from this date that the (tremendously exciting, by the way) first sound clip of the Beatles in performance, singing "Some Other Guy," originates. The footage has been screened and used in videos countless times, and the song can be seen and heard in full on the *Anthology* series. The audio track has long been circulating on bootleg, and it was naturally assumed that it must be a straightforward dub from the soundtrack of the August 22 film clip. Little in early unreleased Beatledom is simple, however, and it's now known that Granada TV returned to the Cavern on September 5 to make additional sound recordings. It's also apparent, even from watching the film clip, that the soundtrack isn't perfectly synced to the performance (and also apparent, incidentally, that both John and Paul appear to be singing, even though only John's vocal really comes through on the audio). Consequently, there's disagreement among researchers as to whether the two circulating live 1962 versions of "Some Other Guy" are from August 22, September 5, or both dates.

This writer will go with the supposition that there's one version from August 22 and one from September 5, the August 22 version signified by the opening announcement of "a midday session at the Cavern" (the only Cavern session on September 5 was in the evening). Whatever the case, though it's in semirough fidelity, there might be no other Beatles recording predating the release of "Please Please Me" that conveys as clearly just what the Liverpool and Hamburg audiences were responding to so strongly, even before the band had a record out. They sound hard and hungry, Lennon's lead vocal seething with energy, the band almost barely able to contain their jumpy, amphetamined forward thrust. Ringo seems to be fitting in with the group immediately, pummeling along with rollicking style (though his presence wasn't necessarily appreciated by everyone that day, as the ghostly male voice shouting, "We want Pete!" after the song makes clear). It's a shame, though, that most circulating copies are afflicted with a varispeed glitch at the end of the first verse—including the one heard on the soundtrack to the clip on the *Anthology* video.

Adding to its appeal among early Beatles collectors, "Some Other Guy"—a great Ray Charles–styled rocker by Richie Barrett that wasn't even too well known in the US (John Lennon referred to it as a "son of 'What'd I Say'"-styled song in a 1974 broadcast on WNEW-FM in New York)—never would appear on an official group release, studio or otherwise. They did, however, perform it three times on the BBC, the last of those versions coming out on *Live at the BBC*. And they'd record another, similar version for Granada TV just two weeks later—though there was the matter of their first proper recording session for EMI to take care of first, just a day before the television network returned to the Cavern. Obviously the song was a huge favorite of John Lennon's; interviewed by *Rolling Stone* a good six years later on September 17, 1968, he declared, "I'd like to make a record like 'Some Other Guy.' I haven't done one that satisfies me as much as that satisfied me."

It's little known, incidentally, that the dramatically ascending notes that open "Some Other Guy"—played on guitar by the Beatles, and electric keyboards on the Barrett original—influenced the brief opening instrumental section of a far more famous song written by John Lennon years later. For as John admitted when he introduced Barrett's single during his slot as a guest DJ on WNEW-FM in September 1974, "You'll notice the intro is slightly like 'Instant Karma.'" Also note how the final chord is very similar to the one the Beatles would use to cap off their arrangement of a far more famous cover they did, "Twist and Shout."

● September 4

Studio Outtake

"Love Me Do" single session
Studio Two, Abbey Road, London

---

*How Do You Do It

    **slightly edited version appears on* Anthology 1

For about 25 years after the event, an almost poetically perfect story of how the Beatles' first chart-topping single arose was accepted as gospel. George Martin, the story went, wanted the Beatles to record "How Do You Do It"—written by Mitch Murray, a songwriter from the British equivalent of Tin Pan Alley—as their second single. The Beatles hated the song. George Martin made them record it anyway. The Beatles, however, insisted they had something better, and played him something they'd written, "Please Please Me." Martin acceded to their will and recorded "Please Please Me"; it went to No. 1 in Britain; not only was the Beatles' judgment vindicated, but their ability to write their own material would never again be questioned. The story crumbled, however, when it was discovered, with the aid of unimpeachable EMI paperwork, that in fact Martin had wanted to release "How Do You Do It" as their *first* single. It was "Love Me Do" that the Beatles persuaded him to release instead. While that song did rise to No. 17 in the charts, that wasn't nearly as decisive a rebuttal as a No. 1 single would have been—especially considering that "How Do You Do It" *did* get to No. 1

when Martin produced it as Gerry & the Pacemakers' debut single just a few months later.

It's been said that the Beatles deliberately fouled up their recording of "How Do You Do It" to roadblock its release. As Paul McCartney said in Barry Miles's biography *Many Years from Now,* "We knew that peer pressure back in Liverpool would not allow us to do 'How Do You Do It.' We knew we couldn't hold our heads up with that sort of rock-a-pop-a-ballad. We would be spurned and cast into the wilderness." As new, unproven recording artists, however, they really weren't in the position to be so obstinate. They *did* learn the number at Martin's request in advance of their EMI session, even performing it (presumably for a very brief period) live. When they did record it, they didn't so much screw it up as sound uninspired, albeit deliberately so.

The studio-quality take escaped onto bootleg by the late '70s, and it's really not so bad. John (who sings lead) and Paul have obviously taken the time to work out characteristic dual vocal harmonies. The guitar solo, however, is another matter, and more than anything else on the track, Harrison's lackadaisical plucking seems to express their lack of interest in this sort of material. The Beatles' Merseyside rivals (and fellow Brian Epstein clients) Gerry & the Pacemakers attacked the song with far more energy, and gave it a bouncier, piano-oriented arrangement, eliminating the almost quizzical guitar licks on the Beatles' instrumental intro, as well as the half-hearted "ooh la la" responsive vocal lines in the bridge and the echoed handclapping in the instrumental break.

The real issue at hand was likely not solely the Beatles' genuine dislike of the song, but also their eagerness to record Lennon-McCartney originals on their singles rather than outside material. As "Love Me Do" was not nearly as strong a tune as "Please Please Me" (and ultimately not nearly as commercial), Martin does deserve credit for both going with Lennon-McCartney material on their first release, and sticking with the songwriting team for their second single, although "Love Me Do" had failed to become a huge smash. Martin did not attempt to supply tunes from outside sources to the group again, and "How Do You Do It" remains the only cover the Beatles recorded that had never been previously released by another artist.

The producer did say in *The Beatles Anthology* book that he "would still have issued 'How Do You Do It' had they not persuaded me to listen to another version of 'Please Please Me.'" It's not clear whether he meant he would have had them rerecord it, or would have actually issued the version already in the can (in which case there would have been little point in summoning them for the November 26 session at which they played him their reworked version of "Please Please Me"). A little more light on the subject was shed by Mitch Murray, who told Spencer Leigh in *Drummed Out! The Sacking of Pete Best,* "The Beatles recorded 'How Do You Do It' and I hated it. I felt that something had been screwed up, perhaps deliberately, although it is now very evocative of the early Beatles. I can't blame them because they were songwriters themselves and didn't want to do it, but it was a waste of a good song. I thought it was terrible, and fortunately, [publisher] Dick James agreed with me. He told George Martin that the Beatles had made a very good demo record. George took it very well and said that he was planning to redo it with the Beatles later on." Some other recent literature has suggested that Martin was considering or intending for the group to rerecord "How Do You Do It" for their second single at the November session, deciding against it when he heard their new, improved arrangement of "Please Please Me" and wisely decided to go with that instead.

Live at the Cavern, not long after Ringo Starr joined the Beatles.

"How Do You Do It" was actually scheduled for official release on a single by EMI (with the 1964 outtake "Leave My Kitten Alone" as the flip side) back in March 1983. That single got canceled, however, and the track wouldn't see the light of day until *Anthology 1,* where it was—for no good reason—edited so that one of the lines at the end ("I'd do it to you") was altered (to "but I haven't a clue"). The original version remains available on uncounted bootlegs. Not so easy to find, however, is the recording on the demo acetate from which the Beatles learned the tune, on which singer Barry Mason is backed by none other than the Dave Clark Five.

● **September 5**

Live Performance
Cavern Club, Liverpool

Some Other Guy
Kansas City/Hey! Hey! Hey! Hey!

The soundtrack of the August 22, 1962, filming of the Beatles in the Cavern hadn't come off too well. So Granada TV had sound technician Gordon Butler go back to the club on September 5 to make a higher-grade recording, with three microphones rather than one. From this recording, a complete version of "Some Other Guy"—similar, but not identical to, the one from August—has made it onto bootleg. The fidelity on this version's a little higher (though not remarkably so), and Ringo's drum fills seem a little more active, but otherwise there's not much difference. It's another exciting performance, though perhaps just a tad less lively than the one they'd played in August.

Also recorded that day was Little Richard's "Kansas City/Hey! Hey! Hey! Hey!" (which Paul introduces as having had a couple of requests for, their audiences still being small enough to make such intimacy possible), which the Beatles would eventually record for their fourth album, *Beatles for Sale.* A half-minute fragment or so popped up in the soundtrack to the *Anthology* video, though some of it's obscured by interviews with McCartney, Harrison, and Brian Epstein. Another pity, as it sounds like quite a strong rendition and the full version is known to exist. For Butler made five acetates containing it and "Some Other Guy," one of the copies eventually selling at a Christie's auction in August 1993 for £15,000. For all the effort Granada TV went to, however, the film was judged unsuitable for broadcast—but, luckily, not destroyed. It was retrieved for its premiere broadcast at the outset of Beatlemania in November 1963, and has been shown countless times since. The two versions of "Some Other Guy" and the fragment of "Kansas City/Hey! Hey! Hey! Hey!" captured by Granada remain the only live concert recordings of the Beatles at the Cavern that have yet circulated.

Epstein, incidentally, had some acetates made of one of the Cavern performances of "Some Other Guy," and it's been reported that they were even sold in his NEMS record shops. That would make it the first Beatles bootleg (even if it was instigated by their own manager), though as only a couple of them have turned up over the years, it seems doubtful that many or any actually made their way into stores. Even more intriguingly, Butler made a full hour-long recording of the Beatles on his September 5 visit—which, tragically, was apparently ordered to be disposed of and does not survive.

● September 11

Studio Outtake

"Love Me Do"/"P.S. I Love You" single session
Studio Two, Abbey Road, London

*Please Please Me
  *appears on Anthology 1

As a kind of adjunct to the story about the Beatles forcing George Martin to record "Please Please Me" instead of "How Do You Do It," it's often been written that Martin first heard the song at their first recording session. He found it lugubrious and advised them to work on it and make it faster, which they did. After they presented the reworked arrangement to him at their second session in November, it was promptly recorded, Martin declaring over the talkback speaker, "You've just made your first No. 1." This version is generally supported by comments made by the Beatles themselves, as early as their first surviving taped interview on October 27, 1962 (see entry below), where John Lennon says of the recording sessions for their first single, "We did record another song of our own when we were down there. But it wasn't finished enough. So, you know, we'll take it back next time and see how they like it then."

This early version of "Please Please Me" was unexpectedly dug up for *Anthology 1,* and while it doesn't sound quite finished, it doesn't sound quite as far from the hit version they'd record in November as we'd been led to believe. For one thing, it actually is about as fast as the arrangement used on the rerecording that made it onto their sophomore release. And it's really not that different from the rerecording, except for the notable absence of the Lennon harmonica that did so much to drive the hit single, a more tentative upswing on the ascending chords that follow the first part of the verse, the absence of backup harmonies during the bridge, and inappropriately busy drumming from session man Andy White. This is, incidentally, the only Beatles recording to feature White, other than the *Please Please Me* album version of "Love Me Do" (Ringo *does* play on the original single take, available on *Past Masters, Vol. 1*) and "Love Me Do"'s B-side, "P.S. I Love You," which were both done at this same session.

It sounds like it really wouldn't have taken that much more polish to get "Please Please Me" in releasable shape at this September 11 session, in which case it would have likely been the Beatles' debut release, rather than their second single. All's well that ends well, however—the Beatles and Martin did produce a better version the second time around, it did become their first chart-topping hit, and Ringo Starr did play on it, never to be replaced by a session drummer again on Beatles recording dates.

● October 25

BBC Session

Here We Go *program (broadcast October 26, 1962)*
Playhouse Theatre, Manchester

A Taste of Honey (fragment)

When the Beatles returned to Playhouse Theatre in Manchester for their third BBC session, there had been significant changes for the group since their second Beeb appearance just four months previously. Ringo Starr had replaced Pete Best on drums, and they now had a single to promote, released by Parlophone on October 5. Accordingly, two of the three songs for this BBC session were the A- and B-sides of that 45, although unfortunately recordings of these performances of "Love Me Do" and "P.S. I Love You" have not emerged. There *is,* however, a mediocre-fidelity 47-second end fragment of the third tune, "A Taste of Honey," done here three-and-a-half months prior to their recording of the song for their debut LP. It's not too different from the *Please Please Me* version—the move into double-time in the bridge is even already in place—save that Paul McCartney's lead vocal is more melodramatic and Presley-styled than it would be in the studio. (Note that there is no agreement about whether this recording was made from this BBC session or from a TV appearance on Granada's *People and Places* just four days later, on October 29.)

On occasion during the course of the Beatles' work for the BBC, recordings made for sessions would not be broadcast due to time restrictions. The song that got the axe for this program was, unfortunately, one of the most regrettable omissions: a cover, with George Harrison on lead vocals, of Tommy Roe's huge late-1962 single "Sheila," which had only entered the British charts six weeks before. It's regrettable because there is no surviving BBC Beatles recording of "Sheila," the only circulating version of the song by the group being the poorly recorded one from the December 1962 Hamburg tapes.

● October 27

Interview

Hulme Hall, Port Sunlight, Birkenhead

As stated at the outset of this volume, this book will not cover the many recordings of spoken-word interviews done with the Beatles between 1962 and 1970. An exception will be made, however, for one of the very most interesting of these—their very first surviving spoken-word interview, lasting just over seven minutes, done just three weeks after the release of "Love Me Do." This was taped for patients of the Cleaver and Clatterbridge hospitals, shortly before the Beatles did a show in Birkenhead near Liverpool, with Monty Lister, Malcolm Threadgill, and Peter Smethurst serving the questions. The interview was then broadcast on the closed-circuit radio station serving the two hospitals.

The Beatles would eventually master of the art of devising more in-depth, articulate responses than they give here. They were, after all, still in their early twenties, with virtually no prior such experiences from which to draw. Still, it's actually an above-average interview for its time, not only for its relatively abundant length, but also because the questions are reasonably intelligent, at least considering the inanities they had to put up with in a great deal of their pre-1967 media interviews. Also, much in the Beatles' individual personalities is already recognizable, though they seem to be taking things a little more seriously here than they would in the insane days of Beatlemania. Paul's the chattiest of the group, though each of the four have his turn.

Much of the conversation's spent establishing basic information (such as who plays what instrument) that's now long familiar the world over, but some less-traveled points are touched upon. McCartney briefly discusses their Germany "My Bonnie" single as the backing group to Tony Sheridan, saying that it actually made No. 5 on the German hit parade, though he adds dismissively, "it wasn't a very good record." Paul also, with surprising readiness, declares that "John is in fact the leader of the group," and claims that he and John have "written about over about a hundred songs. But we don't use half of them, you know." John, as noted in a previous entry, explains that they're in the process of polishing "Please Please Me" (without naming it by title) in hopes that it will be recorded for their second single. For the time being he was certainly excited enough that "Love Me Do" was out, quoting its catalog number (Parlophone R4949) by heart near the end of the chat.

The recording of the interview was officially issued in 1986 as a flexidisc in Mark Lewisohn's book *The Beatles Live*, and has subsequently shown up on a number of bootlegs. A mere 15-second sliver (part of McCartney's comments about "My Bonnie") showed up on *Anthology 1*, but the whole transcript can be viewed on-line on Radio Clatterbridge's website at http://www.radioclatterbridge.co.uk/pages/transcript.htm.

● Circa Late 1962

Rehearsal Tapes
Cavern Club, Liverpool

I Saw Her Standing There
One After 909 (two versions)
Catswalk (two versions)

Of all the 1962 recordings of the Beatles that didn't make the rounds until years later, this five-song rehearsal tape—made in the Cavern Club, without an audience—is by far the most mysterious. The principal mystery is when it was made. In *The 910's Guide to the Beatles' Outtakes: 2004 Edition,* Doug Sulpy makes the logical case that since it's been reported that Ringo has confirmed he's drumming on the tape, and since the arrangement of "I Saw Her Standing There" is much less worked out than it would be on the late-December 1962 Hamburg tapes, it most likely was done between mid-August 1962 (when Starr joined) and mid-December 1962 (when the Beatles left England for their final Hamburg stint). It's not entirely clear, either, *why* it was made. The fidelity is about what you'd expect from a fair portable tape machine in late 1962—listenable, but not great by any means. The performances are a bit rough, sometimes surprisingly sloppy, and the group doesn't quite maintain 100 percent seriousness throughout "I Saw Her Standing There."

An educated guess would surmise that the group was putting some original material on tape for reference as they developed some of their songs—particularly as with the modest chart success of "Love Me Do" it now looked increasingly likely they'd have the chance to record more

of them for EMI. The Beatles would sometimes rehearse in the Cavern when it was closed, and according to some accounts from others around the group at the time, recorded at least some of these sessions. One somehow thinks they'd have been a little too embarrassed, however, to play the tapes to George Martin as works-in-progress to consider at such an early stage in their relationship. There are just a few too many missed notes, lyrical gaffes, and off-keyisms to make such a presentation comfortable. Nonetheless, these are reasonably enjoyable, and certainly very interesting, snapshots of the Beatles at work on their own compositions in late 1962 (and, it should be hastily added, they're *way* better in sound, performance, and quality of material than their 1960 home rehearsal tapes).

Perhaps the most intriguing of the five tracks is "I Saw Her Standing There," captured in a decidedly rawer state than it was in the classic February 1963 studio recording included on their debut album. For one thing, John Lennon is playing harmonica, and quite wheezily at that—an idea that was wisely discarded. The beat's a little slower and chunkier. George Harrison puts in some chords for emphasis near the end of the verses that didn't survive to the final arrangement. The instrumental break is a little chaotic, with Lennon's almost random, atonal harmonica blasts rubbing against George's rudimentary solo riffs. The lyrics aren't quite all there yet, as John and Paul diverge on slightly different words in the bridge. On the second bridge, in fact, the order of the first and second lines is reversed—an apparent mistake, as both start to crack up on the next line, going into near-jokey falsettos at the end of the bridge as they recover from their screw-up. Still, the song's close to a done deal. Most of the vocal harmonies are in place and Paul's singing displays as much enthusiasm as he would in many subsequent performances of the tune in the next year or two, right down to a "one-two-three-four" count-off that's much like the one kicking off the studio version.

"One After 909" is much tighter here than it was back on the 1960 home tapes, but not exactly tight per se. The main culprit, it must be said, is Harrison, whose guitar seems a mite out-of-tune, and who doesn't seem to have a solid idea of what to play, or when to play, adding interjections at nearly every possible pause of the vocals. Otherwise, these are pretty good performances, particularly John and Paul's harmonizing vocals and their exclamatory whoops. The arrangement's similar to the one they'd use when they recorded it in March 1963 (as heard on the outtake included on *Anthology 1*) at the session for the "From Me to You" single, though that EMI recording would have a smoothed-out, slightly slower rhythm. The two versions here aren't drastically different; George's guitar gets a little better on one of them, but unfortunately that's the one where they land, hard, on a bum guitar note when they come back into the verse from the first bridge.

"Catswalk" is a fascinating tune both because the Beatles never released their own version, and because these two particular run-throughs are the only surviving tapes of the band performing the number. Penned by McCartney alone, it was likely one of the earlier originals the band had maintained in their repertoire, having first played it back in the late '50s. It's one of their most atypical relics, too, as it's an instrumental with a snaky motif and a pronounced jazzy beat, rather like a rockified take on the kind of song you might have heard on the soundtrack of a late-'50s detective drama, as hoods and their molls huddled in a dank, smoky club. It's a rather cool if slight oddity, but alas, the sticking point is—again—George's rather stumbling lead work. In fact, it must be said—and this from a big Harrison fan—that George's lead guitar was the most frequent source of flaws in the whole of the Beatles' storehouse of unreleased recordings through the mid-'60s, as heard on numerous subsequent BBC performances and studio outtakes. And as with "One After 909," there's not much difference between the two versions on this tape, each one lasting just a minute and a half.

One does wonder whether the Beatles were seriously considering recording "Catswalk" for release, perhaps as an album track, as the chances of an LP release grew more likely. Those were the days when albums were sometimes seen as showcases for an act's versatility, and maybe the group—who'd actually already recorded an instrumental in the studio, "Cry for a Shadow," in 1961 at the Tony Sheridan sessions—viewed it as possible filler if they were to do a longplayer. Instrumentals were not really where the Beatles were at, though, and "Catswalk" was wisely not attempted in the studio. The group, who would record very few wholly instrumental tracks at EMI, perhaps realized this was a facet of their repertoire that was naturally phasing itself out. The song did eventually find release, however, about five years later in October 1967, when British trad jazz giant Chris Barber gave it an appropriately jazzy arrangement on a single (with Paul contributing keyboards and production assistance), retitling the song "Cat Call." On that single, the composition was credited only to Paul McCartney—the first instance, excepting his contributions to the 1967 *The Family Way* soundtrack, of a commercial release on which music he and/or Lennon wrote was credited solely to one of the two writers, rather than bearing the joint Lennon-McCartney billing.

As these five tracks add up to a mere twelve-and-a-half minutes or so of music, it seems quite possible that it's just an excerpt of a longer rehearsal tape. Even more enticingly, the bottom of a photo of the Beatles rehearsing at the Cavern in January 1963 clearly shows a Grundig tape machine—making it seem likely that other such rehearsals were recorded, though none have yet circulated.

● Circa December 21–31

Live Performance
Star-Club, Hamburg

This set of "lost" Star Club tapes misleadingly pictures the Pete Best lineup on the cover, though Ringo had been in the band for four months by the time the material was recorded.

*Roll Over Beethoven

*The Hippy Hippy Shake

*Sweet Little Sixteen

*Lend Me Your Comb

*Your Feet's Too Big

*Mr. Moonlight

*A Taste of Honey

*Besame Mucho

*Kansas City/Hey! Hey! Hey! Hey!

*Nothin' Shakin' (But the Leaves on the Trees)

*To Know Her Is to Love Her

*Little Queenie

*Falling in Love Again

*Ask Me Why

*Be-Bop-A-Lula

*Hallelujah! I Love Her So

*Red Sails in the Sunset

*Everybody's Trying to Be My Baby

*Matchbox

*I'm Talking about You

*I Wish I Could Shimmy Like My Sister Kate

*Long Tall Sally

*I Remember You

**I Saw Her Standing There

**Twist and Shout

**Reminiscing

**Ask Me Why

***I'm Gonna Sit Right Down and Cry (Over You)

***Sheila

***Where Have You Been

***Till There Was You

A Taste of Honey (unedited version)

I'm Talking about You (alternate version)

Roll Over Beethoven (alternate version)

I Saw Her Standing There (alternate version)

Money (That's What I Want)

Road Runner

Red Hot (fragment)

appears on both the German and US 1977 LP versions of The Beatles Live! At the Star-Club in Hamburg, Germany; 1962

**appears on the German 1977 LP version of* The Beatles Live! At the Star-Club in Hamburg, Germany; 1962

***appears on the US 1977 LP version of* The Beatles Live! At the Star-Club in Hamburg, Germany; 1962

As with some other large chunks of unreleased Beatles recordings, there's enough intrigue behind the material taped for the album originally issued in 1977 as *The Beatles Live! At the Star-Club in Hamburg, Germany; 1962* to fill a book of its own. It still hasn't been established beyond a shadow of a doubt when these tapes were recorded, or whether everything on the tape has come out, officially or on bootleg. Indeed, some people—including, quite possibly, the Beatles themselves—might argue that it was never "officially" legally released in the first place, even though it was easily available in commercial record stores the world over in the late '70s and hit No. 111 on the US *Billboard* charts. Along with the nearly simultaneously issued *The Beatles at the Hollywood Bowl,* it was

the first set of previously unavailable recordings released after the band's 1970 breakup. In various near-whole or partial pieces, it's remained easy to obtain over the last few decades, and can now be found on CD.

For all its wide exposure, however, the *Star-Club* album has seldom been granted the in-depth critical analysis of other items in the group's official discography. It's been widely acknowledged, at the least, as a valuable historic document of the group as they sounded in their Hamburg apprenticeship (albeit at the very end), and at the precipice of fame. Its serious sonic flaws, however, render it unpalatable to a mass audience, and it's fortunate that many other 1962–1963 recordings (legit and illegit) surfaced that were far better-recorded preservations of the group's rock 'n' roll roots.

The long road to the album's release started sometime in late December 1962, during the Beatles' fifth and final stint in Hamburg. At some time or times during this visit (in which they played at the Star-Club nightly between December 18 and 31, save for Christmas Eve), the group and several other acts were taped by the Star-Club's stage manager, Adrian Barber, to test the sound system he'd designed for the facility. (Barber himself had been in the Liverpool combos Cass & the Cassanovas and the Big Three, and after relocating to the US would work as an engineer on recordings by legendary bands such as the Velvet Underground and the Allman Brothers.) Made on a machine with a single microphone, the tapes passed into the hands of one of the fellow acts on the bill, Kingsize Taylor. Taylor led another Liverpool group, Kingsize Taylor & the Dominoes, who'd offered a job to Ringo Starr around the same time as the Beatles had; Starr made his choice, in part, because the Beatles offered £25 a week to Taylor's £20.

A decade later, reports of the tape's existence began to make their way into the press. A full-page feature by Mike Evans in the August 4, 1973, issue of *Melody Maker* described many of the tracks in detail, claiming that "the overall sound quality is remarkably good, much better (for instance) than the many Charlie Parker or Billie Holiday releases from the major companies, which appear for their historic and documentary as much as musical value." That couldn't help but whet the appetite among Beatles fans for an official release, which Taylor and early Beatles manager Allan Williams tried to achieve for years. Apple and the Beatles themselves weren't interested in helping, and ownership of the tapes changed a few times before the Double H Licensing Corporation announced its intention to release it. The Beatles tried to block it in court, but the British High Court ruled against them. After a reported $100,000 of postproduction attempts to improve the sound—which was clearly not as good as Evans's *Melody Maker* story had intimated—a 26-song double-LP of the material came out in Germany in April 1977. Confusingly, when the US version came out in June, it too boasted 26 songs, but included four tracks unavailable on the German version, while taking *off* four that had appeared on the original German release.

The original liner notes to *The Beatles Live! At the Star-Club in Hamburg, Germany; 1962* quite inaccurately state that the recording was done while Pete Best was still in the band, on a night when Ringo Starr just "happened to be 'sitting in'" for Best. This was done to avoid hassles with EMI, who'd taken the Beatles under contract in June 1962. For if the recording was claimed as dating from the Best era, it could also be claimed that it was done during one of their pre-Starr Hamburg residencies (the final of which lasted from April 13 to May 31, 1962). EMI would have done well to enlist some Beatlemaniacs in research for a case against the labels issuing the record, as it soon became pretty obvious that it couldn't have been done prior to June 1962. In addition to references in the between-song patter to Christmas—a holiday which the Beatles spent playing Hamburg only in 1962—there were also covers of some songs (Tommy Roe's "Sheila," the Isley Brothers' arrangement of "Twist and Shout," and Frank Ifield's arrangement of "I Remember You") that did not reach the British charts until after May 1962, making it extremely unlikely the group would have been aware of them before June.

It's now accepted that the tapes were made during the Beatles' two-week Hamburg swan song at the end of December 1962. Disputes about exactly when they were made and what was on them, however, are pursued with a vehemence not often seen outside the halls of academia. In *The Beatles from Cavern to Star-Club*, Hans Olof Gottfridsson deduced that the tapes were actually recorded during four separate sets, two on December 25, one on either December 21 or December 28, and one on either December 30 or New Year's Eve. Other researchers are adamant that the tapes were taken from just three sets, recorded between December 25 and December 30. There is also disagreement about in what order the songs were recorded, and what extra material on the tapes (at least some of it subsequently bootlegged) was passed over for the album releases. There is not even agreement on exactly what kind of tape recorder was used.

These aren't minutiae that cause even most Beatles fanatics to lose sleep at night, but it *has* been established that the albums aren't taken from just one night, as the original liner notes declared. So what you're hearing is not a sequential lengthy Beatles performance. It (like many if not most commercial live albums) is actually a combination of performances that have been reedited and resequenced, and different versions of the record present differently placed (or even different amounts of) between-song crowd noise and onstage banter. Some of the individual *songs* have even been chopped up and restrung (sometimes using composites of two different versions) to create the illusion of greater continuity, particularly as a few of the performances captured on tape were incomplete. And the lead vocals on two of the tunes aren't even by the Beatles.

Producer Larry Grossberg did pull out as many stops as 1977 technology allowed, including, according to *Billboard*, the use of "Burwen, dbx, and Dolby noise suppressors, UREI compressors and limiters, Orban Farasound and API sibillance controllers, API equalizers, Kepex noise gates, Audio Design spectrum analyzer, and an Orban stereo synthesizer." The magazine went on to report that "a special group of new Ashley parametric equalizers capable of suppressing frequencies of .05 of an octave was extremely valuable in recouping practically all the rhythm tracks and bringing out substantial lead voices and background vocals when they were apparently drowned out by general extraneous sounds." For all the money poured into its sonic rehabilitation, however, it still doesn't sound much better than an average audience recording bootleg for the most part. The vocals in particular suffer, sounding somewhat muffled and distant at the best of times, and as if they're bleeding across the wall from the next room at the worst. The blame cannot be laid solely with the primitive recording equipment; the Beatles' late-1962 Cavern rehearsal tapes were likely done on a similar machine, but even those come across with considerably greater clarity (particularly in the vocals).

And what about the music—something that, in all the effort to determine when and how it was recorded and prepared for release, tends to get too overlooked? It's pretty fair and gives a good picture of the Beatles

at the tail end of their raw days. There's much evident improvement from the Decca audition days just a year previously, and Paul McCartney's finally washed all traces of strained Elvis Presley imitation from his voice, even if the music does have its share of sloppiness and fluffed notes (George Harrison, sorry, being the most obvious stumblebum). The Beatles did not want to make this final Hamburg trip, being more eager to promote their budding recording career in Britain, and it's sometimes written that the *Star-Club* tapes capture a tired and dispirited band. But really, for most of the time they do sound quite engaged and energetic, especially McCartney (was there a time when Paul *wasn't* the most engaged onstage?), with an impatient, slightly frantic edge. Had they known these recordings would be heard by millions of people in perpetuity, they might well have tried to be a little tighter—though then again, had they known what was in store, they might just as well refused to have been taped at all, which would have been a big loss.

When the album was first released—long before most of the Beatles BBC sessions had made the rounds—attention naturally focused on the sudden wealth of cover versions that the group had never officially issued. The only two originals were their second B-side, "Ask Me Why," and "I Saw Her Standing There," still about six weeks away from being recorded for their debut LP. (It's odd that their upcoming "Please Please Me" wasn't played, if only to give the group a chance to perfect it onstage as they got ready to promote the single in the wake of its January release, but they'd make up for that omission, likely playing it more than 100 times over the course of 1963.) Of the other 28 tunes, just nine were rerecorded for Beatles records. Most of those nine are pretty close in arrangement to the studio versions, though rawer and never as good (and you can barely hear Ringo's vocal at all on "Matchbox"). The same might be said for the eight songs that were also done for the BBC, "Besame Mucho" having been done, in fact, for the BBC and both the Decca and EMI auditions. (And if that was one of the songs they were doing against their will at the Decca audition, why are they still doing it a year later, at a gig where nothing was on the line career-wise?)

The one song of the nine later reprised for record to differ significantly in its Hamburg incarnation is "Mr. Moonlight," taken not just at a *way* faster pace, but also with deliberately silly lyrical alterations that have John Lennon begging Mr. Moonlight on his nose (rather than his knees). The rolling Latin rhythms of the *Beatles for Sale* arrangement are absent in favor of a straightforward rock beat, and instead of an organ solo in the instrumental break, George peels off some Hawaiian-flavored licks. It can also be said that "Roll Over Beethoven" was never taken at a more breakneck pace by the group than it was here, as if the amphetamines had well and truly kicked in right before the number.

That leaves 11 songs not recorded by the Beatles elsewhere, excepting "Hallelujah! I Love Her So," which they'd done back on the grimy 1960 home tapes. Those are naturally the items of greatest interest today, though "Hallelujah! I Love Her So" and "Be-Bop-A-Lula" are blighted by the artlessly barked lead vocals of Horst Fascher (the Star-Club's manager) on the former, and his brother Fred (a waiter at the club) on the latter (though some believe it's Horst singing on both numbers). (Not that this is common knowledge, even though the vocals sound nothing like any of the Beatles; in his 2000 book *Flowers in the Dustbin: The Rise of Rock and Roll, 1947–1977*, former *Newsweek* popular music critic James Miller would single out "John Lennon['s]" lead vocal on "Be-Bop-A-Lula" as "harsh, adamant, seductively self-absorbed.") Paul's bent for pop standards comes out in pretty tough rocked-up arrangements of "Your

Feet's Too Big" and "Red Sails in the Sunset," the latter of which boasts, like several of the Beatles' covers, an effective move into double-time in the bridge. Less successful are "I Remember You," in which his falsetto can't quite hit all the highest notes and Lennon's mistimed harmonica bleats half-assedly, and "Falling in Love Again," which is let down by some of Harrison's clumsiest leads, despite some nice haunting harmonies on the final verse.

John isn't shown to best advantage on "I Wish I Could Shimmy Like My Sister Kate," where he infamously changes the chorus from "shimmy shimmy" to "shitty shitty," though that does at least preserve some of the early vulgar humor that Brian Epstein would emphatically remove from the Beatles' live presentation. Lennon's love of soul singer Arthur Alexander (original performer of "Anna," done on the group's first album, and "A Shot of Rhythm and Blues" and "Soldier of Love," done for the BBC) is further demonstrated by a Lennon-led cover of Alexander's "Where Have You Been." It's a cool, moody song, but this track has some of the muddiest sound heard on any of the officially unleashed *Star-Club* recordings, to the point where you could never figure out most of the lyrics without referring to the original Alexander recording. Also boasting even poorer fidelity than most of the tape are George's two other lead vocals, covering Buddy Holly's "Reminiscing" and Tommy Roe's "Sheila." "Sheila" was an obvious imitation of Buddy Holly's "Peggy Sue," right down to the galloping-horse drum pattern, and the Beatles would see Roe do it up close just two months later when they supported him on their second national tour. Its inclusion here is—along with Harrison-sung covers of similar watered-down Buddy Hollyisms like Bobby Vee's "Take Good Care of My Baby" and "Sharing You," and Joe Brown's "A Picture of You"—evidence of George's little-noted affection for rather wimpy Hollyesque early-'60s pop.

The real sleeper on the Hamburg tapes might be Chuck Berry's "Little Queenie." McCartney attacks the song here with such infectious (if foggily recorded) zest that one laments the group's failure to perform it for the BBC, where a well-recorded version would have likely been one of the highlights of their radio work. The band, too, is far more on-the-button here than they are on most of the *Star-Club* tracks, and George's guitar is imaginatively thrilling, veering off on some truly wild right angles in the first instrumental break that have no counterpart in Berry's original. The Rolling Stones would eventually release a cover of "Little Queenie" as a 1969 concert recording, but the Beatles, dare it be said, would have done the better one had they had the opportunity to make a technically decent recording.

The 30 songs that found more-or-less official release from the Hamburg tapes are probably enough for even most serious Beatles fans, particularly as it does take some hardiness to put up with the sub-standard recording quality for so long. However, for the hardest of the hardcore, there are—you guessed it—unreleased performances from the tape that have been bootlegged, some of them with yet raunchier sound than anything on the above-ground records. All but two of these are actually different or unedited versions of songs that did make it onto *The Beatles Live! At the Star-Club in Hamburg, Germany; 1962.* The most interesting of those is "A Taste of Honey," which has an additional verse that doesn't appear on either the *Star-Club* or *Please Please Me* album. You also get to hear Paul introduce it as "a Lied [German for 'song'] which John's gonna hate," and hear John shout at the audience, "STOP TALKIN'!!" at the end of the first bridge, cracking up McCartney enough so that Paul has trouble hitting all the words upon returning

to the verse. (If you're keeping a scorecard, note that while the end of this version is identical to the final part of the *Live! At the Star-Club* take, the first part of the *Star-Club* version is edited in from another performance.)

Also booted have been full versions of "Till There Was You," in which you can hear John more obviously sending up the tune with joking spoken lines echoing Paul's lead vocal, and "Where Have You Been," which has a second verse not heard on the *Star-Club* version. There are also different versions of "I Saw Her Standing There," "Roll Over Beethoven," and "I'm Talking about You" that are close to the *Star-Club* takes, except that the fidelity is even worse—*much* worse, though you wouldn't think such a thing possible. At least the unissued "I Saw Her Standing There" has a guitar solo, which the *Star-Club* one does not.

The only bootlegged songs *not* to appear on *Star-Club*, in fact, are "Money (That's What I Want)," its value diminished by the presence of Tony Sheridan on lead vocals, and Bo Diddley's "Road Runner." This is the sole extant Beatles version of the latter tune, but it's execrably recorded, and sounds more like a rehearsal of a fragment of the tune than a proper performance. Finally, a half-minute piece of the rockabilly nugget "Red Hot" (sometimes known as "My Girl Is Red Hot") can be heard on the soundtrack of the Beatles' *Anthology* video (and numerous bootlegs). It is indeed a burning red-hot version with John on lead vocals, but no complete take has yet circulated. And for those who care, there's yet more incidental (and differently placed) between-song chatter and audience noise on bootlegs, proving that there were much longer pauses between at least some of the numbers than reflected on the more tightly edited *Star-Club* album (which clearly rearranges some of the chatter to places it didn't originally occur). As an aside, much of that chatter, particularly Lennon's, was far coarser than they would offer on the BBC (or what the BBC would have stood for) and on all taped live concerts by the group from 1963 onward. It might have been the very last chance for the Beatles to act naturally, or at least wholly naturally, onstage. Both Brian Epstein's influence and the need to polish their image as their audience spread beyond small clubs meant that such tomfoolery would no longer be acceptable, not when the whole country (and soon the whole world) would be watching.

Upon initial release *The Beatles Live! At the Star-Club in Hamburg, Germany; 1962* was, in its commercially released version, most likely a disappointment to both its purchasers and the labels that put it out. It was simply too hard to get past the poor sound quality, which in turn meant that it was rarely played on the radio, even during Beatles A–Z weekends. The release of only slightly differing double-LP packages in Germany and the US soured even many Beatlemaniacs, who resented having to pick up the US version for just four additional tracks. It wasn't long before the material was being carved up for various other reissues, some of them just slapping a few of the cuts onto brief single LPs. Many of those bore exceptionally ugly covers, and one of them included a song, "Hully Gully," that was not even the Beatles but Kingsize Taylor & the Dominoes, though this was not noted in the packaging. Some bootlegs have likewise fueled yet more confusion by tacking on songs by Taylor or other artists recorded in Hamburg at the time, misleadingly billing those to the Beatles, though anyone with half an ear could tell it wasn't the Beatles playing on such cuts.

The multiple versions of the Hamburg tapes, as well as the over-flow of used copies from disappointed listeners, has meant that it's never been hard to find the material in some form or another. The Beatles,

A Brief Guide to the Songs on the Hamburg *Star-Club* Tapes

I n all, 30 tracks from the Beatles' Hamburg *Star-Club* tapes have gained official or quasi-official release, though fans without an encyclopedic knowledge of the group have a hard time keeping straight which songs appear only on these recordings. Here's the basic breakdown.

Star-Club songs also recorded for Beatles studio releases:

"Ask Me Why" (on the B-side of the "Please Please Me" single, 1963; Lennon-McCartney original)

"I Saw Her Standing There" (on the *Please Please Me* LP, 1963; Lennon-McCartney original)

"Twist and Shout" (on the *Please Please Me* LP, 1963; modeled on version by the Isley Brothers)

"A Taste of Honey" (on the *Please Please Me* LP, 1963; modeled on version by Lenny Welch)

"Roll Over Beethoven" (on the *With the Beatles* LP, 1963; original version by Chuck Berry)

"Till There Was You" (on the *With the Beatles* LP, 1963; modeled on version by Peggy Lee)

"Long Tall Sally" (on the *Long Tall Sally* EP, 1964; original version by Little Richard)

"Matchbox" (on the *Long Tall Sally* EP, 1964; original version by Carl Perkins)

"Kansas City/Hey! Hey! Hey!" (on the *Beatles for Sale* LP, 1964; original version by Little Richard)

"Everybody's Trying to Be My Baby" (on the *Beatles for Sale* LP, 1964; original version by Carl Perkins)

"Mr. Moonlight" (on the *Beatles for Sale* LP, 1964; original version by Dr. Feelgood)

Star-Club songs also recorded for the BBC:

"The Hippy Hippy Shake" (original version by Chan Romero)

"Sweet Little Sixteen" (original version by Chuck Berry)

"Lend Me Your Comb" (original version by Carl Perkins)

"Nothin' Shakin' (But the Leaves on the Trees)" (original version by Eddie Fontaine)

"To Know Her Is to Love Her" (original version by the Teddy Bears)

"I'm Talking about You" (original version by Chuck Berry)

"I'm Gonna Sit Right Down and Cry (Over You)" (modeled on version by Elvis Presley)

"Besame Mucho" (modeled on version by the Coasters; also recorded for Decca audition tapes and EMI audition tapes)

Star-Club songs of which no other Beatles version exists:

"Your Feet's Too Big" (original version by Fats Waller)

"Little Queenie" (original version by Chuck Berry)

"Falling in Love Again" (original version by Marlene Dietrich)

"Red Sails in the Sunset" (modeled on version by Joe Turner or Emile Ford and the Checkmates)

"I Wish I Could Shimmy Like My Sister Kate" (modeled on version by the Olympics, who retitled it "Shimmy Like Kate")

"I Remember You" (modeled on version by Frank Ifield)

"Reminiscing" (original version by Buddy Holly)

"Sheila" (original version by Tommy Roe)

"Where Have You Been" (original version by Arthur Alexander)

Also, the *Star-Club* performances that circulate on bootleg include, in addition to alternates of a few numbers listed above and a version of "Money (That's What I Want)" (later recorded for *With the Beatles*) with Tony Sheridan on lead vocals, a couple songs of which no other Beatles version exists:

"Road Runner" (original version by Bo Diddley)

"Red Hot" (original version by Billy "The Kid" Emerson, but likely modeled on a version by either Billy Lee Riley or Ronnie Hawkins)

---

however, never did resign themselves to its availability, and in 1998 they successfully blocked its reissue on Lingasong Music. George Harrison himself gave memorable testimony before the High Court in London on May 6, 1998, spurning the claim that John Lennon had given Ted Taylor verbal permission to make the tape in exchange for some drinks. "One drunken person recording another bunch of drunks does not constitute a business deal," Harrison declared. "If we had been sitting around the table and Ted Taylor was saying, 'Hey lads, I am going to record you and I'll make this live record that will come back to haunt you for the rest of your lives,' and John was saying, 'Great, you can do it,' then I would have said, 'You are not recording me.' We had a record contract, and we were on a roll. The last thing we needed was one little bedroom recording to come out." Interestingly, like many listeners to this day, he was still under the impression that the recordings had been done on one night, rather than on a series of nights.

George went on to give perhaps the most detailed appraisal of the Hamburg tapes ever heard from an ex-Beatle: "The Star-Club recording was the crummiest recording ever made in our name! There was no organized recording. It was a wild affair. We were just a whole bunch of drunken musicians grabbing guitars, and if Teddy Taylor just happened to have a tape recorder and decided to plug it in and tape us, that still doesn't constitute the right to put out a record. It's not whether he bought a pint of beer for John; it's whether people are allowed to make a recording without permission. I could go out tonight and tape Mick Jagger—but it doesn't mean I could go and sell it. The bottom line is that John didn't give permission, and even if he had, he couldn't have given it for us all. We were a democratic band." This time, the court ruled in the Beatles' favor, though that somehow didn't stop a remastered version from appearing on CD in 2000 (missing, like almost every single commercial iteration of this material does, a few of the 30 tracks from the original

1977 releases). Respectfully recognizing the Beatles' objections, for all its deep flaws, *The Beatles Live! At the Star-Club in Hamburg, Germany; 1962* is an invaluable document of the group. It's almost a diploma of sorts for the completion of the five-year apprenticeship that set the foundations in place for Beatlemania. Despite the Beatles and Apple's most strenuous efforts, it will likely always be fairly readily available. And if that's the case, why not at least give it, at long last, a sanctioned release with respectful packaging, historically accurate and astute liner notes, and even those sandstone-rough unreleased outtakes as bonus tracks?

1962 Noncirculating Recordings, Known and Rumored

From 1962 through each succeeding year of the Beatles' career, the known and rumored noncirculating recordings would increase annually, as the group became more heavily documented and their fame grew and grew. There's just one known existing artifact with a lot of unheard material from 1962 itself, however, which hasn't stopped rumors of others from flying over the years.

● Circa Early 1962

Demo Acetate

In *With a Little Help from My Friends: The Making of Sgt. Pepper*, George Martin remembers Brian Epstein playing a demo acetate in their first meeting in February 1962, with recordings that certainly haven't been documented elsewhere. According to Martin, "The quality of the recording was appalling. Not only that, but these Beatles, as they called themselves, were grinding out a succession of ballads that were beginning to sound moldy even then: things like 'Over the Rainbow,' or 'Besame Mucho,' interspersed with the odd blues classic, like Fats Waller's 'Your Feet's Too Big.' . . . In among all the creaky crooning, the band members had worked up a couple of their own tunes. The songs they had written were called 'Please Please Me' and 'Love Me Do.'"

Of the five songs mentioned, only "Besame Mucho" was part of the Decca tapes, igniting hopes that this was an entirely different set of recordings. It seems far more likely, sadly, that Sir George Martin's memory was quite faulty in this instance. He clearly states in this book (co-written with William Pearson) that the acetate disc had just been made of the Beatles' demo tape that had just been transferred to disc at the HMV record shop on London's Oxford Street. That was the *Decca audition tape*, and it didn't include "Your Feet's Too Big" (which Martin had also recalled being on the tape back in 1971 for *Melody Maker*), "Love Me Do," "Please Please Me," or "Over the Rainbow" (nor was it solely "a succession of ballads," or of "appalling" recording quality). "Please Please Me" almost definitely wasn't even written at this point; otherwise, it almost certainly would have been proposed as one of the Lennon-McCartney songs for Martin to hear at their actual EMI audition four months later.

"Over the Rainbow," "Your Feet's Too Big," and "Love Me Do" (as well as "Besame Mucho") *were* on the long *list* of songs that Brian Epstein

had suggested George Martin listen to at their June 1962 EMI audition. Maybe Martin was remembering songs from the list, or remembering hearing the Beatles play some of those songs at the actual audition. Whatever the case, it seems most improbable that Epstein and the Beatles would have managed to make a separate audition demo outside of Decca in the six weeks or so between the Decca audition tape and the first Epstein-Martin meeting, or that Epstein would have made an acetate from a recording of "appalling" quality rather than from the simple but acceptably professional Decca recording.

● May 24

Studio Outtake
Studio Rahlstedt, Hamburg

Swanee River

Though most of the Tony Sheridan/Beatles recordings were done in June 1961, on May 24, 1962, the group made a couple of final recordings for Bert Kaempfert. These were backing tracks and background vocals only for rocked-up arrangements of the standards "Sweet Georgia Brown" and "Swanee River," with McCartney, Lennon, Harrison, and Pete Best joined by Roy Young on piano. This recording of "Sweet Georgia Brown" was released on a German EP in 1962 (and endlessly reissued over the next few decades, along with the other Sheridan/Beatles tracks). However, this version of "Swanee River" was not, and is now presumed lost.

A Beatles-less version of "Swanee River" *was* released by Sheridan in 1962, causing much confusion among researchers over the years, particularly as it was often misleadingly included in compilations as a Sheridan/Beatles recording. To be gauche, however, even if the Beatles version ever turns up, could we possibly be missing much? "Swanee River," like a bunch of other tunes from the Sheridan/Beatles sessions, doesn't lend itself naturally to being made over into a rock tune, and the Beatles wouldn't even be singing lead vocals on it.

● Mid-1962

Live Performance
Cavern Club, Liverpool

Words of Love
What's Your Name
Roll Over Beethoven
Tell Me Why (or Ask Me Why)
The Hippy Hippy Shake
Till There Was You
Hey! Baby
If You Gotta Make a Fool of Somebody
Please Mr. Postman
Sharing You
Your Feet's Too Big
Dizzy Miss Lizzy
I Forgot to Remember to Forget

The Beatles were still playing clubs in the early days of the Ringo Starr lineup, but the group became
so big by the end of 1963 that performing in small venues would no longer be possible.

Matchbox
I Wish I Could Shimmy Like My Sister Kate
Memphis, Tennessee
Young Blood
Dream Baby (How Long Must I Dream)

On August 29, 1985, a tape of a Beatles 1962 Cavern Club performance made by a fan in the audience was auctioned by Sotheby's of London for £2,310. It's the only known relatively full-length recording of a live show predating their December 1962 Hamburg tapes, though it's uncertain as to exactly when it was made. Sotheby's dated it as February or March of 1962, though others have speculated that it was done somewhat later, around June or July. It certainly wasn't done in February or March, as one of the songs covered, Bobby Vee's "Sharing You," wasn't even released until mid-May, not entering the British charts until June. Pete Best would have been the drummer, however, regardless of what exact month the concert took place.

Most of the 18 songs do exist in other Beatles versions, whether on actual Beatles albums, the *Star-Club* recordings, or BBC performances. Most interesting, of course, are the few numbers that *don't* survive in any other form. The classic harmonica-driven shuffle "Hey! Baby" had been a huge Transatlantic hit earlier that year for Bruce Channel, an American singer the Beatles supported at a show near Liverpool on June 21, John Lennon picking up some tips from Channel's harmonica player, Delbert McClinton. The dramatic soul-pop ballad "If You Gotta Make a Fool of Somebody" had been learned from a smaller American hit single by James Ray, and would be taken into the UK Top Five by Freddie & the Dreamers in 1963. "Sharing You," a Gerry Goffin-Carole King composition, was sung onstage by George, who'd covered another Goffin-King-penned Bobby Vee hit ("Take Good Care of My Baby") at the Decca sessions. It's another small indication that the Beatles probably weren't as pressured to include light pop at the Decca audition as is usually believed. Nothing was at stake at a Cavern Club performance, and they were likely doing the song because they honestly wanted to.

Though a few of the other tunes appear at a glance to be unique to this tape, that's not necessarily the case. "I Wish I Could Shimmy Like My Sister Kate" is likely based on the arrangement of this standard by the Olympics, who retitled it "Shimmy Like Kate"; as previously mentioned, a later version was released on the Beatles' *Live! At the Star-Club* album. Sotheby's titled one of the tracks "Tell Me Why," but that's probably "Ask Me Why," which the Beatles were already performing live in mid-1962 (as they did on their second BBC broadcast in June 1962). It's true the group did the Lennon-McCartney original "Tell Me Why" in 1964 on *A Hard Day's Night*, but it's extremely doubtful it had even been written by mid-1962. That leaves "What's Your Name" as the real mystery item. There's no known Lennon-McCartney composition by that name, and while Don & Juan had a Top Ten US doo wop hit with a song of that title in early 1962, it really doesn't seem like the kind of material that best suited the Beatles' style.

Even if the fidelity of the tape is lousy (which one would guess it to be), it would probably at the very least make for very interesting and historically significant listening. The winning bidder for the tape at the Sotheby's auction, incidentally, was Paul McCartney. That would have made it easy for an excerpt to be included on *Anthology 1.* But it

wasn't, raising suspicions that the fidelity might not even be as good as the 1960 rehearsal tapes, as bits of the latter did make the cut for that release.

● July 1

Live Performance
Cavern Club, Liverpool

A live recording of "What'd I Say" appeared on a 1980s Gene Vincent bootleg, *Rarities,* that claimed that the Beatles were the backing band on the track. The Beatles did share the bill at the Cavern with Vincent on July 1, 1962. But here's yet another item that falls in the "seems unlikely" category, especially as there's a saxophone on the recording. Vincent's *Rebel Heart Vol. 3* CD credits this as a live Cavern Club recording from 1965 with the Dyaks as backing band, which is a more plausible scenario.

● September 12

Live Performance
Cavern Club, Liverpool

On this date, the Beatles played at the Cavern both on their own and as a backing group for 16-year-old singer Simone Jackson. *Mersey Beat* reported that Granada's TV unit was at the venue on this night, without specifying as to whether any filming was done. Still, it leads to speculation as to whether yet more Granada-filmed or Granada-recorded movies or music might surface.

● November 26

Studio Outtake
Studio Two, Abbey Road, London

Tip of My Tongue

Mark Lewisohn's *The Beatles Recording Sessions* reported that several takes of the Lennon-McCartney original "Tip of My Tongue" were taped at the November 26, 1962, session that yielded the second Beatles single, "Please Please Me"/"Ask Me Why." It's now thought likely they just played the number for consideration at the session without taping takes, particularly as none are noted in John Barrett's catalog of the EMI Beatles tape library.

George Martin did consider using "Tip of My Tongue" on the B-side, telling *Mersey Beat,* "It's a great number, but we'll have to spend a bit of time giving it a new arrangement. I'm not too happy with it as it is." But the Beatles would never again consider recording it for EMI, most likely in view of the far stronger original material they were coming up with even by the time of the *Please Please Me* album session in February 1963. The song was covered in mid-1963 by Tommy Quickly (see entry on page 342), and it would have been interesting to hear how the Beatles played it, even if it was one of the weakest, most lightweight early Lennon-McCartney songs.

● November 27

BBC Session
The Talent Spot *program (broadcast December 4, 1962)*
BBC Paris Studio, London

Love Me Do
P.S. I Love You
Twist and Shout

The vast majority of the Beatles' BBC broadcasts miraculously survive on tape in whole or part, in one form or another. But four early sessions were lost entirely (five, if, as noted in a prior entry, the fragment of "A Taste of Honey" from their October 25 session is actually from a TV show a few days later). This is the first of those lost sessions, on which they plugged both sides of their debut single and added "Twist and Shout"—which, if it's ever discovered, would be the earliest Beatles recording of that tune, predating the *Star-Club* version by about a month.

● Circa Late 1962

Rehearsal Tapes
Cavern Club, Liverpool

As discussed earlier, it's likely the Beatles recorded themselves rehearsing at the Cavern Club on several occasions, taping more material than the mere five songs from those rehearsals that have surfaced. Paul McCartney's brother, Mike McCartney, evidently taped the Beatles rehearsing there several times, and wrote in his 1981 book *The Macs—Mike McCartney's Family Album* that he still had an unreleased tape from such a session that no one had heard other than himself. Or could that possibly be the same five-song tape that's already been widely bootlegged?

The Beatles performing in 1963.

1963

Today Britain, Tomorrow the World

The Year in Review

In 1963, Beatlemania exploded in Britain. The fine details are in hundreds of other books, the obvious highlights being the Beatles' four chart-topping singles, culminating in two ("She Loves You" and "I Want to Hold Your Hand") that were the biggest rock 'n' roll hits the British Isles had ever seen; two No. 1 albums, holding down the top position on the UK charts in succession for 52 weeks; and the largest, most frenzied outpouring of adulation for popular entertainers experienced in the nation, leading to prestigious concerts at the London Palladium and in front of the Queen Mother at the Royal Variety Performance. As a by-product of their enormous expanding popularity, there was also an explosion in the quantity and quality of their unreleased recordings, though this, of course, was noted only in retrospect. Throughout the year, though even more so in its final months, the Beatles were constantly being recorded in the studio, on the radio, on television, and in live performance. There would be no more substantial gaps, even the several-month ones of 1962, in which little or nothing was taped somewhere by someone. From 1963 until their 1970 breakup, the Beatles' every move would be followed by the media, leaving a trail of unissued music that even today has yet to be fully retraced and cataloged.

For the fan curious enough to look beyond the official record, the Beatles' 1963 unreleased recordings yield an embarrassment of riches. This is mainly due to the almost ridiculous abundance of BBC recordings from that year, in which they undertook 40 separate sessions for the radio network. Most of the music from this survives in some form, often in quite excellent, near-studio-standard fidelity. These tracks comprise some of the most valuable unreleased Beatles music of all, including, as they do so, many covers (and one Lennon-McCartney original) not included on their 1960s releases, as well as more-or-less live versions of many songs from their early records that have a refreshing spontaneity not possible in a studio environment. It was also the year they began their official recording career in earnest, and fortunately quite a few outtakes survive from their first album and the session for their third single, even if there are comparatively few from their follow-up album and 45s. While tapers were slower to capture the Beatles outside of EMI and the BBC, by the second half of 1963, more of their live concerts were starting to get recorded as well, albeit usually under official guise for TV or radio. There are even some private home demos and composing tapes to ice the cake, though less of these than there would be as the '60s progressed.

If there's any downside to the bulge, it's that this is the point where repetition of the same songs in different guises becomes not only inevitable, but excessive. Among Beatles collectors, it's part of what separates the dames from the dilettantes, and the men from the boys. Even many fans with unreleased Beatles recordings in their collection are likely quite content with just a few multiple versions (at most) of any one Beatles song, let alone several dozen each of "From Me to You," "She Loves You," "Twist and Shout," and "Please Please Me," and more than three or four of many others the group released on disc in 1963. And while it's undeniably cool to eavesdrop on recording sessions like a fly on the wall, you'll have to steel yourself for a dozen or more takes of "There's a Place," "I Saw Her Standing There," and "From Me to You," some of them identifiable from each other by the barest of differences.

Understandably, the proliferation of similar performances of the same song is just too much for many listeners to wade through, even for many who love the Beatles. For those who love the Beatles above all else, however, they offer fascinating (if sometimes minute) variations from the familiar recordings, as well as some thrilling, unsanctioned insight into their creative process as record-makers, songwriters, and performers. The unreleased recordings of 1963 are essential to full appreciation of the group's evolution from several angles, more fully revealing their breathtakingly rapid growth as composers; their increasing confidence in and mastery of the recording studio; the astonishing breadth of their repertoire and their underrated genius as interpreters, particularly as demonstrated by the numerous otherwise-unavailable BBC covers; the excitement of their live performances; the rapidly increasing level and sophistication of their instrumental technique and vocal harmonies; and even the wit of their personalities that comes through in the between-song chatter and interviews. As good as they were by the end of 1962, throughout 1963 they made enormous strides on all fronts—more strides than could possibly be documented even by the two albums and four singles they churned out for official consumption that year. And well before year's end, there could be no question that they were the best rock 'n' roll artists in the world.

● January 16

BBC Session
Here We Go *program (broadcast January 25, 1963)*
Playhouse Theatre, Manchester

Chains (incomplete)
Please Please Me (incomplete)
Ask Me Why (incomplete)

The release of the Beatles' second single, "Please Please Me," on January 11 generated almost instant excitement in the UK, particularly as it coincided with a sharp rise in the frequency of their media appearances. Just three days before the taping of this radio broadcast, they had played the song on their first major British television spot. Now they returned to "Here We Go" for their first BBC radio session of 1963, plugging both sides of the 45 and also adding a cover of the

Cookies' "Chains," which they'd record the following month for the *Please Please Me* album.

Unfortunately the tape of the broadcast has primitive fidelity, and is also missing fragments of the three songs. Still, you can hear a spirited performance of "Please Please Me" (with the beginning cut off), taken at a slightly faster pace than the single and lacking the harmonica that graced the studio version, as well as a spot-on recreation of "Ask Me Why" (whose beginning is also chopped off). "Chains," sadly, is missing both the beginning and a big chunk of the middle, as well as (again) the harmonica from the studio version. There's another small, interesting difference, however, in that you can (faintly) hear high backup harmonies on the bridge—harmonies that didn't survive into the arrangement used on *Please Please Me*.

This, incidentally, was one of the sessions on which the group taped a cover of the Coasters' "Three Cool Cats" (which they'd done a year previously at their Decca audition), only not to have it broadcast. No tape of this performance has turned up, and a similar fate would befall the taping of another version for the BBC in July.

● January 22

BBC Session
Saturday Club *program (broadcast January 26, 1963)*
BBC Playhouse Theatre, London

Some Other Guy
Love Me Do (incomplete)
Please Please Me (incomplete)
*Keep Your Hands Off My Baby
Beautiful Dreamer
        appears on Live at the BBC

This is one of the Beatles' more interesting sessions, as it combined their first two hits with three songs that didn't make it onto their early records (as well as one that *still* isn't officially available on any Beatles disc). The sound of the tape making the rounds isn't bad, although it's obviously not an original tape or transcription disc, and at least two of the songs are incomplete.

"Some Other Guy" is taken at a slightly higher key than the versions recorded by Granada TV at the Cavern Club in late summer 1962. While it's not quite as ferociously edgy as the Cavern Club performances, or as definitively nailed as the one they'd do for the Beeb in June 1963 (subsequently included on *Live at the BBC*), it's a fine version of a song obviously dear to their hearts, as well as being a big favorite of several other Liverpool groups. "Please Please Me" is taken at a *real* fast pace, as the band would be wont to do with the song live until they dropped it from their repertoire after early 1964; too bad, however, that just a few brief segments of this particular performance have been bootlegged, rather than the entire performance (or even a continuous lengthy fragment). "Love Me Do" is the first non-EMI version of the song available, and Ringo's clattering drum part comes through much more strongly here, though the track fades out just before reaching the instrumental break. It's interesting to hear presenter Brian Matthew note in his intro, though, that while at this early stage the majority of the Beatles' fans are in their native Liverpool, he accurately has "a very strong suspicion it won't be long before they're all over the country."

"Keep Your Hands Off My Baby" had just been a Top 20 hit for Little Eva, best known in the States for her classic No. 1 hit "The Locomotion." John Lennon puts his all into his lead vocal on this number, written by Lennon-McCartney's songwriting idols Gerry Goffin and Carole King. With appropriate gender alterations to the lyrics, superb background vocal harmonies by Paul and George, a twangy Harrison solo, and an exultant chuckle by John as the band heads into the instrumental break, it was a first-rate cover of a song the Beatles never did get around to putting on their records. Until 1994, that is, when it was the earliest recording to be included on the official *Live at the BBC* compilation, though that track was artificially manipulated to create the impression of an instrumental drums-only opening that actually doesn't exist on the original tape. The Beatles probably did come close to putting this song on *Please Please Me*, as the February 22, 1963, edition of *New Musical Express* reported that it had been recorded for the LP, though EMI recording sheets do not mention it; they also played it live in February 1963 on their first British tour.

The final track from this broadcast, the mid-19th-century Stephen Foster composition "Beautiful Dreamer," is to collectors the most desirable. Not only was it never released on Beatles studio records, but it wasn't included on *Live at the BBC*, probably for fears that the fidelity was just too low to be salvageable (there's also a Brian Matthew voiceover obscuring the intro). One might think the song too inherently corny to lend itself to an effective (not to mention off-the-wall) rock 'n' roll treatment. But it's actually a terrifically exciting version, Paul McCartney giving it a downright raunchy vocal, complete with his patented electrifying Little Richard screams. Taken at a hyper-fast tempo, John and George add good backup doo wop–shaded harmonies, Harrison peels off a sharp rockabilly solo, and a sudden upward key swing for the final verse brings it to the finish line in just under two minutes. It's not known if the Beatles modeled their interpretation on a specific previously recorded version, though Mark Lewisohn's *The Complete Beatles Chronicle* speculates that country singer Slim Whitman's 1954 cover might have been the source. It's also been suggested they drew the arrangement from the version performed onstage by Rory Storm and the Hurricanes (with Ringo on drums) in Hamburg in the early '60s. Quite possibly, however, the song was familiar enough to the general public that the Beatles didn't need to hear it on disc to learn it. It was certainly popular in the Merseyside—fellow Liverpool groups the Searchers, Billy J. Kramer, and Rory Storm and the Hurricanes all released versions of the tune in 1963, and it was another song the Beatles played live on their first British tour, though it was likely never revisited after that.

● **January 22**

BBC Session

The Talent Spot *program (broadcast January 29, 1963)*
BBC Paris Studio, London

Ask Me Why

As an indication of just how quickly things were picking up for the Beatles, on January 22 they did two separate BBC radio sessions—one

for *Saturday Club* (see above entry) and this briefer, less interesting one for *The Talent Spot*. Of the three songs from the broadcast, just one, "Ask Me Why," has found its way onto bootleg. As it's got rather poor sound quality, and as the song's available in several other better-sounding BBC versions, this is one only for those who want every single Beatles BBC recording available. Tapes of the two other songs they did on this program, "Please Please Me" and "Some Other Guy," have yet to be discovered.

● **February 11**

Studio Outtakes

Please Please Me sessions
Studio Two, Abbey Road, London

There's a Place (takes 1–13)
*I Saw Her Standing There (takes 1–12)
Do You Want to Know a Secret (takes 7–8)
A Taste of Honey (takes 6–7)
Misery (takes 1–8)
　　take 9 of "I Saw Her Standing There" appears on the Free As a Bird *CD single*

The first large clump of genuine EMI Beatles studio outtakes all originate from one day: February 11, 1963. Although it's sometimes written that their entire debut album, *Please Please Me,* was recorded in one day, that's not quite true; four of its 14 songs had been recorded earlier at the sessions for the first two Beatles singles. The remaining ten *were* all recorded on this day, an astonishing achievement even given that such haste was relatively standard practice for rock 'n' roll albums at the time.

Alternate takes of five of these ten songs have been widely bootlegged, in sound quality just as good as what was released on *Please Please Me*. The disappointment for the casual collector is that none of them differ too radically from the final versions issued on the album, and that sitting through multiple repetitions of the same song with only tiny variations will prove too taxing. The reward for the more serious Beatles scholar, however, is that it's a great chance to study how the group and George Martin operated in the studio at their first album session; indeed, the first session to take place after the boys had become stars, "Please Please Me" having entered the Top Ten that very week.

These outtakes also reveal both the relative simplicity of the group's recording methods as they got used to the studio, and—even at this early date—their first ventures into use of the tricks made available by studio technology. At this point, recording for the Beatles was pretty much a matter of playing, as an ensemble, the best possible live performance. Much of the day was spent ironing out small glitches in the performances as they worked through take after take. In the cases of "There's a Place" and "I Saw Her Standing There," we're able to pretty much hear that process from beginning to end. They were also, however, able to create yet more perfect (or at least near-perfect) tracks for the final LP by editing together parts of individual performances, or by overdubbing instrumental and vocal parts onto already completed takes. The group would exploit these and many other technological devices to a far greater extent in subsequent years, but the rudiments of the exploration were already starting to grow.

You can also hear that the band are already getting far more comfortable in the studio environment than they had been in 1962, joking, whistling at the end of take breakdowns, making small suggestions and curious inquiries, playing the "Please Please Me" riff before entering take 5 of "There's a Place," and going through rigorous multiple retakes with taut professionalism. And, of course, the music—reflecting Lennon-McCartney's advancement into supremely melodic compositions, the flowering exuberance of their musical harmonies, and their overall mastery of still-raw but infectiously sung and played rock 'n' roll—is excellent, if not quite as excellent as the takes chosen for *Please Please Me*. Compared to the Decca audition tapes from January 1962, the improvement in every facet of their sound is so immense that it's hard to believe that only a little more than a year has passed.

The big difference in takes 1–10 of "There's a Place" is that they're lacking the harmonica overdubs that did much to seal the power of the released version. From take 1, though, it's obvious they have this magnificent early Lennon-McCartney song pretty well down. The chief differences—none of them too major—are in some of the vocal inflections and accents, the harmonies occasionally wavering more than they should, Lennon singing the lyric "there'll be no sad tomorrow" with a more forced, evenly spaced cadence at points. At the end of take 1, you can also hear one of them go into a brief twisting doo-woppy "ooh-ooh"—an idea that was wisely excised by the end. A stray vocal harmony roves in the background at the end of the first verse of take 2; takes 3, 5, and 7 all break down before the first minute as the band realizes it won't be "the one"; some reverb appears to get added to the guitar at the beginning of take 4; Ringo's drums sometimes play a more stumbling fill when entering the bridge. Take 10 would be the keeper, and takes 11–13 are actually three separate passes at superimposing (a term synonymous with "overdubbing") John Lennon's harmonica, take 13 being the one used on the released track (take 12 being an aborted attempt that hardly gets off the ground).

"I Saw Her Standing There" is a rather more interesting series of minor variations, though again the song was pretty much in place at the start. The outtakes reveal that the song was, at its outset, called "Seventeen"; that's the title given in the control room takeoff to take 1, prefaced by muttering from George Martin that "I think it ought to have a different title." In fact, take 1 would be the one selected as the bedrock, with an intro (McCartney's famous "1-2-3-4" count-in) spliced on from take 9, and handclaps overdubbed as a "take 12" superimposition. Harrison's classic solo in take 1 is easily his best work in any of the instrumental breaks—he sounds a little like he's losing track of himself in the others—and they were wise to stick with the first attempt. It's still fun, however modestly so, to hear some odd tics and screw-ups in the alternate takes—Paul slurs the word "just" in the opening line in a strange, elongated fashion, and occasionally John and Paul just can't time their harmonies right. Also amusing: Paul starts to mistakenly sing "*She* wouldn't dance with another" in take 6 before correcting himself, disingenuously asking "Too fast?" when the song stops halfway. A faint voice in the control room tells him he's sung a wrong word, but he unflappably brushes his blooper off: "Yeah, but I mean it's too fast anyway."

Only takes 1, 2, and 9 (the last released in 1995 on the *Free As a Bird* CD single) of "I Saw Her Standing There," incidentally, are complete. Take 6 is a breakdown and takes 7 and 8 false starts, while takes 3–5 are unused "edit pieces," (i.e., song fragments cut with the possible intention of splicing them into another take, with noticeably different incidental whoops and hollers). The first pass at overdubbing handclaps, take 11,

quickly breaks down, much to the merriment of the group, who start breaking into mock-applause; obviously the mere act of overdubbing was still a novelty to them at this point.

The eight early takes of "Misery" are very close to the released version, but lack the piano trills that George Martin would overdub onto the intro and bridge in the band's absence on February 20. That enables you to hear George Harrison's rather weedy guitar work far more clearly, and the boys are certainly having fun with the tune on the fadeout, singing in a more ridiculous falsetto on take 1 than they would on the released version, almost as if they were mocking the excesses of the doo wop vocal style. Takes 2, 3, and 8 are false starts, and 4 and 5 are breakdowns, John and Paul periodically messing up their harmonies, sometimes even singing different words ("I *won't* see her no more" McCartney emphasizes to John before take 6). It would be take 11 that made the final cut, and neither 9 nor 10 have yet surfaced.

The two available outtakes of "Do You Want to Know a Secret" are not actually takes per se, but different attempts at putting superimpositions onto the take (6) used as the foundation for the released version. At a glance that might seem like a trivial variation, but actually take 7 shows that they initially took a substantially different approach to the vocal arrangement. The backup harmonies kick in right at the beginning of the first verse, rather than waiting until the second verse, as they do on the familiar official version. In addition, when lead singer George Harrison reaches the end of the verses, you can hear backup harmonies trailing his vocal that were eliminated from the LP track. As was almost always the case until their split in 1970, the Beatles and Martin made the right ultimate decisions: stalling the backup harmonies for a verse added just a tiny bit of extra drama, and taking out the extra backup vocals kept things from being a mite over-fussy.

In addition, where the LP version fades out, take 7 also comes to a complete rounded ending with a sweet chord (also heard on some BBC session performances of the tune). At that point, John Lennon can be heard muttering something like "I can't get on top"; could that mean that George took the lead vocal in part because John, the primary writer of the song, didn't think he could have done the wordless falsetto vocals at the end of the verses? Obviously some discussion about the vocal arrangement took place between takes, as Lennon asks at the beginning of take 8, "Should we just do it on the second verse, like we said? Okay, so we wait. . . ." (He's obviously still getting used to communicating with the control room as well, emitting a puzzled, echoing "Hello?" after not hearing the initial response to his question.) The overdubs of background vocals and tapped drumsticks onto take 8 would, in fact, comprise the final version; the bootlegged take 8 differs from the LP version only in the inclusion of that pretake chatter.

Completing the available *Please Please Me* outtakes are the relatively uninteresting takes 6 and 7 of "A Taste of Honey," which are just vocal superimpositions onto take 5, which was the base of the official version. In fact, take 7—that is, the track that put vocal overdubs onto take 5—was the track used on *Please Please Me*, though reverb was added for the commercial release that isn't heard on the bootlegged cut.

It's doubtful that any other works-in-progress-type *Please Please Me* outtakes lie in the vaults, as it's believed likely that no more original session reels even exist. Certainly no others have made it into the outside world for inspection, though, owing to the nature of the day's session, it's doubtful than any would vary widely from the end result.

The Beatles at their March 5, 1963, recording session, which produced many bootlegged outtakes from their "From Me to You"/"Thank You Girl" single.

● March 5

Studio Outtakes

"From Me to You"/"Thank You Girl" single session
Studio Two, Abbey Road, London

From Me to You (takes 1–13)
Thank You Girl (takes 1–13)
*One After 909 (takes 1–5)

*an edit of takes 4 and 5, as well as a track combining portions of
takes 3, 4, and 5, appear on* Anthology 1

"Please Please Me" was still at the top of the singles charts, and the *Please Please Me* album still 17 days away from release, when the Beatles convened back at Abbey Road to record their third single. Remarkably, this is one of the most exhaustively documented EMI sessions of all on bootleg. *All* of the many takes of both sides of the single are in circulation, as well as all five takes of "One After 909," though no versions of the latter song were released at the time.

For all the effort put into "From Me to You" in the studio, the arrangement was pretty well in place right from take 1, and none of the takes differ too much either from one another or from the track ultimately issued on the single. The big difference, as might be expected, is the absence of a harmonica prior to the overdubs, with George Harrison's lead guitar playing the familiar opening riff in the instrumental intro (as it usually would, in fact, for the next year or so in concert). George adds a few too many responsive guitar fills to trail the vocal lines in the first couple takes, a tendency that was still cropping up five years later, when Paul McCartney famously nixed the responsive licks he'd devised for the vocals in "Hey Jude." Take 1's a breakdown, in which John and Paul, interestingly enough, sing "so call on me" instead of "just call on me" in the second verse; it would take them a few more takes to settle on "just" for good. Take 2 makes it clear they hadn't yet decided to use a brief instrumental break and extra chorus in the middle section, and Paul has a good-natured jibe at Ringo for missing the drum fills at the end. But by take 3, they're extremely close to the final arrangement, and it was just a bit of spit and polish before they had their second chart-topping single.

It was take 7 that provided the backbone of the final version, with the addition of overdubbed harmonica and intro harmony vocals on take 8. Gilding the lily a little too much, they tried out a few edit pieces on the subsequent takes that went unused. One interesting idea that was discarded, on take 11, was to wordlessly hum, in unison, over the opening intro. On take 13, they try out a really ill-conceived approach that has Paul doing his harmony in the intro in raspy falsetto, somewhat à la the Four Seasons. The ultimate selection of take 8 is early proof they could recognize that "if it ain't broke, don't fix it."

It's surprising that "Thank You Girl" was initially considered for the A-side of the single, as it's clearly inferior to "From Me to You" (and, for that matter, to some of the originals already in the can for *Please Please Me*). As with "From Me to You," however, the group had the basics down right from the first take, and it was just a matter of working out some kinks (including false starts on takes 2 and 3, and a superfluous high winding harmony by McCartney near the end of take 5) and doing some vocal and harmonica overdubs before they had the final version. Also some lyrical adjustments were still taking place on the fly, albeit very minor ones ("all I wanna do is thank you girl" instead of "all I gotta do is thank you girl," "love that seems too good to be true" instead of "love that is too good to be true"). Actually John and Paul are occasionally still singing some different words by the take (6) that would form the nucleus of the released versions, though you have to listen pretty closely to hear it. As long as you're bothering to listen for such things, however, perk up your ears for the ending of take 6, which has a shout near the very end not heard on the released track (which spliced on a take 13 "edit piece" to supply the final part of the song). You won't hear Lennon's harmonica anywhere on these bootlegged takes, however; those overdubs would be done at a separate session on March 13 that hasn't circulated.

It was known that "One After 909" was one of the earliest Lennon-McCartney originals even at the time it was recorded in January 1969 (and eventually released on the *Let It Be* album). However, it wasn't until the *Sessions* bootleg of the mid-'80s that most collectors became aware they'd first attempted the song in 1963 at this session for their third single. On *Let It Be*, the Beatles were revisiting this song as a self-conscious "back-to-the-basics" humorous nod to their earliest roots, but in March 1963, they were still playing it as a totally straight (and pretty Chuck Berry–influenced) rock 'n' roll song. There's an earnest chug to the arrangement, which is considerably tighter than the one they'd done in late 1962 on a private Cavern Club rehearsal tape, though the tune lacks the ultra-catchy melodic sophistication to be heard even on most of the *Please Please Me* Lennon-McCartney originals.

Anthology 1 included take 3 (a breakdown), part of take 4 (another breakdown), and a composite of take 4 and take 5 to simulate what might have been used as a master. All five takes in their entirety were bootlegged, however, and indicate the band might have had some problems getting the number to sound like they wanted. Amusingly, when take 1 breaks down at the end of the second verse, John comes down hard on Ringo: "What are you doing? Are you out of your mind? Do the boom-boom-boom-boom [the kick drum pattern heard at the end of the verses]." Take 2, in fact, is the only complete one they managed, and suffers from some peculiarly anemic George Harrison plucking (listen for the bum note at his solo's conclusion), prompting the ever-lovable Lennon to declare at the end, "What kind of solo was that?" Everything sounds fuller and tougher on take 3, which breaks down in part because McCartney's finding it tough to play without a pick (road manager Neil Aspinall pointing out that Paul didn't ask him to bring in the suitcase in which it was packed). George's solo

still sounds a little directionless on take 4, breaking down when John resumes his lead vocal before the instrumental break's finished. Take 5 is an edit piece that takes up the song right before the instrumental break, probably intended to be combined with another take, though Harrison's solo sounds none too impressive here either. Was he really still struggling with a song that, as its presence on 1960 home rehearsal tapes verifies, the Beatles had been playing for at least three years?

The Beatles would not come back to "One After 909" in the studio for almost six years, and then only as a tribute of sorts to their origins as a primitive rock band. Maybe it was left in the can in 1963 because they and George Martin weren't satisfied with the takes. It seems more likely, however, that when it was time to line up new Beatles releases a few months down the road, it was just considered too weak a song when stacked up against the other available alternatives, so fast were Lennon and McCartney developing as composers.

● March 6

BBC Session

Here We Go *program (broadcast April 12, 1963)*
Playhouse Theatre, Manchester

Misery
Do You Want to Know a Secret
Please Please Me

Excepting the harmonica overdubs for "From Me to You," after the session for their third single the Beatles wouldn't be back in EMI studios for almost four months. But they were caught on tape by the BBC the very next day, and, in fact, would be taped frequently for the BBC until they managed to get back into the studio to record "She Loves You," with many of the broadcasts preserved and bootlegged.

This "Here We Go" date (their last for the program) is notable as the earliest BBC session to survive in very good quality. In fact, it's the very first relatively hi-fi live recording whatsoever of the Beatles, recorded as it was in front of an audience. From the *Please Please Me* album (still two weeks away from release), they enthusiastically previewed "Misery" and "Do You Want to Know a Secret," and presented "Please Please Me" itself. There's not much difference between these and the studio versions, save for the absence of both the piano from "Misery" and the harmonica from "Please Please Me," and "cold" nonfaded endings on both "Misery" and "Do You Want to Know a Secret." It's still great to hear, however, with each tune taken at a slightly faster gait, "Misery" coming to a stop with a nonchalant, downwardly spiraling guitar lick. George Harrison sounds a little more comfortable with the lead vocal of "Do You Want to Know a Secret" here, too, perhaps relieved to be free of the pressure of the studio, and having had a few more weeks to get familiar with the number. "I Saw Her Standing There," incidentally, was performed but not broadcast at this show, though listeners would have to wait just one more week for its BBC premiere.

● March 13

Studio Outtake

"Thank You Girl" single session
Studio Two, Abbey Road, London

Thank You Girl (edit takes 14 & 30)

A miniscule variation of "Thank You Girl" has escaped from this session, which was solely devoted to John Lennon harmonica overdubs. This edit has a few different such harmonica overdubs, so close to those on the record that most listeners wouldn't suspect that anything was amiss.

● March 16

BBC Session

Saturday Club program (broadcast live)
Broadcasting House, London

I Saw Her Standing There
Misery
Too Much Monkey Business
I'm Talking about You
Please Please Me
The Hippy Hippy Shake

As it became apparent the BBC wanted to feature the Beatles regularly, perhaps the group started to realize they'd need to vary their programs more, dipping deeper into their repertoire. Or perhaps they started to draw on songs they hadn't yet recorded in order to make the sessions more interesting for themselves. Or maybe they didn't even think much or at all about such things, just doing what came naturally to them. Whatever the case, sessions such as these were interesting for their inclusion of items the Beatles had yet to (and sometimes would never) record. Although many Beatle fans were probably just glad to hear their heroes on the radio so often, surely even back then, some of the more fanatical were starting to make sure to tune in if only for the chance to hear songs they couldn't purchase on a Beatles disc. Three of the six songs from this *Saturday Club* program, for instance, would not be attempted at EMI. While it's unfortunate the circulating tape marks a return to funky-yet-listenable fidelity, certainly the performances are gutsy enough to be treasured.

The prime catch among this batch is the cover of Chuck Berry's "I'm Talking about You." Probably due to its relatively subpar sound, it was one of the five songs from the BBC sessions not to be represented in any version on either a 1960s Beatles release or the *Live at the BBC* compilation (although an earlier recording does appear on *The Beatles Live! At the Star-Club in Hamburg, Germany; 1962*). This rendition is preferable all the way round: they take it at a slightly slower but far more comfortable pace, Harrison delivers an admirably raunchy but focused solo, and Lennon's aggressively jubilant vocal catches on an ingratiating chuckle as the band launches into the instrumental break. Listen closely, too, to the bassline, which is pretty much identical in parts to the one McCartney plays on "I Saw Her Standing There" (Paul admitting as much even at the time to *Beat Instrumental*). The Rolling Stones might have done a slightly better, more salacious job with their slower and funkier take on the tune on a 1965 album, but the

Beatles do acquit themselves well on this pretty obscure Chuck Berry number.

While BBC airshots of the two other songs from this session (Chuck Berry's "Too Much Monkey Business" and Chan Romero's "The Hippy Hippy Shake") destined not to make an official Beatles '60s release would be included on *Live at the BBC*, these are different, earlier versions. Well, "Too Much Monkey Business" isn't *that* different (and unfortunately the very beginning is cut off), though the group's screams threaten to blow the transistor with their exuberance on this fine, plucky interpretation of one of Berry's wittier numbers. Learned from an obscure American single, "The Hippy Hippy Shake" was a big onstage favorite of the group—it's on *Live! At the Star-Club*, and they'd do it no less than five times on the BBC over the course of the next year. A big hit in both the UK and US for fellow Liverpudlians the Swinging Blue Jeans, it would have fit in well on one of the first two Beatles' albums, enough so that it's a bit of a mystery as to why it wasn't given stronger consideration. For the Beatles' versions are not just superior to the Swinging Blue Jeans' decent cover—they absolutely obliterate the relatively tame Romero original, Paul McCartney unleashing some of his most throat-shredding high, raw rock 'n' roll singing. This first BBC version isn't totally redundant with the others, featuring, as it does, some of the most oddly rudimentary, guttural guitar work to be heard on any Beatle recording, stuttering unpredictably between spiky notes, though Harrison unfurls a pretty good conventional solo. That makes this take of "The Hippy Hippy Shake" markedly less impressive than the other available BBC versions, yet at the same time interesting merely because it's quite audibly *different* from those other performances.

As the other three songs were all on *Please Please Me*, these are of far less note, particularly as higher-fi BBC passes at all three are available. It's the first BBC airing (and a very enthusiastic one, with a more spontaneous-sounding Harrison solo) for "I Saw Her Standing There," *Please Please Me* still being a week away from release (though they decide not to include the second middle eight, or bridge). Perhaps they gave "Misery" another plug here since, as presenter Brian Matthew noted in the between-song patter, it was about to be released as a single by Kenny Lynch—the first ever Lennon-McCartney cover, at a time when the pair were keen to establish themselves as cover-worthy songwriters in addition to being star performers. And it's another time around for "Please Please Me," for which *Saturday Club* had received (as Matthews points out) a "tremendous sack of requests," as it was still hovering around the top of the British charts at the time of this broadcast. Which, incidentally, was one of the relatively few of their BBC sessions beamed out live, leaving no room for foul-ups, the Beatles rising to the challenge with a nearly seamless set.

● April 1

BBC Session

Side by Side *program (broadcast May 13, 1963)*
BBC Piccadilly Studios, London

Side by Side (with the Karl Denver Trio)
Long Tall Sally
A Taste of Honey
Chains

Thank You Girl
Boys

As just the second BBC session to survive in pretty high quality, this is a pleasure to hear, even if it doesn't have any true rarities as far as the song selection. It's most notable for the first BBC airing for "Long Tall Sally" (about a year in advance of the release of the studio version), which is the first good-quality live Beatles performance of the song available (though a prior one appears on *Live! At the Star-Club*). Quite a frenetic one this is, too—though nothing matches the one the Beatles would record in the EMI studio, this one really does have off-the-graph energy. Paul McCartney can barely contain himself in the enthusiasm of the vocal, putting in more frequent interjections of shouts and woos than he does in the familiar studio version (at almost every available turn, in fact). George Harrison's solo work is, as it often was in live performance, rawer than on record, especially when it goes into an almost dissonant jagged riff to finish off the first instrumental break.

The other songs are, for the most part, well-executed harmonica-less facsimiles of the studio versions. Instead of fading out, however, "Chains" has quite a nice ending, with some descending vocal harmonies and an upward-sweeping declamatory guitar chord not heard on record. "Thank You Girl" benefits from an unfaded finish too, though the version of "Boys" here—Ringo Starr's first surviving BBC vocal, with a cracking lickety-split descending Harrison guitar solo—is incomplete, fading out soon after the instrumental break. The between-song interview bits are pretty amusing as well, the group clearly becoming bolder in offering their idiosyncratic humor and horsing around. It may mark the first time fans outside of Liverpool heard the famous explanation of how the name "Beatles" came from a man on a flaming pie, delivered by John Lennon in a fairly hilarious, creaky mock-senile tone. Ringo gets off one of his first public witticisms by saying of "Boys," "They did give me a go on the LP, and between you and me, I think that's the track that's selling it!" Paul, meanwhile, introduces "A Taste of Honey" as "a lovely tune, great favorite of me Auntie Gin's"—the kind of homey touch that would help ensure the group's appeal to several generations, not just teenagers.

Don't get too excited, incidentally, by the presence of the unfamiliar title "Side by Side." It's the show's corny theme song, and is performed not by the Beatles, but by the forgotten yodeling British folk-country-pop group the Karl Denver Trio, with John and Paul adding some vocals. Too, this fragment is of mediocre sound quality, and only lasts ten seconds; an April 4, 1963, session has a longer, near-complete, better-sounding version, if you really need it. Finally, also note that one song from the session, "From Me to You," has never been made available on bootleg.

● April 3

BBC Session
Easy Beat *program (broadcast April 7, 1963)*
Playhouse Theatre, London

From Me to You

Done before a live audience, the brief surviving slice of this broadcast is of very marginal value, though it does have slight historical signifi-

cance as the first surviving live version of "From Me to You." The sound quality's on the crummy side, some of the guitar sounds a bit out of tune, and there would be many better live versions of the song (still a week away from release at the time) recorded over the next year. (We do mean *many*—the Beatles ended up performing the tune no less than 16 times on the BBC alone.) You do get to hear Gerry Marsden of Gerry & the Pacemakers introduce the number, "which I really think is gonna be a hit," adding that there's nothing more to say except "how do you do it"—a lame pun on the song of the same name the Beatles had rejected in 1962 and which, as Gerry & the Pacemakers' debut single, was about to take over the No. 1 spot. Not that the Beatles had too much to be worried about, since "From Me to You" would not only knock "How Do You Do It" from the No. 1 position, but stay there for seven consecutive weeks. Also broadcast were performances of "Please Please Me" and "Misery" that have not yet been retrieved for bootleg.

● April 4

BBC Session
Side by Side *program (broadcast June 24, 1963)*
BBC Paris Studio, London

Side by Side (with the Karl Denver Trio)
Too Much Monkey Business
Boys
*I'll Be on My Way
From Me to You
     appears on Live at the BBC

This session, fortunately preserved in very good quality, would be of great interest simply for the inclusion of the only Lennon-McCartney composition broadcast on the BBC that the Beatles would not release as a studio recording. That was "I'll Be on My Way," which would soon appear as the B-side of Liverpool singer (and fellow Brian Epstein client) Billy J. Kramer's debut single, a British No. 2 hit cover of "Do You Want to Know a Secret," on April 26. Why a tune with some commercial potential was tossed away as a B-side isn't clear, though maybe it was just a matter of the Beatles, Epstein, and George Martin (who also produced Kramer) making sure they could generate some more publishing royalties.

"I'll Be on My Way" may not be among the stronger early Lennon-McCartney compositions, but it's a nice, catchy (if slightly sentimentally corny) medium-paced ballad. It wouldn't have been too out of place as an early Beatles B-side, being about as good as or better than "Ask Me Why" or "Thank You Girl," for example. The influence of Buddy Holly is stronger here than it is on almost any early Beatles original, particularly in Harrison's solo and when the harmonizing voices come together at the end of the verses. It's also graced by a simply beautiful series of dramatically ascending, slightly shifting chords (on which the fifth-note is being augmented, to be technical) with a distinctive yearning quality in a beginning opening instrumental section that does not appear in the Billy J. Kramer version (and is reprised at the very end, underneath repeated vocalizations of the title). That Billy J. Kramer version, by the way, is markedly inferior to this Beatles' BBC take, using a slightly faster, blander (particularly in the vocals), and more Buddy Holly–fied arrangement.

Interviewed by *Playboy* shortly before his death, Lennon claimed the song was the work of McCartney, uncharitably describing it as "Paul on the voids of driving through the country." Even if Paul was the dominant composer, however, one would guess that Lennon had at least some input into the writing, since both he and Paul sing the lead vocals, which rarely occurred on tunes that were solely the work of one or the other.

"I'll Be on My Way" was the only track from this broadcast selected for the official *Live at the BBC* compilation, but the others are certainly well worth hearing, starting with another take on Chuck Berry's "Too Much Monkey Business." This has much better fidelity than the tape of the version they did on their March 16 session, and, if anything, is an even better and more ferocious performance, and about as good as the later one (from September 3) chosen for *Live at the BBC*. John really pushes along the instrumental break with a scream at the halfway mark, after George veers off into some superbly edgy riffs. "Boys" is complete here (with a nonfaded, full-stop ending), and it's one of the best Beatles versions; Ringo really gets into his vocals, and as he did on many BBC performances, Harrison again proves his seeming incapability of delivering the exact same solo on different versions of the same song.

Things wrap up with the first good-sounding live recording of "From Me to You," Harrison's guitar coming through much more prominently than it does on the record, owing to the absence of harmonica. George, incidentally, doesn't sing on this session, a brief comic betweensong bit in which he croaks a bit of "From Me to You," making it clear that he's suffering from a sore throat. And the show kicks off, as noted in the prior entry, with a near-complete version of "Side by Side," though it's much more a Karl Denver Trio performance than a Beatles one.

● April 18

BBC Session
Swinging Sound '63 program (broadcast live)
Royal Albert Hall, London

Twist and Shout
From Me to You

Broadcast live as part of a show including numerous other artists, the Beatles performed their new single "From Me to You" and the song "Twist and Shout" (with a truncated third verse) that would become the opening number of many of their concerts over the next couple of years. The excited audience reaction makes it clear Beatlemania is taking off, but the recording's only of fair quality, though these are spot-on renditions. The most interesting action was actually taking place offstage, as this was the night Paul McCartney met young actress Jane Asher, who'd become his girlfriend for the next five years. In addition, also on the bill was the impressed American star Del Shannon, who'd decide to cover "From Me to You" for the US market. In fact, his 1963 version would become the first Lennon-McCartney song to reach the *Billboard* Top 100, though it would stall at No. 77 at a time when the country remained virtually unaware of the phenomenon erupting across the Atlantic.

● Circa May–June

Demo Acetate

Bad to Me

BBC sessions and (to a lesser degree) studio outtakes would supply the lion's share of unreleased Beatles music in 1963. But another tributary to that stream was opened by John Lennon and Paul McCartney's sudden success as songwriters, not only for the Beatles, but also for other artists. As part of the process of getting their compositions (and particularly ones the Beatles weren't planning to use) recorded, they would cut demos of the songs, probably both to aid the performers in learning the tunes and to supply their publisher with a reference version.

Not many such items have been heard by us common folk, but one that has is a demo of "Bad to Me," a song "given" to Billy J. Kramer & the Dakotas as their follow-up single to "Do You Want to Know a Secret." It might have been a tad too lightweight for the Beatles to consider recording, but "Bad to Me" was one of the best of the songs they gave away to other performers. Its melody was pretty irresistible, its slow strummed opening reminiscent of "Do You Want to Know a Secret," perhaps intentionally so, considering Kramer had just taken that song to No. 2 in the UK.

It should come as no surprise that even this rudimentary, poorsounding recording from an aged acetate is, in some ways, leaps and bounds above Kramer's jaunty reading of the tune. With folky acoustic guitar accompaniment, Lennon invests the song with a winning, knowing tenderness totally beyond the reach of Kramer. For all its sonic imperfections, it's a lovely find, though brief, lasting a little less

A collection of 1962–63 BBC performances that satirizes early Beatles LP art and promotional material.

than a minute and a half. It's sometimes believed this is a Lennon solo demo, but if so, at least some double-tracking was involved, especially since two voices strain in high harmony at the fade. The demo may never even have made its way to Kramer, as the singer recalled (in the liner notes to *The Best of Billy J. Kramer & the Dakotas: The Definitive Collection*) learning the song via Lennon playing it to him on piano.

Dating this acetate's a tricky business, but it almost certainly must have been cut in May or June. In his 1980 *Playboy* interview, Lennon clearly recalled writing the song while on holiday with Brian Epstein in Spain in late April and early May (though Paul McCartney has intimated that he had a role in the composition as well). John also revealed that it "was a commissioned song, done for Billy J. Kramer," who didn't record his own version until June 26. Even if Billy didn't hear the demo, some taped performance of the song was probably desirable for publishing and/or reference purposes before Kramer recorded it. Its origination as "a commissioned song, done for Billy J. Kramer" might also further explain why it was never recorded by the Beatles. The bootlegs are probably sourced from the copy (belonging to Brian Epstein's assistant Alistair Taylor) that was auctioned at Sotheby's on December 22, 1981, for an unbelievably lowly 308 pounds; if it surfaced today, it would likely fetch at least ten times that amount.

● May 21

BBC Session

Saturday Club *program (broadcast May 25, 1963)*
Playhouse Theatre, London

I Saw Her Standing There
Do You Want to Know a Secret
Boys
Long Tall Sally
From Me to You
Money (That's What I Want)

It wouldn't be until fall 1963 that Beatlemania was fully acknowledged by the general British press. But it's clear that it was already getting entrenched by the time of this May 21 session. Why else would host Brian Matthew note, "It seems to be getting to be a habit these days for us to get as many requests for the Beatles as we do for everything else combined"? Requests were coming in from as far and wide as the Royal Sheffield Infirmary, Germany, and even Egypt, read aloud in the song intros by George, Ringo, and John, respectively. But if the Beatles themselves were starting to get tired of repeating some of the same songs within weeks of each other (or even, occasionally, on the same day), it doesn't show.

The entire session survives in just-below-studio-standard quality, yet while quite good (if very slightly thin and distant), none of the individual tracks stand out as the best extant BBC version. "Long Tall Sally," while customarily manic, seems just a bit rushed compared to the earlier BBC take, almost as if the group is sprinting for a finish line, Paul's vocal verging on breathlessness at times. You do, however, have the treat of hearing the first live version of "From Me to You" with harmonica (though John messes up a couple of notes at the beginning of the instrumental break), and another nifty solo from Harrison in "Boys," in which he seems to favor the low notes more than usual. There's also the

first BBC version of "Money (That's What I Want)," the official *With the Beatles* studio recording still being six months away from release. This rendition isn't much different from the one on their second LP, other than lacking George Martin's piano contributions, and it is immensely more sure-handed than the relatively callow one they'd played at the Decca audition—the only earlier high-fidelity recording of the song.

● May 21

BBC Session

Steppin' Out *program (broadcast June 3, 1963)*
Playhouse Theatre, London

Please Please Me
I Saw Her Standing There

After taping a *Saturday Club* broadcast earlier on May 21 (see prior entry), the Beatles stayed on to record a separate one for the "Steppin' Out" program in front of a live audience later that evening. Just two of the five songs have made it onto bootleg, and those suffer from a lot of distortion. Good performances, as almost always, but these have a place only for those committed enough to collect complete Beatles BBC box sets. The other songs, for the record, were "Roll Over Beethoven" (its first BBC airing), "Thank You Girl," and "From Me to You." Though performed, "Twist and Shout" was not broadcast.

● May 24

BBC Session

Pop Go the Beatles *program #1 (broadcast June 4, 1963)*
Aeolian Hall, London

Pop Go the Beatles (intro)
From Me to You
Everybody's Trying to Be My Baby
Do You Want to Know a Secret
You Really Got a Hold on Me
Misery
The Hippy Hippy Shake
Pop Go the Beatles (outro)

As an extraordinary testament to the rapid growth of their popularity, in May 1963 the go-ahead was given for a BBC series of half-hour programs featuring the Beatles. Initially planned to run for just four installments, the network picked up its option for another 11 episodes, the series running for 15 episodes altogether. Proposed by BBC studio manager Vernon Lawrence, the show was broadcast every Tuesday at 5:00 p.m. during its lengthy run, each slot filled out with contributions from a guest group (including such notable up-and-coming British Invaders as the Searchers and the Hollies). Lawrence originally suggested the title *Beatle Time* for the program, which was modified to *Pop Go the Beatles* at the suggestion of a secretary in the production department. The *New Musical Express* reported at the time that "R-and-B material will be strongly featured," and while many R&B-oriented covers *were*

The Dick James Acetates

The Beatles started using Dick James as their publisher with their second single, and for most of the Beatles' career as EMI recording artists, acetate discs of Beatles recordings were pressed bearing the imprint "Dick James Music Limited." Used for copyright, publishing, and demonstration purposes, appreciation for their possible historic (and financial) value appears to have been virtually nonexistent. Nor do the ones that have been found sound very good, as acetates, by definition, can be played only a few times before their lacquer coat wears off the metal core of the disc. The Dick James discs apparently sound even worse than most other such acetates, as blanks were used from the MeloDisc company that did not endure well over time.

Most of the Dick James Beatles acetates that have surfaced are merely acetate pressings of tracks that are identical to the released versions. At least three, however—"Bad to Me" (see entry in this chapter), "One and One Is Two" (see entry in 1964 chapter), and "Goodbye" (see entry in 1969 chapter)—were demos of Lennon-McCartney songs the Beatles never released (or indeed otherwise recorded) in any form. Sold through auctions, their discovery raised suspicions, and wild hopes, that at least a few other such items could be found. It seems reason-able to suppose that the Beatles, particularly John and Paul recording on their own, would have done at least some other such demos for the numerous songs they "gave away" to other artists. Possibly they might even have cut some demos for songs the Beatles actually recorded, both for publishing use and to shop around to solicit cover versions. If they did, however, none have been bootlegged. Acetates featuring different mixes of released tracks *have* been bootlegged, although many listeners will find the differences from the official versions minor to infinitesimal.

Rumors in the underground Beatles-collecting community fly fast and furious about other such gems on Dick James acetates. So specious and confusingly contradictory is much of the research, however, that the author has decided to note in detail only ones whose existence seems probable. It can be noted here that some other demos whose existence have been mooted include a version of "Like Dreamers Do" that's different from and postdates the Decca audition one, a solo demo of Paul McCartney doing "Yesterday," and a McCartney solo demo of "The Long and Winding Road." If there's much more previously unknown Beatles music to be ferreted out, the Dick James acetates might be among the richest wells of such material.

---

featured, so were virtually all of the original songs they'd yet recorded, as well as a number of pop-rock and even straight pop covers. They had to do a lot of covers in order to fill out the programs without repeating themselves too much, though, if anything, the Beatles probably relished the chance (and challenge) to perform material that they likely wouldn't be able to fit onto any of their upcoming releases. There wasn't even an opportunity to work them into any of their concerts, which by this time had shortened to an average length of 20 to 25 minutes, and were usually restricted to a set program concentrating on their most popular recorded material.

Each episode of *Pop Go the Beatles* got off to a roaring start with the series' theme song, a rocked-up 18-second instrumental version of the nursery rhyme "Pop Goes the Weasel." As cringe-inducingly corny as this sounds on paper, typically the Beatles threw their all into it, transforming it into—as hard as it might be to believe—ultra-tough Merseybeat, complete with twangy George Harrison rockabilly riff, grittily bluesy John Lennon harmonica, splashing Ringo Starr drums, and a hair-raising Little Richard–style whoop-shout from Paul McCartney. A much longer version (the first 18 seconds identical to the intro), lasting just over a minute, closed each show, essentially changing into a (fairly good) blues improvisation after the "Pop Goes the Weasel" riffs had been executed. It's been suggested, though not confirmed, that members of the Lorne Gibson Trio (the guest artists on the first episode of the series) played on this track, though for what it's worth, to these ears it really does sound like the Beatles alone. (In the interests of eliminating redundancy, these versions of *Pop Go the Beatles* will be listed only in this entry.)

All of the songs from the first program, except the opening "From Me to You," have been bootlegged in reasonable though not perfect quality. "Everybody's Trying to Be My Baby" predates the recording of the *Beatles for Sale* version by almost a year and a half, and is in some ways more lively, with a slightly faster, purer rockabilly tempo, McCartney's pumping bass really pushing the Carl Perkins tune along. This is the first available performance of "You Really Got a Hold on Me" (to be recorded a couple months later for *With the Beatles*), and it's already in almost identical shape to the studio version, its sound only a shade less full. The second BBC version of "The Hippy Hippy Shake" is an improvement on the first try, those strange, guttural staccato guitar notes eliminated in an arrangement that takes the song at a much faster pace than the later one selected for *Live at the BBC*.

The *Please Please Me* album had been at No. 1 since the beginning of May, but the group would be mindful of continuing to plug it throughout *Pop Go the Beatles*, playing every song from the LP at some point during the series. Inevitably these were less exciting than the numbers the Beatles wouldn't (or at least had yet to) record, but filling out this program was a faithful rendering of "Misery" and "Do You Want to Know a Secret." The latter does make a nice complement to the studio version; the beat really has more of a thump, and George gets into some different falsetto notes at the end. "From Me to You" was also broadcast as part of this program, but hasn't been found (or at least hasn't been bootlegged).

● June 1

BBC Session
Pop Go the Beatles *program #3 (broadcast June 18, 1963)*
BBC Paris Studio, London

A Shot of Rhythm and Blues
Memphis, Tennessee
A Taste of Honey
*Sure to Fall (in Love with You)
Money (That's What I Want)
From Me to You
          *appears on Live at the BBC

Too Much Monkey Business
*I Got to Find My Baby
*Young Blood
*Baby It's You
Till There Was You
Love Me Do
          *appears on Live at the BBC

So hectic was the Beatles' schedule by mid-1963 that they sometimes had to record more than one episode of "Pop Go the Beatles" on the same day, laying down an album's worth (or even more) of material. This day was the first of those occasions, the group actually recording episode three first from 9:30 a.m. to 1:30 p.m., then working on episode two from 1:30 p.m. to 5:30 p.m. (This change in order is reflected in the entries here.) There's no evidence that the group found it tiring, however, as they offered a well-balanced set of two songs from their releases and four covers they had yet to issue (and, in three cases, never would cut in the studio for EMI), preserved in pretty good though short-of-perfect sound.

Although the Beatles put just one Arthur Alexander cover on their studio recordings ("Anna," on *Please Please Me*), the two additional Alexander songs they did for the BBC made John Lennon's love for the somewhat obscure soul singer obvious. This was the first of three versions of Alexander's "A Shot of Rhythm and Blues," and while it's pretty good, it's not the best. It's taken at a faster clip than the best subsequent interpretation, and it's missing some of the bluesy funk of the August 1 performance selected for *Live at the BBC*. Chuck Berry's "Memphis, Tennessee"—curiously described by presenter Lee Peters as a country-and-western number—had been performed way back on their first BBC show (and on the Decca audition tape), but isn't the best Beatles recording of the song, as the fidelity fluctuates notably throughout.

Carl Perkins's rockabilly ballad "Sure to Fall (in Love with You)" is the only track that was selected for *Live at the BBC,* and is a *big* improvement over the Decca audition tape performance. Paul's vocal has escaped the shadow of Elvis Presley, and the tempo's been slowed to a far more appropriate and comfortable pace. This is one of the few instances, however, in which *Live at the BBC* inarguably opted for the wrong version. The one from March 31, 1964, is simply better all around, primarily because it slips into a clever double-time meter in the bridge that gives the arrangement a huge energetic lift.

"Money (That's What I Want)," first played on the BBC just a week before, is much the same here. What's particularly interesting, however, is that unlike the earlier performance, this has John wailing "I want to be free!" on the final verse—an interjection that sounded like a spontaneous addition on the subsequent *With the Beatles* track, but obviously must have been consciously added to the arrangement before that. Filling out the program is another version of "A Taste of Honey," this one very well recorded, and another version of "From Me to You," which has noticeably worse fidelity than the rest of the cuts.

● **June 1**

BBC Session
Pop Go the Beatles *program #2 (broadcast June 11, 1963)*
BBC Paris Studio, London

The *New Musical Express*'s prediction that "R-and-B material will be strongly featured" on *Pop Go the Beatles* was fulfilled by the first three songs on this broadcast (available in excellent quality), all covers of songs by the black American rock 'n' rollers the Beatles admired so much. It's the third BBC time for Chuck Berry's "Too Much Monkey Business," and really, there's no clear-cut choice as to which the best of the four versions are; all are good, though this one's perhaps a little more smoothly executed than the first pass. "I Got to Find My Baby" was taken from one of Berry's more obscure early-'60s records and gives John Lennon a chance to deliver some of his bluesiest harmonica playing ever, as well as putting a lot of soul into the vocals. It's somewhat similar to (though bluesier and less exciting than) a more familiar song the group covered, "Kansas City/Hey! Hey! Hey! Hey!", the Beatles handling the stop-start rhythms with aplomb. This was the take chosen for *Live at the BBC,* though the Beatles would revisit the number on a later *Pop Go the Beatles* episode.

Also on *Live at the BBC* is the Coasters' humorous "Young Blood," originally one side of a 1957 single the Beatles must have worn to death, as they covered its A-side ("Searchin'") back at the Decca audition. The Beatles' cover is a delight, not only for their adept makeover of the saxophone-decorated shuffle into a more guitar-oriented arrangement, but also for the deft, witty interplay between lead vocalist George and backup singers John and Paul; listen especially for McCartney's howl of delight as Lennon warns, "You better leave my daughter alone." Another cool, extra-subtle touch is how they change the major final chord of the original into an altogether more complex, bittersweet guitar slash.

It wasn't all R&B-soaked rock at this session, however, the rest of it was devoted to poppier sounds. This version of "Baby It's You" was included on *Live at the BBC,* minus the celeste that producer George Martin overdubbed into the instrumental break of the *Please Please Me* track. George's solo is a little longer in the BBC arrangement, which also features a different, nonfaded ending reprising that solo, finishing with an upward flourish of a suspended dominant guitar chord—something the group often used as a finale in the early days, especially in live performance. "Till There Was You" gets its first BBC outing, and is only a little less down pat than the one recorded in the studio the following month for *With the Beatles.* The difference between it and the Decca audition attempt is astonishing, making it obvious that George had improved dramatically as a guitarist, pulling off his renowned Charlie Byrd–influenced solo flawlessly (and making a little more use of the vibrato effect here than in the familiar version). As he often would in live versions, Paul's vocal drifts into an extra-high couple of notes at the very end that are not heard on the studio version, while Ringo taps out the rhythm on sticks, rather than the bongos used on *With the Beatles.* "Love Me Do," of course, had already been around for a long time, and is even introduced by Lee Peters as "their very first waxing, from the dark days of 1962." Yet this is, surprisingly, the first well-recorded nonstudio rendition. Though the quality's a little lower than the rest of the tracks from this session, it faithfully reproduces the single right down to the harmonica riffs, played by John Lennon a little more lazily in the instrumental break.

● June 17

BBC Session

Pop Go the Beatles *program #4 (broadcast June 25, 1963)*
Maida Vale Studios, London

I Saw Her Standing There
Anna (Go to Him)
*Boys
Chains
P.S. I Love You
Twist and Shout

appears on Baby It's You *CD-EP*

One of the less interesting sessions, consisting entirely of versions of songs from *Please Please Me*. Very good sound quality, though, making it one of the better sources if you want to compile an "alternate" BBC-performed version of *Please Please Me*. Apple certainly thought so, making "Boys" one of the three BBC tracks exclusive to its *Baby*

It's You CD-EP in 1995. The idiosyncrasies of these well-done renditions are arcane, but include some pretty spontaneous Paul McCartney shouts during the instrumental sections of "I Saw Her Standing There." There's also some slightly different phrasing by John Lennon during the emotive bridge of "Anna (Go to Him)" and Ringo Starr in his "Boys" vocal (chased by a pretty hot George Harrison solo).

This appearance is most valuable for the only surviving BBC version of their first B-side, "P.S. I Love You," which had been performed on two late-1962 broadcasts (though the tapes of these renditions are probably forever lost). A little disappointingly, it's one of the relatively few BBC performances that's decidedly not as good as the studio version. Paul's vocal is a little strained and worn, and Ringo's drumming a little more obtrusive than it should be for this naively charming tune. It does, however, offer the small bonus of an extra melancholy guitar chord at the very end not heard on the single—not much of an extra, admittedly, but one of the small perks that Beatles collectors eagerly take if they can get them.

● June 19

BBC Session

Easy Beat *program (broadcast June 23, 1963)*
Playhouse Theatre, London

All the circulating outtakes from the Beatles' February 11, 1963 Please Please Me *session were crammed onto this single-disc package.*

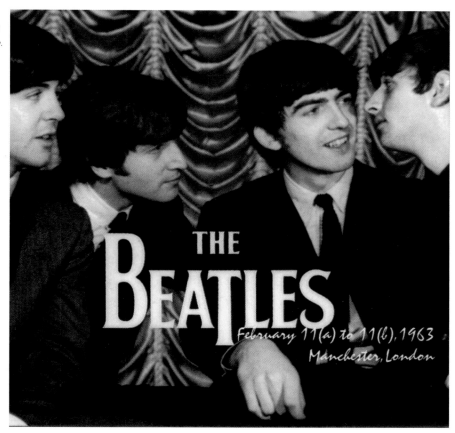

*Some Other Guy
A Taste of Honey
*Thank You Girl
From Me to You
  appears on Live at the BBC

Although the Beatles had now started a 15-week BBC series of their own, the incredibly industrious group continued to fit in occasional sessions for other programs on the Beeb as well. This four-song performance is one of the most exciting of all their radio spots, both for its atmosphere and the excellent performances (and fidelity). Recorded before a live audience, some authentic early Beatlemania comes through in the occasional screams, which aren't yet loud enough to obscure the music. The group seems to respond to the feedback by stepping up the intensity just a notch, in all making this feel somewhat more "live" than most of their other BBC sessions.

This is the best of the four surviving versions of "Some Other Guy," kicking into higher-than-higher gear near the outset with a great John Lennon "Yoww!" George Harrison's solo is a little more powerful and intricate than on the previous performances, and the whole track (also found on *Live at the BBC*) just pounds along with tremendous tightness and energy, making this one of the very best Beatles recordings not to be issued in the group's lifetime.

Also selected for *Live at the BBC* was "Thank You Girl," which might be the only instance in which a BBC version of an officially released Beatles track is better than the corresponding studio recording. As the B-side of "From Me to You," "Thank You Girl" was frankly one of the more mediocre early Lennon-McCartney numbers. But here it transcends some of its limitations with a more ferocious performance of this innocuous tune than you might think possible. Ringo really pounds the daylights out of the skins, much more forcefully than he does on the single, and John in particular lets loose with some wicked screams not found whatsoever in the original. If only they'd been able to include the harmonica part featured on the original single, there'd be no doubt of its superiority. "A Taste of Honey" and "From Me to You" are here too, and aren't as eyebrow-raising as the other two tracks, but are likewise done with sparkle.

● June 24

BBC Session
Saturday Club program (broadcast June 29, 1963)
Playhouse Theatre, London

I Got to Find My Baby
Memphis, Tennessee
Money (That's What I Want)
Till There Was You
From Me to You
Roll Over Beethoven

None of the six tracks from this broadcast are the best available versions, and, in fact, none have been officially issued. Still, as par for the course,

on its own terms it's very good, and the sound on four of the tracks is excellent, though "Money (That's What I Want)" and "Till There Was You" aren't nearly as good, and must obviously have been taken from a different source.

It's the second and final go-round for "I Got to Find My Baby," and though opinions differ, this author's opinion is that this isn't as good as the previous version (see entry for June 1, 1963), which is now available on *Live at the BBC*. There's not a huge difference, but the attack seems a little looser and more nonchalant, the group having demonstrated a bluesier swing on their first attempt. "Memphis, Tennessee" is a slight improvement above all prior passes through the tune, and few would have argued if it had been chosen for *Live at the BBC* in favor of the later one (from July 10, 1963) that was chosen. The harmonica makes a comeback on this version of "From Me to You." Not that anyone's losing sleep over it, but for the BBC sessions, why was the harmonica sometimes used on songs that had featured the instrument on the record, yet not used on others?

Although a recording of considerably later vintage (from February 28, 1964) of "Roll Over Beethoven" was used on *Live at the BBC,* you could make a good argument for having used this earliest surviving BBC version instead. In fact, you could make a good argument that this is one of the very best, most interesting live versions of *any* Beatles song also found on their studio releases. George Harrison's solo is twice as long and quite imaginative, going off on a wild staccato trill at one point, and Paul McCartney's bass is really well recorded, pulsing up and down the scale with majestic grace. *This* is why serious Beatles fans go to the trouble of listening to all 200-plus BBC recordings and braving multiple identical versions; there really is some gold to be found, with a value far above and beyond nerdy archival completism.

● Circa Mid-1963

Private Tape

I'm in Love

Never recorded by the Beatles, the slight but nicely haunting Lennon-McCartney composition "I'm in Love" would be a Top 20 hit for fellow Liverpool band and Brian Epstein clients the Fourmost in early 1964 in the UK, though it never charted in the US. The origin of this slightly muffled tape of John Lennon gingerly performing a not-quite-completed version of the song on piano is uncertain enough to make some doubt whether it was even recorded in the 1960s, though it's sometimes been dated as having been done in July 1963. It does have a somewhat bluesy boogie feel not present at all in the Fourmost arrangement. Also it's nice to hear John sing the tune himself, even if his voice cracks during one of the choruses, he stumbles a bit on the piano, and he hums-mumbles his way through some of the words. The perky Merseybeat of the Fourmost single, however, actually makes a much better listen.

"I'm in Love" was first heard on *The Lost Lennon Tapes* radio series, which had no other musical recordings from as early as 1963, and some analysts think the track was actually recorded in the last half of the 1970s. Why, however, would Lennon be revisiting one of the least known and less impressive songs from his early catalog at such a late date? And how would he be able to remember most of the song when, asked to comment on it in his 1980 *Playboy* interview, he replied, "That sounds like [my composition]. I don't remember a hell of a thing about it"? Whether done in the 1960s or 1970s, the exact date will probably remain a mystery. If it was done before anyone had recorded it in the studio, however, it was almost certainly done before October 14, 1963. That's when Billy J. Kramer recorded his unreleased version, not issued until a 1991 CD compilation, with Lennon present; you can hear John's voice on the session chatter at the beginning of the track.

● July 2

BBC Session

Pop Go the Beatles *program #5 (broadcast July 16, 1963)*
Maida Vale Studios, London

---

*That's All Right (Mama)
There's a Place
*Carol
*Soldier of Love
**Lend Me Your Comb
*Clarabella

> *appears on* Live at the BBC
> **appears on* Anthology 1

Of all the 53 Beatles BBC sessions, this one is the very most interesting and one of the very best, period. Five of the six songs were never attempted by the group at EMI. Apple recognized this when compiling its archival releases in the 1990s, officially issuing all five tracks, none of which the Beatles would do on radio again. With the benefit of hindsight, it's tempting to wonder whether this was a deliberate decision on the group's part, whether to make sure that their interpretations of these tunes got heard at least once; whether to intentionally make one of their programs virtually wholly comprised of, relatively speaking, obscure material; or perhaps even to produce a tape that George Martin could hear when considering what covers to place on the Beatles' second album. The first session for *With the Beatles* was just 16 days away, and while there's no evidence that the Beatles would have been doing something like this, it's an intriguing notion. In all likelihood, they did at least run some of these songs past Martin; asked by Mark Lewisohn in *The Beatles Recording Sessions* whether they'd thought of doing songs available only in BBC versions on record, Paul McCartney responded, "I think we probably played them all to George and said 'How about this one?' 'Clarabella' was one."

That's not to downplay the quality of the music itself, which is superb (and preserved in near-excellent fidelity). The group did relatively few Elvis Presley covers, considering what big fans they were of his early work, but they do a good job with his legendary first single, "That's All Right (Mama)" (actually first recorded by bluesman Arthur "Big Boy" Crudup). Here they capture the free-and-easy rockabilly breeze of the early Sun Records sound while adding something of themselves, particularly in McCartney's muscular basslines and relaxed vocal (exploding into a characteristic Beatle-like whoop before the instrumental break), as well as some stellar rockabilly picking from Harrison. The Sun Sound

gets another homage with Carl Perkins's "Lend Me Your Comb," previously done on *Live! At the Star-Club,* but sounding much better here. The group navigates the tricky time shifts with stop-on-a-dime precision, and makes the most of its vocal assets by having John and Paul closely harmonize the rumba-rhythm verses, yet handing off to Paul for swaggering solo vocals on the more rocking bridge. Apple goofed big-time by leaving this off *Live at the BBC,* and while it does appear on *Anthology 1,* it would have been more properly appreciated in the company of other BBC airshots.

"Clarabella" is one of the most obscure Beatles covers, originally appearing on a noncharting single by the Jodimars, a spinoff band from Bill Haley & His Comets. If you buy the argument that the Beatles did not just almost always at least match the originals they were covering, but often exceeded them, "Clarabella" is one of the best illustrations of your point. The Beatles' rendition is about ten times as good and powerful as the Jodimars', Paul McCartney transforming a pretty formulaic and run-of-the-mill early rock 'n' roll tune into a piercing Little Richard–style screamer, aided and abetted by some wailing John Lennon harmonica. Chuck Berry's "Carol" is handled here by John on solo vocals, and slightly precedes the much more famous delivery of the same song by the Rolling Stones on their debut 1964 album. It's a contentious assertion, but the Beatles' less noted interpretation is yet better than the one by the Stones, who took the song at a much more even, clipped beat. The Beatles' interpretation has a more forward-thrusting groove, Lennon's best cocky rock 'n' roll voice, and propulsive Harrison guitar riffing, especially when he flicks off some cliff-descending notes near the end of the instrumental break.

The best number from this session, however, is Arthur Alexander's "Soldier of Love," which changes the rather gloomy, hesitant original into an almost celebratory exhortation. The early Beatles' swings between harmonized vocal lines and tradeoffs between the lead vocal (John's, of course) and inventive backup harmonies were rarely executed better. The lyrics, mixing antiwar metaphors into an ode to romantic reconciliation, are more sophisticated than anything Lennon-McCartney had yet to come up with, but Lennon's up to the challenge with an ultra-soulful delivery. Most of the songs the Beatles did exclusively for the BBC are readily identifiable as American rock 'n' roll songs even by listeners who haven't heard the originals, but "Soldier of Love" is one instance where quite a few have mistakenly guessed they were hearing a great lost early Beatles original. Of the songs the Beatles recorded only for the BBC that would have made indisputably great early album tracks—such as "Some Other Guy," "Lucille," and "The Hippy Hippy Shake"—"Soldier of Love" is the greatest of all.

Rounding off this "Pop Go the Beatles" episode was the first BBC performance of "There's a Place," minus the harmonica from the *Please Please Me* arrangement. As good as this session was, it could have been even better. Recorded but not broadcast were takes of Chuck Berry's "Sweet Little Sixteen," the Coasters' "Three Cool Cats," and "Ask Me Why." At least there are other well-recorded versions of "Sweet Little Sixteen" and "Ask Me Why," but there isn't a BBC version of "Three Cool Cats"—a real shame, as presumably it would have been much improved from their recording of the same tune at the Decca audition. If unused tape of these tracks is ever discovered, that would have to rank high on the list of desirable finds of "lost" Beatles recordings, though in all probability it's vanished forever or been erased.

● July 3

BBC Session

The Beat Show *program (broadcast July 4, 1963)*
Playhouse Theatre, Manchester

A Taste of Honey
Twist and Shout

In the midst of all these exciting BBC nuggets comes a session barely worth mentioning. The recording quality's not very good, though the live audience is certainly getting into it, and both songs are available in several better different versions. "From Me to You" was also broadcast, though it hasn't yet made the collector rounds.

● July 10

BBC Session

Pop Go the Beatles *program #6 (broadcast July 23, 1963)*
Aeolian Hall, London

---

*Sweet Little Sixteen
*A Taste of Honey
*Nothin' Shakin'
*Love Me Do
*Lonesome Tears in My Eyes
*So How Come (No One Loves Me)
   appears on Live at the BBC

Scarcely any less exciting than the fifth episode of *Pop Go the Beatles* was the next installment, which offered four songs the group would never record for EMI. No doubt due in part to its excellent sound quality, all six of the numbers can be found on the official *Live at the BBC* compilation. Three of the four were also done for the *Star-Club* Hamburg tapes, though the fidelity here is leagues better.

Of those three, the classic "Sweet Little Sixteen" is not a great departure from Chuck Berry's arrangement, but is driven by a typically raucous John Lennon vocal. There's also a George Harrison solo that, as with many BBC cuts, has a distinctive, jaggedly raw, almost maniacally edgy quality that's quite different (though still quite accomplished) from his smoother studio work. "Sweet Little Sixteen" had been a big hit in both the US and UK, but the other covers testified to the Beatles' diligence as record collectors, since Eddie Fontaine's "Nothin' Shakin'" got only to No. 64 in the US in the late '50s. With George on lead vocals and curling rockabilly guitar, it could easily be mistaken for a Carl Perkins cover here. Even more obscure was the Johnny Burnette Trio's "Lonesome Tears in My Eyes," with its beguiling rolling Latin rhythm, cha-cha-flavored Lennon vocal, and yet more distinctive, commendable (and rather Hawaiian-sounding) rockabilly guitar from George. (Those riffs, or variations close to them, would resurface about six years later on parts of "The Ballad of John and Yoko.") Here the song's also joined with one of the most memorably comic spoken bits from the whole Beatles-at-the-Beeb vault, John putting on his best wheezing old man voice to introduce it as "recorded on their very first LP, in 1822!"

The Beatles also deserve kudos for finding the Everly Brothers track "So How Come (No One Loves Me)," which was good enough to have been a single for the great American duo, but ended up as a track on their 1960 LP *A Date with the Everly Brothers*. The great vocal harmonies here (with George to the forefront) make the band's debt to the Everlys evident, and there's yet more notable rockabilly guitar, both in Harrison's responsive licks and his not-a-note-wasted solo. Perhaps to make sure the record-buying public knew that it *was* the Beatles on this program, they also included a couple of songs that would have been familiar from both records and previous BBC airings, on near-letter-perfect takes of "A Taste of Honey" and "Love Me Do."

● July 10

BBC Session

Pop Go the Beatles *program #7 (broadcast July 30, 1963)*
Aeolian Hall, London

---

*Memphis, Tennessee
Do You Want to Know a Secret
Till There Was You
*Matchbox
Please Mr. Postman
*The Hippy Hippy Shake
   appears on Live at the BBC

The Beatles' hectic schedule again demanded they record two episodes of *Pop Go the Beatles* on one day, this one being done later than the session yielding the sixth installment. It's not quite as interesting as some of the previous *Pop Go the Beatles* programs, primarily because the material isn't as exotic. But it's still extremely well recorded, so much so that three of the six tracks were selected for *Live at the BBC*.

This is the third of the five versions of "Memphis, Tennessee" done for the BBC, and about as good a choice for inclusion on *Live at the BBC* as any, since the fidelity's excellent. The same goes for "The Hippy Hippy Shake," though it's notable that for this third BBC version, the Beatles have effectively slowed down the arrangement a little from the previous two passes. As a result it's just that extra bit funkier, and it might be that Paul McCartney never did a better vocal on any other rendition. It's a simply magnificent track that combines the best of Little Richard, rockabilly, and Merseybeat, and would have easily been among the better half of their EMI-recorded covers had they decided to do an official version.

"Matchbox," also included on *Live at the BBC*, holds some interest, as it predates their EMI studio recording by almost a year (though an earlier one is on *Live! At the Star-Club*). Save for the absence of piano, it's very close to the official arrangement, perhaps with a slightly more spontaneous rollicking feel. There are enough small lyric differences—Ringo sings "and everything I do turns out mighty wrong" at the end of the second verse, for instance—to make you wonder how well Ringo knew the song, or if he was given to winging his way through it. This is shorter than the version used for official releases in 1964, too, skipping the verse with all the "dog" references entirely, and going into the instrumental break after the second verse rather than the third.

Also being previewed after a fashion was "Please Mr. Postman," with a full ending rather than a faded one, and predating the *With the Beatles* recording by about three weeks (though they'd done it back in March 1962 on their first BBC session). This version suggests they had yet to work out the distinctive handclap-motored intro from the studio arrangement, with a super-brief intro of descending guitar notes that was eliminated entirely from the one they did for official release. "Till There Was You" also had yet to be recorded at EMI, and this isn't quite the best BBC take, the recording lacking some of the brightness of the best other presentations. And it's the sixth and final time for "Do You Want to Know a Secret"—and quite possibly the final time they ever performed this song, which wasn't reinserted into their repertoire even after it unexpectedly rose to No. 2 in the US when issued as a single in 1964.

● July 16

BBC Session

Pop Go the Beatles *program #8 (broadcast August 6, 1963)*
BBC Paris Studio, London

*I'm Gonna Sit Right Down and Cry (Over You)
*Crying, Waiting, Hoping
*Kansas City/Hey! Hey! Hey! Hey!
*To Know Her Is to Love Her
*The Honeymoon Song
Twist and Shout

appears on Live at the BBC

Somehow the Beatles managed to fit in the recording for *three* episodes of *Pop Go the Beatles* on July 16, taping 17 tracks (of 17 different songs) in a mere seven-and-a-half hours. That's a stupendous feat, almost equivalent to recording an album and a half in a single day, though, of course, each song would have been labored over more intensely had they been in an actual commercial recording studio environment. The first of the sessions was almost the equal of their July 2 recording of episode five in terms of yielding a mini-goldmine of uncommon material, which is probably the primary reason five of the six songs were chosen for *Live at the BBC*. Four of the six would not be attempted by the Beatles for EMI; a fifth predates the EMI recording by a good 16 months.

Starting with the four most off-the-beaten-track tunes, "I'm Gonna Sit Right Down and Cry (Over You)" had been recorded on the *Live! At the Star-Club* tapes in far poorer fidelity. Another of the few Elvis Presley covers recorded by the Beatles, it's a tremendously exciting, even rowdy performance. Ringo Starr particularly excels here—as he does in much of the BBC material, it should be stressed—with his varied opening drum rolls, leading the band through some tortuous tempo shifts (which they execute with stone-cold exactitude). It's a much different, harder-rocking arrangement than Presley's country-boogie-flavored 1956 LP track, with particularly emphatic blasts of twangy Harrison guitar at the end of the verses, and one of his better rockabilly guitar solos. George—who took a notably higher percentage of the lead vocal duties on the 1963 BBC recordings than he did for the band's official releases—is also at the forefront of Buddy Holly's "Crying, Waiting, Hoping," done with affectionate

tidiness and tenderness. The difference between this and the Decca audition run-through from a year and a half earlier is giant, as if a clutch of ill-fitting jigsaw pieces have magically fallen into exactly the right place. This is also one of the better illustrations of how vital Starr's recruitment was to this amazing transformation—where Pete Best's drums on the Decca recording help tilt the band into a too-nervous tempo and too-busy heavy beats, Ringo gives it just the right light, airy touch.

Also coming in for a big improvement over the Decca audition is "To Know Her Is to Love Her" (also done in the lower-fi *Star-Club* tapes). The arrangement actually isn't changed much. The vocals, however, are just so much more together, particularly the three-part harmonies, which have changed from the lugubriously sloppy to the upliftingly Beatlesque, particularly when they fly into the verse. John takes lead here, proving that Paul wasn't the only chief Beatle with an affection for romantic ballads, as is sometimes mistakenly claimed.

McCartney *was* the Beatle with the greatest enthusiasm for straight pop, of course, and fortunately instead of offering yet another rendition of "A Taste of Honey" or "Till There Was You," on this program he opted for one of the very most obscure covers in the whole Beatles canon. "The Honeymoon Song," written by Greek composer Theodorakis as the theme song for the film *Honeymoon,* had been learned from a vocal version by Marino Marini and His Quartet. "I was the force behind that," admitted McCartney to Mark Lewisohn in *The Beatles Recording Sessions.* "The others thought it was a real soppy idea, which I can see now!" No doubt it's too soppy for those who consider the aforementioned "A Taste of Honey" and "Till There Was You"—as beautiful as the Beatles' interpretations of those songs were—aberrant missteps in their career. But "The Honeymoon Song" actually has a lovely, bittersweet melody, sung by Paul in his best understated croon, with a lilting Latin rhythm and a luminous pseudo-rockabilly, Hawaiian-speckled solo from George. Nor would it be forever forgotten by the group after it had been exhumed just this once, as the McCartney-produced debut album by Mary Hopkin, *Postcard,* would include the song in the late '60s.

More intriguingly, in the instrumental tag of the Beatles' own 1969 single "The Ballad of John and Yoko," the guitars play a descending serenading line quite similar to the closing riff of the Beatles' arrangement of "The Honeymoon Song" (and also rather similar to another obscure song the group did on the BBC, the Johnny Burnette Trio's "Lonesome Tears in My Eyes"). Perhaps it's off-base speculation, but could it be that "The Ballad of John and Yoko"—the song about John Lennon and Yoko Ono's wedding and honeymoon—deliberately ended with a musical quote from another tune called "The Honeymoon Song"? If so, that's a pretty darn clever inside joke that very few listeners sussed out in 1969, and very few have noticed since.

This version of "Kansas City/Hey! Hey! Hey! Hey!" is the first well-recorded one available, but is definitely not as impressive as the energetic two-take recording the group did for *Beatles for Sale.* It's just less intense, and though George's almost randomly roving guitar solo is rawer, it's not as effective as the one he laid down in the studio. You can at least hear a nonfaded ending and some differently placed background "woos," and Paul McCartney's vocal is about as amazing in its upper-register power. The only cut from this session *not* to make *Live at the BBC* is a good, brisk charge through "Twist and Shout," which doesn't appear on *Live at the BBC* in any form, despite being done for the Beeb in ten separate versions.

THE BEATLES AT THE BEEB

ELECTRIFYING RADIO PERFORMANCES BY ENGLAND'S
Paul McCartney, John Lennon, George Harrison and Ringo Starr

BB 2173/S

VOL. 2

Including
I GOT TO
FIND MY BABY
TOO MUCH
MONKEY BUSINESS
and
YOUNGBLOOD

*Drawing heavily from the Beatles' pre-*Please Please Me *stage repertoire,
the BBC sessions gave George Harrison more of a chance to sing lead
vocals than he was getting in either the studio or live concerts by 1963.*

● July 16

BBC Session

Pop Go the Beatles *program #9 (broadcast August 13, 1963)*
BBC Paris Studio, London

---

*Long Tall Sally
Please Please Me
She Loves You
You Really Got a Hold on Me
I'll Get You
*I Got a Woman
       appears on Live at the BBC

The Beatles' second *Pop Go the Beatles* session of the day wasn't nearly as interesting as the first, with just one song that didn't end up on their 1960s releases. Again, however, it's a strong set, preserved in excellent sound quality, two of the tracks finding a place on *Live at the BBC*.

Though most often identified with its originator, Ray Charles, the Beatles' Lennon-sung version of "I Got a Woman" was based on the more rock 'n' roll–oriented cover that Elvis Presley put on his debut 1956 LP. This is the better of the two versions the group did for the Beeb, as the stop-start rhythms of the bridge and the delayed entrance of the drums in the first verse (neither present in the subsequent radio recording in March 1964) add to the drama. It was rightfully given precedence over its counterpart for 1990s release, though the same can't be said of the other cut from this episode to belatedly make its way into official circulation. For with seven versions of "Long Tall Sally" to choose from, the compilers of *Live at the BBC* goofed by choosing this particular take, as it's lacking the suspenseful octave-long key jump that does so much (on both the EMI recording and some other BBC versions) to push it over the top.

No Lennon-McCartney originals postdating their "From Me to You" single had been played for the BBC over the preceding three months, and the group must have been excited to premiere both sides of their new single here (not to be released until ten days after the August 13 broadcast of this session). This is the first-ever live performance of "She Loves You," and they sound as if they've been playing it for months, apart from adding an extra word ("so," before the line about apologizing) not heard on the famous hit 45. Its underrated B-side "I'll Get You" is here too, interestingly taken a couple of keys higher than the studio arrangement (as it would be on all its subsequent BBC versions), also lacking the harmonica of the official version. And here they sing all the words on the bridge correctly—on the single, in one of the most noticeable outright mistakes to creep its way onto a Beatles record, one of the harmonies mistakenly opts for the word "make" instead of "change" in the bridge.

Speaking of lyrical gaffes, on "You Really Got a Hold on Me," they make a big error, singing the first line of the second verse on both of the first two verses. Maybe the extreme pressure of fitting three "Pop Go the Beatles" episodes into one day eliminated the luxury of an extra fix-it take. No such miscues blight "Please Please Me," however, which is one of their best BBC performances of the song.

● July 16

BBC Session

Pop Go the Beatles *program #10 (broadcast August 20, 1963)*
BBC Paris Studio, London

Words of Love
*Glad All Over
*I Just Don't Understand
**Devil in Her Heart
*Slow Down
       appear on Live at the BBC
       **appears on* Baby It's You *CD-EP*

If the Beatles' energy was flagging at the end of this marathon day of sessions, it doesn't show on this, the third episode of *Pop Go the Beatles* cut on July 16 to be preserved in excellent quality. Again they took the opportunity to cover a bunch of tunes they hadn't yet presented on record. Two of the five they never would cut for EMI, two predate the recording of the studio versions by quite a while, and four, fortunately, were made available commercially on either *Live at the BBC* or the *Baby It's You* CD-EP.

The two most interesting numbers, as usual, are the ones not found on their official '60s releases. Carl Perkins gets covered yet again on "Glad All Over," and besides doing his usual fine son-of-Perkins guitar picking, George Harrison summons one of his best early lead vocals. George didn't have the vocal chops to compete with John and Paul, and his early lead singing sometimes sounded self-consciously hesitant and restrained. But here he's playfully letting loose to some degree, really sounding like he's enjoying himself. It's also great the way the Beatles hush down a bit near the end before ramping up for a stomping charge through the final chorus.

"I Just Don't Understand" wasn't as obscure as it's sometimes assumed, having made the American Top 20 list in 1961. Still, it's long surprised some Beatlephiles that John Lennon would have covered a song originally performed by starlet Ann-Margret, of all people. Lennon and the Beatles, however, seem to have recognized the inherently bluesy qualities of this sorrowful pop-rock waltz. Their cover, put bluntly, absolutely rips Ann-Margret's tamely pouting prototype to shreds. George puts in some nasty low growling guitar riffs and staccato trills, the background harmonies dolefully swell and swoon, and John's vocal squeezes every ounce of hurt out of the lyrics, changing an innocuous teen idol ditty into a genuinely dark lament.

Larry Williams's "Slow Down" would not be recorded at EMI for almost another year, and while the studio version is better on all fronts, this earlier take is an interesting and fun contrast. At this stage, the arrangement has a faster, more irregular beat, leaning more toward rockabilly than the straighter rock of the track heard on 1964 official releases. There's no great George Martin piano to fatten the attack, but John's vocal is equally vivacious, and George Harrison's guitar more rooted in his formative rockabilly style. Buddy Holly's "Words of Love" wasn't recorded for *Beatles for Sale* until October 1964, and perhaps this earlier version was passed over for *Live at the BBC* because it's very close to its EMI counterpart in most respects, though the beat's a little smoother and more straightforward on the later studio track.

The little-known girl-group gem "Devil in Her Heart" was just two days away from being recorded for *With the Beatles*. The fellows hadn't quite gotten the tune down yet, as they amusingly mess up the lyrics on *both* the bridges, semihumming their way through the final words. Perhaps there really was no time for a retake, given the day's crushed schedule, though it's still a little strange that the *Baby It's You* CD-EP uses this take rather than the more correctly (though not flawlessly) sung BBC version from a couple months later. (By the way, although the tenth episode of *Pop Go the Beatles* also included "She Loves You," this was a repeat of the same version previously recorded for and broadcast on episode nine.)

● July 17

BBC Session
Easy Beat program (broadcast July 21, 1963)
Playhouse Theatre, London

I Saw Her Standing There
A Shot of Rhythm and Blues
There's a Place
Twist and Shout

The day after recording 17 tracks in three sessions for *Pop Go the Beatles*, did the group take a well-earned rest? Nope—they were, unbelievably, right back in the BBC studios, doing four songs for a live audience. The sound's not quite as clean and clear as those *Pop Go the Beatles* sessions, and none of the tracks have been officially issued. But the fidelity's okay, and the performances (the only live-before-an-audience ones of "There's a Place" and "A Shot of Rhythm and Blues") are fine, though just one of the songs is a detour from the standard early Beatles catalog. That song, "A Shot of Rhythm and Blues," shows the band settling into a slightly slower, more suitable groove than the one used on their June 1, 1963, BBC session, and has a slightly bluesier (if short) George Harrison solo during the brief instrumental break than the other versions. Here, too, is a place to hear a non-faded ending to "There's a Place," the group landing on a nice harmony on the chorus.

● Between July 22 and 27

Private Tape
Weston-super-Mare, Somerset

The Lord Is My Shepherd
There Is a Green Hill

July 1963 produced some of the most delightful unreleased music of the Beatles' career. Unfortunately, however, foul-sounding marginalia is never far away when the group's material is excavated. Here we have perhaps the earliest case of Beatle bootleg extremism (though those 1960 rehearsal tapes could qualify on some grounds), harboring gratingly dull sounds of no real interest other than the physical presence of our heroes. Part of the infamous private tapes that fell into the hands of Beatles chauffeur Alf Bicknell, this has Paul McCartney, George Harrison, John Lennon, and Gerry Marsden (of Gerry & the Pacemakers) reading biblical passages in silly voices, the words made largely indecipherable by the lousy recording quality. John does eventually break out into an obviously deliberately abysmal rendition of "The Lord Is My Shepherd," followed

by the not-quite-four-Fabs taking individual and collective duncelike turns on another hymn, "There Is a Green Hill." Perhaps they committed this idiocy to tape (sometime during a week-long gig at the Odeon Cinema in Weston-super-Mare) just to test a new portable recorder? And if that's not enough for you, many bootlegs group these tracks with yet more tortuous snippets of Marsden asking locals for directions. . . .

● July 30

Studio Outtakes
With the Beatles sessions
Studio Two, Abbey Road, London

Please Mister Postman (take 3)
It Won't Be Long (take 7)
It Won't Be Long (second alternate take, unknown take #)
Untitled instrumental

With the exception of one reel of September 12, 1963, recordings (see details under that entry), no twin-track tapes are known to have survived from the *With the Beatles* sessions. That's probably why no *With the Beatles* outtakes appeared on the *Anthology* series, or, for that matter, on bootlegs (other than those alternates of "Hold Me Tight" and "Don't Bother Me" from September 12). We do have, however, off-line tapes of a few outtakes from this session, made from playback speakers rather than copied from the actual session reels. They're poor substitutes for the real deal, but unfortunately, they're the *only* available recordings of these takes, bootlegged after surfacing as part of the Alf Bicknell tapes.

Take 3 of "Please Mister Postman" is extremely close to the arrangement they'd used on their BBC recording of the song three weeks before, complete with the brief intro of descending guitar notes and nonfaded ending of doo wop–like vocals. Obviously some thought must have gone into tinkering with the subtleties between takes 3 and 9, as the latter (released as the *With the Beatles* version) added handclaps, cut off the small intro, and used a more effective fade. Take 7 of "It Won't Be Long" isn't much different from the *With the Beatles* track at all. The main difference is how the fellows periodically come to dead pauses between the verse and chorus instead of playing all the way through; there are some small variations in the guitar and vocal parts as well. A second alternate (take number unknown) from the session is much the same, except John Lennon suddenly breaks into some high wailing whoops and hollers on the last chorus not heard whatsoever in the final version . . . and then the tape breaks off.

Also usually described as coming from this batch of July 30 off-line session tapes is a brief, rudimentary, jazzy piano-drum instrumental. The drumming's so rudimentary, in fact, that it's questionable whether it's Ringo. It's also questionable whether this instrumental was done at EMI—it sounds like it could well be part of the rustic private recordings that comprised the bulk of the Alf Bicknell tapes.

● July 30

BBC Session

Saturday Club *program (broadcast August 24, 1963)*
Playhouse Theatre, London

Long Tall Sally
She Loves You
Glad All Over
Twist and Shout
*You Really Got a Hold on Me
I'll Get You

appears on Live at the BBC

Presumably the Beatles and their management weren't turning down any offers for national exposure in mid-1963 if they could help it, as this *Saturday Club* session was fit in between morning and evening EMI recording sessions at Abbey Road for *With the Beatles*. It's hard to imagine any act putting up with that kind of scheduling today, but the group had put in five long years or so in the trenches before finally reaching fame, and maybe they weren't about to let any opportunity pass to tighten their grip on stardom.

Generally the most interesting BBC performances (and certainly song selections) from this period are reserved for the *Pop Go the Beatles* programs. This *Saturday Club* date is, relatively speaking, among the less essential of their summer 1963 radio broadcasts, and except for "You Really Got a Hold on Me" (which has just one opening instrumental bar instead of two), none of it's been officially released. The sound varies from excellent (on "She Loves You") to less than adequate, and there's just one song, "Glad All Over," not found in their studio discography. This version, too, isn't as good as the previous one from *Pop Go the Beatles*, if only because voiceovers obscure the instrumental intro. The stairs-ascending chords have been put back into the second instrumental break on this pretty ferocious (though only average-fidelity) attack on "Long Tall Sally," by the way. Why had they been taken out for the July 16 session?

So concluded the Beatles' most active month of BBC recording, which had seen them do nine separate sessions, at which they cut 48 tracks (and on August 1, they would do another two sessions and another dozen tracks). Also in July, they recorded both sides of their fourth single ("She Loves You"/"I'll Get You") and much of their second album, *With the Beatles,* and played live concerts on 21 days of the month. Anyone who thinks the Beatles' success wasn't hard earned has it wrong.

● August 1

BBC Session

Pop Go the Beatles *program #11 (broadcast August 27, 1963)*
Playhouse Theatre, Manchester

*Ooh! My Soul
*Don't Ever Change
Twist and Shout
She Loves You (fragment)
Anna (Go to Him)
*A Shot of Rhythm and Blues

appears on Live at the BBC

Three pretty great, only-on-the-Beeb songs were presented on broadcast (the first of two *Pop Go the Beatles* episodes taped on this day), and all three were appropriately placed on *Live at the BBC* (with very good sound quality) three decades later. It's a close call, but perhaps the best of the trio is their positively manic tear through Little Richard's "Ooh! My Soul." Like several BBC performances (also including "The Hippy Hippy Shake," "Clarabella," and "Lucille," for starters), it proves beyond doubt that Paul McCartney is the best raunchy upper-register male rock 'n' roll singer, bar none. The joyful ants-in-the-pants squeal-of-delight vocal is enhanced in no small part by George Harrison's two guitar solos, showing a knack for almost crazed, machine gun–like riffing that doesn't come through too often on his more measured Beatles studio work.

Along with "Soldier of Love," "Don't Ever Change" might be the BBC Beatles cover most likely to be mistaken for a Lennon-McCartney original. The catchy, happy-go-lucky yet major–minor melody, the close harmonies, and even the subtly shifting and ascending opening chords all bear similarities to their brand of early Merseybeat. Compare the opening instrumental intros of "Don't Ever Change" and the Beatles' "I'll Be on My Way," for instance, for a particularly vivid, near-mirror image, down to the augmented fifth-notes on those ladder-climbing chords. But "Don't Ever Change" wasn't written by Lennon and McCartney; it was penned by the songwriting team that was perhaps their greatest compositional influence, Gerry Goffin and Carole King. British listeners would probably not be subject to such confusion, for while the original version was by an American group (the Buddy Holly-less Crickets), it had been a No. 5 hit in Britain in 1962, despite failing to chart at all in the US. Here's another occasion where the Beatles' cover simply blows the rather wimpily sung original away, both via the ingratiating power of the vocals (a rare harmonized duet between Paul and George) and the overall greater punch of the instrumentation, even though the arrangement is pretty similar. By the way, though it certainly does sound like Paul McCartney's singing "your kisses let me know you're not a dumb boy" at the end of the second verse, that's not necessarily an early bout of naughty Beatle humor, as the original (if odd) lyric is "your kisses let me know you're not a *tom*boy."

This episode's "A Shot of Rhythm and Blues" was the one that made the cut for *Live at the BBC*—a sound decision, as it's decisively the best of the three versions. The tempo's slowed down to an effectively earthy grind, Harrison unfurls a lightning flash of a bluesy guitar solo, and overall it's one of the group's better ventures into forceful R&B. It was preceded on the broadcast by another Arthur Alexander cover, albeit one they'd done before on both *Please Please Me* and the Beeb, "Anna (Go to Him)," though the sound quality's not quite as good on this track as it is for the rest of the session. Also heard on this episode: another "Twist and Shout" and "She Loves You," though a mere six-second intro fragment of the latter has been booted.

● August 1

BBC Session

Pop Go the Beatles *program #12 (broadcast September 3, 1963)*
Playhouse Theatre, Manchester

From Me to You
I'll Get You

Money (That's What I Want)
There's a Place
*Honey Don't
Roll Over Beethoven
*appears on Live at the BBC

The second *Pop Go the Beatles* episode taped on August 1 yielded just one item of special interest, and was accordingly slotted into the *Live at the BBC* compilation. That was Carl Perkins's "Honey Don't," presented here about 15 months before it was recorded for *Beatles for Sale.* Whereas Ringo Starr took the lead vocal on the album, however, John Lennon's still doing the singing here, and while both singers did a good job on their respective versions, John did bring a somewhat brasher, more assertive feel to his interpretation. That's especially audible when he goes into a totally different line on the last verse—"Well I love you baby on a Saturday night," not Ringo's "Well sometimes I love you on a Saturday night," and sung higher than Starr's line—and scats "Bop bop bop bop" on the last chorus. On the other hand, there's no unforgettable urge from Ringo to "Rock on George, one more time for me!" and there's just one guitar solo, not two. This arrangement does have a pleasing, slightly rawer vibe as well, though much of the distinctive Harrison guitar work from the EMI recording hasn't been worked out yet.

"Honey Don't" has excellent sound quality, and "There's a Place" and "Roll Over Beethoven" aren't far behind; Ringo's drums are especially crisp on "There's a Place," with a great cymbal crash right before the final line of the last verse. But "From Me to You" (with a very bass-heavy instrumental break), "I'll Get to You," and "Money (That's What I Want)" are significantly fuzzier, putting them at lower priority than the superior BBC takes of those same songs. Also recorded (but not broadcast) for this episode were "Baby It's You," "She Loves You," and Little Richard's "Lucille." "Lucille" had not yet been heard on the BBC, but fortunately would be recorded, broadcast, and saved in decent quality on two subsequent sessions later in 1963.

● Between August 19 and 24

Private Tape
Palace Court Hotel, Bournemouth

Don't Bother Me (two versions)
Tuning

Another segment of the Alf Bicknell tapes that can be dated with reasonable certainty is this one of George Harrison working out his first true solo Beatles composition, "Don't Bother Me." We know this because he remembered writing the song in a Bournemouth hotel, and the only time the group played Bournemouth prior to "Don't Bother Me" getting recorded in the studio was between August 19 and August 24 of 1963. "I was a bit run down and was supposed to be having some sort of tonic, taking it easy for a few days," he told Hunter Davies in *The Beatles: The Authorized Biography.* "I decided to try to write a song, just for a laugh. I got out my guitar and just played around till a song came. I forgot all about it till we came to record the next LP." Actually the Beatles had already started that LP, *With the Beatles,* and "Don't Bother Me" would be recorded just three weeks later.

Relatively speaking, this is one of the more interesting parts of the Bicknell tapes, though the quality's so bad you have a hard time making out the words. That's tough luck on us, as some of them seem to be different at this point. But it *is* "Don't Bother Me," Harrison working out the haunting melody on guitar and whistling and humming where many of the words would be, though it seems like a slightly more doleful (almost Mediterranean-flavored) tune at this point. That's followed by a couple minutes of tuninglike plucking, recognizable tunes failing to emerge from the fussing around.

● August 27

Live Performance
Little Theatre, Southport

Twist and Shout (incomplete)
She Loves You
I Saw Her Standing There (fragment)

The Beatles had been on TV throughout 1963, but the live segments of the BBC documentary *The Mersey Sound* contained the earliest live footage of the group (albeit done live without an audience) that survives, other than their August 1962 clip at the Cavern. As with all of the numerous live telecasts that will be discussed in this book, by far the best and most exciting way to experience this is by watching the film, not just listening to the audio. The audio of this telecast (and others), however, does often show up on bootlegs, offering solid if not quite state-of-the-art fidelity versions of "Twist and Shout" (albeit minus the first part of the song) and "She Loves You." Also heard is a half-minute instrumental frag-

The inner label of an early-'80s bootleg LP with 1963 Beatles broadcasts, made to look like a legitimate transcription LP available only to radio stations.

ment of "I Saw Her Standing There" with a particularly spiky Harrison guitar solo, at one point ascending the scale like the instrumental break in the Beatles' arrangement of "Long Tall Sally."

September 3

BBC Session

Pop Go the Beatles *program #13 (broadcast September 10, 1963)*
Aeolian Hall, London

*Too Much Monkey Business
Till There Was You
Love Me Do
She Loves You
I'll Get You
A Taste of Honey
The Hippy Hippy Shake
     appears on Live at the BBC

After a lengthy (by the insane standards of their summer 1963 work-load) break of one month from radio work, the Beatles were back in the Beeb on September 3 to lay down—incredibly, in one day, although they'd done a three-session day once before, on July 16—the final three installments of *Pop Go the Beatles.* Just two covers never to be heard on their studio releases were done in episode 13, including their fourth and final visitation of "Too Much Monkey Business," which ended up as the one ultimately chosen for *Live at the BBC.* It's the fourth (though not final) time for "The Hippy Hippy Shake," too; maybe it's a hair less fine than the one on *Live at the BBC,* but it's another mighty performance, the group having slipped back into a slightly faster beat. If it's not as accomplished as the one you can hear officially, it's got a neat, slightly rawer edge, George Harrison throwing in a couple off-the-wall upward zooming bent notes during his solo.

If it's a little disappointing that the rest of the session was spent on far more familiar tunes, it's worth noting that the sound is real good, and that this has a particularly good version of "Love Me Do," with bluesy and passionate John Lennon harmonica. There's an indication, incidentally, that all these versions of "A Taste of Honey" were done, at least in part, because of the song's popularity among BBC listeners, presenter Rodney Burke noting in his intro that there were a "stack of requests for Paul to sing" the tune. Weirdly, Paul reads another request for "Till There Was You," but the Beatles don't play it—not that there weren't many other opportunities to hear them do so on other BBC broadcasts. And when a request is read from a boy from Paul and George's alma mater, Liverpool Institute, McCartney seizes on the chance to get a little wicked with his cheekiness, inquiring in a nasty tone, "How's Slimy? Stinky? Pinhead? Weepy?"

September 3

BBC Session

Pop Go the Beatles *program #14 (broadcast September 17, 1963)*
Aeolian Hall, London

Chains
You Really Got a Hold on Me
Misery
Lucille
From Me to You
Boys

The second of the day's *Pop Go the Beatles* sessions is most notable for Little Richard's "Lucille," never recorded by the group for EMI, and sung by Paul in his best take-no-prisoners piercing whoop. Locked in place by a vicious circular guitar riff, it's as hard-hitting a rock 'n' roll cover as the Beatles ever managed—which, considering how many such items they pulled off, is really saying something. A subsequent BBC version (from just four days later) was chosen for *Live at the BBC,* but for my money this earlier one has the edge. Unlike the *Live at the BBC* take, the intro isn't dampened by a voice-over, but also, the performance is fiercer all around. There's a great snarling muffled shout right before the vocal starts; McCartney's vocal threatens to go right off the rails near the end of the first bridge; and George's deranged guitar solo in particular is better in this version, making wild shimmering use of the tremolo effect. Paul is too often lazily caricatured as the softie of the Beatles; "Lucille," among many other recordings, makes it clear that, on the contrary, when opting for the harder stuff, Paul McCartney was among the very toughest rock 'n' roll singers of the 20th century.

This particular performance of "Lucille," as a side note, was requested (if presenter Rodney Burke's intro is to be trusted) by their Liverpool friend Derry Wilkie of Derry & the Seniors, the first Liverpool band that Allan Williams had sent over to Hamburg in 1960. When Williams informed their manager, Howie Casey, that the Beatles were next, Casey urged him (as quoted in Williams's memoir, *The Man Who Gave the Beatles Away*) not to send "over that bum group, the Beatles." McCartney apparently didn't hold any grudges (if he even knew about this slight in the first place), using Casey as a saxophonist in 1973 on *Band on the Run.* As another side note, "Lucille" must be Paul's favorite Little Richard song (except for "Long Tall Sally"), as he's returned to the song throughout his career, singing it on Wings' first tour in early 1972; at the 1979 Concert for Kampuchea; and on his 1988 USSR-only album, *CHOBA B CCCP.*

While the sound quality of the entire session is excellent, the performances on the other cuts are sometimes a tad more ragged than usual, perhaps due to the strain of fitting three sessions into one day. There's a guitar flub in the solo of "You Really Got a Hold on Me"; they seem to slightly mumble their way through the "keep you satisfied" parts of "From Me to You"; and George's guitar, to pick on him again, sounds a bit out of tune on "Misery," which does have a funny, sarcastic-sounding falsetto "la-la-la-la-la-la" at the end.

September 3

BBC Session

Pop Go the Beatles *program #15 (broadcast September 24, 1963)*
Aeolian Hall, London

She Loves You
Ask Me Why

Devil in Her Heart
I Saw Her Standing There
Sure to Fall (in Love with You)
Twist and Shout

This was not only the final of the three *Pop Go the Beatles* episodes taped on September 3, but the final episode of the entire series. As with the second of the September 3 *Pop Go the Beatles* sessions, none of the material appears on *Live at the BBC*. The sound quality is very good, but it's one of the less interesting *Pop Go the Beatles* sessions, more due to the selection (and repetition) of material than the performances, with just one of the six songs failing to appear on their studio releases. That song, "Sure to Fall (in Love with You,)" gets a slightly purer country approach than it does in the earlier version selected for *Live at the BBC*, George really lingering on the rapid staccato strums of his solo.

For their second and last BBC take of "Devil in Her Heart," the lads do (unlike the first time) manage to get virtually all the lyrics right the whole way through. "Ask Me Why" might be one of the lesser Beatles songs, and while the harmonies are really tight on this version, the second bridge has been mysteriously eliminated from the arrangement. You want a surprise, though? Listen to the gnarly "eins, zwei, drei, vier!" that kicks off "I Saw Her Standing There," perhaps in tribute to their now fast-vanishing-in-the-rearview-mirror Hamburg days. The Harrison solo on this number is pretty gnarly too, though effectively so, and it's interesting that George rarely replicated (or even came that close to replicating) the actual brilliant solo on the studio version of the song from *Please Please Me*.

With *Pop Go the Beatles* coming to a close, the Beatles would never again have a chance, in a live or pseudo-live setting, to vary their repertoire so much. John Lennon famously claimed in his marathon early-'70s *Rolling Stone* interview that, in the Beatles' live act, "the music was dead before we even went on the theatre tour of Britain [in early 1963]. We were feeling shit already because we had to reduce an hour or two hours playing, which we were glad about in one way, to twenty minutes and go on and repeat the same twenty minutes every night. The Beatles' music died then as musicians. That's why we never improved as musicians." With all respect to the late genius, this is a fallacy; all of the Beatles improved noticeably and sometimes dramatically as musicians throughout the 1960s, and indeed noticeably and sometimes dramatically just from the beginning of 1963 to the end of 1963. Lennon's specific frustration was more likely with the limitations of improving the Beatles' *live* sound as the setlists became shorter and set in stone, and as Beatlemania made it hard to make the actual music heard.

The evidence of the Beatles' continued improvement as musicians and singers during this time is, luckily, documented in depth by their 1963 BBC sessions, never more so than on the *Pop Go the Beatles* episodes. This constant radio exposure, as has been occasionally noted, was an underrated factor in spreading Beatlemania as a commercial phenomenon. Could it just be, however, that the extreme pressure of putting together 15 episodes in a few months—constantly varying the setlist, with many covers never attempted by the Beatles for their commercial record releases—was also an underrated factor in sharpening and perfecting their musical skills as they became superstars? Their tough multiset, multimonth Hamburg stints had done their part to whip the group into shape prior to 1963, of course. But there, they were just playing to club audiences. Here, they were broadcasting to millions of listeners, needing to summon the goods week after week (and sometimes twice or thrice a day). In that sense, it was a real baptism by fire, and a challenge that the Beatles rose to magnificently.

● September 7

BBC Session
Saturday Club program (broadcast October 5, 1963)
Playhouse Theatre, London

I Saw Her Standing There
Memphis, Tennessee
Happy Birthday Saturday Club
I'll Get You
She Loves You
*Lucille

appears on Live at the BBC

Pop Go the Beatles might have been finished, and the Beatles' media commitments growing in scale as their fame grew, but the group would appear regularly on BBC radio for some time yet. In fact, they did a *Saturday Club* program just four days after their taxing trio of September 3 sessions. "Lucille" was the most ear-catching item here and was chosen for *Live at the BBC,* though, as earlier noted, there are grounds for arguing that the *Pop Go the Beatles* version is more exciting. The instrumental intro of this cut, unfortunately, is obscured by a voice-over from announcer Brian Matthew, and while he states that Paul McCartney's paying tribute to the Everly Brothers (who had a hit with the song in 1960), the Beatles actually learned the song from the Little Richard original. The guitar solo *is* significantly different this time around, though, with a cool, bee-stinging quality not heard on its counterpart. Give George Harrison his due here: he might not have executed all his BBC guitar lines with the smoothness of Mr. Clean, but he did, whether by intention or happenstance, usually find a way to change his riffs around in interesting ways and somehow manage to rarely play the same solo twice.

This is the last of the five BBC presentations of "Memphis, Tennessee," and it might have been the best—the rhythm pummels along really hard—but for yet another Brian Matthew voice-over during the intro, and a spot near the end of the first verse where John Lennon's voice breaks. The other track here not found on the group's studio releases is a trifle, but an amusing one: a half-minute "Happy Birthday Saturday Club" jingle, sung to the tune of "Happy Birthday" but played Eddie Cochran–style. As they did with "Beautiful Dreamer," the Beatles rock this overdone standard up really hard with the usual whoops, though without as much of a melody or lyrical content to work with, it's not nearly as memorable (or long) as that "Beautiful Dreamer" cover.

By the time this session was recorded, "She Loves You" had just hit No. 1 on the British charts, and as Matthew announced, there'd been a "sackful of requests" for them to perform it on this program. That they do, also reprising its B-side, "I'll Get You," and "I Saw Her Standing There." As a whole, the session's good but not great—but take note that the superb sound quality is about as fine as any of the available BBC recordings get.

● September 12

Studio Outtakes

With the Beatles *sessions*
Studio Two, Abbey Road, London

Hold Me Tight (rehearsal)
Hold Me Tight (takes 20–29)
Don't Bother Me (takes 10–13)

The only circulating *With the Beatles* outtakes on par sound-wise with official releases come from this day, with two of the lesser-known songs from the album represented. "Hold Me Tight" had first been attempted during the *Please Please Me* sessions, and the numerous outtakes here (including a half-minute instrumental rehearsal and some false starts, overdubs, and, on takes 25–29, superimpositions of backing vocals) are matters of tweaking. On take 21 John and George aren't singing as many vocal harmonies, and still don't have their backing vocals down cold (John sings "sleep tight" instead of "me tight" at one point!). Too, on the second bridge (or middle eight, as the Beatles themselves call it in their studio chat), they continue chugging away with the same straight 4/4 rhythm of the verses, rather than switching to the more rolling beats and haunting guitar flicks that they (presumably) should.

If you enjoy hearing off-guard Beatle screw-ups, there's a vintage one on the false start that's take 23, with Paul tailing off to moan, "Oh, bloody hell!" after he messes up the second line. Almost as good is take 20, where he brings the track to a dead halt after half a minute by singing the grammatically impossible, "Let me I'm the . . ." His vocal on this track has often been criticized (pretty fairly so) for being out of key, and these series of outtakes make it clear that problem was pretty consistent throughout the session. So why didn't they adjust the key, or return to the song later if Paul's voice wasn't holding up? Was time really that tight?

The series of "Don't Bother Me" outtakes is more interesting to follow, as the structure isn't quite as firmly in place yet. George's vocal is shaky on some attempts through this, the first of the songs he wrote all by himself to be recorded by the group. On take 10 he really does sound nervous, having clear trouble staying on pitch, especially on the last part of the second chorus (and then into the bridge); perhaps he'd caught the same vocal bug infecting McCartney's work on "Hold Me Tight." The guitar solo's not as right-on, and Ringo's drum breaks rhythm midway through the second bridge. On the fade George, probably sensing this complete take is by no means releasable, breaks into a drolly hilarious, sardonic-sounding "Oh yeah, rock and roll now, oh yeah." If you enjoyed those montages in the *Anthology* video series soundtracked by several minutes of humorous outtake-bloopers, this is one for the ages.

Take 11 and take 12 are interesting, as the group slightly alters the rhythm so that the band briefly comes to a dead stop between the instrumental intro and the verse. But neither get far, the small change seeming to confuse both George's vocals and the band's timing. They'd pretty much straighten everything out on take 13, even leaving in the muffled, sour background shout from the intro when it was given overdubs on take 15 (claves, bongo, tambourine, and George double-tracking his

vocal) to create the released track. As an aside, it's strange that George himself always disliked the result, telling Hunter Davies, "It was a fairly crappy song. I forgot about it completely once it was on the album." Many Beatles fans disagree—it's a superbly brooding track with a most unusual minor melody and reverbed guitar, and it's unfortunate that it was never done either live or for the BBC.

● October 9

BBC Session

The Ken Dodd Show *program (broadcast November 3, 1963)*
BBC Paris Theatre, London

She Loves You

The rapid-fire march of good-to-great-sounding BBC sessions in the last half of 1963 is a happy thing. But just to keep you from getting complacent, here's a most nonessential one, due to its one-song brevity, the lousy fidelity, and the availability of "She Loves You" in more superior-sounding versions than almost anyone could want.

● October 13

Live Performance

For television program, Val Parnell's Sunday Night
at the London Palladium
London Palladium, London

From Me to You
*I'll Get You
She Loves You
Twist and Shout
        *appears on Anthology 1

The Beatles' 1963 appearance on the *Val Parnell's Sunday Night at the London Palladium* television program marks, in most accounts of their legend, the point at which Beatlemania became a fully national phenomenon throughout Britain. Unfortunately, despite everyone's best efforts, the actual clip of the performance hasn't been found. When bootlegged, these tracks have boasted poor fidelity, of the kind from someone taping off-line from a television set. So this audio's of mostly historic value (you certainly *can* hear Beatlemania screams from the audience), though the appearance of "I'll Get You" on *Anthology 1* in quite good sound—you can even hear the audience clapping along with the intro chorus—suggests that the other three tracks might exist in decent shape as well.

● October 16

BBC Session

Easy Beat *program (broadcast October 20, 1963)*
Playhouse Theatre, London

*I Saw Her Standing There

Love Me Do

Please Please Me

From Me to You

She Loves You

appears on Live at the BBC

Following the *Sunday Night at the Palladium* success by just three days, the Beatles were already being introduced as "Britain's biggest attraction" when they taped this broadcast in front of a live audience. It seems like this program was deliberately planned as a greatest hits set of sorts, Brian Matthew jovially informing listeners after "I Saw Her Standing There" that "it's almost a year since the Beatles first hit the show business jackpot, so all the rest of the numbers that you're going to hear today are the big hits that the boys have achieved during the past 12 months." True to his word, "the boys" fire off all four of their singles to date in reliably exciting fashion. It's one of the more animated versions of "Love Me Do," coming to a nice jaunty, nonfaded ending distinctly different from the record. The sound quality's just a shade below excellent throughout.

● October 17

Studio Outtakes

"I Want to Hold Your Hand"/"This Boy" single session
Studio Two, Abbey Road, London

I Want to Hold Your Hand (take 1, fragment)

I Want to Hold Your Hand (take 2, fragment)

I Want to Hold Your Hand (take 9, fragment)

I Want to Hold Your Hand (unknown take, fragment)

*This Boy (take 12)

*This Boy (take 13)

This Boy (take # unknown, incomplete)

appears on Free As a Bird *CD single*

You have to be eagle-eyed to spot them, but a few outtakes from the session for the Beatles' fourth single did find official release. By far the most substantial of these are takes 12 and 13 of "This Boy," found as one of the four tracks on Apple's 1995 CD single of "Free As a Bird." Though the arrangement's in place, the faces aren't quite straight enough to play it right the whole way through. Take 12 breaks down in laughter right at the start of the second verse, Paul emitting a show-bizzy "that boy." Take 13, though described as "incomplete" on the sleeve, is actually almost complete, but the timing of the harmonies is off, especially on the middle eight. The group seem to be suppressing giggles at their mistakes by the home stretch, and actually break out laughing at the end, knowing they'll have to go over the whole damned thing again.

It sounds trivial on paper, and maybe it is in real life too, but part of the charm of listening to Beatles outtakes really is hearing their incapable-of-taking-themselves-too-seriously humor come through at points like these. Considering the close connection many have felt to the group through the generations, it's like sharing inside jokes with your family. There's evidence, however, that John Lennon wasn't all

smiles throughout the session, blurting "get this bloody little mike out of the way" before take 12. "Don't be nervous, John," soothes Paul. "I'm not," Lennon defensively shoots back.

The best and easiest place for the average fan to hear such ingratiating studio chatter is on the montages of outtake snippets that soundtrack actual studio images on three separate segments in the *Anthology* video/DVD series. The Beatles rib each other, trip up in false starts and crash endings, mess up their own lyrics, and so forth, occasionally getting annoyed but almost always defusing the tension with jokes. Many of these snippets had never been heard on any bootleg, indicating that quite a bit of digging through the vaults was involved to construct these sound-bite medleys. As another of our early examples of Beatles bootlegging extremism, however, it might come as a surprise even to some avid collectors that these snippets—often lasting no more than five to ten seconds—have actually been individually bootlegged on CD. Not only that, when *Anthology* was issued on DVD with a new stereo and 5.1 surround sound mix, all those brief "tracks" got bootlegged all over again in those formats. Not only *that*—sometimes these blips were issued in formats that allowed you to hear "isolated tracks" (or separate instrumental/vocal components) of these bitty fragments. It's the kind of rabid enthusiasm, frankly, that leads to even dedicated music lovers backing away in alarm from the devotees of such items, and for most sane people, it'll be quite enough to enjoy these on the videos/DVDs themselves.

This overzealous archivism, however, affects the discussion of the recording of "I Want to Hold Your Hand"/"This Boy" because it's the earliest session from which some outtake snatches have leaked *only* via those *Anthology* montages. (These particular ones are on the fifth chapter of episode two on the DVD, titled "Voice Clips from Abbey Road Studios," to be precise.) All the brief false starts of "I Want to Hold Your Hand" on the *Anthology* video tell us is that the guitars weren't in quite as perfect tune, that a slightly more elaborate and bluesier guitar figure was used at the end of one of the instrumental intros, and that Paul seems to be instructing Ringo to "attack" his first drum pattern. Paul even cited, in Barry Miles's *Paul McCartney: Many Years from Now,* the "I Want to Hold Your Hand" outtakes as an example of how "yes, okay, in the studio I could be overbearing. Because I wanted to get it right! I heard tapes recently of me counting in 'I Wanna [sic] Hold Your Hand,' which was our first number one in the States, and I'm being pretty bossy: 'Sssh, Sssh! Clean beginning, c'mon, everyone. One, two. No, c'mon, get it right!' and I can see how that could get on your nerves."

Having duly logged these snippets, completists can get ready to scream in frustration with the revelation that the *Anthology* DVD actually yanks one of the micro-takes (take 9) and substitutes a different one. The *Anthology*-exclusive "This Boy" outtake fragment remains the same in all formats, and it's a funny one, the fellas mixing up the phrases "this boy" and "that boy" to their considerable amusement.

● October 17

The Beatles Christmas Record

Studio Two, Abbey Road, London

With the explosion of Beatlemania, the group's fan club was swelling in membership. As a gesture of both seasonal goodwill and goodwill toward their staunchest supporters, on the same day they cut their fifth

The Beatles' Christmas Records

In the two years or so since Brian Epstein had played Tony Barrow an acetate in late 1961 in hopes of getting some ink in a newspaper column, Barrow had himself risen to a high-ranking position in the Beatles' hierarchy. As their press officer, he had the idea of having the group record a disc exclusively for distribution to their paid-up fan club members (and would end up writing the sleeve notes for the first three of them, just as he had written the sleeve notes for early Beatles LPs). The first Christmas fan club disc in 1963 (actually a one-track single) was an instant sellout and became an annual tradition for the group's entire career, even at the point where all four weren't able or willing to enter the studio at the same time to record it together.

In his authorized Beatles biography, Hunter Davies wrote that on the Christmas discs, "They do little sketches and sing a few corny songs, as in their old Cavern days." Reading this as a ten-year-old in the early '70s immediately fired up this author's curiosity and, indeed, jealousy of those lucky dogs who'd been able to get these "songs" that I hadn't a prayer of hearing. Be cautioned, however, that there really is very little in the way of actual "songs" on the Christmas discs. Even what songs there are bear little relation to conventional Beatles music, consisting mostly of off-the-cuff snatches of holiday tunes or busked variations/satires of same. The records are mostly a chance for the Beatles to indulge their most humorous impulses, the music being secondary to the sketches, rather than the other way around.

Putting them out as not-quite-serious, limited fan club–only editions enabled the Beatles to fulfill some standard show business obligations, yet at the same time steer clear of recording the treacly albums of straight readings of Christmas music that are an embarrassment to many major artists' catalogs. Even credible rock stars that the Beatles admired, such as Elvis Presley, the Beach Boys, and the Everly Brothers, did straight Christmas LPs for the commercial market. As in so many facets of their career, however, the Beatles would not do their holiday discs the usual way. They kept them separate from their commercial catalog so as to avoid diluting their main discography, slipping in some slyly subversive content along the way.

The first Beatles Christmas disc was pressed on "flexi-vinyl" on Lyntone Records in 1963, selling out so fast that a second pressing (without a sleeve) that didn't reach the public until early February 1964 had to be done to satisfy the demand. The print run of about 30,000 was doubled-and-then-some to 65,000 for the 1964 recording, and continued to appear on Lyntone until the group broke up in 1970. That year's fan club "release" was an LP (mastered from fan club secretary Freda Kelly's original flexis, rather than the original tapes) compiling all of the band's 1963–1969 Christmas singles. Listening to that LP compilation

(which has, naturally, often been issued as a bootleg) today, what's striking is how it, as much as any compilation of actual 1963–1969 Beatles tracks, reflects their changing characters, images, and even (to a limited degree) music and studio experimentation. Initially just a vehicle for a more-or-less standard Christmas greeting, even by the mid-'60s they were restlessly expanding beyond the limitations of their initial wholesome moptopness. Becoming increasingly less concerned with keeping up appearances, the "messages" became more and more sardonically humorous, the "music," "sketches," special effects, and editing progressively odder, even avant-garde at times.

By 1968, they were, in keeping with a group starting to fall apart, recording their parts separately. By late 1969, when the group had all but *fallen* apart, even the separately recorded portions seem less personally interconnected. At this point the members seem to have grown so much as solo entities (and drifted so far from one another) that it's hard not to read their final Christmas release, albeit with the benefit of hindsight, as yet another subtle signpost that a breakup was inevitable.

Technically, it could be argued that the seven Christmas fan club records were "officially" released, and certainly they were officially sanctioned. Yet the substantial majority of Beatles fans never did hear them, and many who were too young at the time to join the fan club (or were not even born) never had the chance to get them, particularly as none of them were re-pressed. Whether the group liked it or not, inevitable bootlegs of the material have been primarily responsible for keeping these artifacts in circulation. Though not commercially available, they continue to be played regularly on radio during the holidays today, and not just on specialty shows on public stations; this writer heard excerpts broadcast in prime time on an affiliate of a major syndicated commercial radio network in 2004.

Gordon Anderson, senior vice president and general manager of the largest mail-order reissue catalog (Collectors' Choice Music), estimates that if the 1963–1969 discs were compiled onto one CD for official release, it would sell two million copies. Still, there are no indications that such an anthology is in the works (and announced plans by R/S Distribution to release them as an LP in 1983 were met with a counterannouncement that representatives of the Beatles would sue those responsible for such a product). That's too bad, even though it wouldn't contain "unreleased Beatles music" in the usual sense of the term. It really should, however, be made easily available, preferably with outtakes (yes, there *were* outtakes from the Christmas release sessions) added as bonus tracks and the nifty original cover of the 1970 fan club–only LP compilation, which showed five snapshots of each Beatle in varying (and very visually different) phases of the group's career.

single, the boys recorded *The Beatles Christmas Record,* to be distributed only to fan club members. It was the first of seven such annual fan club releases, which got increasingly wacky and even experimental as the years passed, serving as the primary audio outlet for their most Goonish brand of humor (fashioned after the beloved British "The Goon Show" radio series).

Lasting for five minutes, the first of these records was unsurprisingly the most naive and innocuous of the lot. Here the Beatles seem basically eager to toe the usual Christmas showbiz message line of "thanks so much to everyone for buying all our records," though part of this is no doubt due to the scripted material publicist Tony Barrow supplied. If the message/script had just been read verbatim, as many stars would have done with an affected heartfelt tone, it would make for a dated and likely somewhat painfully boring listen. As usual, however, the Beatles couldn't really even read the straight lines straight, sending up the text with their silly delivery ("Hello, this is John, speaking with his voice"), but not to the point of making any of their young fans suspicious enough to doubt the group's sincerity. As to the "music" contained on this outing, it's limited to some brief snatches of holiday songs and miscellaneous royal themes and jingles. They're sung (and sometimes whistled) in exaggeratedly arch high and low voices, a cappella save some bells heard at the beginning.

Whether it's Barrow's doing or not, though, it's interesting to hear Paul McCartney sound a semi-serious note when he reflects, "Lots of people ask us what we enjoy best, concerts and television or recording. We like doing stage shows, 'cause it's, y'know, it's great to hear an audience enjoying themselves. But the thing we like best—I think so anyway—is going into the recording studio to make new records, which is what we've been doing all day before we started on this special message. What we like to hear most is one of our songs, you know, taking shape in a recording studio, one of the ones what John and I have written, and then listening to the tapes afterwards to see how it all worked out." Even amidst the tomfoolery of a Christmas fan club message, you could hear the heartbeats of true artists. All those great BBC rock 'n' roll covers notwithstanding, it was a sign that original material and records had become the group's focus.

By the way, there was more material done at this session than what you hear on the record, but you'll never hear it. In his 2005 memoir, *John, Paul, George, Ringo & Me: The Real Beatles Story,* Barrow confirmed that when he and Lyntone Records chief Paul Lyntone edited the tape, they "actually cut the tape recording with scissors, patched the pieces together and let the discarded bits drop to the floor. In doing this we destroyed a master tape that at some future date might have raised many thousands of pounds at auction as a unique piece of memorabilia—particularly with all the unused bad language left in!"

● October 24

Live Performance
Karlaplansstudion, Stockholm

---

*I Saw Her Standing There
*From Me to You
*Money (That's What I Want)
*Roll Over Beethoven
*You Really Got a Hold on Me
She Loves You
Twist and Shout

   *appears on Anthology 1

As kind of a Swedish counterpart to a BBC session, the Beatles performed seven songs in front of a live audience in Stockholm, broadcast on November 11 on Swedish National Radio. This was their first show abroad as actual pop stars, and it's one of the best (and most well-recorded) early Beatles concert (or live-in-the-studio, if you prefer) appearances. Apple recognized its quality, putting five of the seven tracks onto *Anthology 1* in 1995.

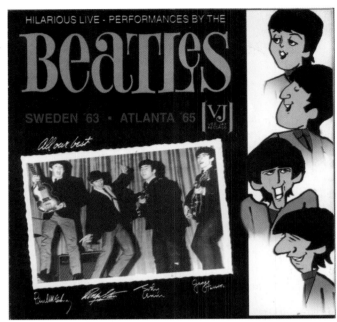

The Beatles' marvelous October 24, 1963, performance for Swedish radio is included in this bootleg, which wittily references both early Beatles LP art and the group's cartoon series.

As Beatles authority Mark Lewisohn observed in *Anthology 1*'s liner notes, the group was "clearly exuberant at playing for the Swedish audience," and the tracks have a slightly more lively feel (particularly in the vocals) than even their by-now-standard excellent BBC sessions. Listen to how Paul McCartney and the group kick off "I Saw Her Standing There," or how John Lennon attacks "Twist and Shout"; they rarely sounded more animated, and the yells at the beginning of "Money (That's What I Want)" were never hungrier. This is the first preserved version of "Roll Over Beethoven," incidentally, where the Beatles introduced a slight but interesting variation into the arrangement, hanging back on the rhythm a bit in the last verse (Ringo Starr's drums sometimes dropping out altogether) before launching into an all-out assault on the final chorus.

This doesn't mean that there aren't some minor glitches to be heard. The guitars aren't in ideal tune at times (most noticeably at points in "From Me to You," "Twist and Shout," and "You Really Got a Hold on Me"); John sings a wrong lyric near the beginning of "You Really Got a Hold on Me" ("my love is wrong now" instead of "my love is strong now"); and the voices aren't in perfect harmony on the opening chorus of "She Loves You." A great audio document nonetheless, it's not as big a find on bootleg now that most of it's officially available, though the two cuts that didn't make it onto *Anthology 1* ("She Loves You" and "Twist and Shout") are just as strong as the rest of the set.

● October 30

Live Performance
For Swedish television program Drop In
Narren-teatern, Gröna Lund, Stockholm

She Loves You
Twist and Shout
I Saw Her Standing There
Long Tall Sally

Recorded for Swedish television before a live audience, this comes from the soundtrack of one of the very most exciting live Beatles performance clips ever, from which two numbers ("I Saw Her Standing There" and "Long Tall Sally") were used in the *Anthology* video series. It's more properly discussed, then, in the accompanying entry in the film section of this book; see part two. The four tracks also show up on audio-only bootlegs, and like the October 24 Swedish radio broadcast, they capture the early Beatles at their very peak as live performers. The Swedish radio show does have slightly better audio and sound balance, and the guitar isn't always in the best tune. There's just one rather than two instrumental breaks in "Long Tall Sally," too, though it's played with the ferocity of a four-headed bulldog.

● November 4

Live Performance
The Royal Variety Performance
Prince of Wales Theatre, London

From Me to You
*She Loves You
*Till There Was You
*Twist and Shout
        *appears on Anthology 1

One of the Beatles' most famous appearances, with the Queen Mother, Princess Margaret, and Lord Snowdon in the audience, televised nationally in Britain. For many years, fans had to put up with mediocre-quality bootlegged recordings of the four tracks. But all save "From Me to You" appeared on *Anthology 1* in good mono sound, complete with Paul's joke preceding "Till There Was You" (introduced as having "also been recorded by our favorite American group, Sophie Tucker") and John's much more famous and wittier one in the intro to "Twist and Shout": "Would the people in the cheaper seats clap your hands? And the rest of you, if you'll just rattle your jewelry."

There are better-sounding live 1963 versions of all of these songs, but the performances are reliably high-grade, George Harrison acquitting himself especially well on the solo for "Till There Was You." Most fans would consider it essential, however, on the grounds of its historic significance alone. While "From Me to You" does not appear on *Anthology 1* (and hence is still not available in the same standard of sound quality as the other tracks), it's readily available on bootleg. Better yet, you can see it as part of the video clip of the performance (see entry in film section), as all the songs except "She Loves You" appear in the *Anthology* video.

As a footnote, the discrepancy between the number of BBC sessions attributed to the Beatles—some sources say there were 52, others 53—might be caused by whether they count this appearance, highlights of which were broadcast on the Beeb on November 10.

● November 9

Live Performance
Granada Cinema, London

I Saw Her Standing There (fragment)

Here we go with the very first of the many terrible-sounding mere scraps of Beatlemania concerts, in which the group's only faintly audible behind a wall of screams—a phenomenon that would really take off in the two years starting from the Beatles' summer 1964 North American tour. This 45-second fragment of "I Saw Her Standing There" was taken from Granada TV's documentary *The Early Beatles*.

● November 16

Live Performance
Winter Gardens Theatre, Bournemouth

From Me to You (fragment)

Another performance with terrible fidelity, nearly drowned out by screams. This audio has some historical importance, however, as its originating film clip was shown (along with another clip from the documentary *The Mersey Sound* of the band doing "She Loves You" on August 27) by Jack Paar on his network television show on January 3, 1964. That marked the first time many Americans had a chance to see the Beatles, predating their *Ed Sullivan Show* debut by more than a month. Unfortunately, not only is the sound on the circulating track awful, but it's further obscured by unfunny voice-over observations by Paar himself, à la "I just show you this in case you're going to England and want to have a fun evening."

● November 20

Live Performance
ABC Cinema, Manchester

She Loves You
Twist and Shout (incomplete)
From Me to You (instrumental reprise)

From the soundtrack of the Pathé News newsreel *The Beatles Come to Town* come these two songs. As the quality's only fair—only the last half of "Twist and Shout" is present, and there's much screaming throughout—it's better experienced on screen as a video clip (see entry in film section). Oddly, a brief snatch of "From Me to You" played as an instrumental (not the version from the record) is also heard on the soundtrack of the newsreel as the curtains close on the Beatles' performance.

● December 2

Live Performance

For television program The Morecambe and Wise Show
Elstree Studio Centre, Borehamwood, Hertfordshire

*This Boy
All My Loving
*I Want to Hold Your Hand
*Moonlight Bay
     appears on Anthology 1

These are the earliest live performances of "I Want to Hold Your Hand,"
its B-side, "This Boy," and the *With the Beatles* highlight "All My Loving," both the single and LP having just taken off for No. 1 at the time
this was done on TV for *The Morecambe and Wise Show.* "This Boy" is
very faithful to the recorded version, though John's voice catches on a
high note in the bridge, and it comes to a full-stop ending rather than
fading as it does on the single. But it's interesting to hear that even at
one of its first public airings, "I Want to Hold Your Hand" has a somewhat chunkier, funkier rhythm than the jerkier one on the single. That
arrangement would stay in place throughout the Beatles' live performances of this tune; perhaps not being able to use the handclaps that
helped keep the record's more irregular rhythm influenced their more
straightforward approach to the song in concert.

Both of those recordings are on *Anthology 1,* as well as the brief bit
where they're put through the paces on the ancient pop standard "Moonlight Bay," Eric Morecambe throwing in bleated references to early Beatles
hits. It's much better experienced on video than record, as is the sole song
not placed on *Anthology 1,* "All My Loving." In fact this strong, faithful-
to-the-record rendition of "All My Loving" (although Paul and George
harmonized on the last verse, upon which Paul had double-tracked his
lead vocals in the studio) would have made much more pleasant listening
on *Anthology 1* than "Moonlight Bay." It was probably passed over in part
because a different, more historically monumental version of "All My
Loving"—the one that opened their first *Ed Sullivan Show* appearance a
couple of months later—appears later on the disc.

● December 7

Live Performance
Empire Theatre, Liverpool

From Me to You
I Saw Her Standing There
All My Loving
Roll Over Beethoven
Boys
Till There Was You
She Loves You
This Boy
I Want to Hold Your Hand
Money (That's What I Want)
Twist and Shout
From Me to You/Third Man Theme (instrumental)

For all the enormous quantity of live music recorded by the Beatles in
1963, this is the earliest existing document (unless you want to count

the *Live! At the Star-Club* tapes) of a relatively full half-hour concert set.
It was the group's first concert in their Liverpool hometown since the
full onslaught of Beatlemania—their final Cavern show having taken
place just four months prior to this event—where the screams of the
audience are louder than anything a club audience could have managed. Unfortunately, the quality's not too good, sounding as if it's been
recorded off-line from the television (though by *those* standards, it's not
too bad). Also, Ringo Starr's vocal for "Boys" is all but inaudible, presumably due to microphone failure. "The boys" give their customary
spirited performance, but the low fidelity means these are among the
less desirable versions of these songs (and if you want to hear almost
the exact same set of songs done a couple of months later, the recordings from their February 1964 visit to America are far preferable).

As for little bits that might distinguish this from other live shows,
there aren't many. But it's funny to hear John, not Paul, introduce "Till
There Was You" as a song from *The Muscle Man* (rather than the actual
musical it came from, *The Music Man*), sung by "Peggy Leg" (i.e., Peggy
Lee). (Acknowledging their Liverpool roots, Lennon also offers that "a
lot of you will remember this from the Cavern.") There's a strange, brief
drum intro to "From Me to You," and it's reprised as an instrumental
for the finale, somehow mutating into a brief passage of Anton Karas's
playful pop instrumental "Third Man Theme," a chart-topper in both
the UK and US after its use as the theme for the popular 1949 movie
The Third Man. Some less-than-visually-optimal fragments of the TV
broadcast are still around, by the way (see entry in film section), but
unfortunately the full program hasn't been discovered.

● December 17

BBC Session
Saturday Club program (broadcast December 21, 1963)
Playhouse Theatre, London

This Boy
I Want to Hold Your Hand
Till There Was You
Roll Over Beethoven
She Loves You
Beatles Crimble Medley

It had been a while since the Beatles had been able to work much new
original material into their BBC programs, and you'd think it might
have come as a relief to have the chance to introduce some new Lennon-
McCartney songs from their new single on this just-before-Christmas
broadcast. If not for the group, it's certainly a relief for listeners two
generations on, after weeding through so many sessions—as enjoyable
as each one is, taken on its own—that repeated so many of the same
songs so many times. Even if the rest of the set was actually given over
to songs that had already been played on the Beeb many times, this
excellent-sounding tape is a welcome addition to the Beatles lover's
library, especially as none of it's come out on official discs.

Before heading into "This Boy," George Harrison makes an unusual
direct reference to the BBC recording radio environment, emphasizing
to listeners that what follows is *not* the record, but an in-BBC-studio
performance. Still, it does follow the record very closely—not that there's

anything terribly wrong with that. "I Want to Hold Your Hand" had already been at No. 1 for a couple of weeks by the time this was taped, and this performance even has the handclaps from the studio arrangement, an effect that would fall by the wayside on most of their non-EMI presentations of this classic.

The new single duly promoted, they turned to tried-and-true material for the rest of the program: "Till There Was You" (the studio version of which had just come out on *With the Beatles*), "Roll Over Beethoven" (ditto), and "She Loves You." There was also a brief snatch of the fellows singing the off-the-cuff, not terribly tuneful or humorous a cappella ditty "All I Want for Christmas Is a Bottle"—so brief, in fact, that it doesn't merit a mention as a separate track. Longer, though not that much more entertaining, was a drumless half-minute "Beatle Crimble Medley" of ultra-short snippets from their five singles to date (plus "Rudolf the Red-Nosed Reindeer)," set to the melody of Duane Eddy's 1960 instrumental hit "Shazam." Although a short excerpt from "All My Loving" opens the program (and appears on some bootlegs), this is not a live performance, but taken from the record; the first BBC version of "All My Loving" would be done at their next radio session the following day.

● December 18

BBC Session

From Us to You *program #1 (broadcast December 26, 1963)*
BBC Paris Theatre, London

From Us to You (intro)
She Loves You
All My Loving
Roll Over Beethoven
Till There Was You
Boys
Money (That's What I Want)
I Saw Her Standing There
Tie Me Kangaroo Down, Sport (with Rolf Harris)
I Want to Hold Your Hand
From Us to You (outro)

There was no way the Beatles could have taken on another 15-part BBC series such as *Pop Go the Beatles* by the end of 1963. But they did make four BBC radio specials under the title *From Us to You*, all broadcast on British bank holidays. The first of these gave them more songs than the half-dozen max to which they'd been accustomed, all of them preserved in excellent sound quality, and none of them issued on official releases.

Even with all that space available, however, there was just one number, "All My Loving," that the group hadn't previously played on the Beeb. Too, by this point their radio renditions were getting ever closer to the familiar studio ones—not that they'd ever been that far apart, but some casual listeners might not even be able to tell the difference between this broadcast's "All My Loving" and the same track on *With the Beatles*. It's a tribute to their growing consummate professionalism, yet at the same time, to be brutally honest, makes such

John, Paul, and George gather 'round the mike at their December 17, 1963,
session to sing '"This Boy" for BBC radio's Saturday Club *program.*

sessions a little less interesting to the seasoned collector looking for something a little more novel or surprising.

That's being a spoilsport for a show that's pretty good, although it sounds better if you're *not* hearing it after plowing through the previous half-dozen CDs of a *Complete Beatles at the BBC* box set at one go. "Money (That's What I Want)," aired for the first time subsequent to its inclusion on *With the Beatles,* might be the most spontaneous-sounding of the tracks, the group screaming their hearts out (albeit faded way down in the mix) on the instrumental intro, John Lennon ad-libbing slightly on the outro. As for the between-song chatter, it's odd to hear Ringo refer to "Boys" as "his one and only number." He'd already sung another ("Matchbox") on the seventh episode of *Pop Go the Beatles,* and *With the Beatles* was already in the shops with his vocal on "I Wanna Be Your Man." It's not one of George's better "I Saw Her Standing There" solos, with a thin, twanging timbre, but hey, at least it's different.

There *are* three small bonuses that aren't as unusual as they appear to be from a glance at the song titles. The group devised a theme song especially for the series "From Us to You" that was just a briefer version of "From Me to You" with the appropriate pronouns changed. A 52-second version opens this program, with a voice-over by host Rolf Harris, ending on a rather sour chord; a different, shorter one, faded out at its end and again with a voice-over, closes it. The Australian Harris had a massive novelty hit in the UK in 1960 with "Tie Me Kangaroo Down, Sport" (which went to No. 5 in the US in 1963), and sings it here, with some assistance on the choruses from the Beatles on backup vocals. He couldn't let it go there, adding "She Loves You"-like "woohs" and changing some of the lyrics to woefully lame satirical jibes at his guests (samples: "cut your hair once a year, boys, if it covers your ear you can't hear," "he can't understand your lingo, Ringo," "George's guitar's on the blink, I think"). Beyond weird, and beyond corny, it's available on too many bootlegs to count—and hard to avoid, in fact, if you want to get this session on disc at all. Harris dispenses more such ageless witticisms throughout the show as well, the bad taste in the mouth thankfully washed out to shore by the "I Want to Hold Your Hand" finale.

● Sometime in 1963

Private Tapes

Instrumental #1

Instrumental #2

Michelle (instrumental)

Instrumental #3

Instrumental #4

Instrumental #5

Three Coins in a Fountain (instrumental)

Rockin' and Rollin' (instrumental backing track)

Rockin' and Rollin' (instrumental backing track with guitar overdub)

Rockin' and Rollin' (instrumental backing track with horn overdub)

Rockin' and Rollin' (instrumental backing track with vocal overdub)

In 1989, ex-Beatles chauffeur Alf Bicknell tried to auction off at Sotheby's five primitively recorded, informal, nonstudio (with the exception of a few playback takes from their July 30, 1963, EMI session) tapes of members of the band. These were given to him, or so it was said, by John Lennon when the group's limousine was being cleaned out. As exciting a find as it might have seemed upon announcement, in reality they're so mundane—and so execrably recorded—as to even make many fervent Beatles collectors wish they didn't have to be examined in the first place. Exist they do, however, and documented they must be, though it's material that nobody in their right mind could stand to listen to much.

Three of the excerpts from the tapes (assorted Beatles and Gerry Marsden reading from the Bible and singing hymns, the playback takes of "Please Mr. Postman" and "It Won't Be Long," and George Harrison working out "Don't Bother Me") can be dated with reasonable certainty, and were detailed in the July 22–27, July 30, and August 19–24 entries. The rest is far harder to pin down with such precision. The tracks listed in this entry were noted at their auction sale as originating from 1963, and while some discographers have assigned a July/August 1963 date to them, the exact date is probably never going to be established. (Another portion of the tape, in which John Lennon sings and plays "If I Fell" on acoustic guitar, is commonly believed to date from early 1964, and so is discussed in an entry in the 1964 chapter.)

By far the most interesting item is a minute-long guitar-only instrumental version of "Michelle," which wasn't recorded by the Beatles until the sessions for the *Rubber Soul* album in late 1965. *Could* it have been played way back in mid-1963? Maybe—the Beatles *did* sometimes keep scraps of ideas around for a long time before fully developing them. In *Paul McCartney: Many Years from Now,* Paul confirmed that the song originated as a "tune I'd written in Chet Atkins's finger-pickin' style," and one he'd first played at parties given by John Lennon's art school tutor Austin Mitchell, years before the Beatles became big. Paul revived it only at John's suggestion years later. For what it's worth, this fragment definitely *is* the melody line of the verse of "Michelle," though it veers off into a completely different bridge with what sounds like an almost unusably strange series of jazzy chords.

The rest of the material is not only unrecognizable as anything the Beatles officially recorded, but much harder going, due to both the fair-to-absymal recording quality and the absence of solid musical ideas. Probably it was just one or more of the group messing around informally while a portable tape recorder was going. Of the five instrumentals, the first (very brief) one has a slight Mediterranean feel, while the second, lasting a good two-and-a-half minutes, is a series of run-of-the-mill bluesy progressions with hints of both jazz and Chuck Berry. The third is a 15-second snippet that sounds like an attempt to simulate stereotypical film soundtracks of scenes taking place in Chinese restaurants; the fourth, with a faint cymbal in the background, again has something of the Mediterranean lullaby vibe, with hesitantly placed jazz chords. The fifth, lasting just over a minute, again taps the dramatic flamenco-Greek ambience of McCartney ballads like "Michelle" and "And I Love Her," though this particular idea was not nearly as developed and would evidently remain in its undernourished state. Then there's a guitar instrumental rendition of the sentimental pop ballad "Three Coins in a Fountain," a movie theme that had been a huge hit for the Four Aces in 1954. The best that could be surmised about these tracks is that perhaps they were done as exercises, at a point where the Beatles or a Beatle—McCartney being the best guess—were consciously trying to introduce some more sophisticated influences into their original material. The jazz and pop colors, rudimentary as they are on these tapes, were some steps removed from the American rock 'n' roll and R&B that served as their main initial inspirations.

"Rockin' and Rollin'"—and here's guessing this was *not* the title given to the song at the time, if any was—is a real oddity, as a generic '50s-styled rock 'n' roll instrumental that was subjected to numerous overdubs. The first version is played straight. On the second, a tape of it plays in the background as someone plays a little bit of undistinguished guitar in the foreground. On the third, a cheesy horn is overlaid on the backing track, again playing away in the background. On the fourth and final one, deliberately doofuslike vocals are added to the backing track; it sounds like that's George singing a lyric that seems improvised in its stereotypical '50s blandness, while backup voices take the mickey out of doo wop clichés. The best that could be said about these is that perhaps they helped get the Beatles' feet wet in the art of double-tracking home recordings. It doesn't seem possible that any of this mucking about could have been done on EMI's time.

Interspersed with these more-or-less actual musical bits are items of such low relevance to the group's art that they just can't quite qualify as "unreleased Beatles music," even though a Beatle or Beatles can sometimes be heard. There's Paul singing along to the radio as it plays recordings of "Tammy" and "Over the Rainbow"; someone, perhaps Paul, doing nursery rhymes with an unidentified small child; and incidental chatter and background radio music. The whole lot's available, should you need it, on numerous bootlegs, despite Sotheby's auctioneer having read a warning from EMI and Apple that anyone making improper use of the recordings would be prosecuted.

And how did that auction go? Bicknell had hoped to raise £60,000, but only sold two of the five tapes. A West German bidder paid nearly £12,000 for both—a great deal more than their actual worth, as even the $20 price they fetch as a bootleg leaves many collectors feeling ripped off.

1963 Noncirculating Recordings, Known and Rumored

From 1963 and each subsequent year, the known Beatles recordings that very few have heard grow in number, as Mark Lewisohn's 1988 book *The Beatles Recording Sessions: The Official Abbey Road Studio Session Notes 1962–1970* documents a great many studio outtakes that have yet to be bootlegged. There are also a number of 1963 BBC sessions that have yet to be discovered on tape, as well as at least one known unreleased demo.

● **February 11**

Studio Outtakes
Please Please Me sessions
Studio Two, Abbey Road, London

In the interests of saving space, and more importantly, avoiding redundancy with Lewisohn's *The Beatles Recording Sessions,* from this point onward this book will be noting and discussing only the very most in-

teresting of the *un*bootlegged outtakes known to exist from the Beatles' EMI sessions. These will be grouped by the overall sessions taking place for specific albums and singles, whether they were completed in a single day or spread over months. It will be emphasized here at the start both that Lewisohn's book documents the existence of numerous Beatles outtakes for virtually all of their sessions, and that *The Beatles Recording Sessions* is essential reading for anyone interested in the unreleased music of the Beatles—and, for that matter, anyone seriously interested in the Beatles, period.

The most interesting known noncirculating *Please Please Me* outtake is an early version of "Hold Me Tight," which would be remade for *With the Beatles.* One wonders whether it was much different at this stage, seven months prior to the recording of the remake, and whether Paul McCartney was having as much trouble staying on key at this point as he was when he sang the tune in September. We'll probably never know, however, as Lewisohn wrote that the tape no longer exists.

Of the other *Please Please Me* outtakes noted in *The Beatles Recording Sessions,* the only one described in much detail is the second (and final) attempt at "Twist and Shout." As George Martin told Lewisohn, "I did try a second take of 'Twist and Shout' but John's voice had gone." It had long been assumed that "Twist and Shout" was accepted immediately as a one-take recording, and, if nothing else, the second take would make for morbidly fascinating listening to hear just how shot Lennon's voice was after this most throat-shredding of vocals. In addition, on the February 20 session at which George Martin (without any Beatles present) overdubbed piano on "Misery" and celeste on "Baby It's You," he also did a piano overdub for "Baby It's You" that's never been heard—a very minor variation, admittedly, but a potentially interesting one.

As a final note, it's curious that perfect-quality outtakes have escaped for about half the *Please Please Me* tracks, but not the other half; it would be great to hear the outtakes of "Twist and Shout," "Anna," "Chains," "Baby It's You," and "Boys," none of them represented on bootleg. But as noted previously, it's doubtful that any even exist, particularly since the original session reels could not be located by John Barrett when he cataloged the Beatles' EMI tapes in the early '80s.

● **February 20**

BBC Session
Parade of the Pops *program (broadcast live)*
Playhouse Theatre, London

Love Me Do
Please Please Me

The first of the three entirely "missing" 1963 BBC sessions, broadcast live and performed in front of an audience.

● **Early 1963**

Private Tapes

Do You Want to Know a Secret
I'll Be on My Way

It's known that a demo tape of "Do You Want to Know a Secret" existed at one point, as Billy J. Kramer remembered hearing it before recording his chart-topping cover of the song on March 21, 1963. "I had this tape given to me, and it was John Lennon singing it with an acoustic guitar," he recalled in Steve Kolanjian's liner notes to the 1991 CD *The Best of Billy J. Kramer & the Dakotas: The Definitive Collection.* "On the tape he said, 'I'm sorry for the sound quality, but it's the quietest room I could find in the whole building.' Then he flushed the toilet."

The survival of a Beatles demo of "I'll Be on My Way" (recorded by Kramer on the B-side of "Do You Want to Know a Secret") is less than 100 percent certain. But Mike Maxwell, guitarist in Kramer's backup band, has claimed ownership of an acetate of the Beatles doing "I'll Be on My Way," which Kramer recorded in March. It hasn't circulated, and if it does, one wonders if it will just turn out to be the Beatles' BBC recording of the tune. Assuming a demo was used by Kramer to learn the song, one thing that *is* virtually certain is that such an acetate demo would *not* simply be the Beatles' BBC performance of the song. For the BBC version was done at an April 4 session, after Kramer had recorded the tune at the same March 21 session where he did "Do You Want to Know a Secret."

● March 21

BBC Session
On the Scene *program (broadcast March 28, 1963)*
BBC Piccadilly Studios, London

Misery
Do You Want to Know a Secret
Please Please Me

Another session of which there seems to be no copy. As it happens, it has the exact same track lineup as their March 6 session for the *Here We Go* program, which *is* preserved in good quality.

● April 1

BBC Session
Side by Side *program (broadcast April 22, 1963)*
BBC Piccadilly Studios, London

I Saw Her Standing There
Do You Want to Know a Secret
Baby It's You
Please Please Me
From Me to You
Misery

The final of the three wholly missing 1963 BBC sessions was the most interesting of the trio due to its greater length and its strong song selection, though hi-fi Beeb versions of each tune exist from other programs. As galling as the loss of these episodes is to the Beatles completist, it's

The Lost Beebs *has sessions that were hard to find when the LP came out in 1988, but a few of the Beatles' BBC sessions are unfortunately truly lost; no tapes have yet surfaced.*

still remarkable just how *much* of the BBC sessions have survived, and how much of it survives in good-to-excellent fidelity. It's especially so, considering that the rock music–collecting community barely existed at the time, and that it would be a good decade or so before home stereo equipment that allowed full-fidelity taping of radio broadcasts became standard. At least none of the "lost" tracks from the BBC sessions were songs of which no other Beatles version exists. The only two real major losses were the previously noted instances in which Tommy Roe's "Sheila" (on October 26, 1962) and the Coasters' "Three Cool Cats" (on January 16, 1963, and July 2, 1963) were taped at BBC sessions but not broadcast, as the Beatles never recorded those songs for EMI (though there's a live version of "Sheila" on *Live! At the Star-Club* and a Decca audition version of "Three Cool Cats").

● Summer

Private Tapes

The earliest of the tapes located when John Lennon's archive was exhumed for the radio series *The Lost Lennon Tapes* includes some untitled songs he played and sang on his own in Liverpool in the summer of 1963. A piano and vocal number titled "It's Different with Me" when the tapes were logged might be the "I'm in Love" composing tape noted earlier in this chapter. There are also reportedly a cappella and French(!) versions of "From Me to You," though as John didn't speak French, one wonders if he's actually singing it in French here or if he's singing made-up gobbledygook.

● July 18–October 17

Studio Outtakes
With the Beatles *sessions*
Studio Two, Abbey Road, London

Few interesting variations among the *With the Beatles* outtakes are noted in *The Beatles Recording Sessions*. One of the reasons few interesting variations might have been noted, however, is that aside from the September 12, 1963, session at which numerous takes of "Hold Me Tight" and "Don't Bother Me" were recorded (and bootlegged—see corresponding entry), none of the session reels are known to exist. At any rate, none could be found when John Barrett did his cataloging in the early '80s. Nor were session tapes found for the "She Loves You"/"I'll Get You" single, recorded only slightly before the *With the Beatles* sessions.

Then why document them at all in this volume, some of you might be asking? Well, although it's probably a long shot that any of these tapes will be located, some such tapes *have* turned up unexpectedly in out-of-the-way places, for the Beatles, Elvis Presley, the Who, and numerous other major twentieth century recording artists. It's always possible the tapes were misfiled, mislabeled, or surreptitiously copied and taken out of EMI back in the 1960s. That's how the June 6, 1962, outtakes of "Besame Mucho" and "Love Me Do" were discovered—the former on a private reel, the latter on acetate, when George Martin's wife was cleaning out his closet. Anything can happen, although we also have to be braced for the very real possibility that the tapes are lost for good. After 1963, luckily, most of the original session tapes *do* survive, even if by no means all of them have been heard outside of Abbey Road.

From the scant information we *do* know about the missing *With the Beatles* outtakes, perhaps the ones that might be the most different are the three July 18, 1963, attempts at "Till There Was You" and the seven September 11, 1963, takes of "Don't Bother Me." For in both instances the songs were redone at later sessions, increasing at least the chance that there might be significant differences in the earlier arrangements. The Beatles also tried a different take of "You Really Got Me" on October 17 (at the session primarily devoted to the "I Want to Hold Your Hand"/"This Boy" single) but ended up using an earlier one, perhaps indicating that they made one attempt at trying a different spin on the number.

● August 21

Live Performance
Gaumont Theatre, Bournemouth

Roll Over Beethoven
Thank You Girl
Chains
From Me to You
A Taste of Honey
I Saw Her Standing There
Baby It's You
Boys
She Loves You
Twist and Shout

This ten-song live tape, recorded by the chief technician of the Gaumont Theatre and said to be of good quality, was auctioned by Christie's on December 10, 1998, for £25,300. Apart from including a few songs for which no 1963 non-BBC live performances are circulating ("Baby It's You," "Thank You Girl," "Chains," "A Taste of Honey"), it's also of interest for containing a prerelease concert performance of "She Loves You," introduced by John as "a new song for us, released on Friday. Buy your copy . . . please."

● October 17

Studio Outtakes
"I Want to Hold Your Hand"/"This Boy" single session
Studio Two, Abbey Road, London

The Beatles Recording Sessions notes that a discarded idea from take 2 of "I Want to Hold Your Hand" (though well short of great) "was to hush the vocal line 'And when I touch you,'" and that outtakes of "This Boy" had a full rather than faded ending. 'Course, you can hear the full ending of "This Boy" on numerous live recordings of the era, including the December 2, 1963, one on *Anthology 1*.

● November 3

Live Performance
Odeon Cinema, Leeds

The Beatles' concert at Odeon Cinema in Leeds was taped, bizarrely, for use as evidence in a legal case between several promoters and the Performing Rights Society. The latter organization wanted more money paid to them for pop music presented in concerts; the promoters were claiming that audiences weren't listening to the music, and thus going to shows for entirely different reasons. The proof? This tape of the Beatles onstage, which was actually played in part during the trial on December 10, 1963, as part of a 15-minute segment that also included snippets of performances by their supporting acts. According to *The Times,* "It would be an overstatement to say that the sound heard was the Beatles. It was much more the sound of 2,000 shrieking teenagers, with a rhythmic, pulsating thud somewhere in the background." The tape's sound engineer, Bernard Weaver, went as far as to offer testimony that "the sound in the auditorium was worse than on the tape. The fans don't listen to the music played. They don't even sit in their seats. They just stand up and go berserk!" The full tape does include the Beatles performing ten songs: "I Saw Her Standing There," "From Me to You," "All My Loving," "You Really Got a Hold on Me," "Roll Over Beethoven," "Boys," "Till There Was You," "She Loves You," "Money (That's What I Want)," and "Twist and Shout." But if it's found, would it even be listenable?

The Beatles' appearances on Ed Sullivan's network TV show in February 1964 sealed Beatlemania's grip on the United States.

1964

The Beatles Conquer America— And the World

The Year in Review

The Beatles Conquer America was the title of one of the better, more popular Beatles bootlegs, featuring the live *Ed Sullivan Show* performances that did so much to cement the group's American superstardom. But the title was not hyperbole—it was truth in advertising. The Beatles *did* conquer America in early 1964, as decisively as any cultural invader has ever vanquished a foreign populace. The statistical evidence alone is staggering. At one point that winter it was estimated that they were responsible for 60 percent of all singles sold in the country, and on April 5, 1964, they occupied all top five positions on the *Billboard* singles chart (and had the top *nine* singles in Canada), as well as the top two slots in the LP listings. Their first appearance on *The Ed Sullivan Show*, days after their arrival in New York on February 7 for their first American visit, broke ratings records with an audience of around 70 million. And while the Beatles had already begun to make some inroads into continental European markets by late 1963, now the phenomenon of Beatlemania repeated itself all over the world.

The Beatles' evolution in 1964 is well documented by their official releases of the year, including two albums, three singles, an EP, and the film *A Hard Day's Night.* While the unreleased recordings from this year don't shed as much additional light on their artistry as the unissued music of 1962 and 1963 does, there are certainly a lot of them. During their quasi-world tour of mid-1964 through parts of Europe and Australia, and then their first full-scale tour of North America a few months later, quite a few full-length or nearly full-length concerts were unofficially captured on tape. More than the recordings of the group's British radio and TV shows under somewhat more controlled circumstances, these reflected the audience hysteria of Beatlemania reaching full volume.

Unfortunately, this excitement was accompanied by a greater difficulty for the group in making themselves heard, or hearing one another, particularly as the sound systems of the day were relatively primitive. It was also accompanied by a certain loss of spontaneity, the group deciding on a certain song list and sequence (and, to a large degree, even a certain between-song banter) for each tour and with rare exceptions sticking to it. It's nonetheless surprising how well and enthusiastically the band usually played at such events. Although part of one 1964 concert did finally get officially issued in 1977 on *The Beatles at the Hollywood Bowl,* there are a number of circulating tapes of additional decent-sounding 1964 shows, fun to hear even if there's the inevitable downside of quite a few multiple versions of the same songs.

There's more to 1964 than live concerts as far as unreleased Beatles music goes, of course. While their BBC sessions were scaled way back from the incredibly prodigious batch they produced in 1963, they still found time to do eight radio programs for the network. Although the song selections and performances on these broadcasts had become somewhat more predictable, they did include the odd surprise cover not found on official Beatles records, as well as some of the few "live" (or at least "live-in-the-studio") versions of some Lennon-McCartney originals from their 1964 discs. There were also a good number of outtakes from the EMI sessions for *A Hard Day's Night, Beatles for Sale,* and all three of the year's singles. Most of them were ironing-out-the-kinks alternate versions of songs that ended up on those records, true, but there were also some in which the structures and approaches changed substantially over the course of the recording. Plus, as in 1963, the lot was rounded off by a bare few demos/composing tapes recorded outside of the studio environment. And it was as composers and studio musicians where the Beatles were making their great artistic strides at this point, their skills as live musicians and interpreters having been so perfected in 1963 that there was little ground to break on those levels.

● January 7

BBC Session
Saturday Club program (broadcast February 15, 1964)
Playhouse Theatre, London

All My Loving
Money (That's What I Want)
The Hippy Hippy Shake
Roll Over Beethoven
*Johnny B. Goode
I Wanna Be Your Man
  appears on Live at the BBC

The Beatles' first BBC broadcast of 1964 was largely devoted to material from their second album. None of those four tracks made *Live at the BBC,* perhaps in part because the sound quality on the surviving tape, while good, isn't quite as good as the fidelity on the February 28, 1964, broadcast (from which "All My Loving," "Roll Over Beethoven," and "I Wanna Be Your Man" *were* chosen). For what it's worth, performance-wise this version of "All My Loving" is rather more interesting than the previous Beeb take (from December 18, 1963); there's just more of a live feel, especially in Paul McCartney's vocal. In fact, there's a little more looseness—to good effect—in the vocals than usual throughout the broadcast, as heard in the closing bars of "Money (That's What I Want)." "I Wanna Be Your Man" is a particularly nice complement to the official recording, with a pronounced Bo Diddley rhythm-and-reverb guitar not present on the *With the Beatles* version, and a full-stop, nonfaded ending.

It's one of the more low key runs through "Roll Over Beethoven," though pleasantly so, George Harrison leaning harder on the bluesier note-bends in his solo than he did on other renditions of this concert staple.

The Beatles were still inserting some covers not represented on their discs into their BBC sessions at this point, and this marks the only appearance of Chuck Berry's "Johnny B. Goode," the only track from this date to make the grade for *Live at the BBC.* Of the many covers the group did on the BBC and elsewhere, however, it's one of the most disappointing. Not that it's at all bad, but it's taken at a slightly lethargic chug, and it's not one of John Lennon's greatest rock 'n' roll vocals; it comes off as subpar only in relation to the usual great job he did with such material. It's also another of those tunes where George seems to meander a little more than he has to in his solos—an approach that sometimes gave some edgy excitement to his BBC work, and at others didn't translate 100 percent well. Also on the program was the fifth and final version of "The Hippy Hippy Shake," where there's a little more boogie in the rhythm guitar lines than usual, a pleasingly raw Harrison solo, and a particularly joyful quality to Paul's concluding shrieks. Paul introduces the song as "one that we used to do a long time ago at the Cavern, and I think it's one that most people will know by now"—perhaps referring not only to the Beatles' four previous BBC presentations of the song, but also the hit version by fellow Liverpool group the Swinging Blue Jeans, which was at that moment rocketing toward the No. 2 position on the British charts.

In a small way, this broadcast marked the end of an era. When it was taped on January 7, the Beatles still pretty much belonged to Britain almost exclusively. Even on that day, however, the "I Want to Hold Your Hand" single had already begun to generate tremendous listener response in the United States, climbing to No. 1 within a few weeks. By the time this session was transmitted on February 15, Beatlemania was in full swing across the Atlantic, the group having made their first television and concert appearances on American soil to phenomenal success. There could be no thought of returning to the Cavern, and opportunities for the band to slot in old Cavern favorites that had slipped out of their stage repertoire such as "The Hippy Hippy Shake" on BBC broadcasts were shrinking, as they'd even grow too big and busy to tape radio sessions within a year or so. Note, by the way, that although a BBC version of "I Want to Hold Your Hand" itself was part of this broadcast (and appears on many bootlegs of this particular session), it was actually just a rebroadcast of the performance of the song from their December 17, 1963, *Saturday Club* session.

● January 12

Live Performance
For television program Val Parnell's
Sunday Night at the London Palladium
London Palladium, London

I Want to Hold Your Hand
This Boy
All My Loving
Money (That's What I Want)
Twist and Shout

The first surviving taped performance of the Beatles in 1964 was a big occasion, and solidly played. Unfortunately, it's not one of the better concert recordings of the era, as it was taped off the television, the sound quality suffering accordingly. "Money (That's What I Want)" is shortened by a verse, and the instrumental break and final verse and chorus are cut from "Twist and Shout"—a truncated arrangement they'd continue to apply to the song throughout most of their remaining stage career.

● Circa January 16

Live Performance
Olympia Theatre, Paris

I Saw Her Standing There
This Boy (introduction only)
Twist and Shout
From Me to You (instrumental reprise #1)
Long Tall Sally
From Me to You (instrumental reprise #2)
From Me to You

There's doubt as to the source and date of this recording, though it had to have been done during their 18-day series of concerts (co-billed with Trini Lopez and French singer Sylvie Vartan) at the Paris Olympia between January 16 and February 4. This series of shows was generally considered a semifailure for the band, Beatlemania not yet having taken off in France. What's most interesting about this and the other Paris Olympia recordings to have surfaced are not so much the performances as the audience reaction. If not quite Beatlemania-like, it's rather more enthusiastic than the many reports of the allegedly tepid reception would have us believe.

The sound on this particular recording—which would have to be the early show of two they did that day, if it is indeed January 16 (since a different tape from their January 16 evening show is in circulation; see below)—is actually very good for a 1964 rock concert tape, Ringo Starr's hard-hitting drumming captured well on "From Me to You," for instance. If the Beatles were miffed at a frosty French house, they weren't letting it affect the quality of the performances, though they're neither better nor more unusual than the many other existing versions of these tunes (and the guitar work on both "From Me to You" and "Long Tall Sally" gets a little sloppy). It could be that they were a little confused by the French manner of haphazardly clapping and singing along with tunes, as opposed to the all-out screaming adulation to which they'd already become accustomed. It does seem, though, like there's a genuine swell of appreciative applause after "I Saw Her Standing There" and "Long Tall Sally." Paul McCartney also appears to be doing his best to fire up the crowd in "Twist and Shout," urging "Come on now!" as they crash into the instrumental break. And there's definitely a loud "Ring-o," "Ring-o" chant at one point.

Note that, although "This Boy" and three versions of "From Me to You" are often listed on bootlegs, "This Boy" trails off right after the spoken introduction, and two of the versions of "From Me to You" are very brief instrumental reprises. Those reprises were apparently a regular, if odd, feature of the group's shows at that point, as one can also be heard on the recording of their December 7, 1963, Liverpool concert.

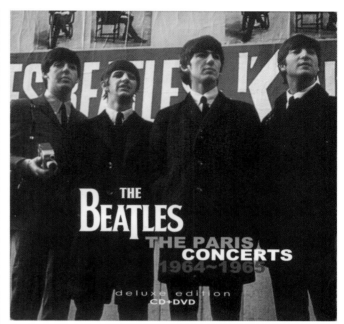

The Beatles supposedly got a frosty reception when they played Paris in early 1964, but tapes of some performances capture an enthusiastic reaction by their French audiences.

● January 16

Live Performance
Olympia Theatre, Paris (evening show)

From Me to You
She Loves You
This Boy
I Want to Hold Your Hand
Twist and Shout
From Me to You (instrumental reprise)

From a French radio broadcast on Europe 1 comes half or so of the set the Beatles were presenting in Paris, in good mono sound. Again, it seems like both the group and the audience are having a better time than is generally remembered, though the reaction is definitely more subdued than it is on the other recording from their French visit. The very beginning of "From Me to You" gets cut off, John Lennon's vocal sounds a little distant and tinny on "Twist and Shout," and there are barely a few seconds of instrumental reprise on "From Me to You," but those aren't major impediments to what's actually one of the better-recorded mid-'60s concert tapes. The lack of all-out screaming (and even French-style handclapping and chanting) means that it's much easier to hear all the instruments and vocals than it is on the average 1964–1966 Beatles live recording; Paul McCartney's high "I can't hide" at the end of the middle eights of "I Want to Hold Your Hand" is loud and sharp. It's one of the better live versions of "This Boy," actually, Ringo's admirably delicate drumwork coming through especially well.

Some of the odd Parisian way of showing appreciation (also sometimes reported to have actually been equivalents of boos) remains audible, however, on "She Loves You," where there are crowd whistles more appropriate to sports arenas than rock concerts. Amusingly, too, one bit of stage banter that was becoming a long-running staple of Beatles shows falls flat on its face. "This one, if you'd like to join in and clap your hands and stamp your feet," Paul urges the audience in his intro to "Twist and Shout," clapping his hands and stamping his feet for emphasis. Puzzled-sounding near-silence follows, where the Beatles are obviously used to adoring fans clapping and stamping as commanded. "Well, if you don't like to join in . . . okay, it's called 'Twist and Shout!'" he shrugs in an on-with-the-show response.

Incidentally, all-out rockers like "Twist and Shout" and "Long Tall Sally" were well received by their French listeners, and John Lennon had hinted in *Melody Maker* at the beginning of their French visit that "we might change the program for the Olympia tomorrow and put in some of the early rock numbers we used to do in Hamburg and the Cavern, things like 'Sweet Little Sixteen' and things we know." If they were so adventurous, however, no evidence survives on the scant material from their 1964 French gigs that has circulated.

● Circa January 18–February 4

Demo Acetate
George V Hotel, Paris

One and One Is Two

Of the many Lennon-McCartney songs "given away" to other artists and never recorded by the Beatles, "One and One Is Two" is possibly the least interesting. Relatively little of the melodic invention gracing even the slightest Lennon-McCartney songs of 1963 and 1964 is present, the verses in particular gliding along with a humdrum, sing-along feel skirting nursery rhymish banality. Things get a little more subtle and tuneful on the arching middle eight, but then it's back to a piece of music that's surprisingly dull for a Beatles-originated tune. Nor was it even successful: when covered by the Strangers with Mike Shannon on a 1964 single, it failed to even make the charts, and probably remains the single most obscure Lennon-McCartney song to find release in the '60s. Likewise, the Strangers with Mike Shannon were probably the most obscure act that ever got first release honors for a Len-Mac tune the Beatles weren't going to do themselves.

The song apparently wasn't originally intended for the Strangers and Shannon, however, but for Billy J. Kramer, who'd already covered a number of Lennon-McCartney castoffs by early 1964 with considerable success. The intention of this demo, sung by Paul and backed with piano and acoustic guitar, was probably to pitch it to Kramer and/or provide a model for Billy's reference. It's been bootlegged from a slightly scratchy Dick James acetate of the demo, and while Paul sings it nicely and enthusiastically, there's just not much you can do with an inherently weak piece of writing. Mike Shannon and the Strangers gave it a more energetic full-band Merseybeatish arrangement (with backup harmonies not heard on this demo) on their single, but that couldn't rescue the song from oblivion. The Fourmost, who'd had British hits with a couple of other Lennon-McCartney giveaways, "Hello Little Girl" and "I'm in

Love," had also considered doing the composition. But as Fourmost lead guitarist Brian O'Hara told Kristofer Engelhardt in *Beatles Undercover*, "McCartney came into the studio and played bass on 'One and One Is Two,' but there just wasn't any meat in the song and we couldn't get anywhere with it."

The exact date of recording of the demo isn't known, but it's been speculated with much certainty that it was done at the hotel where the Beatles were staying during their series of concerts in Paris in early 1964, which means it must have been taped between January 16 and February 4. Probably it wasn't taped until January 18 at the earliest, since it was that date when publisher Dick James requested a demo tape of the song. It did at least generate some vintage wicked John Lennon humor, as he was reported to utter at some point in the proceedings, "Billy J. is finished when he gets this song"; Kramer would avoid the embarrassment by sagely declining the offer. It's also been reported that several versions were recorded at this time, though only one's been bootlegged. If any "outtakes" show up, their entertainment value would no doubt be greatly enhanced if they finally offered that savage Lennonism for all the world to hear.

● January 29

Studio Outtakes
"Can't Buy Me Love" single session
Pathé Marconi Studios, Paris

---

*Can't Buy Me Love (takes 1–3)
Sie Liebt Dich (fragment, take # unknown)
Komm, Gib Mir Deine Hand (fragments, takes 1, 2, 7, 9, 10)
Komm, Gib Mir Deine Hand (fragment, take # unknown)
   *take 2 of "Can't Buy Me" love, with the guitar solo edited in from take 1,
   appears on Anthology 1

"Can't Buy Me Love" is one of the more interesting early Beatles songs of which several outtakes exist, as all of them have an arrangement differing substantially from the version chosen for official release. Take 1, unfortunately, is available thus far only as a "control room monitor mix," or an off-line tape made from studio monitors as a track is mixed or played back. To digress for a minute, get used to that term; it will often, if intermittently, be used throughout the rest of this volume. Control room monitor mixes are, to varying degrees, hollower and tinnier than the actual tape. A rough analogy might be the difference between hearing one of the group's BBC broadcasts as taken from a transcription disc, and one recorded by someone putting their portable machine against the radio speaker, though control room monitor mixes tend to be of substantially better quality than those homemade BBC radio tapes. You'd never want to listen to control room monitor mixes if you had the option of hearing the tapes themselves, but as with the most primitive BBC tapes, they often get bootlegged because they represent the *only* available option of hearing some takes or mixes.

Getting back to "Can't Buy Me Love," it's apparent even from the monitor mix of take 1 that the song's a ways from reaching its final state. It's several keys higher, and George and John add rich, responsive backup harmonies to Paul's lead vocal. George's bee-stinging guitar solo isn't as fully worked out or precise; it sounds kind of clumsy, to be brutal.

Paul doesn't seem to have fully settled on a few of the minor lyrics, a problem that becomes more evident on takes 2 and 3, which have both been booted in full fidelity. On the chorus, he sings what sounds like an awkward "Everybody did it so" instead of "Everybody says it's so," and on the final verse, he jazzily scats his way through the last part of the first line, as if singing dummy syllables for words that haven't quite yet arrived. Harrison's solo is actually worse than on the first take, and while the third take gets the key right and eliminates the background singing, it breaks down in the second verse. McCartney trails off downward on "I may not have a lot to give" and comes to a dead stop, perhaps realizing the guitar work on *this* take isn't going to be salvageable either.

Presumably much discussion and restructuring took place between take 2 and take 3, and perhaps between take 3 and take 4. It's a good illustration of how the Beatles and George Martin were almost always right in their refinements: the backup vocals did make the song too cluttered, those couple of fluffed lyrical lines did need to get polished off, and the guitar solo had to be improved. All of which happened by the fourth take, resulting in another great Beatles A-side. The originally junked take 2 is on *Anthology 1,* but with the better, relatively speaking, guitar solo from take 1 edited into the track.

To digress again, the *Anthology* CD series employed such surgical reconstruction on a number of occasions. While this probably does result in more listenable music for the average listener, some hardcore Beatles collectors are dismayed and even outraged at such decades-after-the-fact tampering, labeling the results "outfakes." That's one of many reasons why the *Anthology* CDs did not make bootlegs redundant, as for songs such as "Can't Buy Me Love" boots offer the chance to hear the separate, unaltered takes used for these composites. It should be pointed out, however, that the Beatles and George Martin themselves very often edited together bits and pieces of various takes for the tracks on their official releases. So it's not as though such an invasive procedure is unique to either the group's authorized reissues (which were also produced by George Martin, for that matter) or to 1990s technology.

Also recorded at this session, held in Paris during the Beatles' Paris Olympia stint, were German-language versions of "I Want to Hold Your Hand" and "She Loves You," with new vocals overdubbed on the same backing tracks heard on those English-language singles. A nine-second snippet of an outtake for "Sie Liebt Dich" is heard in the montage of outtakes used over the closing credits of the *Anthology* video/DVD, and it's actually pretty funny, the take breaking down in hysterical giggles. Taking documentation of this session to extremes, six four-to-nine-second fragments from vocal overdub takes for "Komm, Gib Mir Deine Hand" (originally made available on the www.thebeatles.com website in 2000) have also been bootlegged, though these have mere micro-bits of speech and singing.

● February 9

Live Performance
For television program The Ed Sullivan Show
Studio 50, New York City (afternoon show)

Twist and Shout
Please Please Me
I Want to Hold Your Hand

The Beatles' slots on *The Ed Sullivan Show* in February 1964 are their most famous American television appearances, not to mention among the most famous American television clips of all time. The first of the three shows to be recorded, however, was not the first one that US audiences saw. On the afternoon of February 9, the Beatles taped three songs, to be edited into and shown on the program broadcast on February 23, two weeks later. The Beatles had actually arrived back in England the night before that show was aired, but many (and maybe most) viewers assumed what they were seeing on February 23 was getting beamed out live. Not so, though the performance they gave for Ed Sullivan's cameras on the evening of February 9 *was* transmitted live, and definitely the most celebrated and widely viewed of their three appearances on the program that month.

In 2003, all four of the *Ed Sullivan Show* episodes featuring the Beatles (including their final appearance on the program, on August 14, 1965) were at long last officially issued on DVD. That's the best way to listen to these historic shows, but if you do want to listen to the music in cold isolation, the tracks continue to show up sans video on bootlegs in pretty good (though not great) sound. And while it's great to watch this clip, and the performances are standard-issue excellent, these *aren't* the greatest-sounding recordings of these songs. There's just too much screaming for that, and even if *Ed Sullivan* was about the most widely watched show in the world, it didn't have the greatest sound balance or clarity, for 1964 rock groups at least. It does at least capture one of the only three American performances of "Please Please Me," which was about to be dropped from their live set; one other US version of "Please Please Me" was also captured on video and tape, at their Washington, DC, concert a few days later.

● February 9

Live Performance
For television program The Ed Sullivan Show
Studio 50, New York City (evening show)

*All My Loving
Till There Was You
She Loves You
I Saw Her Standing There
I Want to Hold Your Hand
    appears on Anthology 1

Of all the many historic Beatles live appearances, their live Sunday night broadcast on *The Ed Sullivan Show* on February 9, 1964, might be the very most historic; it did more to spread Beatlemania across the US than any other single event. It would be a little silly, to be honest, to willfully hear the music alone, now that the entire episode has been officially issued on DVD as part of *The Four Complete Historic Ed Sullivan Shows Featuring the Beatles.* We're here to talk about the music, though, and the group played great on an occasion that would have rattled the nerves of almost anyone in their position. Presenting themselves before nearly 100 million viewers, they looked at ease and performed and sang with the locked-in groove that had become second nature at big concerts for months. Their professionalism extended to asking to hear a tape playback of their rehearsals to check the sound balance, though as George complained in a 1977 *Crawdaddy* interview, "Finally when they got a balance between the instruments and the vocals, they marked on the boards by the control, and then everybody broke for lunch. Then we came back to tape the show and the cleaners had been round and polished all the marks off the board."

One slightly odd aspect of this maiden *Ed Sullivan Show* is that the song selection was somewhat weighted toward spotlighting Paul McCartney's vocals, almost to the extent that some seeing the band for the first time might have assumed Paul was the leader. He sings lead on the first two numbers, co-leads with John on "She Loves You" and "I Want to Hold Your Hand" (the vocal mix favoring Paul, especially on the latter tune), and does another lead on "I Saw Her Standing There." John doesn't get any lead features of his own, though the subsequent pair of Sullivan shows that month would redress that imbalance.

Regardless, the sound is quite good (though in mono); in fact, decisively better than on some other Sullivan programs, though John's vocals were undermiked. If the screaming audience does constantly cut across the music, it's an indispensable part of the atmosphere of the occasion. The show's monumental significance to the Beatles' saga was acknowledged by Apple's placement of the opening song, "All My Loving," on *Anthology 1.*

● February 11

Live Performance
Washington Coliseum, Washington, DC

Roll Over Beethoven

From Me to You

I Saw Her Standing There

This Boy

All My Loving

I Wanna Be Your Man

Please Please Me

Till There Was You

She Loves You

I Want to Hold Your Hand

Twist and Shout (incomplete)

Long Tall Sally

The Beatles' first proper American concert was (mostly) captured on film by CBS television, and shown in movie theaters as a closed-circuit broadcast the following month. It's the very most exciting live footage of the early band, and it's available, in part and whole, on both legitimate and illegitimate DVDs (see entry in film section). And for that reason, you should use all means necessary to enjoy the show by seeing that film, rather than settling for listening to a bootleg, which is just a dub of the soundtrack.

This isn't to say that the music is inconsequential on its own. It's another historic occasion, and, along with the recording of their December 7, 1963, show in Liverpool, the first surviving almost-full-length concert set of the group after they'd reached superstardom. And the group is playing with fire and loving it. But—the sound isn't very good, though it's certainly listenable. Apart from contending with an

audience volume they'd likely never experienced in Britain, the sound system was inadequate to the task of yielding a top-grade professional recording, with a muddy and unbalanced mix. At least the singing does come through loudly for the most part, but even this suffers from some problems. George Harrison's vocal mike is obviously out of order during the first part of "Roll Over Beethoven" (at this point still unavailable on US vinyl, though it had come out on *With the Beatles* in the UK), and Ringo Starr's mike basically isn't working at all on his solo turn, "I Wanna Be Your Man." Too, "Twist and Shout" cuts off halfway, perhaps because the film of the event didn't include the whole song either. It's great music in its own way; just be sure to take advantage of the availability of the film to appreciate it to its fullest.

If you want to keep track of the gradual alterations of the Beatles live repertoire now that they'd finally earned the space to do a full half-hour show, it's interesting to note that "Money (That's What I Want)" and "Boys" (both included in the December 1963 Liverpool show) had been replaced by "I Wanna Be Your Man" and "Long Tall Sally." "Boys," nonetheless, would come back into the set by their summer American tour. The finale "Long Tall Sally" was the only song of the 12 the group had yet to release on disc—an advance preview that, even at this early stage of American Beatlemania, many in the audience must have noticed and appreciated.

● February 16

Live Performance
For television program The Ed Sullivan Show
(rehearsal, not broadcast)
Deauville Hotel, Miami Beach

She Loves You

This Boy

All My Loving

I Saw Her Standing There

From Me to You

I Want to Hold Your Hand

It's not well known that a dress rehearsal of the Beatles' Miami *Ed Sullivan Show* appearance (in front of an audience) was filmed but not broadcast. Despite some sound and microphone problems, it would have made a good bonus feature for the official *The Four Complete Historic Ed Sullivan Shows Featuring the Beatles.* The video portion has itself been bootlegged (see film section), as has the audio-only component, which does sound pretty good, if pretty similar to the other *Ed Sullivan* performances. Paul's microphone goes virtually dead for most of "I Saw Her Standing There," however, inadvertently turning much of it into an instrumental where John's occasional harmonies are unaccompanied by the lead vocal it's supposed to be supporting.

● February 16

Live Performance
For television program The Ed Sullivan Show
Deauville Hotel, Miami Beach, Florida

She Loves You
This Boy
All My Loving
I Saw Her Standing There
From Me to You
I Want to Hold Your Hand

The second of the *Ed Sullivan Show* segments to be broadcast (though the third and last to be filmed) actually gave a little more space to the band than the others had. It also gave a much better idea of the humorously informal, yet simultaneously super-polished, stage banter that had become integral to the band's stage shows. Again, that comes through much better on the commercially available DVD of the show than the audio-only portion, especially after "This Boy," where John mocks Paul's smooth, showbizzy patter with mild shouts. John also emits a strange clowning falsetto peep right before the final chorus of "This Boy," which is otherwise a virtually unblemished presentation of that close-harmony near-classic, and quite possibly the best illustration of their remarkable ability to match the complex three-part vocal harmonies of their records onstage. Paul also introduces, oddly, "I Want to Hold Your Hand" as "a great favorite of ours . . . recorded by our favorite American group, Sophie Tucker"—a rather mismatched recycling of a joke he'd used back in November 1963 at the Royal Variety Performance in his introduction to "Till There Was You." The Miami audience doesn't get it, or at least doesn't laugh, leaving Lennon to pick up the slack with forced machine gunlike bursts of "Ha-ha-ha"—whether that's part of the act or a sarcastic jibe at the lameness of Paul's joke, it's hard to say.

The sound on this episode is actually better than on the first and more famous Sullivan appearance, in part because there's less screaming. But it's also because the clarity and balance actually is very good for a 1964 TV broadcast, with more sonic presence on Ringo's drums than there usually would be in such situations. In fact, it would qualify as one of the very best of their live recordings but for a major foul-up on "I Saw Her Standing There," where Paul's vocal is seriously undermiked, John's harmony line coming over at least twice as loud.

● February 21

Private Tape
Deauville Hotel, Miami Beach

Talking Guitar Blues

From the sublime to the less-than-trivial—that's the world of unreleased Beatles music, and a spectrum that can be traversed in a matter of days. For in the midst of some of their greatest triumphs comes this brief, foggily recorded non-nugget of George Harrison playing and singing a rudimentary folk-blues on a poorly tuned acoustic guitar. As much as it sounds like an off-the-cuff improvisation, it's actually a real song, "Talking Guitar Blues," by country great Ernest Tubb, though George and the Beatles probably knew it from Lonnie Donegan's cover version on a 1959 B-side. Played as they were packing to return home from their successful February invasion of the United States, it can be both seen and heard as part of the commercially available *The Beatles:*

The First U.S. Visit video. It's a brief nod to their skiffle roots, which must have seemed like the dark ages as they prepared to return to England as conquering heroes.

● February 25

Studio Outtakes
A Hard Day's Night sessions
Studio Two, Abbey Road, London

*You Can't Do That (take 6)
*And I Love Her (take 2)
     *appears on Anthology 1

The Beatles had probably barely even recovered from jet lag before they were back in the studio again, working on their next album. Two complete outtakes from the day were issued on *Anthology 1*, the more interesting of the pair being "And I Love Her," which fans had wanted to hear since Mark Lewisohn had rightfully cited this early version as being one of the most interesting Beatles alternate takes in *The Beatles Recording Sessions*. With a far rockier (indeed, pre-folk-rockier) arrangement, including full drums and electric guitar, it was some ways away from the superior, softer approach—with a Greek-style acoustic guitar—on the famous LP version (which was also a sizable hit single in the US). It's interesting, though, to hear George Harrison play his newly acquired electric 12-string in the brief instrumental break. It was probably one of the first few times he'd played the instrument in a professional situation, explaining to some extent the tentative nature of the fingering.

A more serious deficiency, actually, was the absence of a bridge, which—along with a McCartney vocal that breaks up in laughter at one point where he stumbles on the words—indicates the composition was actually some ways from satisfactory completion. Beatles publisher Dick James was at the session and, as he told *Melody Maker*, felt that "it was proving to be, although plain and a warm and sympathetic song, just too repetitive, with the same phrase of repeating. George Martin told the boys, 'Both Dick and I feel that the song is just lacking the middle. It's too repetitive, and it needs something to break it up.' I think it was John who shouted, 'OK, let's have a tea break,' and John and Paul went to the piano . . . within half an hour they wrote, there before our very eyes, a very constructive middle to a very commercial song. Although we know it isn't long, it's only a four-bar middle, nevertheless it was just the right ingredients to break up the over-repetitive effect of the original melody."

The final cut was laid down just two days later. As with "Can't Buy Me Love" the previous month, this testifies to just how quickly the Beatles and George Martin were able to substantially rearrange, in a very short period of time, a good song that didn't seem 100 percent written. The spoken discussions over how to do so might, one wagers, be even more interesting than the earlier outtakes.

Harrison also used the 12-string on "You Can't Do That," whose alternate is less assured than the great final version (take 9, used on the B-side of "You Can't Do That") in every way. It's missing the jubilant responsive backup harmonies that do so much to push the official track into near-classic status; John Lennon's vocal phrasing isn't quite as effective, and neither is his guitar break (his first such solo on a Beatles disc) as worked out. In fact, John's spoken "Ah-one-two-three-*faw*uh" intro is about the most enjoyable difference.

● February 26

Studio Outtakes
A Hard Day's Night sessions
Studio Two, Abbey Road, London

I Should Have Known Better (take 8 fragment)
I Should Have Known Better (take 11 fragment)
And I Love Her (take 11 fragment)

It's back to the outtakes montages on the *Anthology* video/DVD for the only available snippets of "I Should Have Known Better" and a "remake" session of "And I Love Her." The bits of "I Should Have Known Better," lasting only about ten seconds each, do provide a chuckle or two, as John's too-hoarse vocal dissipates into laughter on both occasions. "Can we skip the mouth organ [harmonica]?" he asks (they didn't, they kept it in the final version); on the second extract, whether by accident or design, he starts to sing, "And when I whisper . . ."—a lyric not found on the record. For those who lament the absence of a full outtake, fear not; there are full-length "alternate" versions, pretty much, in the form of two performances of the number they'd cut for the BBC in the summer of 1964. The "And I Love Her" fragment (over *Anthology*'s closing credits) is just long enough to hear a real howler of a lyrical goof, Paul singing, "And if you saw my love, *I'd* love her [too]. . . ."

● February 27

Studio Outtakes
A Hard Day's Night sessions
Studio Two, Abbey Road, London

Tell Me Why (take 4 fragment)

In the just-so-you-know category falls this ten-second false start to "Tell Me Why," heard on the *Anthology* DVD. The lads trail off into nothingness, as a voice (it sounds like Paul's) taunts in mock-childishness, "You made a mistake! I know you did!" If you're the kind to thrill to such off-the-wall sound bites, incidentally, a sliver of chatter from take 1 of the recording of "I Call Your Name" at their March 1 session shows up on Paul McCartney's experimental 2000 album *Liverpool Sound Collage*. John Lennon, wondering if it's okay to do a Lennon-McCartney song that Billy J. Kramer had already recorded, asks, "'Cos it's our song anyroad, innit?" Paul replies, "It must be all right." That little crumb is the only unreleased item to have surfaced from that day's work, though it does prove that Paul is a) both aware of some of the minutiae floating around in Beatles outtakes (this particular bit was first reported in *The Beatles Recording Sessions*), and b) must have done some digging through the EMI vaults to extract this brief exchange.

As an almost beyond-incidental note, the late *A Hard Day's Night* producer Walter Shenson said that the six-second snatch of instru-

mental rock music heard in the scene where Ringo whips out a transistor radio on a train was actually played by the Beatles. If so, it probably would have been recorded between February 25 and March 1, during the first batch of sessions for the LP *A Hard Day's Night*. This brief snippet sounds like such generic early British Invasion music, however, that it shouldn't be assumed without a shadow of doubt that it's the Beatles themselves. And speaking of the film *A Hard Day's Night*, for reasons unknown, the incomplete version of "Tell Me Why" heard in the original film (in the concert scene) has a different John Lennon vocal than either the stereo or mono studio versions.

● Circa Early 1964

Private Tape

If I Fell (version 1)
If I Fell (version 2)
If I Fell (version 3)
If I Fell (version 4)
If I Fell (version 5)

The most valuable item to surface from the so-called (and usually near-worthless) Alf Bicknell tapes is this four-minute-or-so sequence in which we hear John, alone on acoustic guitar and vocals, working out the composition of "If I Fell." That song was one of the Beatles' greatest early ballads, and despite the cheap recording quality, it's a fascinating look at its gestation. The first of the five "versions" lasts just through the intro, going even slower than the famous one on *A Hard Day's Night*. The second attempt is the only complete pass, but it's obvious that John's trying to sing too high for his range; it's a little like hearing it done Four Seasons–style, with a dash of Tiny Tim. The song's almost done, but there are small lyrical differences near the end, the most significant being how John worries that his old girlfriend won't be able to stand the pain and will be sad if his new love's in vain, rather than fretting about how *he* won't endure the pain and will be sad.

Then, at the end of both middle eights, comes the kind of moment that makes all the digging through rubble such as this worthwhile. John sings "so" with a high, winding melody that—could it be? Yes! It's almost identical to the melody and phrasing of the words connecting some of the verses of "Imagine." Compare it, for instance, to the way he lingers on the word "you" ("you-hoo, hoo-oo-oo") on that famous Lennon solo track. It would be seven years before "Imagine" would be a huge 1971 hit for Lennon as a solo artist, and here's apparent proof that one of its riffs was tossed around long before the Beatles broke up. There's also reason to believe he might have recycled another idea from this tape much sooner, as at the end of this second version, he drifts into some ad-libbed-seeming patter with a tune identical to the verse of—"I Should Have Known Better." Or perhaps he'd already written or started writing "I Should Have Known Better" too, and was just throwing in a passage from that to mull over?

On the third excerpt, starting mid-song and lasting less than half a minute, John pitches his voice downward, but now it's too *low*. It's back to the strained near-falsetto for the fourth run-through, which starts at the first verse and chops off the intro, and likewise lasts only half a minute or so. The fifth and final fragment has just about a line of the first verse before that, too, breaks off. All five of the versions have a slight lingering, sentimental doo wop feel, somewhat akin to "Do You Want to Know a Secret," that would get washed out of the mix when the song was tightened up (and given crucial Paul McCartney vocal harmonies) in the studio on February 27, 1964. That date makes it virtually certain that this composing tape (sometimes estimated as having been done in January 1964) must have been recorded before the group did it at EMI in late February, though its age will likely never be pinned down with greater precision.

● February 28

BBC Session

From Us to You *program (broadcast March 30, 1964)*
Studio One, BBC Piccadilly Studios, London

**From Us to You
You Can't Do That
*Roll Over Beethoven
*Till There Was You
*I Wanna Be Your Man
Please Mister Postman
*All My Loving
This Boy
*Can't Buy Me Love

     appears on Live at the BBC
     **edited version appears on* Live at the BBC

In the first two months of 1964, the Beatles had toured France and the United States, causing more pandemonium than any other popular entertainers in subduing America; had recorded both sides of their next chart-topping single; and had begun work on their *A Hard Day's Night* LP. In just two days, they were due to start nearly two months of filming for the *A Hard Day's Night* movie. So, as February drew to a close, did they rest? No—they went back into the BBC to record their longest single radio session yet, as part of promotional duty that might have even then started to feel a little low-priority when stacked against their other triumphs and commitments. As the song "A Hard Day's Night" itself declared, they really were working like dogs.

If fatigue was setting in, however, there was no sign of it on this program. Six of the ten tracks were used on *Live at the BBC* (where "From Us to You" is significantly shortened), probably because the sound quality was among the best to be heard on any of the surviving sessions. These aren't necessarily the best radio *performances* of "Roll Over Beethoven," "Till There Was You," and "I Wanna Be Your Man" (the last still bearing the Bo Diddley beat heard on their January 7 Beeb rendition of the tune, if more faintly), but they're dependably fine. And, at long last, a fairly serious question about their music slips into the announcer's links, Alan Freeman asking Paul about his vocal idols. Elvis Presley, Chuck Berry, Carl Perkins, and Marvin Gaye are name-checked, Gaye probably being the biggest surprise to British audiences, as the Motown star was barely known on UK shores at the time. But the Beatles were always hip to the newest hip things, and did take opportunities to plug some of their favorites, praising Motown in several different interviews of the time.

This broadcast would mark the final BBC set oriented toward material from *With the Beatles*, as other, newer songs were beginning to pile up on their EMI releases, like "Can't Buy Me Love" and "You Can't Do That," probably performed on this date for the first time outside the recording studio. (Indeed, John goofs slightly on the lyric of the first line of the latter, singing, "I got something to tell you" instead of "I got something to say.") It's disappointing that the group did not do more numbers from *With the Beatles* on the radio. They'd done every original composition from *Please Please Me* and their 1962–1963 singles on the Beeb, but never did get around to such top-flight *With the Beatles* originals as "It Won't Be Long," "All I've Got to Do," "Not a Second Time," and "Don't Bother Me" (or, for that matter, fun second-tier originals from that LP, such as "Little Child" and "Hold Me Tight"). In fact, they never did any of these songs live in any capacity (although they did sing "It Won't Be Long" on the TV program *Ready Steady Go* in March, mimed to the record). From today's vantage point, one would think the group would have wanted to play those tunes to make the sessions more interesting for themselves, if nothing else. But those were the days of giving the people what they wanted to hear, or, maybe, what the performers thought the people wanted to hear. And by this point, the Beatles' material was evolving at such a rapid pace that they may not have even considered digging further into *With the Beatles* on their BBC programs after early 1964.

● March 31

BBC Session

Saturday Club *program (broadcast April 4, 1964)*
Playhouse Theatre, London

Everybody's Trying to Be My Baby
I Call Your Name
I Got a Woman
You Can't Do That
Can't Buy Me Love
Sure to Fall (in Love with You)
Long Tall Sally

For the first time in at least four years, the Beatles went an entire month without performing live in March 1964, though they did mime a few segments for TV shows and the *A Hard Day's Night* movie. Perhaps that explains why this BBC session was the most interesting and spontaneous-sounding one they'd done since the summer of 1963, almost as if they were airing out the mothballs. You'd never say the Beatles sounded stale in any specific BBC recording, but both the song selection and performance had become more pat and predictable in late 1963 and early 1964. That couldn't be said at all about this session, which—combined with the failure of any of the seven recordings to see official release on *Live at the BBC*—makes it one of the most desirable ones for aficionados to collect.

Four of the cuts were of special interest for not having yet appeared on a Beatles disc, though two would do so by the end of 1964. Carl Perkins's "Everybody's Trying to Be My Baby" had been done on the Beeb once in 1963, but this interpretation has a nice loose, relaxed, almost jaunty feel. The guitar solos are quite different (if more basic) than they are on the *Beatles for Sale* version, and George has rarely seemed to

Another LP collection of BBC performances with an inner label designed to fool the unwary into mistaking it for an authorized BBC transcription disc, this one taken from spring 1964 sessions.

be enjoying the lead vocal position more. Following that number is the only live Beatles version of "I Call Your Name," which was still a couple of months away from release on a British EP when this was aired (though it would come out in the US in April). Billy J. Kramer had released the song first as a 1963 B-side, and naturally the Beatles' version is better on all counts. This BBC performance, too, has a slightly bouncier, more informal feel than the studio counterpart with McCartney's throbbing bass to the fore, though there's an accidental-sounding lyrical switch near the end, where "I can't go on" is sung instead of the title phrase.

"I Got a Woman" had been done on the radio in 1963, and while that version got the justified nod for *Live at the BBC,* this second try is both good and appreciably different. Where the 1963 take has dramatic pauses that draw out the tune's bluesiness, this one is taken at a brisker, more even pace, with a double-tracked John Lennon lead vocal and a very nice Harrison rockabilly solo. And while "Sure to Fall (in Love with You)" had been cut for the BBC twice the preceding year (and before that at the Decca audition), this blows the prior ones away. The secret ingredient's a newly introduced switch into double-time in the bridges, adding some much-needed buoyancy to an otherwise rather ponderous, barely rockabillified country number. It's the recording that should have been chosen for the *Live at the BBC* set, but wasn't.

On more ordinary but wholly acceptable notes were both sides of their current hit single and "Long Tall Sally," which—although this was the fifth time it had been presented on the Beeb—had yet to be issued on a Beatles recording. It's one of the more pedestrian readings of the song, however, lacking that escalator-climbing passage in the second instrumental break, and taken at a calmer gait than usual. Unfortunately, the sound quality's a little variable on the best-booted tape of the session—some of the tracks ("I Got a Woman," "Sure to

Fall (in Love with You)," "You Can't Do That") are close to excellent, and others ("Can't Buy Me Love," "I Call Your Name"), while decent, suffer from a bit of fuzzy distortion.

Present at this session was *Melody Maker* reporter (and future John Lennon biographer) Ray Coleman, who quoted Lennon telling producer Bernie Andrews, "Don't forget, next time we're down I'm going to do some of that Bob Dylan stuff. You know, 'Blowing in the Wind' and that." A fascinating premise, but they never did. Coleman also observed John playing the introduction to the Searchers' hit "Needles and Pins" and telling Paul, "Great song. We ought to do it." They never did that one either, though they were great admirers of fellow Liverpudlians the Searchers, citing them as one of their favorite British groups in several interviews of the period.

● April 16

Studio Outtakes
A Hard Day's Night sessions
Studio Two, Abbey Road, London

---

*A Hard Day's Night (take 1)
A Hard Day's Night (takes 2–9)
    *appears on Anthology 1

A most valuable complete look at the recording of "A Hard Day's Night," from its first take (issued on *Anthology 1*) through its almost-final shape (take 9, which, with a piano overdub, would be issued as a single and the title track of the *A Hard Day's Night* album). Take 1 reveals that the song was pretty much in its finished form at the outset, though George Harrison's universally familiar opening 12-string guitar chord lands with an unearthly shimmering blast, as if it's been processed through an earthquake. John and particularly Paul don't seem to have committed all the lyrics to memory yet, the tempo's a bit slower than it should be, Paul's effeminate way of squealing, "Tight, all through the night" at the end of the first middle eight is pretty ineffectual, and the ending loop of guitar notes was uncertain, dissolving into a wave of reverb. So, too, is Harrison's solo in the instrumental break, which is pretty rudimentary compared to the bursts of notes on the single. So it seemed like a simple matter of adjusting the screws here and there.

For whatever reason, it seemed like a bit of horseplay had to be gotten out of the way before it could really be put in the can. Take 2 is loads o' fun—ten seconds of John Lennon doing a mocking one-two-three-four count-in, followed by an oceanic crash of a reverbed guitar chord. That happens again on take 3 (a false start) and take 4, the lads clearly enjoying the novelty of the explosive, almost movie sound-effect-like crash of that electric 12-string. But Paul seems to be too diffidently carefree when he takes over the upper-register lead vocal for the middle eight on take 4, and John's still singing, "You make me feel all right" instead of "You know I feel all right" at the end. The real problem, however, seems to be George's squawking solo in the instrumental break, as there's no indication he's worked out a suitably memorable, concise series of riffs. To be brutal, the solo on take 4 is abominable, even amateurish, as George is apparently both uncertain of what notes to play and not hitting all of the ones that he *does* know to play. It's perhaps his worst recorded passage with the Beatles ever to surface on their EMI studio tapes. Not that it seems to bother the unflappable McCartney, who lets loose with a joyful "Hey-yeahhh!"—whether in sarcastic mirth or genuine good humor, it's hard to say.

Still, by take 5 things are coming together, the tempo tightening slightly, even though George still doesn't have much of a clue of how to fill out the solo, sounding as if he's laying down a "guide" part, not a proper one. Take 6 breaks down as poor George doesn't quite strike the right chord, prompting John to accuse, "It was him. I heard a funny chord." John's vocal sounds labored at times in take 7, John and Paul are still having a hard time coordinating their harmonies, and George still seems to be following the path of least resistance with a near non-solo and a stumbling pass through the hypnotic 12-string licks of the fadeout.

Take 8 breaks down right at the first chord, but take 9, miraculously, gets it all together, with the help of 4-track recording enabling John to double-track his vocal; bongos to be overlaid on Ringo's drums; and, most crucially, George Martin's electric piano, which (played in duet with Harrison's guitar) filled in the gap that George Harrison couldn't plug in the instrumental break on earlier takes of the song. It proves how absolutely crucial Martin was to making the instrumental section and the song itself work—something he did, to varying degrees, by playing keyboard parts himself on numerous Beatles tracks (such as "In My Life" and "Good Day Sunshine," to take just a couple of examples). One wonders just how much of a factor Harrison's frankly substandard work in the instrumental break on earlier takes of the song was in sparking Martin's marvelously inventive solo. Was this a case where the producer pulled rank and, unsatisfied with what Harrison was coming up with, decided to take matters into his own hands? Or, viewed in a more positive light, perhaps that was the intention all along, and Harrison didn't solo seriously or at all (particularly on latter takes of the number), knowing the plan was to airlift a piano/guitar part into the middle.

● April 19

Studio Outtakes

For British television special Around the Beatles
IBC Studios, London

Twist and Shout
Roll Over Beethoven
*I Wanna Be Your Man
*Long Tall Sally
Medley: Love Me Do/Please Please Me/From Me to You/
    She Loves You/I Want to Hold Your Hand
Can't Buy Me Love
**Shout
*Boys

      appears on Anthology 1
      **edited version appears on* Anthology 1

What to call this: a live performance, studio outtakes, or a television broadcast? It's kind of all of the above, and none of them. For their musical segment on the British television special *Around the Beatles*—filmed on April 28 and first broadcast on May 6—the Beatles mimed to seven songs (one an extended medley) before a studio audience. Yet

The April 1964 TV special Around the Beatles *produced several unreleased Beatles recordings, some of studio quality.*

they weren't miming to the records, but to a non-EMI, non–Abbey Road, non-BBC studio recording of the tracks laid down at IBC Studios in London nine days before the filming, with no audience present. Using records to mime to wouldn't have been wholly possible in any event, as one of the songs, the Isley Brothers' "Shout," hadn't been (and never would be) recorded by the Beatles for EMI. In essence, then, what you have is something like a BBC radio session, but recorded at somewhat better facilities, though not with as much attentiveness as the group gave their proper EMI sessions. They weren't working with producer George Martin, or any producer, on this occasion. But the second engineer/tape operator, Glyn Johns, would work with the group again way down the line for the *Get Back/Let It Be* sessions in early 1969, eventually getting credited as one of three producers on the *Let It Be* album.

Although this music is perhaps best appreciated by viewing the *Around the Beatles* special itself (see entry in film section), hearing the studio recordings alone provides an important advantage. On the television program, the sound quality of the recordings is inferior, due both to the lesser fidelity a film soundtrack can offer and the presence of audio screams. Heard in isolation, the quality is excellent, nearly on par with the Beatles' official releases. None of these well-traveled songs (with one exception) is the definitive or greatest alternative version, but they're typically fine, rather like hearing a good BBC session of the era. Among the more noteworthy things to listen for are the way they flatten out the beat somewhat for "Roll Over Beethoven," where Ringo's cymbals are especially prominent (though the last verse gets cut out); the almost Four Seasons–like high harmony vocals from Paul at the end of "Twist and Shout"; Paul's absolutely great wiggly backing shouts during "I Wanna Be Your Man"; and a most lively "Can't Buy Me Love." "Long Tall Sally" suffers, however, from the omission of the second instrumental break.

Some of the material wasn't quite just a re-creation of a popular record, however. There was a contrived four-minute medley of their first five hit singles, connecting just an excerpt from each (though each segment was indeed a different performance than the one heard on the record), not always with the smoothest of edits. Far more exciting was "Shout"—an entirely different Isley Brothers song, it needs to be noted, than "Twist and Shout." The greatest thing about how the Beatles take on this gospel-rock raver is the way they switch off lead vocals between all four of the members, all the while keeping up tremendous momentum with wild backup group singing, high Beatlesque (not to mention Little Richard–esque) "woo"s to the fore-front. Interviewing the band during rehearsals for the show (see next entry), Murray the K was impressed enough to ask John Lennon why the Beatles didn't make it a single. Replied John in acidic, exaggerated Liverpool brogue, "Because we didn't write it, did we? And it gets rather boring!" For good measure, he added with venom, "Don't call me 'baby,' or I'll smash your face in! Ha ha! [Just] joking. . . ."

One of the finer Beatles covers never to find its way onto disc, "Shout" was remixed and criminally edited when placed on the *Anthology 1* compilation, which chopped out about half a minute for no good reason. *Anthology 1* also contained stereo remixes of "I Wanna Be Your Man," "Long Tall Sally," and "Boys" (with a fiercer-than-usual Harrison solo and minus the final verse) from this soundtrack recording, although the last of the songs was not actually used in the program. All of these tracks (except "Boys"), as well as the songs performed by the numerous guest artists on the program, have also been bootlegged from the soundtrack itself—though if you want to hear it that way, you should just get the video of the actual TV special.

● April 23

Private Tape
Hall of Remembrance, London

Words of Love
Let Me Go Lover
Bo Diddley
Love Me Do
From Me to You
You Can't Do That

In the barely-qualifying-for-inclusion category is this half hour of the band being interviewed by famed American DJ and self-hyped "Fifth Beatle" Murray the K at the rehearsals for the *Around the Beatles* television special (see entry for April 19, 1964). Submerged way in the background, you can hear the band fooling around on bits of some songs that wouldn't be included on the special. "Bo Diddley" and the nonrock '50s pop hit "Let Me Go Lover" would never be recorded by the band elsewhere; there are also a few seconds of George Harrison playing the harmonica, if you want to keep track of every last musical breath the Beatles expelled. But the music is so buried, and the snatches of the tunes so tossed off, that it's arguable as to whether these are even "songs," although you might see them listed as such on some bootlegs. Murray the K (who'd actually briefly appear on the TV special) babbles questions and nonstop hipster patter that not only obscure the music, but are absolutely asinine,

making this material torture to listen to from any angle. Unfortunately, it wouldn't be the last time that all-but-inaudible unreleased Beatles music would be yet further swamped by irritating commentary by a non–band member on subsequently bootlegged tapes. . . .

● April 26

Live Performance
New Musical Express Pollwinners' Concert
Empire Pool, Wembley

She Loves You
You Can't Do That
Twist and Shout
Long Tall Sally
Can't Buy Me Love

For their first show before a live audience in over two months (and their first in Britain since January 12), the Beatles played five songs at the *New Musical Express* Pollwinners' Concert, the *New Musical Express* being one of the two top music magazines in the UK. It's another performance better experienced on video, but the songs sans image do show up on bootleg, in pretty good mono sound. Concentrating on their most popular material (though not, oddly, "I Want to Hold Your Hand"), the group seemed to feed off the energy to give a more kinetic performance (albeit with slightly sped-up tempos) than they were usually summoning for more artificial radio and TV dates by that time. It's not a great sound balance, though, John's vocal part overwhelming Paul's on "She Loves You," and John's guitar solo, in turn getting overwhelmed by George's classic ringing 12-string riff on "You Can't Do That." The rhythm teeters on "Can't Buy Me Love," but it's got a wonderfully gritty McCartney vocal.

● May 1

BBC Session
From Us to You program (broadcast May 18, 1964)
BBC Paris Studio, London

From Us to You
Whit Monday to You
I Saw Her Standing There
Kansas City/Hey! Hey! Hey! Hey!
*I Forgot to Remember to Forget
You Can't Do That
Sure to Fall (in Love with You)
Can't Buy Me Love
Matchbox
Honey Don't
    *appears on Live at the BBC

Like their prior BBC session on March 31, this was another above-average program, perhaps reflecting a fresher attitude toward live performance during those brief months of March–May 1964 when the Beatles did few live concerts. And besides the plugs for both sides of their most recent single and the "From Us to You" jingle theme, it focused on their rock 'n' roll roots, with no less than three Carl Perkins covers, an Elvis number, and a Little Richard tune, as well as their early original "I Saw Her Standing There." ("Whit Monday to You" was also sung a cappella a couple of times to the tune of "Happy Birthday," it being the Christian holiday Whit Monday on the day of this broadcast.)

Elvis's "I Forgot to Remember to Forget" is the most distinctive offering (and the only one selected for *Live at the BBC*), as the Beatles never recorded it at EMI, and it marked the very last time the group would debut a number for the BBC that wouldn't appear on their discs. It's actually not one of their better rockabilly covers, as it's a bit sluggish. But it's quite acceptable, George offering one of his more relaxed vocals and his usual impeccable Sun Records–styled rockabilly picking, the sleepy stanzas contrasted well by the double-time bridges. That's a trick they also used—as they had on their March 31 session—for Carl Perkins's "Sure to Fall (in Love with You)," done here for the fourth and last time on the radio. The fidelity isn't as good on the bootlegged tape as it is for the March 31 session, but dig that very nice Harrison solo, where he does some note-bending not heard on any other version.

All of the other songs had been or would be issued on Beatles records, and some of them had been around the block quite a few times already. Still, it's a very good "I Saw Her Standing There," the rhythm somehow altered just a bit to give it a slightly funk-chunkier feel. "Kansas City/Hey! Hey! Hey! Hey!" was still a few months away from release on *Beatles for Sale*, and benefits from the usual rawer-but-right Harrison guitar solo, as well as a nonfaded ending and some subtly different Paul vocals. "Matchbox" was just a month away from being recorded, and has some delightful variations, principally when Ringo alters the lyric to refer to both himself and John shortly before the instrumental break. It's one of the best vocals Ringo ever laid down—he sounds more spirited, earthy, and joyful here than on the studio version, even if the familiar EMI recording certainly boasts a tighter arrangement. But John, not Ringo, is still singing "Honey Don't" here, on a very nice version that (like the 1963 BBC recording of this Carl Perkins tune) rocks along a little less uninhibitedly than the arrangement on *Beatles for Sale*. (Incidentally, the liner notes of *Live at the BBC* are incorrect when they state that John had handed over the lead vocal to Ringo by the time of this program; you don't have to be a Beatle expert to tell that it's definitely John singing here.)

Unfortunately, the sound quality of this session, while okay, isn't quite as good as it is on most of the group's bootlegged BBC work from around mid-1963 onward. That might explain why only "I Forgot to Remember to Forget" was used on *Live at the BBC*, probably because it was performed just this once. Note, too, that this is the cut whose sonic clean-up for *Live at the BBC* has probably been most criticized by audiofile Beatlemaniacs; it does have a somewhat squashed, lifeless tinge.

● June 1

Studio Outtakes

A Hard Day's Night *sessions*
Studio Two, Abbey Road, London

*I'll Be Back (takes 2–3)
I'll Be Back (takes 12–14)
appears on Anthology 1

As part of the final round of *A Hard Day's Night* sessions, the Beatles' "I'll Be Back," like much of their newly penned material, was stretching into new horizons, this number anticipating folk-rock in some ways. Takes 2 and 3 are on *Anthology 1,* and are among the more valuable alternates in the *Anthology* series. Take 2 reveals how it was originally constructed as a waltz, though it breaks down midway as John complains it's too hard to sing, growling like a bulldog in good-humored frustration. Take 3 is complete (with a fadeout) and actually quite nice, the rhythm evened out and the guitars playing nearly full-blown folk-rock, though a vocal mistake by John early on (plus various other imperfections) meant they knew this take wasn't going to be the one. But that's not all, folks, as a few seconds-long false starts show up on the *Anthology* video, though these don't offer much except more good-natured verbal jousting as each attempt stops almost before it's begun. Some sources list takes 12–15 as appearing on the *Anthology* video, but it's not certain that more than a fragment of take 15 is present, as all that's heard is some spoken joking.

● June 3

Studio Outtakes

Studio Two, Abbey Road, London

*You Know What to Do
*No Reply
appears on Anthology 1

For the first time, the Beatles on this day recorded material at EMI that didn't really belong to any album, single, or EP session, even if "No Reply" would be rerecorded for their *Beatles for Sale* LP in late 1964. Ringo Starr had fallen sick with tonsillitis and pharyngitis that morning, on the eve of a world tour. That meant the afternoon was spent at Abbey Road rehearsing with their hurriedly recruited replacement, Jimmy Nicol, instead of doing a recording session as planned. After the rehearsal, however, John, Paul, and George stayed on to record three songs, two of which saw the light on *Anthology 1*. Given Ringo's absence, it's doubtful these were intended as any more than demos, though it's odd—as Mark Lewisohn observed in his *Anthology 1* liner notes—that there's a drummer on "No Reply." It wouldn't have been either Starr or Nicol (who had gone home to pack); maybe it was Paul McCartney or one of the other Beatles, in an ad hoc lineup in which they'd done some switching of instruments.

"You Know What to Do" is especially intriguing as the Beatles would never return to it, and it's the only recording of a George Harrison song between 1963's "Don't Bother Me" and 1965 to have surfaced. So although Hunter Davies's authorized biography stated that George "forgot about writing songs for almost two years" after "Don't Bother Me," Harrison affirming that "I was involved in so many other things that I never got round to it," obviously he was engaging in at least some songwriting activity during the interim. Not that it deserved enshrinement on a bona fide Beatles album, as "You Know What to Do" is a fairly

The Beatles at a June 1964 press conference with Jimmy Nicol, who replaced an ill Ringo Starr for several concerts, of which a few tapes survive.

bland, good-time, country-influenced tune, somewhat along the lines of a generic Carl Perkins song. It's true the song isn't done full service by the demo-quality recording, on which the only percussion is a tambourine. It's also true the Beatles could be brilliant at making their most meager songs quite listenable in the studio, and maybe "You Know What to Do" would have spruced up considerably had it been given a full-on treatment. But then, it wasn't so outstanding that it demanded such a treatment. In 1965 (as reported in *The Beatles Off the Record*), George Martin might have referred to "You Know What to Do" obliquely when he noted that Harrison "got discouraged some time ago when none of us liked something that he had written."

One does wonder whether George's songwriting confidence was damaged when his song was passed over, though in reality it wouldn't be too long until the Beatles tackled a couple Harrison songs for real (with "I Need You" and "You Like Me Too Much" in February 1965). George certainly *was* continuing to try to compose between late 1963's "Don't Bother Me" and early 1965; asked if he'd written any new songs at a September 3, 1964, press conference in Indianapolis, he confirmed, "I've got about three bits of songs, actually, but nothing for the whole [sic]." And just a few days before recording "You Know What to Do," at a May 30 press conference, he'd said that he'd composed a couple of new songs for the Beatles' next LP. If "You Know What to Do" was one, what was the other?

"No Reply" is close in form to its *Beatles for Sale* version, but the group just doesn't seem to be taking it too seriously. This take has an unsuitably merry ambience, not to mention lyric goofs, a faster rhythm, and unimaginatively basic drumming by whoever was handling the skins on this occasion. The downbeat latter parts of the verses are much less effective, and the "I saw the light" line is sung once instead of twice,

thus lacking the change in the melody on the second line that does so much to add to the drama of the official recording. The song was originally intended as a gift to fellow Brian Epstein client Tommy Quickly, who never did release a cover of the number. Maybe the group started to take it more seriously when they decided to do it themselves—or maybe they decided to do it themselves when they realized the song was worthy of being taken more seriously. The *Beatles for Sale* arrangement certainly does bring out the song's hurt and rejection with infinitely greater power and taste, particularly in John's recast, more personal lead vocal.

● June 4

Live Performance

KB Hallen, Copenhagen

I Saw Her Standing There (incomplete)
I Want to Hold Your Hand
All My Loving
She Loves You
Till There Was You
Roll Over Beethoven
Can't Buy Me Love
This Boy
Twist and Shout

The Beatles never considered replacing Ringo Starr with Jimmy Nicol, who played drums on the June 4–13 shows in Denmark, the Netherlands, Hong Kong, and Australia. He was chosen only because he was the session drummer recommended by George Martin and able to fill in at a moment's notice. Wild rumors being constant fodder for the gossip columns of the day, that didn't prevent there being speculation that Ringo was out for good. What's not usually realized is that there are actually live recordings of the band with Nicol in the lineup, though unfortunately the fidelity on all of them is flawed.

This is the first of the Nicol tapes, and the quality's pretty bad, not only from the perspective of listening to the Beatles as a band, but also from trying to zero in on the drumming in particular. From what you can hear of the drumming, it's not too distinguished, with a more generic, ordinary sound than Ringo's characteristically joyous, uplifting playing. It would be too much, to be fair, to expect anything else: this was just Nicol's first night with the group, and he'd only had the chance to rehearse with them once, going through a few songs the previous day at EMI. It's safe to say, however, that Ringo's job was never in jeopardy, though the other three Beatles carried on with an on-with-the-show determination that made the Nicol concerts sound otherwise much like other gigs they were doing in mid-1964. Note that one of the tracks on this tape, "I Saw Her Standing There," is so badly recorded that it's virtually unlistenable; the others are better, but still badly recorded.

Although Nicol has not often spoken about his brief stint with the Beatles, he did tell Austin Teutsch in a 1987 interview, "I think I was accepted by most of the fans 'cause I fit in. I wore the suit and hair and tried to play like Ringo in his nonchalant fashion." In the same interview, he did disclose that at this particular show in Denmark (the only night the Beatles played in that country in their entire career), John Lennon's "head was a balloon! He had drunk so much the night before, he was on stage sweating like a pig." Yet as Paul McCartney later remembered in a conversation taped during the Beatles' January 1969 *Get Back/Let It Be* sessions, Nicol was having his own problems: "It was the first time that we'd had this new drummer because Ringo was sick, and he was sitting up on this rostrum, just eyeing up all the women. We'd start 'She Loves You,' '1, 2,' and nothing. '1, 2,' still nothing." For the record, Nicol doesn't seem to be missing count-ins on this particular tape, though the screaming and fuzzy sound make it hard to tell one way or the other on some of the intros.

● June 5

"Live" Concert

For Dutch television program The Beatles in Nederland
Cafe-Restaurant Treslong, Hillgom, The Netherlands

She Loves You
All My Loving
Twist and Shout
Roll Over Beethoven
Long Tall Sally
Can't Buy Me Love

This Dutch television broadcast qualifies as an "unreleased" set of Beatles music by the merest of margins. For although the group did mime to their records before a studio audience, the vocal mikes were left on, allowing the band to, in effect, sing along with their own recordings. It's an odd novelty, but surely a much more splendid time for all to see as a

video—which is just as easily available as the audio bootleg of this event, and quite entertaining (see entry in film section). It doesn't change the sound all that much; it just thickens the vocals, creating a strange reverb-like effect, though the pseudo-double-tracking is most obvious on "Long Tall Sally." And yes, Jimmy Nicol was playing drums with the group on this program, but that's *not* his drumming you hear in the music—it's Ringo's, from the original released tracks of these numbers.

● June 6

Live Performance

Vellinghal Op Hoop Van Zegen, Blokker,
The Netherlands (afternoon show)

I Saw Her Standing There
I Want to Hold Your Hand
All My Loving
She Loves You
Twist and Shout
Long Tall Sally (fragment)

This material is available in different parts as recorded via separate different sources, including an audience recording, a TV recording, a PA recording, and others. All of which makes it difficult to evaluate in one condensed entry, though you can find all the multiple versions from different sources combined into one disc on certain bootlegs focusing on the Beatles' live Holland performances. It's barely worth the effort, as their sole redeeming quality is to give us some idea of how the group sounded with Nicol in the drum seat. Some of the songs are on an audience recording on which a few of the instruments actually come through okay, but you can barely hear the singing whatsoever—though you can hear the *audience* singing along with gusto, language barrier be damned, coming in with the chorus a full verse early on "All My Loving." You *can* hear Nicol pretty well on that audience recording, and he just doesn't fit in as well as Ringo does, hitting too bluntly and putting in too many beats. Listen to the instrumental break of "I Saw Her Standing There," for example, or the hammers he lays down right before the chorus in "I Want to Hold Your Hand" and the first chorus of "Long Tall Sally." The vocals do come through fairly clearly on the TV recording of "I Saw Her Standing There." But it takes some teeth-gritting to even sit through a compilation of all the source tapes available, due both to the meager fidelity (some songs can only be heard way in the background underneath screaming or a Dutch spoken commentary!) and the availability of some of the songs in mere fragments on the nonaudience tape sources.

● June 6

Live Performance

Vellinghal Op Hoop Van Zegen, Blokker,
The Netherlands (evening show)

I Saw Her Standing There (incomplete)

Yet another, different performance of "I Saw Her Standing There," this one from newsreel footage of their evening concert on this date. The fidelity's actually not too bad, though it's missing the first part of the song and there's plenty of football-cheering-crowd-like noise.

● June 12

Live Performance
Centennial Hall, Adelaide, Australia

I Saw Her Standing There
I Want to Hold Your Hand
All My Loving
She Loves You
Till There Was You
Roll Over Beethoven
Can't Buy Me Love
This Boy
Twist and Shout
Long Tall Sally

For all you Jimmy Nicol obsessives, here's the holy grail of sorts: a reasonably fair-quality recording (though well short of great) of a full set with your boy on drums, three days before Ringo Starr rejoined the group. Well, maybe not; while you can hear the vocals and guitars pretty well, the drums are pretty faint. You can hear the drumming much *better*, actually, in some of the recordings made in Holland on June 6, even though the overall quality of those is pretty miserable. From what you can make out, though, Nicol does seem to be settling into the band better, doing an adequate job on an adequate concert recording (from the Australian radio broadcast of the event) for the standards of the era. But the two concerts they gave in Melbourne a few days later would be recorded in substantially superior audio, and with Ringo back on drums. About the only not-in-the-usual-program note here is struck when Paul's voice breaks during his spoken intro for "Long Tall Sally"—that and the Australian MC's manic exhortations for the audience to scream for "MAHW!"

● June 17

Live Performance
Festival Hall, Melbourne (matinee show)

I Saw Her Standing There
You Can't Do That
All My Loving
She Loves You
Till There Was You
Roll Over Beethoven
Can't Buy Me Love
This Boy
Twist and Shout
Long Tall Sally (spoken intro only)

Ringo had returned to the Beatles on June 15, and two of the concerts from their three-day, two-shows-a-day stint at Melbourne's Festival Hall were recorded in decent-quality mono. For both shows, the setlist they'd just played in Adelaide was tinkered with slightly, "You Can't Do That" replacing, strangely, "I Want to Hold Your Hand," which had to have been (with "She Loves You") their most globally popular number of the time. This is about the time they made an adjustment to "You Can't Do That" for live performance, too; where Paul and George had sung their responsive harmonized line "Gonna let you down and leave you flat" on just one note in the studio version, Paul would jump to a higher note for the second "you" onstage. A mighty small thing in the big scheme of things, sure, but it's something Beatles fans notice—even if the way Paul holds the note all the way through the line on the record works better.

Though comparable in quality to the other recording of the Beatles in Melbourne, the set that includes a complete version of the finale "Long Tall Sally" (see entry below) gets the nod for better audio fidelity. The lead guitar might be even less audible at some points (it's virtually absent in "I Saw Her Standing There") than it is on the other Melbourne tape, which is not a good thing. The recordings can be easily differentiated by a false start to "I Saw Her Standing There" in this one that does not occur in the other.

● June 17

Live Performance
Festival Hall, Melbourne (evening show)

I Saw Her Standing There
You Can't Do That
All My Loving
She Loves You
Till There Was You
Roll Over Beethoven
Can't Buy Me Love
This Boy
Twist and Shout
Long Tall Sally

Though similar to the earlier tape of the Beatles in Melbourne (see entry above), this set is preferred for its better sound quality. It's the best full-set recording of the band playing live in a noncontrolled (i.e., non-radio/TV studio) environment that had been made to this point. Not that it's great, actually; just that the fidelity's better than the relatively primitive and flawed ones that had preceded it.

Perhaps understandably buoyed by the return of Ringo, the performance is very good, though the musicians are contending with industrial-strength Beatlemania screams and a less-than-perfect sound balance. You can barely hear the guitar solo on "Roll Over Beethoven" (which jumps into a near-ska rhythm for part of the instrumental break) and some other songs, for instance. It's one of the more ear-catching versions of "Till There Was You," the mix giving more prominence to the rhythm guitar than usual, and Ringo—maybe unknowingly taking a page from the Jimmy Nicol book—hitting the drums much harder than he usually did on this ballad. Indeed, Ringo seems audibly delighted

This CD included two June 1964 concerts in Melbourne, Australia, on one disc.

to be back in the band again, slashing his kit with fiery abandon. And the audience seems delighted to see him, responding to Paul's "It's very nice for all of us to have back with us now—Ringo!" with a huge roar of squeals. Ringo doesn't, however, do his usual cameo lead vocal, perhaps under doctor's orders after his bout with tonsillitis.

This concert was also filmed (see entry in film section), nine songs appearing on the Australian TV special *The Beatles Sing for Shell.* This recording, however, has a different and, to some ears, superior mix. It also contains one song ("This Boy") not included on the television program—maybe because one of the singers sputters "uh-oo-buh!" at the end.

● June 18–20

Live Performance
Sydney Stadium, Sydney

I Saw Her Standing There (fragment)
You Can't Do That (fragment)

That *is* the Beatles playing, somewhere down there, underneath a waterfall of screams on this soundtrack to a newsreel clip. And isn't it fortunate we have several vastly superior documents of their Australian tour instead of having to settle for this one!

● June 23

Private Tape
Hotel St. George, Wellington, New Zealand

Bouree

During an interview in Wellington, New Zealand, Paul played almost half a minute of the Johann Sebastian Bach classic "Bouree" on guitar, sing-scatting in an exaggerated operatic voice for a few seconds of this "performance." It's reading too much into this to say that, in hindsight, "Eleanor Rigby" was just around the corner, but it is evidence that he had some passing knowledge of classical music before classical influences made their way into Beatles recordings. He and George used to play "Bouree" as something of a "party piece" in their early days, and as he recalled in July 2005 for his television special *Chaos and Creation at Abbey Road,* this doodling around actually did have an influence on a Beatles song that was way off in the future, as the acoustic guitar work on "Blackbird" used a similar technique in its combination of bass and melody lines. As he elaborated in *Paul McCartney: Many Years from Now,* "I developed the melody [to 'Blackbird'] on guitar based on the Bach piece and took it somewhere else, took it to another level, then I just fitted the words to it."

● July 14

BBC Session
Top Gear program (broadcast July 16, 1964)
Broadcasting House, London

Long Tall Sally
*Things We Said Today
*A Hard Day's Night
And I Love Her
If I Fell
You Can't Do That
        appears on Live at the BBC

The purpose of this day's session was probably to promote the Beatles' latest record releases, as five of the songs were on their just-issued *A Hard Day's Night* LP, and one the title track of their June EP *Long Tall Sally.* So, no points for originality as far as offering items without official counterparts, but on the other hand, four of the songs were making their BBC debut. The surviving tape has excellent sound quality, with the exception of "You Can't Do That," which is slightly distorted. And one of the songs, "And I Love Her," was played outside EMI for the only time *anywhere,* despite its huge popularity. It's given a nice light treatment, though Paul McCartney changes the phrasing of the end of the final chorus, strangely rushing out the words of the song's title. "If I Fell," the other popular ballad from the *A Hard Day's Night* film, *would* make it into their stage repertoire, and is taken just a little faster than the studio version on this faithful rendition.

Both sides of their current UK single, "A Hard Day's Night"/"Things We Said Today," were presented, and both also appear on *Live at the BBC.* For "A Hard Day's Night," the fellows made an emphatic point of repeating the final riff (which fades out quickly on the studio version) over and over, to prove that it wasn't the record. Great idea, but they rather sabotaged the point they were trying to make by ham-fistedly editing a George Martin electric keyboard solo into the instrumental break, from—*the record.* Even upon the initial broadcast, lots of listeners must have noticed this not-so-smooth sleight of hand. (The show's producer, Bernie Andrews, has said that George Martin was supposed to play his keyboard part for the BBC version but did not show up at the session.) This mild embarrassment might have vanished into the ill-lit corridors of bootlegdom if not for Apple's curious decision to use this take on *Live at the BBC,* even though another version, without grafting from the official recording, was done for radio later in the month. For the version of "I Should Have Known Better" used on this broadcast, they went one better and just played the record, though they'd make a genuinely different radio-only one for their next BBC session just a few days later.

The between-song chat is rather more interesting on this session than most, not only because they were able to talk about their just-completed *A Hard Day's Night* film, but also because it was revealed that Ringo was working on composing a song. "I've written a good one, you see, but no one seems to want to record it," he disclosed without rancor. Then Paul proceeds to recite an extract: "Don't pass me by, don't make me cry, don't make me blue, baby, 'cause you know why. . . ." The passage would, almost verbatim, comprise the chorus of the first Ringo Starr solo composition on a Beatles release, "Don't Pass Me By"—but not until four years later, on *The White Album.* (Ringo had first mentioned the song in the press in 1963, and Paul actually sang a bit of the tune a few weeks earlier, on June 26, during a radio interview in Dunedin, New Zealand.)

Striking, too, is the measurable rise in confidence of the group when speaking on the radio. They were never ill at ease in such situations, even back in early 1963, but now it's almost as though they're running the show and allowing the announcer his two cents every once in a while, rather than the other way around. The foursome obviously no longer felt the need to play so hard at their "eager to please" roles—and, soon, would feel no need to record BBC music sessions at all.

● July 17

BBC Session
From Us to You *program (broadcast August 3, 1964)*
BBC Paris Studio, London

Broadcast:
From Us to You (with announcer voice-over)
Long Tall Sally
If I Fell
I'm Happy Just to Dance with You
Things We Said Today
I Should Have Known Better
Boys
Kansas City/Hey! Hey! Hey! Hey!
A Hard Day's Night
"Session Tape," Not Broadcast:
From Us to You (without announcer voice-over)
From Us to You (outtake)
Kansas City/Hey! Hey! Hey! Hey!
Long Tall Sally
If I Fell
Boys
I'm Happy Just to Dance with You (backing track)
I'm Happy Just to Dance with You
I Should Have Known Better (false start)
I Should Have Known Better (single-tracked vocal, missing harmonica overdub)

I Should Have Known Better
Things We Said Today
A Hard Day's Night

This is about as neat as a Beatles BBC session without any songs not to show up on their studio releases can be, for a few reasons. Several of the songs are from *A Hard Day's Night,* and not often done for the BBC; these are the *only* non-EMI versions of "I'm Happy Just to Dance with You" and "I Should Have Known Better" that exist anywhere, in fact. The sound is good (though not quite as good as it is on the best of the surviving radio tapes of the group), and the performances a bit more animated than usual on some of the well-traveled items. And not only have none of the tracks been officially released, there's also a "session tape" of material from the date that wasn't even broadcast (although most of these are just missing vocals or announcements later dubbed onto the recording, rather than being wholly different performances/outtakes).

"I'm Happy Just to Dance with You" is the most noteworthy cut, and not just because it's a good song of which no other alternate is available. It's also the home of some of the most charmingly blatant vocal mistakes to be heard on any BBC recording, George Harrison obviously not being accustomed to singing it (maybe understandably, as it was one of only two Lennon-McCartney songs on which he sang lead, the other being "Do You Want to Know a Secret"). The foul-ups between different words of his multitracked vocal are apparent at several points, particularly in the intro. But those are kid stuff compared to the misstep he makes when he sings, "If somebody tries to take *your* place, let's pretend we just can't see his face." A *guy,* trying to cut in on a dance between George and his girl, and take the *girl's* place? Hmmm. . . . George also switches the order of the last two lines. For all that, it's quite a good version.

The quartet sounds happy to get the chance to give several other new songs an airing, playing them with just enough of a certain bounce to distinguish them from the classic studio recordings. It's the only complete non-EMI version of "I Should Have Known Better," though John Lennon might have overdone it a bit with his harmonica overdubs. This second and final BBC pass at "A Hard Day's Night" eliminates the clumsy, edited-in instrumental break from the record they'd used on the first broadcast of the number. In its place, George Harrison delivers a sterling, nearly note-for-note emulation of George Martin's keyboard solo on his guitar, with a cool, slightly echoing effect. It makes you wonder why they felt the need to edit in Martin's solo the first time around, though some smart alecks might counter that given Harrison's abysmal solos on early takes in the session for the single back in April, maybe it took him three whole months to get that part down to perfection.

The program was filled out with a few covers, with both "Boys" and "Long Tall Sally" given their seventh and final BBC presentations. "Boys" comes off better than "Long Tall Sally," on which the backing's a little workmanlike and plodding compared to the studio take (or several other live versions, for that matter). Not so for "Kansas City/Hey! Hey! Hey! Hey!" which is a really superb version. The guitar solo's a little down-and-dirtier than on the *Beatles for Sale* arrangement, and the call-and-response vocals between Paul and the rest of the band have an almost loosey-goosey, improvised atmosphere.

Also available is a lower-fidelity tape, with some varispeed wobble in places, of the session before the final touches were laid onto the broadcast tape. In some cases, the variations are extremely minimal,

CRINSK DEE NIGHT?

amounting to no more than a bit of tune-up/chatter or the absence of a voice-over from the announcer. In other cases, the differences are more noticeable, though not exactly exciting. There's a brief false start to "I Should Have Known Better" that breaks down when John begins his vocal on the second verse rather than the first, and another that's missing the harmonica and has a single-tracked vocal (rather than the double-tracked one used on the broadcast). The "From Us to You" jingle—on which, by the way, the bridge is played without vocals—is heard without the voice-over, and also as a wholly different alternate take on which John sings "from me to you" instead of "from us to you" near the end. And "I'm Happy Just to Dance with You" is heard in its backing-track-only state. That's the first such instance, in fact, in which a full-length unreleased Beatles track of any sort is missing its vocals, an occurrence which became far more common on the outtakes of later EMI recordings as the group's method of layering components became more sophisticated.

Finally, some bootlegs of this session also include a performance by Cilla Black of "It's for You" that was used as part of the original broadcast. That was keeping things all in the family, to some degree: "It's for You" was a Lennon-McCartney song the Beatles never released, and Cilla Black was a friend of theirs from their Cavern days, likewise managed by Brian Epstein.

● July 19

Live Performance
For television program Blackpool Night Out
ABC Theatre, Blackpool

A Hard Day's Night
Things We Said Today
You Can't Do That
If I Fell
Long Tall Sally

A good if brief set that essentially offers about half the program the Beatles would present on their upcoming summer American tour. The highlight's probably "If I Fell," where John and Paul, for reasons lost to time, have a laughing fit that necessitates a relaunch into the song after a false start. Note that George takes the harmony part for "Things We Said Today" (as he would whenever the song was performed live), unlike on the studio recording, which has a double-tracked McCartney vocal. It was the same sort of rejigging that had already taken place for "All My Loving," recorded with a double-tracked Paul in the studio, but done with George on harmonies in concert.

● August 14

Studio Outtakes
Beatles for Sale *sessions*
Studio Two, Abbey Road, London

I'm a Loser (takes 1–7)
I'm a Loser (take 8 intro)

*Mr. Moonlight (takes 1, 4)
Mr. Moonlight (take 2)
Leave My Kitten Alone (take 4)
*Leave My Kitten Alone (take 5)
   *appears on Anthology 1

Much of the first day's work on *Beatles for Sale* has made its way into circulation, starting with the complete roll of takes (some of them false starts or quick breakdowns) for "I'm a Loser." While this was very much a "tweaking" sequence with the skeleton of the song firmly in place from the start, it does reveal how much restructuring went on before the number was ready to take its place as one of the strongest selections on the LP. The dramatic, drumless, pause-laden introduction was at first totally absent, the band just charging into a single declaration of the title/chorus. Also, Paul McCartney's singing harmonies throughout the chorus, instead of letting John sing the final line alone to create a touch more dramatic gravity.

John's still hiding behind his mask rather than beneath it on take 2, and there's none of the Dylanesque harmonica that gave so much somber weight to the final product. Instead of letting John's mournful harmonica and George's sympathetic guitar take the song into an instrumental fade-out, John and Paul happily harmonize on the title phrase over and over, changing the melody slightly and drifting into woozily joyous falsettos. It's also the spark for one of the more memorable asides on an early Beatles session, Paul happily acknowledging at the end, "There's a frayed edge for you." But it's an unsuitably jolly conclusion for a song about rejection and donning false smiley faces, and the group seemed to realize the song was deserving of a more serious treatment the further they got into the session. A few Dylan-ish bleats in the false start of take 5 lets us know John's whipped out his harmonica, though he'd definitely planned to use that instrument all along, as Paul refers to "where you'll come in with the mouth organ" at the end of take 1. Take 6 has another intriguing bit of lyric jiggling, John twisting a phrase so that he should have known *he* would *lose* in the end, rather than that *she* would *win*. It also has a full harmonica solo, which remained when the group nailed the track on take 8—not before an entertaining bit at the start of take 7 where John and Paul yelp the title, à la some of Monty Python's more eccentric characters. (A very small bit of chatter and music preceding the proper start of take 8 has been bootlegged as well.)

The Beatles' arrangement of Dr. Feelgood's "Mr. Moonlight" had changed considerably since they did it on *Live! At the Star-Club*. Issued on *Anthology 1*, take 4 has the faux-Hawaiian feel of the final version in place. It differs substantially only in a different order of the lyrics and the instrumental break, which features a high, almost wracked guitar solo; its place would be taken by a not-entirely-serious-sounding organ on *Beatles for Sale*. (The opening solo vocal of the title phrase by John on this take was grafted onto the eventual master version after the song was re-recorded at a later session.) Also on *Anthology 1* was the mere ten-second take 1, where John only has time to wail the title a cappella before it breaks down. And if you want more of that, head to the *Anthology* video, which allows you to hear him doing the exact same thing just as briefly on the beginning of take 2.

The day's most interesting rarity, however, was the cover of "Leave My Kitten Alone," which was the first complete, full-band outtake recording of a song never to be issued in any form during the life of the group since "How Do You Do It" back in 1962. Though first recorded by Little

Willie John in the late '50s, it's believed the group might have modeled their arrangement on Johnny Preston's subsequent cover, as both were small US hit singles in early 1961. Whatever record they learned it from, the Beatles transformed it into an altogether tougher song, wisely getting rid of the cutesy "meow, meow" backing vocals heard on each version. (If you have this track on *Anthology 3* and bootlegs, you might find John's vocal to be more upfront on the bootlegs; according to a 1996 *ICE* article, engineer Geoff Emerick mixed it down "so that it might sound more in balance with the instruments," at George Martin's suggestion.) There is another "version" of "Leave My Kitten Alone" that's escaped (take 4), but that's just a four-second false start of a count-in and a couple of guitar notes—recorded off-line, for that matter.

So why wasn't "Leave My Kitten Alone" placed on *Beatles for Sale*? There's no obvious explanation. It's not the greatest rock 'n' roll cover the band did, but it's pretty good. John Lennon's double-tracked vocal is strong and committed; George's guitar solo has the kind of stinging, high-pitched, wiry feel he'd perfect on "Drive My Car"; and the piano (played by Paul here) sits comfortably in the mix, as it did on other Beatles rockers of the period like "Slow Down." Maybe they thought it wouldn't fit into the album as well as the other six covers they did eventually include. They could have added "Leave My Kitten Alone" as well, but that would have perhaps been bumping the length up too much (to 15 songs), and/or putting more weight on covers for the album as a whole than the Beatles would have liked.

Still, as Mark Lewisohn rightly speculates in *The Beatles Recording Sessions*, "Hindsight shows that perhaps it might have made a better LP track than, say, 'Mr. Moonlight,' most people's least favorite song on what was to become the *Beatles for Sale* LP." In fact, "Mr. Moonlight" is probably one of the least popular Beatles tracks, period; in a 1971 poll in which Howard Smith of New York radio station WPLJ and *The Village Voice* asked listeners to name their least favorite Beatles song, "Mr. Moonlight" came in second, "beat" only by "Revolution 9."

● August 19

Live Performance
Cow Palace, San Francisco

Twist and Shout (fragment)
She Loves You
A Hard Day's Night

Three songs from the first show of the Beatles' summer 1964 North American tour were recorded as part of a KCRA-TV documentary on the group's San Francisco visit. The quality's terrible, the band sounding as if they're playing under glass a football field away, one excited screamer in particular almost drowning out everything else from time to time. That may indeed be how it sounded to those in the cheap seats, but that doesn't mean it's any joy to listen to, even if you're only doing so for its documentary value.

● August 21

Live Performance
Seattle Coliseum, Seattle

Twist and Shout
You Can't Do That
All My Loving
She Loves You
Things We Said Today
Roll Over Beethoven
Can't Buy Me Love
If I Fell
I Want to Hold Your Hand
Boys
A Hard Day's Night
Long Tall Sally

Considering that full-length rock concerts were seldom recorded for any purpose in 1964, it's remarkable that no less than half a dozen tapes of complete or near-complete shows were made of the Beatles' 1964 North American tour. This is the worst of the lot, however, and if it's any indication of how it actually sounded up in the rafters, you really *would* have had a hard time telling which song from which unless you were really familiar with the material. As for the wild audience reaction, the most ear-opening passage arrives at "Can't Buy Me Love," where the crowd, for some reason, decides to clap along madly.

● August 22

Live Performance
Empire Stadium, Vancouver

Twist and Shout
You Can't Do That
All My Loving
She Loves You
Things We Said Today
Roll Over Beethoven
Can't Buy Me Love
If I Fell
Boys
A Hard Day's Night
Long Tall Sally

Now this is more like it: a show in listenable (though hardly sparkling) sound, and, more importantly, one that isn't just a near-identical companion to other tapes made during the same tour. It is pretty much the same as the others for the first few songs, though there's some brittle distortion (particularly on the vocals) until partway through "She Loves You." Something's obviously greatly amusing the group, however—or maybe they're just happily overwhelmed at the wild reception they're getting, this being just their fifth show of the tour—as John Lennon bursts into a triumphant cackle near the end of "She Loves You." Perhaps it was the trouble they were having on timing their vocals, Paul coming

Unreleased Beatlemania Live

By mid-1964, crowds at Beatles concerts were becoming so big, and so loud, that the way the group played their music (and the clarity with which it was heard) was inevitably affected. In part because of the Beatles' own retrospective comments, the impression has sometimes been fostered over the years that the shows were subpar, sloppily played, and occasionally downright inaudible. To the fan hungry enough to seek out the evidence on many unissued live 1964–1966 Beatles recordings, there's both reward and frustration. The reward is that, contrary to myth, there's actually some pretty good stuff to be heard on those tapes. The frustrations are that some of the recordings are so lo-fi as to be absolutely excruciating to endure; that, on some of the shows, the group did indeed fail to play or sing well; and that, even on the better gigs, there was such a rigidity to the setlist, arrangements, and stage announcements that listening to more than one or two shows per tour can become a repetitious experience.

Back in the Cavern and Star-Club days, part of what drew audiences to the Beatles was the very unpredictability of their live sets. They drew from a huge repertoire, though as surviving setlists attest to, even back then there was usually a planned order of presentation. They clowned around onstage and bantered with the audience. That began to change when Brian Epstein cleaned up their image, but became especially curtailed when they started to go on national tours in early 1963, where their sets were usually limited to four to six songs, usually specifically chosen and unaltered from night to night. At least there were those frequent BBC sessions that gave them a chance to play lots of cover versions, and even some Lennon-McCartney originals, that weren't part of their stage show. There were also some nontour smaller gigs (their last Cavern show didn't take place until August 3, 1963) that might have allowed them to vary their program. But by late 1963, even those were out the window, replaced pretty much permanently by sets of ten-to-twelve-song duration that were specifically tailored and sequenced for each tour, only occasionally deviating from the plan. To a certain degree, the Beatles were now approaching touring as a job, giving the crowds a selection of their most popular material, and reserving their musical creativity and experimentation for writing and studio recording.

From a 21st-century perspective, listeners sifting through the live Beatles tapes might be puzzled as to why the group didn't play longer sets or perform a wider range of tunes, particularly as the band often cited sheer boredom as one of the reasons they retired from touring permanently after the summer of 1966. It needs to be stressed, though, that this was common practice in the mid-'60s. Even acts with a more antiestablishment, rebellious image such as the Rolling Stones and the Who usually stuck to a preset selection (and order) of songs on their tours (and, even in the 2000s, still often do). Though a dozen songs and a half hour seems like short value today, actually that was more time than many touring rock acts of the era were given onstage, even the headliners.

Similarly, it was (and, again, still often is) standard show business to get an onstage routine down and repeat it night after night. The Beatles worked out between-song patter that, while made to sound spontaneous (and probably perceived as such by their largely teenage audiences), verged on the carefully scripted. On tape after tape, unofficial group MC Paul McCartney urges the audience to "make as much noise as you like" and "join in and clap your hands and stamp your feet" (seconded by John Lennon's mock-spastic claps, stamps, and mutters), hoping before each closing number that the audience has enjoyed the show. "Have you enjoyed the show?" he then shouts/pleads, as if he expects anything less than a roof-rattling cheer to arise from the seats. (Viewed in this light, the song "Sgt. Pepper's Lonely Hearts Club Band" almost seems like a loving satire of their own onstage audience-endearing proclamations.) Even the funny, seemingly ad-libbed asides—"If I Fell" being introduced as "If I Fell Over," "Baby's in Black" as "Baby's in Blackpool," the "One-two-three-four-five!" count-in to "All My Loving," John announcing "She Loves You" in an exaggerated Liverpool accent as "She Loves YOO!"—were repeated at different shows. George and Ringo got one vocal lead per show, all four except Ringo (save on rare occasions) introduced various songs, and there was always a point where someone was introduced who didn't often get the chance to sing, as if it were a big secret, before "*Ringo!*" was announced (and the crowd roared in response as if on cue). Entire bootlegs have been named after sound bites from the McCartney spiel, such as *We'd Like to Carry On* and *Make As Much Noise As You Like*.

Years later, the Beatles came clean and admitted they often rushed through the shows if they weren't in the best of moods. That, and the adrenaline of being in the eye of the hurricane even when they *were* in the best of moods, account for the frequent sped-up tempos. It's not quite true, however—at least, on the tapes that have survived—that they managed to pare down the time by five minutes by charging through the songs at the speed of light on certain occasions. Songs like "Twist and Shout," "Ticket to Ride," "She's a Woman," and "Things We Said Today" were shortened by cutting out a verse or so, even though they weren't that long in the first place, and one wonders whether it would have taken that much more effort to play them all the way through. The Beatles have so often complained about how hard it was to hear one another in these situations that it's hard to pick one or two representative quotes, but here are a couple. Ringo, talking to *Goldmine* in 1988, admitted, "If you look at films, you'll see I'm looking at their mouths—I'm lip-reading where we're up to in the song because I couldn't hear the amps or anything . . . just to find out where we were up to in the song, and just carrying a beat." And Ringo again, about 20 years earlier, in Hunter Davies's authorized biography: "It was wrecking our playing. The noise of the people just drowned anything. Eventually I just used to play the offbeat, instead of a constant beat. I couldn't hear myself half the time, even on the amps, with all the noise. We'd get put in silly positions in the halls so we'd be too far away from each other. Onstage we used to play things faster than on the records, mainly because we couldn't hear what we were doing. I used to come in at the wrong time sometimes because I'd no idea where we were at. We just used to mime half the time to the songs, especially if your throat was feeling rough."

For all that, remarkably, the singing, harmonizing, and playing on many of their live tapes is pretty good, especially considering the obstacles they were up against, though there is a notable deterioration in the 1966 shows. Also, even when they were obviously coming in at the wrong places, and even though they griped about what a drag touring had become, the Beatles rarely sounded anything less than totally enthusiastic and thrilled to be there. If it was a simple matter of professionalism or just an act, it was a damned good one.

There are decent-quality (if scream-shrouded) tapes of at least one show from all of their major tours from early 1964 through the summer of 1966, with the odd exception of any of their British tours from this period. (At the bottom end of the rung, be warned that there are also absolutely execrable-sounding fragments of numerous concerts from the era, usually found as part of radio and television documentaries or recorded from the audience, that are solely of value as proof that the events actually occurred.) For those who want to collect selectively rather than indiscriminately, the problem is not finding listenable concerts, but good ones, avoiding shows that are pretty much identical to one another. If that's your approach, your best bet is to pick up just one or two of the best concerts from each one of the tours represented on tape. That avoids the redundancy that's the biggest impediment to consistent enjoyment of their live work, as the setlists (and, to a lesser degree, style) *did* change from tour to tour, though not as radically as they might have.

The following shows are particularly recommended, and taken as a whole give you some idea of the Beatles' musical evolution in the mid-'60s, albeit photographed from a specific, limited angle:

February 1964 American visit: February 11, Washington Coliseum
June 1964 world tour: June 17, Festival Hall, Melbourne (evening show)
Summer 1964 American tour: August 23, Hollywood Bowl
    (complete, unedited version)
Mid-1965 European tour: June 20, Palais des Sports, Paris (evening show)
Summer 1965 American tour: August 30, Hollywood Bowl
    (complete, unedited version)
Summer 1966 world tour: July 1, Nippon Budokan Hall, Tokyo
Summer 1966 American tour: August 29, Candlestick Park, San Francisco

Honorable mentions:

All three Ed Sullivan Show performances, February 1964 (none of which
    are full-length concerts, but which together equal about one concert)
September 2, 1964, Convention Hall, Philadelphia

in with the final chorus a fraction of a beat too early. The trouble multiplied on "Things We Said Today," Paul uncharacteristically screwing up a lyric in the second verse, sing-mumbling something along the lines of "Be my one and only, yes, you'll say you're mine." And George's voice cracks on a roughly if enthusiastically sung "Roll Over Beethoven."

Then the real fun starts, however, when MC and Vancouver radio DJ Red Robinson suddenly takes the stage, threatening to cancel the show unless the crowd simmers down. Which is immediately followed by—with no sense of irony—Paul urging the masses to "join in, clap your hands, stamp your feet!" before charging into a somewhat breathlessly sung "Can't Buy Me Love." Then John and Paul, whether as a reaction to the alleged crowd rowdiness or bemusement at the difficulty at hearing each other over the din, get absolutely giddy during "If I Fell," apparently trying to get each other to crack up in front of the assembled 20,000. Surprisingly it's Paul, not John, who's the chief joker in this pack, barely managing to get through the second middle eight, and it's hard to tell whether his singing here is deliberately making fun of himself or the best he can manage while suppressing his giggles. Paul keeps the giddiness going during "Boys," with what certainly seem like some intentionally overexuberant backup harmonies, adding in more over-loud, extraneous "Yeah yeah yeah"s and "Talk about boys"s than you'll hear in any other version of the song. And on the last verse, those backup harmonies are changed to "Be-bop-a-lula," capping a rendition that's undeniably sloppy but in its own way wonderful, Ringo himself chuckling through his lead vocals at one point.

The crowd frenzy evidently hadn't dimmed, however, as Beatles press officer Derek Taylor takes the stage briefly to again warn that the program will be cut short unless people move back. "They're very worried about the situation at the front," he chides, which seems contradicted by John Lennon's mumbled comment a few seconds later, "Oh, come on, let's go!" That's followed immediately by a count-in to "A Hard Day's Night," and the show does get to its conclusion without the group getting overrun by fans. But the evidence on tape argues that the Beatles, if anything, fed off the hysteria and worked it to their advantage, reveling in

the absurdity of the conditions and riding the wave to actually make the performance *more* fun for themselves, rather than allowing themselves to become unnerved or stop the show. So while this is far from the group's most impeccable full-length concert tape from a purely musical point of view, it's one of the more entertaining, supplying a small window into the humor and camaraderie that enabled them to take stressful and perhaps even dangerous situations like this in stride. It's missing "I Want to Hold Your Hand," though, possibly omitted to shorten the concert, given the unstable crowd situation.

Speaking in his office to the Canadian magazine *Maclean's* in March 2003, Red Robinson disclosed that threatening to stop the concert certainly wasn't the Beatles' idea. After interviewer Ken MacQueen noticed a picture of Robinson with the Beatles, the DJ confirmed, "That's John Lennon telling me to 'fuck off.' And I'm saying to the crowd, 'Listen, calm down or the Beatles are going to leave the stadium . . .' 'Fuck off,' he said. 'Nobody interrupts a Beatles concert.' I've got another shot where I'm leaning over talking to John and he's saying 'OK, mate, carry on,' because I'd said, 'Brian Epstein, he sent me up here.'"

The show was broadcast live on the Vancouver radio station CKNW, and at least two other gigs on the tour would be transmitted as they happened on local radio outlets. It's unimaginable today that such a big act would permit several concerts to be broadcast in such a short span, and we have the naïveté of that era to thank for the existence of these relatively high-quality bootlegs of not only this Vancouver stop, but also performances in Philadelphia and Indianapolis in early September.

● August 23

Live Performance
Hollywood Bowl, Los Angeles

Twist and Shout
You Can't Do That

*All My Loving
*She Loves You
*Things We Said Today
*Roll Over Beethoven
Can't Buy Me Love
If I Fell
I Want to Hold Your Hand
*Boys
A Hard Day's Night
*Long Tall Sally

appears on 1977 LP The Beatles at the Hollywood Bowl

Although this was the first Beatles concert (and one of the very few) professionally recorded with the intention of producing an authorized commercial release, it was not actually the first time such an endeavor was given serious consideration. Way back in January 1963, George Martin told *Mersey Beat* he was "thinking of recording their first LP at the Cavern, but obviously I'm going to have to come to see the club before I make a decision. If we can't get the right sound we might do the recording somewhere else in Liverpool, or bring an invited audience into the studio in London. They've told me they work better in front of an audience."

Martin and the Beatles decided to record the debut album in the studio instead, but there was another near-attempt at a live recording when Capitol Records planned to tape their Carnegie Hall concert in New York on February 12, 1964. This project even got as far as getting announced in a January 29 press release, with permission obtained from both Brian Epstein and concert promoter Sid Bernstein, and was planned to be issued in April 1964. That show was never recorded, however, due to objections from the American Federation of Musicians. That organization did give permission for Capitol, however, to record their August 23 show at the Hollywood Bowl, with the label's Voyle Gilmore acting as producer and Hugh Davies as recording engineer.

Remembered Gilmore in a 1977 interview with *Melody Maker*, "When the Beatles were first coming here, we would love to have a live album. I think Epstein would have gone for it, but the boys didn't go for it. They came from a poor background, you know, and they were always conscious of that. They felt a live album would be a rip-off because all the tunes were already recorded. I did know we could do it right, so I asked if we could do it anyway. Sometimes you just can't tell with these things. . . . We took a sound truck up there and plugged directly into the board with our mikes. Hollywood Bowl has a pretty good stereo sound system." Gilmore added that George Martin, though in attendance, didn't take much of an interest in the proceedings: "We parked several blocks away and took a cab up together. He wasn't around the sound truck that much. Oh, I think he stuck his head in and said, 'that sounds terrible,' or something like that. He was more interested in hanging out backstage with the boys or going out front to see how it sounded out there, that sort of thing."

It's no real mystery as to why the album didn't come out back in the mid-'60s. The Beatles and George Martin didn't think the sound quality was good enough. As Martin straightforwardly explained in the liner notes to the album on which some of the tapes were eventually used, 1977's *The Beatles at the Hollywood Bowl*, "Frankly, I was not in favor of taping their performance. I knew the quality of recording could not equal what we could do in the studio, but we thought we

would try anyhow. Technically, the results were disappointing; the conditions for the engineers were arduous in the extreme. The chaos, I might almost say panic, that reigned at these concerts was unbelievable unless you were there. Only three track recording was possible; the Beatles had no 'fold back' speakers, so they could not hear what they were singing, and the eternal shriek from 17,000 healthy, young lungs made even a jet plane inaudible."

Apart from the sound quality, there are indications the Beatles weren't wholly pleased with the performances. "I didn't like Hollywood Bowl," John Lennon told *Rolling Stone* shortly after the group broke up. "If we knew we were being recorded it was death, we were so frightened. I mean 'cause you knew it was always terrible, your voice was always, you could never hear yourself and you knew that they were fuckin' it up on the tape anyway, and there was no bass and they never recorded the drums, you could never hear 'em. The sound . . . those places were built for fuckin' orchestras, not groups." In the unreleased director's cut of *Anthology*, Paul McCartney was more succinct: "We listened to that back and we wouldn't let 'em release it." (It must also be added that according to a 1964 quote by the ever-contradictory Lennon used in *The Beatles Anthology*, "The Hollywood Bowl was marvelous. It was the one we all enjoyed the most, I think, even though it wasn't the largest crowd . . . it was a big stage, and it was great. We could be heard in a place like the Hollywood Bowl, even though the crowd was wild: good acoustics.")

"It wasn't that bad," claimed Voyle Gilmore in *Melody Maker*. "I kept thinking maybe we were going to get permission [to release it], so I took it back into the studio and worked on it awhile. I worked with the applause, edited it down, made it play, and EQ'd it quite a bit. The boys heard it and they all wanted tape copies. So I had five or six copies made and sent over. That's where the bootlegs must have got out, from the Beatles themselves. . . . They said they liked it, that it sounded pretty good, that they were surprised. But they still didn't want to release it."

Of course, some of it *did* get released in 1977, when Martin and frequent Beatles studio engineer Geoff Emerick transferred the 3-track tapes to modern multitrack ones and put them through the grinder of remixing, filtering, and equalization. That album, however, was a composite of six tracks from the 1964 Hollywood Bowl show, and seven from the evening concerts they gave at the same venue a year later in August 1965 (though an early report had suggested it would be a double-LP set). The entire 12-song 1964 Hollywood Bowl show circulates on bootleg, the six unissued tracks boasting the same sound quality (i.e., pretty good, though not perfect) as the six included on the LP. (Note, too, that a 48-second excerpt of "Twist and Shout" came out on Capitol's November 1964 Beatles documentary LP *The Beatles' Story*; the version of "Twist and Shout" on *The Beatles at the Hollywood Bowl* is an entirely different one, recorded on August 30, 1965. And the Beatles themselves *did* use some of the audience screams from one of the Hollywood Bowl recordings they made in the mid-'60s, interestingly enough, in *Sgt. Pepper*'s segue from the title track to "With a Little Help from My Friends"!)

Background, recording, and release details aside, how does this show *sound*? Well, there is something of a smothered, blanket-over-the-canopy feel, the imbalance meaning that certain elements tend to jump out at you while others seem submerged. The lead vocals and Harrison's 12-string guitar in "You Can't Do That" are sometimes far more to the front than the other elements, for instance. The scream-

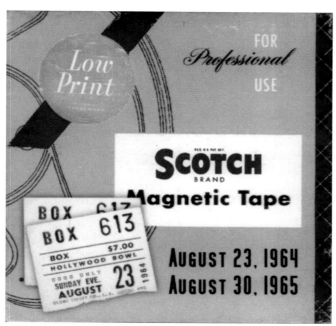

The complete versions of two shows excerpted for the official The Beatles at the Hollywood Bowl *LP, here combined onto one illicit CD whose cover gets the point across without even mentioning the Beatles by name.*

ing, while considerable, has an artificially squashed-to-the-back shape. It adds up to an ambience where the separate parts seem oddly isolated, rather than carrying the all-out punch you imagine the band could have generated if they weren't struggling with the recording and sound equipment's technical limitations. There are undeniably points at which they're struggling to keep in time with one another; listen to Ringo's drumming in parts of "All My Loving," for example. And the set-opening "Twist and Shout" has been perfunctorily rearranged (as it would in concert from this point onward), with a more even, rollicking tempo and a cruelly shortened length, clocking in at about a minute and 20 seconds.

All this is, in the end, nitpicking at what's ultimately a good listen, even if it's not the undisputed No. 1 live Beatles recording you might expect, given that it's one of their few concerts granted official release in even a piecemeal fashion. The enthusiasm's there, and "Things We Said Today" in particular gets a certain charge in its live setting, especially when Paul yells, "Yeah!" as the band slams into the bridge. And of the six tracks not retrieved for *The Beatles at the Hollywood Bowl*, three were of songs not included on that 1977 LP in any form—"If I Fell" (where sped-up rhythm becomes especially noticeable), "I Want to Hold Your Hand," and "You Can't Do That." The other three—"A Hard Day's Night," "Can't Buy Me Love," and "Twist and Shout"—*are* on *The Beatles at the Hollywood Bowl*, but in their 1965 versions. Perhaps the 1964 "A Hard Day's Night" was passed over because John and Paul don't even seem able to hear each other when they come in with the chorus after the instrumental break. At least that instrumental break of lickety-split riffs, played by George Martin's electric keyboards on the studio single, is executed by George Harrison on 12-string guitar with brash assurance.

So for all its drawbacks (painfully idiotic five-minute introduction by local L.A. announcers included), the complete version of this August 23 concert is an essential part of any collection of unreleased Beatles music. And, it might be noted, one of the most bootlegged ones, having first shown up in that form way back in 1970, when rock bootlegging was still in its infancy. It's often packaged with the August 29, 1965, and August 30, 1965, shows that were also recorded at the Hollywood Bowl, putting all of the recordings of the group at this celebrated venue into one handy collection.

● September 2

Live Performance
Convention Hall, Philadelphia

Twist and Shout
You Can't Do That
All My Loving
She Loves You
Things We Said Today
Roll Over Beethoven
Can't Buy Me Love
If I Fell
I Want to Hold Your Hand
Boys
A Hard Day's Night
Long Tall Sally

Broadcast live on local radio station WIBG, this very good-quality tape really isn't all that far behind the August 23 Hollywood Bowl one in terms of sheer entertainment value. True, it's in mono and not stereo, the typical sound imbalances permeate the proceedings, and the performance is a little more ragged. Yet, perhaps because (unlike at the Hollywood Bowl) the group knew this was not being taped with an eye for a release, they sound just a bit less uninhibited and more at ease. In some ways, the sonic ambience is a little more natural, and somehow the screaming, while certainly audible, is mixed low enough so that it doesn't get in the way of the music at all. There are plenty of musical misalignments to pick on if you're so inclined, and the backup vocals on "Twist and Shout" are almost buried. But that's more than made up for by the obvious joy the group is taking in playing their music, and moments like the way the crowd goes wild when the band hushes parts of the final verse of "Roll Over Beethoven" before leaning hard into the beat. Dig, too, how Ringo sings "All right" instead of "Hey" a couple of times during the final verse of "Boys," the kind of variation that's admittedly tiny, but treasured by Beatles fanatics all the same.

As it had in Vancouver, "If I Fell" proves to be troublesome. John and Paul were again unable to get through the whole song without suppressing some giggles, and (perhaps distracted by someone on or near the stage yelling, "Easy now!" shortly after the song starts) maul the first line of the second verse into something like "If I give in you." "If I Fell" was probably the hardest song in the tour's set to pull off under Beatlemania conditions, as it was the only ballad in the program, and thus the one most subject to the singers getting overrun by crowd noise. Perhaps that's why, in part, the Hollywood Bowl tape of "If I Fell" was passed over for inclusion on the official 1977 *The Beatles at the Hollywood Bowl* release. John's spoken intro to the song in Philly and on other occasions, by the way, asks the audience to wait a minute while George Harrison changes guitars, as George used both Rickenbacker 360-12 and Gretsch Country Gentleman models during the tour.

There's been lots of criticism levied at the Beatles' live performances by some writers over the years. But harping on some missed notes and vocal harmonies (which were inevitable, given the crowd noise and problems suffered by every other popular British Invasion band, from the Rolling Stones on down) is missing the larger picture. More than any other group, the Beatles excelled at having a good time and projecting their good humor onstage. And the 1964 Philadelphia concert, for all its flaws, is one of the best documents of those attributes.

● September 3

Live Performance
Indiana State Fair Coliseum, Indianapolis

Twist and Shout
You Can't Do That
All My Loving
She Loves You
Things We Said Today
Roll Over Beethoven
Can't Buy Me Love
If I Fell
I Want to Hold Your Hand
Boys
A Hard Day's Night
Long Tall Sally (partial)

Somehow this hasn't circulated as much as the two other live radio broadcast shows from the 1964 North American tour. But the sound quality on this recording, beamed out on Indianapolis's WIFE, is about as good as the better-known tapes of the Vancouver and Philadelphia concerts. In fact, it could be a little better; not that it's great, of course, but you can hear all the voices and instruments, and the sound's reasonably full, given the technical limitations of the era. The performances are a little scratchier, though, particularly in the vocal department, with John having an especially hard time making the high notes at the end of the verses in "I Want to Hold Your Hand." Ringo's voice shows some wear on "Boys," and it's another bumpy ride through "If I Fell," a cracked falsetto and fluffed lick marking the end of the verse, and more giggles infecting the John-Paul harmonies. For his part, George totally fluffs a note on the intro to "Roll Over Beethoven," though he makes a nice recovery with a deft bluesy flourish right before the vocal starts. It's also missing about the last half of "Long Tall Sally" (which has slightly worse fidelity than the other songs), though for all the tape's shortcomings, it's not bad at all as a whole.

If the group didn't sound as fresh here as they did the previous day in Philadelphia, there might be good reasons for that. America's most famous (if not most accurate) psychic, Jeane Dixon, had predicted their plane would crash on the Philadelphia–Indianapolis flight. It didn't, of course, and you couldn't tell from the tape that the group was stressed

We've Got Combs

Philadelphia and Indianapolis 1964

Two surprisingly hi-fi recordings of concerts from the Beatles' summer 1964 North American tour, combined onto one CD.

out about that incident in the least. But a listen to John's vocals on "A Hard Day's Night" and the chorus of "She Loves You" confirms that his voice was fraying noticeably as the tour marched onward. In fact, he was coming down with a sore throat that prevented him from attending the following day's press conference in Milwaukee (though he somehow made it through that night's concert), and the whole band got antibiotic shots in Milwaukee to combat their colds.

● September 5

Live Performance
International Amphitheater, Chicago

Twist and Shout (fragment)
You Can't Do That (fragment)

You can hear precisely the last three seconds of "Twist and Shout" and first five of "You Can't Do That" on this soundtrack to TV coverage of their Chicago appearance. Just so you know, in case you see these on bootlegs and expect something more substantial. . . .

● September 6

Live Performance
Olympia Stadium, Detroit, Michigan

Can't Buy Me Love (fragment)

From a sound clip broadcast on WKNR-AM in Detroit, this is another barely audible Beatlemania memento. As an announcer said when it was rebroadcast years later, "It sounded like this at Olympia Stadium. The Beatles? Well, they were in there somewhere."

● September 7

Live Performance
Maple Leaf Gardens, Toronto, Canada

You Can't Do That (fragment)
She Loves You (fragment)
All My Loving (fragment)

While these don't appear on the notorious *Make As Much Noise As You Like!* bootleg (devoted to the very worst-sounding Beatlemania concert recordings), they might as well have, being parts of two songs heard in the background on a CBC-TV documentary. There's no way of telling at which of the two Toronto shows they gave that day these were recorded—but does it matter?

● September 8

Live Performance
Forum, Montreal

Twist and Shout
You Can't Do That
All My Loving
She Loves You
Things We Said Today
Roll Over Beethoven
Can't Buy Me Love
If I Fell
Boys
A Hard Day's Night

"I Want to Hold Your Hand" and "Long Tall Sally" aren't here, the beginning of "Boys" is clipped off, and "A Hard Day's Night" is missing its last verse, but otherwise everything the Beatles usually played on their American tour is present. It's not much fun to hear, however, as the fidelity's pretty blurry and a hum runs throughout the tape, though the voices and (for the most part) instruments are there. You can't tell from the tape, but as reporter Larry Kane told it in his memoir, *Ticket to Ride: Inside the Beatles' 1964 Tour That Changed the World,* "Sharpshooters and uniformed officers of the Royal Canadian Mounted Police stood watch in the upper stands, making sure that no [anti-British] protesters [from Quebec's separatist movement] could get in and make worldwide news by disrupting the concert with violence." A plainclothes officer specifically assigned to guard Ringo was next to the stage. From what you can hear, however, it was just another Beatles concert, the threats not audibly affecting their playing whatsoever. Perhaps to ease their nerves, John and Ringo engage in (for Beatles concerts) extended repartee after "Boys": "Thank you Ringo." "Thank you, John." "Thank *you*, Ringo." "Thank *you*,

John." "No, thank *you*, Ringo . . ." Adding to the silliness, John continues, "The next song we're going to sing, we're gonna sing the next song, we're gonna sing the song," before bursting into giggles.

● September 12

Live Performance
Boston Garden, Boston

Twist and Shout (fragment)

Thankfully completing the series of barely audible concert morsels from radio and television documentaries of the summer 1964 North American tour is this half-minute front end of "Twist and Shout," heard *way* underneath the screams in this documentary on Boston's WBZ-AM.

● September 30

Studio Outtakes
Beatles for Sale *sessions*
Studio Two, Abbey Road, London

What You're Doing (take 11)
No Reply (take 1)
*No Reply (take 2)
        appears on Anthology 1

After playing the same dozen songs almost every day in the most hectic of conditions for a month in North America, Abbey Road must have seemed like a sanctuary when they returned to the *Beatles for Sale* sessions at the end of September, both for its relative calm and the opportunity to work on some new, different material. The Beatles had started work on one of the album's more obscure songs, "What You're Doing," with seven takes on September 29. Continuing with five additional takes the following day, they determined that take 11 was the best, though they'd redo the number from scratch on October 26 to come up with the track included on the final LP.

Take 11 ultimately made it into bootleg circulation in 1999, and while it's among the best and most complete substantially different alternate takes not to have been chosen for the *Anthology* series, it's easy enough to hear why they decided to opt for a more effective re-arrangement. This earlier version is missing the dramatic rolling, extended Ringo Starr drum introduction, and has a considerably more jangly 12-string guitar, rather in the mode of the Byrds—though the Beatles certainly wouldn't have heard of the Byrds at this point, still nine months before the California folk-rockers had an international hit single with their debut 45, "Mr. Tambourine Man." Too, while Paul sings much of the *Beatles for Sale* version of "What You're Doing" on his own, at this point John and Paul sang the verses (as well as the end of the bridge) in unison. There's also a dramatic one-and-a-half-second pause before the instrumental coda, and weirdest of all, a sudden jump to a higher key for the instrumental break, which, unlike the final arrangement, doesn't have a piano as well as guitar.

When "What You're Doing" was remade the following month, it benefited from newly devised strong background harmonies in the verse, the distinctive Ringo Starr rolling drum pattern added to both the intro and outro, a longer instrumental break, and a sharper focus on McCartney's lead vocal. But take 11 of "What You're Doing" is one of the more enjoyable of the Beatles' alternate takes, not least because it really is different from the familiar version, not just a very minor variation.

Steered to completion on this session was "No Reply," with take 2 making its way onto *Anthology 1*. The song had been way more light-hearted than it should have been when they'd first demoed it back on June 3, and was still not being taken wholly straight-faced here. Though the tempo's been changed to approximate the near–bossa nova that appears on the early parts of the verses in the final version, the piano interjects notes at points with a lilt more suitable to a cocktail lounge than a Beatles record. John and Paul's vocals are disjointed enough to suggest this particular take was intended only to have a guide vocal all along; they laugh and stumble periodically, and throw in a doo wop-pish, downward-trailing "Door door door door" at the end of one line. There are other differences to be smoothed out: Ringo's drums are far harder and more straightforward in the second verse, the first verse is reprised at the end instead of the second, they're undecided as to whether to keep the bossa nova tempo going in the bridge, and John sings, "You walked hand in hand with another blank" before heading into that middle eight. Could he really have forgotten such an obvious rhyme as "another man," which he'd sung way back on the June demo version? That's what it sounds like.

Take 1 is heard on the *Anthology* video, and is much the same as take 2, except that it breaks down as soon as they crash-land into the end of the first verse. The reason? John's losing the upper range of his voice at the end of the session, muttering, "[I'll] never make it. . . . STOP! . . . He'll [Paul] have to do it . . . just can't get anywhere near [sings the word 'light'] now . . . so he'll have to do it." Which must be why, at least in part, those lines were divided between low John and high Paul harmonies on the finished version—just one small illustration of how perfectly the two backed up each other when one of them needed a helping hand.

● October 3

Live Performance
For television program Shindig
The Granville Studio, London

Kansas City/Hey! Hey! Hey! Hey!
I'm a Loser
Boys

In a rare instance of the US getting to see and hear a British Beatles performance never broadcast in the UK, the group filmed these three songs live before a studio audience specially for the American *Shindig* television program (broadcast four days later on October 7). Well, sort of live; though they weren't miming to records, they *were* miming, using tracks specially recorded for the program, à la what they'd done for their April 1964 special *Around the Beatles.*

Refreshingly, they didn't trot out "Can't Buy Me Love" or "She Loves You" yet again, instead offering some material that had yet to

be issued on a Beatles disc on either side of the Atlantic. "Kansas City/Hey! Hey! Hey! Hey!", still a couple weeks from being cut at EMI for *Beatles for Sale,* is distinguished from the recorded version by a slightly bluesier George Harrison solo and some different vocal inflections in the extended "Hey! Hey! Hey! Hey!" section—which actually isn't as "extended" in this live rendition. "I'm a Loser" follows the record closely, though it's interesting that it was included on a broadcast that went out (on October 7) two months before it was issued on an LP. That's something that would probably never be allowed to happen for such a big act these days, when there's great fear of an as-yet-unissued original composition getting exposed to the world before it's been blessed with an officially sanctioned CD release.

Probably to give Ringo a chance to sing, the program also included "Boys," with a powerfully sharp George Harrison solo that was, again, rather bluesier than the more familiar LP cut. The entire segment also circulates on video (see entry in film section), and two variations of "Kansas City/Hey! Hey! Hey! Hey!" have been bootlegged, one with more audience screams than the other (though it's the same performance underneath).

● October 6

Studio Outtakes
Beatles for Sale sessions
Studio Two, Abbey Road, London

---

*Eight Days a Week (take 2, incomplete)
*Eight Days a Week (take 4, incomplete)
*Eight Days a Week (take 5)
  appears on Anthology 1

With the increased status of being the world's number one recording act, the Beatles were being granted more time to experiment and tinker with their arrangements in the studio, though hardly on the order of *Sgt. Pepper* just yet. The outtakes of "Eight Days a Week" on *Anthology 1* testify to this, with the incomplete takes 2 and 4 (strung together as a medley on that compilation) trying handclaps and high vocal harmonies on the intro, somewhat (though only faintly) in line with what the Beach Boys were doing in the mid-'60s. There's also a slight reverb on the vocals, which comes through as well on Paul's cheeky spoken declaration, "I'll try to remember, John, but if I don't, well it's just too bad, isn't it?" declaimed with a ridiculously exaggerated Northern accent. The complete take 5 keeps the high opening harmonies, as well as what sound like occasional tone pedal guitar effects, and reprises those harmonies near the end on a brief instrumental coda.

The group eventually opted for a more striking faded-in, vocal-less intro of strummed guitars, as well as moving those handclap rhythms to the end of the verses. Take 5 would have been a good recording on its own merits, but here we have one of many illustrations of how the Beatles could take a good song and make it better. Considered as a single, "Eight Days a Week" was eventually passed over for that honor in the group's native UK, "I Feel Fine"/"She's a Woman" being issued instead. But if all that work went into the recording under the assumption that it might be a single, it wasn't totally for naught; issued as a single in the US in early 1965, "Eight Days a Week" went to No. 1. (Note that while the liner notes for *Anthology 1* say that take 1 is also on that record, it doesn't seem to be present.)

● October 8

Studio Outtakes
"She's a Woman" single session
Studio Two, Abbey Road, London

She's a Woman (take 1, incomplete)
She's a Woman (takes 2–7)

"She's a Woman" was another late-1964 song that was given over to substantial in-studio tinkering, the evidence fortunately escaping via unreleased takes that let us hear it take shape from start to finish. All seven takes, in fact, have been bootlegged, though take 1 is incomplete, and take 6 simply a slightly longer, differently mixed version of the one that was used on the released single.

Take 1 lasts just over a minute, and while the lyrics seem finished (aside from a mistake from McCartney near the end of the second verse in which his love "give her" instead of "gives me"), the backing is little more than a skeletal blues-funky vamp. By take 2, the song's distinctive introductory choppy, faux-Cajun opening guitar slashes are in place. But Paul has trouble with a line in the verse right before the instrumental break, his voice breaking up and then breaking down into a chuckle. The vamped chords then become oddly sour and dissonant at times, and there's no solo in the instrumental break. The ending futzes around instead of coming to a solid fadeout, McCartney playing around with bluesy vocalizations of the title phrase, throwing in a desperate-sounding "Woo!" at the end.

After a couple of false starts, take 5 gets all the way to the finish line. Yet the Beatles are still having quite a bit of trouble keeping on the same chords—a little surprisingly, considering that for a Beatles original, there are relatively few—and Paul trips up on a lyric again, singing "non't" instead of "don't." The backing simply sounds far more underwhelming, klutzy, and simplistic than this powerful rocking song and lead vocal deserve, and McCartney seems to realize the take's unusable on the fade, where he gurgles the title phrase like a baby at one point. Take 6 (including some overdubs) makes all the right fixes, however, fattening the rhythm with a chocalho shaker and adding some much-needed texture with Paul's piano and a sharp, bluesy Carl Perkins–styled guitar solo. This is what's heard on the single, though the bootlegged version has a count-in not heard on the commercial release and a longer fade.

The group did give the song one more try, however, and take 7 is the most interesting variation of the bunch. The intro (after a false start) has slightly elongated guitar chords that cut off some of the choppiness. Otherwise it's much the same as take 6 (if a bit sloppier), but then it detours into an instrumental rave-up at the end that takes the song past the six-minute mark. The Beatles rarely went in for blues-rock improvisations in the studio, but for whatever reason, they decided to do so here, Paul singing (usually sing-screaming, in fact) the title over and over, then raising his pitch to wordless Little Richard–style pitches, howls, and grunts. The rhythm breaks up and loosens, and the guitar roves all up and down the scale, from low growls and bee-sting jabs to strangled upper-register runs. The Beatles weren't

the Yardbirds, and they were wise to excise such jams from their records (and their live performances, for that matter). It's nonetheless intriguing to hear them letting their hair down and getting a little self-indulgent, even if they knew all the while it would almost certainly end up on the cutting room floor. Ringo Starr knew it, announcing at the end, "Well, we got a song *and* an instrumental there."

● October 18

Studio Outtakes
Beatles for Sale *sessions, "I Feel Fine" single session*
Studio Two, Abbey Road, London

*Kansas City/Hey! Hey! Hey! (take 2)
I Feel Fine (takes 1–2, 5–6)
I Feel Fine (take 7, fragment)
I Feel Fine (takes 8–9)
    appears on Anthology 1

Extended hours on a single track were not luxuries granted to the Beatles on this mad day of work, which saw them record or polish almost half the *Beatles for Sale* songs, as well as cut the A-side of their next single. Of the *Beatles for Sale* numbers, the only outtake to have made it out of Abbey Road is the second and final take of "Kansas City/Hey! Hey! Hey!" which closes *Anthology 1*. Other than some variations in Paul McCartney's vocal inflections (particularly when he shouts "Kansas City" near the end of the instrumental break), a less spot-on George Harrison guitar solo, and a full-stop, nonfaded ending, it's barely different from the released version, but not as good.

More interesting are the half-dozen takes of "I Feel Fine" in circulation, both because you can hear more evolution in the arrangement, and because it was one of the group's most creative explorations into new territory in late 1964. Take 1 bears solid evidence that the most experimental element, the opening feedback guitar, was in place right at the beginning. But the key's a step higher than the final version, and the intricate guitar lines aren't as slickly woven together, breaking down at the instrumental break. For take 2, the key's been adjusted downward to its familiar level, but the high harmonies that do so much to ice the official single are still absent, and this again breaks down in the instrumental portion after a high-pitched squeak and a clumsy drum pattern. The sound is basically there, however, as it is on take 5, though John Lennon's vocal isn't as focused or effective as it would be by the final run-through.

Take 6 is just an instrumental backing track, testifying to the working method that was becoming more common on Beatles sessions: laying down a vocal-less take upon which superimpositions could be made. It's pretty similar to the backing used on the final take, though a bit of spice is provided by George Harrison warming up with a few rapid "She's a Woman" licks before the band starts playing for real. The bit of take 7 that's been heard is not the actual complete take, but just a few seconds of the band jamming/warming up on a few bars of the Champs late-'50s instrumental hit "Tequila," which they'd played back in their early days. (Obviously they still remembered it well even in March 1967, when authorized biographer Hunter Davies watched Lennon and McCartney suddenly break into a joyful snatch of the tune in the middle of a songwriting session for "With a Little Help from My Friends" at Paul's house.) Take 8 is just a brief false start; you'll see take 9 on bootlegs, too, but the only difference between this and the released version is an ultra-brief additional opening guitar feedback note.

● October 26

Studio Outtake
Beatles for Sale *sessions*
Studio Two, Abbey Road, London

What You're Doing (take unknown)

From the final *Beatles for Sale* session, just this 18-second scrap of an unknown take—possibly a breakdown, possibly an excerpt from a longer take—has been made available (as part of the first outtakes montage on the *Anthology* video/DVD). "What You're Doing" had been first attempted in the studio back on September 30, but was remade this day, producing the version used on the LP. It's just long enough to hear a couple runs through the main 12-string guitar riff—one that sounds like it might have been quite influential on the guitar style to be popularized in folk-rock by the Byrds within a few months. A humorous exchange at the end signifies the Beatles were getting more informally comfortable, even cheeky, with their producer, Paul asking the control room in a ludicrously rapid-fire tumble of words, "George what did it sound like, was the bass doing a funny thing, did it sound good or did it sound just [indecipherable] crap." Over the talkback speaker, George Martin confirms that it sounded fine, to which McCartney responds in his best nyah-nyahing schoolboy voice, "Did it, well, see, told ya, hello to you, see how you like it!"

● October 26

Another Beatles Christmas Record
Studio Two, Abbey Road, London

Another Beatles Christmas Record (fan club disc)
Another Beatles Christmas Record (takes 1–4)
Another Beatles Christmas Record (unknown take)
Hello, Dolly!

Demand for everything by the Beatles multiplied in 1964, all the way down to their Christmas fan club discs. Where in 1963 about 30,000 had been in print, the next year 65,000 were needed to satisfy the growing membership. Far from viewing this as a burdensome obligation, according to press officer Tony Barrow's *John, Paul, George, Ringo & Me* memoir, "The following year [1964] it was the boys themselves who prompted me into continuing the tradition. 'When are we doing this year's Crimble record?' they asked me. They also wanted another script. I knew they needed my words simply as a security measure in case they dried up. In the event they made everything I wrote much funnier by their distinctively zany, Goons-style presentation."

Oddly, this particular Christmas disc was never issued in the US during the 1960s, where no holiday record had come out in 1963, Beatle-

THE BEATLES
COMPLETE CHRISTMAS COLLECTION
1963 PLUS BONUS OUTTAKES **1969**

[1] **Christmas Time Is Here Again** [November 28 1967]   5:44
[2] **The Beatles Christmas Record 1963** [October 20 1963]   5:02
[3] **Another Beatles Christmas Record 1964** [October 26-28 1964]   4:03
[4] **The Beatles Third Christmas Record 1965** [October 19 1965]   6:22
[5] **The Beatles Fourth Christmas Record 1966** [November 25 1966]   6:39
[6] **Christmas Time Is Here Again 1967** [November 28 1967]   6:10
[7] **The Beatles 1968 Christmas Record 1968** [Fall 1968 Seperately]   7:53
[8] **The Beatles Seventh Christmas Record 1969** [Fall 1969 Seperately]   7:42
[9] **Christmas Message Outtake 1964** (Bonus) [October 26 1964]   4:40

All Words And Music: Lennon, McCartney, Harrison & Starr. Total Time: 54:34

YDCD 031   ®1992 Yellow Dog Records

This anthology not only includes all of the Beatles' 1963–1969 Christmas fan club discs, but also contains an outtake from the session for the 1964 edition.

mania having not even started there yet. So in 1964, the curious decision was made to issue the *1963* Christmas record as the first one made available to American fan club members. The 1964 material would not come out in the US until 1970, when it was used as part of the fan club LP compilation of all of the band's 1963–1969 Christmas singles.

Another Beatles Christmas Record, as the 1964 edition was called, was actually edited together from five separate takes. The group did sound less wide-eyed and bushy-tailed than they had the first time around, and more given to knowing wisecracks. Still, the holiday disc—for the last time—is more or less in line with their moptop personas. Paul thanks fans for buying their records; John thanks them for buying his first book, *In His Own Write;* George thanks them for coming out to see the *A Hard Day's Night* film; and Ringo, in what seems like an afterthought by comparison, wonders at how much they've traveled while touring over the past year. It's funnier to hear than read about on paper, though, as they make it clear they're reading from (and sending up) a script, John coughing loudly when introduced by Paul, all the boys laughing like mock Jack-in-the-Boxes at one point.

As for the best of the modestly amusing wordplay this disc has to offer, Paul entreats, "We hope you've enjoyed listening to the records as much as we've enjoyed melting them," while John "plugs" his next book with, "It's the usual rubbish, but it won't cost much." He adds, "It's been a busy year, Beatle peedles"—few listeners likely aware that "peedles" was a German slang word for "penises." (On their 1961 German single "My Bonnie," their billing had even been changed from "Tony Sheridan and the Beatles" to "Tony Sheridan and the Beat Brothers" because "Beatles" was feared too close in pronunciation to "peedles," though the subsequent mass marketing of Beatles product in Germany did not seem to invite any obscenity charges.) George announces their next film will be in color, on which John elaborates, "Green." The package was dressed up with sound effects, from the marching feet of the opening bars to the crashing glasses underneath Ringo's speech. As for what "music" is here, it's not much—a piano-harmonica-kazoo-backed snatch of "Jingle Bells," and another silly few seconds of piano-anchored Christmas caroling on the outro.

Another Beatles Christmas Record is one of two Beatles fan club recordings of which—believe it or not—multiple outtakes (takes 1–4, plus a brief fragment of an unnumbered one) have been bootlegged. These don't, however, include much different content than what ended up on the final disc (and, sadly, very little in the way of the "cusses and rude jokes" that Mark Lewisohn refers to having been edited out in his book *The Beatles Recording Sessions*). One of the ideas that was discarded was to have the group hum-singing "Hello, Dolly!" in the background during Ringo's bit. Other crumbs of "music" that didn't make the final cut (from take 2) were an a cappella round of "One Plastic Bag" sung (flatly) to the tune of "A Partridge in a Pear Tree," plus a passage of "Jingle Bells" whistled wordlessly to xylophone accompaniment. Other not-so-gemlike cuttings include a few (again, flatly sung) lines of "A Partridge in a Pear Tree" and a brief Jimmy Stewart imitation. The payoff, such as it is, comes at the end of take 2, when one of the four sincerely utters, "And I'd just like to say—we hate you all, you little skroks [sic]! Get out!" the rest of the band cackling in delight.

Also from the session, and lasting just a little over a minute, is a shambolic kazoo-piano attack, instrumental save a few moronically intoned "Dolly"s, on Louis Armstrong's "Hello, Dolly!"—the record that had been responsible for ending the Beatles' 14 consecutive weeks atop the American singles charts in spring 1964. And if you *still* can't get enough, what purports to be an "alternate mix" of the finished disc has also been booted, along with a halfminute of Paul's segment under which the record of "She's a Woman" plays. Even taken in the frivolous spirit in which *Another Beatles Christmas Record* was intended, however, grouped together these outtakes are a bit too much chaotic levity for even the merriest holidaymaker.

● November 17

BBC Session

Top Gear program (broadcast November 26, 1964)
Playhouse Theatre, London

*I'm a Loser
Honey Don't
*She's a Woman
*Everybody's Trying to Be My Baby
**I'll Follow the Sun
*I Feel Fine
Not broadcast:
I Feel Fine (false start)
I Feel Fine (incomplete, single-tracked vocal)

    *appears on Live at the BBC
    **appears on Baby It's You CD-EP

What with the summer 1964 North American tour and recording their next album and single, there had been an unprecedented four-month gap since the Beatles' last BBC session. When they returned to the Beeb for this November program, they focused exclusively on songs from their new single and album. As it happened, the two covers, Carl

Perkins's "Honey Don't" and "Everybody's Trying to Be My Baby," had already been played on the BBC a couple times each prior to their inclusion on *Beatles for Sale*. The sound quality on this tape is among the best of any surviving Beatles sessions, so it's no surprise that five of the six tracks found official release when Apple issued BBC material in the 1990s. There's nothing revelatory here, just good, fairly faithful approximations of the records, even down to the echo on George's vocal for "Everybody's Trying to Be My Baby." At least they were records that would have not been overly familiar to much of the audience at the time of the broadcast, since the "I Feel Fine"/"She's a Woman" single wouldn't come out until the day after it was transmitted, and the *Beatles for Sale* LP wouldn't be available for another week after that.

As for minor points of interest, "I'm a Loser" has a slightly longer fade than the record, and the opening feedback of "I Feel Fine" is recreated for the radio, though in a detectably less powerful fashion than they'd managed in EMI's studios. There are also some odd, faint, organlike high tones on "I Feel Fine" not heard on the classic 45 recording. "I'll Follow the Sun" is the only version of the song (discounting the primitive one from their 1960 home tapes) other than the track on *Beatles for Sale* to have surfaced. The only one of the six cuts not to have been issued officially, "Honey Don't" differs from the previous two BBC performances in that Ringo's taken over the lead vocals from John (as he did on the *Beatles for Sale* album version).

There's a fair amount of chat with Brian Matthew between the songs, some of it of the teeth-grittingly trivial variety—could it really have interested either the Beatles or the audience as to whether it bothered them to be so famous they couldn't take public buses? At long last, however, comes some actual, if brief, discussion about the *music* on one of their hits—something that's far rarer on BBC Beatles session chatter

The front cover of The Beatles at the Beeb Vol. 9 *showed the group in action at the BBC studios during their November 17, 1964, session.*

than you'd expect. Paul reveals that "She's a Woman" was "written the morning of the session," John adding in his best mock-upper-class-BBC-announcer voice, "Actually in the studio! Most of it—we had about one verse, you see, and we had to finish it off rather quickly. That's why there's such rubbishy lyrics." Finishes Paul: "Just a bit of soul in the studio, you see?" They further disclose that one of the songs on *Beatles for Sale* was nearly a single—presumably "Eight Days a Week," though the tune isn't named—but ultimately wasn't considered as good as the 45 that came out. As to whether it might be later released as a single, Paul McCartney observes, "In America they do that, and it's a bit of a drag." Which Capitol Records did, keeping it off *Beatles '65,* the rough US parallel LP release to *Beatles for Sale,* and making it a No. 1 American single in early 1965. Despite its genuine quality, it doesn't seem to have been among the group's own favorites from *Beatles for Sale,* as they never would perform it live or on the BBC.

Just a couple of minutes of unbroadcast takes of "I Feel Fine" from the session reel have also escaped. After some session chatter, the first of these quickly breaks down when the tricky guitar riff gets tangled up in itself, followed by laughter and a few seconds of loungeish vamping. The second, an incomplete version lasting just over a minute, differs from the broadcast version only in that its lead vocal is single-tracked, not double-tracked. An additional stray 40 seconds of session talk is mostly interesting for a bit of Lennon gobbledygook after a voice in the control room asks, "Do you want to have a listen before we go on to the next one?" Sez John, in part, "If it's all right here, it'll be better in there, so it'll be better out there than in here, 'cause this is crap, innit?"

● **November 25**

BBC Session

Saturday Club program (broadcast December 26, 1964)
Aeolian Hall, London

---

*Rock and Roll Music
Kansas City/Hey! Hey! Hey! Hey!
  appears on Live at the BBC

As a sign that BBC sessions had slipped much lower on the Beatles' list of priorities, they recorded just two songs for what would turn out to be their second-to-last specially recorded music program for the network. Although six numbers *were* broadcast, four of them—"I'm a Loser," "Everybody's Trying to Be My Baby," "I Feel Fine," and "She's a Woman"—were simply retransmissions of the exact same recordings of those tunes that had been included in their November 17 session for the "Top Gear" program. "Rock and Roll Music," included on *Live at the BBC,* is actually distinctly inferior to the explosive *Beatles for Sale* version; this take lacks George Martin's wonderful boogie-woogie piano, and is weighed down by a slower, chugging rhythm. Nor is "Kansas City/Hey! Hey! Hey! Hey!" as good and high-energy as either the *Beatles for Sale* take or previous BBC performances of the tunes, though it's certainly respectable, and has a bit more snakiness to the George Harrison solo than usual.

The Beatles on Tour in Britain, 1964

As previously noted, no recordings have surfaced of any of the full-length concerts the Beatles played in their native Britain in 1964. They did actually alter their setlists on those occasions, first for their fall 1964 British tour, and then for the three weeks they played as headliners of "Another Beatles Christmas Show" at the Odeon Cinema in London from Christmas Eve through mid-January. Two of the songs from the fall tour, "I'm Happy Just to Dance with You" and "I Should Have Known Better," were never performed live at any other time; the Christmas shows were the only occasions on which Ringo Starr sang "Honey Don't" onstage with the band. Should any tapes of these performances be discovered, here's what to expect:

Setlist, Fall 1964 British Tour
Twist and Shout
Money (That's What I Want)
Can't Buy Me Love
Things We Said Today
I'm Happy Just to Dance with You
I Should Have Known Better

If I Fell
I Wanna Be Your Man
A Hard Day's Night
Long Tall Sally

Setlist, "Another Beatles Christmas Show" at Odeon Cinema, London, December 24, 1964–January 16, 1965
Twist and Shout
I'm a Loser
Baby's in Black
Everybody's Trying to Be My Baby
Can't Buy Me Love
Honey Don't
I Feel Fine
She's a Woman
A Hard Day's Night
Rock and Roll Music
Long Tall Sally

1964 Noncirculating Recordings, Known and Rumored

● Circa January

Private Tape

World Without Love

In an interview with Bill DeYoung (posted at www.billdeyoung.com/pete ash.htm), Peter Asher said he had a tape of Paul McCartney's demo of "World Without Love" without the bridge. As half of Peter & Gordon, Asher took "World Without Love" to No. 1 in the UK in April 1964; it reached the same position in the US a couple months later. As Paul was living in the same house as Peter (brother of McCartney's girlfriend, Jane Asher) at the time, and wrote a few other hits for Peter & Gordon, one imagines that there might be some other such demos lying around in Asher's attic as well. Peter & Gordon recorded it on January 21, 1964; the demo might well date from sometime earlier than January 1964, if it was still missing a bridge.

● February 25–June 2

Studio Outtakes
A Hard Day's Night *sessions*
Abbey Road, London

The most intriguing-sounding outtakes from *A Hard Day's Night* described in *The Beatles Recording Sessions* include the first three takes of "I Should Have Known Better," described by Mark Lewisohn as opening "with a very Bob Dylan-ish harmonica solo and George ending it with his lead guitar." The first couple takes of "If I Fell" apparently had a lighter drum sound, and the first seven takes of "Any Time at All" did not have the middle eight section of the final version. And, weirdly, George Martin overdubbed a piano part on "You Can't Do That" on May 22, while the Beatles were out of the country on vacation. While that unheard piano-ized version is probably not very different from the official one, why was he even overdubbing at all—especially considering that "You Can't Do That" had already been released as the B-side of the "Can't Buy Me Love" single? Did he think a new version should be done for the *A Hard Day's Night* LP, on which "You Can't Do That" was also issued?

● June 1

Studio Outtakes
Studio Two, Abbey Road, London

Blue Suede Shoes
Honey Don't

Everybody's Trying to Be My Baby
Your True Love
Sawdust Dance Floor
(Others?)

On this evening, rockabilly great and Beatles idol Carl Perkins was in the studio to watch as the band covered his 1957 single "Matchbox." In a December 1968 issue of *Rolling Stone*, Perkins told Michael Lydon that "I was in the studio when they did 'Matchbox' and played guitar with George on one cut of it, but it's never been released." In the chapter on Perkins in Lydon's book *Rock Folk*, the singer phrases his recollection slightly more vaguely, claiming he "played on a cut they never released." If that's so, its existence is not supported by EMI session documentation.

Furthermore, according to his 1996 autobiography, *Go, Cat, Go!* (written with David McGee), Perkins stayed at the studio until almost three in the morning, playing "Blue Suede Shoes" "with the stop-time pauses, and each Beatle taking a line of the intro, with Ringo having the honor of shouting 'Go, cat, go!' As night melted into day, other Perkins songs were given vigorous treatments, including 'Honey Don't,' 'Everybody's Trying to Be My Baby,' and 'Your True Love.'" In an interview quoted in Keith Badman's *The Beatles Off the Record*, Perkins specifically praised "Your True Love" as "by far the best thing" they cut at the session, adding, "Their harmony was terrific on that song. They really threw their 'yeahhhhh' in there. It was great." In yet other sources, Perkins claimed the Beatles covered his compositions "Sure to Fall" (which, of course, they'd done at the Decca audition and several times at the BBC) and "Sawdust Dance Floor."

Possibly Perkins played with them in the studio, but probably not while the tape was running. No Beatles recording session officially ran past midnight until October 13, 1965. In the event they and Perkins were allowed to stay on and jam for a few hours, it's extremely unlikely that any EMI personnel were on hand to operate the tape machines.

In April 1998, confirmation of the session seemed at hand when *Record Collector* reported the incredible discovery, "from the vaults of a diehard Sun collector," of an EMI disc acetate from the session of Perkins and George Harrison dueting on "Your True Love." A photo of the acetate itself even accompanied the story, complete with handwritten label attributing the disc to "Beatles/Karl [sic] Perkins." Furthermore, the anonymous collector revealed he'd obtained the rarity "off a collector in a pub about 20 years ago" who had about half a dozen acetate singles from the session, also including "Everybody's Trying to Be My Baby" (which would have been different from the *Beatles for Sale* version, as that wasn't cut until October 18). Alas, the piece turned out to be a carefully constructed hoax. It had, after all, been printed in the April 1998 issue—and was, in the end, nothing more than an elaborate April Fool's joke, instigated by the magazine itself.

● June 3

Studio Outtake
Studio Two, Abbey Road, London

You're My World

John Lennon, Paul McCartney, and George Harrison demoed three songs at this session, versions of two ("No Reply" and "You'll Know What to Do") eventually showing up on *Anthology 1*. The third was a mere 33-second version of Cilla Black's "You're My World," which had just taken over the No. 1 position on the British charts, "a haphazardly busked" version with Paul on lead vocal, according to John C. Winn's *Lifting Latches*.

In July 1964, a ghost-written interview with Paul McCartney in *The Beatles Book* magazine reported that he'd composed a song called "Always and Only" while on vacation in late May, and recorded it after coming back to England. That would have placed its recording right around the date of this demo session. But as Mark Lewisohn notes in *The Complete Beatles Chronicle*, "Conclusive session documentation at EMI proves that no recording of the latter title was ever made, neither by the Beatles nor by anyone else; also, no McCartney song of this title was copyrighted, even though . . . Dick James registered all new Beatles compositions whether released or not. So it could be that 'Always and Only' was really the ghost-writer's misinterpretation of 'It's for You'"— a Lennon-McCartney song, never recorded by the Beatles, which Cilla Black had a hit with a couple of months later.

● June 9

Live Performance
Princess Theatre, Hong Kong

What was described as "the only existing recording of a Beatles concert at Hong Kong's Princess Theater in Kowloon in 1964" was put up for auction by Christie's in London on September 28, 2005, but failed to sell.

● Circa Mid-1964

Demos

It's for You
No Reply

Cilla Black has recalled getting a demo of "It's for You," featuring just Paul and guitar, before recording her cover of this Lennon-McCartney song on July 2, 1964. And Colin Manley, who played guitar on Tommy Quickly's unreleased cover of "No Reply," told Kristofer Engelhardt in *Beatles Undercover* that "I don't think the *Anthology 1* version is the demo we heard; it's too complete. I wish it would have been the one we heard. I'd back my life that the demo we used had no middle eight; it didn't have any clue as to the rhythm we should use. It contained the

sound of a toilet flushing at the end which we thought was hilarious because it was typical of John's humor. I think we were told it was recorded in a hotel room. We immediately noticed when the Beatles put it on their album *Beatles for Sale* that it had a middle eight."

● July 14

BBC Session Tape
Broadcasting House, London

The House of the Rising Sun

According to Kevin Howlett's *The Beatles at the BBC*, during the first episode of the *Top Gear* program (broadcast on July 16, 1964), host Brian Matthew "made a tantalizing reference to having 'a smashing little bit of tape that the lads don't know anything about, that we recorded at rehearsal, with Paul and the other three giving a fabulous impression of the Animals and "The House of the Rising Sun" but . . . we daren't play it!'" The Animals' "The House of the Rising Sun" was released in June, and the Beatles did not tape any BBC sessions between May 1 and July 14. So it can be reasonably assumed this version—if it actually was taped—was laid down at the July 14 session, where the Beatles made their contribution to *Top Gear*. It would certainly be something to hear, as would, in fact, anything else from a Beatles BBC rehearsal session tape. However they did "The House of the Rising Sun" in mid-1964, it must have been better than the fairly diabolical version they'd do during the interminable *Get Back* sessions/rehearsals on January 9, 1969.

● August 11–October 26

Studio Outtakes
Beatles for Sale *sessions*
Abbey Road, London

The most significant variations logged in *The Beatles Recording Sessions* include experiments by George Harrison on the bent notes on "Baby's in Black"; early takes of "Leave My Kitten Alone," take 1 of which had a "subdued" John Lennon vocal, take 3 a *searing* vocal; and John strumming the "I Feel Fine" guitar riff between takes during the session for "Eight Days a Week," 12 days in advance of the actual "I Feel Fine" session. It's a good bet that the "searing vocal" version of "Leave My Kitten Alone" would be the most exciting of these. But as *no* version of "Leave My Kitten Alone" came out before take 5 turned up on *Anthology 1*, it might have been felt that putting out two takes of the song at once would have been excessive.

THE BEATLES

LIVE!

TICKET TO RIDE

1965

Beatlemania, More and Less

The Year in Review

In many respects, 1965 was a year brimming with almost exactly the same accomplishments the Beatles had logged in 1964. There were two No. 1 albums, three smash singles, a hit movie, and tours in Europe, North America, and Britain. It wasn't identical music, of course, the group branching out by absorbing folk, soul, increasingly personal and sophisticated lyrics, additional instruments, and other new elements into their compositions. They were also spending more time experimenting with and perfecting their work in the studio, and less living up to the wholesome cheeriness of their initial public image. While their schedule was still insanely busy even by the pump-out-the-product standards of their era, there was a little more time to relax and reflect.

In some ways they were industrious as ever, but as a by-product of their evolution, there was just a little less in the way of unreleased Beatles recordings than there had been in 1963 and 1964. BBC sessions, such a reliable fountain of bonus Beatles in their early days, were virtually discontinued, with just one program recorded during the year—a program that would turn out to be their last of music especially taped

for Beeb transmission. With a less hectic round of touring and television appearances, fewer concert tapes were made as well, though fortunately several decent-quality ones survive. And although a fair number of studio outtakes were generated, a growing proportion were of instrumental backing tracks and barely different mixes, mirroring their burgeoning technical savvy as recording artists.

There may be a drop in quantity of unissued Beatles from 1965, but that doesn't mean it's accompanied by a drop in quality. Some of their more interesting unreleased songs and alternate takes were cut in this year, though it's true the best of these were cherry-picked for the official 1996 *Anthology 2* compilation. While some of the innocent, exuberant edge of their live act was wilting, they remained more entertaining and accomplished stage performers than has usually been acknowledged, and there are good documents of 1965 shows in the US, UK, and Continental Europe. Plus there are the usual odds and ends: the last BBC session, the third Christmas fan club disc, and scraps of home recordings.

● February 15

Studio Outtakes

Help! *sessions*
Studio Two, Abbey Road, London

Ticket to Ride (take 2, longer version)
Ticket to Ride (take 2, mono film soundtrack mix)
Ticket to Ride (take 2, production acetate mix)

The Beatles had not been wholly inactive between the end of November 1964 and mid-February 1965, doing a few weeks of concerts as part of the "Another Beatles Christmas Show" production at the Odeon Cinema in London from December 24 through January 16. However, that period did mark the first gap of more than two months between any surviving recordings of Beatles music since mid-1962. But in mid-February, they returned to the studio to start working on their new single and film soundtrack album, and the next week would generate a spate of new recordings, both released and unreleased.

As a reflection of the different methods the Beatles were beginning to favor for studio recording, the three "different" versions of "Ticket to Ride" that have been bootlegged are actually slight-to-minuscule variations on the same version (take 2, which itself incorporated numerous overdubs) used for the classic single. The most significant of these does not fade out as the official track does, but goes on for about ten seconds longer, allowing us to hear a little more improvised-sounding, bluesy Paul McCartney riffing. (That *is* Paul on lead here; on "Ticket to Ride," he played the lead guitars on both the end of the bridges and the fade.) In fact, the track ends abruptly, rather than with a graceful cold stop, as if the guitar and tambourine have run out of ideas simultaneously.

This session marks an occasion—and get used to it, there are many—in which variant mixes of the same track were produced, some of which never found official release. While such items are often bootlegged as "different" versions, fans should prepare themselves for cuts that bear only slightly detectable differences from the official ones that have been familiar for decades. It's this author's opinion that they're the least interesting of unreleased Beatles rarities, not to mention the ones most apt to get sad, incredulous shakes of the head from less Beatles-besotted friends who can't believe you don't have better things to do in your life than acquire these kinds of items when you could just hear the nearly identical (and better-sounding) official version. For the record, though, a mono film soundtrack version of "Ticket to Ride" with the drums mixed lower exists, as does a production acetate (with an engineer's pretake announcement) for the *Help!* film that de-emphasizes the tambourine and puts the vocals further out front.

● February 16

Studio Outtakes

Help! *sessions*
"Yes It Is" single session
Studio Two, Abbey Road, London

I Need You (take 5, mono film soundtrack mix)
I Need You (take 5, production acetate mix)

Another Girl (take 1, mono acetate mix)
*Yes It Is (takes 1–11)
*Yes It Is (take 14)

*portions of takes 2 and 14 of "Yes It Is" were edited
together into a single track on* Anthology 2

Although recorded in the midst of the sessions for the *Help!* album, "Yes It Is" would not make that LP, but instead be used as the B-side of "Ticket to Ride." Most of the 14 takes are in circulation, and comprise one of the more entertaining instances in which we can hear a Beatles recording take shape almost from start to finish. Take 1 obviously seems intended as a trial run-through, as John Lennon's only doing a "guide" vocal (i.e., one that's done only to help the band keep track of where they are, and not as consideration for use in the final version). His singing here is as rough and scratchy as you'll ever hear it—perhaps he's conserving his resources—and at times he seems to be making fun of himself by putting on a mock-effeminate voice, particularly when he slurs through some words and drifts into a drama queen falsetto at the end of the middle eights. While George Harrison had first experimented with the softly swelling sounds produced by a tone pedal guitar in 1964 on "Baby's in Black," he put it to much more prominent use on "Yes It Is," and can be heard testing it out as John's counting in the take. His tone pedal work throughout the take itself has the aura of a test, as if he's afraid of getting his fingers burned if he leans on the notes too hard. Combined with Lennon's uncertain vocal, the overall effect is that of a band gingerly maneuvering a song through the oven with kid gloves, and while it's no match for the excellent finished track, it does have a tender charm of its own.

Take 2 takes much the same approach, but breaks down at the end of the middle eight, John starting to sing some delightfully childish nonsense ("dun-dee-dee-dee, dee-dee-doi, dee-dee-doi") where the words should be. The problem could be, as he comically announces a few seconds later, that "the string broke. Did you hear it?" Takes 3 and 4 don't get much past the count-ins, which—after John explains something about making sure there's enough space between the verses—get silly in their inimitably Lennonesque way on take 5, introduced with "One, two, three, bread!" John's vocal gets so soft it can barely be heard on take 7, which breaks down in the troublesome middle eight again, and he's scatting his way through the bridge, apparently just conserving his energy for the "real" vocal. After a take 8 breakdown, take 9—John's vocal all but inaudible—makes it all the way through, and seems to have the distinctive ending (where the key briefly changes) in place for the first time, complete with the same wistful four tone-pedal notes from George's guitar.

Take 14 is the one used for the single, though the lovely three-part vocal harmonies were overdubbed onto a backing track, not sung live with the instrumental portion. In the increasingly complicated world of how variations make their way onto bootleg the later a Beatles recording was made, however, a slightly more complete take 14 has circulated with some strange circus-like organ right before the song's proper beginning. And let's not forget the version of take 14, with voices raised and percussion lowered in the mix, that appears on a production acetate made for the *Help!* film (indicating it was, at one point, under consideration for the *Help!* soundtrack, though it made neither the soundtrack nor the *Help!* LP). In addition, portions of takes 2 and 14 were edited together into a single track for the *Anthology 2* compilation. But a listen to the near-whole session is the best way to hear the gestation of "Yes It Is," whose outtakes give us a sneak look at the group while their guard is down, and some of the better snatches of the irreverent humor John Lennon brought to the recording studio.

On more trivial notes, some unreleased mixes have circulated of a couple other songs finished in the studio on February 16. There's a mono film soundtrack mix of "I Need You" with less reverb on George Harrison's vocal and lower percussion presence, and a mono mix on the production acetate that accentuates those differences more. The mono production acetate mix of "Another Girl" de-emphasizes the drums too, but at least this offers a blink-and-you'll-miss-it bonus of a particularly animated count-in: "Ah-one, ah-two, ah-three!"

● February 17

Studio Outtakes

Help! *sessions*
Studio Two, Abbey Road, London

The Night Before (take 2, mono film soundtrack mix)
The Night Before (take 2, production acetate mix)
You Like Me Too Much (take 8, production acetate mix)

Continuing the march of don't-you-have-better-things-to-do-in-your-life *Help!* outtakes are these alternate mixes of "The Night Before" and "You Like Me Too Much." In common with other *Help!* alternates from these sources, there's not much to say about them, other than that the production acetate gives the material a drier, more vocal biased sound. "The Night Before" was actually not used in beginning-to-end whole in the *Help!* soundtrack, but on one of the pieces that was used, Paul's aside of "Yes!" right before the instrumental break is louder. And, again, the mere presence of "You Like Me Too Much" on the production acetate proves the song was considered for the soundtrack at one point. It ultimately didn't make the film—maybe it was thought that one George Harrison composition, "I Need You" (which did make the soundtrack), was enough—though unlike "Yes It Is," it did find a place on the *Help!* LP.

● February 18

Studio Outtakes

Help! *sessions*
Studio Two, Abbey Road, London

---

*You've Got to Hide Your Love Away (takes 1, 5)
*You've Got to Hide Your Love Away (take 2, fragment)
You've Got to Hide Your Love Away (take 9, production acetate mix)
*If You've Got Trouble (take 1)
    *appears on Anthology 2

Some genuinely interesting complete outtakes arose from the sessions on this day, as opposed to mere mix variations (though there was one of those, too). Take 5 of "You've Got to Hide Your Love Away," issued on *Anthology 2*, was the only complete take of that song other than

the one (take 9) used on the record. The biggest differences are the absences of the flute and tambourine heard on the end of the *Help!* version, but John Lennon's vocal phrasing also seems more hesitant and uncertain. It's not a bad performance at all, and perhaps closer to the roots of the song in the Bob Dylan–esque folk that was starting to heavily influence the Beatles at this point. The slightly more pop-oriented official version, however, has the edge in every respect. Also on *Anthology 2* is take 1, which has just a waltzing count-in and a few guitar strums before it breaks down, and some surreal spoken chatter from the beginning of take 2, which basically amounts to John repeating the phrase "Paul's broken a glass" in full or part several times fast. And for the true gotta-have-it-alls, there's that trusty production acetate mono mix, on which the flute's louder and the tambourine's lower.

"If You've Got Trouble" marked the first time a Lennon-McCartney composition was taped at EMI but not released in the '60s. ("One After 909" was still in the can from the March 5, 1963, session, but at least that would be revived six years later and eventually heard on the *Let It Be* album.) Sung by Ringo Starr, the song's been soundly derided by many critics, yet while it's certainly understandable it didn't make the cut for the *Help!* album, it's really not that bad. The circular lead guitar riff and ringing rhythm guitar put it more in the *Rubber Soul* sonic era than the *Help!* one. The tune's moderately catchy and gritty, though far from brilliant. Ringo's drumming is splashing and solid, there are a couple nicely witty interjections of backup harmonies, and the lyric exerts an odd fascination by the virtue of its very daftness. Maybe that's why it was given to Ringo, the whole "If you think *you've* got troubles, wait till you get a load of mine" vibe and the "You think I'm soft in the head" line being somewhat in keeping with his hangdog image. He certainly sings it as though he's amused by the lyric's very ludicrousness, right down to the highlight of the whole track, when he declares, "Oh, rock on, *anybody!*" before George Harrison's fairly rote guitar solo.

The failure of the band to perform more than one take, however, was evidence enough they found the song hard to take seriously. "The lyrics are the most ridiculous lyrics I've ever heard," laughed George in a 1996 *Billboard* interview. "It's a pretty bizarre song, but it was quite nicely played and recorded." And they *did* take it seriously enough to give it three overdubs, Ringo double-tracking his vocal. In the end, though, it was appropriately decided to make Ringo's token lead vocal on *Help!* a cover of Buck Owens's "Act Naturally." "If You've Got Trouble" wouldn't see the light of day until *Anthology 2.*

● February 19

Studio Outtakes

Help! *sessions*
Studio Two, Abbey Road, London

You're Going to Lose That Girl (take 3, mono film soundtrack mix)
You're Going to Lose That Girl (take 3, production acetate mix)

More extra mixes from the film soundtrack and production acetate, but of greater value than usual, as such things go. For the production acetate mix—introduced, by a stentorian EMI production staff voice, as simply "Lose That Girl"—features an entirely different guitar solo.

Not one that's better or as good, mind you, but a noticeably different, less fluent one. You can also hear, though far down in the mix, a stuttering electric piano in the instrumental break that seems missing altogether from the released version. And as what might be called in the DVD age another "bonus feature," you also get a "one-two-three" count-in. The mono film soundtrack mix makes for duller dissection, putting the usual higher-vocals/lower-percussion twist on the track.

● February 20

Studio Outtakes

Help! *sessions*
Studio Two, Abbey Road, London

---

*That Means a Lot (take 1)
That Means a Lot (take 1, unedited)
That Means a Lot (edit piece)
    appears on Anthology 2

For the second time in three days, a Lennon-McCartney composition was recorded to completion in the studio, only to remain in the can for three decades. "That Means a Lot," however, had a stronger case for release than "If You've Got Trouble." As a nice if corny song with a typically haunting Paul McCartney vocal, there are some good things to say about this track. It has a rather complicated, catchy tune, a nicely dramatic downturn in the bridge that ends with a dead pause, good winding backup harmonies, and a skipping martial drum rhythm, though the lyric "love can be suicide" in the bridge is one of the most awkward and peculiarly downbeat phrases in a Beatles recording. There's also a fadeout that, slightly at odds with the poppy tenor of the number, features some rather frenzied, extemporized James Brown–Little Richard-styled screaming from Paul. The production, strangely, has more reverb than virtually anything else the Beatles had recorded up to this point, almost as if they were trying to emulate Phil Spector's simulated orchestral ambience.

So why wasn't it released on a Beatles disc? At the time, John Lennon explained that it was a ballad the group wrote for the *Help!* film, but found they couldn't sing well. So they ended up giving it to P.J. Proby, the expatriate UK-based American who made ballads a big part of his stock in trade. That wasn't before, however, trying one more time to record the song in the studio (see March 30, 1965 entry), though those rerecordings were probably even less to the satisfaction of the group than the first go-round.

Though the group didn't state it, maybe they just didn't feel "That Means a Lot" was quite strong enough for a Beatles release, or just wasn't suitable for one. A decent enough number by most artists' standards, it was—like virtually all of the Lennon-McCartney songs they "gave away" to others—more lightweight and sentimental than what they reserved for themselves. As to how the group managed to suddenly record two songs in three days that weren't deemed up to snuff, it could have been that the pressure of having to write and record material for the *Help!* soundtrack and album in a short time was pushing tunes into consideration that ordinarily might not have been deemed appropriate or robust enough. For just two days later, the Beatles left Britain to begin filming *Help!* and would only be able to return to EMI for one day (ironically, to try "That Means a Lot" again) during the next two months or so. None-

theless, the Beatles' version of "That Means a Lot" is much better than P.J. Proby's somewhat lugubrious, overorchestrated one, which wasn't even all that commercially successful, topping out at No. 30 in Britain and failing to chart in the US at all.

Although it was a one-take recording (albeit a take adorned with overdubs), there are several variations from this session floating around. The standard one is on *Anthology 2,* but there's a much "drier" mix, minus the weird reverb and plus a few seconds of chatter at the beginning. Some collectors prefer this mix, but to these ears, it's distinctively less lively than the *Anthology 2* one, even if that officially available mix does have a peculiar, transistor radio–like tinniness. Much harder to find is the "dry" mix that adds about 30 seconds of a nonfaded ending (punctuated by a few Little Richard–like woos and shouts from McCartney), where the other versions fade out early. And there's also a 25-second "edit piece" (perhaps taken from one of the four rehearsals the Beatles were known to have recorded of the song on this date) which seems intended for the fadeout of the track, Paul improvising a vocal even heavier on rather heavy-handed "whoos," screams, and croons.

● Circa March

Private Tape

Twickenham Film Studios, London

Am Sonntag Will Mein Suesser Mit Mir Segeln Gehn

As part of an interview with Radio Luxembourg's German-language branch, George Harrison was asked (in German) if he could sing a German song. "Probably," George responded, in German, before launching into a couple of lines of this jaunty, folksy ditty (a hit in Germany for the trad jazz group the Old Merry Tale Jazzband in 1961), accompanying himself on guitar. Abruptly halting, he explains, "That's all I know" in English. When this most informal (not to say dispensable) scrap has been bootlegged, it's been on at least one occasion strung together with another brief snippet in which George, again, sings, whistles, and plays a melancholy, folksy tune, "Belle of the Ball," on guitar. On that snippet, he stops to address a radio audience for 12 seconds, in German, in a bit clearly meant for use on Radio Luxembourg. It's not known whether these two pieces of tape are related or from the same day, and indeed there's some dispute as to what day "Am Sonntag Will Mein Suesser Mit Mir Segeln Gehn" was recorded, though March 1965 is the date most frequently cited. It's pretty much some ado about nothing, but for what it's worth, George's German accent and delivery are fairly passable, no doubt improved by the Beatles' lengthy stints in Hamburg.

● March 30

Studio Outtakes

Help! *sessions*
Studio Two, Abbey Road, London

That Means a Lot (takes 20, 22–24)
That Means a Lot (test)

It wasn't unknown for the Beatles to rerecord a track weeks after first recording it in an attempt to do it right, as they did in late 1964 with "What You're Doing," for instance. It's remarkable how much effort they put into "That Means a Lot," however, considering it would never be used on a 1960s Beatles release. Yet the more they tried to play around with it, the further away they seemed to get from a satisfactory arrangement, leading them to abandon it altogether.

All of this day's attempts at remaking the song—the first of which was tagged take 20, though only one take had been done the first time around—are in circulation. Take 20 shows the tune had been recast in a far more straightforward, pop-rock-oriented approach, with a faster 4/4 rhythm, a higher key, and much more prominent guitar by George Harrison, who filled out the sound with rather overbusy responsive fills. It's too bright and cheery an approach for a track that originally had a slightly melancholy tinge, and breaks down after a minute. Take 22 reverts to the key and tempo of the version they'd recorded in February, but still gives more weight to the guitar, this time played by George with a slightly reverberant tone, executing particularly spiraling riffs at the end of the verses. It's better than take 20, but still sounds like they're trying to fit a square peg into a round hole, especially in the bridge, where Ringo Starr switches between skipping beats and a more straightahead attack. It seems like they're trying to bend the number into a harder-rocking song somehow, but it's just too gentle to be suited for that mindset, and the end refrain breaks down as if they're unsure of how to wrap it up.

Take 23 doesn't get beyond the first couple beats, and take 24 goes back to the inappropriately upbeat vibe of take 20, actually holding together fairly well for a spell. But for one of the few times on Beatles sessions, Paul McCartney audibly seems to be losing faith in the song. Perhaps feeling discouraged by the trouble he's having singing the high notes in the bridge, upon returning to the verse he suddenly starts singing "whew" like an up-and-down rollercoaster, as if giving up on the prospect of getting a usable take. Following his lead, the band breaks into a "that's all folks" jazzy tempo.

The take marked "test," most unusually for a Beatles outtake of any kind pre-1966, appears to be a deliberate cock-up. The tempo slows to a turgid jazz waltz, Paul sings with a strained crooner's bellow, and the whole mess collapses with a show-bizzy finale less than a minute into the track. While it might have been recorded in rehearsal before takes 20–24 began, it comes off less as a preparation to take the song onto the battlefield than a determination to send it off to its grave with a middle-finger salute. Funny and entertaining in its sheer awfulness, in light of its ultimate fate it's difficult to hear as anything other than the raising of a white flag on the whole troubled enterprise. The Beatles must have decided to give the song away almost immediately, for P.J. Proby recorded it just over a week later in Abbey Road, on April 7.

● April 11

Live Performance
New Musical Express *Pollwinners' Concert*
Empire Pool, Wembley

I Feel Fine
She's a Woman
Baby's in Black
Ticket to Ride
Long Tall Sally

The Beatles' five-song set at the 1965 *NME* Pollwinners' Concert was their first live appearance in three months, and the source of the first surviving tape of the group onstage since September 1964, as well as the first surviving concert versions of "I Feel Fine," "She's a Woman," "Baby's in Black," and "Ticket to Ride." The whole set was caught on film too (see entry in film section), which is double the pleasure of just hearing the music, though the tracks are found in decent sound on audio-only bootlegs. Perhaps happy to be onstage again after a comparatively long layoff, the group puts on a good show, though unfortunately Paul's and George's mikes don't seem to be working for the first part of "I Feel Fine," as only John's lead vocal is heard. George's lead guitar coming out of the first bridge of "Ticket to Ride" is kind of sloppy, maybe because it was Paul and not George who played that passage on the single. He makes up for that, however, via a very upfront solo with almost zany flourishes on the second instrumental break of "Long Tall Sally."

● April 13

Studio Outtakes
Help! *sessions*
Studio Two, Abbey Road, London

Help! (takes 1–12)
Help! (mono film soundtrack mix)
Help! (production acetate mix)

By 1965, the Beatles were becoming accustomed to recording instrumental backing tracks over which vocals (and other parts) could be overdubbed. This is the first session from which a large clump of instrumental-only backing tracks is most of what's escaped onto bootleg. The plus, if a marginal one, for listeners is that such groupings accurately illustrate the increasingly layered, piece-by-piece approach the band was taking toward recording, and give us a chance to hear the underlying dynamics of a classic, famous track. The harsher truth is that such backing tracks also make for duller listening than ones with vocals, especially when heard one version after another where only minor adjustments are being made.

Such is the case with these dozen takes of "Help!" None of the first eight have vocals, and some of them break down very quickly. How odd it is, at points (such as take 5, a complete run-through), to hear nothing but Ringo's drumbeats where we're so used to rich vocals and spidery guitar webs filling in the space. The arrangement is pretty much there from the get-go, and the imperfections are fairly minor problems with guitar tunings and rhythm-keeping. It's a modest pleasure to hear these guitar parts unobscured by singing, which let the folk-rock at the song's core hit you full in the face. Some discussion at the beginning of take 4 (you have to turn the volume *way* up to make it out) indicates that George Harrison is having a little trouble executing the complicated, fast riffs; he's also worried about having to play and sing at the same time, though Paul assures him that won't be necessary, as there are two voice tracks available.

Otherwise, it's one of the less interesting, near-full documents of the recording of a Beatles track, even if it is one of their great songs.

THE BEATLES

mono

SPECIAL BONUS: NME Poll-winners' Concerts 1964 & 1965!

VOL. 13

THE BEATLES
AT THE BEEB

BB 2184/S

BEEBrecords

"he Beatles mimed to "The Night Before" in the Help! scene where they play in the open air, filmed in
arly May of 1965. A few weeks later they would play the song on their last BBC session (included on
his LP), broadcast two months before the studio recording was first released on the Help! album.

Voices and additional overdubs are heard on takes 9, 10, and 12, none of which have the precise mix of the single version, though all are similar. ("Take" 11 is just a false start of the playback tape.) Also available are the usual rather superfluous extras common to numerous *Help!* tracks, including a mono film soundtrack mix with double-tracked Lennon vocals on the intro and more prominently placed backing harmonies, and a mono mix from a production acetate that mixes out part of the drums linking the intro to the first verse.

As long as we're on the subject of the *Help!* soundtrack mix, it can be noted that the Beatles are heard not-very-seriously singing and whistling to the famous Rossini classical piece "Barber of Seville" in the closing credits of the film. Recorded at an unknown date (though it must have been around spring of 1965), this "track" has shown up on bootlegs, though it's debatable as to whether it should be considered a "recording" or "performance."

● May 26

BBC Session

For program The Beatles Invite You to Take a Ticket to Ride *(broadcast June 7, 1965)*
Piccadilly Theatre, London

Everybody's Trying to Be My Baby
I'm a Loser
The Night Before
Honey Don't
*Dizzy Miss Lizzy
She's a Woman
*Ticket to Ride

appears on Live at the BBC

It had been six months since the Beatles' last BBC session when they recorded this special program in late May of 1965, titled—with a forced pun on the group's current single—"The Beatles Invite You to Take a Ticket to Ride." Though not planned as such, it would be not only the group's sole 1965 radio session, but their final Beeb session whatsoever. Perhaps if they'd known it was the finale, the group might have chosen a somewhat more imaginative selection of tracks to perform than this grab bag of songs from their last two LPs, *Beatles for Sale* and *Help!*, four of which they'd already performed on the BBC. John Lennon, for one, seems a little less inclined to put up with the contrived between-song chatter expected of these get-togethers. When Paul McCartney jokes in his intro to "The Night Before," "This song . . . was written by Denny Piercy, you know him," and host Denny Piercy fishes for a compliment by countering, "Of whom you once said," John then responds with a retching sound—a sound bite which, we can probably be assured, will likely not make it onto any officially sanctioned Beatles vault releases in the near future.

It's not a great Beatles BBC session, but it's a decent one, preserved on tape in good-to-excellent fidelity. "Everybody's Trying to Be My Baby" has more of an easygoing bounce than some of the other numerous versions of this oft-played George Harrison lead vocal feature, particularly in the second instrumental break, where he plays more languidly than usual. "I'm a Loser," compared to the other non-EMI recordings of the song, is a real standout for its injection of some irreverent humor in the way John Lennon twists a key lyric into "beneath this *wig*, I am wearing a *tie*"—the only time, really, the mid-'60s Beatles were caught on tape significantly and knowingly changing words to one of their songs in a non-EMI performance. Almost as surprisingly, this session marked the only non-EMI airing of "The Night Before," one of the less celebrated songs from the *Help!* film and LP, taken just a tad faster and more funkily than the studio version. This amounted to a sneak preview for British listeners, as the *Help!* album on which the song was first released wasn't issued until August 6, a good couple of months after this program was broadcast.

"Honey Don't" has a nice cocksure feel, George injecting a little more countryish spinning into his riffs than usual, Ringo throwing in some "bop-bop" vocal scats on the outro as John had in the days when he sang lead on the number (and as John had on the version the group did for the Beeb back on August 1, 1963). "Dizzy Miss Lizzy"—again predating its release on *Help!* by a couple of months, though the group had done it onstage before they had a recording contract—has a slightly bumpier, more boogying feel to the rhythm than the LP version. Fans of Paul's bass playing will enjoy this version of "She's a Woman" for its particularly well-recorded bass parts, while hounds for small lyric variations will note how he changes a couple of lines in the first verse to tell us how his love don't "buy" (rather than "give") him presents. He yelps a great "Ooh-hoo!" right before the guitar solo, too, and there's a little more improvised vamping on the nonfaded outro than there is in most live versions of this tune. "Ticket to Ride" is a little disappointingly milder, however, than the great single version. It and "Dizzy Miss Lizzy" were the only tracks from the session to make the grade for the *Live at the BBC* compilation.

Part of the Beatles' failure to do any more BBC sessions after this date may have been due to some dissatisfaction with the relatively primitive recording conditions the radio network allowed. Even for this final installment, the group had expressed a desire to record the program at one of their EMI recording sessions, though in the end they did it at one of the BBC's London studios. Brian Epstein indicated to BBC executive Donald MacLean in October 1965 that the Beatles would be able to do a Christmas morning *Saturday Club* special, and there were further discussions about using EMI's studios during their *Rubber Soul* sessions to record music for a radio program. But while the Beatles did appear on *Saturday Club* on Christmas Day (and would be interviewed by the BBC often during the next five years), it was only via some chat with Brian Matthew, though the session tape (according to Kevin Howlett's *The Beatles at the BBC*) caught Paul McCartney musing whether listeners to the program might wonder "why we didn't happen to play on this one."

Even if reluctance to record in simpler settings might have played a part, however, it's most likely that the Beatles never did another BBC session because they had simply gotten too big and busy. There were global touring commitments, acting in feature films, increasingly elaborate EMI recordings, new marriages and families, and a need for more rest and privacy. The BBC sessions had served their purpose of helping to make the Beatles huge in Britain, as well as producing a ton of great music. But the Beatles frankly didn't need the publicity those sessions gave them anymore, especially as they continued to set their sights on ever more widening and bolder commercial and artistic horizons.

● June 14

Studio Outtakes
"I'm Down" single session
Help! sessions
Studio Two, Abbey Road, London

---

*I'm Down (take 1)
*Yesterday (take 1)
     **appears on* Anthology 2*

This was a great day in the studio for Paul McCartney in particular, as three fine and stylistically varied songs for which he was the prime/sole author were recorded: "I'm Down," "Yesterday," and "I've Just Seen a Face." Outtakes of "I'm Down" and "Yesterday" are on *Anthology 2,* with take 1 of "I'm Down" being very similar to the version that turned up on the B-side of "Help!" It lacks the backup harmonies of the single, George Harrison's guitar work is less distinctive, and there are some superfluous son-of-Little Richard vocal injections in the instrumental breaks, coming to a cold, nonfaded end on a sour minor chord. So it's less effective than the final version in every respect. As pre- and postsong chat goes, however, it does serve up a couple of unexpected goodies, Paul opening the take by declaring in a mock American accent, "Let's hope this one turns out pretty darned good, huh?" And at the end, he utters, "Plastic soul, man, plastic soul"—a possible seed for the idea of the title of their *Rubber Soul* album later that year.

Take 1 is "Yesterday" without the string quartet—and a look at how the track might have sounded if the Beatles had decided to issue the song as a Paul McCartney solo acoustic guitar-backed performance. Within the context of what the Beatles had released up to that point, this would have been almost as radical as the string arrangement they did use. It sounds a little more like a folk song in this early version, which is nice even though Paul's vocal is more tentative at this point, and the order of the two lines at the beginning of the second verse is reversed.

● June 15

Studio Outtakes
Help! sessions
Studio Two, Abbey Road, London

---

*It's Only Love (takes 2–3)
     **appears on* Anthology 2*

"It's Only Love" is one of the more fully formed outtakes to make its way onto the *Anthology* series, yet also one of the less interesting. That's not due to any shortcomings in the song itself, but because the take chosen for *Anthology 2* (take 2) isn't much different from the familiar *Help!* LP track at all. It's a little more rushed, and John's vocal is a little more hoarse and less comfortable—it even sounds like his mind is wandering a little from the task at hand during diffidently phrased parts of the first chorus. Also, there's none of the George Harrison tone pedal guitar that does so much to enhance the official version. The *Anthology 2* version places the whole of take 3 (a brief false start) before the beginning of take 2.

● June 20

Live Performance
Palais des Sports, Paris (afternoon show)

Twist and Shout
She's a Woman
I'm a Loser
Can't Buy Me Love
Baby's in Black
I Wanna Be Your Man
A Hard Day's Night
Everybody's Trying to Be My Baby
Rock and Roll Music
I Feel Fine
Ticket to Ride
Long Tall Sally

Broadcast on the French radio station Europe 1, this is the first known recording of a full concert set by the group since their 1964 North American tour, in decent though not stellar sound quality. Much had changed since the Beatles first visited France in January 1964 to a cool reception. Beatlemania had now gripped France, as is obvious from the enthusiastic reception of this Parisian crowd.

It might be a little rust, or just a little fatigue as the group set out on the road yet again after completing the *Help!* film and album in just four months, but there's not quite as much joie de vivre as there had been on their 1964 shows. And while the setlist had changed to reflect their more recent recordings, one can't help but think it might have been a bit of a letdown for the group to go back to playing things like "Twist and Shout" and "I Wanna Be Your Man." Both then and now, it wouldn't be considered anachronistic for rock bands to play material that had been recorded more than a year earlier. But the Beatles were evolving so quickly that they might have felt at odds with what they were singing when the original material they were laying down in the studio was becoming distinctly more advanced.

The show is only average, relative to the Beatles' high standards, as they deliver a credible if workmanlike set that includes the first-before-a-live-audience versions of "I'm a Loser" (here given a truncated, cold full-stop ending on the instrumental outro, as well as what sounds like some very subdued tone pedal guitar swells at the beginning) and Chuck Berry's "Rock and Roll Music." There aren't many tics to report, but it's interesting to hear Paul, as he had in late May on the BBC, change the opening verse of "She's a Woman" to have his love "buy" rather than "give" him presents. This points to a deliberately introduced variation (repeated on various other shows from that time onward), not a one-time slip-up. There are some very halting, elementary attempts to address the audience in French between some of the songs, and their tendency to speed things up gets pronounced on "Rock and Roll Music," which is taken at quite a fast clip (ironically so for a song that castigates modern jazz for being too darn fast). The vocals sometimes have a slight distant hollowness, and the sound balance wavers, particularly in the vocals. Make no mistake, however: it's a much better-than-average Beatlemania-era concert recording from a technical standpoint, gremlins and all.

The evening concert of this date would also be broadcast on Europe 1, and also filmed for French television (see next entry).

● June 20

Live Performance

Palais des Sports, Paris (evening show)

Twist and Shout
She's a Woman
I'm a Loser
Can't Buy Me Love
Baby's in Black
I Wanna Be Your Man
A Hard Day's Night
Everybody's Trying to Be My Baby
Rock and Roll Music
I Feel Fine
Ticket to Ride
Long Tall Sally

As this show was not only broadcast on the French radio station Europe 1 but also filmed for the French television channel 2, it's another one of those situations where it's more fun to watch the program (which survives on film in its entirety) instead of just listening to it. Maybe because they'd gotten the first show of this European tour out of the way in the afternoon, or maybe because they knew it was going out on TV, the Beatles sound better here than they do on the tape of the afternoon show (see previous entry). The technical ends of things go more smoothly too. That doesn't mean everything comes off without a hitch, as Paul loses his way on "She's a Woman," putting some lines from the second verse into the end of the first.

Yet as a whole, it's one of the better mid-'60s concert tapes, and certainly the best of the few that have surfaced from their mid-1965 European tour. The French propensity for singing along with rock bands rears its head on "Can't Buy Me Love," where the crowd belts out the chorus with gusto. "Rock and Roll Music" has been slowed down from its too-fast afternoon tempo, though it's a shade less frenetic than the classic *Beatles for Sale* recording, and McCartney emits an uncharacteristically gruff, almost spoken "Everything's all right" during the final chorus of "Long Tall Sally." "Everybody's Trying to Be My Baby" (which has a markedly enthusiastic George Harrison vocal), "A Hard Day's Night," "Baby's in Black"—all (and some other songs here) are hugely enjoyable, showing the Beatles remaining close to their arena-era live peak.

● June 27

Live Performance

Teatro Adriano, Rome (afternoon show)

Twist and Shout
She's a Woman
I'm a Loser
Can't Buy Me Love
Baby's in Black
I Wanna Be Your Man
A Hard Day's Night
Everybody's Trying to Be My Baby

Rock and Roll Music
I Feel Fine
Ticket to Ride
Long Tall Sally (fragment)

Asked about live recordings of the Beatles in his 1970 *Rolling Stone* interview, John Lennon mentioned, in addition to the Hollywood Bowl and Shea Stadium sets, "one in Italy apparently that somebody recorded there." Probably John was remembering seeing an official 1965 Italian LP titled *The Beatles in Italy,* which, despite the title, was not a concert recording, but a haphazard collection of 1963–1965 singles and EP tracks. Though it was buried in a long, long interview, the remark inspired a search for a live Italian album, bootleg or legitimate, and it's likely that a few poor souls still labor under the delusion that an official one exists.

Funnily enough, however, there *is* a bootleg of one of their Italian shows, though it's not 100 percent complete, it didn't circulate until 1985, and it's far, far below release quality. It's an audience recording, and given that you can hear the band play the same material in vastly better fidelity at their Paris shows just a few days before this one, it's only necessary if you're dying to hear them utter a few Italian phrases in their between-song announcements. Too, parts of some songs are missing—most of "Long Tall Sally" is cut off, in fact.

● June 27

Live Performance

Teatro Adriano, Rome (evening show)

Contrary to rumor, there was never an official release of a live June 1965 Italian Beatles concert, and the recordings that have been bootlegged aren't nearly as good as tapes of the Paris shows from the same month.

Twist and Shout
She's a Woman
I'm a Loser (fragment)

Though it seems like it's taken from an in-line recording, and thus sounds much better than the circulating recording of their afternoon show at the same venue, the sound on this brief portion of their evening Rome concert is thin and blurry. "I'm a Loser" fades at the end of the first verse, but that's enough time to hear John insert some of his speaking-in-tongues gibberish in a pause during the first lines of the tune.

● August 1

Live Performance

Television program Blackpool Night Out
ABC Theatre, Blackpool

*I Feel Fine
I'm Down
Act Naturally
*Ticket to Ride
*Yesterday
*Help!

> *appears on* Anthology 2

From a musical viewpoint, this was one of the Beatles' finest telecasts, enough so that four of the six songs were included on *Anthology 2*. The whole shebang's on film too (see entry in film section), and the evidence is that—with the possible exception of the rooftop concert at the end of the *Let It Be* movie in January 1969—the Beatles would never sound or play as good in a live situation again. It helped, of course, that while there were screamers in the audience, it was nothing on the level of their stadium shows, enabling the Beatles to hear one another well (and us to hear them well on the tape). Admittedly, it's not note-perfect, as George Harrison again has a little trouble recreating the solo that ends the bridge of "Ticket to Ride," and John sing-mumbles the end of the second verse of "Help!", which receives its live premiere on this occasion. And there's no pretense of recreating the record on "Yesterday," performed by Paul on solo guitar with an offstage backing tape of strings.

The two songs not included on *Anthology 2* are not toss-offs by any means, as these are the best live versions of "I'm Down" and "Act Naturally" available. (As it happens, too, they were the *first* live versions of those songs ever performed.) "Act Naturally" moves along with a real kick to the rhythm, George introducing enough variations on the guitar licks to let us know beyond a shadow of a doubt that it's not the record. It's also quite a welcome change to at long last hear Ringo sing something live *besides* "I Wanna Be Your Man" and "Boys," though, as it turned out, "I Wanna Be Your Man" hadn't quite been permanently retired.

● August 14

Live Performance

Television program The Ed Sullivan Show
Studio 50, New York City

I Feel Fine
I'm Down
Act Naturally
Ticket to Ride
Yesterday
Help!

For their final *Ed Sullivan Show* appearance, the Beatles sang the same six songs, in the exact same order, as they had a couple of weeks before on *Blackpool Night Out*. The *Blackpool* show is better, though, due both to a tighter performance and slightly superior sound. There are also a couple of major lyrical screw-ups here, the first when Paul McCartney switches the order of the first and second verses on "I'm Down." That doesn't affect the power of that particular number, but then John's still doing battle with the lyrics of "Help!", mangling-mumbling part of the second verse. As in *Blackpool*, too, "Yesterday" is done by Paul alone on acoustic guitar with a prerecorded backing track of strings. And for some reason, the instrumental intro for "Ticket to Ride" is about twice as long as normal. It's not because of a vocal mike failure; looking at the video clip, it seems like it was planned, so that the camera had time to cross-fade between individual shots of all four Beatles before the singing started. Overall it's not as sensationally memorable as their 1964 *Ed Sullivan Show* spots, not so much because of any notable gap in quality, but because the February 1964 broadcasts carried a sense of historic occasion that could never be repeated.

The entire performance (along with the rest of the *Ed Sullivan Show* episode that evening) was legitimately reissued on DVD in 2003 on *The Four Historic Ed Sullivan Shows Featuring the Beatles*. Viewing this slightly flawed but still very good program, it's evident that the group had, as usual, worked out a fairly established routine for introducing the songs. Ringo himself introduces "Act Naturally"—a nice touch, as it had been left to others to introduce his vocal numbers when he did "I Wanna Be Your Man" and "Boys" onstage—with the self-deprecating, "Now we'd like to do a thing that we don't often do, [singing] 'Act Naturally,' all nervous and out of tune—Ringo!" And he does sing a little out of tune at the beginning. George introduces "Yesterday" as "a song off our new album in England, and it will be out in America shortly." As when *Help!* came out in the US, it had been cut to seven songs plus incidental soundtrack music and "Yesterday" had been taken off, the track instead issued as a September single that soared to No. 1. John gets his dig in at Paul at the conclusion of "Yesterday": "Thank you, Paul. That was just like him!"

Incidentally, this was not a live broadcast; it was taped on August 14 and not transmitted until nearly a month later, on September 12. So few, if any, of the teenagers in the audience would have previously heard "Yesterday" or "Act Naturally," neither of which came out in the US until they were released on a single on September 13. That doesn't stop them, however, from screaming for the songs as enthusiastically as if they'd heard them hundreds of times.

The Beatles at Shea Stadium, August 15, 1965.

● August 15

Live Performance

Shea Stadium, New York City

Twist and Shout

I Feel Fine

Dizzy Miss Lizzy

Ticket to Ride

*Everybody's Trying to Be My Baby

Can't Buy Me Love

Baby's in Black

A Hard Day's Night

Act Naturally (fragment)

Help!

I'm Down

     appears on Anthology 2

Presented for 55,600 fans, the Beatles' first US concert in almost a year was one of their most famous, setting an attendance record for a popular music concert. It was also filmed for a television special (see entry in film section), and it's from that soundtrack that bootlegs of the show have often been made. It was another considering-the-circumstances-very-good performance by the group, clearly energized by the sheer scale of the event, though the huge crowd also presented a new scale of difficulty in hearing one another. Partially for that reason, it was deemed necessary to overdub and rerecord new parts and even entire songs. In the early '70s, John even observed that if you look at the film, you'll see that he and George aren't even bothering to play half the chords.

Fuller details are in the entry for this concert in the film section, but for now, it's important to stress that circulating versions of the Shea Stadium concert—as enjoyable as the music is—are, for the most part, not entirely, truly "live." For on January 5, 1966, at CTS Studios in London, Paul overdubbed new bass parts on "Dizzy Miss Lizzy," "Can't Buy Me Love," "Baby's in Black," and "I'm Down"; John over-dubbed a new organ track on "I'm Down"; and wholly new versions of "I Feel Fine" and "Help!" were done. The fix-it work was so extensive, in fact, that a case could be made for dating this recording as having been done on August 15, 1965, August 30, 1965, *and* January 5, 1966, though for the sake of convenience this book will discuss it within just this August 15 entry.

There are additional clouds keeping this out of the list of the very top unreleased Beatles live recordings. Much of "A Hard Day's Night" is obscured by bits of spoken interviews with John, Paul, George, and Brian Epstein that were used over the song on the soundtrack. Two of the songs played at the concert, "She's a Woman" and "Act Naturally," are not included at all (although "Act Naturally" is seen being played in the film, what's heard on the soundtrack is the studio recording, not the Shea Stadium rendition). And "Twist and Shout" is not the unadorned Shea Stadium version, but one, according to Mark Lewisohn's *The Beatles Chronicle*, that used a recording of the song made at their August 30, 1965, Hollywood Bowl concert "to bolster the sound, causing—in one place—John's live vocal to be double-tracked." Some screaming from that

Hollywood Bowl recording was also employed, especially on the newly cut studio versions of "I Feel Fine" and "Help!", which, of course, had no screaming at all in their original state.

Most bootlegs of the Shea Stadium concert/soundtrack do not have "Everybody's Trying to Be My Baby," as it wasn't included in the film. But that track does appear on the legitimate *Anthology 2* in its undoctored, slightly ragged-and-out-of-tune state. The two other songs from the show that have never appeared in any form ("She's a Woman" and "Act Naturally") are likely somewhere in the vaults as well, as might be a recording of the original performances in their unoverdubbed form. A genuinely live 15-second bit of "Act Naturally" *has* been bootlegged, taken from the soundtrack of a television program.

● August 18

Live Performance

Atlanta Stadium, Atlanta

Twist and Shout

She's a Woman

I Feel Fine

Dizzy Miss Lizzy

Ticket to Ride

Everybody's Trying to Be My Baby

Can't Buy Me Love

Baby's in Black

I Wanna Be Your Man

Help!

I'm Down

Though it's not often remembered in Beatles histories, three days after Shea Stadium, the group gave a concert in an equally large baseball park, though "only" 30,000 of the 55,000 seats were filled. As recordings of Beatlemania stadium concerts go, this is above average, but not great. You can hear the instruments and voices pretty well, and the band seem to be tighter, actually, than what you can glean of what might remain of their Shea gig on the film soundtrack of that event. There's some harsh distortion, though, particularly on the voices, and parts of "Ticket to Ride" and "Dizzy Miss Lizzy" (on which John stumbles on the first part of the second verse) are missing (though only a very small part in the case of "Ticket to Ride"). "A Hard Day's Night" isn't here at all, though it was usually a part of their sets during their 1965 North American tour.

That imperfection in the tape notwithstanding, apparently the Beatles themselves were pleased with the sound at this particular show. According to Tony Barrow's *John, Paul, George, Ringo & Me: The Real Beatles Story,* "A brilliant sound system (by '60s standards) at a newly built baseball stadium outdid the one at Shea and, for the first and only time on the '65 tour, I remember being able to hear voices and instruments clearly amplified and beautifully balanced. I wondered at the time why one venue could get it so right while most of the others got it so wrong and I came to the conclusion that the sound system was way down the average concert promoter's priorities because it was assumed that the screaming of the audience would drown out whatever the loudspeakers had to offer. I also noticed that in Atlanta and one or two other places

where we had OK sound, the Beatles gave a musically superior performance. If a promoter cared, the boys cared too." Even at the time, Barrow enthused to reporter Larry Kane, "For the first time in three years, I hear a complete Beatles performance because of a very fine loudspeaker system which lets every note and every word come over clearly and ring 'round this super stadium. The Beatles were talking about it to people around them for days, particularly comparing it to less adequate setups in places as we went on."

The Beatles do seem to be putting a lot of heart into this particular show. John really blasts out the lyric for "Help!", goosed along by an atypical (for this particular number) joyful shout of encouragement from Paul in the background at one point. Whether or not it's because the mikes are picking up vocals more closely than they customarily did on live Beatles concerts, Paul's vocal is overwhelmingly searing on the "I'm Down" finale. George's solos in both "Can't Buy Me Love" and "I Wanna Be Your Man" are a little different and more animated than usual, and the most reticent (relatively speaking) Beatle gets his chance to be a bit silly by introducing his vocal number with the machine gun–patter utterance, "Everybody's-Trying-to-Be-My-Baby-Now!"—a routine he used throughout this tour. As he had at Shea Stadium, John introduces a line at the end of the second verse of "Dizzy Miss Lizzy"—"Love me till I'm satisfied"—not heard in the Beatles' recording (or even the Larry Williams original), and apparently used regularly on the 1965 North American tour. And John goes into some seemingly unscripted chat before "Help!", chuckling, "We'll have to wait a minute now while Paul changes his bass, he's broken a string. What are you gonna do?" "Keep talking," somebody (Paul?) faintly retorts, though John's improvisational clowning fails him somewhat: "Keep talking. What should I say? It's simply wonderful to be here. . . . I can't think of anything to say, so why don't you just . . . talk to yourselves for a bit. . . . Go on. . . ."

● August 19

Live Performance

Sam Houston Coliseum, Houston (afternoon show)

Twist and Shout

She's a Woman

I Feel Fine

Dizzy Miss Lizzy

Ticket to Ride

Everybody's Trying to Be My Baby

Can't Buy Me Love

Baby's in Black

I Wanna Be Your Man

A Hard Day's Night

Help!

I'm Down

It's not known for certain, but it's generally assumed that both of the Beatles' 1965 concerts in Houston were broadcast on local radio—almost certainly KILT, who sponsored the event. Those broadcasts would be the probable source of the tapes of both shows, which are both among the better unreleased Beatlemania live recordings from a purely sonic viewpoint. The sound is not far below *The Beatles at the Hollywood Bowl* standards, and there's none of the kind of distortion that afflicts the otherwise comparable Atlanta tape (see previous entry). The main problem, unfortunately, is that the Beatles' voices, especially John Lennon's, are showing some signs of wear, perhaps due to having just tried to project themselves in the two of the largest venues they'd ever played (Shea Stadium and Atlanta Stadium). The first warning bell sounds just a dozen seconds into the opening song, "Twist and Shout," where John's faltering vocal sounds half-shot, and the other Beatles' ascending harmonies don't quite manage to stay in tune. John gamely soldiers on through the rest of the show—and it was just the first of two they gave that day! But the higher the note and the louder he sings, the more cracked his delivery usually is, especially on parts of "Ticket to Ride" and "Dizzy Miss Lizzy."

That doesn't mean, however, that the Beatles don't make the best of it, and that the performance isn't pretty fun despite its shortcomings. The lads themselves seem quite amused about something—whether the considerable level of audience hysteria, John's rasp, or something else—and Paul puts some quite unexpected semicomic vocal mannerisms into "Can't Buy Me Love," particularly when he almost speaks the end of the second chorus in exaggerated Liverpudlian. It's also a good occasion for semi-improvised humorous intros, John admitting in his announcement for "Dizzy Miss Lizzy," "I think the album's *Beatles 5* or *'65* or *'98* or something," no doubt confused by how Capitol was retitling and resequencing their releases for mass consumption in the United States. He also has a bout of echolalia in his preface to "A Hard Day's Night," described as "our last but one single, but one single, but one single, but one single." "Baby's in Black" is announced with the Welsh pronunciation "Baby's in Blach," followed by a performance where they drive right to the edge of cracking up in laughter, maybe instigated by their not-so-tight vocal harmonies on this specific number. And despite their frenzied schedule, the Beatles did know where they were on this particular date, Paul greeting the throngs of Texans with "Howdy y'all" almost as soon as he first took the microphone.

This was one of the rowdier Beatlemania audiences, the MC admonishing the screamers to quiet down with an almost schizophrenically over-the-top tone. He bellows like a teacher in the midst of an out-of-control school cafeteria food fight one minute and a showbiz "The Beatles are here!" pride the next. One imagines the Beatles found it as painful to listen to then as we do today, especially when he threatens to pull the plug with two songs to go, scolding, "People are getting hurt on the front two rows. The show will be stopped if you don't move back. This is the Houston Security Beatle Division." To which John Lennon immediately rejoins, with sarcastic contempt that says it all: "Thank you very much, that was wonderful."

● August 19

Live Performance
Sam Houston Coliseum, Houston (evening show)

Twist and Shout
She's a Woman
I Feel Fine
Dizzy Miss Lizzy
Ticket to Ride

Everybody's Trying to Be My Baby
Can't Buy Me Love
Baby's in Black
I Wanna Be Your Man
A Hard Day's Night
Help!
I'm Down

"Quiet! Ladies and gentlemen, quiet, quiet! Quiet! I bring to you, through KILT, the Beatles! The Beatles!" So goes the bizarrely grating introduction to the evening half of the group's Houston gig, almost certainly taken from the same source of the afternoon tape detailed in the previous entry. The sound is again good—very good, really, given the standards of the era, although Ringo's vocal mike either gives out or moves out of his range halfway through "I Wanna Be Your Man." But John Lennon's voice is yet more hoarse than it had been in the afternoon, and by the middle of the first verse of "Twist and Shout" even Paul and George are audibly laughing through their vocals as John's loss of tonal control becomes obvious. Say this about John, though—despite his image (sometimes propagated by himself) as an often lazy sod, on this particular night he was a trouper, throwing himself into demanding hard rockers like "Dizzy Miss Lizzy" and "I Feel Fine" with abandon, heedless of the damage he might have been inflicting upon his greatest musical asset. And he continued to find new ways to inflict damage upon the lyrics to "Help!", at one point singing, "Now I find I've changed my mind, I've never done before."

Some frays around the edges are heard on Paul's "She's a Woman" and "I'm Down" vocals, too; listen especially to how his shout almost breaks in two when he comes in for the final refrain of both songs. But, likewise, he seems to be willing to jeopardize his voice, to lose himself

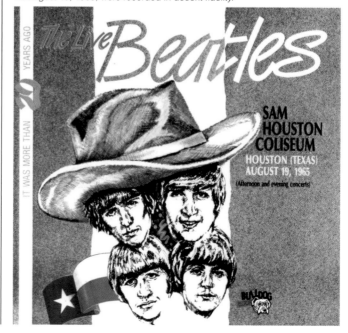

Both of the raucous shows the Beatles gave in Houston on August 19, 1965, were recorded in decent fidelity.

in the sheer joy of performing, slipping into uncharacteristic casual grammar by singing one line as "I know she ain't no peasant." By "I Feel Fine," it's obvious it's not going to be a night of all nights for musical tightness, John's voice sounding as if it's manning a sinking ship, he and his backup harmonizers singing different lines at one point. Some critics might savage the Beatles for such sloppiness, and there *is* sloppiness. But here's a difference between Beatles-sloppy and most other sloppy live rock. When the Beatles knew they were off, they didn't let it get them down; they laughed it off, laughed at themselves, charged on as if it didn't mean a lick, and, if anything, made the gaffes work for them to some degree. That aspect of the group rarely comes through better than it does in this concert.

● August 21

Live Performance

Metropolitan Stadium, Minneapolis

She's a Woman
I Feel Fine
Dizzy Miss Lizzy
Ticket to Ride
Everybody's Trying to Be My Baby
Can't Buy Me Love
Baby's in Black
I Wanna Be Your Man
A Hard Day's Night
Help!
I'm Down

On this poor-fidelity audience tape, you can pick up the screaming (and even some of the incidental chatter of the people sitting near the recorder) better than the distant, blurry sounds of the group onstage. And "Twist and Shout" is missing (in fact, it wasn't performed at all, due to John's sore throat), as well as the last part of "I'm Down" and some bits of other songs. There's even an airplane soaring overhead in the midst of "A Hard Day's Night." With no less than half a dozen other shows from the 1965 North American tour of much, much superior sound quality, is there any reason to put up with this? You *can* tell, however, that John Lennon switches the order of the verses on "Dizzy Miss Lizzy," and as he had at Shea Stadium, introduces a line at the end of the second—"Love me till I'm satisfied"—not heard in the Beatles' recording (or even the Larry Williams original). And he's *still* having trouble getting all the words of the second verse of "Help!" right. . . .

● August 29

Live Performance

Hollywood Bowl, Los Angeles

Twist and Shout
She's a Woman
I Feel Fine
*Dizzy Miss Lizzy

**Ticket to Ride
Everybody's Trying to Be My Baby
Can't Buy Me Love
Baby's in Black
I Wanna Be Your Man
A Hard Day's Night
**Help!
I'm Down

> *the second half of "Dizzy Miss Lizzy" appears on 1977 LP The Beatles at the Hollywood Bowl
>
> **appears on 1977 LP The Beatles at the Hollywood Bowl

Undeterred by their failure to gain a release with their tape of the Beatles' Hollywood Bowl performance from August 23, 1964, Capitol Records tried again to record a satisfactory show at the same venue—twice—in August 1965. The first of their two concerts there on August 29, however, produced a substantially worse recording from the technical end. The big goof was the failure of Paul's vocal mike on the first three songs, which had the effect not only of making "She's a Woman" sound like an instrumental, but also eliminating crucial vocal harmonies from "Twist and Shout" and "I Feel Fine." Whether because they felt inhibited by the knowledge they were being taped or not, it wasn't the Beatles' most comfortable-sounding performance either. Some slightly out-of-tune guitars on "I Feel Fine" and "Baby's in Black" didn't help. Nor did fluffed guitar licks on "Ticket to Ride" and "I'm Down" (on which John and George don't always sing the backup vocals together as they should), or some muffed harmonies on "A Hard Day's Night" and "Help!" Then there was Ringo's apparent failure to sing the word "man" on the first line of the choruses of "I Wanna Be Your Man," though George introduced some very nice bluesy responsive guitar licks to the vocal on this version. John made the best of another equipment snafu before "Help!", announcing, "I think we're having a bit of trouble with Paul's amplifier, so I'll just whistle to you for a bit." Which he does.

Most of the 1965 Hollywood Bowl material that was eventually used on the 1977 *The Beatles at the Hollywood Bowl* LP would be taken from the following day's concert on August 30. Capitol's effort didn't go to total waste, however, as "Ticket to Ride" and "Help!" were both used on the album, and the version of "Dizzy Miss Lizzy" that appears on that LP was actually edited together from both 1965 Hollywood Bowl shows. Although the LP gives August 30 as the date for the "Dizzy Miss Lizzy" track, the second half of it was, in fact, taken from the August 29 performance, complete with an arching George Harrison lick at the end that's totally different from the one on the studio version.

Even if it's not up to the standards of the August 30 Hollywood Bowl recording, the August 29 show is still an above-average live Beatles tape, if only because it was actually being professionally (if not wholly competently) recorded with an eye for possible release. And there are a few fun spins on the spoken song intros, George announcing "Everybody's Trying to Be My Baby" (which had appeared on the US LP *Beatles '65*) as a song from *Beatles '93*. Yet some exasperation with the equipment, performance, or the whole strain of battling the screaming masses with another heavily routined presentation might be coming through in John's sardonic intro to "Baby's in Black": "We'd like to do another number, 'cause that's what we're here for . . . while Paul fiddles with his amplifier. . . . I hope you can hear me. . . . I'd be awfully disappointed if you couldn't. We'd like to do another one from one of our LPs, albums, long-players, records . . . it's

The entire Hollywood Bowl concert from August 29, 1965, was recorded by Capitol Records, though not much was used on the 1977 LP The Beatles at the Hollywood Bowl.

a slow number, and it's a waltz for all of you over ten. Some people play fast waltzes, and some people play slow waltzes. So we're gonna play a slow one. And it's called 'Baby's in *Black!*'" he finishes, expelling the word "black" like a dog biting off the hand that feeds it. This intro was used when a Hollywood Bowl version of "Baby's in Black" was issued on the *Real Love* CD single in 1996, though the track that followed was actually taken from the August 30 performance the following day.

● August 30

Live Performance
Hollywood Bowl, Los Angeles

---

*Twist and Shout
*She's a Woman
I Feel Fine
**Dizzy Miss Lizzy
Ticket to Ride
Everybody's Trying to Be My Baby
*Can't Buy Me Love
***Baby's in Black
I Wanna Be Your Man
*A Hard Day's Night
Help!
I'm Down

    appears on 1977 LP The Beatles at the Hollywood Bowl
    **the first half of "Dizzy Miss Lizzy" appears on 1977 LP* The Beatles at the
      Hollywood Bowl
    ***appears on* Real Love *CD single*

This is the show from which Capitol drew most of the 1965 Hollywood Bowl material for its 1977 *The Beatles at the Hollywood Bowl* LP. It's better than the August 29 tape in all respects, particularly the techni-

cal ones. Crucially, the Beatles themselves are also performing better and generally in a better mood. It also seems like the sound is a little more balanced and fuller than it had been for the August 23, 1964, Hollywood Bowl recording, though nothing could fix that errant off-key guitar note at the end of the solo on "A Hard Day's Night," or John swallowing some of his words in "Help!" But it still wasn't good enough for the Beatles, and none of the material came out until the 1977 LP.

The whole show's in circulation, including the six songs that remain officially unreleased: "I Feel Fine," "Ticket to Ride," "Everybody's Trying to Be My Baby," "I Wanna Be Your Man," "Help!", and "I'm Down." There aren't many obvious reasons why they weren't chosen for *The Beatles at the Hollywood Bowl,* but whether it's in the original tape or not, there's a varispeed tape glitch on "I Feel Fine." Paul repeatedly comes in with his vocals too soon on the second chorus of "I'm Down"—he must have been unable to hear where the rest of the band was, the missteps are that obvious—and Ringo's still not singing his "man" on the first lines of the chorus of "I Wanna Be Your Man." Still, though this likely wasn't the best Beatles *performance* during their 1965 North American tour—the one in Atlanta is more enthusiastic, on the whole—it's certainly the best-*sounding* one, and, as such, a necessary listen for those collecting the group's unissued music.

Some Hollywood Bowl material may have been readied for release as early as 1971, with Apple telling *Melody Maker* in May of that year that it had tentative plans to release a *The Beatles at the Hollywood Bowl* LP (though EMI disavowed any knowledge of it). It's also been reported that John Lennon gave Hollywood Bowl tapes to Phil Spector, who got them to an acetate stage in preparation for a release on Apple that year. Nothing officially came out, however, until *The Beatles at the Hollywood Bowl* was released in May 1977, hitting No. 2 in the US and No. 1 in the UK. (One additional track from the August 30 show, "Baby's in Black"—where you can hear John suppressing a laugh in the opening chorus—gained low-profile official release on the 1996 *Real Love* CD single.) Yet, as of this writing in 2006, *The Beatles at the Hollywood Bowl* has, for unexplained reasons, never been issued on compact disc. In polls, it regularly scores at or near the top of the list of rock albums collectors most want to see reissued on CD, and there are even on-line petitions circulating on the Internet to ask Apple/Capitol for its release. But it's failed to appear, despite obvious demand.

No official explanation has issued from the Beatles camp, but expert collectors speculate it's never made the transition to CD owing to one or more of several possible factors. It could be the Beatles were/are simply unhappy with their performances and/or the sound quality; Paul and John certainly stated their dissatisfaction in various interviews. It was, too, a release they didn't approve in the first place back when it was originally taped, although George Martin claimed that John had been delighted with the recordings when he'd sent them to Lennon for approval in 1977. Perhaps the surviving Beatles and their estates are concerned about it causing confusion among fans as to whether the versions of the songs on the album are the familiar studio ones or the live ones, though that's frankly underestimating the average intelligence of the people who buy Beatles records. Or maybe it wouldn't even be considered a sound business move; it would probably sell much less on CD than their standard catalog does, possibly even less than *any* other CD in their standard catalog, though it's hard to imagine it failing to turn a profit (or failing to sell at least a million or two units). It's still easily findable as a used vinyl LP, of course. But if only as a piece of history (though it's musically more interesting than that), it really should be made available in the CD format, preferably in an expanded version that uses all three of the shows recorded in 1964 and 1965.

● August 31

Live Performance
Cow Palace, San Francisco (afternoon show)

Twist and Shout (incomplete)
She's a Woman (incomplete)
Can't Buy Me Love (fragment)
Baby's in Black (fragment)
I Wanna Be Your Man (fragment)
A Hard Day's Night (fragment)

Taken from the soundtrack of a newsreel, these three song fragments add up to three and a half minutes. You *can* hear it's the Beatles through the cacophony, but the timbre's so harsh and tinny that it's a most unpleasant experience.

● August 31

Live Performance
Cow Palace, San Francisco (evening show)

Twist and Shout (incomplete)
She's a Woman (incomplete)

More atrocious 1965 San Francisco recordings, this from a radio report of the evening concert.

● Circa Late Summer–Early Fall

Private Tapes

We Can Work It Out
Michelle

It's hard to date these brief snatches of Paul McCartney solo demos of these two songs. The Beatles would start recording "We Can Work It Out" in the studio on October 20 and "Michelle" on November 3, so these demos of the songs almost certainly would have been done before October 20. The most logical guess would place the dates between September 1, when the group returned to Britain from their North American tour, and October 12, when the *Rubber Soul* sessions started.

Both tapes have circulated in good fidelity, Paul accompanying his singing on acoustic guitar for "We Can Work It Out" in a nicely gentle, folky performance lasting a mere 45 seconds. We don't hear the *whole* performance, unfortunately, because John Lennon evidently erased the rest of it on the tape from which it is sourced, replacing it with one of his home tape experiments, "Lucy in Littletown." A shame, especially as it would have been interesting to hear if the song had a

different form at this point, since the anguished bridge that contrasts so nicely with the sunny verses is widely assumed to have been largely John's doing.

"Michelle" had been around in some form long before the *Rubber Soul* sessions, and another circulating private tape of the song has been dated as originating from 1963 (see entry discussing the "Alf Bicknell tapes" in the 1963 chapter). This version, lasting just under a minute in reasonable sound, is also a guitar instrumental. Its melody is closer to, but not precisely the same as, the one used on the recording, veering into a section that sounds close to—but, again, not exactly the same as—the variation used on the very final lines of the *Rubber Soul* track. As with "We Can Work It Out," John was instrumental in devising the middle eight used on the released version. So maybe this predates John's input, and maybe it even predates September–October 1965; if it really was done shortly before the song was cut at EMI, it's odd that it's still lacking any lyrics.

● October 12

Studio Outtakes
Rubber Soul sessions
Studio Two, Abbey Road, London

Run for Your Life (take 5, incomplete, with different lead vocal)
*Norwegian Wood (This Bird Has Flown) (take 1)
　　　appears on Anthology 2

There had been a gap between how much more quickly the Beatles were musically progressing in the studio than they were progressing onstage almost ever since they began recording albums. The gap was getting much wider than ever, however, by the time the *Rubber Soul* sessions began. Much of the material was devoted to arrangements, and introspective and personal sentiments, that would not only arguably be too quiet and reflective to work in a Beatlemania live setting, but at times would be impossible to recreate outside of the studio. There was still almost a year of touring ahead, but if only in hindsight, it's obvious that the Beatles were almost becoming different groups for touring and recording purposes by late 1965.

The first day of *Rubber Soul* sessions was split between one of its least progressive songs and one of its most adventurous. The less daring of the pair was "Run for Your Life," and an incomplete take has circulated, containing only about the first minute and 20 seconds, with the same instrumental backing track (from take 5) as the released version. John Lennon's vocal's different, however, though not substantially so, and the backing harmonies are missing. Some trivial informal chat and guitar strums preceding take 1 have also been bootlegged, but not take 1 itself.

Of far more consequence is take 1 of "Norwegian Wood (This Bird Has Flown)," one of the very most interesting and entertaining alternate studio versions of a Beatles song, and thus a natural for inclusion on *Anthology 2*. Done a couple of keys lower than the LP track, it's also taken at a slightly brisker, nearly waltzing pace and has a distinctly less folky feel, finger cymbals and maracas adding to the more insistent tone. There's only one verse rather than two before the first bridge, and the order of the lines about biding time and drinking wine are reversed. George Harrison's sitar is on this track as well, played a little more sloppily than on the LP version. It's actually more prominent to some degree in this arrangement, as the instrument's drone is heard more often throughout the song, whereas the sitar on the *Rubber Soul* version is played principally to supply twangy riffs for punctuation. The bit at the end of this unreleased take, with its disoriented sitar playing in isolation, presumably would have been chopped off had this attempt been released; a bootlegged version is slightly longer, with an additional sitar strum at the start.

With its slightly sinister air, this earlier take would have been a fine track had it been issued on *Rubber Soul* itself. The Beatles, however, reconsidered and gave it a folkier, more acoustic sound on a remake nine days later, in the process laying down *another* alternate take that's been bootlegged, though unlike take 1, it's never been officially issued (see entry for October 21).

● October 16

Studio Outtakes
"Day Tripper" single session
Studio Two, Abbey Road, London

Day Tripper (takes 1–3)

With the Beatles increasingly favoring a method of recording an instrumental backing track on top of which to lay multiple overdubs, there were less and less instances of substantially different alternate takes as their career progressed—unless, as in the case of take 1 of "Norwegian Wood," they brought an entirely different approach to the arrangement for an early take. So while the opportunity to hear all three takes of "Day Tripper" sounds enticing, in actuality all of them sound very similar to the one used on the hit single. In fact, one of them, take 3, *was* used on the hit single, though the bootlegged version is a bit longer. Takes 1 and 2 both break down, take 1 just before the two-minute mark, take 2 (after some tuning and a count-in) after less than half a minute. The lack of vocals does allow us to hear the counterpoint rhythm guitar and Ringo's brilliant drumming much more prominently, if you have an appreciation for the underlying dynamics of classic Beatles recordings. Take 3 offers the small bonuses of a count-in and a slightly longer, non-faded ending, where the circular guitar riff suddenly breaks out of its loop as if it has no idea where to go when set free.

● October 18

Studio Outtake
Rubber Soul sessions
Studio Two, Abbey Road, London

In My Life (take 3, incomplete, different keyboard part)

Take 3 of "In My Life" was the one used for the *Rubber Soul* LP track, yet an incomplete version with a different mix has shown up on bootleg. The big attraction is a different (though not too different) keyboard part in the instrumental break. As is well known, the keyboard passage

on the released version was a sped-up piano, but George Martin's playing a Hammond organ here.

● October 19

Studio Outtakes
The Third Beatles Christmas Record *(12-minute session outtake tape)*
The Third Beatles Christmas Record *(seven excerpts)*
Marquee Studio, London

Although the Beatles didn't really put much creativity into their Christmas records until their 1966 disc, there are indications they took some initiative in making the 1965 edition a more artistic endeavor than the one that ultimately resulted. On this date, they gathered at London's Marquee Studio, Tony Barrow again acting as producer and scriptwriter. Much material from this session found its way into circulation in the early 2000s, though strangely none of it was used on the actual 1965 Beatles Christmas disc, *The Third Beatles Christmas Record*. (A small part of it *was* used for a flexi-disc, *Sound of the Stars,* that Barrow produced to promote the British music weekly *Disc and Music Echo*.)

There's evidence that, for at least part of this session, the Beatles were using Barrow's script as at least a loose model for the content, as John Lennon's heard griping about it in a sound clip of about a minute and 20 seconds stringing together seven brief excerpts from the session. With piano backing, the Beatles are also heard singing "Silent Night" (as "Bonfire Night") and "The Twelve Days of Christmas," the very sort of Christmas carols they'd informally massacred on their previous Christmas outings.

A much longer 12-minute session outtake tape has surfaced on which the Beatles don't sound like they're sticking to planned repartee. Yet neither do they summon anything particularly witty to say, despite a surreal passage in which they discuss dismembering babies. Perhaps that was a seed of the idea for the infamous photo session a few months later for the "butcher cover" (the original and subsequently withdrawn sleeve of the US *Yesterday . . . and Today* LP, on which they're pictured holding butchered baby dolls). Otherwise it sounds like a failed, right-off-the-top-of-me-head series of attempts to emulate Goon show sketches, complete with sound effects, without any complete or particularly funny ideas, and lacking any overriding narrative structure. (In that respect, it was perhaps a seed for the *Magical Mystery Tour* film, without the visuals.) There's also a snatch of "Dixie," which is, alas, halted with sardonic fears of treading on the copyright.

Finally, there's also a 26-minute tape from the session that's been offered for auction, described as including five-and-a-half minutes of the Beatles singing the Christmas carols "The Holly and the Mustard," "Silent Bonfire Night," "Christmas Is Coming, The Goose Is Getting Fat," "Jingle Bells," and "The Twelve Days of Christmas." On the last of these, Ringo improvises the lyric, "On the third day of Christmas, my true love sent to me, one bird a hummin', two sailors coming"— undoubtedly too off-color a witticism to have made the cut for any Beatles product in 1965, even their Christmas record. Possibly this 26-minute tape could also be the source of all of the outtakes that have circulated; certainly it's the source of some of the material. As Beatles mysteries go, however, it's near the bottom rung of the ladder.

● October 20

Studio Outtakes
"We Can Work It Out" single session
Studio Two, Abbey Road, London

We Can Work It Out (takes 1–2)

It was the same deal for "We Can Work It Out" as it had been for "Day Tripper": an instrumental backing track was quickly established, upon which overdubs could be laid. It was recorded even more quickly than "Day Tripper" had been, and while both takes are in circulation, take 1 is just an instrumental backing track that's nearly identical to the released version. After a bit of presong warm-up and chat, however, it breaks down in the midst of its second bridge, where it sounds like Ringo's lost the beat. Take 2 is the one used for the hit single, except the harmonium note at the end sustains much longer, followed by a brief guitar lick (there's also a spoken count-in at the start). There's also a bootlegged take 2 mix that has a "thinner" Paul McCartney vocal, lacking some additional vocals that were later superimposed onto the track.

● October 21

Studio Outtakes
Rubber Soul sessions
Studio Two, Abbey Road, London

Norwegian Wood (This Bird Has Flown) (takes 2, 4)

Though "Norwegian Wood" was entirely remade in this session, take 2 makes clear that the group didn't have the rearrangement finalized when work on the song resumed. Though the key has lowered close to the one used on the final version, it still has a waltzing beat, with a heavily accented Ringo Starr drumbeat. George's sitar is still more to the fore, droning softly in the background through much of the track, with an additional bit of quizzical riffing at the very beginning that didn't survive to the released cut. It's more of a rock song at this point than the near-folk one it would become; it has some harmonies on the last line, where the released version would not; and the lines about biding time and drinking wine are still in the reverse order of the finished lyric. For that matter, the song's still going by the title "This Bird Has Flown," as the announcement before the take reveals.

While the much folkier, more acoustic-oriented arrangement of take 4 would be used as the actual *Rubber Soul* track, the bootlegged version is a bit longer, with a take announcement and a couple of false starts strumming through the opening guitar chords. There was likely some involved discussion about rearrangement between takes 2 and 4, with Lennon and the other Beatles perhaps concluding that a plaintive mood was a better fit for the composition than the somewhat more exotic earlier run-throughs. In his early-'70s *Rolling Stone* interview, John accurately if somewhat exaggeratedly recalled, "We went through many different sort of versions of the song, it was never right and I was getting very angry about it, it wasn't coming out like I said. They said, 'Well, just do it how you want to do it' and I said, 'Well, I just want to

do it like this.' They let me go and I did the guitar very loudly into the mike and sang it at the same time."

● October 24

Studio Outtake
Rubber Soul sessions
Studio Two, Abbey Road, London

*I'm Looking through You (take 1)
  *appears on Anthology 2

The Beatles did not often record unissued, substantially different alternate versions that could be considered on par (or at least nearly on par) with the ones they chose to release. Yet *Rubber Soul*, remarkably, produced two of them—the previously discussed take 1 of "Norwegian Wood (This Bird Has Flown)" and take 1 of "I'm Looking Through You," which is, if anything, even more different from the one that ended up on the LP. It's far funkier, with a nearly proto-reggae rhythm, unaccompanied maracas setting the beat at the start before an acoustic guitar joins the mix. Paul's vocal, too, is top-notch; it's more forceful and rocks harder than the one on *Rubber Soul*, almost as if he's bringing more anger and less gentle wistfulness to the table. There's an elementary, bluesy guitar solo, and an ending that gives him the chance to wield the upper-register, semi-improvised hard rock vocal chops he liked to flash from time to time on extended fadeouts, as he had on "She's a Woman," for example. The only big handicap is the absence of a bridge, something that would be fixed when the Beatles decided to remake the track in November. The take can now be heard legitimately on *Anthology 2*, though a slightly longer version has been bootlegged. This has a "take 1" announcement and, more crucially, a non-faded ending, with about ten more seconds at the tag that allow appreciation of McCartney's high, grainy vocal improvs in all their glory.

● November 4

Studio Outtakes
Rubber Soul sessions
Studio Two, Abbey Road, London

*12-Bar Original (takes 1-2)
12-Bar Original (rehearsal)
  *edited version of take 1 appears on Anthology 2

It's still a mystery as to what the Beatles were thinking when they recorded "12-Bar Original," a long and, to be harsh, monotonous blues-rock instrumental. As has been noted elsewhere, it's very much in the style of the great Memphis soul-rock instrumental band Booker T. & the MGs, with the same sort of walking beat they used on their classic 1962 hit "Green Onions." But the riffs on "12-Bar Original" aren't anywhere near as compelling as the ones on "Green Onions." They follow a generic, plodding blues pattern, over and over, and while George Harrison's tone pedal lead guitar and George Martin's harmonium were unusual touches, in this context they sound misplaced. It was a *long* track, too, with take 2 meandering along for a full six minutes and 36 seconds; the version used on *Anthology 2* edits it down, mercifully, some would say, to a mere 2:54. The full take 2 (count-in intact) has been bootlegged, as has take 1, which (although following the same arrangement) chugs along (after some pretake warm-up) for only about a dozen seconds before breaking down. If you need yet more, a further minute and 45 seconds or so from an unknown take is much the same, but has a somewhat brighter, more active vibe, with a busier harmonium presence. It's speculated that this might be from a rehearsal, as only two takes are documented in Mark Lewisohn's *The Beatles Recording Sessions*.

As for the more interesting speculation as to why the group spent so much time on such a humdrum piece in the first place, it might have been a desperate move to fill up space on *Rubber Soul*. The album's release date was just a month away by the time of this November 4 session, and they still didn't have enough material for a full LP. Jam-type instrumentals were used as fillers on albums by many other leading bands of the day, all the way up to the Rolling Stones and the Who. But the Beatles were simply not as given to blues-type jams as the Stones or some other British Invasion bands. While "2120 South Michigan Avenue" (on the second American Rolling Stones LP, *12 X 5*), for example, was a genuinely excellent R&B instrumental with its own debts to Booker T. & the MGs, "12-Bar Original" would have stuck out as the gravest misstep in the Beatles' recording career had it gained a place on *Rubber Soul*. It would have dragged down a classic album not only because of its musical mediocrity, but also because it wouldn't have fit in at all with the surrounding material, much of which was folk-rockish and mellow in nature. Perhaps it was even a stall tactic, to buy time as the group scrambled to write new material? And was its very title, "12-Bar Original," a self-deprecating pun on the derivative tune itself, this being perhaps the *least* original Beatles original to be attempted at EMI to date?

Had it been issued at the time, "12-Bar Original" would have been the first Beatles composition credited to all four members of the band. As it happened, that honor fell a couple of years later to another instrumental, *Magical Mystery Tour*'s "Flying"—on which the group also used a Booker T. & the MGs–like base, but took it in much more imaginative directions.

● November 8

Studio Outtakes
Rubber Soul sessions
Studio Two, Abbey Road, London

Think for Yourself (rehearsal)

One of the weirdest extensive segments from any Beatles session to have circulated is this 19-and-a-half-minute tape (actually several portions edited together, not a continuous recording) of "rehearsals" for "Think for Yourself." "Rehearsals" might be too formal a label, for while they do rehearse their three-part vocal harmonies at various and numerous junctures, most of this tape is incidental chat and joking (and no musical instruments whatsoever are heard). According to *The Beatles Recording Sessions*, this was taped with the Beatles' knowledge in hopes that some of the banter could be used for their 1965 Christmas fan club disc, which would be recorded the same night (see following entry). Its

musical value isn't negligible, as it affords a fly-on-the-wall perspective of John, Paul, and George working out their three-part harmonies, John in particular taking a while to get it right. Some of these attempts are quite out-of-tune, and while there's much giggling and tomfoolery, they're clearly putting a lot of work into it as well. Then, suddenly, almost 11 minutes into the tape, they hit on a rich, magical blend. And they know it, one of them announcing, less with surprise than matter-of-fact observation, "That was it."

Of perhaps greater interest is the chatter, which more than any other outtake yields a relatively in-depth glimpse of the Beatles having fun in the studio. It sounds much better on tape than it reads on paper, but the funny voices and mock teasing illustrate just how close they were as friends, not just musicians. Much of the humor, perhaps to the surprise of some listeners, comes from Paul, who could be a match for John as a witty mimic. Here he imitates both fundamentalist preachers with exaggerated Northern English dialect and posh upper-class British theatrical directors, adopting a fake aggressive American accent in challenging Lennon (not seriously) to a fight. Much of John's acerbic personality informs his own repartee, including brief vocal send-ups of "Yesterday" and an X-rated twist on a line from "Do You Want to Know a Secret" (which he sings as "do you want to hold a penis? Do-wah-ooh"). There are also less-than-wholly-complimentary references to his then-wife Cynthia, and some mildly self-deprecating jabs at his struggle in getting his own vocal part down ("You'll have to bear with me or have me shot"). George, perhaps understandably more preoccupied with the recording than the others as it's his composition, is heard less than John or Paul; Ringo, unfortunately, is absent altogether.

More than for its content, however, the tape's value is in its illustration of how well the Beatles were getting along and enjoying one another's company at this point. (It would *not* be this way, with rare exceptions, in the uncomfortable hours of dialogue captured on tape during the marathon January 1969 rehearsals for their ill-fated *Get Back* project.) It has its share of dead air and inconsequential exchanges too, but in a way it's funnier than their actual Christmas discs, if only because it seems less contrived and closer to the way they really were.

For all the effort that went into making this lengthy tape, none of it was actually used on the Beatles' 1965 Christmas record. It wasn't 100 percent wasted effort, however, as a six-second excerpt of the trio practicing their vocal harmonies was used in the *Yellow Submarine* soundtrack. Sung by the cartoon Beatles in the film to awaken the Lord Mayor of Pepperland from his slumber as he's being uncovered from an avalanche of apples, it's heard just past the 56-minute mark on the *Yellow Submarine* DVD. And if you want to get more of an idea of what the rest of the tape sounds like, as of this writing in 2006, a transcript of much of it could be read on-line at http://www.vex.net/~paulmac/beatles/bts/beatle _speech.html. It's also discussed in some detail in Mark Hertsgaard's book *A Day in the Life: The Music and Artistry of the Beatles*.

● November 8

The Third Beatles Christmas Record
Studio Two, Abbey Road, London

If the Beatles sounded a bit fatigued on *The Third Beatles Christmas Record*, it wasn't solely due to the wear and tear of Beatlemania. The three takes used (with judicious editing) to construct the final disc were recorded at the end of a session lasting until 3:00 a.m.—at a point where they had just a few days to somehow finish writing and recording *Rubber Soul* to make its early December release date. It could also be that they were in no mood to conjure up a Christmas disc out of little more than thin air after apparently having invested so much effort for naught on the exact same project back on October 19.

The thank-yous for presents, Christmas cards, and the like do sound more mechanical and dispirited than they had in 1963 and 1964. But there are flashes of passable Fab Four humor, as well as some what-the-heck music, including a glorious din of an off-key stagger through a few lines of "Yesterday" and some rapidly busked holiday folk sing-along. Some genuine disenchantment with the novelty of fame wearing off creeps into their acoustic rendition of the Four Tops' hit "It's the Same Old Song," abruptly halted, quite amusingly, when the others archly warn John to stop because of possible copyright problems. But the momentum flags and the proceedings veer near anarchic chaos about halfway into the "track," Paul shrugging, "That looks like as though it's about it for this year. We certainly tried our best to please everybody. If we haven't done what we could have done, we've tried." That's not all, though: some low-energy caroling, and a couple more deliberately wretchedly sung snatches of "Yesterday," haul the disc past the six-minute mark like an out-of-shape Santa Claus dragging behind his reindeer. They do slip in a surprisingly overt reference to the Vietnam War in their desecration of "Auld Lang Syne," complete with "bodies floating in the river Jordan"—in turn a reference to a similar line in Barry McGuire's then-recent hit "Eve of Destruction."

If you're somehow in the mood for more of this particularly forced holiday horsing around, a 12-minute outtake from their previous unsuccessful attempt to make a 1965 holiday disc (see October 19 entry) has surfaced on which the Beatles don't sound quite as grumpy, along with a minute and 20 seconds of other snippets from that same session.

● November 11

Studio Outtakes

Rubber Soul sessions
Studio Two, Abbey Road, London

I'm Looking Through You (take 4)
Girl (take 2, backing track)

The final day of *Rubber Soul* sessions saw the completion of the "remake" of "I'm Looking Through You," with vocals superimposed onto a take actually done the day before. The bootlegged take 4 is identical to the one heard on the *Rubber Soul* album, except that it has an announcement of the take number and a longer fadeout with a disorganized ending (as well as the false starts that actually made it onto the mix used for the US stereo LP). Both "I'm Looking Through You" and "Norwegian Wood (This Bird Has Flown)," as an aside, started with somewhat more eccentric arrangements before being given folkier, more acoustic, and relatively more normal remakes. (In the case of "I'm Looking Through You," there was also the insertion of a key bridge missing from the first recording.) Most likely the Beatles were just following their instincts, but one also wonders whether it's possible they were influenced by a wish to

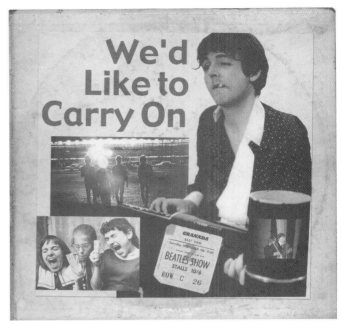

Even as early as late 1965, the Beatles were starting to tire of touring. The group would cease to play live within a year, in part because of the excessive crowd noise documented on this CD of low-fidelity, mid-'60s concert tapes.

make these two tracks more consistent with the sound of the album as a whole. While both available versions of "I'm Looking Through You" have their merits, if the bridge of the final take had been incorporated into its structure, arguably the earlier arrangement might have been even better than the one that was ultimately used.

As a final peripheral extra from the year 1965, what is known as a "rough monitor mix of the backing track" of "Girl" has been bootlegged, though you can get the same effect by playing the vocal-less channel of the original stereo release. Which has led some to believe this is in fact an "outfake," not an "outtake."

1965 Noncirculating Recordings, Known and Rumored

● February 15–June 17

Studio Outtakes

Help! sessions
Abbey Road, London

Uncirculating outtakes noted in *The Beatles Recording Sessions* include ten edit pieces for "Another Girl" in which George played a guitar figure with a tremolo effect, intended for the end of the track but never used; several rehearsals for the first go at "That Means a Lot" on February 20; and "Wait," before the track was retrieved for *Rubber Soul* and embel-

The 1965 British Tour

Although there is no circulating Beatles music from 1965 recorded later than November 11, they weren't quite done making music for the year. On December 3, they launched their next British tour—a short, ten-day jaunt that would turn out to be their *final* British tour, though they did one short concert in the UK in 1966 and the famous concert atop their Apple headquarters roof in London in January 1969. No tapes have emerged of this late-1965 British tour, a particular loss as one of the songs, "We Can Work It Out" (on which Paul played electric piano live), was never done onstage elsewhere. In addition, although they did do "Yesterday" in concert in 1966, the arrangement for this particular tour was different, Paul accompanying himself on organ instead of playing bass as he would the following year.

Maybe the performances on this tour wouldn't have been that great, as they rehearsed for it just once, and perfunctorily, at the flat of their road managers Neil Aspinall and Mal Evans. If a tape of a full show were to surface, however, it would follow this setlist:

"I Feel Fine"

"She's a Woman"

"If I Needed Someone"

"Act Naturally"

"Nowhere Man"

"Baby's in Black"

"Help!"

"We Can Work It Out"

"Yesterday"

"Day Tripper"

"I'm Down"

---

lished with tone pedal guitar, tambourine, maraca, and additional vocals. Paul McCartney also divulged some interesting chatter in the *Anthology* book, where he revealed, "In an outtake I heard recently—recording 'Dizzy Miss Lizzy'—John is saying, 'What's wrong with that?' and George Martin says, 'Erm . . . it wasn't exciting enough, John,' and John mumbles, 'Bloody hell'—that kind of thing was creeping in a bit—'It wasn't exciting enough, eh? Well, you come here and sing it, then!'"

There was a song considered for but not included on *Help!* that, while never taped, has an interesting enough story behind it that it deserves discussion. According to Norman Smith, the principal engineer on the Beatles' EMI recordings from 1962 to 1965, the group almost recorded one of his compositions when they were looking for material to fill out the *Help!* album. This would have taken place in mid-June 1965, as the *Help!* sessions were concluding. Despite some initial enthusiasm, they explained to Smith that they needed to record a track for Ringo to sing on the album ("Act Naturally") instead. Although they also told him they'd do it for the next LP, by the time of that next album, *Rubber Soul*, "they'd progressed so much that my song was never even considered again," as Smith told Mark Lewisohn in *The Beatles Recording Sessions*. If it had been cut, John would have been the singer, Smith having penned it specifically with John in mind for that purpose.

Had they recorded the song and put it on *Help!*, it would have been the only time a Beatles release included a nonoriginal composition never previously recorded by anyone else. The only other time this had come close to happening was when George Martin instructed the band to record Mitch Murray's "How Do You Do It" in 1962, though as explained in an earlier chapter, this remained in the vaults until *Anthology 1*. That does leave Beatleologists to wonder, however, what would a song from such an unexpected outside source have to sound like to impress the group (Lennon and McCartney particularly) enough to consider recording it for an album? The possibility cannot be discounted that John and Paul were humoring or stringing along their longtime studio colleague, but as Smith told the story (on more than one occasion), their enthusiasm for the tune was genuine.

Unfortunately, the demo that Smith recorded for the group no longer exists. "Not only could I never ever find that damned manuscript or the little demo that I gave them, but I can't even remember the blasted title either!" confessed Smith in Richard Buskin's *Inside Tracks*. "It was a good song with a solid beat, almost like the solid beat of 'Twist and Shout,' but with a bit of romance, too. . . . I try not to think about it too much." Still, his inability to even remember the name of the song or that much about it begs the question, could it have been all that good?

While Smith lost his chance to get a song on a Beatles LP (and the substantial royalties that would have gone with it), he hardly vanished into obscurity after ending his association with the Beatles at the end of 1965. He not only produced Pink Floyd's first albums and the Pretty Things' 1968 psychedelic rock opera *S.F. Sorrow*, he also had a couple big hits as a recording artist in the early '70s under the name Hurricane Smith, with "Oh Babe, What Would You Say" making No. 3 in the US in early 1973.

Weirder still, this might not have been the only outside composition the Beatles were offered at this time. In June 1965, as quoted in Mark Paytress's *The Rolling Stones Off the Record*, Mick Jagger told the press that he and Keith Richards had written a song for the Beatles, claiming, "A long time ago, me and Keith wrote something called 'Give Me Your Hand and Hold It Tight,' but the Beatles wouldn't do it. They wrote one for us as well, called 'Outside 109' [possibly meaning 'One After 909,' which the Beatles had written years before and recorded at EMI in March 1963, though they didn't release their own version until *Let It Be*]. We said we wouldn't do the song until they did ours. So nothing happened on either side. We're still waiting." (Of course, the Rolling Stones already *had* done a Lennon-McCartney song way back in late 1963, when they made "I Wanna Be Your Man" their second British single.) Strangest of all, in January 1966 *Melody Maker* reported an announcement from Motown that the Beatles had commissioned two songs from the label's foremost songwriting team, Eddie Holland–Lamont Dozier–Brian Holland, though it's difficult to imagine why the group would want to ask for that kind of help.

● October 12–November 11

Studio Outtakes

Rubber Soul sessions
Abbey Road, London

The Beatles Recording Sessions revealed that take 3 of "Norwegian Wood (This Bird Has Flown)" had only two acoustic guitars, bass, and John and Paul's vocals. On the same day, an early version of "Nowhere Man" was done using an intro with three-part vocal harmonies that were apparently higher than those used on the final version, though this particular try (take 2) had only an electric rhythm guitar as musical backing. There was also an intermediate attempt at "I'm Looking Through You" done (on November 6) between the earliest and final versions, with two takes described by Lewisohn as "perhaps a little too fast and frenetic," though similar to the LP version.

● Circa Late 1965

Private Tape

In My Life

In his 1980 *Playboy* interview with David Sheff, John Lennon said he probably had an original (presumably home) tape of "In My Life." John's memory wasn't always faultless, but in the same answer, he also remembered having tapes of "Strawberry Fields Forever" and "We Can Work It Out," both of which *did* turn up. Like "Strawberry Fields Forever," "In My Life" is known to have mutated considerably in the course of its composition—in an early draft, it referred to numerous Liverpool landmarks by name—which could make prestudio tapes of the song fascinating.

● Circa Late 1965

Private Tape

What Goes On

In the April 1966 issue of *The Beatles Monthly Book*, Neil Aspinall reported that "when Paul wanted to show Ringo how 'What Goes On' sounded he made up a multi-track tape. Onto this went Paul singing, Paul playing lead guitar, Paul playing bass and Paul playing drums. Then Ringo listened to the finished tape and added his own ideas before the recording session." Like most McCartney private tapes from the Beatles era, it seems unlikely to make its way into circulation, if it even still exists.

● Circa December 25

Private Tape

Unforgettable
57 Wimpole Street, London

For years, it had been reported that Paul McCartney recorded an album at home around Christmas 1965 specifically for the other Beatles. Supposedly, it included singing, acting, and sketches, and only three copies were pressed, one each for John, George, and Ringo. In a 1995 interview with Mark Lewisohn, Paul confirmed this in some detail, explaining, "Yes, it's true. I had two Brenell tape recorders set up at home, on which I made experimental recordings and tape loops, like the ones in 'Tomorrow Never Knows.' And once I put together something crazy, something left field, just for the other Beatles, a fun thing which they could play late in the evening. It was just something for the mates, basically."

Continued McCartney, "It was called *Unforgettable* and it started with Nat 'King' Cole singing 'Unforgettable,' then I came in over the top as the announcer: 'Yes, unforgettable, that's what you are! And today in *Unforgettable . . .*' It was like a magazine program: full of weird interviews, experimental music, tape loops, some tracks I knew the others hadn't heard, it was just a compilation of odd things. I took the tape to Dick James's studio and they cut me three acetate discs. Unfortunately, the quality of these discs was such that they wore out as you played them. I gave them to the fellas and I guess they would have played them for a couple of weeks, but then they must have worn out. There's probably a tape somewhere, though." If it ever turns up, it might be the earliest evidence of the Beatles using home recording equipment for specifically experimental/avant-garde purposes—something that both John and Paul did in the last half of the 1960s, though John's ventures in this field are more widely known than Paul's.

Too, there may be similar tapes from 1965 or even earlier. As Paul told biographer Barry Miles in *Paul McCartney: Many Years from Now*, he used to make tapes in the home of the family of his girlfriend, Jane Asher, where he lived between 1963 and 1966. "I used to have a couple of Brenell tape recorders I got through Dick James's son," he elaborated. "I used to experiment with them when I had an afternoon off, which was quite often. We'd be playing in the evening, we'd be doing a radio show or something, and there was often quite a bit of time when I was just in the house on my own so I had a lot of time for this. I wasn't in a routine. I could stay up till three in the morning, sleep through till two in the afternoon, and often did. It was a very free, formless time for me . . . So I would sit around all day, creating little tapes." He also spelled out the contents of *Unforgettable* a bit more: "I did one once called *Unforgettable* and used the 'Unforgettable'—Nat King Cole—'Is what you are . . .' as the intro. Then did a sort of 'Hello, hello . . .' like a radio show. I had a demo done by Dick James of that, just for the other guys because it was really a kind of stoned thing. That was really the truth of it."

The Beatles made only one British concert appearance in 1966, as they concentrated more of their resources on studio recording. This photo was taken from their final British concert appearance, at the NME Pollwinners Concert on May 1, 1966, which was sadly not filmed for posterity.

1966

The End of Touring and a Retreat to the Studio

The Year in Review

Though there was no advance plan to retire from the road and become a studio-only band, by the end of 1966, that's essentially what the Beatles had become. Purely in terms of music released, it was their least productive year since 1962, yielding "just" 16 tracks, used on one No. 1 album and two chart-topping singles (the second of which was also included on the LP). And while the group did tour the world in the summer, there was just one truncated concert on their native soil. Furthermore, various calamities and hassles on that summer tour sealed the group's decision to put an end to touring for good. It was a decision they stuck to, and there were no more Beatles concerts before a paying audience. During the rest of their career they played live in public on only a few occasions in rather manufactured circumstances, those being a couple of television performances and their rooftop concert for the *Let It Be* film in January 1969. This was an unprecedented way of doing things in pop music in 1966, with the arguable exception of Elvis Presley's cessation of live performances in the early '60s to concentrate on movies. There was even speculation

that the Beatles were finished as a group, though that proved to be far from the case. They would remain a unit and continue to evolve creatively, but do most of their work in the recording studio.

Unsurprisingly, there was also a significant drop in unreleased Beatles recordings in 1966. The nature of the way they were painstakingly building tracks in the studio also means that most of the *Revolver* outtakes that escaped prior to the mid-'90s were pretty meager table scraps, mostly being isolated tracks or variant mixes rather than markedly different alternates or outtakes. And while a few of their 1966 shows were recorded in listenable-to-decent sound, there's no escaping the evidence that the group's playing had deteriorated onstage, with an accompanying audible loss of enthusiasm.

It's not all downbeat ends and cuttings as far as unreleased 1966 Beatles music goes, however. One of the major achievements of the *Anthology 2* compilation was to unearth a few genuinely different, interesting, and even enjoyable alternate versions of *Revolver* songs that had never made their way into circulation. The few tapes of unreleased

139

live shows from the summer tour may not display the group at their best in performance, but they're at the least very interesting documents of how they sounded onstage in their final touring days, and do contain some better music than some of their harsher critics have acknowledged. There are also a number of interesting John Lennon home recordings from this era, including the beginnings of "Strawberry Fields Forever." And when that song was taken to the studio in late 1966, its numerous outtakes would round off the most interesting instance in which the evolution of a Beatles classic is documented virtually from start to finish.

● Circa Late 1965–Early 1966

Private Tape
Kenwood, Weybridge

He Said, He Said (five versions)
She Said, She Said (two versions)

It's pretty hard to pin down the date of these work-in-progress John Lennon solo home recordings, and, in fact, pretty hard to date many of the home recordings he did from the mid-'60s onward. This particular batch must have been started in September 1965 at the earliest, as the incident inspiring the song (Peter Fonda saying, "I know what it's like to be dead" to John during an acid trip) didn't take place until late August, and the Beatles didn't return home until early September. And these home recordings couldn't have taken place any later than June 21, 1966, when "She Said, She Said" was recorded in Abbey Road. An educated guess would surmise that none of them predate December 1965, since the Beatles were scrounging for material to fill out *Rubber Soul* in November, and "She Said, She Said" might have been offered as a song for the LP if John had already started writing it. It's placed in the 1966 chapter as the song itself is more conveniently grouped near discussion of the album on which it eventually appeared, *Revolver*, than with the 1965 recordings.

Whenever these were made, they offer valuable if slightly lo-fi glimpses of how the song changed during construction. An obvious difference in the first five versions—reportedly taken from a composing tape lasting about ten minutes, although these five excerpts only add up to about two minutes—is that the title itself is different. Maybe John changed "He Said, He Said" to "She Said, She Said" to ward off suspicion that Fonda was the nattering character portrayed in the song, rather as he would later use "Sexy Sadie" instead of "Maharishi."

These five "He Said, He Said" fragments, with John on acoustic guitar, are all very short and in a much lower key than the *Revolver* version, lasting between ten and 45 seconds. The first two, with a folky gallop to the guitar, are little more than the line, "He said, I know what it's like to be dead," with a gentler, less acidic melody (and vocal delivery) than the LP track would use. In fact, only two chords are used, though John does jump to a higher key at the end of the third fragment; it also adds a second line, "I must be out of my head" (which did not survive to the recorded rendition). The fourth (merely ten-second) pass has a far more insistent, steady rhythm, and the fifth—the longest, at 45 seconds—shows him starting to approximate the much more memorable melody of the final version, though there are some rather bland, reas-

suring chord changes that would eventually fall by the wayside. There are also a few more lyrics that, again, wouldn't make the final edit: "I know what it's like to be sad," which would be only slightly altered, and a consolatory "That's what he said," which wouldn't be used at all.

The other two versions, also done solo on acoustic guitar, almost certainly come from a later date, as not only has the title been changed to "She Said, She Said," but the song is in a higher key and much closer to its final form. On the first version, lasting a mere 40 seconds or so, John makes the odd alteration of singing an elongated "I" instead of "she said," almost as if he's having second thoughts about ascribing the dialogue to a third person at all. The second version actually commences with two false starts before the song proper starts, with the first verse exactly the same as the one on the *Revolver* track, albeit with a folkier lilt. The first and last lines of the second verse, however, are totally different: "I said, who put all that crap in your head . . . and you're making me feel like my trousers are torn"(!). After a move into the bridge with more lines not heard on *Revolver* ("She said, I will love him more when he's dead, I said, no no no no, it's wrong"), the tape cuts off.

The second verse is so radically different, in fact, that there's doubt as to whether it could have been seriously intended for the track to be recorded at EMI. No big pop acts were putting words as controversial (by the era's staid standards) as "crap" into their lyrics in 1966; no rock groups at all were using words like that, actually, except the underground New York band the Fugs. The line about the torn trousers is rather racy too, and maybe that's a knowing Lennon joke, not something that he expected to get cleared for release. These lines aside, overall the tapes show "She Said, She Said" to be a folkier, milder song in its inception. That's something true of many demos, naturally, but this particular composition really gained a lot of vitriol in its studio arrangement.

Altogether, these home-taped fragments last a mere four minutes and 20 seconds or so. It's known, however, that at least 20 more minutes of "She Said, She Said" composing tapes exist. On April 30, 2002, a 25-minute cassette of the material—described as having been recorded at John's home in early spring 1966—was auctioned for £58,750 at Christie's. It's not known for certain whether all the fragments that have been bootlegged are on this tape, but the cassette certainly contains a lot of material that's never circulated, including the lyrics, "When I was a little boy, I never had no toy . . . and I might be green, I might be green." Paul McCartney's voice has been reported to be heard in the background, with John—frustrated with the endless tinkering, evidently—griping at one point, "God, I just don't know what I'm doing. I'll have to give up. I'm going crazy with it!" As to how this material escaped the Lennon archives, John would have only himself to blame, as he gave the tape to Yoko Ono's ex-husband, Tony Cox, while he and Yoko were visiting Cox's family in Denmark in early January 1970.

● Circa March–April

Private Tape

Eleanor Rigby

A mere 16-second fragment of a Paul McCartney home demo of "Eleanor Rigby" escaped in 2001, when those auctioning the complete tape put up a clip on the Internet. In slightly blurred fidelity, this simply has

Beatles bootlegs don't shy away from using titles that major labels would almost certainly find too controversial. Here's one example, with a surrealistic photo of John and George taken at the same March 25, 1966, session that produced the infamous withdrawn "butcher cover" on the first edition of the US LP Yesterday . . . and Today.

him running through the refrain once on acoustic guitar, with double-tracked vocals. It couldn't have been done earlier than March, as it was recorded over the first two minutes of a tape containing the audio of the March 1 BBC television airing of the documentary *The Beatles at Shea Stadium,* and almost certainly predates the recording of the backing track for the song for EMI on April 28, 1966.

The mere existence of this busk, however, is significant if only because there are so few McCartney home tapes from the '60s (particularly in comparison to the relative wealth of ones by John Lennon). It would also be fascinating to hear the entire "Eleanor Rigby" tape, particularly as at this stage reportedly the lyrics were not finalized, referring to Father McCartney rather than Father McKenzie. In *The Autobiography of Donovan: The Hurdy Gurdy Man,* Donovan quotes another unused lyric from an early version, "Ola Na Tungee, blowing his mind in the dark with a pipe full of clay—no one can say" (the phrase "Ola Na Tungee" possibly having been inspired by the great Nigerian drummer Babatunde Olatunji). What's more, some other work-in-progress tapes of the song were made, Barry Miles reporting in *Paul McCartney: Many Years from Now* that Paul recorded several demo versions of the song, most of them at the basic recording studio he'd set up at 34 Montagu Square in central London.

● **April 6**

Studio Outtake
Revolver sessions
Studio Three, Abbey Road, London

*Tomorrow Never Knows (take 1)
   *appears on Anthology 2

With the exception of an overdub session for the TV documentary *The Beatles at Shea Stadium* on January 5, 1966, and some home tapes, the Beatles did not record or perform any music between December 12, 1965 (the last date of their British tour) and April 6, 1966 (the first session for *Revolver*). While a four-month gap from musicmaking for a big rock band is nothing by 21st-century standards, it was a mammoth one for the Beatles, who had been either playing live, recording, or making movies since around the spring of 1960, with only brief holidays to break up the grind.

For the most part, the gap was probably because they just needed a long time-out from the breakneck schedule. If only subliminally, however, it might have been a major assertion of independence from the rigorous schedule that Brian Epstein had been setting up for them since he started managing the band. Pop groups had been expected to work nonstop, but here, as in many other areas, the Beatles—having paid their dues with years of grueling multitasking—would pioneer a new path. They had already defied Epstein, who had wanted them to tour more extensively in Britain in late 1965 and do another extended Christmas engagement, by drastically scaling down the live concerts he'd hoped to plan. The nearly four-month rest, too, must have been an enormous help creatively at a time when they wanted to marshal most of their resources into the studio. Not only must it have recharged their batteries, but it likely also gave them far more time to write material than they were accustomed to, and probably for doing some home taping, experimental and otherwise, when the inclination struck. The extra time might have been particularly valuable at a point when they were forging into new, more demanding methods of recording and composition.

These new directions were immediately evident when they convened at Abbey Road to start *Revolver,* beginning with its most experimental track, "Tomorrow Never Knows." While the song would undergo much embellishment via the addition of overdubs and tape loops over the next couple of days, take 1 proves it was quite far-out right from the start. When it was released on *Anthology 2,* it was a pleasant surprise to hear that it was quite different from the version (based on take 3) that ended up on *Revolver,* and equally avant-garde. With a much steadier though very heavy Ringo Starr drum pattern (compared, amusingly, to a rumba by George Harrison when the John Lennon-less Beatles listen to a playback in 1995 on the "Special Features" disc of the *Anthology* DVD), it's something more of a standard rock song, though only just. Distorted, sinuous, Indian-like notes not used in the subsequent arrangement flutter, drone, and bend in the background, though John Lennon's vocal already has the distant megaphone timbre of the official LP track. Most arresting are the shockwaves of sound emanating from the backing track, as if supersonic gulps are rising from a huge subterranean fish bowl. ("What's that underwater sound?" asks a genuinely curious George Harrison during the *Anthology* playback.) It's more doom-laden and dirgelike than the *Revolver* version, and partially for that reason, not as propulsive or as ultimately impressive. It's also missing the great stuttering Ringo drum lick and the multitude of tape loops, effects, and mock seagull voices that so distinguish the final mix. Yet it still counts as one of the most exciting, even inspirational cuts to have been excavated as part of the *Anthology* project.

● April 7

Studio Outtakes
Revolver *sessions*
Studio Three, Abbey Road, London

---

*Got to Get You into My Life (take 5)
Got to Get You into My Life (take 5, fragment)
    *appears on Anthology 2

By 1966 it was becoming more common practice for the Beatles to build up a recording via multiple overdubs on a rhythm/backing track, rather than record take after take, as they'd done in earlier days. Yet as several *Revolver* outtakes on *Anthology 2* demonstrated, a song could still change significantly in structure and arrangement between an early take and the final recording. One nice example was take 5 of "Got to Get You into My Life," which at this stage had a gentler, more subdued feel, with a celestial organ and nice John/George backing harmonies that were not present on the official *Revolver* version. Also eliminated was a section where ascending harmonies sing the phrase "I need your love," and Paul's interjection of the words "somehow, someway" at the end of the chorus. It's got a seminaked feel, as if it's still missing some overdubs, and its grace is unfortunately somewhat diminished by the funny-voiced, clowning-around vocals on the fade. The released arrangement, with a brass section, would do much more to bring out the Motown-ish soul of the song. But this early version retains a glowing, more sedate effervescence worth appreciating. In the tradition of blink-and-you'll-miss-them extras, the mix of the 20-second fragment from the end of take 5 used on the *Anthology* video has some more of the loopy vocals heard on the fade.

● April 13

Studio Outtakes
"Paperback Writer" single session
Studio Three, Abbey Road, London

Paperback Writer (take 1)
Paperback Writer (take 2)

Take 1 of "Paperback Writer" lasts less than a minute, even counting the clumsy vocal and instrumental warm-up sounds before the band really starts. Then it takes only 30 seconds for the take to break down, though that's enough to allow you to hear the erupting bass and searing guitar in all their glory, unobscured by vocals, as well as soft, ascending guitar notes behind Ringo's opening drum taps. Although take 2 was the one used on the single, a version has circulated with a different mix, the most notable difference being the absence of the echoing-into-infinity effects on the vocals at the end of the verses. That "dry" vocal mix allows you to hear those light Ringo drum taps during those sections, and the fadeout's a few seconds longer, reaching a point where the vocals flag, one singer sing-speaking the title phrase as though fatigue is setting in, leaving a lone falsetto to carry the lead. The intro's longer, too, though that's mostly presong dead air as the group prepares to launch into the proper take.

● April 20

Studio Outtake
Revolver *sessions*
Studio Two, Abbey Road, London

---

*And Your Bird Can Sing (take 2)
    *appears on Anthology 2

Another in the string of notably different alternate *Revolver* takes unearthed for *Anthology 2*, take 2 of "And Your Bird Can Sing" was in a much lower key than the *Revolver* version. It was also much, *much* more specifically Byrds-influenced in its arrangement, particularly in George Harrison's 12-string guitar work. Had it been released, in fact, it would have rivaled Harrison's "If I Needed Someone" as the most explicitly Byrds-influenced Beatles recording of all. Otherwise, it's not far off the rearrangement recorded six days later, though there are some subtle differences: a greater concentration of John/Paul vocal harmonies, a less polished guitar solo, and a brief bit before the instrumental refrain/fade-out where John and Paul end up on unaccompanied a cappella harmonies on the last word of the last verse. It's a solid arrangement, but the remake is better sung, better played, and not nearly as Byrdsy. It might be overspeculating, but take 2 sounds *so* Byrdsy that one wonders whether the remake might have been specifically motivated by a desire to make the track less obviously derivative, in its arrangement at least, and more distinctly Beatlesque. And if you want to go in for more tenuous speculation, could the song's very title—"And Your *Bird* Can Sing"—itself be an inside joke-pun on the song's Byrds-heavy guitars and vocals?

The vocals in the *Anthology 2* take, incidentally, are almost drenched in giggles, sputtering laughter, whistling, and joking spoken asides. For that reason, Paul cited it as one of his favorite *Anthology* cuts in the *Anthology 2* electronic press kit, in which George Martin added, "You can't help laughing with them, it's so funny." While this book is deliberately not examining the numerous artificially doctored takes that have shown up on Beatles bootlegs, in this case an exception must be made to note that a version has been manufactured that eliminates those giggles and chatter, just by taking the signal out of phase (which isolates all the sound not heard in both stereo channels). Though the *Anthology 2* mix does supply some fun (and stoned-sounding) Beatles humor, this artificial variation might actually be the better one, allowing us to hear the alternate take as a straightforward rock song.

● April 21

Studio Outtake
Revolver *sessions*
Studio Two, Abbey Road, London

---

*Taxman (take 11)
    *appears on Anthology 2

Another highlight from the small batch of officially issued *Revolver* alternate takes, this take of "Taxman" is actually mostly comprised of the same tracks used to construct the *Revolver* version. The chief differences are that John and Paul sing, "Anybody got a bit of money" super-fast on their responsive vocals in the last verse, instead of singing "Mr. Wilson" and "Mr. Heath." The "anybody got a bit of money" phrase (dismissed by composer George Harrison as "a novelty" in a 1996 *Billboard* interview) sounded a little forced in its hyperactivity, and the correct decision was made to replace it with something more natural and spacious—a small touch, but a vital one.

Even if the *Revolver* "Taxman" is superior, this variation is valuable, and not just for the novelty of hearing something unexpected. It's also an illustration of how no detail was too small for the Beatles to re-examine and improve, and perhaps of how much more time they were now afforded to try slightly different arrangements in the studio. In addition, this version uses a pretty short, abrupt ending, instead of using the long fade with excellent rowdy Paul McCartney lead guitar work—another small but crucial adjustment that worked in the track's favor.

● April 22

Studio Outtake

Revolver sessions
Studio Two, Abbey Road, London

Tomorrow Never Knows (take 3 end fragment)

To be technical, the scene on the *Anthology* DVD "Special Features" disc with George Martin and the then-three surviving Beatles listening to a playback of "Tomorrow Never Knows" has a little bit of unreleased music from take 3 (whose mix was completed on April 22). This consists of only a few more wildly scattered notes on the piano at the very end, however, and is obscured by dialogue on the DVD.

● April 28

Studio Outtake

Revolver sessions
Studio Two, Abbey Road, London

*Eleanor Rigby (strings only)
    *appears on Anthology 2

It could be argued that this backing track for "Eleanor Rigby" isn't even a Beatles recording at all, since none of the Beatles actually plays or sings on it. It's merely the instrumental track upon which the Beatles overlaid their vocals, performed by four violinists, two violists, and two cellists, scored and conducted by George Martin. The earliest instrumental backing track from the Beatles' recording sessions to be officially released, it's certainly one of the more peripheral items presented on the *Anthology* series. But it should be mentioned that it was not unknown, even back in the mid-'60s, for admirers of the group to put on just one largely-to-wholly-instrumental channel to enjoy pseudo-isolated, vocal-less Beatles recordings. In *The Rolling Stone Illustrated History of Rock & Roll*, for instance, Greil Marcus remembers how "the dynamics of 'I'm Looking Through You' . . . were so striking that many fans delighted in listening to the stereo version of the tune with the vocal track off."

● April 29

Studio Outtakes

Revolver sessions
Studio Two, Abbey Road, London

*I'm Only Sleeping (rehearsal)
*I'm Only Sleeping (take 1)
    *appears on Anthology 2

"I'm Only Sleeping" was one of the most complicated recordings the Beatles had worked on up to this point, especially in the overdubbing of backward guitar parts. Oddly, these unreleased outtakes were laid down two days *after* the basic rhythm track had been recorded (as take 11) and six days *before* the backward overdubs were done. So obviously the group must have given a good amount of thought and time to various ways they could tinker with the arrangement, to a degree that they'd probably rarely if ever been granted in the past.

The 40-second rehearsal on *Anthology 2* is interesting primarily for its use of vibraphone, a notion that would not survive into the final track. Take 1 is a rather sloppy, choppy, acoustic guitar busk with rudimentary percussion. It's hard to imagine why they would have thought this might have led to or constituted an improvement over what they'd recorded a couple of days before; it sounds more like an initial studio pass at the song (or rehearsal) than a remake. It's no match for the great *Revolver* version, but it's "I'm Only Sleeping" unplugged, and, as such, carries its own measure of appeal. Incidentally, according to Mark Lewisohn's liner notes for *Anthology 2*, we'll almost certainly never get to hear any of the rehearsals recorded on this date, as all of them were recorded over, save that rescued 40-second bit.

● May 9

Studio Outtakes

Revolver sessions
Studio Two, Abbey Road, London

For No One (rehearsal)
For No One (take 1)
For No One (take 2)
For No One (unknown take #1)
For No One (unknown take #2)
For No One (unknown take #3)

For the earliest time in reviewing the Beatles' EMI outtakes (aside maybe from the preponderance of *Help!* soundtrack and production acetate mixes), this is a point where merely sorting out what's what gets to be grueling. First off, these are not even taken from the source tapes; they're monitor mixes, with the accompanying tinny sound quality, which alone lends some unpleasantness to the listening experience. Plus, even among experts who've studied unreleased Beatles recordings for years, there's no agreement as to whether these should be classified as five takes, five takes plus a rehearsal, or one continuous outtake plus three bits and pieces. It's all a little incomprehensible for those not steeped in either underground recordings or studio technology,

Believe it or not, there are entire CDs of "monitor mixes" of Beatles tracks. This particular volume includes numerous such mixes of "For No One" and "Here, There and Everywhere."

particularly when the rehearsal and the first two takes are sometimes grouped together on bootlegs as one "unreleased track," and the excerpts from the following three takes are sometimes grouped together with recordings done at a May 16 session.

Here we're going with the assumption that the first 30 seconds or so before Paul McCartney counts in the first take constitute a "rehearsal," followed by two "takes." Those first 30 seconds have him going over some of the piano parts near the end, rather approximating the style used in Derek & the Dominos' "Layla" a few years later. On take 1, Paul plays piano and Ringo plays drums, with no vocals or additional instruments heard. That breaks down within about a minute, take 2 starting with about 40 seconds of loose warm-up until it really gets going again. Which it does, for about another minute, except at one point everything drops out except for the drums, as the technicians working with the recording were apparently "isolating" tracks from the take as part of their work. There's not much difference between the parts heard on these takes and those heard on the *Revolver* recording, other than the rhythm seeming steadier in the absence of the other instrumentation and vocals that would be overdubbed.

The next three items from this session are fragments from three separate unknown tapes. The first two, again with just Paul's piano and Ringo's drums, last about 40 seconds each. They're again not much different either from each other or from the parts used on the *Revolver* version except that the final rhythm is still yet to be worked out. Following these are two separate, *very* short (about six and two seconds, respectively) excerpts from a third unknown take, interrupted by sounds of the tape being reversed or fast-forwarded. Taken as a whole, these May 9 monitor mixes cough up pretty meager rewards for the home listener, though the

more extensive circulating monitor mixes of "For No One" from the May 16 session (see entry below) are yet more challenging.

● May 16

Studio Outtakes
Revolver sessions
Studio Two, Abbey Road, London

For No One (monitor mix take 10, excerpt #1)
For No One (monitor mix take 10, excerpt #2)
For No One (monitor mix take 10, excerpt #3)

Listening to the approximately four and a half minutes that constitute the three circulating excerpts from monitor mixes of take 10 of "For No One" (with Paul's overdubbed lead vocal) is an even more headache-inducing exercise than weeding through the monitor mixes from the May 9 session. As a translation for the lay listeners out there (the bootlegs certainly don't provide one), what you're hearing is studio technicians playing parts of take 10 back, and isolating certain tracks (or instrumental/vocal parts) of the recording as the tape plays. So the sounds coming out of the speakers may suddenly switch from a vocal-with-drums track to an isolated clavichord track to an unaccompanied vocal track to an isolated piano track. Listening to just one isolated track all the way through the take would at least have some scholarly purpose for audiophiles wanting to hear how each part sounds on its own. But being led like an ox by the nose through this back-and-forth zigzag is an invitation to aural seasickness.

If you're up for the task, you won't find many significant variations from the final arrangement, other than just a few seconds of Paul informally practicing a bit of the vocal line. It's too taxing an endeavor for anyone but Beatles fanatics to endure. But like a cat who wraps itself in the nearest available bedding when the electric blanket is snatched away for cleaning, such fanatics are willing to put up with whatever's available for the time being, even when it's a clearly inferior substitute for the real thing.

● May 19

Studio Outtakes
Revolver sessions
Studio Two, Abbey Road, London

For No One (monitor mix take 14, #1)
For No One (monitor mix take 14, #2)

We're not quite done with the enervating round of "For No One" monitor mix tapes, these two being ones in which parts of the final take (14) are isolated in the course of playback. The first mix doesn't quite make it to the end of the song; the second does, and includes the French horn part overdubbed at this session. This makes it possible to hear bits and pieces of component tracks in isolation from one another. But again, because those component tracks are unpredictably added and subtracted in the course of playback, not much insight or entertainment is provided, other than hearing the final chord sustain for slightly longer than it does on the record.

● June 1

Studio Outtakes
Revolver *sessions*
Studio Two, Abbey Road, London

---

*Yellow Submarine (take 5, remix)
Yellow Submarine (take 5, alternate mono mix)
      *appears on Real Love CD single

Literally dozens of sound effects and spoken sound bites were recorded for use on "Yellow Submarine," which means that there were an almost infinite number of options as to how to mix these into the take (5) used as the bed for the released track. In 1996, a new mix was done for the version used on the *Real Love* CD single, the major difference being a 15-second intro of marching feet in which Ringo recites a few lines about marching from Land O'Groats to John O'Green to see a yellow submarine. Although it might sound like there are additional effects sprinkled into this mix, there aren't. They're just mixed way, way louder, making it into even more of a novelty track than it was in its original incarnation.

Making the rounds in the underground is a mono alternate mix of take 5. This has a different, and quite cacophonous, brass section in the first instrumental break, though some collectors/experts have doubted whether this is an authentic alternate mix or an outfake. If it was authentic, here perhaps the Beatles' burgeoning avant-garde impulses were getting the better of them, and it was wise to use the more conventionally tuneful burst of brass heard on the *Revolver* track. For that matter, it was wise to lop off Ringo's spoken intro, as the song was commercial enough to be used on a single, where such embellishments might have been a distraction to both airplay and sing-alongability.

● June 16

Studio Outtakes
Revolver *sessions*
Studio Two, Abbey Road, London

---

*Here, There and Everywhere (edit of takes 7 and 13)
      *appears on Real Love CD single

This edit is largely comprised of take 7 of "Here, There and Everywhere," with some vocal harmonies (also used on the released *Revolver* version) from take 13 superimposed for the final part of the track. Most of the track, then, has only a guide vocal from Paul, unaccompanied by background harmonies. It might be partly due to the unfamiliarity of hearing his unadorned high vocals on this number, but his singing sounds a trifle shaky and a little prissy here, to be honest. The instrumental backing is much the same as it is on the take ultimately used on *Revolver*.

● June 17

Studio Outtakes
Revolver *sessions*
Studio Two, Abbey Road, London

Here, There and Everywhere (monitor mix #1)
Here, There and Everywhere (monitor mix #2)
Here, There and Everywhere (monitor mix #3)
Here, There and Everywhere (monitor mix #4)

As with the monitor mixes of "For No One" cited slightly earlier, be wary when you see discs purporting to have four "different" versions of "Here, There and Everywhere." For these are also monitor mixes—not even of alternates, but of the take (14) used on *Revolver*. (These mixes are complete in length except for the third one, which is missing about the first 25 seconds.) And like the monitor mixes of "For No One," they vary the mix *as the song is playing,* so that different components are constantly dropping in and out of the track. You do get a few slivers of incidental pretake guitar strums and chatter, but basically you'll be trying to shake that nagging feeling that you're listening to the same thing over and over on a transistor radio, with minimal variations for perking your interest.

● June 24

Live Performance
Circus-Krone-Bau, Munich (early evening show)

I Wanna Be Your Man (fragment)
I'm Down

Since they wrapped up their British tour in late 1965, the Beatles had done just one live show. Even that one—on May 1, 1966, at the *New Musical Express* Pollwinners' Concert (their last British concert, with the tenuous exception of their January 1969 *Let It Be* rooftop performance)—wasn't a full set, lasting a mere five songs. So they were rusty when they set out on the first leg of their 1966 world tour, and indeed probably rustier in a live situation than they'd been since early 1960. There was to be no hiding in out-of-the-way venues while they got their act into shape, however, as the late show from their very first date was filmed for West German television (see entries below and in the film section). Part of the early show was filmed for a German TV newscast, and it's from that we get this 45-second end slice of "I Wanna Be Your Man" and complete version of "I'm Down," both drenched in screams. The sound on these is actually significantly better than it is on most Beatles live recordings taken from newsreels, though that's not saying much. The arrangement of "I'm Down," incidentally, would be different onstage in 1966 than it had been in 1965, with John on rhythm guitar rather than organ.

● June 24

Live Performance
Circus-Krone-Bau, Munich (late evening show)

Rock and Roll Music
She's a Woman (fragment)
Baby's in Black
I Feel Fine
Yesterday
Nowhere Man
I'm Down (incomplete)

The second show of the tour (the first having been done at the same venue earlier in the day) was filmed for West German television, although only a little more than half of the Beatles' set was used in the broadcast. The entire film is also in circulation (see entry in film section), which is the best way to appreciate this subpar Beatles concert. Even listening to the audio alone, however, you can tell the vocal harmonies in particular, and the in-tuneness in general, aren't as sharp as they should be. It's not truly awful—you'd be hard-pressed to find awful Beatles live stuff before an actual audience—but it's pretty sloppy by their own high standards.

As for particular flaws to pick on, "Rock and Roll Music" is slimmed down to just a minute and a half (as it would be for the entire tour); Paul's half of the vocal chores on "Baby's in Black" is terribly strained; the intro guitar riff to "I Feel Fine," never an easy one to play, hits some flat bumps on the road, as does Paul's harmony vocal; and George incorrectly introduces "Yesterday" (the earliest available full-band rendition) as a song from *Beatles for Sale*. Paul doesn't sing that one all that well either, and his vocal performance overall might be the worst to be heard on any Beatles concert tape. While they pull off the three-part harmonies at the start of "Nowhere Man" well, they don't remain glitch-free. And, as he had back on *The Ed Sullivan Show*, Paul mixes up the order of the verses of "I'm Down," but where that performance was otherwise done well, this one is almost a shambles. Paul messes up a lyric on the second verse, coming to a brief chuckling dead stop, and George's blues guitar riffs seem lazily executed. Virtually the entire section after the second instrumental break is missing from the TV program soundtrack, and almost *all* of "She's a Woman" is missing, except a six-second intro that's clumsily grafted onto the beginning of "Baby's in Black."

Looking at the show from the Beatles' point of view, it must have been a comedown of sorts to go back to singing "Rock and Roll Music" just days after finishing an excellent album on which their material had evolved far beyond such rock 'n' roll roots. Some critics have interpreted their failure to perform *Revolver* material on this tour as a sign of laziness. But it should be pointed out that after rising to stardom, the Beatles customarily did not play original songs in concert that had yet to be released, and *Revolver* was still about six weeks away from being issued.

● June 25

Live Performance
Grugahalle, Essen, Germany (afternoon show)

Rock and Roll Music
She's a Woman
If I Needed Someone
Day Tripper
Baby's in Black
I Feel Fine
Yesterday
I Wanna Be Your Man
Nowhere Man
Paperback Writer
I'm Down

The last of the lousy-sounding audience recordings of a complete Beatles concert was not a landmark audio document. As there are much better-sounding complete shows from their Tokyo shows a few days later (and a far better-sounding audience recording of their final concert in San Francisco in August), don't labor under the illusion that this is anything unique or special.

● June 25

Live Performance
Grugahalle, Essen, Germany (evening show)

Paperback Writer (fragment)

A just-for-the-record incomplete version of "Paperback Writer" from the evening show, captured in the background of a radio report of the event.

● June 26

Live Performance
Ernst Merck Halle, Hamburg

Baby's in Black (fragment)
I Wanna Be Your Man (fragment)
Nowhere Man (fragment)
Paperback Writer (two separate fragments)

Poor even by the standards of mid-'60s audience tapes, you can make out the Beatles playing underneath a welter of screams on the first two performances, "I Wanna Be Your Man" being the much longer of the pair. The half-minute-or-less fragments of "Nowhere Man" and "Paperback Writer" remain unheard by this writer. Not all collectors agree upon which songs belong to which of the two performances they did on this date, but does it really matter?

● June 30

Live Performance
Nippon Budokan Hall, Tokyo

*Rock and Roll Music

*She's a Woman

If I Needed Someone

Day Tripper

Baby's in Black

I Feel Fine

Yesterday

I Wanna Be Your Man

Nowhere Man

Paperback Writer

I'm Down

appears on Anthology 2

Two of the five concerts the Beatles gave in Tokyo between June 30 and July 2 were filmed, the soundtracks to these resulting in two of the most frequently circulated unreleased live Beatles concerts. On the one hand, they're among the best-sounding live Beatles shows from a pure technical standpoint. The mix is balanced, clear, and full. Owing to different standards of conduct at such events in Japan (not to mention the 3,000 police on hand to enforce them), there's not nearly as much screaming competing with the music as there is on Beatlemania-era shows elsewhere, though there's certainly some. But the Beatles didn't play too well, here of all places—within the technical situation that afforded the most decent-sounding, professionally recorded, full live concerts that they ever encountered in their career (with the exception of their January 1969 Apple rooftop performance, which wasn't done before a conventional audience). Nor did they come off too well in the films of the two con-

certs, which are also in circulation (see film section) and preferable to the naked audio. Nonetheless, two of the tracks from this day's performance ("Rock and Roll Music" and "She's a Woman") were chosen for *Anthology 2*, possibly because the Japanese TV soundtracks are really the only 1966 live recordings of the group with reasonably release-standard fidelity.

As we are focusing solely on the music for this entry, it must be noted that these performances have often been derided by critics (even those who don't usually collect unreleased music), and in fairness, they do have a point. Out-of-tune vocal harmonies are the biggest problem. But so to some degree are the lead vocals of George (on "If I Needed Someone," the only Harrison composition the Beatles ever performed live) and John, which sometimes have a half-hearted, half-moaned delivery, as if they've even lost the will to paste smiley faces on their dimmed enthusiasm for going through the motions. The biggest offenses include George's careless lead vocal on "If I Needed Someone"; his anemic rubber band–twanging solo on "Day Tripper," which he plays worse than some of the teenage garage bands that were probably butchering that exact riff in basement practices at that very moment; the preposterously mistimed vocal harmonies of "I Feel Fine"; and John's dolefully woeful backup harmonies on "Paperback Writer." It couldn't wholly be put down to boredom with trotting out old material, as "Paperback Writer" had just come out, and "Day Tripper" and "If I Needed Someone" weren't all that old.

And yet . . . even if it's playing devil's advocate to some degree, this show (and the one from July 1, discussed in the following entry) really

Though prominently featuring a Japanese show from the Beatles' 1966 tour, this CD not only mixed it with material from a 1964 Ed Sullivan Show program, but also used a circa-early '64 picture of the group.

isn't *that* bad, and is not without its enjoyable aspects. No other recordings, perhaps, demonstrate so well that Paul McCartney was clearly the most enthusiastic performer in the band and the most determined to try his best to please an audience even when the other three were not wholly along for the ride. He sings his leads with real fire and freshness, and if only from a historical viewpoint it's great to hear "Yesterday" done with a full rock arrangement, rather than the acoustic guitar-with-strings one heard on the studio recording. True, the Beatles seem to handle it with uncertainty, giving it a moderate rock tempo that sits ill at ease in such a sentimental ballad, but at least it's a definite contrast to the very familiar released track. Speaking of different arrangements, George summons a weird, almost pseudo-Eastern wailing, winding sound from his guitar on "I Wanna Be Your Man"—not really that good an effect, but again, at least different from the same old versions we're used to hearing. These are also among the few live versions of *Rubber Soul*–era material ("If I Needed Someone," "Day Tripper," and "Nowhere Man") anywhere, and if they're not that well-executed, well, at least they'd be performed somewhat better on the following day.

● July 1

Live Performance
Nippon Budokan Hall, Tokyo

Rock and Roll Music
She's a Woman
If I Needed Someone
Day Tripper
Baby's in Black
I Feel Fine
Yesterday
I Wanna Be Your Man
Nowhere Man
Paperback Writer
I'm Down

The second of the Tokyo shows to be filmed for Japanese television went better than the first, in part because the problems of poorly placed and secured microphone stands that had plagued the initial concert had been rectified. It still wasn't a great show, lowlighted by "If I Needed Someone," where George sings the end of the first bridge in a half-muted, half-serious tone, almost as if he can't be bothered to finish it. "Nowhere Man" is almost a good performance, except that John gets lost in the lyrics, ending up singing something like "Isn't he a bit like me at all?" On the other hand, "Day Tripper" has a real guitar solo, rather than an indifferent afterthought of one—even if John isn't up for doing the falsetto vocals of the last chorus. Ringo puts more energy into his singing for "I Wanna Be Your Man," inserting a couple of encouraging shouted asides to his band mates, though he muffs the lyrics of the final verse, doing the same line four times. "Paperback Writer" is also done with more zest, almost as if the Beatles needed that extra day to get over jet lag, though Paul's vocal seems seriously undermiked.

Although many of the criticisms about the Tokyo concerts that have made the rounds over the years are justified, they've been blown out of proportion by some as evidence that the Beatles were an inferior live band. It was really only on this 1966 tour that the group's enthusiasm was audibly (and visibly) flagging (with the exception of Paul, who seems about as enthusiastic as ever), and the performances sometimes verged on the truly ragged. These are the shows that are more widely circulated than almost any other unreleased live Beatles recordings, however. That may be why they're sometimes incorrectly assumed to be characteristic of their live performances by listeners who haven't heard many or any other such documents of the group onstage.

Incidentally, it's sometimes been written that John insensitively mocked his fans in Tokyo by doing some stage announcing in ridiculously exaggerated fake Japanese. The evidence is, however, that it wasn't a routine he specifically cooked up for Japanese audiences. He can be heard doing much the same thing at the Beatles' evening concert in Houston on August 19, 1965 (see corresponding entry), where he improvises the following ditty as George changes guitars prior to "A Hard Day's Night": "Sa-ya-kan-ha-yamoto . . ."

● August 14

Live Performance
Cleveland Stadium, Cleveland

I Feel Fine (fragment)

This concert was interrupted for a half hour when several thousand fans rushed onto the baseball field where the Beatles were playing. An on-the-scene report by a DJ covering the tour includes this 42-second fragment, heard faintly in the background, as usual on such recordings, of "I Feel Fine," the number they played when the show resumed.

● August 18

Live Performance
Suffolk Downs Racetrack, Boston

She's a Woman
Long Tall Sally

The first 20 seconds of "She's a Woman" are heard way in the background as a reporter for local radio station WBZ-AM gives the play-by-play on a spectator getting intercepted by the police while rushing the stage.

● August 19

Live Performance
Mid-South Coliseum, Memphis (afternoon show)

I Wanna Be Your Man (incomplete)
Paperback Writer (incomplete)
Long Tall Sally

A terrible-quality report from their first Memphis show, in which you can't properly make out either the background Beatles music or what the woman doing the commentary is saying. This isn't the infamous concert at which a cherry bomb explosion gave rise to momentary fears that someone had taken a shot at the group; that was the evening show (see the August 19 entry in this chapter under "1966 Noncirculating Recordings, Known and Rumored").

● August 23

Live Performance
Shea Stadium, New York City

She's a Woman (fragment)
If I Needed Someone (fragment)
I Feel Fine (fragment)
Yesterday (fragment)
Paperback Writer (fragment)

Five half-minute fragments of tunes are heard in the background of this fairly histrionic, on-the-scene radio report of their last Shea Sta-

dium concert—mercifully, the last such audio verité recording of the Beatlemania era in which the music's incidental to the event.

● August 29

Live Performance
Candlestick Park, San Francisco

Rock and Roll Music
She's a Woman
If I Needed Someone
Day Tripper
Baby's in Black
I Feel Fine
Yesterday
I Wanna Be Your Man
Nowhere Man
Paperback Writer
Long Tall Sally (fragment)

The Beatles' final official performance, Candlestick Park, San Francisco,
August 29, 1966. It was taped by their publicist, Tony Barrow.

THE BEATLES

SHEA! / CANDLESTICK PARK

THE BEATLES

SHEA! / CANDLESTICK PARK

Two of the Beatles' most famous concerts (Shea
Stadium in 1965 and Candlestick Park in 1966)
were combined onto this CD.

The only recording of a (virtually) full-length set from the Beatles' 1966 North American tour turned out to be a quite historic one, as the performance ended up being the last true concert the group ever played. While it wasn't announced as such at the time, indications are that the Beatles themselves knew that it would be the last onstage hurrah. For one thing, Paul McCartney specifically asked press officer Tony Barrow to record it on the tape player that Barrow carried with him on tour. None of the Beatles had requested such a souvenir tape before, and probably Paul did so at least partly because he knew, or had a strong hunch, that it would be the final Beatles show of all.

It was hardly the most sophisticated technology available for such a momentous occasion, but at least the person operating the equipment would be conscientious about trying to do the best job he could under the circumstances. "Although I didn't fancy my chances of making a brilliant recording of the concert, one thing in my favor was the great distance between the stage and the stands at this particular venue," explained Barrow in *John, Paul, George, Ringo & Me: The Real Beatles Story.* "Because of this, I guessed I might be able to capture sound from the stage without picking up too much of the nonstop screams and shouts of the fans coming from the stands. The fact that it was an open-air gig also helped. In an enclosed auditorium it would have been impossible to pick up the sound of the music without picking up too much crowd noise."

The resulting fidelity was rough, and certainly a few steps below the professionally recorded Tokyo concerts, for instance. Yet it's listenable, the voices and instruments all getting captured on the tape for the most part, even if the sound's brittle and tinny, especially on the high end. And the Beatles' performance does sound significantly better than it had in Tokyo, for a couple of likely reasons. Even if their heart wasn't in touring anymore, it *was* a couple of months since the June Munich shows, and they'd had some time to get the rust out of their systems. Plus, they really do sound as if they're putting more oomph into this particular performance—Paul more than anyone, of course—with the likely knowledge that it could be their last. The vocal harmonies are still problematic, though that might be in part due to the unavoidable sonic difficulties of hearing one another when playing a baseball stadium in front of tens of thousands of screamers. Too, George's guitar sometimes has a strange, unappealing, dour-sour tone, most audibly on sections of "Rock and Roll Music" (when he throws in a responsive lick near the end of the first verse), "She's a Woman," "Day Tripper" (whose growling riffs never came across live nearly as well as they did on the record), and "I Wanna Be Your Man."

With the possible knowledge that it was no longer necessary to keep up appearances, the boys' onstage patter varies from the usual routine more than it does on any other live Beatlemania-era recording. Some spontaneity seeps into the music as well, especially "Baby's in Black," with some whoops and shouts *from* the stage, not directed *to* the stage. The announcements are refreshingly loose and off-the-cuff in an almost carefree manner, as if the foursome are making some jokes for themselves rather than sticking to scripted ones for the benefit of their paying audience. John, before "Day Tripper": "We'd like to carry on now . . . carry on together . . . and we're all one together and all for one . . . with another number that used to be a single record back in, a long time ago . . . and this is about a naughty lady called Day Tripper!" George, before "I Feel Fine": "We'd like to carry on with something that's very old indeed. And this one was recorded about 1959." John,

before "Nowhere Man": "We'd like to do another song now from our BBC [sic] album, and this one's called [adopts silly jocular voice]: 'He's a real nowhere man, sitting in his nowhere land, oh yeah!'" Paul, before "Paperback Writer," using the "we'd like to carry on" bit in concert for the umpteenth and final time: "We'd like to carry on, I think. Not really sure yet. I'd like to carry on, certainly. Definitely. Well, should we just watch this for a bit?"

Paul also took a risqué swipe that likely sailed over the heads of almost all of the teenagers in the audience: "We'd like to do the next number now, which is a special request from all the backroom boys on this tour . . . 'I Wanna Be Your Man.'" Unfortunately the backroom boy who might have most appreciated that joke, Brian Epstein, was not in the audience on this night. He was in Los Angeles, dealing with the theft of his briefcase—containing a large sum of money, sensitive personal papers, and barbiturates—by an ex-boyfriend who was trying to blackmail him, threatening to make its contents public unless Epstein paid him off.

It's Paul, of course, who handles the final stage announcement as always, though this is a strange one: "Thank you very much, everybody. Everybody, wonderful. Frisco. Butchered. [A sly reference to the banned "butcher cover" of *Yesterday . . . and Today*?!] We'd like to say

The poster for the Beatles' final official concert.

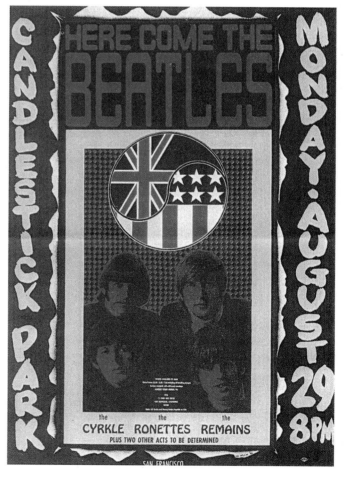

The End Of Touring

After taking their bows at Candlestick Park, the Beatles never gave another concert in the standard sense of the term. Yes, there was that rooftop concert in January 1969 for *Let It Be;* television presentations of "All You Need Is Love" and "Hey Jude," which actually combined live performances with prerecorded tracks; and many "live" tracks recorded without overdubbing in a film or recording studio during the endless January 1969 *Get Back* sessions. But wholly live performances that members of the public could attend were finished, as was the plentiful stream of illicit concert recordings that had been made of the band between 1962 and 1966.

The reason most often trotted out for the Beatles' decision to stop touring was a dissatisfaction with the grind of playing set programs before screaming audiences with inadequate equipment, all of which made it hard for either the crowd or the band to hear the music properly. Close behind were the unusual stresses the band had endured during their 1966 tours in particular, especially in the Philippines, where a perceived snub of an invitation to visit the royal family had endangered their actual physical safety. John Lennon's controversial, if flippant, remark to a journalist that the Beatles were bigger than Jesus Christ had also generated hostility and threats throughout the United States, though no violence was actually committed against the band.

There was also the overall feeling that touring under these conditions was stunting their growth as musicians. Though it's tempting to view this as something the Beatles felt only in hindsight many years later, in fact they had clearly expressed such sentiments at least a year before they stopped performing live. In a July 30, 1965, interview with Dibbs Mather for the BBC Transcription Service, George Harrison had observed, "We used to improve at a much faster rate before we ever made records . . . because we used to get so fed up playing the same things so we'd always learn new songs all the time." Added John Lennon in the same interview, "You'd have to improvise every time. Even with the old songs you'd do 'em different anytime but when you make records you've got to reproduce, as near as you can, the record—so you don't really get a chance to improvise or improve your style."

Even Paul McCartney, apparently the only Beatle with true second thoughts about coming off the road, told *TeenSet*'s Judith Sims on the flight to Los Angeles after the San Francisco show that "we're not very good performers, actually. We're better in a recording studio where we can control things and work on it until it's right. With performing there's so much that can go wrong, and you can't go back over it and do it right." A few months later, interviewed on film on December 28, 1966, outside Abbey Road shortly after the *Sgt. Pepper* sessions were under way, Paul was yet more negative, saying it wouldn't worry him if the group didn't tour again, as "it's gone downhill, performance, 'cause we can't develop when no one can hear us." In the same footage, Ringo added, "We can't do a tour like we've been doing all these years because our music's progressed, we've used more instruments. It'd be soft us going onstage, the four of us, and trying to do the records we've made with orchestras and, you know, bands and things. So if we went onstage, we'd have to have a whole lineup of men behind us."

Questions that have seldom been analyzed by the Beatles and others, however, are: Why *didn't* they put more of an effort into changing the conditions of their live performances so that the music would sound better? And how *would* it have sounded if they had made that effort? Even at the time, the group was sometimes criticized for not featuring more recent material in their sets—one condition they *did* have control over, and which presumably could have made the gigs more interesting for both themselves and their audiences. In his *San Francisco Examiner* review of the Candlestick Park concert, for instance, Phil Elwood lamented the absence of "Yellow Submarine" (then on its way to No. 2 in the US charts), adding, "As a matter of fact, nothing from the new, delightful album was on the show, probably because special sound effects and backgrounds are impossible in ballpark appearances."

The difficulty of recreating their increasingly complex studio recordings onstage is often cited as one reason for their lack of interest in continuing to play live. It is true that *Revolver* tracks like "Eleanor Rigby," "Tomorrow Never Knows," "Love You To" (with its prominent sitar), and "I'm Only Sleeping" (with its backward guitar) would have been impossible to present onstage in arrangements duplicating the sound of the record. So, for that matter, would have the deceptively simple "Yellow Submarine," which was, in fact, crowded with overdubbed sound effects. Yet other, relatively straightforward guitar-oriented rockers on *Revolver* such as "And Your Bird Can Sing," "Dr. Robert," and "Taxman" would not have presented any such obstacles, and would have worked well in a live setting. Ditto for some *Rubber Soul* goodies that were never played live, such as "Drive My Car" and "Think for Yourself." And just because some of their recorded tracks used instruments or effects the Beatles themselves couldn't bring on tour, that didn't necessarily mean they couldn't work up different arrangements for live versions, as they did for "Yesterday" (though admittedly that song wasn't wholly convincing when rearranged for guitars, bass, and drums on their 1966 tour).

The truth seems to be that the Beatles just did not want to pour a great deal of energy into rehearsing and reshaping their live set, though the extenuating circumstances of the enormous pressure they were under on their world tours makes that understandable, to some degree. A big part of this was certainly the difficulty they had even making themselves heard, and frustration that no one might be able to hear the music properly even if they did go to such lengths. It wasn't until the end of the 1960s and early '70s that acts such as the Rolling Stones, the Who, Jimi Hendrix, Pink Floyd, and the Grateful Dead truly began to develop the massive, technologically advanced sound systems necessary to project rock music well to large arena and festival crowds. It wasn't until that time, too, that fold-back speakers that could enable musicians to hear themselves under these circumstances became more common.

All of those acts, however, leaned more on the sheer volume of their music than the Beatles did to get their music across. And none of them contended with the frenzied screaming that the Beatles did, both because none of them were as popular as the Beatles, and because the rock audience itself had matured by the end of the '60s—as the Rolling Stones, who had dealt with plenty of screaming themselves on their mid-'60s tours, found out when they toured the US in late 1969 after a three-year absence. It's tempting to blame the Beatles, if only slightly, for underestimating the intelligence of their audience and its capacity to evolve in such a fashion. But it has to be remembered that no one was anticipating how much the demographic for rock would change over the next three or four years, with not only the age of the average rock fan rising from the mid-teens to the late teens and early twenties, but also the tastes of the average Beatles fan becoming far more intellectual and sophisticated.

If anyone *did* have the financial resources and creative vision to surmount the challenge of presenting rock music to stadium audiences with excellent sound, of course, it was the Beatles themselves. Had they decided to spend an enormous amount of time and money reconfiguring their sound and PA systems from top to bottom, selecting and soundchecking smaller arena-sized venues that could offer superior acoustics, upgrading their security so that they weren't in fear for their lives, augmenting their lineup with other instrumentalists and sound effects, and tailoring their sets to older and more adventurous audiences, one suspects they could have done so successfully. But they didn't. Instead, they poured those resources primarily into spending more time and money on *studio* music than anyone ever had. And considering the astonishing quality and quantity of the music the Beatles made over the next three years, that was indisputably the right decision.

---

that it's been wonderful being here in this wonderful sea air." (Candlestick Park, right on the San Francisco Bay, is notorious for its whipping winds, Paul in fact having noted, "It's a bit chilly" after "Yesterday.") Resumes McCartney, "Sorry about the weather. And we'd like to ask you to join in and, uh, clap . . . sing . . . talk. In fact, go on, do anything. Anyway, the song is—good night."

And with that, Paul launches into what is almost certainly the song he most enjoyed singing with the Beatles, "Long Tall Sally." Contrary to some reports, this wasn't done as the finale on this tour just this once to mark the special occasion. Although "I'm Down" had been the usual closing number of Beatles concerts over their final year of touring, "Long Tall Sally" was occasionally substituted during the 1966 North American jaunt. It starts off like it's going to be the mother of all monster versions, Paul summoning a positively superhuman bellow of an intro he'd done hundreds of times, going straightaway to upper register notes he didn't customarily use right off the bat. And then, right after he finishes the second verse and goes into his scream to cue the instrumental break—the music abruptly cuts off. Cassettes were only 30 minutes per side in those days and Tony Barrow's tape had run out, missing not only the last part of "Long Tall Sally," but the opening guitar line of "In My Life," played by John as a punctuation mark at the very end of the show. Maybe it was all that between-song improv, but this particular Beatles concert did not conform to the legend of lasting only 20–25 minutes, and one half hour of tape wasn't quite enough to capture all of it.

As a footnote, according to Barrow, just two copies of the tape were made—the original, given to Paul, and a copy Barrow made for himself, kept locked in his office desk. Yet eventually bootlegs of the show appeared, obviously made from one of these copies. So which one of you wise guys reading this was responsible?

● Circa September 19– November 6

Private Tapes

Santa Isabel, Spain

Untitled (instrumental warm-up)
Strawberry Fields Forever (six versions)
Strawberry Fields Forever (demo fragment)

In September 1966, one door had slammed closed on the first half of the Beatles' recording career—with the end of touring and the approximate midpoint of their stint as an EMI act—and another had been opened. The very first recording known to have been made by any of the Beatles after their final concert could hardly have more decisively reflected the change in mood. Not only was the placid tone of these John Lennon acoustic composing tapes of "Strawberry Fields Forever" worlds removed from the ear-shattering madness of their summer tours, but the song's structure and subject pointed toward directions more psychedelic than anything the Beatles had previously done. Too, it would be the very first beneficiary of the group's new determination to spend unprecedented numbers of hours on their songs in the studio, evolving into something wholly different than these relatively primitive home recordings after numerous arduous recording sessions. But for all the effort and expense that followed, "Strawberry Fields Forever" started as a relatively simple, unfinished folky tune. (As an interesting trivial note, John might have had some of the melody in his head for years before these recordings. In the documentary *The Beatles: The First U.S. Visit,* Lennon can be seen playing a riff on a melodica in a New York hotel room in February 1964 that resembles the chord progression heard in the verses of the "Strawberry Fields Forever" single.)

This initial group of recordings was done by John solo on a nylon-stringed acoustic classical guitar, and the fidelity is so low that it's hard to make some of the words out. It's possible to date them as having taken place between September 19 and November 6, as it's known John did these in his hotel room in Santa Isabel, Spain, his base while filming his role in Richard Lester's *How I Won the War.* The brief, 24-second instrumental warm-up bears no resemblance to "Strawberry Fields Forever" and more to the riffs of "Paperback Writer" being played on classical guitar. And the first version, lasting only about 45 seconds, has no more than a seed of the song, John twice singing lines that approximate the second verse, the chords of the melody strummed dolefully as accompaniment. Yet most of those lines are very close to their final form; the one about tuning in exactly so, though there's nothing about his tree yet. Although most of the tune is there, the end of the verse winds up rather blandly and diffidently. At this point, it's something of a melancholy dirge.

But John kept working at it and adding to it, and over the course of the next few versions we can hear the song starting to take familiar shape. In the second one, lasting a little over a minute, he's still having trouble with the first line of this verse, humming it at one point as if he's resigned to using it as a dummy line for the time being. The

John started writing "Strawberry Fields Forever" while he was filming his part in Spain, as heard on several early acoustic composing tapes he recorded at the time that were included on this CD.

home recordings upon his return to England as he prepared to take the song into the studio.

● Circa November 8–23

Private Tapes
Kenwood, Weybridge

Strawberry Fields Forever (guitar overdub #1)
Strawberry Fields Forever (guitar overdub #2)
Strawberry Fields Forever (demo playback #1)
Strawberry Fields Forever (vocal overdub #1)
Strawberry Fields Forever (demo playback #2)
*Strawberry Fields Forever (eight demos)
Strawberry Fields Forever (Mellotron overdubs)
Strawberry Fields Forever (backward talking and Mellotron flutes)

*an edit comprising the sixth of these versions, and fragments of the fourth
and seventh, appears on Anthology 2*

---

third time around, he has the keeper introductory line for the verse, "No one I think is in my tree," and though it's still winding up with a too-hurried, relatively melodically undeveloped "I mean it's not too bad," he ends with an instrumental chord sequence almost exactly replicating the tune used on what would become the song's chorus. The fourth version puts words to that chorus, though these are uncertainly sung and still a ways from their final form.

The fifth try has an echo, suggesting John might have been doing it in a stairwell or bathroom, and after the first verse he stops, interrupted by a thumping noise. Starting again almost immediately, after repeating that verse he introduces a new line that made the final cut, "Always no sometimes think it's me." In the absence of any more new lines, he just repeats the other lyrics he's worked out to finish the next verse. The words to the chorus, however, are getting closer to completion, although at this point there's nothing to get "mad" about rather than "hung" about. The last line of the chorus, too, isn't there, John singing, "Strawberry Fields and nothing" as if he might mean to fill in the words later, the melody at this point taking a brief sentimental turn that was eventually discarded. There's also a snatch, lasting just a dozen seconds, of John singing the line about tuning in a couple of times, in a slightly higher key than the other versions; some collectors believe this might be from an earlier taping session that was largely erased by the attempts that comprise most of these circulating made-in-Spain recordings.

As fragmentary and lo-fi as these Spain tapes are, clearly John had a gem in the making, and as with many early demos—no matter who the artist—there's an attractive embryonic fragility quite different from the mood of the released studio track. As it clearly needed more work, however, John would undertake a yet more extensive series of

Working in his home, "Kenwood" in suburban London, in the two weeks or so before the first EMI recording session for "Strawberry Fields Forever," John made this somewhat elaborate series of refinements and tinkerings to his new song. John was never the most sophisticated gearhead, and the two guitar overdubs were relics of his crude approach to home multitracking, in which he'd play back a tape over speakers, play along with the tape, and record the whole thing on a second tape machine. On the first, lasting about a minute, we hear an instrumental sequence of electric guitars running through the song's melody issuing from speakers—the home recording equivalent of a "control room monitor mix," if you will—as, live, John overdubs almost random chords and licks. It sounds like he doesn't quite know what he's doing, frankly. Nor does he sound better on a second, similar attempt, this one lasting for two minutes. John's approximating some of the guitar parts used on the studio recording, but the evidence is that he needs the two Georges, Martin and Harrison, to properly execute those ideas.

Working in a similar fashion, John played back a "Strawberry Fields" guitar-vocal demo—not one of the ones he'd done in Spain, but a different one, in a higher key—and sang along with the playback live, as a rudimentary way of double-tracking his vocal. As a pure listening experience, to be honest, it would be better to hear the unadorned demo (which you do, for brief bursts and through a playback speaker, on the two separate unaccompanied demo playbacks). Still, it proves that the song structure and lyrics are virtually in their final form, and gives some insight into the way John was working as he became more acquainted, in his own fashion, with the new avenues opened up by overdubbing and multitracking.

Finally, we then get to the most musically edifying of the prestudio "Strawberry Fields" demos-of-sorts: a series of takes, eight in all, in which John sings along with his electric guitar as sole accompaniment. The fidelity is clear and the song has been almost fully written, so basically you have nearly pristine-sounding solo performances of the composition that can be enjoyed simply as music, and not primarily/solely for their historical significance. John's not known as the most technique-obsessed instrumentalist, but the primary purpose of this sequence seems to have been to work out the most suitable approach for the guitar in the arrangement. The first version breaks down after about half a minute, and on the second, John alters his playing to an arpeggiated style more in line with the studio recording. This too breaks down quickly, John chuckling that "it just sorta goes too quiet," also making one wonder who else might be in the room with him—Paul, perhaps? He reverts to a more conventional style for versions three and four, strumming with a rhythm rather close to what McCartney had used on "Yesterday," though this too breaks down as John mutters something like "I cannot do it." Then he tries a more lilting, fingerpicked style for a couple more partial run-throughs, and although the effect is more pleasing than the strumming, he's not satisfied with this angle either, feeling like "it doesn't work like that."

Then follows—on the seventh version—a more or less complete performance, on which John reverts to a more basic strummed technique, not all that far removed from the tapes he'd made in Spain. Assuming this is the complete version of the song as it stood at that point, however, it's interesting to hear that there are still some lyrics that would be changed and added before the single was recorded.

It starts with the second verse, not the chorus (the section used as the first verse on the final recording is still missing altogether); the chorus is not inserted between what would be used as the second and third verses on the record; the order of some words on the second line of the third verse is transposed; and in one chorus John wants to take us "back" not "down" to Strawberry Fields. Components of the fourth, sixth, and seventh versions on this home tape—John's spoken comments at the end of "take 4," a complete "take 6," and a considerably edited "take 7"—would be edited together for the "Strawberry Fields Forever" "demo sequence" that appears on *Anthology 2*. But it's necessary to hear the whole lot to appreciate just how involved a process this series of home recordings was.

There's yet an eighth version, about two minutes long, similar in nature (though not quite as well-recorded) to the seventh, in which John gets the order of that line in the third verse right. He also strums wordlessly at one point, as if in silent knowledge that he really needs some new words to fill in the lyric before the song can be considered complete. There's also a four-minute tape of John, again using his primitive multitracking method, overdubbing Mellotron effects to a playback of his composing tape (which now has double-tracked vocals). On a surface level, this is almost as hard to listen to as his earlier attempts to overdub guitar parts onto a playback. The Mellotron effects enter irregularly and occasionally cacophonously, the fidelity of the playback track is mediocre, and John himself interjects some sardonic comments over the earlier segments: "I must say, I don't think much of that. . . . Please, have a bit of respect, will you? . . . Shut up, I'll smash your face in." It's more significant than those earlier flubbed guitar overdubs, however, because the Mellotron would end up being a significant (and innovative) part of the studio recording. John became one of the first musicians in Britain to purchase the instrument just before he left for the Beatles' North American tour in August 1965, and while Paul remembered composing on John's Mellotron while working on "In My Life," these recordings likely represent some of Lennon's first efforts to apply it constructively. Here John adds ghostly effects produced by the Mellotron's "wine glasses" and "pipe organ" settings that do much to point the way to the far more psychedelic ambience of the final production. The higher tones sprinkle astral fairy dust on the verses, while the pipe organ adds a sense of more earthly gravity, particularly when it enters with a *Phantom of the Opera*–like vengeance right after the chorus starts.

Also grouped together with these "Strawberry Fields Forever" private tapes on bootlegs is a 38-second fragment of John uttering backward gibberish, interrupted by eight seconds of swirling Mellotron emulations of a flute sound, almost as though it were a tape loop of flutes. While this might not have been recorded with "Strawberry Fields Forever" specifically in mind, these are the exact same effects (from the Mellotron's "Cha Cha: Swinging Flutes" setting) that ended up on the eerie instrumental fadeout of the single, qualifying this fragment (if only peripherally) as part of this most interesting batch of "Strawberry Fields" home recordings. As much work as John had put into the song in Spain and at Kenwood, however, there would be much more work (and accompanying unissued tapes) to follow when he recorded it with the Beatles, starting in late November.

● November 24

Studio Outtake

"Strawberry Fields Forever" single session
Studio Two, Abbey Road, London

---

*Strawberry Fields Forever (take 1)
  *appears on Anthology 2 in remix that removes backing
    vocals and second track of John Lennon's vocals

The first attempt by the Beatles to record "Strawberry Fields Forever" was quite good, though markedly lighter, in a vaguely folk-rockish fashion, than the one that would emerge after a further month's work. The Mellotron was a strong element in the arrangement from the start, though played by Paul McCartney rather than John Lennon. The version that's circulated on bootleg has a few seconds of Paul making spooky sounds on the instrument, as if he's testing its settings, both before and after "Take 1" is announced. Then the Mellotron, on the "flute" setting, supplies the sole accompaniment to John's vocal on the first verse before the more standard rock instruments of guitars, drum, and bass join in. There's no Mellotron intro, and the track is still not beginning with the chorus, as it does on the familiar classic recording. It's also in a higher key than the final version, and much shorter, the extended instrumental tag consisting of quite lovely, haunting Mellotron riffs, arpeggiated guitar weaving sympathetically in the background. Other exceptionally pretty features of this first take are George Harrison's gliding, stinging guitar slides and, on the final verse, helium-high backing harmonies.

More than almost any Beatles outtake, had it been issued in this form, it would have been fine, and it has a certain delicate sensitivity, gentleness, and sweet sadness that's not present on the official track. "It was the way I heard it originally, when John sang it to me," remembered George Martin in the 1992 television documentary *The Making of Sgt. Pepper*. "It was a sweet, gentle, simple song. I think that version is very charming. A very simple version of a very simple song." But it wouldn't have been as killer as the single that was eventually issued, which—with added orchestration, effects, and restructuring—carried far more ambiguity, depth, and almost frightening power.

Although take 1 of "Strawberry Fields Forever" (minus the pre-song Mellotron tones) is on *Anthology 2*, it's a remixed version that, for unexplained reasons, removes the backing vocal harmonies. It also takes off the second track of the double-tracked vocals heard at the end of the first chorus and throughout the third verse. So here we have an instance where a project (the *Anthology* CD series) meant, at least in part, to counteract unauthorized product ends up having exactly the opposite effect. For the mix with these overdubs can still be heard only on bootlegs, which some listeners might not even have thought to hunt down had not the *Anthology 2* mix whetted their curiosity. Further muddying the line between which mix should be considered "correct," the bootlegged mix sometimes runs at a slower speed (in the lower key in which it was originally performed) than the *Anthology 2* one, though the tape was, in fact, deliberately sped up at the time it was recorded in 1966. Finally, for the curious, George Martin is seen and heard isolating a fragment of the slide guitar/vocal track in the television documentary *The Making of Sgt. Pepper*.

● November 25

Pantomime—Everywhere It's Christmas

Dick James House, London

Cut in the basement studio under the office of their publisher, Dick James Music, the Beatles' 1966 Christmas disc was the first that they approached as a creative studio recording, rather than just a semiscripted audio greeting card. Instead, it was constructed fairly tightly as a radio play of sorts, mixing music, dialogue, sound effects, and a (very) loose narrative. In this manner, it reflected, if only indirectly, the group's own increased immersion in studio recording and psychedelic songwriting. There were even titles for each of the ten parts of this six-minute, 40-second skit of sorts: "Everywhere It's Christmas," "Orowayna (Corsican Choirs and Small Choir)," "A Rare Cheese (Two Elderly Scotsmen)," "The Feast," "The Loyal Toast," "Podgy the Bear and Jasper," "Felpin Mansions: Part One (Count Balder and Butler)," "Felpin Mansions: Part Two (the Count and the Pianist)," "Please Don't Bring Your Banjo Back," and "Everywhere It's Christmas (Reprise)."

Pantomime—Everywhere It's Christmas isn't incredibly funny or musical, but it's an admirable, carefully edited slice of mildly surrealistic Beatle seasonal whimsy. The "music" is mostly limited to the peppy pub sing-along-style songs "Everywhere It's Christmas" and "Please Don't Bring Your Banjo Back," and the choral vocal bits on "Orowayna (Corsican Choirs and Small Choir)," Paul playing piano throughout. The narrative, giving each Beatle a chance to speak in normal storytelling or put-on funny voices, shifts without rhyme or reason between a choir in Corsica, two elderly Scotsmen in the Swiss Alps, a medieval feast, the ship H.M.S. *Tremendous*, the fairy tale of "Podgy the Bear and Jasper," and a posh mansion. It was obviously modeled on sketches that had appeared on the British "The Goon Show" radio series, but that was appropriate enough, considering that George Martin had done a lot of production work for "Goon Show" star Peter Sellers. Martin produced this 1966 Beatles Christmas disc too, though the actual editing was done on December 2 at Abbey Road by engineer Geoff Emerick and overseen by Beatles press officer Tony Barrow.

The Beatles' drastically increased creative input into the Christmas disc even extended to the sleeve, a florid psychedelic-influenced color illustration designed by Paul McCartney himself. Also heard on the disc, incidentally, is Beatles co–road manager Mal Evans, who utters, "Yes, everywhere it's Christmas" right before the reprise of the title song.

● November 28

Studio Outtakes

"Strawberry Fields Forever" single session
Studio Two, Abbey Road, London

Strawberry Fields Forever (takes 2–4)

Having thought about it over the weekend, the Beatles decided they wanted to remake "Strawberry Fields Forever," putting it in a lower key and moving the chorus to the front. Right from the start of take 2 (at least after some drum beats and guitar noises), it's recognizable as the arrangement used for the nonorchestrated sections of the final studio track. The Mellotron flute introduction is there, as are the smoothly flowing arpeggiated guitar and Ringo Starr's highly underrated, powerful, varied, and thundering drum part. There aren't any vocals, and the Mellotron and guitar aren't as honed as they would be in the final version, particularly when the guitar hits some wrong notes at the end of the second chorus. There's no extended fadeout, either, the instrumental tag abruptly cutting off. But basically, it's quite similar to the bulk of what became the bedrock of "Strawberry Fields Forever," and it's amazing that the group could so substantially restructure an already excellent song for the better so quickly.

Take 3 gets only about ten seconds into the Mellotron intro and cuts off, John Lennon heard remarking, "Too loud." Take 4 is complete with double-tracked John Lennon vocal, and makes some subtle, important alterations, George Harrison putting on some swooping guitar slides and interesting telegraphlike guitar blips. It still sounds a little hollow, particularly in the transitions among verses, and there's no chorus between the first and second verses. Also a better, more decisive fade has yet to be worked out—something the Beatles would address on their next session.

● November 29

Studio Outtakes

"Strawberry Fields Forever" single session
Studio Two, Abbey Road, London

Strawberry Fields Forever (takes 5–6)
*Strawberry Fields Forever (take 7)
    *appears on Anthology 2

The Beatles were now basically refining the new arrangement they'd given "Strawberry Fields Forever," though take 5 is nothing more than some practice riffs and a false start on the Mellotron intro. Take 6 was the one they wanted, however, with the key addition of a slowed-down John Lennon vocal that added a druggy, sleepy effect. The fadeout was longer, too, though at this point it was still melodically different from the one eventually concocted for the single, even briefly moving into a jazzy bit at the very end that presumably would have been chopped off had this take been the complete basis of the final track. Which was still the apparent plan at this point, as take 7 was merely a reduction of take 6 onto three tracks, leaving room for John to thicken his vocal, as well as for bass and piano overdubs. An especially vital, almost subliminal touch was the addition of a single strummed guitar chord at the end of the Mellotron intro, brilliantly closing up a momentum-dragging gap where just a lone Mellotron note was heard. The coda was shortened, however, fading out earlier than it had on take 6, and the ending at this stage was simply no match for the far more imaginative one that would soon be dreamed up.

Take 7 was issued on *Anthology 2,* although there it's cross-faded into an edit piece of percussion and vocals recorded on December 9 (see following entry). You can also see and hear George Martin isolating the rhythm track for a few seconds in *The Making of Sgt. Pepper.* Minus the few opening warm-up notes of Mellotron on some bootlegs, take 7 was apparently intended as the version that was going to be released at this point. Indeed, its first minute would end up being used as the first minute of the released version. But John Lennon and the Beatles would have second thoughts a second time, and do yet another remake.

● December 6

Studio Outtakes
Studio Two, Abbey Road, London

*Christmas Messages for Radio London and Radio Caroline
  four messages from this tape appear as superimpositions on "Christmas Time (Is Here Again)" on the Free As a Bird *CD single*

In the midst of their early sessions for the album that would become *Sgt. Pepper's Lonely Hearts Club Band,* the Beatles recorded a series of Christmas messages for the British pirate stations Radio London and Radio Caroline. The three and a half minutes from this session tape that have shown up on bootleg are not taken from the source but from a monitor mix, though as monitor mixes go, the quality's very good and listenable. It's admittedly a little arguable as to whether this recording qualifies as an "outtake." It doesn't contain much music, and it wasn't done for a single or album, or even as part of their Christmas disc. On the other hand, it does have a little music, and it *was* done at their usual Studio Two facility at Abbey Road, with George Martin producing.

The tape consists of each of the four Beatles reciting basic, short holiday greetings, often trying to make them a little more unique by using unusual accents or humorous deliveries. While there's not much in the way of entertainment value, you *can* hear a bit of music underneath some of the messages. The Beatles, and especially John Lennon, seem to have been quite immersed in the Mellotron at this point—particularly as this was bang in the middle of the "Strawberry Fields Forever" studio revisions—and what little music's here is taken from Mellotron tapes, including snatches of cocktail piano, cha-cha lounge sounds, be-bopping jazz, and horror movie–like effects. It's likely John was primarily or solely responsible for the Mellotron bits, as he was using the instrument in similar ways on quite a few of his doodling-around home tapes of the period, and can be heard asking for certain things to be played on a brief snatch of between-take chatter.

If this sounds like something too marginally arcane even for the average collector of unreleased Beatles music to be concerned with, consider that if you're reading this, it's quite possible you have a bit of it in your collection already. For one greeting apiece from John, Paul, George, and Ringo was overlaid as superimpositions onto the edited version of

their 1967 outtake "Christmas Time (Is Here Again)" that was used on the official 1995 *Free As a Bird* CD single. The Radio London and Radio Caroline messages have sometimes been listed as outtakes from their 1965 Christmas disc session on bootlegs, but you don't have to consult a reference book to know that's a mistake, as a few of the greetings specifically refer to 1967 as the upcoming New Year.

● December 9

Studio Outtake
*"Strawberry Fields Forever" single session
Studio Two, Abbey Road, London*

*Strawberry Fields Forever (edit piece)
  appears on Anthology 2

On this date, several "edit pieces" were recorded from which the creepy instrumental tag of "Strawberry Fields Forever" (the wordless one that comes in after the false ending) was constructed. In a somewhat convoluted archival rescue mission, an "edit piece" from this session lasting about one minute and 20 seconds was used on *Anthology 2,* as part of the track given the awkward title "Strawberry Fields Forever (Take 7 and edit piece)." Basically, what that means is that take 7 of the song (see entry for November 29, 1966) is cross-faded into this edit piece, where Ringo Starr flails ominously on his drums, accompanied by some backward cymbals effects and distant, disturbed shouting from John Lennon. It's much like the avant-garde section that concludes the "Strawberry Fields Forever" single; it just goes on longer. The cross-fade was probably done so that this more closely simulated a full alternate take of the released version, though, in fact, the two sections were recorded separately, about ten days apart, and not edited together until the *Anthology* project.

There's some confusion about when this edit piece was recorded, some sources listing December 8 and others December 9. As *Anthology 2* gives December 9 as the date, so will we, though the Beatles' authorized releases do occasionally present inaccurate information for details such as these. Not all of the strange noises John made on this edit piece were used in the released version, but the most famous one, of him saying, "Cranberry sauce" (according to the official accounts), did make it. All those official explanations to the contrary, however, it still sounds more like he's saying "I'm bored" or (as became famous as a clue in the Paul McCartney death rumors of late 1969) "I buried Paul."

● December 15

Studio Outtakes
*"Strawberry Fields Forever" single session
Studio Two, Abbey Road, London*

Strawberry Fields Forever (take 25)
Strawberry Fields Forever (RM9)

As exhaustively documented as the "Strawberry Fields Forever" sessions are, there's a significant missing piece of the puzzle in the absence of any takes from 9 through 24, where the Beatles recorded an entirely new rhythm track. This December 15 session saw overdubs of four trumpets and three cellos onto that rhythm track, the result labeled "take 25." Basically, it's an instrumental version of the "orchestral" section of the released track, minus the very important component of John Lennon's vocals. Oddly, the decision's now been made to revert to a structure that starts with a verse rather than a chorus. As such, it's no match for the finished experience, but it's nearly stunning nonetheless to hear the stately brass and strings in such an upfront fashion. The fadeout does contain some sounds not heard on the final recording, including some of the crazed Ringo drumming and John's shouting from the edit piece they'd done a week before, and sirenlike horn bleats. A control room monitor mix, despite its vastly inferior fidelity, adds a smattering of pretake instrumental sounds, a wiggling guitar (or guitarlike noise), and a very brief blast of *Phantom of the Opera* Mellotron at the end.

"Strawberry Fields Forever" took its next big step toward completion not with a conventionally numbered "take," but when take 25 was reduced from a four-track recording to a two-track recording, making two other tracks available for additional vocals and instrumentation. This allowed John Lennon to add vocals, and George Harrison to add svaramandal, the Indian instrument that makes the guitarlike sounds heard on the released track at the end of one chorus and on the first of its instrumental fadeouts. A mono mix of this new recording was made, labeled "RM9," whose single-tracked Lennon vocal was not used in the final version. His singing on that vocal's a bit rougher than what you hear on the single, though not drastically different. Otherwise, it's getting close to the finish line, although it's still about a minute shorter than the ultimate single, as the decision to combine an excerpt of an earlier, less elaborate version with this orchestral one had yet to be made.

Although many of the components of this "RM9" version are also heard on take 26 of "Strawberry Fields Forever," RM9 and take 26 are not identical to each other. The track labeled "take 26," with a different Lennon vocal, is discussed in the following entry.

● December 21

Studio Outtake

"Strawberry Fields Forever" single session
Studio Two, Abbey Road, London

Strawberry Fields Forever (take 26)

Take 26 of "Strawberry Fields Forever" was not a "take" in the sense of the term the Beatles had usually used. Rather, it was an alteration to the four-track recording that had been done on December 15, from which the mono mix known as RM9 had been made (see previous entry). Track three of RM9 was erased and replaced with a new vocal by John, enabling him to harmonize with himself on the last chorus.

Much of John's singing from take 26 was also used on the released version, although his vocals are largely absent from the first verse. A few more, but still incomplete, vocals in the opening verse can be heard on a control room monitor mix. This has led to reasonable speculation that perhaps John knew at this point that he wanted to join together the first minute of take 7 with most of take 26 (starting at the first chorus) to construct the final track. That would account for his failure to sing all of the lyrics in the section of take 26 where the first verse should have been.

The last task in polishing off "Strawberry Fields Forever" is its most famous one. John liked some aspects of two different versions the Beatles had recorded of the song, takes 7 and 26. He asked George Martin to join the beginning of take 7 to the end of take 26, even though they were in different keys and tempos. Martin and engineer Geoff Emerick managed to do this, as—by an almost divine miracle—speeding up take 7 and slowing down take 26 enabled the different versions to mesh together virtually seamlessly. The final mix also made a smaller, yet also important, change to the "take 26" portion of the track by fading the volume down during the instrumental tag and fading it back in a few seconds later, creating the impression of a false ending in which the track was interrupted by virtual complete silence. In the bootlegged take 26, there's no such gap. The bittersweet svaramandal is gradually overtaken by Ringo's clattering drums, sirenlike notes (said by John's *How I Won the War* co-star Michael Crawford to have been inspired by the night train to Madrid, claiming that Lennon had declared plans to write a song about the train), John's distant strangled shouts, and swirling Mellotron flutes without interruption, creating a somewhat more cacophonous outro. As with other takes of "Strawberry Fields Forever," Martin can be seen and heard isolating tracks of a few segments of take 26 in *The Making of Sgt. Pepper.*

Even at the time it was released, "Strawberry Fields Forever" was acknowledged as by far the most complicated recording the Beatles had yet done. Even though the story about the takes being joined and speeded/slowed to match was revealed shortly afterward, few listeners had any idea of just *how* long and winding a road it was from start to finish. It might be excessive to listen to *all* the outtakes of "Strawberry Fields Forever," one right after the other—and there *are* bootlegs consisting of nothing but "Strawberry Fields" outtakes, from the acoustic solo tapes in Spain to take 26. But their availability gives us extraordinarily valuable insight into the evolution of one of their greatest songs—an evolution which will probably never be documented in such absorbing step-by-step detail by a commercial release.

An entire CD of nothing but alternate versions of "Strawberry Fields Forever," documenting its evolution from acoustic solo John Lennon tapes to its completion at Abbey Road.

John Lennon/The Beatles

It's Not Too Bad
the evolution of strawberry fields forever

December 29, 1966–
January 17, 1967

Studio Outtake
"Penny Lane" single session
Studio Two and Studio Three, Abbey Road, London

---

*Penny Lane (**Anthology 2** mix)
   *appears on Anthology 2

Although "Penny Lane" was not as complicated a recording as "Strawberry Fields Forever"—few recordings are—it too needed several complex Abbey Road sessions before becoming an equally brilliant final result. As another indication of how the Beatles' studio process was entering a whole new phase, it's not even possible to describe this different version of "Penny Lane" as a specific "take" or even a combination of "takes." Rather, it's a mix specifically prepared for *Anthology 2* in the mid-'90s, drawing from recordings made on December 29 and December 30 of 1966, and January 4, 5, 6, 9, 10, 12, and 17 of the following year.

The previous sentence makes it sound like something of interest only to techno-nerds, but actually, it does comprise a pretty interesting alternate version, albeit one that was artificially manufactured. The big difference is the instrumental solo, which features cor anglais and trumpets where you expect the familiar, classic piccolo trumpet from the released version. The substitution of David Mason's piccolo trumpet, however, was both inspired and far superior to the instrumentation it erased. The cor anglais and trumpets sound more middle-of-the-road and dated, particularly the trumpets, which have a slightly corny, swinging London tinge. As a more subtle difference, much of Paul McCartney's vocal is single-tracked and his wordless, singing sighs are missing from the instrumental break.

Also included in the *Anthology 2* mix was the trumpet coda that was heard on North American promo copies of the "Penny Lane" single, but taken out of the track on official releases. Where the single ends with an eerie cymbal wash, however, the *Anthology 2* version then cross-fades into weird, rubberlike wobbling noises and some guitar, piano, and drum doodling, a deliberately silly voice announcing, "And soon it will end." It's arguably one slice of tomfoolery that would be better consigned to bootlegs, puncturing the otherwise dreamily picturesque ambience of the song, and that seven-note trumpet coda is better heard unobstructed on the original promo single mix (issued on numerous bootlegs). There are a couple of other subtly different "Penny Lane" mixes that have shown up on bootleg too, but those will be discussed in the following chapter, as they're all mixes actually done in January 1967.

● Circa Late 1966–Early 1968

Private Tapes
Kenwood, Weybridge

Mellotron Improvisation #1
Mellotron Improvisation #2
Mellotron Improvisation #3
Mellotron Improvisation #4
Mellotron Improvisation #5
Breakdown
Chi-Chi's
Daddy's Little Sunshine Boy
Down in Cuba
Lucy from Littletown
Pedro the Fisherman
Stranger in My Arms

Few other Beatles recordings are as hard to date, title, describe, or even listen to as this batch of John Lennon tapes, recorded in his Kenwood home with his Mellotron and, sometimes, the assistance of Ringo Starr. Blending avant-garde experimentation and slightly demented comedy, they were likely in no way intended as prototypes for Beatles records. Nor are they even conventionally constructed "songs," which is why even the titles of some of the tracks remain uncertain. They most likely functioned as outlets for John's most outrageous, oddball, free-form ideas, as well as vehicles for amusing himself at a time when he was largely just sitting around in his suburban London home when he wasn't recording with the Beatles.

As to when they were recorded, all that can be stated with reasonable certainty is that they were probably done between late 1966 and early 1968 (though as the Mellotron features prominently on most of these, it's possible the first could have been as early as August 1965, when Lennon bought the instrument). And they are not likely to have been done later than May 1968, when John and Yoko Ono became an item (and hence recorded together on virtually all of John's experimental tapes), John moving out of Kenwood shortly afterward. It's just an educated guess, but these tapes are more apt to have been done in the earlier part of this roughly year-and-a-half time frame. John didn't have the longest attention span, and he might have been more inclined to fool around on the Mellotron when it was a new toy, rather than keep at it for months after the novelty wore off. It's anyone's guess as to the exact sequence in which these tracks were recorded, although the way in which John's archive was logged in preparation for the radio series *The Lost Lennon Tapes* intimates that "Pedro the Fisherman" and "Stranger in My Arms" were done in November 1966. In the interest of neutrality, in this entry they'll be discussed in alphabetical order. Other than the Mellotron improvisations, that is, which will be addressed first, considering the possibility they were done as tests or warm-ups for John to get a feel for the instrument before he graduated to more involved experiments.

Now on to the music. The five instrumental pieces that have been usually titled "Mellotron Improvisation"(s) on bootlegs are all brief, adding up to only a bit more than six minutes; the shortest is a mere 20 seconds, and none are as long as two minutes. The first of them, after a jokey "one-two-three-four" intro, settles (after a bit of cocktail piano) into a rather pleasing, dreamy cha-cha, rather like a synthesized counterpart to a soundtrack you might hear in the Latin nightclub scene of a '40s/'50s B-movie. The second, lasting only half a minute, goes in a much more pronounced avant-garde direction, with stabs of sustained, disquieting notes that fade in and out like a light being switched on and off. The third, lasting just 20 seconds, is much like a tape loop of a three-second burst of a record revving up and immediately grinding to a halt as a turntable's turned on and instantly unplugged. An insistent tape-looped, low chamber-of-death tone forms the foundation of the fourth improvisation, over which a horror movie violin curls, stuttering and then giving way to an upwardly spiraling flute riff. That same chamber-of-death tone anchors the fifth improv, though the higher notes that augment it are more random and ethereally soothing, with a vibraphonelike timbre.

More than any other of the Lennon home Mellotron experiments, these demonstrate that the avant-gardeisms of "Revolution 9" (particularly its repeating ominous violinlike sounds) and the albums he did with Yoko Ono didn't come out of nowhere. They were just felt not to be releasable at the time; they probably *still* aren't releasable, though they're actually a little more accessible to the average listener than those oft-grating Lennon-Ono LPs. It could well have been material such as this that John recalled (in his early-'70s *Rolling Stone* interview with Jann Wenner) playing to Yoko the first time she stayed the night at his home in the spring of 1968, when "I didn't know what to do; so we went upstairs to my studio and I played her all the tapes that I'd made, all this far out stuff, some comedy stuff, and some electronic music. She was suitably impressed and then she said well let's make one ourselves so we made *Two Virgins*."

Ringo is the only Beatle other than John heard on these recordings, although he was the member of the group with the least avant-garde leanings. Possibly he turns up on some of these tapes because he lived closest to John at the time, and was the one who most often went over for social visits. He's John's sparring partner on "Breakdown," not so much a piece of music as a quite-tough-to-listen-to, rapid-fire volley of vaudevillian spoken lines, like has-been Blackpool comedians on laughing gas. The exchange that gets the biggest laugh, to give you an idea, has John asking, "Have you got a minute for an old-timer?" To which Ringo snaps back, "No, I've got an hour for a young man, though." The only "music" here is heard in some distorted, music-hallish sounds in the background, Ringo setting the mood by urgently yelling several times over at the outset, "The mike's not on!"

"Chi-Chi's" is not an actual continuous track, but a string of fragments edited together especially for *The Lost Lennon Tapes* radio series (and, it has been reported, overlaid with applause not part of the original tapes). Also with both John and Ringo, it's a moderately amusing send-up of cabaret culture. One part takes place in an imaginary Edgehill Country Club, and a subsequent one shifts the scene to Chi-Chi's Bar with deliberately awful and ridiculous operatic singing, as well as heavy mock Latin accents. (As an aside, there are quite a few Latin influences to be heard on this set of Lennon-Mellotron home tapes; perhaps he was especially taken with the settings on the instruments that produced Latin rhythms.) There's a faint possible link to an actual Beatles recording, maybe, in how the sleazy Latin nightlife vibe would also surface—to much, much greater, well-constructed, and well-produced comic effect—in the section of "You Know My Name (Look Up the Number)" that takes place in the imaginary "Slaggers" nightspot, crooned to a rumba rhythm. Ringo gets something of a solo feature on the half-minute, almost a cappella "Daddy's Little Sunshine Boy," sung like a vaudeville piece, except the last half adds some loud thumps and insistent shouts of "C'mon" in the background, as if daddy's little sunshine boy's getting spanked.

"Down in Cuba" has yet more ersatz Latin Americanisms as, like "Chi-Chi's," it takes place in a cabaret club of the mind, or perhaps a cabaret club from hell. As a fake American voice announces at the outset, "I'd like to think that now, this time of year, we can bring you a more broader . . . you know, something bigger and better. And this year,

we've got for you, straight from Havana, Cuba . . . we've got a swinging little trio, bass, maracas, and bass [sic]. Each one of them are gonna do their ut [sic] to entertain you in that inimit [sic] Latin American way." The ensuing rumba will not win any awards for politically correct satire: "In down Cuba we get many bananas, we get the coffee too, we don't have many cigars, 'cause we've sold them all." And following that gem is a minute or so of nonsensical, operatic, pidgin Spanish croon, the Mellotron backup laying down a nonchalant rumba. Again, a possible foreshadowing of the "You Know My Name (Look Up the Number)" rumba sequence here, and again, not nearly as good—not least because "You Know My Name (Look Up the Number)" benefited from noncanned instrumentation and Paul McCartney's considerable vocal and comic input.

"Lucy from Littletown" is not a bona fide John Lennon original, but John reading an excerpt from Beatrix Potter's classic children's story "The Tale of Mrs. Tiggy-Winkle." For what it's worth, he does put acidic melodramatic menace into his delivery, the muted Mellotron backing sounding like late-'40s radio play Muzak stuck in a haunted house. Lennon probably did have a mock radio presentation in mind with whatever he was doing here, prefacing the fairy tale by declaring like an old-time radio announcer, "There's a young couple living [in] Sussex, and they've won this week's golden breast! Are you ready for it?" It's a low-glimmer reflection of John's love of children's fairy tales, which he sometimes drew upon for lyrical inspiration in the Beatles' psychedelic phase.

John borrows from Latin music of a slightly different sort on a minute-plus folk-flamenco tune in which he takes on the role of "Pedro the Fisherman." "I'm Pedro the Fisherman, I fish by night and day," he intones in a silly, Spanish-accented, unnaturally low vibrato. The lyrics are pretty silly too, and not all that uproarious: "Unfortunately I live in Bristol, far far away. And there ain't no fish to be caught. . . . I've got a hook and a line, a Mac, a big axe, and socks, and a pair of Wellingtons, and a bit of wire." Then some scary penetrating organlike tones intrude, John launches into the next line with operatic bravado . . . and the track, perhaps thankfully, cuts off. Maybe this was indeed done in late 1966 shortly after he returned from Spain, where he might have heard music vaguely like this (or seen an actual Spanish fisherman). Maybe he was just taking the piss out of self-consciously authentic folk balladry. Or maybe he was just terribly bored.

It's back to faux Latin croonery yet again for "Stranger in My Arms" (titled "You're a Stranger in My House" in the logging for *The Lost Lennon Tapes*, though John's clearly singing, "You're a stranger in my arms"). At three minutes and 33 seconds, it's actually the longest of these Kenwood tapes, and is structured a bit more as a conventional song. It's still neither too developed nor too Beatlesque, John singing this mellow cha-cha in another phony Latin lounge lizard voice. The sporadic pangs of originality, such as they are, sail in via the keening high tones of the instrumental breaks, one passage crossing the timbres of mandolins and organ, another landing midway between an organ and a trumpet, the last offering a brief breeze of jazzy piano before Lennon mutters something like, "Uh, it's gone out." And that's where the track ungracefully cuts off.

A few of these recordings were actually aired in public on *The Lost Lennon Tapes* radio series, but the rest have been heard only on bootleg. Other than the tenuous hints of "Revolution 9," "You Know My Name (Look Up the Number)," Lennon's psychedelic fairy tale lyrical imagery, and the avant-garde albums John Lennon and Yoko Ono did as a duo, there's no strong connection to the music the Beatles were making during this time (unless you figure John was putting at least something of what he was learning to use on the few Beatles tracks that featured a Mellotron). It's really for serious fans only—and, maybe, only for fans who are even more serious than the usual fans serious enough to collect unreleased Beatles music. And, believe it or not, there are yet other similar Lennon home recordings from this era that might make the rounds some day (see corresponding entry later in this chapter).

● Circa 1966

Private Tapes

Probably made at one or more of the following locations:
57 Wimpole Street, London; 7 Cavendish Avenue, London;
and 34 Montagu Square, London

John Lennon is perceived by most of the public as the most avant-garde Beatle, but each of the other three also made experimental excursions. George Harrison's 1969 solo album *Electronic Sound* contained early Moog synthesizer ramblings, and his journeys into Indian music and the sitar were themselves avant-garde in the context of the 1960s. Ringo Starr participated in John's home Mellotron tapes, and while that might have been more of a social activity than an artistic endeavor, he was the Beatle who worked most closely with John Tavener after the contemporary classical composer was briefly signed to Apple in the late '60s. (Starr also made a brief vocal appearance on Tavener's Apple album, *The Whale*, recorded a few months after the Beatles broke up, and referred to having recorded an experimental album at home on Moog synthesizer with Maurice Gibb on vocals in a 1971 interview.) And while Paul McCartney has the straightest public image of the four, like John he made some avant-garde home tapes, and was also the main force behind one of the group's most experimental outtakes, "Carnival of Light," in early 1967.

In Barry Miles's biography *Paul McCartney: Many Years from Now*, Paul went to some length to establish his credentials in this realm, even devoting a 57-page chapter to his activities in avant-garde London. In this section, he remembered that he used to make experimental tapes in the mid-'60s with a couple of Brenell tape recorders in the home of the family of his girlfriend, Jane Asher, where he was living at the time (at 57 Wimpole Street in central London). The 1965 Christmas recording *Unforgettable* was one of these (see entry in 1965 chapter), and after that he made tape loops "mainly with guitar or voices, or bongos," some of which he brought into Abbey Road for use on "Tomorrow Never Knows." He continued doing similar tapes in the music room of the home he bought for himself near Abbey Road at 7 Cavendish Avenue in 1966. He also set up a small, basic demo studio the same year for the use of poets and avant-garde musicians, including William Burroughs, at 34 Montagu Square, a flat that had been vacated by Ringo. Paul used the Montagu Square studio to make some tapes for himself as well, though the equipment was gone by late 1966, when Ringo let Jimi Hendrix, Hendrix's manager Chas Chandler, and their girlfriends move into the flat for a few months.

Whether many of them still exist or not, it's definite that Paul made a number of home tapes at these various locations in 1966 (and probably for some time before and after that year). A couple of untitled

excerpts were aired on June 12, 2004, as part of a documentary, *Z for Zapple* (about the short-lived late-'60s experimental Apple subsidiary label, Zapple), produced for BBC Radio 4's *The Archive Hour* series. Adding up to only about four minutes (much of which is obscured by narration done specifically for the program by Barry Miles), these sound more like tryouts of ideas and equipment than definite pieces. Paul fiddles with echo, spews nonsensical phrases ("My mother was a seaman, and my father was a Jew," "I'm afraid there's a crinkle in the tea") in funny accents (à la some of the Beatles' Christmas fan club recording sessions), scats like a spaceman singing sea chanteys, and inserts a bit of super-sped-up tape winding. "It's amazing what it does to your voice, isn't it?" he exclaims dryly at one point.

Naive stuff indeed, though Miles confirmed in the program that he and Paul "discussed the idea of releasing an audio equivalent of the avant-garde magazines where, instead of reading a review of a poetry reading, listeners would hear extracts from the reading itself, or maybe clips from concerts, rehearsals. . . . It was agreed that what we needed in order to do this was a small studio where writers and musicians could record without the overheads of a commercial facility. . . . Our first release was to feature a long electronic piece by Paul McCartney," as well as a poem by Pete Brown (later to help write some of Cream's songs) and a story. This project never got off the ground, however, and even when the idea was picked up a couple of years later for the Zapple subsidiary, the label released just two albums (John Lennon's *Unfinished Music No. 2: Life with the Lions* and George Harrison's *Electronic Sound*) before folding.

For all the innocuous weirdness of the brief excerpts broadcast on the documentary, however, it may be that Paul made less such off-the-wall excursions than he'd originally envisioned. In *Many Years from Now*, he confessed that he thought he would use the Montagu Square studio "for cut-ups. But it ended up being of more practical use to me, really. I thought, let Burroughs do the cut-ups and I'll just go in and demo things. I'd just written 'Eleanor Rigby' and so I went down there in the basement on my days off on my own. Just took a guitar down and used it as a demo studio." That could well be where the snippet of a home-taped "Eleanor Rigby" (see entry earlier in this chapter) comes from. But nothing else, either conventional or far-out, has surfaced from Paul's home tapes of this period, though his memories were a bit more specific in an October 1986 interview with *Musician*, where he recalled sitting in Montagu Square "with William Burroughs and a couple of gay guys he knew from Morocco and that Marianne Faithfull-John Dunbar crowd doing little tapes, crazy stuff with guitar and cello." Thought of as a generally more guarded individual than John, perhaps Paul has been more conscientious about keeping this material in the vault than Lennon's estate has, knowing that it might be too inaccessible or undeveloped to merit public airing.

It's also known for certain that Paul did have acetates pressed of some of his early tape loop adventures, though when he played one for Bob Dylan, it was not well received. According to Marianne Faithfull (as related in *Faithfull: An Autobiography*, co-written with David Dalton), "I saw him come in once with an acetate of a track he'd been working on which was very far out for its time, with all kinds of distorted electronic things on it. Paul was obviously terribly proud of it. He put it on the record player and stood back in anticipation, but Dylan just walked out of the room. It was unbelievable. The expression on Paul's face was priceless. . . ."

1966 Noncirculating Recordings, Known and Rumored

● January 5

Studio Outtakes
CTS Studios, London

I Feel Fine
Help!
Ticket to Ride

As noted in the August 15, 1965, entry, on this date the Beatles gathered at CTS Studios in London to overdub and rerecord new parts and entire songs for use in the soundtrack to the television documentary special about their Shea Stadium concert. Paul overdubbed new bass parts on "Dizzy Miss Lizzy," "Can't Buy Me Love," "Baby's in Black," and "I'm Down"; John overdubbed a new organ track on "I'm Down"; and wholly new versions of "I Feel Fine" and "Help!" were done. In *The Complete Beatles Chronicle*, Mark Lewisohn wrote that "documentation also suggests that John wished to record a new version of 'Ticket to Ride,' and that it was done during this CTS session, but close study of the film indicates that the original Shea version was used (although perhaps a little instrumental overdubbing was effected)." So there might well be a tape somewhere from this session with January 1966 studio versions of "I Feel Fine," "Help!" and "Ticket to Ride" without the screams heard on the TV special soundtrack, though it's not wholly certain that "Ticket to Ride" was entirely remade.

● Circa Early 1966

Private Tapes
Kenwood, Weybridge

Hold On, I'm Comin'
Mr. Moonlight

In his book *The 910's Guide to the Beatles' Outtakes: 2004 Edition,* Doug Sulpy briefly describes these two John Lennon home recordings, sequencing them in a position suggesting they were done around early 1966. The acoustic "Hold On, I'm Comin'" is apparently no relation to the classic Sam and Dave soul hit of the same name (released in March 1966), lasting just a minute and two seconds. According to Sulpy's book, "It's a pretty tune, but obviously little more than a sketch." It was taped over a part of John's home recordings of "She Said, She Said," supporting the theory that it probably dates from early 1966.

Early 1966 seems a little late for John to be doing "Mr. Moonlight," which the Beatles had recorded for *Beatles for Sale* in late 1964 (and performed onstage for a couple of years before that). But John returned to early rock 'n' roll classics at times throughout his entire life, and maybe he was just doing it here as informal fun. Again according to Sulpy, this is a "laidback, tropical-flavored version," lasting a little more than five

Home tapes of the Beatles, and particularly of John Lennon, grew significantly in number after the group retired from touring in late 1966.

minutes, with John unable to remember all the lyrics. That tropical flavor fits in with the Latin-tropical ambience John would use on many of his Mellotron-dominated home tapes a little later on, though even the *Beatles for Sale* version of "Mr. Moonlight" had an island-Hawaiian feel.

● April 6–June 21

Studio Outtakes
Revolver sessions
Abbey Road, London

The most intriguing of the *Revolver* outtakes known to have been taped start with an acoustic version of George Harrison's "Love You To" with Paul McCartney on backing vocals that must have been considerably different in this early form than the Indian-flavored final album track. Although a different take of "And Your Bird Can Sing" was used on *Anthology 2*, Mark Lewisohn's *The Beatles Recording Sessions* cites yet another alternate (take 3) as "a *very* heavy recording."

● August

Live Performance

Yesterday (incomplete)
I Wanna Be Your Man
Nowhere Man
Paperback Writer
I'm Down

A nonbootlegged audience tape, heard by this writer, consists of about half of one of their 1966 North American concerts. It must be from that tour, as "Paperback Writer" is in the set and the audience is speaking English. But the sound quality is about what you'd expect (i.e., not very good, the band heard faintly amidst lots of crowd noise and talk). From what you can make out of it, this might be a better performance of "Nowhere Man" than the one in San Francisco, but it's impossible to tell from behind this all-but-iron curtain. There are probably numerous such undocumented, noncirculating audience tapes of the Beatles, by the way; even in the film of the group's very first American concert in Washington, DC, you can see a fan quite openly taping the show on a portable recorder.

● August 19

Live Performances
Mid-South Coliseum, Memphis (afternoon and evening shows)

This was a more noteworthy Beatles concert than most, if for the wrong reasons. They'd received death threats in Memphis in the fallout from John's remark about the group being bigger than Jesus, and at one point during the evening show a firecracker was thrown onstage. The Beatles looked at one another, fearing that one of them had been shot. Legend would have it that none of them missed a note, so used were they to playing under stressful conditions after three years of Beatlemania.

In 1998, tapes of the Beatles on this date were taken out of storage by Gloria Allen and Noreen Prouty. Thirty-two years before, the two Jackson, Mississippi, teenagers had brought a portable reel-to-reel recorder into the Mid-South Coliseum, attending both shows. After being made aware of the tapes, Michael Heatley, general manger of EMI's International Catalogue Development, actually flew to Nashville to listen to them. While he did offer to buy them for an unspecified lower-than-six-figure sum, the owners declined, instead putting them up for auction on eBay in early 2003. Chris Larkin, who'd contacted Heatley on the tapers' behalf, thought that the offer was made only to keep the music out of the bootleg circuit. And as of early 2006, the tapes *still* haven't made their way onto bootleg.

As with many such "discoveries," however, it was likely hardly worth the fuss. As an audience tape, it's probably not nearly up to the standards of either the Capitol-recorded Hollywood Bowl shows, or more than half a dozen other 1964–1966 concert tapes (Philadelphia, Vancouver, and Indianapolis in 1964; Houston and Atlanta in 1965; Tokyo in 1966) that have made the rounds for years. Indeed, as *Rolling Stone*'s Robert Gordon confirmed in his small piece on the tapes in February 2003, "The fidelity is low, and the shrieking of teenage girls often drowns out the band." However, they do capture that tense moment when fireworks were hurled onstage while George Harrison was singing "If I Needed Someone." According to Gordon's description of the tape, "When the explosion occurs, the audience reacts with intensified screaming, as if the boom was stage pyrotechnics." Just after that explosion, as reported in a December 30, 2002, article in the Mississippi newspaper *The Clarion-Ledger,* Allen can be heard screaming, "Get them off the stage!" Confirmed Allen in the same article, "The Beatles never missed a beat when that cherry bomb went off. Not one single note. They might have been scared, but they never showed it. They just kept right on playing. It was wonderful."

● Circa Late 1966–Early 1968

Private Tapes
Kenwood, Weybridge

Mellotron Improvisation #1
Mellotron Improvisation #2
Mellotron Improvisation #3
Mellotron Improvisation #4
John and Ringo
Kenwood Sequence

In *The 910's Guide to the Beatles' Outtakes: 2004 Edition,* Sulpy details yet more Mellotron-dominated home tapes recorded by John Lennon in his Kenwood home. The similarity to the circulating recordings of this nature documented in a prior entry in this chapter seems strong enough that it's reasonable to also estimate these as dating from between late 1966 and early 1968. Within this batch are four more Mellotron improvisations, the first lasting 0.34; the second, 2:25; the third, 5:16; and the fourth, 2:02. Apparently, like the improvs that have made it onto bootleg, they're not too structured or melodic, also using dissonant tones and textures, Latin rhythms, sustain, and timbres suggestive of horror film soundtracks. The most interesting of them might be the one lasting 2:25, as Sulpy reports it uses "occasional baby doll squeaking and backwards sounds similar to those used in 'Flying.'" There's also a solid ten-minute tape, titled simply "John and Ringo" by Sulpy, in which the pair play some records, sing, comically banter, and otherwise fill up the space.

Sulpy also describes a 14-and-a-half-minute tape titled "Kenwood Sequence," compiled by John from some of his favorite excerpts of his home recordings. Of the 21 segments into which he breaks it down in his analysis, three ("Lucy from Littletown," "Down in Cuba," and "Pedro the Fisherman") have escaped onto bootleg, although the version of "Down in Cuba" used on this tape is actually an excerpt of a longer version that circulates on bootleg. Of the remaining 18 portions, again, none seem either too exciting or too different from the similar tapes that have come out on bootleg. There's singing, poetry, comedy, surreal storytelling, bossa nova, and backward sounds. When the most interesting bit seems to be a passage that, in Sulpy's words, "sounds frighteningly like Syd Barrett at his most incoherent," you know this is not something you'd be apt to play often or for pleasure. And this is Lennon's *favorite* stuff—imagine what the rest of it might sound like.

As this is a compilation, obviously there's yet more where this came from, and there's a possibility that yet more of it might come to light someday, though it's doubtful such material would be of anything but scholarly value. And some such material was indeed noted when John's tapes were logged for *The Lost Lennon Tapes,* including such unappetizing titles as "John Clowns Around [Mellotron]," "John Sings A Capella/Clowns," "Acoustic Guitar Piece," "John Messing Around [Plays Organ, Sings and Talks]," "Hello Dolly [Sung Off Pitch w/Mellotron]," and "John and Ringo Messing Around." There's also "Danny Boy [A Capella]"—and, funnily enough, John *would* eventually sing a brief a cappella snatch of that tune on a Beatles record, when "One After 909" fades on the *Let It Be* album.

The entrance to EMI Studios on Abbey Road in London, where the Beatles retreated to concentrate on studio recording, having retired from touring.

1967

The Studio Year

The Year in Review

The year 1967 was far from the dullest year of the Beatles' career, what with a mammoth-selling album, *Sgt. Pepper's Lonely Hearts Club Band,* roundly recognized as one of the most significant and influential popular music recordings of all time. There were also three classic, huge hit singles, and another commercial smash in the soundtrack to their *Magical Mystery Tour* film (issued as an EP in the UK and, with the addition of all the tracks from their 1967 singles that didn't appear on British LPs, an LP in the US). The *Magical Mystery Tour* film didn't fare well with either the critics or the public, yet that was a minor blemish at a time when they were not only recognized as major innovators of psychedelic rock, but also as spokesmen of sorts for the entire countercultural lifestyle. Beyond the studio, it was an exciting and tumultuous year as well, with the formation of Apple, the death of Brian Epstein, their continued exploration of drugs, and their growing interest in the transcendental meditation taught by the Maharishi.

Yet 1967, somehow, was the *least* interesting year for unreleased Beatles music between 1962 and 1969. In part, that was because they'd stopped touring, and there were absolutely no live performances, with the arguable exception of their presentation of "All You Need Is Love"

(combining live music and studio tracks) on television in June. In at least as large measure, however, it had much to do with the way they were now recording their music in pieces and layers that could be combined in different ways, and not so much as group performances that could be altered or perfected (with the increasing help of overdubs) in the course of a session. As a consequence, there are relatively few instances of significantly different alternate versions of songs that ended up on their studio releases. There's also virtually nothing in the way of outtakes of songs that didn't make it onto Beatles records. What variations exist are often differences in the way parts were mixed, or what parts were used for mixes.

At the risk of upsetting the most vociferously audiophile-oriented Beatles collectors, it can be contended that at this point a certain joylessness often creeps into the process of both listening to and analyzing unreleased music by the group that's made it into circulation. When you sometimes have to do A–B comparisons, often several times over, to specify the differences between the released version and the "unreleased" version/mix, the larger point of listening to music itself—to enjoy and be inspired by it—is in danger of getting lost. Occasionally, too, the "differences" are, though real, so subtle as to be missed altogether by average Beatles fans. It *is* interesting to track how the Beatles made such decisions (and how such small details were obviously not too small to escape their and George Martin's attention), and sometimes there are substantial differences that make the tracks worth appreciating on their own merits. But the mundane effort of picking through the track to studiously identify micro-deviations and components will outweigh the reward for many listeners. So will listening to the various "isolated" parts of tracks (i.e., vocals only, or horns only) that have been made available from the *Sgt. Pepper* sessions. It's a process that does take some joy out of the listening, and if there's any such thing as an antonym to what the Beatles were all about, "joylessness" is it.

Thankfully, it's not all gloom for lost treasure-seekers in Pepper-land. *Anthology 2* came through with some genuinely interesting alternate versions of 1967 Beatles tracks, though some weren't so interesting, and some have been criticized as being artificially manufactured long after the event. There are also a few odd circulating alternates never included on official Beatles releases that *are* significantly different from the familiar version. A few home recordings round off this slimmest of annual pickings from the unreleased Beatles crop.

● January 9

Studio Outtakes
"Penny Lane" single session
Studio Two, Abbey Road, London

Penny Lane overdub session

Getting right into the spirit of how 1967 outtakes sometimes make for challenging, mostly-of-academic-value Beatles listening, these tapes are not really of the "Penny Lane" track itself. Lasting nearly seven minutes, they were made at an overdub session for the song. And they're not even of isolated overdub tracks, or from official takes, or even recorded by EMI staff. Rather, they were recorded by John Lennon in the control room, basically making an audio verité document of sounds in the studio while the session was in progress.

In the more interesting section, Paul plays the piano for about two-and-a-half minutes, largely sticking to the part heard on the final track. He can be heard faintly scat-singing, as if he's illustrating where some of the brass instruments might be inserted. Near the end of that section, distorted tape varispeed effects and echo are introduced, presumably by mischievous joker John in the control room. If these were seriously intended as psychedelic flourishes to be overdubbed onto the track, it was an idea that was thankfully discarded.

Also heard are bits of the session men playing brief riffs that don't appear in the recording, perhaps as a warm-up rather than anything intended specifically for "Penny Lane," although the flutes at one point *do* play something that approximates their parts in the song. Then comes a yet tougher part to wade through, as an early version of the actual "Penny Lane" track is played back through speakers, while the hired hands are simultaneously heard "live" playing stray riffs of their own and faintly chatting. They don't sound too interested in what they're doing, though maybe that's to be expected from jobbing session men for whom this was just another day's work, albeit probably one of their more stimulating ones.

Two and a half minutes of these tapes were aired on an episode of *The Lost Lennon Tapes* radio series, and the six minutes and 52 seconds that have been bootlegged offer more, but not everything. The full tape runs 13 minutes, though judging from what's here, it's hard to imagine the unheard six minutes containing anything of revelatory significance.

● January 12

Studio Outtake
"Penny Lane" single session
Studio Two, Abbey Road, London

Penny Lane (RM8)

As the mixing and remixing steps in Beatles recordings became ever more involved by 1967, it becomes more common for some unreleased circulating tracks from around late 1966 onward to be identified by "RM" and "RS" prefixes, rather than take numbers. Those abbreviations will be used throughout the rest of this book, "RM" signifying a mono remix, and "RS" a stereo remix.

The RM8 mix of "Penny Lane" is much the same as the released version, except it has a different solo in the instrumental break—the same solo, in fact, as you'll hear on the *Anthology 2* mix. So why do you need this one? Well, because it has some low oboe parts in the last section—on the last two choruses, to be exact—that aren't heard on the single or *Anthology 2* mixes. It's also missing the piccolo trumpet David Mason added to the final chorus on January 17. So while this mix is not as good as the final "Penny Lane," it does allow us to hear just how Paul McCartney and George Martin altered the arrangement to fit in that piccolo trumpet, and verify that their decisions on these small but critical details were very much the correct ones.

● January 17

Studio Outtakes
"Penny Lane" single session
Studio Two, Abbey Road, London

Penny Lane (RM9)
Penny Lane (RM10)

Both of these mixes are very close to the final "Penny Lane" track, other than containing some false starts and count-ins. So why bother with them? Well, there's one very important difference. At the very end, instead of hearing nothing but harsh, swelling and ebbing cymbal-like tones, you hear those *plus* a seven-note piccolo trumpet coda (right after the final piano chord). That same coda was also used on the North American promo copies of the actual "Penny Lane" 45—the RM11 mix, if you're keeping track. But a yet different mix, RM14, was made on January 25 at the eleventh hour that took that final trumpet flourish off. Again, we're talking small details, but as interesting as that variation is, the Beatles made the correct move in eliminating the trumpet; the song's conclusion is far spookier when the cymbals swell on their own. Like

The Beatles' Mixology

As a witty wordplay on the Beatles' *Anthology* projects, there's an actual series of *Mixology* bootlegs devoted to nothing but uncommon mixes of Beatles songs, all of which have been officially released somewhere in the world at one time or another. If you're wondering how in the world there can be enough such items to fill four CDs totaling 93 tracks, think again. For even those CDs, as lengthy as they are, don't come close to collecting all the commercially issued mixes of Beatles recordings that don't appear in their current EMI catalog.

The most common source of Beatles mix variations are the different mixes that were prepared for stereo and mono releases in the 1960s. From a 21st-century standpoint, the sheer number of differences that slithered into these mixes—ranging from the infinitesimal to ones that are quite noticeable even to fans who never make a point of listening for this kind of thing—is both astonishing and inexplicable. The main difference between mono and stereo, to the layperson at least, is that the mono format has the same music coming from each speaker, while the stereo one separates different parts of the track into different speakers. Yet the Beatles discography is awash with instances where some sounds, instruments, and vocals are heard in the stereo version but not the mono, and vice versa. How could the Beatles and EMI's technical staff have come up with so many apparent mismatches?

First, it must be understood that in constructing mono and stereo mixes, technicians were often working from a pool of available components to individual tracks, and sometimes even from multiple takes. While separating sounds into different channels (or combining them into one channel) of a recording is one of the overriding tasks involved in making a stereo or mono mix, it's not the only one. Musicians, producers, and engineers were also conscious of using the specific parts that would make the best stereo or mono recording, not just in separating and setting the level of the instruments and voices. So they might have decided that a certain part of a vocal or guitar was appropriate for the mono version, but not for the stereo, or mixed out something in one of the formats that they felt worked in stereo, but not in mono.

It should be noted, however, that the process likely wasn't always that careful or deliberate. Record companies were under great pressure to manufacture product quickly for many different regions of the world in the 1960s, and never more so for the Beatles, as demand for their records was unprecedented. It's quite possible that in some or many instances, mixes vary because they had to be done very quickly with the raw studio tapes available, without any time (or maybe inclination) to compare them with previous mixes to see if certain parts were identical or missing. So there may well have been times when different parts were used for a stereo mix where the people responsible for the assembly hadn't even listened to the mono mix of the same track—not just for Beatles records, but for records by many artists.

The Beatles themselves were not even involved in the mixing process at the beginning of their career, their records often being mixed when they weren't even in the studio. Remarkably, in one instance, George Martin overdubbed piano (on "Slow Down") when the Beatles were not only not in the studio, but not in the country. In some cases, mixes were done at EMI when they weren't even on the same continent. This changed considerably from the mid-'60s onward, as the group began to take a much stronger interest in the technical side of their recordings. Even so, however, until the late 1960s, they were far more concerned with their mono mixes than their stereo ones.

That surprises some fans, who rightly think of the Beatles as studio pioneers. But the mono format was by far the more common one for most home record players in the early and mid-'60s, especially in Britain, which wasn't as affluent as the US, and where home stereo systems took considerably longer to become common household items. It wasn't until the *Abbey Road* album, in fact, that a Beatles LP was issued only in stereo (for the US market, that honor went to the slightly earlier *The White Album*). Even as late as *Sgt. Pepper,* far more time was spent mixing the mono version than the stereo one, the Beatles not even attending the sessions at which George Martin and engineers Geoff Emerick and Richard Lush did the stereo mixes.

After the '60s, the group might have wished they'd had more active control over the mixing end, both for first-time releases and reissues. No less a figure than John Lennon was alarmed when variations in which he was not involved surfaced, sometimes long after the recording. "If you mix something in mono and then try and fake it, it just . . . you lose the guts of it," he complained on New York's WNEW-FM in September 1974, when discussing the stereo mixes used on the 1973 compilations *1962–1966* and *1967–1970*. "The fast version of 'Revolution' [from the Beatles' 1968 single] was destroyed. I mean, it was a heavy record. And then they made it into a piece of ice cream!"

The Beatles were also not directly involved in instances in which some mixes were prepared specifically for foreign markets. Most notoriously, Capitol Records, under the supervision of Dave Dexter, Jr., did mixes for early US Beatles releases that added a little-to-a-lot of reverb and echo to the recordings. Though these mixes have been roundly derided by most critics, and few listeners would be as bold as to declare they actually *prefer* them, quite a few do at least want to own them, in many cases if only because the Capitol mixes represent the tracks as these American fans first heard the Beatles. EMI, unusually, recognized this demand and issued the first four Beatles Capitol LPs on CD in both stereo and mono in 2004 on the box set *The Capitol Albums Vol. 1*. That was followed by the next four Beatles Capitol LPs in stereo-mono on 2006's *The Capitol Albums Vol. 2,* the first pressing of which, in turn, generated yet *more* collectibles when incorrect "reduced mono mixes" were used on *Beatles VI* and *Rubber Soul*.

Prior to the appearance of the officially sanctioned *The Capitol Albums Vol. 1 & 2,* demand for the Capitol-mixed LPs on CD was so great that they were actually bootlegged on compact disc. Post–*Rubber Soul* LPs continue to get bootlegged in their Capitol-ized form, as do many other uncommon, once commercially available mixes of Beatles tracks, even if those bootlegs do not often (if ever) use the best EMI source tapes. Unauthorized circulation of hard-to-find commercially released Beatles mixes, often placed side-by-side with actual unreleased tracks on bootlegs, is a common enough phenomenon that some people might wonder why such mixes are not covered in this book. It's a judgment call, but for one thing, these tracks *were* commercially released, often while the Beatles were still active, even if many of them might be hard to find these days.

In addition, there are so many such tracks, and so many variations are contained within them, that it would be difficult to cover them in detail without expanding this volume to an unpublishable size. Many of them are so minor that they can't be spotted without an aural magnifying glass, such as the absence of the word "only" from one of the lines in the double-tracked vocal in the stereo "It's Only Love," and the restoration of the second syllable of that missing "only" in the stereo CD remix. Even far more audible ones have escaped the attention of Beatles fans who've heard the tracks literally hundreds of times, such as the extra "woo!" near the end of the stereo "Slow Down," the extra note at the beginning of the stereo "Misery," the extra backing vocal on one word on the mono "Julia," and the extra tambourine beat at the beginning of the stereo "Sexy Sadie." These are not made-up, exaggerated examples. There are many, many more such details, and the difference in actual length of many tracks often varies between stereo and mono versions, usually in the fades. Sometimes, too, the tracks actually run in different speeds in mono and stereo, the stereo mix of "She's Leaving Home" lasting nine seconds longer than the mono one, for example.

But as jolly a pastime as it is to discover such hidden idiosyncrasies, the simple truth is that many of these mix variations and stereo-mono differences are so small as to be nearly undetectable to the average Beatles fan, or at least so small as to merit a shrug of "So what?" even from many dedicated enthusiasts. Some of them are so subtle, in fact, that even some Beatles experts who've spent years studying the matter dispute whether they're different from certain other mixes, or what, exactly, those differences are. Critical assessments as to the relative value of the stereos vs. the monos can vary from each other even as widely as the mixes themselves do. You will find one treatise on why the mono version of *The White Album* is by far superior to the stereo one, and another equally authoritative piece contending—as the book *Every Little Thing: The Definitive Guide to Beatles Recording Variations, Rare Mixes and Other Musical Oddities, 1958–1986* does—that "the overall sound quality of the mono mix . . . suggests it was nothing more than a rough dub. The sonic range is very limited in comparison to the stereo version."

There are, however, a number of tracks on which the variance between mixes is so apparent, and rather interesting, that the very most blatant of them deserve at least a mention in a volume such as this. A list of the three dozen such tracks with the most noticeable variations follows (not even getting into the different mixes used on the *Let It Be . . . Naked* release, which are briefly detailed in the 1970 chapter), along with brief descriptions of the most audible respects in which they part ways from each other.

(Several of these were actually reissued on Capitol's 1980 *Rarities* LP compilation, though even there the legitimacy of some of them was compromised, as a few of the tracks were actually newly produced combinations of previously issued mixes/versions. Those looking for extremely in-depth investigation of all known Beatles mix variations should look for Doug Sulpy's *The 910's Guide to The Beatles' Outtakes 2004 Edition* and John C. Winn's *Way Beyond Compare: The Beatles' Recorded Legacy, Volume One, 1957–1965* and *That Magic Feeling: The Beatles' Recorded Legacy, Volume Two, 1966–1970*, all of which examine the subject in exacting detail.)

"**Please Please Me**": On the stereo version, John messes up some words in the last verse, where it sounds like he suppresses a chuckle at his mistake.

"**From Me to You**": There's harmonica on the intro of the mono mix, but not on the stereo one.

"**Thank You Girl**": There's much more harmonica in the stereo mix.

"**All My Loving**": The mix on the German-Dutch compilation *The Beatles Greatest* starts with five taps of the hi-hat from Ringo.

"**I Call Your Name**": The cowbell starts at the beginning of the song in the mono version, but not until the first line in the stereo mixes. The intros of the stereo and mono versions have different guitar parts.

"**And I Love Her**": Some mixes have a single-tracked vocal; on others it's double-tracked. On the German version of *Something New*, the instrumental coda lasts six bars instead of four.

"**I Should Have Known Better**": Different harmonica overdubs are used for the instrumental intros of the stereo and mono versions.

"**If I Fell**": A most entertaining one, as Paul's voice cracks on his high harmony on the word "vain" in the stereo version, though it doesn't in mono.

"**Tell Me Why**": Double-tracked John Lennon vocal in stereo, single-tracked John Lennon vocal in mono.

"**I'll Cry Instead**": Some US mixes have a reprise of the first verse not found in others (such as the one currently available on CD).

"**Matchbox**": Ringo sings a longer line at the end of one of the verses in the mono version; in the stereo version he throws in a "well" not in the mono mix at the start of one verse. The guitar solo is also different in mono than it is in stereo.

"**Words of Love**": The fade on the mono mix is ten seconds longer than the stereo one.

"**Help!**": The stereo version uses an entirely different lead vocal track than the mono one, and also has tambourine in the chorus that's absent from the mono.

"**The Word**": The only mix on which John's lead vocal is double-tracked is on the US stereo LP.

"**I'm Looking Through You**": One of the most obvious differences in any Beatles mix—the US stereo LP has two false starts of guitar strumming, missing from other versions.

"**What Goes On**": The mono version's missing the guitar riff heard on the stereo mix's instrumental outro.

"**Paperback Writer**": Ringo's drum taps on the choruses of the mono version are not in the stereo counterpart.

"**Taxman**": The cowbell enters a few lines earlier in the mono version than it does in the stereo one.

"**I'm Only Sleeping**": A knotty one, as four different mixes put backward guitar sounds in different places.

"**Got to Get You into My Life**": The fade on the mono mix is eight seconds longer than the stereo one, with a different vocal by Paul on the last few words.

"**Tomorrow Never Knows**": The mix on the first mono British pressings of *Revolver* lasts about three seconds longer, with different placement of the special effects.

"Penny Lane": Seven-note trumpet coda on North American mono 45 promo copies not heard elsewhere.

"Within You, Without You": The mono version has different laughter effects at the end.

"Sgt. Pepper's Lonely Hearts Club Band" (reprise): There are four extra drumbeats at the beginning of the mono version, and the audience effects are placed differently in the mono and stereo mixes.

"All You Need Is Love": The fade on the mono mix is ten seconds longer than on the stereo one.

"I Am the Walrus": Some mixes use a four-beat intro, others a six-beat intro; the US single has an extra bar of instrumental music before the "yellow matter custard" line not heard in other versions.

"The Inner Light": The part played by the shenai on the Indian instrumental intro is different in the mono and stereo versions.

"Across the Universe": The first two mixes that were issued were so different that they're considered essentially different tracks. The first, much lighter one, with bird effects and no strings, was first issued in 1969 on the *No One's Gonna Change Our World* various-artists charity LP, and is now on the *Past Masters, Vol. 2* CD compilation. The second, from which Phil Spector removed the bird effects and added strings and a slowed-down John Lennon vocal, was used on the *Let It Be* album, and is currently on the *Let It Be* CD.

"Hey Jude": The mono version is eight seconds longer at the fade than the stereo one.

"Back in the U.S.S.R.": Different jet effects used in the mono and stereo versions.

"Blackbird": Different bird effects in the mono and stereo.

"Piggies": Different pig sounds in the mono and stereo.

"Don't Pass Me By": Different and longer fiddle solo on the mono version than the stereo one; the mono also runs at a slightly faster speed than the stereo mix.

"Honey Pie": The guitar solos are different in the mono and stereo mixes.

"Yer Blues": The mono version is ten seconds longer than the stereo one.

"Helter Skelter": A very strange one to have slipped past quality control, with the mono mix running a full 53 seconds shorter than the more familiar stereo one. In addition, there are numerous other differences in the drumming, guitar, and vocal parts in mono, as well as some beeping noises not heard in the stereo version.

"Savoy Truffle": The guitar parts differ in the mono and stereo mixes.

"Let It Be": The mixes of the single and album versions are so different that even EMI considers them to be essentially different tracks, putting the single version on the *Past Masters Vol. 2* CD compilation and the album version on the *Let It Be* CD.

---

the brief passage of clamoring drums and demented, distorted speech that follows the false ending of "Strawberry Fields Forever," it adds an ambiguous, sinister aura to the placid nostalgia on the tune's surface, suggesting that such apparently cozy childhood memories are never as idyllic as we imagine them to be as adults. Through no fault of trumpeter David Mason, that effect would have been totally absent had his jaunty, gracefully reassuring coda stayed in place.

The RM11 mix of "Penny Lane" from the North American promo 45 might be considered unreleased by hard-liners as well. Although a version of the song with the trumpet coda was issued in 1980 on Capitol's *Rarities* compilation, that track was, for the most part, not taken from the mono mix found on the rare promo 45. Instead, it was mostly taken from a stereo mix first released on the West German *Magical Mystery Tour* LP in 1971, with the coda (in the words of the liner notes themselves) "tagged on." The preponderance of released and unreleased mixes of Beatles studio tracks such as "Penny Lane" is dreadfully confusing to novice collectors (and even some veteran ones), which makes this as good a time as any to address the topic in the adjoining sidebar.

● January 19

Studio Outtakes

Sgt. Pepper's Lonely Hearts Club Band sessions
Studio Two, Abbey Road, London

A Day in the Life (take 1 fragments)
A Day in the Life (take 4 fragment)

Compared to the final recording, take 1 of "A Day in the Life" was simple, with just piano, bongos, maracas, and John Lennon on vocal and acoustic guitar. The way in which excerpts from the take have scattered onto various authorized and illicit sources, however, is anything but straightforward.

A little over a minute of the beginning of the song can be heard on the television documentary *The Making of Sgt. Pepper,* with George Martin isolating the vocal track for a few seconds. As early on as this is in the process, it's not much different from the first part of the final track as it appeared on the *Sgt. Pepper* album, other than John's singing being a bit more reserved. The most delightful bonus, in fact, is nonmusical, John counting in the track with the druggily phrased words "sugar plum fairy, sugar plum fairy." A bit more of the opening part of the take is heard, though as heard on monitor speakers, on the bonus disc of the *Anthology* DVD. About a half minute from the third verse has also appeared on bootleg. And a little less than half a minute of the beginning of take 1—the presong chatter, ending at the "sugar plum fairy" count-in—is used as the beginning of the *Anthology 2* version, discussed in the next entry.

Finally, about a minute from the beginning of take 4 can be heard on the unreleased rough cut of the *Anthology* video series. This isn't much different from take 1, and isn't quite an unfettered excerpt, as George Martin works the mixing board to highlight certain aspects of the track at points while the fragment plays.

The Beatles posing in their Sgt. Pepper *finery on a grab bag bootleg of various rarities.*

● January 19–February 10

Studio Outtake

Sgt. Pepper's Lonely Hearts Club Band *sessions*
Studio One and Studio Two, Abbey Road, London

---

*A Day in the Life (**Anthology 2** mix)
  *appears on Anthology 2

One of the more artificially reconstructed tracks in the *Anthology* series, this mix combines parts of takes 1, 2, and 6 of "A Day in the Life," as well as some orchestral pieces recorded slightly later, into a five-minute facsimile of a complete alternate version. The procedure was nearly headspinning in its intricacy, the cut beginning with the presong banter and "sugar plum fairy" count-in from take 1—but not including anything from the song proper as performed in that take. The track then switches to take 2 (taped on January 19), which is what we hear from the first guitar strum to the point at which Paul McCartney starts singing his middle section (from take 6, taped on January 20).

From what we hear in this mix, take 2 was similar to take 1, with a sparser, folkier feel than the opening section of the *Sgt. Pepper* track. Otherwise it's similar, with the notable exception of the absence of Ringo's thundering drum accents; there's also a tinge of awkward insistence to the piano not in the final version. The big difference arrives in the ominous build-up to the middle section. Not only are there no swimming orchestral instruments at this stage, but you can clearly hear Beatles roadie Mal Evans counting off all 24 bars of this section in a ghostly voice, the echo of his declarations steadily mounting until he sounds as if he's shouting from the bowels of a cavern. You can also hear the discordant piano on this section a lot more clearly here than in

the album mix, and while it's no match for the drama of the orchestral crescendo, it does have an undeniably spooky (if sparer) ambience all the same.

Paul's middle bit is likewise rather similar to the section as it was presented on the *Sgt. Pepper* mix, except he's singing a guide vocal here. This guide vocal isn't too different from the released version, other than a markedly different vocalizing of the phrase about grabbing his hat, on which he suddenly reaches for high notes near the end. He hasn't settled on the final lyrics yet, as he "made" rather than "found" his way upstairs, where "everybody" rather than "somebody" spoke. Or maybe it's an actual mistake, as he chuckles and then mutters cheerfully, "Oh, shit"—score one for the integrity of the corporations coordinating *Anthology 2,* as that expletive was, a little surprisingly, *not* deleted on this official release. The subsequent, brief instrumental conclusion of this middle section sounds pretty hollow without the graceful orchestration and John's haunting, high, wordless vocals, leaving only a rather uninteresting piano-led rhythm track, during which a cough is plainly heard.

When John returns to sing the final verse, we switch back to take 2. But only for a bit, as after John finishes the verse—singing the word "how" more like "now"—there's (quoting from the *Anthology 2* liner notes) "a new mix of the orchestral crescendos recorded on 10 February." And no slam-the-coffin piano chord at the end, as instead we hear a bit of ill-fitting studio chat from Paul, indicating he was a bit concerned about the Beatles' growing experimental ambitions being perceived as pretentious: "The worst thing about doing something like this, is that I think that at first, people sort of are a bit suspicious. Y'know, just, c'mon, what are you up to?"

Those behind *Anthology 2* likely went to such elaborate efforts to piece together this mix under the perception that the greater record-buying public would prefer a composite mix that approximated the sound and structure of the familiar released *Sgt. Pepper* track, rather than hearing separate, rougher pieces. That may be, but it's also likely that those who seriously collect anything they can of the Beatles would prefer to hear the original, separate takes in their complete form. It would give a much clearer insight into the process of how masterworks like "A Day in the Life" were built.

● January 20

Studio Outtake

Sgt. Pepper's Lonely Hearts Club Band *sessions*
Studio Two, Abbey Road, London

A Day in the Life (take 6)

Speaking of which, a complete take 6 *has* been bootlegged that gives us a clearer idea of at least one step in the process that "A Day in the Life" took in its evolution. This early version is still considerably sparer than the final one. But it's taken things much further along from where they were at takes 1 and 2 just one day before, with the addition of drums and bass. The orchestral build-up to Paul's middle section, and the middle section itself, are still relatively undeveloped, as they are in the *Anthology 2* mix. The most interesting difference between this and that *Anthology 2* version, however, comes at the end, when Mal Evans enters for another chamber-of-horrors, echoed count-off, hellish piano thumps and bashes keeping pace. An eerie, high-pitched whistle sounds, the piano veers higher and higher into atonality, and a pulsating, nervous bass pushes the rhythm, the whole track reaching for but not falling into an anarchic abyss. Just when things seem about to fall apart, with rapid descending bass runs and piano glissandos, all the instruments come to a simultaneous stop, the clamor dissolving in a brief burst of laughter.

The Beatles almost certainly knew there was much work to be done yet on the song, especially in raising the instrumental crescendo passages to the level of the rest of the track. That would be accomplished with the overdubs recorded by a 40-piece orchestra on February 10, and there's no question that the final version was much improved. Yet this skeletal prototype is certainly a much more accurate snapshot of the song in its formative state than the *Anthology 2* mix is, and is in that respect a more interesting (and certainly more organic) "alternate version" of this most famous of Beatles songs.

In the rough cut of *Anthology,* incidentally, George Martin plays about three minutes of excerpts from take 6, isolating some aspects of the track while it's in progress.

● Circa Early 1967

Private Tape
Kenwood, Weybridge

Good Morning, Good Morning

"Good Morning, Good Morning" wasn't one of the better *Sgt. Pepper* tracks, but it's the only one where a 1966–1967 version exists that was *not* recorded at EMI. That comes in the form of this John Lennon home demo, lasting just a tad over a minute, which gives him just enough time to finish the bridge before he comes to a dead-stop chord. It's another home outing on which he accompanies himself on the Mellotron, accounting for the mechanical, pianolike texture of the instrumental backing. That also explains its metronomic rhythms, almost as though he were thinking of having the beat of a ticking clock as a timekeeper. It would have been in keeping with the song's theme of going through the paces of everyday life with all the crushing predictability of a bus making all the scheduled stops on its timetable.

Although the two verses and bridge have lyrics virtually identical to the ones heard on *Sgt. Pepper,* John doesn't seem to have worked out the chorus yet. At the end of the first verse, he sings "Good morning" just once, almost as an afterthought, using notes wholly unlike those sung by the Beatles on the studio version. That's followed by a muffled chuckle-snigger, as if he's a little embarrassed by the knowledge that this stopgap chorus won't cut the mustard. The people he sees in the bridge are "fast" rather than "half" asleep, too.

Assuming this was almost certainly taped shortly before the Beatles started work on the song in the studio on February 8, it shows that the bulk of its final structure was in place. It's actually part of a larger 14-minute tape with the kind of John 'n' Ringo fiddling about that typified the experimental home Mellotron tapes Lennon was doing in this period, though this "Good Morning, Good Morning" run-through is the only part to have been bootlegged.

● February 2

Studio Outtake
Sgt. Pepper's Lonely Hearts Club Band sessions
Studio Two, Abbey Road, London

Sgt. Pepper's Lonely Hearts Club Band (RM1)

This mono rough mix of the title track from *Sgt. Pepper's Lonely Hearts Club Band* is actually substantially different from the released version, as there are no brass overdubs or sound effects. Heard in this state, it's more of a straightforward *rock* song, rather than a slightly contrived theatrical curtain-raiser. Too, the band continues to play "Sgt. Pepper" for about 20 seconds after you're expecting them to segue into "With a Little Help from My Friends," even if that extra section's just a monotonous tag anchored by a repetitious throbbing chord.

● February 10

Studio Outtakes
Sgt. Pepper's Lonely Hearts Club Band sessions
Studio One, Abbey Road, London

A Day in the Life (orchestral overdub onto take 7)
A Day in the Life (edit piece, take 11)

In an inspired brainwave, the Beatles decided to fill up the spaces leading up to the middle section and end of "A Day in the Life" with the discordant, ascending maelstrom of a 40-piece orchestra. George Martin discusses and plays about half a minute of these orchestral overdubs in the rough cut of *Anthology,* observing, "It was no good just playing the notes as written. These were the finest musicians you could get in London, and for years they'd been taught to play as one man. I suddenly said to them, 'Don't listen to the fellow next door to you. Make your own way up this huge climax. And if you're playing anything like the fellow next door to you, you're playing a wrong note.' It worked!"

A more interesting, if very brief, excerpt from this day's session was also played by Martin in this sequence. "We still needed a finish . . . and it had to be something that wasn't orchestral," he explained. "We had already done that. And this was one of those bright ideas that just didn't work. We thought of all the ideas of Buddhist monks chanting, thought it would be a great idea to have everybody massed in the studio doing 'Ah-ummm' and hanging onto it, and multiply that many times. And the result was . . . pathetic." Whereupon he punches a button and we hear the Beatles singing, en masse, for seven seconds from one of the edit pieces they recorded that day: "Ah-UMMMMMM." It's not "pathetic," but it would be replaced by a more effective, and *much* longer, piano chord recorded 12 days later.

● February 13–April 20

Studio Outtake
Yellow Submarine sessions
Studio Two, Abbey Road, London

*Only a Northern Song (**Anthology 2** remix)
   *appears on Anthology 2

Many fans with complete collections of standard Beatles albums still don't realize that George Harrison's "Only a Northern Song" is a genuine *Sgt. Pepper* outtake, retrieved for use on the *Yellow Submarine* soundtrack after it had been rejected. The decades-after-the-event mix on *Anthology 2* is another of its more patchwork reconstructions, combining take 3 with unused vocal tracks "flown in" from take 12. At casual listening, it seems like nothing more or less than the *Yellow Submarine* version without the fanciful overdubs of trumpet and other strained far-outisms, making it sound much more like a standard rock song. Listen more closely, however, and you'll hear a number of differences in the lyrics. Specifically, here George takes responsibility for the song's wrong words, harmony, and chords. On the final version, those flaws are largely attributed to a third person and a band. Maybe that's George's dig, if a subconscious one, at John and Paul, whose compositions (like George's) were published by Northern Songs. Probably, however, that's reading too much into something that was, like the title said, "Only a Northern Song."

Whatever the case, George's alterations couldn't make one of the Beatles' most (and few) mediocre songs into a good one. George's contribution to *Sgt. Pepper* ended up being "Within You, Without You," which was not only a better composition, but a far better fit into the album's exotic-eclectic ambience.

● February 16

Studio Outtake

Sgt. Pepper's Lonely Hearts Club Band *sessions*
Studio Three, Abbey Road, London

*Good Morning, Good Morning (take 8)
   *appears on Anthology 2

Actually incorporating recordings from both February 8 and February 16, take 8 of "Good Morning, Good Morning" was the backbone of the much-overdubbed recording that eventually produced the *Sgt. Pepper* version. Issued on *Anthology 2*, it's essentially a rhythm track with John Lennon vocals, lacking the singing on the chorus, the brief but burning guitar solo, and the many animal noises of the final mix. As such, it's a dissatisfying, bare-bones listen; you're constantly waiting in vain for voices, instruments, and cockle-doodle-doos to fill up the empty spaces. You do hear the band vamp all the way to a dead stop for quite a while at the end, giving the song a more straightforward rock 'n' roll flavor than the ornately decorated *Sgt. Pepper* recording.

● February 17

Studio Outtakes

Sgt. Pepper's Lonely Hearts Club Band *sessions*
Studio Two, Abbey Road, London

*Being for the Benefit of Mr. Kite (take 1)
*Being for the Benefit of Mr. Kite (take 2)

Being for the Benefit of Mr. Kite (rehearsal take 7)
   *appears on Anthology 2

The two super-brief takes of "Being for the Benefit of Mr. Kite" that appear on *Anthology 2* aren't much to shout about. Take 1 goes at such a languid, spacey gait that one must assume the Beatles used the rhythm by collective mistake, perhaps because they weren't yet familiar with the song. This seems especially true because take 2, which starts just a few seconds later, has an arrangement and rhythm almost identical to that used in the final version. It doesn't get far, however, as John's voice breaks badly on the word "trampoline." But at least you get to hear him sing the title line in an old man's voice in the pre–take 1 chatter at the very beginning.

There's a yet less consequential "outtake" from this session in the form of a largely instrumental ten-second end fragment of one of the day's "rehearsal" takes, heard during the end credits to the *Anthology* DVD. And if you want to burrow even further, a two-second snatch of John Lennon dialogue from the session ("Well, we'll have the Massed Alberts on by then") appears on Paul McCartney's *Liverpool Sound Collage*.

● February 17–20

Studio Outtake

Sgt. Pepper's Lonely Hearts Club Band *sessions*
Studio Two, Abbey Road, London

*Being for the Benefit of Mr. Kite (**Anthology 2** mix)
   *appears on Anthology 2

The *Anthology 2* cut 'n' paste of "Being for the Benefit of Mr. Kite" is mostly drawn from take 7, which provided the base backing track for the released version. John's vocal here is different, however, especially during the instrumental break, where he can be heard hum-scatting wordlessly before singing half-heartedly about Henry the Horse dancing the waltz. That bit during the instrumental break is sung as though he knows it's a guide vocal that will be erased from the final mix, but it does indicate that maybe he was still thinking of using some lyrics during that section instead of making it wholly instrumental. Otherwise, this is much like hearing the *Sgt. Pepper* track minus some overdubs, sounding oddly skeletal, as though the circus the song describes has yet to arrive in town.

Near the end, this *Anthology 2* track crossfades from take 7 into an organ and calliope effects tape made on February 20. According to the *Anthology 2* liner notes, those effects are "clearer in this new mix"—which doesn't explain why the effects fade out here, rather than coming to a dramatic, sweeping close as they did on the end of side one of the *Sgt. Pepper* LP.

● February 22

Studio Outtakes

Sgt. Pepper's Lonely Hearts Club Band *sessions*
Studio Two, Abbey Road, London

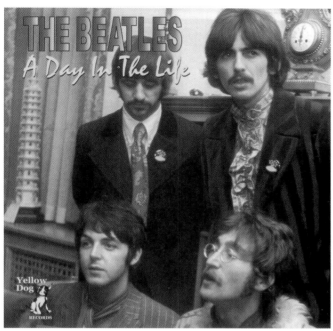

The A Day in the Life *CD, with nine mixes of "A Day in the Life" that differ only slightly from one another.*

A Day in the Life (RS1–RS9)

The final, magnificently reverberant piano chord that finishes "A Day in the Life" (and the *Sgt. Pepper* album) having been recorded earlier that day, the track was then mixed into stereo at Abbey Road. These outtakes are both an audiophile's dream and his or her significant other's worst nightmare: no less than *nine* stereo mixes of the song from that one mixing session, differing from one another in only the slightest of nuances. The most audible differences as far as the content, in fact, are nonmusical: small bits of applause from the orchestra at the end of the mixes (for which you'll have to turn the volume *way* up to hear), and faint chatter and take announcements from the engineers before each mix. None of the nine mixes include the final piano chord, by the way; some are aborted just a minute or two into the track. The primary variations are in the positioning of the instruments within the stereo picture. As the fidelity's pristine, that might make them a fascinating document for musical engineering students. But they quickly wear out their welcome when taken out of the control room and into the living room, particularly heard nine in a row.

Incidentally, one tiny extra bit from the edit pieces of the final piano chord recorded at this session is heard on the rough cut of *Anthology*: Paul McCartney counting "one, two, three" before the assembled hands land on several pianos at once.

● **March 1**

Studio Outtake
Sgt. Pepper's Lonely Hearts Club Band *sessions*

Studio Two, Abbey Road, London

Lucy in the Sky with Diamonds (take 6 fragment)

It's back to the TV documentary *The Making of Sgt. Pepper* as a source for this excerpt from "Lucy in the Sky with Diamonds." It's actually pretty similar to the *Anthology 2* mix of the song (see entry below), which used take 6 as its basic track. However, here you can hear the chorus as an instrumental section without the overdubbed vocals, albeit under dialogue by George Martin and Paul McCartney. Also, at one point the mix is tweaked so that John's vocals are way out front. Microscopic bonuses, then, but for the most studious of Beatles scholars, they're there.

● **March 1–2**

Studio Outtake
Sgt. Pepper's Lonely Hearts Club Band *sessions*
Studio Two, Abbey Road, London

*Lucy in the Sky with Diamonds (**Anthology 2** mix)
*appears on Anthology 2

Marching onward with *Anthology 2*'s artificially manufactured *Sgt. Pepper* outtakes, this mix of "Lucy in the Sky with Diamonds" was taken from elements of takes 6, 7, and 8. The big, obvious difference is John's singing, deliberately intended as a "guide vocal" rather than the finished article. Still, even as guide vocals go, it's strangely expressionless, using a mechanical staccato rhythm that drains the song of much of its seductive, hallucinogenic beauty. John, of course, gave a much more rhythmically varied, nuanced vocal when it came time to finalize the recording.

It's easy to take potshots at this little army of *Sgt. Pepper* "outfakes," as some specialized collectors have ungraciously dubbed them. To be fair to the compilers, however, they did face a daunting task here. *Sgt. Pepper*'s immense popularity must have dictated that they find *some* unused material. Yet at this particular point in the Beatles' career, the group was so consciously layering their tracks in stages that there was little in the way of complete-sounding, interesting alternate takes/versions. If creating new mixes from bits and pieces of separate takes/mixes wasn't as "honest" as just presenting them in their original, unaltered states, the product was likely more listenable. And the *Anthology* CDs weren't made exclusively for the scholarly collector—they were made for the more general Beatles fan, who likely would have found the truly naked original takes and mixes even more confusing and piecemeal than these newly strung-together concoctions.

● **March 6**

Studio Outtake
Sgt. Pepper's Lonely Hearts Club Band *sessions*
Studio Two, Abbey Road, London

Sgt. Pepper's Lonely Hearts Club Band (take 10 fragment)

Not so much an outtake as a manipulation of the mix, this is taken from *The Making of Sgt. Pepper's* soundtrack. While playing back much of the title song, George Martin isolates the vocal and horn tracks for small snatches, allowing us to hear these elements on their own rather than within the mix.

● March 15–April 3

Studio Outtake
Sgt. Pepper's Lonely Hearts Club Band *sessions*
Studio One and Studio Two, Abbey Road, London

*Within You Without You (instrumental)
        appears on Anthology 2

As *Anthology 2* had done with "Eleanor Rigby" so it did with "Within You Without You": presenting an "instrumental" version by mixing out the vocal, the backing track itself subjected to a new remix. Without George's singing, it becomes much less of a pop song—not that it was a standard pop song to begin with—and almost purely Indian in feel. But that rather defeats part of George's original point in writing the tune, which was, as he said in *The Making of Sgt. Pepper,* "just my way of trying to make a Western pop song, using some of those instruments and some of those sounds."

● March 29

Studio Outtake
Sgt. Pepper's Lonely Hearts Club Band *sessions*
Studio Two, Abbey Road, London

Good Morning, Good Morning (take 11 fragment)

Perhaps the most peripheral of the sequences in *The Making of Sgt. Pepper* in which George Martin toyed with the mix was this one, in which he worked the board so that some of the animal effects on "Good Morning, Good Morning" were more easily audible than they were on the released version. By the way, it's not exactly a Beatles recording, but the entire minute-and-a-half tape of animal noises that John Lennon put together for use in "Good Morning, Good Morning" has been bootlegged. As have, for that matter, the tapes of audience noise and applause that were used at different points on the *Sgt. Pepper* album.

● March 31

Studio Outtake
Sgt. Pepper's Lonely Hearts Club Band *sessions*
Studio Two, Abbey Road, London

Being for the Benefit of Mr. Kite (take 9 fragments)

Yet another instance in which the only way to hear a *Sgt. Pepper* song broken down into separate components is on *The Making of Sgt. Pepper's* soundtrack. Here George Martin variously highlights/isolates the vocal, cymbals, and circus effects of "Being for the Benefit of Mr. Kite."

● April 1

Studio Outtake
Sgt. Pepper's Lonely Hearts Club Band *sessions*
Studio One, Abbey Road, London

*Sgt. Pepper's Lonely Hearts Club Band (reprise) (take 5)
        appears on Anthology 2

In the midst of all these isolated tracks, slim fragments, 1990s mixes combining various takes, and whatnot, how refreshing it is to come upon a complete beginning-to-end, substantially different alternate version of a *Sgt. Pepper* song. Granted, it's the album's shortest and perhaps least remarkable song, this "reprise" mainly serving the purpose of bookending the loose concept unveiled at the beginning of the record. But it's a more conventionally harder-rocking number than anything else on the album, which might explain why its recording was fairly straightforward, yielding this earlier take with a Paul McCartney guide vocal. The absence of animal sound effects (from the fade of "Good Morning, Good Morning") and crowd noise also allows us to hear the very beginning of the track as it might have originally been envisioned, with a clock-ticking, chicken-scratch guitar rhythm and a small glissando flourish of the piano.

Although similar in many respects to the final take (take 9) recorded later that day, this earlier version is surprisingly rudimentary in some ways. It's different enough to suggest that, in a throwback to the old days, some relatively on-the-spot rearranging might have been taking place. The ascending chord change in the beginning of most of the song's lines is missing, making the tune sound much less developed (and more monotonous). Paul's guide vocal, while enthusiastic, is similarly a ways off its final form, the phrasing more casual and laidback. The stabbing organ's more prominent in the mix, especially at the end, where its slightly cheesy sustained tone rings like a refugee from an American garage band 45. Most of all, it's missing the three-part vocal harmonies that did so much to lift this slight tune into an altogether more satisfying, punchy rock 'n' roll track on the *Sgt. Pepper* album.

● April 3

Studio Outtake
Sgt. Pepper's Lonely Hearts Club Band *sessions*
Studio One and Studio Two, Abbey Road, London

Within You Without You (take 2 fragments)

The last of our entries for the *Sgt. Pepper* album is also the last that cites *The Making of Sgt. Pepper,* the TV documentary on which George Martin, as he does for several of the album's songs, isolates certain parts of the track. In the case of "Within You Without You," that means

A collection of 1967 outtakes that almost, but not quite, replicates the actual Sgt. Pepper *cover.*

brief sections in which we hear the dilruba, sitar, pizzicato strings, cello, and vocals highlighted or isolated in the mix so that the individual parts can be more clearly heard. It's much more interesting to hear and see Martin and the Beatles doing and discussing these mix variations on screen than as audio-only soundtrack excerpts, of course. As of this writing in 2006, however, *The Making of Sgt. Pepper* has not been issued for the home video market, meaning that both the film *and* the soundtrack continue to be accessible only via bootleg. That's too bad, for although many of the stories on this program have been around the block several times in assorted documentaries and books, it's a pretty entertaining and informative overview of the evolution of the *Sgt. Pepper* album, with interviews of Martin, McCartney, Harrison, and Starr.

● Circa Spring

Private Tapes
Kenwood, Weybridge

She's Walkin' Past My Door
You Know My Name (Look Up the Number)

Acknowledging we'll probably never know when these John Lennon home tapes were recorded, among those who've considered the matter there's not much agreement. Some think a late 1967–early 1968 date makes the most sense, particularly as there are a bunch of roughly similar-sounding home tapes of other Lennon compositions that were probably done at that time. Others believe they were done earlier, the giveaway being the presence of "You Know My Name (Look Up the

Number)," which the Beatles started recording at EMI in mid-1967. It's not an easy call, but here we'll go with a spring 1967 estimate, musing that John would have been more likely to record "You Know My Name (Look Up the Number)" at home before the Beatles began working on it in the studio.

Whatever the date, it's pretty certain that these solo piano-plus-vocals outings were recorded at the same time, since they segue into each other. "She's Walkin' Past My Door" is the first of the pair, and while that's the title it's usually been given on bootlegs, it's not at all certain that's the title John had in mind, especially since it's hard to even hear his vocal for much of the minute-and-a-half performance. It's not much of a song at this point, to be honest, anticipating some of his drabber, slow-to-mid-tempo, piano-based compositions of the early '70s. At one point early in the recording, the chord sequence stumbles toward something strongly resembling "Imagine," but it stays there only briefly before detouring into something else entirely. At another point the chord sequence drifts into a progression close to the one used in "You Know My Name (Look Up the Number)," so it's possible that these two "songs" were, in fact, just one tune that John was working on.

In the cut lasting just over a minute that's usually identified as "You Know My Name (Look Up the Number)," John starts to wander close to the song's slightly jazzy melody with the same sluggish tempo he's using on "She's Walkin' Past My Door." Perhaps sensing the rhythm's dragging a lead weight, he suddenly speeds into a perky, almost music-hallish pace, singing the song's one and only line, "You know my name (look up the number)," over and over. He's having so much trouble hitting the right piano chords, however, that it's reminiscent of that Monty Python sketch where John Cleese's Beethoven character can't get the opening notes to his Fifth Symphony right (not that this is anything on the order of the Fifth Symphony). Maybe John took it to the other Beatles in this ultra-primitive state realizing that he couldn't take it any further, and might as well have some off-the-wall fun with it. It's been theorized that, if this was taped in late 1967 and early 1968, John's actually having trouble remembering the song, which the Beatles had started recording in the studio in May, but abandoned for the time being.

It's also been theorized that a piano-Mellotron-vocal tape containing barely recognizable seeds of "Across the Universe" was done around this time. That could be, but just taking a guess that John wouldn't have wanted to sit on the song for so long, that recording (as well as other home tapes of that tune) will be discussed in an entry dealing with numbers he may have done at Kenwood in late 1967 and early 1968.

● April 20

Studio Outtake
Yellow Submarine sessions
Studio Two, Abbey Road, London

Only a Northern Song (RM6)

Quirkily, the mono version of the original *Yellow Submarine* album (issued in the UK but not the US) used not the original mono mixes of the four songs released for the first time on that LP, but "bouncedowns" that blended both channels of the stereo "duophonic" mixes into one. While casual listeners aren't likely to worry about this apparent carelessness (or notice much difference among the various official and unreleased mixes), it's the cause of great consternation to the most audiophile-oriented Beatles collectors. It's also meant that the original mono mixes of these four songs (except "Hey Bulldog") have been available only on bootleg, such as this one of "Only a Northern Song."

As to why the original mono mixes were never used, perhaps the UK mono edition was simply not given much attention, issued as it was at a time (in early 1969) when mono was on the verge of getting phased out altogether in favor of stereo. Or perhaps the whole *Yellow Submarine* LP mixing process was given relatively low priority by the Beatles and the EMI staff. After all, the LP featured just four new Beatles songs, all of them slightly substandard (by the group's very high standards, at any rate), and all of them recorded quite some time before its January 1969 release date. *The Beatles* (aka *The White Album*), released less than two months before *Yellow Submarine,* was a much more important project to both the Beatles and their record label. Plus, during January 1969, the Beatles were busy recording a yet additional new album, *Get Back,* not to mention trying to hold themselves together in the midst of unprecedented internecine tensions. As another indication of *Yellow Submarine*'s low-man-on-the-totem-pole status, the stereo "duophonic" mix was done by boosting the treble in the left channel and the bass in the right, rather than via the more subtle and creative methods customarily granted to Beatles product in the last half of the 1960s. As the 1999 *Yellow Submarine Songtrack* CD created fresh stereo remixes for the four songs (plus other Beatles recordings used in the *Yellow Submarine* movie), it's that version that most audiophile Beatlemaniacs prefer.

● **April 27**

Studio Outtake
Magical Mystery Tour *sessions*
Studio Three, Abbey Road, London

Magical Mystery Tour (RM4)

Right up until 1969, the Beatles were always working ahead of themselves, often writing new songs and forging new directions even while some of their latest innovations in the recording studio were still awaiting release. *Sgt. Pepper* was still more than a month away from going public when they started work on the theme song to their next movie–slash–television special, *Magical Mystery Tour.* Though the material they cut from this point onward through the end of 1967 is less celebrated than *Sgt. Pepper,* if anything, the tracks they made in this period were recorded in an even more layered and intricate fashion.

Such was the case with the sessions for the "Magical Mystery Tour" song itself, which have spawned several different mixes that have made it into circulation. The one labeled RM4 is the first of these, taken from a notably scratchy acetate. Other than the absence of trumpet overdubs and sound effects of a bus rushing by, it's not much different from the familiar version at all. The basics of the track were already in place, but the group would tamper with the trimmings quite a bit by the time they were finished.

● **May 3**

Studio Outtake
Magical Mystery Tour *sessions*
Studio Three, Abbey Road, London

Magical Mystery Tour (RM7)

"Magical Mystery Tour" was mostly completed with this mix, with the addition of four trumpets and (on the instrumental fade) glockenspiel. The only things missing are the mock carnival barking speech over the intro and the bus sound effects, which wouldn't be added until November 7, when the television program was much closer to its air date.

Incidentally, the version you hear on the soundtrack itself is yet different from the officially released ones and these unissued mixes. On the soundtrack, it's John, not Paul, who rallies the troops to join up for the Magical Mystery Tour on the intro, adding a few words ("Hurry, hurry, hurry") not heard on the album. Too, John adds a frankly sardonic-toned, spoken huckster pitch over the brief instrumental break: "When a man buys a ticket for a Magical Mystery Tour, he knows what to expect. We guarantee him the trip of a lifetime, and that's just what he gets." And then, just to remind us he isn't any old used car salesman, some serious psychedelic echo distorts his next few words: "The incredible Magical Mystery Tour!" There are some extra crowd noises and motor vehicle sound effects on the soundtrack too, and while you can hear this version on the film (newly mixed into stereo for the 1988 home video), it's made its way onto a few bootlegs too.

● **May 12**

Studio Outtake
Yellow Submarine *sessions*
Studio Two, Abbey Road, London

All Together Now (RM6)

The original, unissued mono mix for "All Together Now," complete with pretake engineering announcement (as is the case for the original mono mix of "Only a Northern Song").

● **May 17, 1967–April 30, 1969**

Studio Outtake
"You Know My Name (Look Up the Number)" single session
Studio Two and Studio Three, Abbey Road, London

---

*You Know My Name (Look Up the Number) (**Anthology 2** mix)
  *appears on Anthology 2

After the Beatles finished *Sgt. Pepper* in April 1967, they were, for the first time, really, recording at their own pace as their whims took them, with no particular album or single release in mind. Some of the material they worked on over the next few months found its way onto the *Magical Mystery Tour* soundtrack, some of it was eventually used on

Yellow Submarine, some of it was never released, and some of it became another global smash single. They'd certainly earned a few months' respite from more dedicated recording, having just completed a masterwork in *Sgt. Pepper* and having, indeed, worked like dogs in general for most of the past five years. This might partially account for the aimless goofiness of some of the numbers they tackled that spring and summer, none goofier than "You Know My Name (Look Up the Number)." And one of the goofiest things about this quite comical track was that it wasn't finished until almost two years after the Beatles began recording it—and not issued until almost another year after that, on the flipside of their "Let It Be" single in early 1970. George later said he thought it had been originally recorded for a fan club Christmas record, but it seems doubtful they'd be working on such a thing in May.

Although it's one of the most obscure tracks the Beatles issued during the group's lifetime, the recording of "You Know My Name (Look Up the Number)" was relatively complicated. Four sessions, two producers, two engineers, and two years were involved. The 1970 B-side, running four minutes and 17 seconds, was actually edited down from a mix lasting six minutes and ten seconds. The mix that was reconstructed for *Anthology 2* lasts considerably longer than the single—but, sadly, does *not* include the entirety of the original mix, despite adding nearly two additional unreleased minutes. For while nearly two minutes were added, about half a minute was taken *out* of the original mix—half a minute that, as it happened, *had* appeared on the original single release. Of all the new mixes created for the *Anthology* CDs, this is one of the few that is nothing less than a hack job.

To start with the positives, the *Anthology 2* version does add entirely new sections. The first, lasting from the 45-second mark to 2:15, tags on about 20 seconds to the intro-chorus (actually nothing more than the title line of the song). Then, after it awkwardly halts for a moment, there's a rather inelegant transition to a few frenetic ska reiterations of the chorus. Ska wasn't a form the Beatles referenced often, probably for good reason, as it wasn't one for which they had a natural feel. It's still fun to hear them do so here, if for nothing more than the sheer novelty of it. There's also (starting at about the 3:50 mark) an additional 20 seconds of the cuckoo-clock-like nonsense from the middle of the song, which when excised for the version used on the 45 tightened the track considerably.

In the meantime, however, 27 seconds of that pretty riotous cuckoo-clocking section of the original single was cut *out* for the mix prepared for *Anthology 2*. Just as bad, the *Anthology 2* mix fades, clumsily, a few seconds earlier than the single. In so doing, it entirely misses much of the incomprehensible, drunken-sounding John Lennon ranting that takes the track to a cold close—including the shouted "Hey!" that brings the curtain down on this lunacy with a glorious bang.

There's no question that the official single version of "You Know My Name (Look Up the Number)" is better than the original, uninterrupted six-minute, ten-second mix from which it was edited. It flows better, it's quicker-paced, and it's funnier. The whole point of making an "alternate" version available, however, should be to hear the whole thing as it originally sounded, not an arbitrary cut that makes decisions even goofier than the song itself. And it seems we can't lay the blame on some wet-behind-the-ears junior engineer for this, as it's been reported that the scissors were wielded by none other than George Harrison himself. That speculation was reinforced by his comment during a 1996 *Billboard* interview that the *Anthology 2* version "still has an edit out of

it, because it did go on a lot, particularly at the end. There was a bit Paul was doing that just went on and on." It's true that George wasn't a fan of "You Know My Name (Look Up the Number)," and perhaps he was unhappy that John and Paul did the vocals without his participation. But if that's what really happened, why leave the editing in the hands of someone who didn't even like the song?

Here's one of the few instances, as a footnote, where an artificially reconstructed Beatles "outfake" comes to the rescue. For a crafty bootlegger has edited all of the different segments of both the single and the *Anthology 2* versions together in sequence, creating a seamless facsimile of how the unadulterated original six-minute, ten-second mix should sound.

● June 2

Studio Outtake
Yellow Submarine sessions
De Lane Lea Recording Studios, London

It's All Too Much (RM1)

Although technically this is an alternate *mix* of "It's All Too Much" and not an alternate take, ultimately it amounts to one of the more interesting available alternate versions of a 1967 Beatles recording. For it contains nearly two minutes that were edited out of the *Yellow Submarine* version, including an entire verse not heard on the album. It's also the original, unissued mono mix, though it's the extra length that incites the most interest.

Had it been issued in its original form in 1967, this George Harrison song would have been—at eight minutes and 15 seconds—the longest track the Beatles had ever issued, by a good three-minute margin. To be frank, even in its edited (six-minute, 22-second) *Yellow Submarine* incarnation, the song suffered from some drift and structurelessness, despite some very admirable elements. Most of those—the scorching opening feedback passage, the heavenly organ that follows it, and the gently cosmic lilt of the verses—were retained in the final edit. However, that final edit still went on too long, with some extraneous instrumental sections and a way-too-long fade. It's difficult to see where the full 8:15 version could have fit in 1967—certainly not on the *Magical Mystery Tour* project, or a single. Maybe it was recorded with eventual placement on a proper Beatles LP in mind, but it ended up as one of the refugees scraped off the cutting room floor for the *Yellow Submarine* soundtrack.

Oddly, the clumsy two-and-a-half-minute extract edited together for inclusion in the *Yellow Submarine* film *did* include one of the key elements missing from the version on the soundtrack LP—the fourth verse, with a couplet about having time to take the opportunity for "me to look at you, and you to look at me." Neither the film nor the LP caught the third chorus, whose line "the more you give, the more you get" faintly foreshadowed "the love you take is equal to the love you make" on *Abbey Road*'s "The End." And more than a minute was lopped off the extended coda/fade, in which the Beatles keep chanting in disorganized fashion as feedback ebbs and flows in the background and random rhythms are shaken.

The main problem with "It's All Too Much," as this outtake reinforces, is not the song, which is certainly better than "Only a Northern

Recording "All You Need Is Love," June 1967.

Song." It's the length. "It's All Too Much" is no "Hey Jude," and even the six-minute version needed some trimming, not just this eight-minute-plus mix. All the same, as long as *Yellow Submarine* was being remixed for *Yellow Submarine Songtrack,* it's too bad it wasn't seen fit to include this long version as a bonus cut.

● June 25

Studio Outtakes

"All You Need Is Love" single session
Studio One, Abbey Road, London

All You Need Is Love (take 58)

All You Need Is Love (unknown take)

To most appearances, "All You Need Is Love" was performed live on this date as the BBC's contribution to *Our World,* the first television program to be broadcast all around the world by satellite. Many people assumed, in fact, not only that the Beatles and their accompanying orchestra were performing entirely live, but also that what they played on the program was identical to the track subsequently issued as a Beatles single. The truth was more complicated. The Beatles were actually playing live to a rhythm track containing previously recorded parts. Also, John would rerecord some of his lead vocal later that day, and Ringo would add a drum roll for the opening section on June 26. So it was a slightly contrived and manufactured live performance, with a safety net. Yet it was still an undeniably exciting highlight of their career, and

much of the performance as seen on the broadcast *was* live, including much of John's lead vocal, all of Paul's bass, George's guitar solo, Ringo's drums, and the 13-person orchestra.

All of this is preserved on film (see entry in film section), and viewing that footage is the best way to experience this semi-outtake. Still, the nearly seven-minute BBC tape of the proceedings has been bootlegged in excellent sound quality, including not only "All You Need Is Love," but some warm-up, studio chat, and commentary preceding the performance. Steve Race's narration actually makes clear that it's not a wholly live recording in the opening bit, in which we hear an orchestra-less snatch of the tune, Race noting that "the boys began by making a basic instrumental track on their own. Then they added on top of that, a second track of vocal backgrounds, and they just added a third track. Now comes the final stage. It brings in a solo vocal from John Lennon, and, for the first time, the orchestra." Underneath some banter between George Martin and his engineers, we hear a bit of jazzy busking. There's also a pretty hilarious, brief Lennon a cappella warm-up vocal of the chorus of "She Loves You," his voice virtually breaking in two, whether to be intentionally funny or from the sheer nervousness of getting ready to sing before hundreds of millions of viewers.

As for the performance of "All You Need Is Love" itself, you have to listen pretty closely to detect differences from the record. An obvious one, however, is the tambourine shake in the instrumental intro, to be replaced by a drum roll on the single. John's vocal is just a tad shakier in spots, which would be fixed by some rerecording later in the day. The fade also goes on a bit longer than it does on both the record and the TV program, ending with some hesitant attempts to play the "La Marseillaise" theme on guitar.

Also escaping from this day's work was a half-minute vocal rehearsal take that can be heard as the very final outtake snippet playing over the end credits of the *Anthology* video/DVD. Here John's more casual vocal is egged on by Paul's interjections, à la "I believe you, Johnny" and "You're right there, boy"—a touching tidbit from the days, soon to come to an end, when John and Paul were best mates as well as band mates. This bit finishes with John declaring, in a heavily echoed voice, "I'm ready to sing for the world, George, if you can just give me the backing. . . ."

● August 22

Studio Outtake

Magical Mystery Tour *sessions*
Chappell Recording Studios, London

Your Mother Should Know (take 8)

After an absence of two months, the Beatles returned to the studio to start work on just the second of their recordings that would be used on *Magical Mystery Tour* ("Magical Mystery Tour" itself being the first). This mono rough mix of "Your Mother Should Know" is basically the final version without overdubs of backing vocals, organ, bass, and tambourine which decorated the final track. It's another one of those 1967 Beatles specials—an outtake that sounds almost identical to the released track to untutored ears, almost as though it's the album version playing through speakers that are stubbornly rejecting signals from some of the more minor elements. The absence of those heliumlike vocal harmonies does iron out the song's almost grating, smiley-faced cheeriness a bit, making it a little graver in tone.

● September 5

Studio Outtakes

Magical Mystery Tour *sessions*
Studio One, Abbey Road, London

I Am the Walrus (monitor mix takes 7, 8, 9, and rehearsal/unknown take)
*I Am the Walrus (take 16)
    appears on Anthology 2

Although the circulating recordings of takes 7–9 of "I Am the Walrus" were recorded off-line, the quality's pretty good considering the source, giving us a fair idea of how the song was played as it was taking shape. One thing that's striking about these vocal-less run-throughs is how much more of a gritty, funky, elemental rock song "I Am the Walrus" sounds like without the orchestration, the eerie swooping backup vocals from the Mike Sammes Singers, and the interjections of dialogue from the BBC *King Lear* radio play. Another aspect this brings to the fore is how much more involved the tempo and chord changes were than you'd guess from a casual listen. The Beatles navigate them pretty well, but they're obviously still getting used to them on take 7, with Ringo's rock-solid drums occasionally hesitating or even stopping altogether. In fact, the take itself stops altogether after about two minutes, disintegrating

into some John Lennon electric piano noodling when they approach the detour into the section about sitting in an English garden.

Take 8 breaks down pretty quickly after John hits an apparent not-quite-right chord. But take 9 is complete and fairly tight, though they steer themselves through the elongated transition into the fourth verse pretty hesitantly. This extra bar of music might have confused even the engineering/production/mastering team, as it made it into the mix officially released on the US single version, but went missing from other official versions of the track. Rather than fading out gradually, this take also comes to a drawn-out close, like a marathoner crawling across the finish line, ending with a flourish of a bent guitar note. Another minute of "I Am the Walrus" from these sessions has also surfaced (with a big drop-out that mutes the volume to almost next-to-nothing halfway through), though it's unclear whether this is from a different take or from a rehearsal.

Take 16 (with vocals), issued on *Anthology 2*, served as the basic track for the released version, minus the numerous overdubs of orchestra, backup singers, and radio noise yet to come. Again, this is like hearing "I Am the Walrus" as more of a conventional rock song, albeit with some empty-sounding, drums-only transitions between the verses. In addition, it's still not without its hiccups in terms of the tricky rhythms. There's a longer, slightly stumbling electric piano intro, and John comes in too early in the section with the extra bar before the fourth verse, catching himself with an "Oo." That gaffe would be mixed out of the final track, as would an exceptionally awkward mini-transition into the "English garden" section where Ringo's drums are accompanied by a couple of straying-off-the-path, descending electric piano notes.

● September 6

Studio Outtakes

Magical Mystery Tour *sessions*
Studio Two, Abbey Road, London

*The Fool on the Hill (demo)
I Am the Walrus (RM4)
    appears on Anthology 2

With so many 1967 outtakes being different mixes or partial works-in-progress, what a joy it is to hear an outtake/alternate version that is a) complete, b) in excellent sound quality, c) performed well, and, most importantly, d) quite different from the familiar final track. That's what we get with Paul McCartney's solo piano demo of "The Fool on the Hill," essentially allowing us to hear his major contribution to *Magical Mystery Tour* unplugged. Though it's sung well, perhaps Paul's not entirely certain of the lyric, mumbling a bit of the second verse (particularly on the first line). And he obviously hasn't worked out the final verses, scatting his way through the last half of the song on everything except the choruses. As something of an acknowledgment that it's unfinished, perhaps, he tops things off with showbizzy "That's all, folks"–type piano flourishes.

The lyric would be finished when "The Fool on the Hill" was recorded for real later in the *Magical Mystery Tour* sessions, but this earlier demo does prove it was taking Paul quite a while to complete the composition. As part of the research for his authorized biography, *The Beatles,* Hunter Davies was present at a mid-March Lennon-McCartney songwriting session (for "With a Little Help from My Friends") at which Paul, on guitar, "started to sing and play a very slow, beautiful song about a foolish man sitting on the hill. . . . Paul sang it many times, *la-la*-ing words he hadn't thought of yet. John said he'd better write the words down or he'd forget them. Paul said it was okay. He wouldn't forget them." Or maybe he did at least forget some, considering how many were still missing nearly six months later? As another aside, this piano demo also makes one wonder why there weren't many other such items recorded by Paul, John, or George at Abbey Road, which presumably offered much better facilities even for simple demos such as these than their home recording equipment. Maybe they felt more comfortable working out songs-in-progress at home; it might also have been a matter as mundane as EMI being unwilling to spend precious studio time on demos, rather than songs that were being recorded and worked on specifically for studio releases.

Also on this day, a mono mix (RM4) of "I Am the Walrus" was done that's not much different from the mix of take 16 used on *Anthology 2*—except it actually got rid of the section with John's vocal blunder, and trimmed the intro to the form it took on the official single. It *didn't* get rid of the faint cough heard in the background in the turnaround into the "English garden" bit. It's the closest you can get, however, to hearing a version of "I Am the Walrus" that approximates the official track in every way save for the absence of orchestral, backing vocal, and radio drama overdubs.

● September 7

Studio Outtake

Magical Mystery Tour *sessions*
Studio Two, Abbey Road, London

Blue Jay Way (RM1)

Another it's-all-over-but-the-overdubs recording from *Magical Mystery Tour*, this mix of "Blue Jay Way" is similar to the track that made the record, except the cello and tambourine added a month later are missing. "Blue Jay Way" may be a minor entry in the Beatles' catalog, but this early mix does illustrate how crucial orchestral overdubs—even minimal ones such as this cello part—were in making numerous tracks they cut more interesting. Indeed, in the case of "Blue Jay Way," it might be said that it helped the track to avoid monotony. This simpler mix also enables us to more clearly hear a randomly shouted "Hey" about three-and-a-half minutes into the song (during the nearly interminable refrain/fadeout), and the distorted swirling effects at the very end are more pronounced.

● September 8

Studio Outtake

Magical Mystery Tour *sessions*
Studio Three, Abbey Road, London

Flying (RM4)

Of all the alternate mixes flying around from the *Sgt. Pepper–Magical Mystery Tour* era, "Flying" itself is one of the very most interesting, as unlike many such animals it actually sounds quite a bit different from the official version. And quite enjoyably and surprisingly so, as even though the solid rock-soul rhythm track is the same as what we're used to hearing on record, the Mellotron parts are *very* different at the beginning and end. The difference is particularly striking in the first 30 seconds or so, which have some dreamy, descending riffs and high-pitched squeals (actually produced by slide whistle) unheard on the official release. The innovations being forged in modern jazz in the '60s had little effect on the Beatles, but these squeals in particular are rather reminiscent of some of the soprano sax lines heard on the wildest jazz records of the age.

There's a yet bigger shock in store, however, for the final 30 seconds. On the standard *Magical Mystery Tour* cut, we're used to the Beatles' semioperatic scatting vocals being immediately followed by wafting-cloud passages of the most ethereal Mellotron sounds. This mix, however, segues right into a brief, cheery, circuslike riff that in turn gives way to a brisk, cartoonish, Dixieland jazz vamp, like a hot New Orleans '20s combo dosed with '60s drugs. You can just picture the four grinning with delighted dementia as they both pay homage to and take the mickey out of this quaint early 20th-century form of entertainment, dancing the Charleston around the Studio Three control room as an amused George Martin lets them hear the playback. Drunken-sounding voices scat faintly in the background before the rhythm goes into curtain-lowering-finale mode, punctuated by a final arms-spread shout of "Yeah!" from the boys.

Or so it was, for years, assumed. For as it turned out, this "Dixieland" tag—though it sounded amateurish enough to be the work of musicians who rarely played Dixieland, such as the Beatles—was *not* the Beatles. Rather, it was taken right off a Mellotron tape, the final "Yeah!" exclaimed not by the Fab Four, but by one of the Mellotron's inventors, Bill Fransen! Even if it's a letdown to find this zanily inspired tag was not only not even the Beatles but essentially ripped right off the machine, it's nothing less than a gas to hear.

This earlier mix of "Flying" is not better than the one that was on *Magical Mystery Tour*, but it's about as good. It's one of the few alternate mixes/takes, in fact, that inarguably should have been chosen for the *Anthology* CD series, yet inexplicably was not. Is it possible that someone eventually realized that the finale was not the work of the Beatles?

● September 16

Studio Outtake

Magical Mystery Tour *sessions*
Studio Three, Abbey Road, London

---

*Your Mother Should Know (take 27)
  appears on Anthology 2

Right from the start of their career, the Beatles had occasionally rerecorded songs from scratch; even "Love Me Do" had been remade a week after the first attempt to record it as a single. Sometimes the remakes took, and sometimes they didn't. "Your Mother Should Know" was one case where it did not. Although the track's foundation had already been recorded (see August 22 entry), the Beatles tried a different

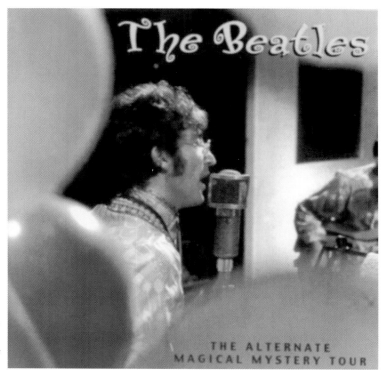

A collection of unreleased Magical Mystery Tour *alternates and outtakes, including some incidental music used in the* Magical Mystery Tour *soundtrack that was taken from unreleased Beatles recordings.*

arrangement at this session. Take 27 was released on *Anthology 2,* and based on its evidence, they really didn't have much of an idea of what, if any, refinements were needed. The main alteration is the peculiar use of stilted, martial drumming by Ringo, and prominent harmonium (by Paul) that lent an even more archaic air to Paul's tribute to songs of his mother's generation. Possibly Paul wanted to make the recording more in line with the song as he'd originally heard it, as he'd composed the tune on an actual harmonium in the dining room of his London home. Paul also threw in an extra "know" when singing the song's title during the final refrain, though it frankly seems like one "know" too many.

Although this was marked the "best" take from the session, it obviously would have endured a number of fixes and editing had it been chosen as the basic track. The first bit to go would have been Paul's falsetto query to George Martin at the start, "Do you want us to do it again, George?" Also, Paul comes in too early with his vocal, trailing off on his first line, making it necessary for him to repeat it immediately. The instrumental tag crumbles dispiritedly in a clamor of harmonium, piano, and drums, Paul remarking, "It should fade out at the end anyway, so there was enough to fade out, is that all right?" It wasn't all right; they wisely decided to stick with the earlier, far less awkward August 22 recording, topping it off with some overdubs to construct the final *Magical Mystery Tour* track.

● Circa Fall

Private Tape

Jessie's Dream

In the background of the *Magical Mystery Tour* dream sequence in which Ringo's Aunt Jessie eats mounds of spaghetti, a bizarre but appropriate piece of music plays on the soundtrack, mixing spooked-out Mellotron weirdness with bad cocktail jazz and monkish chanting. It has the distorted, wobbly focus associated with both nightmares and the music usually employed to accompany nightmares in horror films, though with a slightly campier and more psychedelic touch. And it was actually written by the group, and even jointly copyrighted to all four members. It was one of the few constructive adaptations of the kind of Mellotron home tapes John was making at home during this period for Beatles purposes, the *Magical Mystery Tour* instrumental "Flying" being the other, far more famous one. It's likely that John was the prime mover behind this incidental music, and also *un*likely it was recorded at Abbey Road, as it's not on any of the EMI Beatles session reels that have been logged. Hence it's not known where or even exactly when it was recorded, though it was almost certainly done between September and November 1967, while the *Magical Mystery Tour* film was being shot and produced.

● September 25

Studio Outtakes

Magical Mystery Tour *sessions*
Studio Two, Abbey Road, London

*The Fool on the Hill (take 4)
The Fool on the Hill (rehearsals)
     appears on Anthology 2

Although he was a great and prolific songwriter, Paul McCartney could sometimes take a while to finish his compositions. "The Fool on the Hill" had been started in mid-March at the latest; the lyrics were still about half incomplete when he recorded his demo on September 6; and they still weren't in their final form when the fully arranged version on take 4 was cut on September 25. Issued on *Anthology 2,* there are a number of lyric variations from the familiar *Magical Mystery Tour* track, though admittedly minor ones. The Fool is sitting still, not keeping still; he's a man of empty mind, not a man of a thousand voices; and nobody goes quite near him. Had this particular set of lyrics made it all the way to the final mix unchanged, it's likely there would have been little or no difference in the public acclaim it received. But it's one example of Paul's perfectionism, with no detail too small to escape scrutinizing, even if it means inserting the word "his" so that a line flows better, or changing a "the" to an "an."

We *would* have noticed, however, a lower level of accomplishment had the Beatles stuck with this particular take, even though it, too, is quite similar to the ultimate arrangement. The rhythm's too regular and unvaried. There's still a sad, minor-keyed sequence of notes on the piano at the very beginning, as there had been on the demo. Paul's phrasing remains a bit too mannered, with an "Oh!" exclamation before one of the recorder breaks, and some gratuitous lower and higher extremes in the vocal melody of one of the verses that were later evened out. And the song's fade has yet to be fully worked out, going on too long and allowing Paul's voice to shake too much. It's all a bit clunky, and no match for the official version, though very much an interesting glimpse of a Beatles song in its not-quite-there state.

Also circulating from this session is a very fuzzy, approximately 15-minute tape of "The Fool on the Hill" rehearsals. Unfortunately, not only is the sound quality supremely hissy, but much of the music is obscured by Japanese commentary from a journalist in attendance at the session. You can tell it's "The Fool on the Hill" they're rehearsing in the background, particularly by the piano and recorder parts, but you can't tell much more than that.

● September 28

Studio Outtakes
Magical Mystery Tour *sessions*
Studio Two, Abbey Road, London

Flying (take 8)
Flying (overdub takes 1–5)

When the Beatles remade "Flying" sans pseudo-Dixieland ending, they created much more in the way of odd Mellotron sounds than actually made their way onto the relatively short *Magical Mystery* track. The evidence is on this quite interesting series of outtakes, usually grouped together on bootlegs so that take 8 is combined with five additional overdub takes into one nine-and-a-half-minute track. In other words, it's basically a superlong version of "Flying," with only the opening (and most conventional) section being used for commercial release.

If we're to listen to this as one continuous track, the first two and a quarter minutes is basically the same as the released version (though it's in mono). On *Magical Mystery Tour,* the blues-soul instrumental jam that takes up most of the song gives way at the end to some delectable astral Mellotron loops, which swirl only briefly before fading out. On this version, however, the Mellotron loops keep going . . . and going . . . and going. For John and Ringo compiled quite a few additional Mellotron loops—about seven minutes' worth—in the course of constructing five takes of potential overdubs.

As a consequence, "Flying" changes from an off-the-wall and imaginative but relatively normal psychedelic rock instrumental into a piece that's almost avant-garde in nature. The Mellotron loops play on and on, unaccompanied by vocals or rock instruments, fading in and out occasionally. They strike far more melancholy, even disquieting, electronic head-in-the-clouds moods than the brief snippet of loops at the end of the released track have time to do. It could even be argued that these recordings represent the Beatles at their very most psychedelic and tripped-out, such is the air of disconnection from earthly matters (and rock 'n' roll music). Never again would they delve into insular psychedelic bliss so determinedly, reining in their impulses and steering them into equally satisfying but far more earthbound, rock-bound directions.

It's interesting that John and Ringo were the pair responsible for these extended Mellotron passages, as Ringo probably has the image of the least experimentally inclined Beatle. At a guess, they probably took the wheel for this particular exercise because they were likely the Beatles most familiar with the instrument, from all those shambolic Lennon home Mellotron recordings. "Flying" may thus have been the one Beatles track where all that tomfoolery was put to constructive use, even if just a hint of that Mellotron madness escaped onto the severely edited released version. Some more of this much longer recording did actually find commercial release, incidentally, though not on disc, as a few of the excised Mellotron passages were used as background music on the *Magical Mystery Tour* film soundtrack.

● October 2

Studio Outtake
"Hello Goodbye" single session
Studio Two, Abbey Road, London

Hello Goodbye (take 1)

With all the wild and sometimes loosely structured experimentation flying around Abbey Road in the post–*Sgt. Pepper* months, George Martin and EMI might have been wondering if the Beatles were ever going to come up with another straightforwardly commercial single. Not to worry, as "Hello Goodbye" was tailor-made for that purpose, and perhaps unco-incidentally was less complicated a recording than many of the group's recent endeavors. Fourteen takes were actually done on this date, though only the first—an instrumental backing track—is in circulation. Despite the numerous subsequent takes, the approach taken on the ultimate single version was pretty defined on the very first run-through, though the song's a little longer in this earlier state, especially on the extended coda (some pre-song piano/drum warm-up is also heard). If you do like hearing the underlying dynamics of a keyboard-driven Beatles song, however, the sound quality on this outtake's superb, though it's in mono.

● October 2–19

Studio Outtake

"Hello Goodbye" single session
Studio Two, Abbey Road, London

---

*Hello Goodbye (take 16)
     *appears on Anthology 2

Actually take 14 with overdubs, this newly fleshed-out recording of "Hello Goodbye" was retrieved for *Anthology 2,* though yet more tinkering would be done when recording and mixing were completed in early November. This version of "Hello Goodbye" is more different from the single than you might think, with a far more active guitar presence. That's particularly so in the opening part of the first verse, where George adds descending responsive licks to each line of Paul's vocal. Too, the brief instrumental break has a pretty conventional guitar solo that went totally missing from the final cut, where it was replaced by some inspired Paul scat-tinged singing.

The Beatles were right to downplay the guitar in the final recording, as it's a little too busy in this earlier version. As an aside, the tension and musical differences between Paul and George are often assumed to have mushroomed in early 1969, particularly as one especially testy exchange was caught in the *Let It Be* film, where George sarcastically says he'll play or *not* play whatever Paul wants. When hearing outtakes such as these, however, one wonders from afar if such frustration over not being allowed to play guitar as he wanted had not been brewing considerably earlier (and Norman Smith, engineer on Beatles sessions from 1962–1965, has confirmed that such tension existed between George and Paul even before 1966). Paul's known to have vetoed George's idea to play responsive guitar licks on "Hey Jude"; "Hello Goodbye" is a much less celebrated instance in which such responsive riffs might have been removed against George's wishes. George really didn't have as much to do, guitar-wise, on Beatles recordings in 1967 as he had in years past, so much had their sound moved away from a more conventional rock foundation. That would change in 1968 and 1969, but could it be that he was starting to get frustrated even earlier with the limitations imposed on some of his contributions?

● November 1

Studio Outtakes

From the Sgt. Pepper *and "All You Need Is Love" single sessions*
Room 53, Abbey Road, London

Lucy in the Sky with Diamonds (RM20)
All You Need Is Love (RM11)

Although "Lucy in the Sky with Diamonds" and "All You Need Is Love" had been in general release for months, on November 1 new mixes were made for potential use in the *Yellow Submarine* film. The very idea of erasing John's vocal from the first verse of "Lucy in the Sky with Diamonds" in favor of a new sing-song, laughing prattle by the movie's Jeremy Boob character is so ludicrous that some collectors assumed the version had to be a fake. It isn't, however; it was actually done by

Beatles engineer Geoff Emerick, the new vocal supplied by the actor who voiced Jeremy Boob in the film, Dick Emery. The new lyrics for this verse were penned by *Yellow Submarine* co-scriptwriter Erich Segal, best known as the author of *Love Story.* Segal was no John Lennon, however, and one can only imagine John and the other Beatles' apoplectic reaction to Emery/Jeremy warbling, "Somebody quotes you, you read from a sourcebook, a concept with microscope eyes" . . . followed, as if that weren't enough, by a burst of maniacal laughter. Thankfully, this must-be-heard-to-be-believed monstrosity was not used, and this track, which barely qualifies as an "outtake," remains mostly unheard.

Also prepared on this day was a new mix of "All You Need Is Love" that, while far less wrongheaded, was about as artificial an enterprise. An extra repetition of the chorus was edited in right before the coda, removing the saxophone so that you can (very briefly) more clearly hear some of the other instruments. For all the effort involved in lengthening the track, the edited version used in the *Yellow Submarine* film was actually *shorter* than the one released on the single.

● Circa Late 1967

Private Tape

7 Cavendish Avenue, London

Step Inside Love

It's been said many times elsewhere, but it bears repeating: the Beatles, while always exploring new directions, never truly abandoned the more traditional rock and pop dimensions of their craft, even though it must have seemed they were determined to do so at times on their most ambitious 1967 psychedelic experiments. In the wake of *Sgt. Pepper* and *Magical Mystery Tour,* not to mention an introduction to the Maharishi and transcendental meditation, it might have been assumed that they wanted nothing to do with commercial showbiz conventions ever again. Yet this was precisely the time that Paul wrote a showbizzy TV theme song for one of the most middle-of-the-road British pop stars of the age, Cilla Black. John and Paul had rarely donated *any* unused compositions to other artists since 1964, but Black was in a unique position to benefit from such a favor. She'd known the Beatles since the Cavern days, and by 1967 was the biggest star on Brian Epstein's roster other than the Beatles themselves. It's just speculation, but Paul might have been particularly motivated to lend Cilla a hand at this particular time. Brian's recent death (in late August) could have made Paul particularly keen to help an old friend and fellow Epstein client out, especially as Brian's business empire was in an up-for-grabs state. The Black-hosted variety television series for which the song would serve as a theme had been arranged by Epstein before his death, and such details as finding a suitable theme song might have been in danger of getting lost in the shuffle.

It's not known when this home demo (unfortunately circulating in quite scratchy, muffled, acetatelike state) was done. But it must have been recorded before November 21, the date on which Black made a studio demo of the song, with assistance from Paul on acoustic guitar and vocals. On Paul's own demo, with double-tracked vocals and acoustic guitar, he sounds quite happy and content to be singing a breezy, romantic tune with no pretensions to plowing artistic frontiers. In common with most songs Lennon and McCartney gave away, it's a slight tune

Strawberry Fields Forever

An assortment of psychedelic Beatles outtakes and alternates, with a cover
photo of the group as they appeared in their promo film for "Hello Goodbye."

by the composers' high standards. But it's a pleasant, fairly effervescent number with ever-shifting chords and more than a hint of the kind of bossa nova–flavored pop sung by the likes of Sandie Shaw in the mid-'60s. There's also a hint of the acoustic troubadour persona Paul would increasingly adopt on some of the Beatles' lighter fare in the final two years of their career, on songs like "Blackbird," "I Will," "Mother Nature's Son," and "Her Majesty." And it's certainly less strident than the characteristically brassy, orchestrated version that Cilla Black released, on a British hit single in early 1968.

● Circa November

Private Tape

All Together on the Wireless Machine

This approximately minute-long jingle, recorded for the BBC radio series *Where It's At,* has long been assumed to have been the work of Paul McCartney. And it does sound like Paul on piano (the only instrument on the recording), particularly at the very beginning, where he plays the chords heard on the verses of "Hello Goodbye." It really *doesn't* sound like Paul on vocals, however; the voice is too pinched, mannered, and limited in range and depth. Could it be Paul, an accomplished mimic, deliberately singing in a phony, stagey voice? Could it be BBC DJ Kenny Everett, who's referred to in the lyrics? It's sometimes assumed it's Everett singing along with Paul in the last part, but could it be Paul (or someone else) singing along with Everett?

It's enough to cast some doubt as to whether this is an actual Paul McCartney recording. Not that it's worth losing much sleep over, as after the "Hello Goodbye" part (with a recitation about writing a jingle for the BBC) ends, it devolves into a typical British music-hallish number with extremely basic lyrics, dominated by repetitions of the title phrase. ("The Wireless Machine," for all you Americans born after World War II, was the British term for a radio back in the pretelevision days.) A few crashing sound effects at the end make it seem rather like an outtake from the Beatles' Christmas records, and, in fact, the group were soon due to record the 1967 holiday disc. This is definitely not from those sessions, however, as at least part of it was broadcast on the BBC on November 25, a few days before their 1967 Christmas record was cut. Assuming this jingle was recorded shortly before that broadcast, it was probably done earlier in November.

● November 28

Christmas Time (Is Here Again)
Studio Two, Abbey Road, London

---

*Christmas Time Is Here Again (fan club disc)
*Christmas Time (Is Here Again) (outtake)
        excerpt appears on Free As a Bird *CD single*

In only the most general sense, the Beatles' 1967 Christmas fan club disc did follow the structure of their previous ones, mixing silly sketches with tossed-off music. Yet it was, in many respects, quite different from what

they'd done in 1963, or even 1966. For one thing, this is the most *musical* of their Christmas records, as it's the only one to make heavy use of an actual (if slight) Beatles-composed song, professionally recorded with full instrumentation at EMI. For another, it captures them in the most intense movement of their psychedelic phase, its jumbled series of surreal sketches and sound effects interspersed with snippets of the bona fide, recorded-just-for-you-fans studio track "Christmas Time (Is Here Again)." Sketch-wise, the group had tried something along the same lines for their 1966 holiday disc, *Pantomime—Everywhere It's Christmas.* But *Christmas Time Is Here Again* is more smoothly produced (by George Martin) and much more tightly edited. It's perhaps the most creative of their fan club records, even if the sketches are way too nonlinear to challenge, say, Monty Python in terms of both sheer comedy and satisfying repeated listens.

The humor and inventiveness are more a matter of the rapid-fire impact of hearing so much weirdness flung at you with such lightning-speed transitions, rather than the slighter quality of the individual bits. It's a sequence that plays better than it reads, but to give novices some idea of what's in store, the narrative and scenery rapidly switches from BBC studios to tap-dancing, a brief manic jangle for "Wonderlust," a mock-TV chat show, another jingle ("Plenty of Jam Jars"), a fake game show, a noirish radio drama, echoing voices reminiscent of Mal Evans's eerily distorted count-in during early versions of "A Day in the Life," a more-or-less-standard holiday greeting from the boys (albeit with psychedelic echo added), and John Lennon speaking in a Scottish accent as wind howls and "Auld Lang Syne" plays on an organ. All four of the Beatles have prominent speaking parts, with cameos granted to Mal Evans, George Martin, and their friend Victor Spinetti (who'd acted in *A Hard Day's Night, Help!,* and *Magical Mystery Tour*). Yet it would, somewhat sadly, be the last Christmas disc the Beatles recorded together. Christmas records would be issued in 1968 and 1969, but the four recorded their parts individually for those.

Though only herky-jerky bits and pieces of the song "Christmas Time (Is Here Again)" are heard on the actual fan club disc, these were, in fact, taken from a six-and-a-half-minute recording of the song that has since circulated in full. It's very much a 1967 Beatles production in the rich vocal harmonies, hard, funky Ringo drums, and mid-tempo piano. Yet the song, with all four Beatles sharing the composer credit, is so insubstantial it's something like hearing a one-dimensional snapshot of the band in their psychedelic era. It's extremely repetitious, both melodically and lyrically, amounting to little more than the title, and variations of same, sung over and over. Occasionally the verses pause for Ringo to offer the interjection "O-U-T spells out" (though it can sound like "hold your tea spells out" at a casual listen), followed by a mildly bluesy guitar riff. Paul, John, and George each get chances to sing one of the lines in the "verse" alone, and more loose joking around is introduced as the number progresses.

But despite the genuine good cheer of the tune, and despite being far preferable to the usual half-hearted, sub-jugband style carols of their previous discs, it quickly not only wears out its welcome, but becomes downright wearisome over the course of six minutes-plus. Perhaps the Beatles found it tiresome as well by the end, as the cut finishes with manic "the party's over" slides up and down the keyboard. As a footnote, that hard-to-decipher declaration by a chuckling John at the beginning of the track is "Interplanetary remix . . . thr . . . page 444"—not that this makes much more sense when it's decoded and spelled out.

Undoubtedly the Beatles never intended the track to be heard as a whole, uninterrupted piece. They must have recorded such a lengthy repetition of a theme-without-much-variation so they had a lot to choose from when they selected bits to insert into the actual fan club disc. It might be considered a blessing for the average Beatles fan, though a curse for the completist collector, that only a little more than two minutes were used when an edited version was officially issued on the *Free As a Bird* CD single. Furthermore, the latter part of that truncated version was overdubbed with some of the holiday messages they'd recorded for Radio London and Radio Caroline back on December 6, 1966 (see corresponding entry). Finally, the shorter edit of "Christmas Time (Is Here Again)" from that CD single was cross-faded into the John Lennon recitation and "Auld Lang Syne" organ passage that had concluded the actual 1967 *Christmas Time Is Here Again* fan disc.

For all its relative dispensability, one thing that does come through in this final documented 1967 Beatles recording is the sense of fun and unity still enjoyed by the group when the four came together, even for such sideline projects as these. Those qualities had been a huge feature of virtually everything they'd done for the past five years. Remarkably, that unrivaled unity—if not, for the most part, the fun—would soon start to disappear, not only from their Christmas records, but in various degrees from many of the recordings they would make in the final two years of their career.

● Circa Late 1967–Early 1968

Private Tapes
Kenwood, Weybridge

Cry Baby Cry (piano version #1)
Cry Baby Cry (piano version #2)
Across the Universe/Cry Baby Cry
Cry Baby Cry (guitar version)
Hey Bulldog (two versions)
Across the Universe

Like all home John Lennon tapes, this batch is impossible to date with total accuracy. It's a reasonable supposition, though, that these recordings were made in late 1967 and early 1968. If so, they probably predate the Beatles' first studio recording sessions of 1968, which took place in early February, and at which the group did two of these three songs ("Across the Universe" and "Hey Bulldog"). And they probably postdate the wrapping up of the recording, filming, and postproduction work for *Magical Mystery Tour,* which left John and the Beatles with light work schedules in both December 1967 and January 1968.

Two of these three versions of "Cry Baby Cry" (all of which last less than a minute) have John singing and playing piano, though the vocals are pretty distant. These fragments take an approach pretty similar to the one he'd use when the song was recorded on *The White Album,* though there the arrangement was considerably more elaborate, and John (perhaps by mistake) ends the first verse of one of these prototypes with the word "queen," not "king." More interesting, perhaps, is a brief medley of sorts where John sings the "jai guru deva" part of "Across the Universe" on piano with a brisk, jaunty tempo and a flash of Mellotron strings. He soon reverts to working on "Cry Baby Cry," however. Was

he thinking of using both of these sections in the same song before splitting them up, or just going into the "Across the Universe" fragment for light relief before resuming the heavy lifting of working out "Cry Baby Cry"?

Another less-than-a-minute tape of "Cry Baby Cry" is yet more satisfying, at least in terms of looking for something that wasn't simply replicated and embellished in the EMI studio. On this fragment, John plays not piano but heavily distorted, almost grungy electric guitar, singing a good octave higher. The Beatles were on the verge of getting back to harder, more fundamental rock 'n' roll, and while they'd opt to give "Cry Baby Cry" a fairly gentle treatment, this particular excerpt sounds rough, almost angry. Viewed in that light, it could be a vague foreshadowing of the rougher and angrier path John would often pursue in the late '60s and early '70s.

Some vitriolic Lennon bite came yet further upfront on these two composing tapes of "Hey Bulldog," with John on piano and double-tracked vocal. He's gone no further than the chorus at this point, and while its menacing chord sequence and pounding piano are in place, the lyrics aren't finalized. It's not a "you" but a "she" who can talk to John, and in the first version, he introduces a lyric—"Lonely sitting Sunday in my room, I'm a-lonely"—that didn't make the studio cut, wandering off into a bit of piano boogie near the end. The second version adds some cool blasts of Mellotron, but John still hasn't gotten further than repeating the chorus a few times, adding another eventually discarded lyric with "Nothin' doin', something she can say." With what we know about John's personal life at this point, he might have been venting some veiled frustration with both his stale marriage to Cynthia and the boredom of sitting around his suburban home. Those references would be yet more veiled in the Beatles' studio recording, but, if only in hindsight, perhaps they represent a subconscious yearning to break out of his unhappy, isolated domestic cocoon, which he'd do with a vengeance after taking up with Yoko Ono in the spring of 1968.

As mentioned in an earlier entry in this chapter, there's another minute-and-a-half home tape, usually identified as a working version of "Across the Universe," that might be from around this period, though some think it's from the spring of 1967. Actually, this piano-vocal-Mellotron performance—in which the vocals are all but indecipherable—isn't much like "Across the Universe." It's more of an affable, structureless ramble, with that slightly lethargic, steady keyboard rhythm Lennon so often favored over the next few years. But there are patterns like the "jai guru deva" section of "Across the Universe" that, if little else, specifically resemble the Beatles' version of the song.

All of this material, incidentally, is found on longer tapes that also contain some far less song-oriented instrumental jamming, as well as more of the kind of John/Ringo experimental doodling that filled numerous other Lennon home recordings of the era. The producers of *The Lost Lennon Tapes* radio series must have sifted through these tapes very selectively, wisely extracting the fragments that were real *songs,* or at least songs in development. Naturally these extracts were soon bootlegged, although some of the songs were broadcast in less complete form than the longest versions that are in circulation.

This group of fairly interesting songs-in-progress may well have been the last such items that John did at his Kenwood home. Soon after they were recorded, he'd take a long trip to India with the other Beatles; almost right after returning, he'd leave his wife and move out of the house. He'd continue to make home tapes throughout the rest of the Beatles' career, but all of these would be quite different in nature than the ones he'd done at Kenwood between late 1966 and early 1968, informed by the huge influence (and, often, actual musical and sonic contributions) of his new partner, Yoko Ono.

1967 Noncirculating Recordings, Known and Rumored

● January 4–April 21

Studio Outtakes
Sgt. Pepper's Lonely Hearts Club Band *sessions*
Abbey Road, London

There are actually some *Sgt. Pepper* outtakes of Beatles songs that have never circulated. The problem is, none of them seem to have been *real* songs. Rather, judging from the description in *The Beatles Recording Sessions*, these are the group's most avant-garde indulgences, perhaps recorded as experimental exercises rather than with any serious intent to develop them for release. Still, at least one of them is among the most discussed never-heard Beatles recordings, even if it probably wouldn't be a popular or much-listened-to item if it ever saw the light of day.

That track is "Carnival of Light," a nearly 14-minute experimental collage that was played at the countercultural multimedia event of the same name at the Roundhouse Theatre in London on January 28 and February 4. The cut was recorded at Abbey Road on January 5, and though John Lennon is usually credited as the originator of the group's furthest-out excursions, Paul McCartney was actually the man behind this enterprise. Combining distorted drum, organ, and lead guitar with church organ, sound effects, tape echo, crazed Lennon-McCartney screaming, and tambourine, it hasn't been played for the public since it was aired at the Roundhouse. If nothing else, it proves that the Beatles' explorations into the furthest reaches of the avant-garde predated "Revolution 9" by a good year and a half or so, and that John wasn't the only Beatle interested in such risky endeavors. In fact the chief engineer on the recording, Geoff Emerick, remembered small excerpts from the session being used in "Revolution 9" itself in his memoir, *Here, There and Everywhere: My Life Recording the Music of the Beatles.*

In his book *The Unknown Paul McCartney: McCartney and the Avant-Garde,* Ian Peel devotes an entire 12-page chapter to the recording. It's recommended reading for those who want to investigate further, as there are far too many details surrounding the genesis of the track (and the "Carnival of Light" event) to summarize in just one concise entry. It can be noted, however, that McCartney biographer Barry Miles compares the track to the Mothers of Invention's searingly jarring, side-long 1966 *Freak Out!* LP cut "The Return of the Monster Magnet" in *Paul McCartney: Many Years from Now,* if you want to get some frame of reference for how this most uncommercial enterprise sounded.

As Paul explained in a 2001 interview with Mark Ellen for the website The Rocking Vicar, he was asked to do "Carnival of Light" by his friend Barry Miles, then a prime mover in the London underground as the publisher of *International Times.* Elaborated McCartney, "I went

Although the Beautiful Dreamer *LP boasted a nice, infrequently seen picture of the Beatles in the studio during their psychedelic era, all of the tracks were actually recorded for the BBC in 1963!*

into the studio and said to the guys, look, we've got half an hour before the session officially starts, would you mind terribly if I did this thing? . . . And they all just fell in with the spirit of it and I just said, 'Would you go on that?' and 'Would you stay on that?' and 'Would you be on that?' and 'We'll just take 20 minutes to do it in real time.' And they all just got into it." Asked whether it was in the running for the *Anthology* series, Paul confirmed, "It was up for consideration on the *Anthology* and George [Harrison] vetoed it. He didn't like it. Maybe its time hadn't come." Although Paul also mentioned he was considering using part of it on a soundtrack of a film he was doing, as of this writing in 2006, none of the track's circulated in either part or whole.

A less in-demand *Sgt. Pepper* outtake is the 22-minute "Anything," recorded on February 22, consisting almost entirely of Ringo's drums, with tambourine and conga. Like his experimental Mellotron collaborations with John, it could be viewed as evidence of his hidden avant-garde side. On a more prosaic note, maybe it was just a way for Ringo to kill time during sessions where, as he's recalled, he often had nothing to do while the songwriters worked on parts of the recording in which he wasn't involved.

● May 11

Studio Outtakes
"Baby You're a Rich Man" single session
Studio One, Olympic Sound Studios, London

Baby You're a Rich Man (takes 1–12)

According to Bob Spitz's *The Beatles: The Biography,* at this session for the B-side of the "All You Need Is Love" single, "there were numerous aborted takes owing to [John Lennon's] frisky, even scandalous improvisations. He took some wicked shots at Paul, Ringo, and Mick [Jagger, who attended the session], according to one observer; otherwise, 'Everyone else was spared.'"

● June 1–2

Studio Outtakes
De Lane Lea Music Recording Studios, London

Untitled (several unnumbered takes)

When the Beatles recorded for EMI, it was virtually always with a purpose, even if it was taking them longer and longer to make their records as time went on. In the gap between *Sgt. Pepper* and *Magical Mystery Tour,* however, there were, as previously noted, several sessions that were directionless by Beatles standards, the results often not targeted toward any specific single or album. And on June 1, 1967 (*Sgt. Pepper*'s actual release date), there apparently weren't even any songs that the Beatles had in mind to work toward. Instead, as Mark Lewisohn reported in *The Beatles Recording Sessions,* they "recorded nothing but untitled, unplanned, highly tedious and—frankly—downright amateurish instrumental jams, with a bass guitar, an organ, lead guitar with reverb, guitar strings being scraped, drums and tambourine." Such wastes of time were highly atypical of the group, yet the very next day, they did it again, though on that date some trumpet and clarinet superimpositions were made to an actual Beatles track ("It's All Too Much").

George Harrison in San Francisco's Haight-Ashbury, August 7, 1967 (with Beatles publicist Derek Taylor, also smoking a cigarette, at his side): a "performance" that doesn't seem to have been taped.

It can only be guessed that the Beatles were only showing up because the studios were booked ahead of time, and, finding themselves without material to work on, filled up the hours with improvisation. Or perhaps it was booked on the spur of the moment, since it was not done at Abbey Road as usual, but at De Lane Lea, elsewhere in London. Maybe they were hoping that some ideas might arise from such an unstructured environment, as it might have not been taped otherwise. As low as our expectations should be, these tapes might make interesting listening, if only to see if they were any better than (or even similar to) the hideous, lengthy instrumental jams the Beatles had done seven years before on their spring 1960 home tapes. And they might not have been totally useless, as Geoff Emerick's memoir noted that the jams might have contained some elements of what became the *Magical Mystery Tour* instrumental "Flying."

● June 7

Studio Outtakes
"You Know My Name (Look Up the Number)" single session
Studio Two, Abbey Road, London

"You Know My Name (Look Up the Number)" (takes 20-24)

According to *The Beatles Recording Sessions*, the boys weren't done with making an improvised racket. This session for "You Know My Name (Look Up the Number)" deviated so far from the original song—itself a pretty unusual, loosely focused Beatles composition—that these takes were eventually noted as "Instrumental—Unidentified" on the tape box. Including flute, electric guitar, drums, organ, and tambourine, these outtakes might be further proof of the group's curious creative malaise in the late spring of 1967, even as the release of the *Sgt. Pepper* album was boosting public acclaim of the band to an all-time high.

● June 14

Studio Outtake
"All You Need Is Love" single session
Studio One, Olympic Sound Studios, London

"All You Need Is Love" (take 10, rough mix)

After the first day of work on "All You Need Is Love," a rough mix of take 10 with an instrumental basic rhythm track was made for the Beatles to take home. It's known to still exist; an acetate of the mix was auctioned by Christie's in May 1994 that, according to *The Beatles Book*, "sounded nothing like the completed record."

● October 12

Studio Outtakes
De Lane Lea Music Recording Studios, London

Shirley's Wild Accordion (takes 1–15)

It's debatable whether these qualify as "studio outtakes," since the Beatles are actually not the featured artists. But "Shirley's Wild Accordion," principally performed by accordionist Shirley Evans and percussionist Reg Wale, was an actual copyrighted Lennon-McCartney instrumental. The session was produced by John Lennon, and Ringo and Paul did make some modest musical contributions to the track (Ringo on drums, Paul on maraca and doing, according to *The Beatles Recording Sessions*, "a little yelling"). The finished track was intended to be incidental music in the *Magical Mystery Tour* film, but it wasn't, even though Evans did play accordion in the movie. Considering the performer and the cut's intended use, we shouldn't expect much of the song (described in *The Beatles Recording Sessions* as "a jaunty ditty") should these recordings ever emerge.

Paul McCartney, Donovan (center), and Mike Love of the Beach Boys (right) smear each other's faces with paint in India in preparation for the Holi festival in March 1968. Much of the Beatles' unreleased material from early 1968 was influenced by their study of transcendental meditation with the Maharishi, as well as the other celebrities who were in tow during their aborted stay at his ashram in Rishikesh, India.

1968

Out of the Cosmos, and Back to Earth

The Year in Review

As much fine psychedelic music as the Beatles made in 1967, at times it seemed they were in danger of losing their tether to earthbound rock 'n' roll entirely. For the most part, the music they made in 1968 embraced—indeed, helped lead—the "back to basics" movement sweeping over much of the rock community that year. Even before they decamped to India to study transcendental meditation with Maharishi Mahesh Yogi in February, they'd already recorded the Fats Domino–inspired "Lady Madonna." The two-LP set *The Beatles* (hereafter referred to by its informal but more widely used title, *The White Album*) would have quite a few funky, even occasionally bluesy, down-home rock 'n' rollers, as well as a good portion of their folkiest, most acoustic-oriented tunes.

Yet although the Beatles were rediscovering their rock roots in a sense, they continued to plow some innovative, at times uncharted waters in their songwriting, arrangements, and production. And, remarkably, they continued to be hugely popular. *The White Album* topped charts 'round the world, as did their first release on their new Apple

label, "Hey Jude"/"Revolution"—a contender for the best double-sided single issued by anyone, at any time. They were also doing this in the midst of enormous tensions that, if only in hindsight, were starting to endanger the group's long-term survival. There was the chaotic, financially volatile launch of Apple, the entry of Yoko Ono into both John Lennon's life and most of the Beatles' recording sessions, and the growing divergence of all four of them as both musicians and personalities.

Partly as a consequence of their new musical directions, there was substantially more, and substantially more interesting, unreleased Beatles music recorded during 1968 than there had been in the previous year. Much of this is due to the two-dozen-plus acoustic-based, "unplugged"-like home demos they recorded just prior to the start of the sessions for *The White Album*, which are among the most fascinating and fun commercially unavailable Beatles music ever discovered. Unlike any other large body of unissued Beatles work in nature, this intimately performed, often wonderful material—which, in turn, often has quite different arrangements from those used on *The White Album*

191

itself—would alone make 1968 a notable year for unofficial Beatles recordings. Yet there was much else of value eventually retrieved from the 1968 vaults, including some outtakes of songs that didn't make *The White Album, White Album* alternates that vary from the official tracks in interesting ways, and some scrappy but intriguing home recordings from the last half of the year. Their reversion to more traditional rock instrumentation was partly responsible for this, as the Beatles were now somewhat less enamored of the layer-cake methods and special fairy dust effects they'd often used to build their tracks in 1967.

It has to be emphasized, however, that although the group's recordings were more earthy and organic, they were no less technologically sophisticated than they'd been in the psychedelic era. They were more so, in fact, after the group finally got access to eight-track equipment near the end of the *White Album* sessions. So there are still the kind of minute mix and overdub variations that might drive the less patient collector up the wall—as there would be, in fact, until the end of their career. Even the more taxing of these, however, are revealing in their illustration of how attentive the Beatles were to sonic detail, even as many of their recordings became more "live"-sounding than they had been in quite some time. Many of these variations, too, show the Beatles working increasingly in ones, twos, and threes—a shift that didn't lower the quality of the recordings whatsoever, but portended some big trouble in their quest to continue creating music as a tightly bonded unit.

● February 3

Studio Outtake

Let It Be *sessions*
Studio Three, Abbey Road, London

---

*Across the Universe (take 2)
Across the Universe (take 2, monitor mix)
    appears on Anthology 2

A *Let It Be* session, in early 1968? Not exactly—at this point, *Let It Be* was more than two years away, and "Across the Universe" was in the running for placement on the Beatles' next single. It would end up, however, being used to fill out *Let It Be* after going through a confusing plethora of different mixes and overdubs, rather in counter to the gentle, folky simplicity of the song itself.

For all the subsequent attempts to improve upon it, take 2 of "Across the Universe," issued on *Anthology 2,* was almost as good as any of the available versions. It's certainly the least cluttered of them, lacking any backup female vocals, or the bird sound effects used on the first released version (on the December 1969 various-artists charity album *No One's Gonna Change Our World*). In this early state, it's almost an acoustic folk song, and quite a lovely one. It's probably the version that comes closest to capturing John Lennon's original vision of the song, the acoustic guitars accompanied by tastefully understated table harp and tamboura. It would be going too far, however, to say they should have released this take. The timing's a bit off in places (particularly the instrumental intro), and John's singing sounds a little more like a guide vocal than a final one.

A slightly longer control room monitor mix of take 2 has been bootlegged, though all it adds is some bluesy warm-up riffs and a few more bars of instrumental guitar at the end. It also "isolates" the guitar and harp parts for brief snatches, if that's your kind of thing.

● February 4

Studio Outtakes

Let It Be *sessions*
Studio Three, Abbey Road, London

Across the Universe (take 7, rough mono mix)

"Across the Universe" grew much closer to the shape it took for its initial release on this session, with the addition of backup vocals from two teenagers hanging around outside Abbey Road, backup hummed vocals, and some backwards tape effects. Some feel that these additions subtracted more than they added, and while that's a valid viewpoint, they were rather interesting ways of embellishing the track to add a more exotic ambience. This rough mono mix isn't too different from the *No One's Gonna Change Our World* version, except it runs slower, and is missing the bird noises.

John, however, wasn't satisfied with the track as it turned out in early 1968, later charging Paul McCartney (in his 1980 *Playboy* interview) of subconsciously sabotaging it. "The Beatles didn't make a good record of it," he felt. "It was a *lousy* track of a great song and I was so disappointed by it." That accounts for why he donated it to the charity album (benefiting the World Wildlife Fund), though it was considered for revival in January 1969 when it came up again during the *Get Back* sessions, and an early 1968 version was going to be an additional track when the group considered putting out all four songs exclusive to the *Yellow Submarine* album on an EP. But additional "alternate" versions of "Across the Universe" were in the group's future, particularly when it was overdubbed yet again in 1970 for inclusion on the *Let It Be* LP.

● February 6

Live Performance

For television program Cilla
Television Theatre, London

Nellie Dean
Do You Like Me?

For all his zany Mellotron home tape experiments with John, Ringo hadn't abandoned his affection for good old-fashioned sentimental show business. So it was that, less than two weeks before flying to India to study transcendental meditation with the rest of the Beatles, Ringo made a guest appearance on the second episode of Cilla Black's variety series—the same series for which Paul McCartney had recently penned the theme song. An off-air audio recording has circulated containing, in addition to some typically dreary variety show humor skits, our Ringo dueting with Cilla on the pop tunes "Nellie Dean" (done sans

Ringo Starr and Cilla Black dueting on Black's British TV show, Cilla, *on February 6, 1968.*

musical accompaniment) and "Do You Like Me?" (backed by light orchestration). Both of them dated back to the early 1900s, and both are excruciatingly corny, though "Do You Like Me?" does have *real* singing, on the kind of tune you could have heard in a 1930s film musical.

Throughout this book, we've seen that some surprising left turns the Beatles took did in fact have hidden antecedents in unissued recordings they'd done a year or two earlier. It may be that few fans have been very curious about the origin of Ringo's surprising decision to devote his early-1970 debut solo album, *Sentimental Journey,* to pre-rock pop standards. But here we have an early hint of his apparently genuine love for this kind of all-around-entertainer schmaltz.

● February 6

Studio Outtakes
"Lady Madonna" single session
Studio One, Abbey Road, London

Lady Madonna (take 4)
Lady Madonna (take 4, rough mix)

Lady Madonna (take 4 monitor mixes)
Lady Madonna (take 5)
*Lady Madonna (***Anthology 2*** mix)
    *appears on Anthology 2

While "Lady Madonna" was very much a return to the Beatles' rock 'n' roll roots, it was *not* a return to the nearly-live-in-the-studio way they'd made records back in 1963. That much is clear from the surprising abundance of alternate takes and mixes of the track. None, perhaps sadly, are much different from the familiar hit single, but they do give us glimpses of some ideas that were discarded in the final product.

Take 4 is floating around in various guises, and is mostly identical to the official track, except it's missing the overdubbed saxophone parts and some background harmonies. That does at least allow you to hear the piano in the instrumental break better than you can on the single. There are, however, some parts that didn't make it into the final mix, starting with a most annoyingly overbearing laugh over the first line. More interestingly, you can hear some faint Mellotron washes in the background during the "see how they run" refrains, some muted whoops and spoken chatter, and some jokingly high-pitched vocals on the instrumental outro that couldn't have been seriously intended for the released track.

There's a full-fidelity stereo take 4 in circulation, but there are also different mixes of this same take, starting with a rough mix that positions the parts differently, and misses out on the Mellotron and some other minor extraneous noises. An exhausting nine-and-a-half-minute monitor mix of take 4 being played and replayed isolates various bits of the recording as it goes along, including Paul's voice, tambourine, handclaps, Paul's voice plus Mellotron, chatter, laughter, and a strained closing vocalization of "Lady Ma-da-nah-ah-ah-ah." It's not all that interesting, but it does prove that the Beatles were having silly fun in the studio on this, the last group of sessions before Yoko Ono's attendance became commonplace. The Mellotron on the last parts of the bridge actually sounds rather nicely haunting. Perhaps it was mixed out of the final version because such a then-futuristic instrument would have been considered out of place on a record with such a '50s rock 'n' roll feel.

Take 5 doesn't vary much from take 4, except for the addition of real brass and background vocal harmony overdubs (as well as some chatter and food munching as the tape is wound back and forth before playing in its entirety). It's admittedly a confusing exercise to sort out these not-too-different "Lady Madonna" outtakes from each other, and the less patient listener will probably settle for the *Anthology 2* mix, which draws from elements of takes 3, 4, and 5. That's a smoother listen, but one from which some of these various differences—including the Mellotron—have been removed. But it does at least have an additional sax riff at the very end.

● February 11

Studio Outtakes
Yellow Submarine *single session*
Studio Three, Abbey Road, London

Hey Bulldog (RM2)

Though it's the most highly regarded package of the Beatles' White Album *demos, the graphics on* From Kinfauns to Chaos *were themselves chaotic.*

It might only matter to the very most obsessed Beatles collectors, but it's a fact that "Hey Bulldog" has never been issued in mono. A mono mix *was* used in the soundtrack to the initial release of *Yellow Submarine,* and has been bootlegged, but it's sullied by some non-musical noises heard in the film sequence that features the song. While a supposed "true" studio mono mix minus those soundtrack superfluities has also been bootlegged, some experts suspect it's not an authentic one.

● Early to Mid-March

Private Tapes
Rishikesh, India

When the Saints Go Marching In
You Are My Sunshine
Jingle Bells
She'll Be Comin' Around the Mountain
Happiness Runs
Blowin' in the Wind
Untitled Acoustic Guitar Instrumental
Hare Krishna Mantra
O Sole Mio
It's Now or Never
Catch the Wind

While the Beatles were in Rishikesh, India, studying TM with the Maharishi, they, their instructor, and other students were filmed for an Italian television program that aired on March 15. The soundtrack for this footage (including some Italian narration) was actually made separately, and overdubbed for the purposes of complementing the on-screen images.

Ringo, however, had already left India by the time the film crew arrived, giving the Maharishi a mere ten days before deciding he'd had his fill. But you can see all three of the remaining Beatles in this sequence, as well as fellow celebrity pupils Donovan, Mike Love of the Beach Boys, Mia Farrow, and new age musician Paul Horn, along with Beatle companions Cynthia Lennon, Patti Harrison, and Jane Asher. Unsurprisingly, considering the setting, the songs are convivial, folky acoustic sing-alongs of the sort that any group of young adults might entertain themselves with on an outing to the beach or the woods. Granted, not many such groups would have sung "Hare Krishna Mantra," but otherwise they largely opted for folk songs that would have been familiar to almost anyone in the Western world. Exceptions—though by 1968 they were almost as familiar as those folk songs—were Bob Dylan's "Blowin' in the Wind" and brief snippets of "O Sole Mio" and Elvis Presley's "It's Now or Never." "Catch the Wind" had been Donovan's first hit, and "Happiness Runs" would appear on his 1969 album *Barabajagal.*

Musically, also unsurprisingly, this fair-quality recording is unexceptional, with all three of the Beatles present participating, but none of them dominating the proceedings. It might have been interesting to hear them working on the *White Album* songs they were writing in India, but they probably didn't want to perform any of those on camera months before they would make it onto record. It does offer both visual and aural evidence that, to all appearances, this was a happy and serene time for the group—perhaps the last such time they were enjoying together. Or mostly together, since Ringo and his wife had already left.

● March 15

Private Tapes
Rishikesh, India

Spiritual Regeneration
Happy Birthday to You/Spiritual Regeneration

As another relic of that brief happy time out of the eyes of the world's media in Rishikesh, we have these slight but amusing acoustic recordings from mid-March. From the sound of them, they were probably written off the cuff, "Spiritual Regeneration" honoring Maharishi teacher and TM founder Guru Deva (the same guru name-checked in "Across the Universe"). It's basic, three-chord '50s rock 'n' roll meets folk-busk, with a Beach Boys flavor giving it a slight resemblance to "Back in the U.S.S.R.," particularly in the brisk chugging rhythm and Chuck Berry–styled guitar break.

After a minute and a half of this, the musicians—including Paul, George, Donovan, and others, but apparently not John—segue into "Happy Birthday to You" without breaking rhythm, before getting back into the "Spiritual Regeneration" lyric. (Unfortunately about 20 seconds of this, from the juncture at which the songs segue into each other, are obscured by narration from famed DJ Wolfman Jack, as the tape originated from a Beach Boys radio special.) The birthday boy was fellow Maharishi student/Beach Boys singer Mike Love, whose influence can be felt both in the high harmonies of this particular ditty, and more substantially in the Beach Boys–like harmonies of "Back in the U.S.S.R." itself. The happy glow of the Beatles' respite in India, however, was probably soon to fade. Paul returned to London about ten days after this recording, and a disenchanted John and George followed a few weeks later, before they'd finished their planned course with the Maharishi.

Mike Love, incidentally, told *MOJO* that he helped Paul write the bridge of "Back in the U.S.S.R.," and that "a tape still exists of he and I playing around with the song." One wonders if he might be getting this confused with the "Spiritual Regeneration" tape, though he might indeed be referring to an entirely different recording that has yet to escape into circulation.

● Circa May 19

Private Tape
Kenwood, Weybridge

Holding a Note

The meeting between John Lennon and Yoko Ono that took place at his Kenwood home, probably on this night, was of monumental significance to both of their lives, as well as to the Beatles. For the next few years, the two would rarely be apart. Yoko, too, influenced much of John's songwriting for the final Beatles records, and his absorption in his new relationship would be a key factor in both destabilizing the group dynamic and leading to his decision to start a solo career.

The recordings they made to commemorate their new affair, however, were *not* of monumental artistic significance. Released as the *Two*

Virgins album, they did at least give John his first commercial outlet for the avant-garde home tapes he'd been messing about with since around 1966. Critically panned at the time (not without reason) as self-indulgently unlistenable, there's been little demand for "outtakes" from the session. But a brief one, titled "Holding a Note" on bootleg and lasting just under two minutes, was aired on "The Lost Lennon Tapes" radio series. It's more a relic of John and Yoko getting used to being around each other in intimate circumstances than it is an artistic creation, and comes from a six-minute recording "full of chirping birds and more madness," according to Chip Madinger and Mark Easter's *Eight Arms to Hold You: The Solo Beatles Compendium.*

● Circa Late May

Private Tapes
Kinfauns, Esher

Julia
Blackbird
Rocky Raccoon
Back in the U.S.S.R.
**Honey Pie
Mother Nature's Son
Ob-La-Di, Ob-La-Da
***Junk
Dear Prudence
Sexy Sadie
Cry Baby Cry
I'm Just a Child of Nature
The Continuing Story of Bungalow Bill
I'm So Tired
Yer Blues
Everybody's Got Something to Hide Except Me and My Monkey
What's the New Mary Jane
Revolution
While My Guitar Gently Weeps
Circles
Sour Milk Sea
Not Guilty
*Piggies
*Happiness Is a Warm Gun
*Mean Mr. Mustard
*Polythene Pam
*Glass Onion

    *appears on Anthology 3
    **edited version appears on Anthology 3
    ***remixed version appears on Anthology 3

In late May of 1968, the Beatles gathered at George Harrison's home, Kinfauns, in the London suburb of Esher, to make rough demos of material under consideration for *The White Album*. There really isn't any other parallel in the unreleased Beatles catalog for the 27 known recordings that resulted. At no other time, to our knowledge, did the Beatles so methodically rehearse and make demos for an upcoming album outside of EMI's studios. And there's no other set of tapes that

John and George with Mike Love of the Beach Boys in Rishikesh, where the Beatles wrote many of the songs they recorded as demos at George's house in May 1968 shortly before starting work on The White Album.

show the Beatles, as a group, making demos for a large batch of songs in a mostly acoustic setup. Although it doesn't include every song that made it onto *The White Album* (but does include a few songs that didn't make the cut), this is very much like hearing *"The White Album Unplugged,"* even if the "unplugged" concept didn't really exist in those days. While seven of the tracks would eventually find release on *Anthology 3,* the great majority of them still lie unheard by the mass audience. Aside from their hundreds of hours of unissued rehearsals and studio outtakes from the *Get Back/Let It Be* sessions in January 1969, it's the largest body of unreleased work to be recorded by the band in one gulp. It's far more enjoyable than the *Get Back* outtakes, though, and it could be argued that these home demos—as rough and imperfect as they are—constitute the most interesting and, yes, fun chapter of all in the unreleased Beatles canon.

It's still something of a mystery as to what led the group to be recording this set of demos in the first place. Certainly it was an interesting, exciting, and in many ways tense juncture in the Beatles' career. They and their wives (and Paul's fiancée) had just completed their lengthy sojourn in Rishikesh, India, to study transcendental meditation with the Maharishi. The plan had been to complete an eight-week course with their new guru, and such was their enthusiasm for TM that there was even thought of staying longer should the spirit move them, release schedules and business pressures be damned. But the trip had ended in disarray. Ringo left after ten days, unhappy about the spicy food and the absence of his children. Paul left after a few weeks, not especially disappointed with the Maharishi or meditation, but not feeling like there was any urgent need to pursue the matter

further. John and George departed in mid-April shortly before the course was due to finish under cloudy circumstances, the Maharishi having come under suspicion of making sexual overtures to one of the students.

Upon their return to the Western world, the Beatles were immediately immersed back in the world of high-powered hype and the very tensions they'd traveled to India to escape. Their Apple Records music and business empire was just rolling up to its serious launch, and in mid-May Lennon and McCartney made a hectic trip to New York to publicize it, with mixed results. Just days after returning to London, Lennon began an affair with Yoko Ono, in turn immediately bringing his marriage to Cynthia Powell to an end. The very day John and Yoko consummated their romantic relationship, they also recorded the first of their avant-garde albums, *Two Virgins*—beginning an artistic and personal collaboration that would do much to pull Lennon out of the Beatles' orbit, and much to destroy the internal harmony that had kept the band together. For his part, McCartney (though officially still engaged to Jane Asher) had met with his future wife Linda Eastman in New York. With all the personal and business complications weighing upon them, it's something of a wonder that they even managed to find the time to demo several dozen songs in late May.

Yet, as George Harrison told the press at the time, they had about 35 songs in the running already for the next album—which, he mused, might be a double album, or even a triple. (By the time of the press screening of *Yellow Submarine* on July 8, George's estimate had risen to 40, ten of them being his own compositions.) For the time spent in Rishikesh had yielded what might have been an unexpected bonus.

Free for the first time in years from the distractions of the media and fans, the group had found the weeks in India especially productive for songwriting. Furthermore, as they had only their acoustic guitars with them for instrumentation, much of their compositions had a folkier, less electric base than what they'd usually devised in the past.

"While the Beatles and I were in India they wrote the *White Album* songs," recalled Donovan, who was also on the Maharishi's meditation course in Rishikesh, in an interview with the author. "It was obvious *The White Album* would have a distinctive acoustic and lyrical vibe. Paul, John, George, and I all had our acoustic guitars with us. George would later say that my music greatly influenced *The White Album*. I played all my styles, and the Beatles were exposed to weeks of Donovan. John was influenced to write romantic fantasy lyrics on the two songs he wrote, 'Julia' and 'Dear Prudence,' after my teaching him my finger-style guitar method. He was a fast learner." Jazz and new age musician Paul Horn, also in Rishikesh on the meditation course, has theorized that the meditation study itself helped spur and shape the group's songwriting in India. "You find out more about yourself on deeper levels, when you're meditating," he said in Steve Turner's *A Hard Day's Write: The Stories Behind Every Beatles' Song*. "Look how prolific they were in such a relatively short time. They were in the Himalayas away from the pressures and away from the telephone. When you get too involved with life, it suppresses your creativity. When you're able to be quiet, it starts coming up."

It's worth recounting this backdrop to the *White Album* demos in some detail, as it might explain to some degree both why the Beatles decided to record them, and why they recorded them the way they did. It could be that, for all their staggering productivity between 1962 and 1967, at no other time did they have such a backlog of material ready for recording, especially now that Harrison was writing more than ever. It may also be that, having written much if not all of the material in informal, acoustic circumstances in India, they felt most comfortable doing "work-in-progress" versions outside of EMI's studios, in a low-pressure home environment, using mostly acoustic instruments. Why George's home was chosen isn't clear; more Beatles-business-related meetings tended to take place at Paul McCartney's house than anywhere else, as Paul (unlike the others) lived in London itself, just a few minutes' walk from Abbey Road Studios. Perhaps it was felt that meeting in a busy area of London wouldn't have the mellow atmosphere the songs seemed to call for. John's house (where he and Paul had often met to work on songs) might have been off-limits given the breakup of his marriage at the time. Cynthia Lennon had just returned from a trip to discover John and Yoko together a few days before, and having the Beatles over on top of that might have been too much to even consider. Or it might have been as simple a matter as Harrison having the best home taping equipment.

Whatever the state of the Beatles' nerves when they recorded their demos on Harrison's Ampex 4-track machine, they certainly don't sound anxious or distracted. In fact, the performances have a remarkably carefree, jolly quality, almost as if it's a campfire sing-along and song-swapping session rather than the initial work on the most eagerly anticipated album of 1968. Unpredictable, joyous whoops punctuate the proceedings, as well as ensemble backup vocals and all manner of crack-up asides and spontaneous scatting, often but not always from the mouth of John Lennon. Far from just laying down the tapes as a work aid, the Beatles are quite obviously having fun—having a blast, actually. Maybe the group, and par-

ticularly Lennon, welcomed these quasi-sessions as a safe haven of sorts from the hassles of the outside world, their music being the one thing they always guarded as inviolable.

It is possible that these songs weren't entirely, or even mostly, recorded at George's house at all, or recorded as a group in some or many instances. Though the seven tracks that appear on *Anthology 3* are all noted as originating from Esher in the liner notes, some feel it unlikely that all of the recording for the nearly 30 demos was done at George's home. It's been theorized, not without reason, that some or many of the songs could have been recorded by Lennon, McCartney, and Harrison individually. As another possibility, the songs could have been largely recorded as solo works, and then brought to George's house for both the songwriter of a specific tune and other members to add overdubs (which would have been easily done on a 4-track recorder). As these recordings weren't subject to EMI's usual detailed record keeping, however, it's unlikely it will ever be definitely sorted out what was recorded when and where.

Ultimately, "only" 19 of the 27 songs known to exist from these sessions found a place on *The White Album* in a re-recorded studio version. For all their wealth of available titles, the Beatles weren't quite yet done with the writing for the upcoming album. Eleven of the tracks on *The White Album* have no Kinfauns counterparts, including "Helter Skelter," "Long, Long, Long," "Martha My Dear," "Birthday," "Savoy Truffle," "Wild Honey Pie," "Revolution 9," "Good Night," "I Will," "Why Don't We Do It in the Road," and "Don't Pass Me By"—several of which are among *The White Album*'s more popular numbers. On the other hand, the tapes do give us the chance to hear no fewer than eight songs that did *not* find a place on *The White Album* and half a dozen that the Beatles would not release at all before breaking up, though all of them except one ("Sour Milk Sea") would appear on some post-Beatles compilation or solo Beatle release. The fidelity is on the crude side (though it's way better on the seven tracks included on *Anthology 3*), the arrangements rudimentary, and the timing of the voices and the instruments sometimes slightly off, especially when some of the overdubbed tracks get out of sync with each other. The tapes are also rather skewed toward songs for which John Lennon was the primary or sole composer; he was the force behind 15 of the tunes (with Paul McCartney tallying a mere seven, and George Harrison five). Yet they're a hugely enjoyable listen and quite different in tone than *The White Album*, though it would be a mistake to say they're just as good as that finished product.

Naturally, the most intriguing items are those the Beatles didn't see fit to record for a release while an active unit. The best of them is "I'm Just a Child of Nature," which Lennon would rework for "Jealous Guy" on his second proper solo album, 1971's *Imagine*. In this early state, the lyrics are quite different, and quite a bit more influenced by Rishikesh than Yoko, as the opening line about the road to Rishikesh makes clear. It's something of a Lennon counterpart to McCartney's "Mother Nature's Son," John sounding at his most pastoral and peaceful, though he typically punctures the mood by drawing out the last line of the second verse with a jokey vibrato that makes one question just how sincere his back-to-nature crusade might have been. As to why it didn't make it onto *The White Album*, maybe it was felt to be too lyrically close to "Mother Nature's Son," or maybe John thought it was too naive, particularly in the company of such Lennonesque, realist screeds as "Yer Blues" and "Revolution." As to why it didn't make it onto *Anthology 3*, maybe there would have been a squabble over

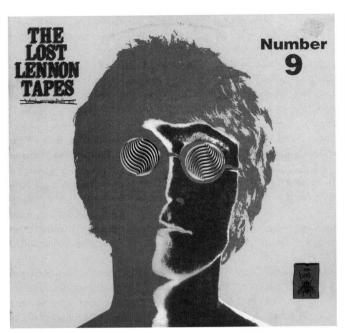

This volume of the long-running "The Lost Lennon Tapes" bootleg radio series was among the first albums to present some of the May 1968 tapes made at George's house, though it only included songs for which John was the principal or sole author.

the songwriting credits—should it have been considered a Lennon solo composition, a joint Lennon-McCartney credit, or had the parties concerned forgotten exactly where the credit should go? Anyway, Lennon at least knew not to let a good melody go to waste, even if it took him three years to resuscitate it for "Jealous Guy." (Note that while this number is usually titled "Child of Nature" on bootlegs, John himself referred to it as "I'm Just a Child of Nature" in his 1980 *Playboy* interview.)

The other Lennon song never to make it onto a pre-breakup Beatles album, "What's the New Mary Jane," is the source of much controversy among fans. Certainly it's one of the most minimal and discordant songs in the Lennon-McCartney catalog, and one of the most inscrutably eccentric. It would indeed be recorded in a studio version for *The White Album,* with a whole gallery of rattling percussion and echo effects, though the track was omitted from the running order at the last minute. It's sometimes thought to be the Beatles song (other than "Revolution 9") that most strongly bears Yoko Ono's avant-garde influence. But if that's true, Ono's influence must have been immediately ingested, as this gentler, less elaborate version from (at the latest) just a few days after they became a couple proves. Many will find this surreal tune—with its sing-along (if not terribly catchy) series of faux Indian-Anglo non sequiturs in the verses, leading to the even more nonsensical non sequitur of the chorus, lamenting what a shame Mary Jane had a pain at the party—more palatable in this arrangement than in the studio outtake that surfaced on *Anthology 3.* It's still not much of a song, however, even if it's a kinda cool example of Lennon's Goonish humor coming stronger to the fore than it did on almost any other Beatles recording. The Beatles certainly sound like they're taking the mickey out of themselves on the near-falsettos of the chorus, especially when the song dissolves into a near-anarchic

mix of voices on the fade. It is, incidentally, the only version in which you'll hear the title actually mentioned, as John does in the improvised-sounding spoken parts at the end.

The only McCartney song from the demos not to make it onto a regular Beatles album was "Junk" (titled "Sing-along Junk" on some bootlegs), which Paul would redo for his first solo album, 1970's *McCartney.* He and the Beatles made the right decision in passing it over—it's a pleasant, slight, and inconsequential folky song about nothing in particular, more like an off-the-cuff lullaby than a fully baked tune. Note, incidentally, that the remix included on *Anthology 3* is actually missing some vocal parts heard on the bootlegged version that were probably ironed out for some unknown reason when *Anthology 3* was prepared for release. As another oddity, on *Anthology 3* the songwriting credit reads "McCartney" rather than "Lennon-McCartney," probably since it had already been copyrighted to Paul alone when it appeared on *McCartney.*

Harrison fared far worse than Lennon or McCartney in the leftover department, as no fewer than three of the five songs he offered for consideration failed to find a place on *The White Album*—in spite of his seeming generosity in letting the Beatles use his home and tape machine for the sessions in the first place. The strongest of the three was "Not Guilty," his defensive rebuttal to criticisms of his own brand of counterculture, here presented in a much less tense arrangement than the more forceful one he'd devise when it was cut (in numerous different takes) at the *White Album* sessions. While "Circles" isn't as good a song, it's a pretty neat, if droning, reflection of Harrison's more somber spiritual sensibilities. Its instrumentation is supplied not by guitar, but by an eerie organ that seems to have been dragged out of a dusty, disused church closet. Harrison would re-record it much, much later for his 1982 solo album *Gone Troppo,* though it's this earlier arrangement, for all its primitivism, that exerts by far the greater fascination. While the last of these Harrisongs, "Sour Milk Sea," is far more uplifting and uptempo in mood than either of the other two (and a rare showcase for extended falsetto in a lead Harrison vocal), in all honesty it's a pretty insignificant, easygoing, slightly bluesy rock song, the lyrics unfortunately delivered in muffled fidelity on the available recording. George himself later admitted the song only took about ten minutes to write. This tune too would eventually find a home, not on a Beatles or Harrison solo album, but on Jackie Lomax's 1968 solo debut single, released on Apple and produced by George, with Paul on bass and Ringo on drums.

The only two other home *White Album* demos not to make the grade for the 1968 double LP were "Mean Mr. Mustard" and "Polythene Pam," both of which were of course revived in 1969 for the side two *Abbey Road* medley. It wasn't until *Anthology 3* that these were even known to exist, and it came as quite a shock to even Beatles experts to find that these songs had been written and demoed as far back as May 1968, over a year before *Abbey Road*'s release (though George had specifically remembered them being penned in India in a late-1969 interview). They're pretty close in feel to the *Abbey Road* versions too, other than being acoustic, though "Mean Mr. Mustard" does leap into a brief, basic blues-rock bridge that was wisely excised when it was redone the following year, and refers to Mustard's sister as "Shirley," not "Pam." "Polythene Pam," too, has a very slightly different, more sour chord progression at the end of its verses, as well as some different lyrics.

So that leaves 19 tracks that are in essence early home acoustic demo versions of songs that actually made it onto *The White Album.*

Only four of these—"Glass Onion," "Happiness Is a Warm Gun," "Piggies," and "Honey Pie"—would be rescued for *Anthology 3,* the rest only surfacing on bootleg thus far. Are they much different from the *White Album* versions, and are they worth hearing?

The answer is an emphatic yes, even if you're not a nutty completist for this sort of thing. True, some of the songs—particularly the slower and folkier ones, like "Blackbird," "Cry, Baby, Cry," "Rocky Raccoon," "Julia," "Mother Nature's Son," and "The Continuing Story of Bungalow Bill"—are pretty close to *The White Album* save for the absence of fuller arrangements. Yet others are noticeably to radically different. Lyric changes abound, from the almost invisibly minor to the nearly extensive. Starting with the most amusing major lyric change, you haven't lived until you've heard the fadeout on "Dear Prudence," which follows the recorded version pretty closely until Lennon launches into a satirical spoken mini-monologue: "Who was to know that [suppressed giggle] sooner or later she was to go completely berserk in the care of Maharishi Mahesh Yogi. All the people around were very worried about the girl, because she was going insane. So we sang to her." So there you have a more direct explanation of what exactly "Dear Prudence" is about than you'll find in the song itself, though the Beatles were wise to make the lyrics more universal by excising this literal explanation. Running a close second is another spoken bit near the end of "I'm So Tired," where John slowly and rhythmically deadpans, "When I hold you in your [sic] arms, when you show each one of your charms, I wonder should I get up and go to the funny farm?" Some particularly great background whooping graces that track, where it's hard to believe the guys aren't having a whale of a time.

As for some more interesting remaining cuts, "Back in the U.S.S.R." has a gloriously funky, down-home feel, McCartney referring here to an "awful" flight rather than a "dreadful" one—a minor variation to be sure, but an example of how no detail is too small to escape the masters as they finish their work. Paul also leans really hard into some of his "R"s when singing "U.S.S.R.," almost as if he's making fun of an American accent; the bridge has more jovial doo wopisms than the studio take; and the fade benefits from some delightful high scatting. "Revolution," too, is a real highlight of the entire Beatles unreleased discography, where the "party" or "campfire" feel reaches its peak, with a clap-along beat, sing-along harmonies, scatted high-harmony verse, and overall giddiness that's far lighter and more joyous than the (itself highly estimable) down 'n' dirty version that ended up on the flip side of "Hey Jude." Like "Back in the U.S.S.R.," it's another recording where a slight Beach Boys influence can be detected, even if that would all but vanish by the time the two different Beatles versions of the song were released (on *The White Album* and the B-side of "Hey Jude"). "Piggies," too, is very different from the *White Album* version, soaked in gentleness and played entirely on guitars (with whistling rather than sung words taking up one obviously incomplete verse), as opposed to the far more acerbic studio arrangement, where strings and harpsichord gave it a hard kick in the backside. And here the piggies clutch their forks and knives to cut their pork chops, instead of eating their bacon—another wise lyric substitution, when it finally came time to record it at EMI down the road.

"Honey Pie" is not so much different as incomplete, some wordless humming and scatting taking the place of words that McCartney would fill in by the time it was recorded for real. (The *Anthology 3* version, incidentally, is severely edited, cutting out about 35 seconds from the song's middle.) In an even sketchier state is "Happiness Is a Warm Gun," afflicted by false starts and stops, missing the final doo woppy section, and obviously not really ready for consumption, Lennon getting stuck in repetitions of the phrase about Mother Superior jumping the gun. The lyrics to "Glass Onion" aren't in final form either, though it's entertaining to hear John plugging some nonsense syllables into some of the lines, and dramatically dragging the rhythm in the final verse. Considering the unfinished state of all three of these songs, it's odd indeed that they were all chosen for *Anthology 3,* when so many other far more polished numbers for the session were presumably available. Of course, several of the other songs were still in an unfinished state as well—"Cry Baby Cry" lacks its intro, "Rocky Raccoon" its opening and closing verses, and "Back in the U.S.S.R." its final verse, while "Julia" changes the order of the lyrics, goes into some whistling at the end, and is played in a higher key to boot.

"Gentleness" is an almost unavoidable byword when discussing these demos, and "Yer Blues" is another instance where the approach is more laidback, easygoing, and rootsy than the one employed for *The White Album.* It's not necessarily a better approach, but it's a very refreshing and different one, particularly after you've heard *The White Album* a thousand times. (Note also how at this stage John is merely "insecure" rather than "suicidal.") This is also true of "Everybody's Got Something to Hide Except Me and My Monkey," which sounds friendlier and less vicious here, though the verse has a more skeletal melody that would be improved upon by the time the Beatles got down to work on it at EMI a month later. Dig also how Lennon repeats "take it easy" on the long, long outro ad infinitum before lapsing into lascivious "make it, make it, make it" as the track collapses to a halt. Speaking of collapsing, "Sexy Sadie" almost seems to run out of gas when it comes to the fade, lacking the long instrumental coda that would finish it off on *The White Album.* "While My Guitar Gently Weeps," the only Harrison song here other than "Piggies" to get a hearing on *The White Album,* is suffused with the same ghostly organ as the one heard on "Circles," giving it an almost funereal quality. The lyrics would undergo some revision by the time the final version was recorded at EMI—at this point, most noticeably, it declares "the problems you sow are the troubles you're reaping" in the first verse.

And what was Ringo's role in these sessions? There's certainly no full drum set in evidence, and no percussion at all on some tracks. What percussion there is tends to be handclaps, thumps (on guitars and furniture, perhaps), and the odd tambourine and miscellaneous rattle. What's more, there was no demo made of "Don't Pass Me By," his sole composition on *The White Album* (and, in fact, the first song wholly written by Starr to be recorded by the Beatles). Is it possible he didn't attend these sessions, leaving the work to principal songwriters John, Paul, or George? One also wonders whether Yoko Ono was in attendance, as she certainly was at almost all of the Beatles' official Abbey Road sessions from this point onward, occasionally even contributing an eccentric vocal snippet (as she did on "The Continuing Story of Bungalow Bill," "What's the New Mary Jane," and "Revolution 9"). Certainly one of the distant background voices on some of the more fully harmonized Kinfauns demos, like "Revolution," could be Yoko's, or, for that matter, another non-Beatle who was part of the group's inner circle, like George's wife, Patti. Both roadie/personal assistant Mal Evans and publicist Derek Taylor are addressed at various points, and it's possible they added to the clamor in low-key fashions as well.

After they were completed, the tracks were mixed to mono by George, with John, Paul, and Ringo each getting copies of this reduction

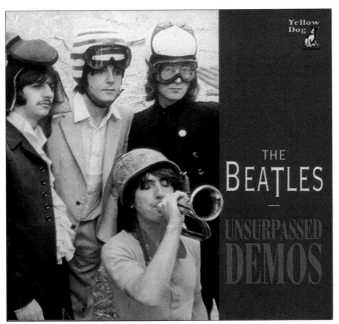

Unsurpassed Demos was the first bootleg to present most of the May 1968 tapes known to have been made at George's house.

tape. Their existence remained unsuspected by Beatles fans until some of the demos first found radio broadcast in the late '80s as part of "The Lost Lennon Tapes" series, John's copy of a tape with much of the material having been found in his archives. These Lennon-dominated tracks and a few others quickly found their way onto bootleg, and as welcome as those were, the focus on Lennon songs exclusively gave listeners an unbalanced portrait of those sessions, which included so many additional compositions from McCartney and Harrison. Twenty-two of the tracks finally circulated in the early '90s as part of the *Unsurpassed Demos* bootleg, with other subsequent bootlegs offering slightly longer versions.

That seemed to be the last word on the matter, except that in 1996, seven Kinfauns recordings—four of them never previously bootlegged—appeared on *Anthology 3*. As these had far better sound than anything heard on illegitimate CDs, that naturally led to speculation that the entire body of 27 tracks existed in much better fidelity than what had been previously available on bootleg. And, naturally, it engendered speculation that if four Kinfauns demos suddenly popped up out of nowhere, there might be yet more where those came from. Some even wondered if Apple were deliberately taunting the bootleggers by selecting material that had never made it out in any form, when there were so many other, previously circulated Kinfauns recordings they could have chosen instead.

Following that line of investigation, it's known that the tape of Kinfauns material found in John Lennon's archives contains the songs from the *Unsurpassed Demos* bootleg on side A, and versions (identified as "*White Album* demos") of "Cry Baby Cry," "I'm Just a Child of Nature," "Yer Blues," "Everybody's Got Something to Hide Except Me and My Monkey," "What's the New Mary Jane," "Revolution," "While My Guitar Gently Weeps," and "Piggies" on side B. These could just be the same versions as the much-bootlegged ones heard on side A—or they could be yet different versions of the same numbers, also recorded as part of the Kinfauns sessions (or even from an entirely different source).

The absence of the four previously unbooted tracks that surfaced on *Anthology 3* ("Happiness Is a Warm Gun," "Mean Mr. Mustard," "Polythene Pam," and "Glass Onion") from this Lennon archive tape in turn adds ammunition to the speculation that those four recordings might not have been part of the Kinfauns batch at all.

Several years before the *Anthology* series got on track, Harrison told *Musician* magazine, "I just realized that I've got a really good bootleg tape—demos we made at my house on an Ampex 4-track during *The White Album*." Harrison's tacit stamp of approval raised hopes that the entire set might find official release, particularly as it was George, and not EMI or the other Beatles, who owned the copyright on these recordings; when seven were used on *Anthology 3*, the small print noted that all of them had been licensed to Apple from Harrison. George's death in 2001 perhaps complicates the matter, however, and though his estate presumably still controls the material, as of 2006 its appearance seems as far away as ever. That's unfortunate, because a thorough compilation of all 27 (or more, if they exist) Kinfauns demos, with the best available fidelity and cleaned-up sound, would be a solid contender for the best collection of (largely) unreleased Beatles material that could be envisioned at this point.

● June 4

Studio Outtakes
The White Album sessions
Studio Three, Abbey Road, London

Revolution 1 (take 20 overdubs and playback)
Revolution 1 (rehearsals)

In the mammoth body of unreleased Beatles music, there are to numerous incredibly strange and off-the-wall recordings. There were those Alf Bicknell–auctioned 1963 tapes of Biblical recitations and hymns, the 19 minutes of screwing around at the "Think for Yourself" session, and all those John Lennon home Mellotron experiments between 1966 and 1968. None, however, is as bizarre as this 67-minute tape of playbacks, overdubs, and jamming from the "Revolution 1" sessions. For it's not so much a tape of the music itself—though there's music to be heard—as a tape of Yoko Ono, relaying her stream-of-consciousness impressions of the moment into a portable recorder. All these "Revolution 1" outtakes can only be heard coming through playback speakers in the background. That makes for enough of a loss in fidelity to devalue the experience right there. But when the music's fighting it out for supremacy with Ono's largely unrelated monologue, it only compounds the frustration of having otherwise unavailable Beatles studio outtakes so tantalizingly close to our ears, yet ultimately all but out of reach.

This was one of the first recording sessions where Yoko was present, her relationship with John having become serious just weeks before. She would be a regular visitor to Beatles recording sessions throughout the rest of 1968 and 1969, her constant presence often later cited as an unwelcome, tension-heightening factor in the group's breakup. The Beatles *had* let visitors into some of their sessions in the past, including not only insiders like Brian Epstein and publisher Dick James, but also musicians like David Crosby of the Byrds and Brian Jones of the Rolling Stones, biographer Hunter Davies, and others from their social circle;

George's wife, Patti, had even contributed to the sound effects of "Yellow Submarine." For the most part, however, they had deliberately excluded visitors so they could concentrate on their recordings without distraction. Although Ono does not seem bent on interfering with John or the group at this particular session, evidenced by this tape, one can only guess what the other Beatles and the EMI staff thought at the sight of her rambling almost continuously into her recorder as everyone else set about trying to perfect the first song cut at the *White Album* sessions. (Even Yoko acknowledges at one point that "I must really look crazy" recording herself in the midst of all this.) For what it's worth, it's rarely pointed out that Paul McCartney was also bringing in a girlfriend, Francie Schwartz, to some sessions around this time (as can be seen in the *Anthology* video in the clip of the recording of "Blackbird" on June 11)—though he was, as far as the world knew, still officially engaged to Jane Asher.

Almost as soon her tape's rolling, Yoko declares, "John, I miss you already." That sets the stage for an hour-plus disquisition taking in a log of their day's activities, the state of their relationship (regarding which she's still feeling precarious and uncertain), her worry about Cynthia Lennon's impending return to Kenwood, a new apartment near Hyde Park she's considering renting, the attempted assassination of Andy Warhol in New York (which had just occurred), the *Two Virgins* album, and more. Sample extracts: "The only time that I remember about my promiscuity is when I feel so insecure that I feel potentially that I have to bring that out in me to sort of protect myself . . . I'm starting to miss you again . . . it's so important you come inside me, instead of coming in my hand or something, you see, and then you say that there's no difference[!] . . . I wonder all this makes sense to you . . . I wish I could get rid of my paranoia . . . I feel like running out of this room . . . I'm the most insecure person in the world right now." And then we have Yoko Ono as John Lennon's graphologist: "Your handwriting, it's always been like all your letters were going backwards, leaning backwards, which means tremendous insecurity . . . leaning backwards handwriting is typical of sort of insecure, terribly insecure high school girl or something like that . . . when I first saw your handwriting, I was really amazed, 'cause you very rarely see that in a man . . . why that insecurity?"

It's psychobabble, really, and one imagines that if Yoko knows this tape has been bootlegged for years, she's mortified at having her naked inner mental state of the time so widely available for examination. True, as an avant-garde artist of repute, she was used to doing pieces and generally behaving in a manner that many others would find embarrassingly self-revealing. This particular document, however, crosses the line from life-as-art to a sneak peek at a diary never meant to be read by anyone else. As for any potential use it might have for Beatles historians, she's pretty oblivious to the Beatles or the "Revolution 1" recording throughout, though she makes passing and fairly positive references to the other Beatles and George Martin (who "looks much better now to me, now that I found out he's from a working-class [background]"). For all the supposed dislike between her and McCartney, interestingly, her impressions of Paul are quite favorable at this point: "After the initial embarrassment, Paul has been very nice to me. He's nice on a very on-the-level, straight sense . . . he's treating me with respect. I feel like he's my younger brother or something like that. I'm sure that if he had been a woman or something, he would have been a great friend, because there's something definitely very strong between John and Paul(!)"

As interesting (if uncomfortably voyeuristic) as this document of Yoko Ono's early interactions with the Beatles (and early stage of

romance with John Lennon) is in some respects, it makes it far more difficult to get at the music on this tape—in which most Beatles fans are more interested. For there *is* music going on almost all the time, of one of *The White Album*'s most notable songs, and *none* of it was released, or available elsewhere. For starters, it's long puzzled fans as to how the last six minutes of take 18 of "Revolution 1" (recorded a few days earlier, on May 30) could have been cleaved off for use in "Revolution 9," so unrelated do the songs seem to be in their released state. But in the playbacks of take 20 (actually take 18 with some overdubs), you can detect this much more clearly (albeit with some struggle on this particular Ono-overlaid tape), particularly in the first of the playbacks. The shaky shouts of "riiiiiighht," the shivering "ooh-ooh-oohs," the skin-crawling siren-like sounds, miscellaneous odd scrapes and electronic pings—all can be heard, but within the context of an instrumental jam on the "Revolution 1" fadeout riff, rather than within the amelodic sound collage that was "Revolution 9."

As for the main body of the "Revolution 1" track, there are also some differences in the mixes and overdubs they were considering at this point. It's pretty hard to wholly dig them out in the midst of this chaotic mixture of Ono monologue and fragments of tape playback, but we can often hear a far more prominent organ part. Played by Paul, it has a celestial feel, almost reminiscent of early Pink Floyd at points. Some more aggressive guitar and drum parts that didn't make the final cut can also be heard in various sections. Interspersed with all these playbacks and overdubs are rehearsal/jams with a moody, bluesy, and almost tuneless flavor, almost as a preview of some of the interminably sloppy improvisation that filled up so much space in the January 1969 *Get Back* sessions. Snatches of "Lady Madonna" and a progression highly reminiscent of the Ventures' classic instrumental "Walk Don't Run" can be heard, while Paul sings an a cappella part of the pop standard "Stairway to Paradise" near the end of the tape, for reasons unknown.

The Beatles do seem to be going about their business without being disturbed or impeded by Yoko's presence, though of course it was one of her first visits, and no one likely had any idea of how often she'd be with John in the studio. Still, this document would be *much* more valuable (and listenable) if it was possible to isolate the music from the monologue, and vice versa. Regardless of one's feelings about Yoko and her art, you're constantly wishing she'd shut up so you could hear the music without interference. As it is, it's like trying to listen to two radio stations at the same time. As a final irony, though it couldn't have been planned as such (or even planned to be heard by anyone but John or Yoko), this unclassifiably weird tape might be more authentically avant-garde than any of the actual albums John and Yoko did together—where they were *trying* to be as avant-garde as possible.

● June 5

Studio Outtake
The White Album *sessions*
Studio Two, Abbey Road, London

Don't Pass Me By (take 3 excerpt)

Good old Ringo. Who else could bring us as solidly back to earth, just a day or two after arguably the oddest and (in some ways) most cacophonous recording of Beatles outtakes of all time? That's what he does (if you're reading this book in chronological order, at any rate) with this outtake of his first recorded solo composition. There's not much, however, to this 15-second bit of take 3 (used as part of the montage of *White Album* outtakes in the *Anthology* video/DVD) except a crashing tumble of piano and drums.

● June 5-6

Studio Outtake
The White Album sessions
Studios Three and Two, Abbey Road, London

---

*Don't Pass Me By (**Anthology 3** mix)
  *appears on Anthology 3

The *Anthology 3* version of "Don't Pass Me By" mixes together elements of takes 3 and 5, and it's rather clunky, the vocal and the backing track falling out of time with each other. It's also missing the country fiddle that added so much to the *White Album* version, and also lacking the extended instrumental fadeout. So why bother with it at all? Because it does at least have a few additional asides in Ringo's vocal, adding an extra "don't make me blue" in the chorus and some half-serious, improvised romantic dialogue at the end.

● June 6

Radio Broadcast
The Kenny Everett Show interview
Abbey Road, London

What to call this 14-minute tape—an outtake, a BBC session, or something else? It was recorded at Abbey Road on June 6, while the Beatles were working on *The White Album,* but not by or for EMI. It was played on BBC Radio 1, but it wasn't a BBC session. As awkward as it might be to classify, basically it was a radio interview containing not just speech, but also bits and pieces of music.

Everett was probably the BBC personality closest to the Beatles, and was able to access them here as the *White Album* sessions were getting underway. Bits of instrumental music are heard in the background throughout, and while these are actual musical instruments producing notes and percussive sounds, there's nothing in the way of actual songs. But the Beatles, individually and in pairs, do break into snippets of tunes on and off. John's the first to take a crack, doing a couple of almost atonal improvised jingles (using only the words "goodbye jingle"), one in an American accent, guitar notes careening and sliding as backup. Far more satisfying is his brief mauling of the folk standard "Cottonfields," the lyrics changed to "when I was a little baby, my mama used to *smash* me in the cradle" as he hastily strums his guitar.

Another barely musical jingle follows, John wailing, "It's the Kenny Everett show," as his fretless guitar executes some deathbed trills. "Are you composing this straight out of your head?" Everett unnecessarily inquires, which John promptly confirms, going into some more skin-crawling fretless guitar strums and slides. Paul then joins John for a

"duo harmony jingle," John singing, "Goodbye to Kenny Everett, he is our very pal," as Paul adds loose harmonies. Particularly in conjunction with the entertaining non sequitur Everett–Lennon interview, it's like hearing a "rootsy" counterpart to their chaotic Christmas fan club disc songs: fun, not terribly musical, and not something that can be listened to for pleasure often.

They're not done yet, though: John offers an a cappella, just-barely-in-tune "Tiny Tim for president, Tiny Tim for queen!"; Ringo sings an off-the-cuff jingle as a cross between a show tune and football cheer; Paul croons an easy-listening snatch of "Strawberry Fields Forever"; and a very faint bit of "Christmas Time (Is Here Again)," the very same song they'd written for their 1967 Christmas record, is heard as a sleigh bell rattles. In hindsight, it was one of the last times the Beatles were caught, as a group, on tape, in a happy-go-lucky mood.

● June 10-11

Live Performance
Raga soundtrack
Big Sur, California

Well, it might be hard to call this a live performance, as it was done only before film cameras. But George Harrison *can* be seen playing sitar with Ravi Shankar for about a minute and a half in the Shankar documentary *Raga*. For all the press George got in the late '60s for playing the sitar, this is the only footage of him actually playing the instrument. And for all his genuine lifetime love of Indian music, he must have dropped serious sitar study shortly after this was filmed, as he never would play it again on Beatles records.

● June 11

Studio Outtakes
The White Album sessions
Studio Two, Abbey Road, London

Blackbird (rehearsal takes)
*Blackbird (take 4)
Blackbird (RM10)
Congratulations
Helter Skelter
Gone Tomorrow, Here Today
Mother Nature's Son
  *appears on Anthology 3

The session at which Paul McCartney recorded "Blackbird" was extremely well documented, as it was filmed by Apple. A small part of it was used in an Apple promotional film (see entry in film chapter), but a full 41 minutes were recorded in good sound as part of the process. It's true that 15 versions or so, often incomplete, of "Blackbird" (the exact number differs according to who's counting, and which stops and starts are considered different performances) are too much at once for non-dedicated Beatles fans. But as it's a lovely song, and the sound quality is perfect, it really does make for a nice lengthy look at a work-in-progress, particularly at a time when so many Beatles songs are just available in one or two alternate versions, or one or two different mixes.

It's not 100 percent certain, from what this author can reckon, but probably the alternates on the tape sourced from the filming were rehearsals rather than official takes (of which there would be 32 on this evening). The song is very much in place and essentially quite similar to the *White Album* version, even on these rehearsal run-throughs, though Paul tinkers a little with the tempo and phrasing, sometimes adopting a strained, self-conscious tone that one presumes wasn't entirely serious. For a minute or so, a few stabbed piano notes play along with the acoustic strumming, though it's unknown whether that's John, Yoko, or someone else; whoever it is, it sounds as if it's not an accomplished keyboardist. On the whole, however, these performances probably were useful insofar as Paul eventually started to work toward a way to end the song by repeating the last line, which he wasn't doing at the outset.

Paul also flies off into half-formed improvisations, probably in the knowledge that none of these passes will be used for the final recording. "Take these broken wings and learn to biscuits," he sings at one point, as a nonchalant non sequitur. At another juncture he uses a different melody, though a similar acoustic, folky tone, and sings a slightly bluesy, fairly nondescript song usually identified as "Gone Tomorrow, Here Today" on bootlegs. There's enough of a structure to the tune to suggest it might have been the germ of an actual composition he was considering finishing rather than a total improvisation. If so, however, it was not developed for consideration on *The White Album* itself.

The studio chat confirms that alternate arrangements were being considered for the song at this point, with Paul thinking of bringing in a string quartet after the second verse, John suggesting a "bit of brass band," and George Martin getting strangely abstract: "The way I was thinking of it, in that stop here, there should be something coming from a distance, a rain sound playing in the distance. A fairly complicated one, like a bit of decoration if you've got on the back of a painting. It suddenly comes up, and as it comes up close, you start again." Whatever Martin was audiovisualizing here, Paul would end up doing the song himself on acoustic guitar, without any such embellishments. In fact, he was probably recording "Blackbird" on this date precisely because he knew it might not need any other Beatles, since George and Ringo weren't in attendance (and, in fact, weren't even in the country). Although John was indeed at the studio and apparently taking a genuine interest in the recording, he himself would work on sound effects for "Revolution 9" at this session, and not play or sing on "Blackbird."

As part of these performances, Paul occasionally drifts into other tunes, including a little of "Congratulations," a then-recent No. 1 British single for Cliff Richard. More intriguingly, he also previews a bit of "Helter Skelter" and "Mother Nature's Son." "Helter Skelter" had probably been very recently composed, as it wasn't included on the Kinfauns tapes, and at this early stage is a much gentler folk-blues of sorts, with far more softly crooned vocals. "Mother Nature's Son" wouldn't be properly recorded for another couple of months, but Paul sounds as if he's already prepared to do it on this fragmentary version, which (like these "Blackbird" rehearsals) sound very much like the *White Album* arrangement in approach. Interestingly, while he plays the tune, he muses to himself, "*That'd* be nice with a brass"—which, indeed, he'd use when it came time to finalize the studio track. Perhaps he got the idea during this informal banter for the "Blackbird" session, keeping it in mind when it finally came time to tackle "Mother Nature's Son" in the studio for real.

More than a dozen takes of "Blackbird," all recorded on June 11, 1968, were included on this CD, along with some additional material recorded during the same era.

Also done at this session was a proper numbered take of "Blackbird" (take 4) that appeared on *Anthology 3*. This too isn't much different from either the prior rehearsals or the *White Album* track, though it does have an extra repetition of the first verse and a fadeout. Too, the vocal's more casual than, and not as good as, the one on the released rendition. There's also an early mix of the take (32) eventually chosen as the basis of the *White Album* version, differing from the final product only in the presence of a few more guitar strums on the intro and some additional echo on Paul's vocal. Beatles assistant Alistair Taylor also recalled getting an acetate with a different version of the track, though apparently the only big variation from the *White Album* mix was the absence of over-dubbed bird noises.

● June 20

Studio Outtake

The White Album *sessions*
Studios One, Two, and Three, Abbey Road, London

Revolution 9 (mono mix)

The most avant-garde track the Beatles released while they were an active unit, "Revolution 9" was such a densely layered collage of sound that it's easy to imagine that mix variations might differ substantially from the official end result. This mono mix is indeed different from the *White Album* version, though owing to its difficult, harsh nature and its general unpopularity even among many Beatles fans, relatively few listeners will want to spend the time to pick out the deviations. It's 25 seconds shorter than the *White Album* track, and set apart not so much by what it contains as what it *doesn't* contain. Namely, it's missing some elements from the original long version of "Revolution 1," particularly John's chilling, wracked shouts. That alone makes it inferior to the familiar stereo mix, although in tandem with the absence of some effects used on the *White Album* track, this does allow you to hear some of the underlying effects more clearly. The bootlegged version seems to have been taken from an acetate and has some surface noise, but not so much that it seriously affects the sound quality, although there's unfortunately a skip along the way. And it's a different mix, incidentally, than the mono mix on the British *White Album*, which is just a mono reduction from the stereo mix.

● Circa Summer

Private Tapes

Julia (instrumental)

Julia (vocal #1)

Julia (vocal #2)

John made a few home tapes of "Julia" that are sometimes erroneously assumed to have been done at the same time as the Kinfauns sessions, as they have a similar low-key, acoustic feel. The Kinfauns tapes *do* include a version of "Julia," but these three additional renditions—one instrumental, two vocal—were recorded elsewhere. Exactly where is uncertain—John was living in a few places in the summer of 1968, as his relationship with his first wife ended and his romance with Yoko Ono blossomed.

The instrumental rendition, on acoustic guitar, offers no surprises, but does emphasize what a pretty melody the song has, even absent the delicate poetry of John's vocal and lyrics. His singing's a bit hoarse on the first vocal version, and he still hasn't worked out how to end all of his verses with the extended phrasing of "Julia," some of the final lines ending too abruptly or jamming up with too many syllables (sometimes even before he can sing Julia's whole name). He stumbles on the guitar for a bit at the end as well.

The second vocal attempt is much the same, but rougher, as he changes the order of the verses and flubs many more notes this time around. At any rate, he seems to give up on his singing a little more than halfway through, when his voice creaks to the breaking point as he winds through the descending melody at the end of one of the verses. Soon after that, he trails off on one of the lines as if realizing he can't make a good complete work tape out of it. That's the cue for him to take some liberties with the tune, singing some of the final lyrics with much higher notes than we're accustomed to, then lowering to a "what the hell, let's call it a day" bass tone at the very end.

June 28

Studio Outtake

The White Album *sessions*
Studio Two, Abbey Road, London

Good Night (unknown take, excerpt)

As originally conceived, the lush *White Album* closer, "Good Night," was to feature a spoken intro from Ringo in which he gently prepared his little ones for bed. About 20 seconds are heard in the *White Album* outtakes medley in the *Anthology* DVD/video, backed by gentle, folky guitar strumming, a feature that would get lost by the time the ultimate orchestral arrangement was finished. He's not quite able to finish his narrative, however, before he starts singing—and he sings only a few words before the excerpt cuts off. Ordinarily one might say the Beatles were wise to cut such sentimental gush out of the picture, but the violin-drenched version that took its place was yet more excessively saccharine, though probably intentionally so.

● June 28–July 22

Studio Outtake

The White Album *sessions*
Studios One and Two, Abbey Road, London

*Good Night (**Anthology 3** mix)
  appears on Anthology 3

Constructed mostly from a June 28 rehearsal take, most of this *Anthology 3* mix backs Ringo's vocal with piano only. While this makes the shakiness of his singing far more audible, it also removes the orchestral excess and allows us to hear the song for what it might have started as—a simple, sweet, sentimental tune. It's also far less of an ironic statement in this uncluttered condition than it is on *The White Album*, where the quasi-Muzak arrangement directly followed "Revolution 9," closing the double LP on a subversively soothing note. There's a little contrivance to the *Anthology 3* version, however, as the rehearsal crossfades into the final section of the released track—a decision made, according to the liner notes, because the rehearsal take "meandered to an indefinite close."

● July 3–15

Studio Outtake

The White Album *sessions*
Studio Three, Abbey Road, London

Ob-La-Di, Ob-La-Da (unknown take or takes, excerpt/s)

It's not known for sure from which take (or takes) the section of "Ob-La-Di, Ob-La-Da" in the Beatles *Anthology* DVD/video *White Album* outtakes medley originates. It would have had to be from between July 3 and July 15 (when the recordings for the song were done), and was probably from a session or sessions postdating take 5 on July 5, 1968 (see entry below), judging from the sound. As with all the snippets used on the *Anthology* DVD/video outtakes medley, however, there's not much music—in fact, only about ten seconds' worth, just enough to confirm it's not the actual *White Album* version. In fact, there's more incidental chatter in this section—including John's Al Jolson shout, "Yes sir, that's my baby!" and Paul's lively "1, 2, 3, 4" count-in—than there is actual music. And it's another one of those painful instances in which the mixes used for the DVD and video versions were different, the DVD mix taking off one of Paul's double-tracked vocals.

● July 5

Studio Outtake
The White Album *sessions*
Studio Two, Abbey Road, London

---

*Ob-La-Di, Ob-La-Da (take 5)
    appears on Anthology 3

One of the Beatles' most happy-go-lucky recordings was subject to days of arduous studio remakes. If only in retrospect, it might have been a small factor in the general discontent beginning to fester amongst the group, both because John and George weren't too enamored of these kind of all-ages McCartney crowd-pleasers, and also because Paul's perfectionism could grate on his band mates. This earlier version of "Ob-La-Di, Ob-La-Da" is a good one, though, with three saxophones, conga drums (by Jimmy Scott, originator of the "ob-la-di, ob-la-da" phrase in the first place), and a slightly faster, more standard rock rhythm than the decidedly reggae-influenced arrangement that would eventually take its place. It's missing the distinctive manic honky tonk piano intro of the *White Album* version, as well as the short line used as a coda. For those reasons and others, the *White Album* version's a little more fully developed and idiosyncratic. But unlike many outtakes on *Anthology*, this could have easily been included on an official '60s Beatles release without standing out as something that necessarily needed refinement or more work. (A different mix of this take has been bootlegged with different before-and-after chatter.)

● July 10

Studio Outtake
"Revolution" single session
Studio Three, Abbey Road, London

Revolution (take 15)

"Revolution" underwent a lot of changes from the time it was demoed acoustically at Kinfauns to its use as the B-side of "Hey Jude" (where it became a big hit in its own right). First there was the long, long (approximately ten-minute) version of "Revolution 1." Then there was the decision to radically shorten "Revolution 1" to a more standard length, using some of the sounds of the extended ending to form part of the foundation for "Revolution 9." And then there was the single version, titled simply "Revolution," which was much faster, rowdier, and ultimately superior to its *White Album* "Revolution 1" counterpart.

No other Beatles song was released in two entirely different studio arrangements during the group's career. "Let It Be" and "Across the Universe" are often thought of as having been released in two wholly different studio versions, but they are in fact radically different mixes sharing some similar parts; the single and *Let It Be* LP versions of "Get Back" are different, but that's because the 45 was a studio recording, and the album track is from their live rooftop concert.

Take 15 of "Revolution," retrieved from John Lennon's archives for broadcast on "The Lost Lennon Tapes," is essentially an early mix that's much the same as the single, save for missing Nicky Hopkins's exceptional electric piano overdubs. Which makes it much less impressive than the official version, though it allows you to hear some of the guitar parts more clearly, especially in the instrumental break.

● July 12

Studio Outtake
The White Album *sessions*
Studio Two, Abbey Road, London

Don't Pass Me By (RM4)

As much as some rock stars grouse about bootlegs, often the source of the leaks can be traced right back to the musicians themselves. This seems to have been the case with some rough mixes of *White Album* cuts, which originated from a tape Ringo Starr gave to Peter Sellers, with whom he would star in the 1969 movie *The Magic Christian*. (Actually Starr and Sellers had first struck up a friendship back in late 1965, when Sellers did a pseudo-Shakespearean reading of "A Hard Day's Night" on the British TV special *The Music of Lennon & McCartney*.) Sometimes overhyped as being virtually an entirely different listening experience than the familiar *White Album* versions, in actual fact this material—auctioned in 1988 for a mere £2300—is usually not remarkably different from the final mixes. This rough mono mix of "Don't Pass Me By," however, does offer the substantial bonus of a reprise of the entire first verse near the end, plus some out-of-place-sounding bass notes during the piano intro. It wouldn't be a great shock, incidentally, if more such rough mixes from throughout the Beatles' career turned up in the future, since, as George admitted in the *Anthology* book, "Usually if we were working on a song we'd take a little rough mix of it home."

● July 15

Studio Outtake
The White Album *sessions*
Studio Two, Abbey Road, London

Ob-La-Di, Ob-La-Da (RM21)

Also from the Peter Sellers tape is this rough mono mix of "Ob-La-Di, Ob-La-Da," differing from the *White Album* version by virtue of a brief (four-note) false start on the piano and very brief incidental before-and-after noises.

● July 16

Studio Outtake
The White Album *sessions*
Studio Two, Abbey Road, London

---

*Cry Baby Cry (take 1)
    appears on Anthology 3

As a welcome interruption from these small mix variations, we have a complete, live alternate take of a *White Album* song. A nice one, too—not superior to the final version, but one that uses a more down-to-earth rock arrangement, Ringo's drums in particular being positioned more assertively. The melody also comes to a slightly more downbeat conclusion. It does, however, lack the keyboard and vocal overdubs that did much to bestow some whimsy onto the official track.

● July 18

Studio Outtake
The White Album *sessions*
Studio Two, Abbey Road, London

---

*Helter Skelter (take 2, edited)
    appears on Anthology 3

Like a number of *White Album* songs, "Helter Skelter" toughened up considerably from its first available skeletal prototype. When Paul had busked it back on June 11 between rehearsals of "Blackbird," it was a softly sung, folk-bluesy ditty. More than a month later, it had changed into a lumbering, almost metallic blues-rocker. Like "Revolution 1," it might have been originally envisioned as a long, long, long track, as the three takes done on this day lasted 10:40, 12:35, and 27:11 respectively.

The picture on this collection of outtakes might have been taken from a mid-'60s photo session, but the title was definitely taken from a notorious phrase many claimed to hear when playing The White Album's *"Revolution 9" backward.*

The Beatles
Turn Me On Dead Man:
THE JOHN BARRETT TAPES

This *Anthology 3* track took some liberties with the original recording, editing take 2 so that it lasts a relatively short four and a half minutes or so—about only a third as long as the whole take, in other words. Remarkably, whereas some *White Album* numbers (such as "Cry Baby Cry," as outlined in the previous entry) changed relatively little in structure and vibe from first take to final mix, this pass through "Helter Skelter" is *way* inferior to the classic final version. It's far too slow, plodding along at an elephantine pace, as though the Beatles were succumbing to their worst instincts and trying to emulate the overlong heavy blues jams becoming so fashionable in the psychedelic hard rock world in mid-1968. The guitar riffs border on tediously unimaginative blues-rock clichés. At least Paul's vocal, however, has made the leap from near-crooning to raunchy belting. The lyrics are largely there, too, though at this point he's repeating "dancer" over and over at the end of one of the verses, as well as substituting "hell for leather" for the title in one of the choruses.

● July 19

Studio Outtakes
The White Album *sessions*
Studio Two, Abbey Road, London

*Sexy Sadie (take 6)
Sexy Sadie (monitor mix, unknown takes)
　appears on Anthology 3

The Beatles had surprising trouble coming to grips with "Sexy Sadie" in the studio, considering that the Kinfauns version illustrates that the song had been relatively complete for at least two months. This may have been due at least in part to a gradually worsening atmosphere in the studio, engineer Geoff Emerick (who'd worked with them since *Revolver*) having quit a few days earlier. The outtakes from this day are certainly no match for the admirable final recording, but are still quite interesting listening, if only as documentary proof of their struggles with both the tune and their own group situation.

Take 6, issued on *Anthology 3*, has a yet slower tempo than the final version, starting off with some nice, almost jazzy guitar chords that didn't survive in the final arrangement. Although it's really not too different in mindset from the *White Album* version, somehow the performance seems sluggish, mostly devoid of the extraordinary uplifting small details the Beatles had become masterful at inserting into their studio productions over the last two or three years. The distinctive authoritative piano that graces the official track is absent, giving Paul's rather halting organ more prominence. Most crucially, an ending hasn't been worked out for the tune. In fact, a traditional ending would never be worked out, *The White Album* covering that up with an extended atmospheric instrumental fadeout. This take just meanders in its latter part, however, and fades out (after a little more than four minutes) before its actual end, as it's known that all 21 takes recorded at this session lasted at least five and a half minutes.

Also escaping—and not likely to ever surface on an official release, owing to its overweening lewdness and abundant profanity—is a shambling but fascinating seven-and-a-half-minute monitor mix of extracts from other "Sexy Sadie" takes of the evening (numbers un-

known). To start things off, a seemingly hysterical, on-the-edge John improvises maniacally on a generic blues riff, sing-shouting-cackling "Fuck a ducky, fuck fuck a ducky" and variations thereof. That steam having blown out of his ears, he then guides the band back into a relatively sane snatch of "Sexy Sadie." Then he's off the leash again, this time on a crude '50s rock 'n' roll–style ditty (often titled "Brian Epstein Blues" on bootlegs) about the group's less-than-a-year-in-the-grave ex-manager. An instrumental jam follows, vaguely along the lines of Chuck Berry's "Little Queenie," John throwing in the nursery rhyme "I saw Mary sitting on the dairy" apropos of nothing.

Then comes the big payoff: an excerpt from a different version of "Sexy Sadie" where John attacks the song's target explicitly and acerbically, with lyrics that in no way could have been issued officially, not on EMI in 1968. "Who the fuck do you think you are?" he sings, quite joyfully, in place of the line about the Maharishi having made a fool of everyone. "Oh, you cunt," he mumbles, for good measure. This section also has the bit, as reported in *The Beatles Recording Sessions*, where Yoko suggests the Beatles could do a better job with the song, John quick to smooth things over by immediately rejoining, "Well, maybe *I* can." John and Paul *do* sound like they're having a good time and getting along, but the unrelated John-sung improvs indicate that the pressure might have been getting to Lennon.

It's also been surmised that a particularly tense exchange between George Harrison and George Martin in the *White Album* outtakes medley on the *Anthology* DVD might be from this session. Turn the volume *way* up, and you'll hear Harrison almost shout at Martin, "I mean, you're very negative!" Things would get worse before they'd get better, however.

● July 23

Studio Outtakes
The White Album *sessions*
Studio Two, Abbey Road, London

Good Night (RM6)
Everybody's Got Something to Hide Except Me and My Monkey (RM5)

More Peter Sellers tape specials here. This rough mono mix of "Good Night" is missing a few notes of music at the beginning of the instrumental break, which makes the transition from chorus to break way too abrupt, as if the two parts are accidentally overlapping each other. There's also a little more whispering by Ringo over the final section. As for "Everybody's Got Something to Hide Except Me and My Monkey," John's vocal is not double-tracked throughout as it is on *The White Album,* and there's some more jabber and screaming at the end.

● July 24

Studio Outtake
The White Album *sessions*
Studio Two, Abbey Road, London

Sexy Sadie (take 28, fragment)

From the medley of *White Album* outtakes on the *Anthology* video/DVD, this is just long enough to hear this take break down, John then asking the others to "reach for this one," also inquiring whether any of the night's previous takes were any good.

● July 25

Studio Outtake
The White Album *sessions*
Studio Two, Abbey Road, London

*While My Guitar Gently Weeps (take 1)
   *appears on Anthology 3

This alternate take of one of George Harrison's greatest songs is almost unique within the Beatles canon in several respects. It's one of the few completed alternate takes not issued during the Beatles' lifetime that's a) as good as the official version; b) very *different* from the official version; and c) an excellent recording on its own merits, even when viewed in isolation from the official version or a study of the Beatles' unreleased music. This is George at his most hauntingly spiritual and melancholy, delivering a languorous, folky performance using only acoustic guitar and harmonium. While those qualities would also be present in the far harder-rocking *White Album* arrangement (with Eric Clapton on guitar), this more plaintive one is more personal and probing, almost as though we've opened a window into the most fragile corners of George's very soul. While the melody is identical to the later re-recording, as are most of the words, it's almost like hearing two entirely different songs, so different is the effect upon the listener. There's also an entire verse that didn't make the final cut, this being a suitably reflective rumination about aging.

You wouldn't think that such an on-the-surface-simple recording would be subject to many bootlegged mix variations. But this is the world of late-'60s Beatles mixdom, and sho' nuff, it turns out that the mix prepared for *Anthology 3* tinkers a little with the original one by unnecessarily creating an artificial loop of a repeated guitar sequence to serve as the fadeout. The real ending, which worked well enough on its own, comes to a cold close with a slowly picked chord, wafting harmonium, and a few rapid anguished guitar strums, George then declaring, "Let's hear that back." (This ending can be heard, in its best available fidelity, in the *White Album* outtakes medley on the *Anthology* DVD/video.) Monitor mixes of the song also isolate some tracks as the recording plays.

● July 29

Studio Outtake
"Hey Jude" single session
Studio Two, Abbey Road, London

*Hey Jude (take 2)
   *appears on Anthology 3

"Hey Jude," recorded during the *White Album* sessions but issued as a single prior to the LP to help launch Apple Records, was another song that wasn't a heck of a lot different from the final version in its early stages. What's missing on take 2, issued on *Anthology 3*, is the sense of epic structure that would so strongly inform the barrier-breaking seven-minute single. Also missing are the mournful backup vocal harmonies and most of the majestic "na na na" tag, although there's a bit of that at the end. Nor does Paul sing those "na na na" syllables to get from one verse to another. He also comes in with the ascending "better better" between a verse and a bridge, rather than waiting until the instrumental break.

In this version, too, the song's woman has found Jude, rather than the other way around. And Paul's vocal is a little prissily loose, perhaps intended as a guide rather than a serious attempt at a usable take. George is trying to insert some useful guitar lines, but they're muted and superfluous, Paul soon vetoing George's idea to play responsive licks to the lead vocal. All told, then, there was actually quite a bit of work yet to be done on the song's structure, though at a casual listen it sounds almost like the single in many respects.

The escalating tensions in the band at sessions from this time are well documented. Yet it should be noted that numerous *White Album*–era outtakes prove the guys *were* still having fun in the studio at least some of the time—such as this one, which starts with John announcing, "In the heart of the Black Country," leading into a 15-second McCartney cabaretish busk/ditty about when he was a robber in Boston Place.

● July 30

Studio Outtakes
"Hey Jude" single
Studio Two, Abbey Road, London

Hey Jude (unknown take #1)
Las Vegas Tune
St. Louis Blues
Hey Jude (take 8 fragment)
Hey Jude (take 9)
Hey Jude (unknown take #2)
Hey Jude (unknown takes, from soundtrack of *Music!* film)

Quite a lot of work went into making "Hey Jude" the studio masterpiece it eventually became. Much of it was done on July 30—some, remarkably, in front of film cameras—and much of the day's labor has gone into circulation. While it's a bit of a confusing pain to sort out what's what, we're lucky so much is available for examination, illustrating some of the song's gradual evolution into its final state.

The earliest of the circulating takes (the exact take number is uncertain) lasts about five minutes, and has more ideas that would fall by the wayside. John is trying to put guitar behind Paul's vocal in the opening section before the full band comes in, but roves around without adding much of use. Paul's now singing, albeit tentatively, his scatting "na na na"s between bridge and verse, and there are hints of the backup harmonies that would eventually get solidified. It's taken a tad too fast, though, and the Long John Silver way Paul and John sing about the movement on the shoulder suggests this might be a guide vocal, as does

Paul's leap into falsetto for part of the final verse, followed by a whoop (John) and a giggle (Paul). The extended tag lasts a good two minutes, sung with such hearty irreverence (and, often, deliberately silly voices) that it again seems unlikely they were intending this as consideration for part of the final record.

Take 2 of "Hey Jude" on July 29 had an unrelated music-hallish intro and, for whatever reason, McCartney takes the same path here, vamping on a 15-second nightclubish improv that bootleggers usually titled "Las Vegas Tune" after the most prominent phrase in the lyrics. Following that is nearly a minute of noodling around on a recognizable standard, "St. Louis Blues." "Hey Jude" isn't a song that comes to mind as an all-around-entertainer vehicle, but it seemed to spark, perhaps subconsciously, some of Paul's leanings in that direction, if only as a way to keep the atmosphere light between takes.

A very short end fragment of take 8 reveals that the arrangement's gotten much closer to its proper place, particularly in the way Paul's hitting the piano keys. That's confirmed by take 9, where the subtle but distinctive lilt to both the keyboards and the vocal that graced the single is much more pronounced. Some cracks still have to be filled—the song's woman is still finding Jude, the vocal is a bit self-conscious, and those nagging bridge–verse transitions still sound awkward, Paul almost hum-mumbling a note on the first such changeover. The Beatles keep straight faces on for the most part, but they start to crumble on the extended tag, Paul urging, "Everybody sing it, children . . . thank you!" and climbing into some ill-advised falsetto slightly afterward. Perhaps still uncertain of how to wrap things up, Paul grandly slides up and down the piano and the track all but screeches to a halt, Paul and John comically exclaiming, "Boo-gie woo-gie! Boo-gie woo-gie!"

But it's getting there, a movement reinforced by a later six-minute take (number unknown, again), where the mood is slightly more stately and the musicians a little more together. Paul has the vocals linking bridge and verse down now, too, though his voice breaks on the first of these, and he adds an extraneous "Yeah!" at the end of the third verse. He has a shredding scream for the stairs-climbing climax of the main vocal, too, though he trembles on the final note like a cartoon character on a crumbling ladder. Oddly, there aren't any backup vocals on this version until the tag, and even those are faint. But Paul's obviously gaining confidence in his decision to scream throughout much of the coda, the final section of the song gaining a lot of life as a result. He varies the piano lines much more in this version than he does in the final arrangement, going into some '50s-styled rock 'n' roll boogie before some more exaggerated runs up and down the keyboard signal it's time to close the curtain. Perhaps carried away by the spirit of the ad infinitum finale, John keeps thrashing away at his guitar for a good dozen more seconds all by his lonesome.

As if this wasn't enough, the Beatles were also filmed on this day for the documentary movie *Music!* (see entry in film section), performing parts of some of the "Hey Jude" takes described above. This clip includes brief sections of other takes that seem unfinished enough to suggest they were done earlier in the session. There aren't any revelations to be heard, though Paul throws in a reference to Little Richard's "Tutti Frutti" at one point, and John a more off-the-wall enunciation of the "Beep beep yeah!" exclamation from "Drive My Car." And there's yet another tossed-off "St. Louis Blues," this one lasting just 15 seconds. That clip also shows how poor George Harrison didn't play at all on these sessions, instead sitting in the control room.

Had the Beatles left the arrangement at where it stood at the end of this session and refined the vocal, they still would have had an excellent recording. It's a tribute to their diligence that they kept at it for a couple more days, smoothing out some more wrinkles and adding orchestration to make the coda that much more powerful.

● August 9

Studio Outtakes
The White Album *sessions*
Studio Two, Abbey Road, London

---

*Mother Nature's Son (take 2)
Mother Nature's Son (unknown take fragment)
    appears on Anthology 3

"Mother Nature's Son" was another in a line of apparently simple, folky, one-take-sounding *White Album* songs for which a number of variations exist. Take 2, from *Anthology 3,* features just Paul's vocal and his acoustic guitar. There's no brass overdub, as there would be on *The White Album,* but other than that the versions are quite similar. Paul does put in another (unnecessary) elongated round of wordless humming at the end, not having yet concocted the neat coda that brings the official track to a conclusion. (As an aside, that's one of an almost infinite number of illustrations of how the group's attention to such seemingly trivial details worked in their favor—there were quite a few tracks where they devised a brief but memorable ending in which melodic patterns were used that appeared nowhere else in the song.) The opening intro of guitar chords on this early take of "Mother Nature's Son" is also blander, lacking the distinctive descending picked notes that were eventually worked out. Plus Paul slips into his all-around-entertainer persona at the end to give a homey introduction to a number he announces as "Londonberry Air"—only to go into some more folky strumming.

There's also a small bit of another take (number unknown) in the *Anthology* DVD/video *White Album* outtakes medley, but it's of little consequence, consisting of a single line about sitting all day writing songs. Paul does add a dry spoken footnote right after that: "And this is one of them."

● August 12

Studio Outtakes
The White Album *sessions*
Studio Two, Abbey Road, London

---

*Not Guilty (take 102)
Not Guilty (RM1)
    an edited version appears on Anthology 3

One of the most fully formed studio outtakes of a Beatles song never released in any form in the 1960s was George Harrison's "Not Guilty." That it sounds complete should be of little surprise—it went all the way up to 102 takes, the most ever logged for an EMI Beatles recording. Why it was not used on *The White Album* after so much effort isn't clear. It's a decent enough chunky rocker, with some very inventive back-and-forth switches between a standard heavy rock rhythm and merry-go-round-like turnarounds. It also benefits from some strong, thickly textured ominous electric lead guitar, George just starting to assert himself on the instrument again after a couple of years or so where it had been less prominent on Beatles tracks than it had through mid-1966. Lyrically, the tune's less straightforward, projecting a vague surliness that some have surmised was directed toward John and Paul in particular, as George was having trouble getting more room for his growing songwriting catalog on Beatles albums. Confirmed Harrison in a 1987 *Musician* interview, "It was me getting pissed off at Lennon and McCartney for the grief I was catching during the making of *The White Album*. I said I wasn't guilty of getting in the way of their careers. I said I wasn't guilty of leading them astray in our all going to Rishikesh to see the Maharishi. I was sticking up for myself."

Indeed, "Not Guilty" would be a victim of the space crunch, although it's about on par with most of *The White Album*'s secondary tracks. The problem might have been—what could have been removed to free up space? Aside from the 52-second "Wild Honey Pie," perhaps, there was no obvious extraneous material. The other Beatles and George Martin probably would have been happy enough to keep "Revolution 9" under wraps, but John Lennon was probably determined to get at least one of his avant-garde outings on the record, particularly as his second-most-experimental *White Album* recording ("What's the New Mary Jane") *was* excised from the final running order. Even such semi-throwaways as "Why Don't We Do It in the Road" and "Birthday" had their place, both as fun tunes and valuable mood-lighteners for varying the pace. "Not Guilty" might not have been obviously inadequate—but it might not have been as indisputably strong enough to demand a place on the album as something like, say, "While My Guitar Gently Weeps."

The mix of "Not Guilty" on *Anthology 3* is more roundly castigated than almost any other of the *Anthology* reconstructions. For although it does work from take 102, it cuts out a few lines and a solo, inserts edits that repeat a few notes in the solo and a drum pattern in the instrumental fadeout, shortens that fadeout, and adds phasing effects not present on the original. The original, untampered stereo version has been bootlegged, and is not only preferable to the *Anthology 3* bastardization, but is an uncommon instance of a mix variation where even non-completists will value its availability. And if you want a mono mix (RM1), the Peter Sellers tape comes through again, the only difference of note being less harpsichord, though a drop and surge in volume near the end suggests that a false ending or earlier fadeout might have been considered.

● August 13

Studio Outtake

The White Album *sessions*
Studio Two, Abbey Road, London

Untitled Improvisation

There's some disagreement about the date, but it was probably during this session for "Yer Blues" that this brief (1:15), instrumental, rather nondescript bluesy jam was recorded. A rather darkly foreboding, at times descending, basic chord progression provides the backing for some enthusiastic but unfocused, non-fluid lead guitar.

● August 14

Studio Outtakes

The White Album *sessions*
Studio Two, Abbey Road, London

What's the New Mary Jane (take 2, fragment)
*What's the New Mary Jane (take 4)
    edited version appears on Anthology 3

Though unfamiliar to the general public, few songs are as controversial—and, to some degree, unpopular—among serious Beatles fans as "What's the New Mary Jane," one of the group's most widely bootlegged outtakes. And it *continues* to be bootlegged, part of the controversy being the massive headache involved in sorting out the various versions and mixes that have appeared over the years in one form or another. The biggest controversy, however, rages over the merits of the song itself, often attacked as the worst exponent (save perhaps "Revolution 9") of John Lennon's most self-indulgent avant-garde impulses.

Some also see it as evidence of Yoko Ono's negative influence upon John's music, though it had been recorded back in the spring as part of the Kinfauns demo and written when John was still in India, before his relationship with Yoko had become serious. Though the composition was credited to John Lennon and Paul McCartney (the latter of whom probably contributed nothing whatsoever), John said in 1969 that it was written with Alex Mardas. (Mardas, aka "Magic Alex," was head of Apple's electronics department and is infamous in Beatles lore for his strange and largely useless inventions, including a 72-track recording studio that proved unusable when the group tried to record with it at Apple in January 1969.)

"What's the New Mary Jane" probably did not deserve a place on *The White Album*, though it very nearly made the final cut. However, judged as an ephemeral outtake, it's really not that bad, and not without its entertainment value. For starters, there *is* something of a tune, in comparison to "Revolution 9" at any rate, even if it's childishly sing-songy. Too, it's about as druggily hallucinogenic a production as the Beatles managed, even if it's at least as much a bad trip as a good one. It's like falling into an alternate Beatles Christmas disc where John's documenting his *real* inner state, not one manufactured to please fans, what with vibes, bells, a ratchet, slide whistle, hand-strummed piano strings, discordant accordion, creepy echoed murmurings, and maniacal laughter tumbling all over each other. The lyrics are certainly incoherent, but that adds to the track's deliberately surreal aura, one where both the musicians and listeners fall into a distorted sonic black hole of sorts. And John (joined by Yoko, George, and Mal Evans) does seem to be having a whale of a time, albeit telling the kind of joke that seems much funnier to a stoned originator than to his audience. Certainly he knew it was a mad exercise, exclaiming in closing, "Let's hear it before we get taken away"—some jaded fans' favorite part of the whole recording.

This is best heard on the six-and-a-half-minute take 4. Unfortunately, the version on *Anthology 3* not only doesn't include the full six and a half minutes, but also tampers and re-edits the track so that the introduction is halved, and vocals from the first verse and final chorus are overdubbed onto other parts of the track. There were yet more mixes of "What's the New Mary Jane" to come—one made, strangely enough, in late 1969 when the Beatles had all but ceased to exist as a group.

In the half-minute of take 2 on the *Anthology* DVD/video *White Album* outtakes medley, John's barely able to sing, such are his fits of laughter. It does yield a glimpse at the song in its original simpler state, the only instruments being John's piano and George's acoustic guitar.

● August 15

Studio Outtakes
The White Album *sessions*
Studio Two, Abbey Road, London

---

*Rocky Raccoon (take 8)
Rocky Raccoon (take 9, fragment)
Rocky Raccoon (RM1, unedited)
   appears on Anthology 3

You wouldn't guess that take 8 of "Rocky Raccoon," issued on *Anthology 3*, was the last take done before the one used as the basis of the final track. The lyrics still aren't finalized, especially in the opening narration, where Rocky comes from Minnesota (rather than Dakota, as he would just one take later), and the whole scenario is laid out in rather more formal terms. The next-to-last verse all but disintegrates after Paul sings of a doctor "sminking" of gin. Other differences: a mock (and rather weak) gunshot is mimicked on the snare drum, there are no hymnal harmonies on the final verse, there's no honky tonk piano, and Paul wraps the tale up with a that's-all-folks "That's the story of Rocky Raccoon." It sounds more like a lackadaisical tryout than an eighth take, but obviously things came together pretty quickly after that.

Though John has the image as the lazier partner in the Lennon-McCartney creative partnership, one thing this alternate take brings to light is that it could take Paul quite a long time to finish his lyrics as well. "Rocky Raccoon" had been demoed a good three months earlier as part of the Kinfauns sessions, yet here it almost sounds in parts as if he's still singing any lyrics that come to mind to fill in the gaps. The Beatles were, of course, working on a lot of songs at once during these unprecedented double-album sessions, and in combination with other stresses (his breakup with Jane Asher and the launch of Apple), maybe Paul just didn't have time to revisit the song for polish before its number was up in the studio. Or maybe the pressure and excitement of being in the studio was the stimulus he needed to finish it off. Or maybe "Rocky Raccoon" was meant to have an improvisational flavor all along, some of that surviving into the final track, particularly in the opening narration and Paul's scatting and urges of encouragement to the song's hero at the very end.

A dozen seconds of that ending (from take 9) are on the *Anthology* DVD/video, with one crucial difference that was cut out of the final mix: Paul's triumphant shout, "I wanna hear that, boy, I wanna hear that!" A yet more trivial extra is at the beginning of the rough mix on

the Peter Sellers tape, where John and Paul sing a few notes in some made-up tongue.

● August 20

Studio Outtakes
The White Album *sessions*
Studios Two and Three, Abbey Road, London

Yer Blues (RM3, unedited)
Mother Nature's Son (RM8)
Wild Honey Pie (RM6, unedited)

The mix variation on this version of "Yer Blues" (the only one of this trio done in studio three, if you're curious) is about as minor as it gets, with a slightly longer count-in and fade. "Mother Nature's Son," from the Peter Sellers tape, is missing an acoustic guitar overdub, the only other differences being a couple faint taps at the very beginning. "Wild Honey Pie," also from the Sellers tape, is another disappointment if you're looking for something completely different, with some extra incidental studio noise at the beginning and end. So beware: Next time you're offered the Peter Sellers tape, it might not be something that'll knock you off your chair—no matter what the packaging promises.

● August 21

Studio Outtake
The White Album *sessions*
Studio Two, Abbey Road, London

Sexy Sadie (RM5, unedited)

And yet, just when you're ready to dismiss the Peter Sellers tape as more trouble than it's worth, here comes a mono mix from that source which actually *does* offer something completely different—namely, the ending instrumental section is a good 38 seconds longer, wordlessly reprising the bridge and part of the verse. "Sexy Sadie" never did have a particularly well-defined finish—even the bootlegged early outtakes verify the Beatles were struggling with it all along—and it was wise to cut out a good chunk of a coda that verged on the meandering, even on the *White Album* version.

● August 23

Studio Outtake
The White Album *sessions*
Studio Two, Abbey Road, London

Back in the U.S.S.R. (RM1, unedited)

The final *White Album* relic from the Peter Sellers tape has slightly longer jet plane effects at the beginning and end, though otherwise it's about the same as the official mono version.

● August 29

Studio Outtakes
The White Album *sessions*
Trident Studios, London

Dear Prudence (take 1, mono mix #1)
Dear Prudence (take 1, mono mix #2)
Dear Prudence (vocal overdub)

Though quite similar to the *White Album* versions, these two boot-legged mono mixes do have a little more to offer the discerning Beatles scholar than, say, the average "Peter Sellers tape" track. In both cases, oddly, John doesn't sing the title phrase during the final verse, leaving only the instrumental backing in those brief sections. There's notice-ably more reverb on John's singing in each mix, foreshadowing his hearty appetite for the effect in his early solo recordings.

The first of those, found in his private tapes cache and broadcast on "The Lost Lennon Tapes," has a burst of applause at the end, followed by an "All Together Now"–like emission of flügelhorn. The second of them has a few extra stray bass notes in the beginning and ending, and comes to a cold close, followed by a drum roll. It also allows us to hear the intro unobscured by the crossfading effects between it and "Back in the U.S.S.R." that were used to segue the tracks at the beginning of side one of *The White Album*. The drum roll, incidentally, was not Ringo, but Paul—Ringo had quit the group briefly during the August 23 session for "Back in the U.S.S.R." (though he'd be back in the fold by the beginning of September). A mere ten-second overdub of high vocal harmonies is also floating around, necessary only to complete your Beatles checklist.

● Circa Late August

Private Tapes
"Peter Sellers Tape" sound effects
Sunny Heights, Weybridge

Ringo might be the last Beatle that comes to mind for making experi-mental home tapes, or indeed home tapes of any sort. But he did have that experience as John's foil of sorts on several of Lennon's Kenwood home Mellotron exercises, and he made some brief effects/music col-lage tapes of his own as part of the compilation of *White Album* rough mixes he made for Peter Sellers. The first of these, found on the end of side one of the original tape, lasts just under a minute, devoted mostly to sardonic clapping and shouts by Ringo of "Wonderful," a dog bark-ing in the background. After a brief expulsion of distorted tape echo, Ringo maniacally shouts/instructs, "If you wanna hear some more, you've got to turn the tape over!" Assuming Sellers did, he would have heard something yet more unusual: a collage of sounds, lasting about 100 seconds, seemingly taken from field recordings of Third World singers and musicians, overdubbed with the kind of weird noises, elec-tronics, and utterances heard on John Lennon's home experimental tapes ("It's a raid!" a voice shouts at one point).

It's believed that Ringo compiled this tape for Sellers around the end of August, and as none of the *White Album* rough mixes it contains

postdate the August 23 session for "Back in the U.S.S.R.," that seems logical enough. If so, that does indicate that he softened his resolve (at that very August 23 session) to quit the Beatles fairly quickly. If he was truly bitter, it's unlikely he'd be spending his downtime making a compilation tape for a celebrity friend of rough mixes from the group he'd just left. Nor is it likely he'd include a song—"Back in the U.S.S.R." itself—on which the drums were played not by himself, but by Paul.

● September 4

Live Performance
For television program The David Frost Show
Twickenham Film Studios, London

By George! It's the David Frost Theme (take 1)
By George! It's the David Frost Theme (take 2)
By George! It's the David Frost Theme (take 3)
Hey Jude (take 1)
Hey Jude (take 2)
Hey Jude (edit of takes 1 and 3)
Hey Jude (edit of takes 1, 2, and 3)
Revolution (take 1)
Revolution (take 2)
Revolution (unknown take, fragment)

This appearance on *The David Frost Show* was the Beatles' first live per-formance of any sort since their June 25, 1967, "All You Need Is Love" television broadcast, and also produced promotional clips that were shown on various programs (see entry in film chapter). The qualification "of any sort" is vital, for these renditions of "Hey Jude" and "Revolution," both sides of their then-new single, really weren't close to being wholly "live." Rather, they use the instrumental tracks from the studio record-ings, with the Beatles adding live vocals. For all the pseudo-liveness, the clips *were* exciting, and gave the group a chance to perform in front of a live audience for the first time in what seemed like ages. It supplied evidence to the rest of the world—who hadn't seen the Beatles in a true concert setting for two years—that the group was indeed still very much alive, functioning, and capable of interacting with real human fans.

Before getting down to business, the Beatles *did* manage a few wholly live performances, though not of the kind of songs anyone would expect out of them. These were jazz-loungeish, probably deliberately cheesy instrumental versions of the less-than-minute-long theme to Frost's program—"A perfect rendition," as Frost says cheekily in his intro. After which the Beatles, with their genius for puncturing the pomposity of any occasion, butcher a line from Elvis Presley's "It's Now or Never." Frost is wholly on board with the whimsical silliness of the moment, referring to the Beatles as "the greatest tea-room orchestra in the world." One would have thought that one witty deconstruction of this tune would have been enough for Frost and the group's purposes. But no, they shambled through a couple of other even briefer renditions, the first including some sarcastic vocals mostly consisting of the phrase "David Frost." As sloppy (perhaps intentionally so) as these are, they're a minor testament to the band's versatility, able to make entertainingly humorous fare out of a task that many others in their position would have been unable to handle so adroitly.

Before Ringo starred with Peter Sellers in The Magic Christian, *he made his pal a special tape of rough*

The live versions of "Hey Jude" (which vary according to the takes and edits used in the different promotional clips that were assembled from the footage) are, as you'd guess, not too distinguishable from the record. There are some differences of note in the vocals, though. In take 1 John neglects to harmonize where he should in the third verse, Paul putting in that extra "Yeah!" before the bridge that he'd used early on in the "Hey Jude" sessions. It becomes most obvious that it's a live vocal, however, in the extended tag, where Paul's clearly relishing the chance to let loose with his peerless upper-register scream-singing. There's plenty of improvisation here that deviates from the studio prototype, including some phrases not found at all on the single: "The whole world smiles with you," a dopey "Yeah yeah yeah" (a knowing reference to "She Loves You," perhaps?), "Take a load off Fanny" (from the Band's recent "The Weight"), and "You must be joking, Jude" (!) being the highlights of those. It's much the same sort of thing on the other takes/edits—in fact, Paul sings "Take a load off Fanny" on all three codas. But the vocals on each of those *are* different, not just the same track matched to different footage. (Unfortunately the edit of takes 1, 2, and 3, used on the *Anthology* DVD/video, is more than a minute shorter than the other versions.)

The two takes of "Revolution" (performed in the same studio, but sans audience) are the same vocals-live/everything-else-studio deal. But these are more interesting than "Hey Jude," as the backing vocals are quite a bit different than they are on the single. Paul adds a lot more *extremely* enthusiastic backup and harmony vocals, and Paul and George add doo wop–like harmonies during the verses, as if to transplant one element of "Revolution 1" that didn't make the transition to the single version. The first version does have a slip by John in the first verse, where he sings, "We all love to see the world"; the second version is marred, though only very slightly, by a bit of feedback. It's the first version you see in the *Anthology* DVD/video, though there it's marred in a different way, as a portion of a John Lennon interview is played over the second chorus. (There's also a seven-second sound bite of the group playing the intro that's been attributed to this filming, though it's uncertain if that's truly the source.)

● September 5

Studio Outtakes
The White Album *sessions*
Studio Two, Abbey Road, London

Lady Madonna (monitor mix)
While My Guitar Gently Weeps (take 40, monitor mix)

While this session was devoted to an attempt to remake George's "While My Guitar Gently Weeps," at one point (technically part of take 40), Paul slipped into a jam on "Lady Madonna," accompanying himself on organ with minimal support from his band mates. As off-the-cuff as it is, in this author's view it's more interesting and entertaining than yet another minor mix variation, as it's quite a bit different from the single. Ever wondered how "Lady Madonna" might sound played at a circus fairground? Here 'tis, with distant, half-hearted vocals and an ending with some interesting, slightly ominous stretched-out twists on the chord sequence used on the official version.

This CD had an ironic title, considering its material was mostly drawn from The White Album *era.*

Paul also plays organ on take 40 proper of "While My Guitar Gently Weeps," and, more intriguingly, sings. The take only lasts a minute prior to breaking down, and as a gloomy organ's the only instrumentation, the effect is to make the tune into something of a funeral dirge. The Beatles were having a lot of trouble settling on an arrangement, and if this was any indication of where they were headed with the tune, it was on such a wayward path that it might have been on the verge of being discarded as unworkable. Recalled George of this session in the *Anthology* book, "We tried to record it, but Paul and John were so used to just cranking out their tunes that it was very difficult at times to get serious and record one of mine. It wasn't happening. They weren't taking it seriously and I don't think they were even all playing on it, and so I went home that night thinking, 'Well, that's a shame,' because I knew the song was pretty good." Fortunately, the problem was solved when George recruited his buddy Eric Clapton to play lead guitar on a far heavier, more standard rock version recorded the following evening.

● September 10

Studio Outtake
The White Album *sessions*
Studio Two, Abbey Road, London

Helter Skelter (RM1, unedited)

A version of the "Helter Skelter" mono mix taken from an acetate differs from the officially issued mono versions merely by virtue of including a few squealing guitar notes before the start. Another mono *White Album* mix taken from acetate, "Birthday" (recorded about a week later), is also technically different from the official mono release. It's not given an entry here, however, as the only additions are a John Lennon track announcement and Paul McCartney count-in. You gotta draw the line somewhere.

● September 16

Studio Outtakes
The White Album *sessions*
Studio Two, Abbey Road, London

---

*I Will (take 1)
Can You Take Me Back (aka "I Will" take 19)
Down in Havana (aka "I Will" take 30)
**Step Inside Love/Los Paranoias/The Way You Look Tonight
    (aka "I Will" takes 34–36)
       appears on Anthology 3
       **edited version appears on* Anthology 3

During the recording of "I Will," the Beatles slipped into several other songs as they worked toward the take (65) that would form the base of the studio track. That's made it difficult for completist collectors to keep straight how many outtakes there are from this session drifting around, as some are variously titled "I Will" or something else, depending on where you find them.

But there's only one real alternate version of "I Will," and that's take 1, officially available on *Anthology 3*. Like the similarly folky "Blackbird," this wasn't all that different from the ultimate recording in its very first take. But, like "Blackbird," it would be recorded over and over as Paul McCartney and the Beatles sought to nail down every last feature. Paul tosses in a superfluous "yeah" between the first and second line, and the picked guitar riff overdubs that did much to flesh out the end of the verses are missing. So's the harmony vocal, and the main vocal itself is more hesitant than the *White Album* one. There's also a muted cymbal crash near the end that didn't last the course, and a slightly extended finale. Overall, however, the performance is nothing to be ashamed of. A few seconds of the take's beginning can be heard on the *Anthology* DVD/video *White Album* outtakes medley, and, quirkily, it's obviously a different mix, as there's another cymbal crash from Ringo as well as his request for the volume in his headphones to be turned down.

The three other outtakes from this session are where things get really confusing, since all were logged as "I Will" takes at EMI, though in fact they're entirely different songs. On take 19, Paul devised the ghostly, disturbing, minor-keyed, uncopyrighted folk tune known as "Can You Take Me Back." Almost a half-minute of this was used as an untitled track on *The White Album*, between "Cry Baby Cry" and "Revolution 9," though fans just assumed (and many probably still do assume) that it was a part of "Cry Baby Cry" that somehow didn't get transcribed onto the LP's lyric poster. Actually this take/song lasted almost two and a half minutes, and much—but not all, to compound the headaches involved—of it has surfaced on bootleg. The unused sections, though, are pretty redundant, consisting mostly of repetitious rephrasings of

the one line's worth of melody the song contains. There is one lyric variation of modest note: "I ain't happy here, my mommy can you take me back." That's the kind of primal, lost-childhood line you'd associate more with John than Paul. Give the group credit, however, for making creative, concise use of an improvisation that most acts would have immediately forgotten about.

Giving full vent to the easy-listening bent that Paul and the other guys usually submerged on proper Beatles releases, on takes 34–36 they breezed into a three-song medley kicking off with "Step Inside Love." Paul had first demoed this almost a year earlier, but here we have a nearly complete full Beatles version (minus George, who did not play on this session), albeit a pretty casually sung, low-energy one. "Step Inside Love" had a bossa nova–like rhythm, and perhaps that's the cue for the three to indulge in their affection for Latin pop pastiches, on "Los Paranoias." It's not much more than a nonsensical make-it-up-as-you-go-along time-filler, though Paul mimics speedy trumpet runs most amusingly and effectively in his scat vocals. After a few minutes of this—which, even as a valve-releasing exercise, was starting to get tiresome—they ease back into the "I Will" chord progression, more or less, though Paul substitutes lyrics from the pop music standard "The Way You Look Tonight."

Lasting a total of six and a half minutes, the medley was drastically pared down to little more than a third of its original length for *Anthology 3*. Four minutes were chopped out altogether, and nothing whatsoever was used from the final three and a half minutes. For all but the most intense Beatles fans, however, it's not a notable loss, being more of a casual (and not particularly inspired) jam than a serious studio recording, even if the first part *was* a British Top Ten hit in the hands of Cilla Black.

Finally, yet another pseudo-Latin-tropical jam has escaped from the evening's proceedings. Lasting a mere half-minute, and usually titled "Down in Havana" on bootlegs, it features Paul singing in a vocal suggestive of a dissolute Elvis Presley before the group bolts back into the "I Will" melody.

Taken as a whole, these "I Will" outtakes are no great shakes. What they do indicate is that, although the bad vibes starting to fester in the group have been harped upon by numerous biographers, the Beatles often *were* still managing to have some relaxed fun in the studio. Even if George wasn't around to share it on this particular occasion.

● September 19

Studio Outtake
The White Album *sessions*
Studio One, Abbey Road, London

Piggies (unknown take fragment)

Just a few seconds of an unknown take of "Piggies" are heard as part of the *White Album* outtakes medley in the *Anthology* DVD/video. It's probably an early take, as a guitar and faint percussive thump serve as sole instrumentation. George's voice goes wildly out of tune as he starts the bridge on this, one of the most embarrassing—and yet, for that reason, one of the most entertaining—of the many *White Album* snippets cobbled together for the soundtrack of this montage sequence.

● September 25

Studio Outtake
The White Album *sessions*
Studio Two, Abbey Road, London

Happiness Is a Warm Gun (isolated tracks, take 65)

As Beatles "isolated tracks" mixes go, this is one of the more interesting ones, enabling us to hear some of the overdubs placed on "Happiness Is a Warm Gun" in their naked, separated state. This two-minute, 45-second tape begins with an organ so churchily downcast it would do the Zombies proud, though you can faintly hear some singing and guitar buried way down in the mix. Then the fierce fuzz guitar preceding the section about needing a fix is heard all by its lonesome, followed by less interesting tambourine and hi-hat drum. The final part spotlights the piano heard on the song's last, doo woppish section, again with some other components of the track heard way in the distance. It's certainly not an "outtake" in the traditional sense, nor is it something that can be heard as a standard "song." But the pungency of that cloudy-day organ alone makes it worth hearing, just about.

● September 26

Studio Outtake
The White Album *sessions*
Studio Two, Abbey Road, London

*Glass Onion (alternate mono mix)
   appears on Anthology 3

This early, unnumbered mono mix of "Glass Onion" is missing the swooping string overdubs that did much to add a sense of whimsical wit to the track. Perhaps sensing the onion could use another layer but not sure what that might be, John added various sound effects, including a ringing telephone, shattering glass, and, strangest of all, BBC television soccer commentator Kenneth Wolstenholme's shout, "It's a goal!" All of those sounds, in fact, were heard in tandem at the song's conclusion, running over and over for almost 20 seconds. John and the Beatles had used sound effects quite imaginatively over the course of the preceding two years, but here they were not so much embellishments as non sequiturs.

John would sometimes denigrate the contribution of George Martin to the Beatles' productions, and indeed Martin wasn't even present at some *White Album* sessions, including this one. Here was an instance, however, in which Martin's later input would prove vital to both curbing John's more excessive tendencies and giving a Lennon composition a valuable extra boost. It was Martin who devised the string arrangement that graced the *White Album* version, this rough mix remaining unheard until it was excavated for the *Anthology 3* compilation.

● October 8

Studio Outtake

The White Album *sessions*
Studio Two, Abbey Road, London

*I'm So Tired (Anthology 3 mix)
I'm So Tired (take 14, fragment)
I'm So Tired (take 14, mono rough mix #1)
I'm So Tired (take 14, mono rough mix #2)
I'm So Tired (take 14, mono rough mix #3)
I'm So Tired (take 14, mono rough mix #4)
I'm So Tired (take 14, mono rough mix #5)
   appears on Anthology 3

The last of the *White Album* sessions to generate a large batch of circulating outtakes was this one, which spewed forth a number of "I'm So Tired" alternates so hard to keep straight that even top Beatles experts don't agree as to how many they total. Even the most accessible and conventionally structured one, on *Anthology 3*, isn't a straightforward alternate take, but an "amalgam" (in the words of the compilation's own liner notes) of takes 3, 6, and 9. There's not much to compare/contrast here, though it's generally not quite as tight as the album version, and the guitar work's a little bluesier and busier. Too, John doesn't reach quite as high into the upper reaches of his vocal register, to the track's detriment.

Take 14 was the one used for the final release, and a head-spinning number of mix variations have escaped into the outer world to confuse (but not necessarily delight) us all. About a dozen seconds from the end are on the *Anthology* DVD *White Album* outtakes medley, with somewhat more upfront guitar. One of the five (!) available mono rough mixes actually isolates the tracks so that all you hear is organ, some searing if slightly undisciplined lead guitar, and a snare drum. So it's nothing like hearing a complete song, but does let you hear some riffs that actually didn't make the final mix, particularly on the organ, which sounds decidedly spookier here than it does on the *White Album* cut. A second rough mix is close to the released track, with the bonus of our ever-favorite minuscule addition, a spoken count-in. Then comes a series of three rough mixes, including two playbacks, a breakdown, and a couple of false starts, accounting for why some scrutinizers count these as anything from two to five individual mixes. There's not much difference from the familiar arrangement to be heard in any of these, making this an exercise in which—dare we say—"I'm So Tired," for all its excellence in its finished state, becomes downright tiresome.

It's a testament to just how much of a marathon the *White Album* sessions ended up being that it took the Beatles more than four months to get through the pile of songs ("I'm So Tired" among them) they'd demoed back in May at Kinfauns. Indeed, the *White Album* sessions were such a marathon that—if you count those Kinfauns demos as *White Album* sessions of sorts—virtually a full CD of outtakes was eventually officially issued, as disc one of *Anthology 3* consists of almost nothing but Kinfauns demos and *White Album* studio surplus.

● October 9

Studio Outtake
The White Album *sessions*
Studio One, Abbey Road, London

*Why Don't We Do It in the Road (take 4)

  *appears on Anthology 3

"Why Don't We Do It in the Road" was, both lyrically and vocally, Paul McCartney's most (quite literally) ballsy performance. When take 4 was issued on *Anthology 3,* however, it was clear that he hadn't quite decided to let it all hang out before the final track was laid down. Not only is there no instrumentation besides acoustic guitar, but Paul switches between a soft, almost effeminate croon and the more familiar throat-shredding declarations that we're used to hearing on this song. He earnestly asks at take's end whether the assembled listeners think he can do it better, and on the very next take he did just that, putting the pedal to the metal that this salacious rocker deserved. Pounding piano, bass, and Ringo's drums were then overdubbed to make it a full-out rocker. All of which makes the *White Album* version quite superior to this earlier take, which is nonetheless a highly instructive and reasonably entertaining look at the song in a formative (and quite different) shape.

● October 10

Studio Outtake
The White Album *sessions*
Studios One and Three, Abbey Road, London

Why Don't We Do It in the Road (takes 4 and 5, fragments)

Lest the reader get the wrong impression, it should be stressed that the four-and-a-half-minute medley of the *White Album* outtakes on the *Anthology* DVD/video really is a fun and valuable thing, stringing together rejected odds and ends in a way that's entertaining—and educational—to hear and watch. It's much better heard all in a row than individually. And by the same token, when it comes to doing the detective work to determine what comes from where, it's proof of the old adage that some mysteries are better left unsolved. Like the origin of the medley's brief fragment of "Why Don't We Do It in the Road," which on the video, weirdly, had sound bites from takes four *and* five playing simultaneously. Only the beginning and end snippets of take 5 (the basis of the official version) were used on the DVD, but even there it's a different mix, distinguished principally by a few spoken McCartney mutterings ("Hello? Yeah, okay") at the start that aren't heard on the album track. There—aren't you glad you asked?

● October 13

Studio Outtakes
The White Album *sessions*
Studio Two, Abbey Road, London

*Julia (take 2)
Julia (take 3 fragment)
  *appears on Anthology 3

Take 2 of "Julia" is largely instrumental, so that John could concentrate on recording his acoustic guitar part. He messes up a note in the

second verse that would have rendered this take unusable, but keeps on going anyway, until the take breaks down just shy of the minute-and-a-half mark after a pause. John chuckles and tries to petition Paul, observing in the control room, for permission to keep on going. Take 3 would nail down the guitar part and, with overdubs, form the official *White Album* track. It's the end of take 3 that plays in the *Anthology* DVD/video *White Album* outtakes medley, with one crucial and quite endearing difference, adding John's explanation that "the last mistake was entirely when I just took me mind off it for a second."

Another aspect of this recording that take 2 makes clear is that although *The White Album* is viewed as a time when the Beatles were fragmenting and recording some tracks wholly by themselves (as John was for "Julia"), that didn't necessarily mean that those not playing on specific recordings were uninterested in what was going on without them. For Paul was in the control room offering feedback, and he and John seemed to still be getting along okay for the moment, on a professional level at least.

● October 14

Studio Outtake
The White Album *sessions*
Studio Two, Abbey Road, London

What's the New Mary Jane (stereo remix)

As one of several remixes done on this day as *The White Album* neared completion, "What's the New Mary Jane"—still planned for inclusion

The Off White *album, with unreleased* White Album*–era Beatles material, both paid homage to and mocked the graphics used on* The White Album *itself.*

on the release at this point—was drastically shortened, from six and a half minutes to about half that length. Maybe John, knowing it was (with "Revolution 9") the least popular number of the whole *White Album* batch, was prepared to compromise so as to make it an easier fit into the running order. (If that was the plan, it didn't work: "What's the New Mary Jane" was dropped from the album at the last minute a few days later.) This edit did make it more listenable, sort of, by concentrating on the beginning part of the song, where there was at least an approximate tune and lyric. This was the version of the song that was first bootlegged (making its first appearance way back in the early '70s), though oddly it's quite hard to find on unauthorized CDs nowadays.

Before taking leave of *The White Album*, it's interesting to note that had George Martin gotten his way and convinced the group to make it a single LP rather than a double, that would have made for an unforeseen major headache years down the road. As George Harrison pointed out in the *Anthology* book, "There were a lot of songs that maybe should have been elbowed or made into B-sides. Having said that, there would just have been more bootlegs today because all of those that weren't put on the album would be out there."

● November 4–25

Private Tapes
Queen Charlotte's Maternity Hospital, London

*Song for John
*Mulberry

*appear as bonus tracks on 1997 CD reissue of
Unfinished Music No. 2: Life with the Lions

Immediately after *The White Album* was finished in mid-October, John and Yoko suffered a traumatic month together. On October 18, they were busted for marijuana possession. John's guilty plea at the end of November would create untold hassles when he tried to visit and then live in the United States, a problem that didn't get cleared up until the mid-'70s. For three weeks in November, Yoko was hospitalized with complications in her five-month-term pregnancy, which ended with a miscarriage on November 21. The Beatles and the group's future, understandably, might have at this point not exactly been foremost in John's mind. In keeping with their seeming intent to merge their lives with art, recordings made at the hospital were issued as part of the *Unfinished Music No. 2: Life with the Lions* LP in 1969.

As sympathetic as many Beatles fans might have been to the couple's misfortunes, the album, like its predecessor, *Two Virgins,* was so avant-garde as to largely be deemed unpleasantly unlistenable by the vast majority. Back in 1969, it would have seemed unthinkable that there would be any desire for outtakes from the album. When Yoko Ono's artistic and musical reputation rose (if only on a somewhat cultish level) in retrospect, however, her vintage catalog was reissued with bonus tracks by Rykodisc. A couple of unused hospital recordings were tacked on to *Unfinished Music No. 2* as bonus tracks. "Song for John" was much more song-oriented than most of the material on the album proper, John supplying nice acoustic finger-picked guitar as

Yoko sings a forlorn (indeed, gloomy) minor-keyed, folky ballad. Not so the nine-minute "Mulberry," Yoko singing of finding mulberries in her trademark high, keening, roving wail as John discordantly slashes away at his fretless guitar. Eventually she drifts off into the wordless, grating improvisations and grunting that she employed on many of her musical pieces.

Also recorded at the hospital was an acoustic guitar–backed duet by John and Yoko on the bluesy, repetitious "Don't Worry Kyoko (Mummy's Only Looking for Her Hand in the Snow)," which would later be recorded in the studio for use as the B-side of John's "Cold Turkey" single. Technically speaking, this did come out in 1969, though only as part of a flexi-disc in the spring/summer issue of *Aspen* magazine; it was later added to the 1997 Rykodisc CD reissue of John and Yoko's *Wedding Album* as a bonus track.

● Circa Late November

Private Tapes
New York State

Nowhere to Go
I'd Have You Anytime

George Harrison and Bob Dylan started to develop a strong friendship in the late '60s, particularly after George hung out with Dylan and the Band in Woodstock in late 1968. Just after the Beatle breakup in 1970 sent shock waves throughout the rock world, George traveled to the States in the brief gap between the end of the group and the beginning of his solo recording career in earnest, and naturally hooked up with Dylan again. It seemed like a good combination: George could teach Bob a thing or two about developing better melodies and more attractive arrangements, and there was no more venerated figure than Dylan to give Harrison the respect and confidence boost he'd never fully received from Lennon and McCartney. Yet it never really produced as much as it promised, other than one excellent songwriting collaboration that led off George's *All Things Must Pass,* "I'd Have You Anytime." The musicians just had too much to express as solo artists to enter into a more extensive partnership, though of course they did eventually do so in the late '80s as part of the Traveling Wilburys, with fellow travelers Roy Orbison, Jeff Lynne, and Tom Petty.

A brief, rickety-sounding tape of the pair singing a couple of songs together with acoustic guitar accompaniment *has* long made the bootleg rounds, and even the rough date at which it was recorded is in dispute among experts. Some believe it was recorded at the end of April 1970, when George and Bob spent some time together in New York. Others believe it was done when Harrison, the Band, and Dylan were spending time together in Woodstock, New York, around Thanksgiving 1968. This general time frame was confirmed by George in a February 15, 2001, interview he gave with Chris Carter to discuss the 30th anniversary reissue of *All Things Must Pass,* in which he was asked about writing "I'd Have You Anytime" with Dylan. "I just happened to be invited to Woodstock by the Band," responded Harrison. "I spent some days with Bob and I suppose we just got round to picking up guitars and he was saying, 'Hey show me some of those chords, those weird chords.' And that's how that came about. It's like a strange chord, really. It's called G Major seventh. It's got all these major seventh chords. You know, we just turned it into a song. So, it was really nice."

It's unfortunate the tape seems to have been recorded very badly on cheap equipment, as these are both pretty, humble, reflective tunes. "Nowhere to Go" has a wonderfully bittersweet descending chorus, and "I'd Have You Anytime," here close to the form it would take on *All Things Must Pass,* is likewise more melodic than virtually all of Dylan's work. Bob seems very tentative with his harmonies, however, almost as if George is teaching him the song, rather than performing something both have written as equal contributors. "Nowhere to Go," sadly, did not make it onto *All Things Must Pass* or any other album, but luckily was recorded by George in a more polished form on the May 1970 demos he did just prior to beginning work on the album (see late May entry in the 1970 chapter).

● Circa Late November

Studio Outtakes
London

How Do You Do
Blackbird
The Unicorn
Lalena
Heather
Mr. Wind
The Walrus and the Carpenter
Land of Gish

The Beatles, as individuals, had made some scattered guest appearances on other artists' official recordings since the mid-'60s—an area that this volume does not cover (Kristofer Engelhardt's *Beatles Undercover* is the most detailed book examining that topic). This session, however, is an exception as it was a first of sorts: an unreleased studio recording, not related to a Beatles session, in which one of the members took a prominent role as guitarist, occasional lead vocalist, and occasional composer. Oddly, the artist of record for these sessions—new Apple Records star Mary Hopkin, who was working on her debut *Postcard* album that night—barely appears on the tape at all. Instead, it's something of an acoustic duet between Paul McCartney and Donovan, both of whom contributed to *Postcard,* Paul as producer and Donovan as a composer of several of the LP's songs.

Paul McCartney and Donovan in the studio, late '60s. A tape from a Mary Hopkin session contains unreleased informal, folky recordings by the pair.

Donovan's influence on the Beatles in the 1960s, like Donovan's influence on the 1960s rock scene as a whole, has been somewhat under-estimated by historians. He'd helped Paul out a bit with the lyric for "Yellow Submarine," and, as previously noted, had some influence on the acoustic direction and guitar styles they used on *The White Album* as the Beatles wrote songs for the the album in Rishikesh in early 1968. While there, George Harrison also wrote a verse for Donovan's hit song "Hurdy Gurdy Man" that was not used in the studio recording; Donovan in turn helped George write "Dehra Dhun," an unreleased version of which Harrison recorded in 1970.

Although this was officially a Mary Hopkin session (precise date and location uncertain), Paul and Donovan apparently used some studio time to informally record together, both playing acoustic guitars. Mary Hopkin has recalled Donovan coming to the studio to play some songs for her to consider using on the album, which might have been why he was at the session in the first place. While it's a little more of a Donovan tape than a McCartney one, Paul does sing a few of his own songs, a couple of which would never reappear, though these were probably improvised ditties for which he had no grand plans. Starting things off is Paul's "How Do You Do," which like some of Donovan's late-'60s material is something of a folky children's song, halting and drastically speeding up at various points. With an agreeably nondescript melody, there's a trace of naughtiness to the lyric, with its references to sitting on a woodpecker and sucking on a "lollipopper"—not exactly G-rated material. Then comes a version of "Blackbird," sung a little slower and lazier than the *White Album* arrangement. Paul scats in a high voice for part of it, Hopkin faintly singing along at points as well. A decent enough relic, most interesting not for the performance but some incidental comments, in which Paul reveals, "I sang it to Diana Ross the other night. She took offense. Not really . . . but I didn't mean it like that originally! I just read something in the paper about riots" (presumably some of the race riots erupting in the US at the time).

Then it's time for Donovan to play some of his work, starting off with a minute-long "The Unicorn," which like much of his writing has a fairy tale feel. He wouldn't release that song until 1971's *H.M.S. Donovan,* though the next song, "Lalena," was his latest American Top 40 single. Paul takes the stage again for "Heather," which sounds very much like a basic nursery rhyme he would have written to play for the five-year-old daughter of his new girlfriend, Linda Eastman. Like "How Do You Do," it's pleasant but bland, and quite repetitive, though Heather would soon have a minor cameo of her own on an actual Beatles session (see entry for January 26, 1969). Donovan then runs through a couple of more previews of material from *H.M.S. Donovan* with brief versions of "Mr. Wind" and "The Walrus and the Carpenter," as well as an incomplete "Land of Gish," which he'd never put on record.

Overall, the tape—with good sound—is an enjoyable document of a musical and personal friendship, though not one that offers any stunning moments musically, the material being on the slight and light-weight side. Some sourpusses might see it as an early warning sign of the direction McCartney would take in much of his early solo career, where he'd increasingly favor light and airy tunes with a cozy, feel-good ambience. Viewed more positively, it might be an early reflection of the domestic tranquility he was finding with his new partner and her daughter, soon to lead to marriage and a family.

● Circic Late 1968

The Beatles' Sixth Christmas Record

The Beatles' Sixth Christmas Record (fan club disc)
Jock and Yono (rough mix)
Once Upon a Pool Table (rough mix)

Unlike the Beatles' five previous Christmas records, the 1968 edition was recorded by the four individual members separately. That's often cited as one small sign of the group's fragmentation, but it was probably due to the fragmentation of their lives into increasingly independent and far-flung activities rather than a product of any genuine animosity toward each other. For one thing, in late 1968 it would have been hard to logisti-cally even get all four of them in the same place. George was in the midst of a six-week trip to the United States; John was preoccupied with his drug bust and Yoko's miscarriage; Paul, his romance with Linda Eastman rapidly intensifying, was traveling with her to New York and Scotland; and Ringo was moving with his family to a new home.

Paul had indicated in the *New Musical Express* that the disc might contain some unreleased home recordings of actual Beatles songs that had not been used on any LP (from the Kinfauns sessions, one wonders?), which perhaps might have been briefly considered as a quick shortcut to assembling material for the record. In the end, though, they individually taped musical scraps and wacky odds 'n' ends in line with what they'd done on previous Christmas discs, but in keeping with the mood of the times these were freakier than ever. Nor would they edit the various parts together themselves. That task was delegated to their DJ friend Kenny Everett, who was well familiar with the Beatles' brand of cutup humor through some of the jingles and interviews he'd recorded of the group for radio broadcast.

Perhaps surprisingly, considering his recent trials and tribulations, it's John who seems to have put the most effort into his contribution. His poem "Jock and Yono," about John and Yoko of course, is known even beyond Beatles collecting circles for its jab, "But they battled on against overwhelming oddities, including some of their beast friends"—often taken to mean the other Beatles, whose acceptance of Yoko was less than wholehearted. Paul, in line with his jams with Donovan at the Mary Hopkin session, donates the most musical passage, with a pleasant, repetitive, off-the-top-of-his-head acoustic guitar ditty with miscellaneous, perfunctory holiday greetings. George offers greeting card homilies with dry sarcasm that make it clear he's making fun of the whole smiley-face pretense that Beatles Christmas fan club discs started as—and certainly, by this time, were *not.* Ringo, perhaps inspired by his home tape collaborations with John in the Kenwood days, puts a lot of energy into his fairly witty one-man, two-sided phone conversation, half of it done in a silly voice that would have made a credible Monty Python character.

Although the Beatles taped their parts separately, Everett edited the final disc in a suitably manic manner that switched between the individual contributions. The whole was overlaid with stop-on-a-dime transitions, excerpts from actual Beatles records (super-sped-up in the case of "Helter Skelter"), and various sound and reverb effects. In the latter half of the disc, John got time to offer another surrealistic poem ("Once Upon a Time") and George was able to introduce Tiny

Tim, who performed a brief rendition of "Nowhere Man" on ukulele in his trademark trilling falsetto. (The Beatles' admiration of Tiny Tim seemed genuine, with John and Paul affirming as much back on their June 6 BBC Radio One interview with Everett.) After George thanks Tiny Tim with a "God bless you," the disc comes to a mock-solemn close. If those final drumbeats sound familiar, that's because they ended side one of *The White Album*, where they brought "Happiness Is a Warm Gun" to a finish. While this montage wasn't wholly the work of the Beatles (certainly insofar as the editing and production went), it's a pretty interesting, entertaining, quasi-psychedelic fun house of a ride—albeit a fun house on the verge of spinning out of control, just as the group's Apple empire and very career was starting to do by Christmas 1968.

Also available are "rough mixes" of John's "Jock and Yono" and "Once Upon a Pool Table" poem/segments. "Jock and Yono" is just slightly longer, with a little more piano (by Yoko) at the beginning, while "Once Upon a Pool Table" has some more lines at the finish.

● Circa Early December

Private Tapes

Kenwood, Weybridge

Oh My Love (take 1)
Oh My Love (take 2)
A Case of the Blues
Everyone Had a Hard Year
Don't Let Me Down (take 1)
Don't Let Me Down (take 2)

Late 1968 may have been the most hectic time ever in John's personal life, what with his drug bust, Yoko's miscarriage, his divorce from his first wife, and problems with the Beatles and Apple. He was also fending off miscellaneous wrath from much of the public regarding his affair with Yoko, his drug use, and his generally growing image as something of a crazed weirdo. At the end of the year, he briefly (with Yoko) moved back into his former Kenwood home, now up for sale in ex-wife's Cynthia absence. Somehow he summoned the energy to record a few home tapes of new compositions on acoustic guitar, as plans for what would become the *Get Back* album were starting to brew, as well as an accompanying concert and/or television special.

"Oh My Love" is actually a John Lennon–Yoko Ono composition, and not just in the token honorary sense; its genesis lay with a Yoko poem. John's got a good, unusual, constantly shifting, wistful melody already on these two brief takes. But he doesn't have a good sense yet of an appropriate rhythm to wed to it, strumming hastily, slowing things down, and (at the end of take 1) resignedly commenting on how hard it is. The second attempt sounds even more hesitant and uncertain in those regards, almost approaching a jazzy unpredictability. It's a moving, tender tune, and only needed some work before it was something of real quality. It's so gentle, in fact, that it can be easily overlooked (particularly in combination with John's mumbly vocal) that it's actually about the baby that died in the miscarriage, Lennon singing almost distractedly in take 1, "You had a very strong heartbeat, but that's gone now. Probably we'll forget about you." At the end of that take, he offers the enigmatic

spoken comment, "It's just too a bit hard, to go through it all like"—and then the tape cuts off.

For whatever reason, however—maybe it was just too painfully personal, or maybe problems were foreseen in giving Yoko any part of the songwriting credit—there's no evidence that John ever did present it to the Beatles for consideration as a group recording. It's not one of the hundreds of songs played in some way, shape, or form during the January 1969 *Get Back* sessions, for instance. When it did finally show up in 1971 on John's *Imagine* LP, some of the chord progressions from this rudimentary demo can still be detected. But by that time, the song had been placed in a much more graceful, quasi-classical setting, the lyrics about their lost child gone, with an extensive bridge wholly missing from this home tape.

John sounds ground down-and-out on "A Case of the Blues," the only song from this tape never to re-emerge in any form on an official release. Against a tense, bluesy chord sequence with an insistent rhythm, John sings, not too distinctly, phrases conveying a definite sense of weary frustration, but little in the way of cogent lyrics. If you're looking for another Lennon song to compare it to, musically it's got a little of the chugging angst of "Mean Mr. Mustard," though the melody's far less focused. If you're looking for a non-Beatles song to compare it to, the descending melody used throughout much of the number bears a strong resemblance to the riff anchoring the Ventures' classic 1960 instrumental "Walk Don't Run." At the end, he slows down the tempo drastically and really drags it out, adding some blues instrumental riffs for punctuation. There's the spark of a decent song here, but it just needs more work, particularly in the lyrical department. And while he didn't completely abandon it, playing bits during the *Get Back* sessions, he apparently never did finish it.

While the Lennon-McCartney writing partnership is often typecast as having completely fizzled out by 1968, in fact the pair were still helping fill in small bits and pieces of the other's songs on occasion. There was even at least one occasion where they joined together two fragments to make a whole, as this less-than-two-minute "Everyone Had a Hard Year" makes clear. For this would soon be absorbed into Paul's "I've Got a Feeling," just as Paul's undeveloped song about a guy going through the paces of everyday life had been absorbed into "A Day in the Life." In this early version, it's more plaintive and folky than it would be as heard in the final "I've Got a Feeling," with a hypnotically circular guitar riff. Characteristically, John doesn't just stick to one mood here: while there's a sense of burned-out resignation about the hard year he's gone through, there's also a sense of hope and optimism. As promising as this fragment is, as it stands it would have been too repetitive, basic, short, and undeveloped to be a workable full Beatles track. Typically, the Beatles found a way to make productive use of it, though prior to that, John and Yoko found yet another use for it in one of the experimental films they made together (see entry later in this chapter).

Certainly the best of this batch was "Don't Let Me Down," though here it's in a relatively primitive state. In the first version, for one thing, it's lacking a bridge *or* a chorus, or indeed any vocalization of the title phrase. At various points John drifts into brief descending and ascending chord sequences that would find no place in the finalized song. Very briefly, he hits upon seeds of the bridge and the chorus, particularly at the end, where he plays an instrumental riff that *almost* captures the melody of the chorus. By the second take, remarkably enough, he has the bridge largely figured out, though he's still uncertain how to fit it into the rest of the song, and intersperses some jazzy chord changes that wouldn't end up being used in the finished composition. As the *Get Back* session tapes in January 1969 demonstrate, Paul and the Beatles supplied invaluable input for giving "Don't Let Me Down" the structure it sorely needed, though John had already figured out most of the building blocks on his own.

Incidentally, a Lennon acoustic demo of "Look at Me" is sometimes billed on bootlegs as having been done at the same time as the other songs detailed in this entry. It's *possible* that's the case, especially as in his early-'70s *Rolling Stone* interview John confirmed that it had been written around the time of *The White Album*. It's more likely, however, that this demo was done shortly before it was recorded for John's 1970 *Plastic Ono Band* album, since the tape from his archives that includes all the other songs listed above does *not* include "Look at Me."

● December 11

Live Performance
Stonebridge House, London

Yer Blues (a cappella)
Instrumental Jam
*Yer Blues (take 1)
Yer Blues (take 1, mono)
Yer Blues (take 2)
Yer Blues (take 3)
Whole Lotta Yoko

appears on the soundtrack CD The Rolling Stones Rock and Roll Circus

---

As part of the ill-fated television show *The Rolling Stones Rock and Roll Circus,* John agreed to perform, backed by an ad hoc band featuring Eric Clapton on lead guitar, Keith Richards on bass, and Mitch Mitchell (of the Jimi Hendrix Experience) on drums. "Mick [Jagger] thought it would be great to have a supergroup made up of musicians, 'cause there hadn't been many," remembered director Michael Lindsay-Hogg on his commentary track to the DVD version. "They didn't exist, really, then, that idea—musicians from other bands who wanted to play together." Stevie Winwood was Jagger's first choice for fronting such a supergroup, and Paul McCartney was also considered. Mick ended up, however, asking John Lennon to fill the role shortly before the show.

Dubbed "the Dirty Mac," the ensemble performed "Yer Blues," and (with Yoko on vocals and Ivry Gitlis on violin) the blues-avant-garde improvisation "Whole Lotta Yoko." The special—which, aside from headliners the Rolling Stones, also featured the Who, Jethro Tull, Marianne Faithfull, Taj Mahal, and classical pianist Julius Katchen—was never broadcast as planned, for murky reasons. Speculation varied from theories that the Stones were unhappy about their performance (the most oft-circulated one), to their jealousy of the fine spot turned in by the Who, to a reluctance to air the special after the death of Stones guitarist Brian Jones (who was still in the band, barely, at the time of the filming) in July 1969. Whatever the reason, the film sat on the shelf for decades until it was finally issued on home video in 1996, though copies of both the film and the soundtrack had been bootlegged for years.

Take 1 of "Yer Blues" is on both the video/DVD and the official soundtrack CD, and it's both a powerful performance and one that's

quite different from the Beatles' *White Album* version. There's a heavier, bluesier rock feel, as could be expected from a lineup including Clapton and Mitchell. John was wise to select a song that such players would be instantly comfortable with, not to mention not too hard to remember or play, it being melodically simple by Beatles standards. His vocal is just as searing as it is on *The White Album,* and generally he seems not just happy to be playing live, but quite at ease with being the spotlighted performer onstage. The audience and players were likely not as happy with the subsequent rudimentary jam "Whole Lotta Yoko," which apart from not being much of a song (though you can hear Bo Diddley's "Roadrunner" riff at its root) goes on way too long. "They cope for John," observed Marianne Faithfull on her commentary track for *The Rolling Stones Rock and Roll Circus* DVD, by way of explanation as to how these superstar musicians ended up backing Yoko Ono's characteristically wordless screeching vocals on this track. "*Everybody* coped for John."

A slightly longer, bootlegged take 1 (in mono) only adds some incidental noise at the beginning, mostly from the film crew, apparently. The mix also gives the instrumental backing such a boost that John's singing can hardly be heard. A similar take 2, sadly, only exists in this quasi-instrumental state as well. Take 3 (seen and heard in the DVD bonus footage) restores John's vocal to the mix, but was probably passed over for use due to his mistaken switch of the words "sky" and "earth" at one point. John was never the best at remembering his own lyrics, and according to *Rock and Roll Circus* photographer Michael Randolph, a lyric sheet had to be taped to the microphone, ripped right from the back of the poster packaged with *The White Album.*

Also available from the day's filming is a silly, yet fun, half-minute a cappella version by John and Mick Jagger, interspersed with some deliberately cretinous American showbiz-like banter. There's also a basic blues jam that, like most unreleased supergroup blues jams, is pretty low on both structure and melody.

Though it's unlikely he intended this as a statement of independence from the Beatles, John's appearance on *The Rolling Stones Rock and Roll Circus* was the first known time a member of the band had performed live as a featured singer with a separate backing unit—as a solo act, essentially. It was another in a pile of small mounting signs that the group was not as united as they had once been, and that solo careers—real solo careers, not just the soundtracks and avant-garde LPs that John, Paul, and George had already released apart from the Beatles—of some sort were probably not too far off in the future. Viewed from another angle, however, it's also possible it fired John's appetite for performing in some sort of live situation with the Beatles. Which they would indeed do, albeit chaotically, in front of film cameras the following month, using the same director as the Rolling Stones had for their *Rock and Roll Circus.*

● Circa Mid-December

Private Tape
Kenwood, Weybridge

Everybody Had a Hard Year

Having expanded their multimedia activities to film, John and Yoko found a use for an embryonic Beatles song in their movie *Rape (Film*

No. 6). In a short scene following the credits, John and Yoko sang "Everybody Had a Hard Year" in the garden of Kenwood, John on acoustic guitar. While the precise date is uncertain, it definitely postdates the "Everyone Had a Hard Year" home recording, as the title's changed slightly, as have a bit of the other lyrics (with a reference to a "soft dream" rather than the more explicit "wet dream" used on the final Beatles studio recording of "I've Got a Feeling"). Lasting just over a minute, it's a delicate, melancholy performance, interrupted after about 20 seconds by John declaring, "Surprise, surprise"—an interjection that makes much more sense on film, where John points at the camera. There's a sunny chord progression more than halfway through that didn't make the transition when the tune was blended with a more developed Paul McCartney song to form "I've Got a Feeling." Then John drifts into the "Julia" melody—a similarity that would likewise be removed when the Beatles worked with it.

1968 Noncirculating Recordings, Known and Rumored

● May 30–October 17

Studio Outtakes

The White Album *sessions*
Abbey Road, London

As pointed out earlier, the presence of nearly a full CD of *White Album* outtakes and related demos on *Anthology 3* has skimmed off the cream of the vault pickings. Too, owing to the Beatles' late-'60s methods of overdubbing layers of different voices and instruments, some of the unheard outtakes described in *The Beatles Recording Sessions* are more interesting on paper than they would be to hear on disc. For example, some tape loops that were never used for "Revolution 1," one of which, as Mark Lewisohn wrote, had "all four Beatles singing, at length, 'Aaaaaaah,' very high register." Or numerous unused sound effects for "Revolution 9," or Ringo's various spoken intros for "Good Night," when that track was still envisioned as a much less ornate production.

There *are* a few unheard *White Album* alternates, however, that might make for historically instructive listening at the very least. Between the first and third conceptions of "Ob-La-Di, Ob-La-Da," there was an initial attempt at a remake that differed from both the first approach to the tune and the final arrangement. At the first "Sexy Sadie" session, some of the takes had some no doubt colorfully foul Lennon curses, and that same session included a six-minute instrumental jam on George Gershwin's standard "Summertime," which had already been adapted by rock acts ranging from Gene Vincent and the Zombies to Big Brother & the Holding Company (with Janis Joplin on vocals). Like "Ob-La-Di, Ob-La-Da," "Sexy Sadie" was also subject to a failed remake session before the Beatles tried it yet again and finally got it right.

However, the most famous—or infamous, depending on your perspective—locked-up *White Album* outtakes of all have to be the three ultra-long versions of "Helter Skelter" recorded on July 18, lasting 10:40 (take 1), 12:35 (take 2), and an unbelievable 27:11 for take 3. Particularly

as Lewisohn noted that "each take developed into a tight and concisely played jam with long instrumental passages," fans were ravenous to hear these, especially as such long jams weren't at all typical of Beatles tracks. Still, there are virtually *no* 27-minute rock tracks, by any band at any time, that come off well or remain interesting throughout the entire performance. The four-and-a-half-minute edit of take 2 on *Anthology 3* alone lowered expectations, as even this truncated version both veered on tedium and was far inferior to the final arrangement, with its dragging tempo and rote blues-rock guitar licks.

Explaining why a longer version was not chosen for the *Anthology* CD compilations in a 1995 Dutch interview (as seen in the bonus disc of the bootlegged director's cut of the *Anthology* documentary), George Martin was blunt: "I think it gets boring." His elaboration perhaps gave away more than he would have liked about the core philosophy behind the *Anthology* collections: "In making these records, my consideration has been to put in works that are interesting to the majority of people. *Not* to Beatle fanatics. And I have to look at the public as a broad, interesting thing. And I don't want to put anything that people are going to say"—here he yawned for emphasis—"'I wonder when this is gonna finish.' And that's what that would do. Now, there are the hardcore Beatle fanatics who would love to have this. But they already have it on bootleg."

Most Beatles fanatics love George Martin for what he did with the group, but most could have told him that he was wrong—we *don't* have it on bootleg, as none of the long versions have ever made it onto that format. (In fact, the over-halved edit of take 2 on *Anthology 3* is the *only* version of "Helter Skelter" from this session to have made it into circulation.) It can also be added that Martin did not have an affection for improvisation or rock jams in general, dating all the way back to the *Sgt. Pepper* sessions, when he would get put off by some of the Beatles' lengthier, less structured improvisational outtakes. Speaking of the *White Album* sessions specifically on the *Anthology* DVD/home video, he observed, "A lot of the recordings, they would have a basic idea and then they would have a jam session to end it, which sometimes didn't sound too good." While Martin's judgment might be a bit harsh, there's some merit to that observation—a number of other *White Album* recordings meandered into a lengthy instrumental jam in their original state, like "Revolution 1" and "Sexy Sadie," and did benefit from much judicious pruning.

The second most sought-after outtake from *The White Album* is Paul McCartney's "Etcetera," recorded as a one-take demo by the composer. Recalled by EMI technical engineer Alan Brown as a beautiful ballad, the tape's apparently no longer in EMI's vaults. That could be because Paul, contrary to Brown's estimation, didn't rate the song highly when he spoke about it in Barry Miles's McCartney biography *Paul McCartney: Many Years from Now,* where he remembered it as having been written with a Marianne Faithfull cover in mind: "I knew Marianne so it was natural that I would be asked to write a song at some point. I did write a song but it was not a very good one. It was called 'Etcetera' and it's a bad song. I think it's a good job that it's died a death in some tape bin. Even then I seem to remember thinking it wasn't very good. There was always the temptation to keep your better songs for yourself and then give your next-best songs to other established people, so when it was someone like Marianne, who at that time was a newcomer, those people would tend to end up with fairly dreadful offerings of mine.

"I suppose, thinking back on it, after 'As Tears Go By' maybe they were looking for more sort of a 'Yesterday,' something more poignant, more baroque. I probably thought, well, this is really all I've got at the moment. I'll send it round and hope it's all okay, and maybe they'll put a baroque thing on it and that'll make it okay. She probably did 'Yesterday' because they figured, 'Well at least it's better than "Etcetera."'"

Interesting stuff, but Paul's comments here seem to indicate that it was written around 1965. "As Tears Go By" had been a hit for Faithfull in 1964, and she would cover "Yesterday," presumably in preference to "Etcetera," on a single in October 1965. (And with little success, it might be added; her recording only made it up to No. 36 in the British charts.) If so, "Etcetera" would have been about three years old by the time Paul did it in August 1968, and quite an odd number to revive at such a late date, especially if he himself didn't even like the song much in the first place. Further confusing the chronology, *Many Years from Now* reported that Paul played "Eleanor Rigby" to Faithfull and Mick Jagger after she had rejected "Etcetera." In that book, McCartney remembers how "Marianne was much more interested in 'Eleanor Rigby' but I had to say, 'No, I want that one'"—which would place the composition of "Etcetera" closer to early 1966.

It's also known that Paul, playing piano, did a demo of "The Long and Winding Road" at some time during the *White Album* sessions. According to longtime Beatles assistant Alistair Taylor (as quoted in Steve Matteo's *Let It Be* book), "Late one Friday night we were all packing up at Abbey Road and I was looking for Paul to say goodnight. I eventually found him in Studio One picking out a melody and adding some lyrics. 'That was fantastic,' I said. 'Lesley (my wife) would love that.' He said it was just an idea and then he motioned to the control room for them to run the tape. He ran through the song and then we said our farewells. Monday afternoon and Paul walks into my office. He hands an acetate record to me. 'Present for Lesley,' he said. It was the recording from Friday. He then took the tape from his pocket and cut it into pieces before lobbing them into the waste bin. 'Now you've got the only recording,' he said. 'What's it called?' I asked. 'The Long and Winding Road,' he said." Even if it's survived, the acetate might never circulate, Taylor having died in June 2004.

Other than that, some of the more interesting unbooted items noted in *The Beatles Recording Sessions* include earlier versions of "Rocky Raccoon" with more improvised lyrics that didn't survive into the final take. While no *White Album*–era outtakes of "Her Majesty" have been

The BEATLES
The 1968 Demos
1

This collection of demos featured another takeoff on The White Album*'s design.*

found in official logs, Radio Luxembourg DJ Tony Macarthur said that Paul played him a tape of the song when he interviewed McCartney for a program on November 20, 1968. Plus some tapes were specifically compiled of some of the more amusing ad-libs that took place during the *White Album* sessions, a few of which have made it into circulation, such as Paul McCartney's medley of "Lady Madonna" and "While My Guitar Gently Weeps" (see September 5 entry).

Finally, Beatles engineer Geoff Emerick's memoir, *Here, There and Everywhere: My Life Recording the Music of the Beatles* (co-written with Howard Massey), mentions that John made a demo of "Good Night" for Ringo that was played back a couple of times in the studio. "It's a shame that this particular tape has been lost to the world, and that nobody will ever hear the gorgeous way John sang his tender little song," wrote Emerick. "In comparison, I really don't think Ringo did the song justice."

THE BEATLES SOUNDCHECK

1969

One of innumerable compilations of material from the Get Back/Let It Be sessions and rehearsals recorded by the Beatles during January 1969. Some of these used images of the group that weren't even from 1969, such as the LP pictured here, which shows the band at a mid-1968 photo session.

Get Back to Abbey Road

The Year in Review

While 1969 is often portrayed in Beatles histories as a bitter, sour year in which the group began to crumble, it's important to remember that to the vast majority of the world, it didn't appear that way at all. In many important respects, it was a year full of the typical Beatles triumphs everyone had come to expect of the band since 1963, with huge, classic hit singles and albums exhibiting their usual genius for reinventing themselves and plowing new artistic ground. Well, a huge classic *album* in *Abbey Road*, at any rate. Part of the problem eating away at the band's core was that, although the group *had* recorded two albums, only *one* came out. The greater public, however, remained unaware of that impossibly complicated imbroglio. Instead, it reveled in the *Abbey Road* LP and three great hit singles, as well as George Harrison's belated emergence as a songwriter on par with John Lennon and Paul McCartney on *Abbey Road*'s two most popular tracks, "Something" and "Here Comes the Sun." As media personalities and cultural icons of the world's youth movement, the group continued to fascinate and inspire as well, their hold on the collective unconscious of the counterculture morbidly mirrored by the unchecked spread of the "Paul Is Dead" rumor across the globe. Increasingly, however, they were undergoing their personal growth as individuals rather than as a team,

via John and Yoko's marriage and peace activism, Paul's marriage to Linda Eastman, Ringo's bid for movie stardom in *The Magic Christian*, and George's low-key return to the concert stage at the end of the year as part of Delaney & Bonnie's band. And for all the fine records that Apple was releasing by the Beatles and others, the financial and organizational chaos it had fallen into directly resulted in a three-against-one split as to who should sort it out—a split that, in combination with other factors, would help lead to the very destruction of the group.

For perhaps the only time in the Beatles' career (with the possible exception of their failed 1962 Decca audition), unreleased music was at the front and center of the band's collective concerns and troubles. For in January 1969, the group recorded (and, often, filmed) an unimaginably immense quantity of rehearsals and sessions, as well as an actual, live performance. Virtually all of them would eventually be bootlegged; some of them, actually, would comprise the very first documented Beatles bootlegs within a year. Inadvertently, these act as an interminable yet oft-fascinating document of what might have been their tensest month—and as a document of most of the primal forces that were tearing the band apart. Aside from capturing, in dialogue and song, heated musical and personal disagreements between the band members themselves, confusion over the very purpose of these sessions was the source of much of the conflict. Were they being done for an album? For a TV show? As rehearsals for a live performance? For the cameras, for the audiotape, or for both? Or for some, all, or none of the above? No one could quite figure it out, let alone agree. Inevitably, much of the music was dispirited and disorganized—though the best of it was as good as any Beatles music. In the end, with the group unable to make up their minds what to do with it, most of it would remain in the can for the time being. And when it was excavated for an LP release more than a year later, fights over how and when to mix and package it would drive the final nail into the Beatles' coffin.

These are the infamous *Get Back/Let It Be* sessions, a body of work so gargantuan that even obsessed Beatles collectors often haven't made total heads or tails of it. From these recordings alone, 1969 would be a milestone year for unreleased Beatles music, at least in terms of significance to the group's history. Soundly derided by most critics, the sessions nonetheless contain some good performances, and even when the band's not playing well (which is often, unfortunately), insights into their musical influences and creative process abound—and not just in the context of explaining some of the forces behind their breakup. The rest of the year couldn't hope to yield unissued material of the same magnitude, at least in terms of sheer quantity and psychodrama. Yet there were some very interesting, and at times very good, *Abbey Road* outtakes and alternates, as well as some cool home recordings and other miscellany. Such a high percentage of those non-studio recordings, however, were done by John (often with Yoko) without the others, that even these serve as a reflection of the band's impending separation. As does the absence of any unreleased group recordings after August 1969—the last month, as it happened, that the group recorded as a foursome, or were even photographed together.

● January

The *Get Back/Let It Be* Sessions: An Overview

As the song listing alone for the very first entry (January 2) of this chapter reveals, the Beatles' January 1969 sessions would be like no others in their career, released or otherwise, whether in the studio or some other environment/context. So confusing is this juncture of the Beatles' evolution that it's necessary to detour for a long preamble to explain what exactly they were up to this month, and how, in even a rough sense, to *make* sense of the hundred-plus hours of music that has made it into circulation—most of it still unreleased.

Very broadly speaking, these sessions resulted from a notion the Beatles were now entertaining: a return to the live concert stage. The rough idea was to give just one show, or just a few, under circumstances in which the Beatles were most comfortable. The idea would have been to arrange the event so the group would enjoy it as much as possible, and so that the music and performance could be truly heard and appreciated. This would have been a big step forward from the Beatlemania days, in which the group trotted maniacally all over the globe under tremendous pressure, unable to even hear themselves well, playing for audiences who couldn't (or didn't want to) hear the music well either.

These were the days of Apple's overambitious multimedia projects, and this commendable brainstorm got complicated by a plan

to use it as a springboard for a record and television show as well. If everything had been pulled off smoothly somehow, the Beatles would have rehearsed for a live concert—highly advisable preparation, considering they hadn't played live, sans backing tracks of any sorts, before an audience in more than two years. The concert would be filmed for a television special, which in turn would incorporate footage of the rehearsals for the show. The concert, perhaps including some other material from rehearsals and other sources, could in turn spawn their next album. As the most unusual and perhaps most challenging aspect of the whole project, the rehearsals and concert would concentrate on new material, intentionally recorded (with that upcoming album release in mind) "live," in utter contrast to the way the Beatles had grown to rely upon painstakingly layered overdubs and studio trickery over the preceding few years.

With the exception of the *Magical Mystery Tour* film, the Beatles had become used to matter-of-factly pulling off artistic feats of this sort that most mortals would dismiss as impossible. The group as a whole was becoming more mortal by the time 1969 dawned, however, and almost immediately the whole enterprise began to go awry. No one could agree on where and how to hold the concert; that idea, at least insofar as making it a conventional concert in front of an audience in a large venue, was scrapped. The rehearsals continued to drag on interminably, the group (and indeed the camera crew filming the rehearsals) becoming increasingly uncertain of whether they were going through these motions for the sake of a TV show, preparation for an official album, or both. Worst of all, arguments among the group, musical and personal, resulted in George Harrison quitting the band for a few days before matters were just about patched up.

At the end, compromises were reached that likely didn't excite anyone too much. There would be no live concert. The band would record some of the new material they'd been working on in a real recording studio, hoping to get an album out of it. Cameras would continue to film them, hoping to get some kind of television program out of *that*. There *was*, thankfully, an impromptu live concert on the rooftop of their Apple headquarters on January 30, 1969, that provided the show the filmmakers were hoping for, even if only a few people could see and hear the band. There was enough material for an album, too, but the Beatles weren't sure how to mix it or when, or even whether, to release it. Indecision over the matter dragged on for more than a year, though two of the strongest tracks *did* become their next single, and another of the highlights would become the last single they released before they split up.

As long an explanation as that is, that's the short version. At least three books have been written about this short but volatile era of the Beatles, focusing on the recording of those January 1969 sessions. And, in large part because so much of those rehearsals and studio sessions were being filmed—and, thus, recorded on state-of-the-art movie sound equipment—there were simply tons of unreleased tapes being generated. Perhaps because they were not subject to even the nominal security of the EMI vaults, tons of these were bootlegged, in very good sound—hours upon hours, from all 20 days of the month in which the Beatles were filmed.

As the old cliché goes, that's enough stuff to generate a book of its own—and it *did*, with Doug Sulpy and Ray Schweighardt's 332-page *Get Back: The Unauthorized Chronicle of the Beatles' Let It Be Disaster.* So detailed is that play-by-play rundown of the audio documents of the sessions, in fact, that this author has opted not to give as detailed a track-by-track analysis for this month of recordings as there is in the rest of *The Unreleased Beatles: Music and Film*. That alone would, like a track-by-track analysis of Beatles official mix variations, expand this volume to an unpublishable size. Instead, the most unusual/interesting/illuminating moments will be highlighted, with general discussions of the progress (or lack thereof) made on each day as the group attempted to get their act together. Sulpy and Schweighardt's book is recommended for further examination if you want to go that route (though quite a few additional tapes that the volume does not cover surfaced after its 1997 publication).

Even after the *Get Back* sessions have been examined in some depth in mainstream biographies and documentaries, there still exists a great deal of confusion as to what they constitute, and what's found on the many bootlegs they spawned. Here, then, is a checklist of sorts to clear up many misconceptions about this material, before we dive into the deep end.

To start with the most elementary mix-up: novice Beatles collectors, and even some veteran Beatles listeners, are still baffled by the appearance of so much material in these early 1969 tapes that ended up on the spring 1970 album release *Let It Be*. If you know nothing else about the whole *Get Back* mess, you should know this: it was recorded *before Abbey Road*, though most of what was eventually released came out *after Abbey Road*. Although *Let It Be* was the last Beatles album to be *released*, it was, with the exception of just a little 1970 recording and overdubbing, *not* the last Beatles album to be *recorded*—*Abbey Road* was. The main body of the *Let It Be* album lay in the can for more than a year, with *Abbey Road* both recorded and released long before the *Let It Be* LP was finally issued.

That ties directly into the next logical question: why are the January 1969 recordings commonly referred to as the *Get Back* sessions, not the *Let It Be* sessions? Because *Get Back* was the original title of the album, in honor of one of its strongest songs (which was indeed selected as the Beatles' next single). The full title, in fact, was supposed to be *Get Back, Don't Let Me Down, and 12 Other Songs*, in homage to the full title of their debut album (*Please Please Me with Love Me Do and 12 Other Songs*), and by extension a nod to the whole back-to-basics ethos of the project. The Beatles even took pictures in the same location and poses (though with much longer hair and more casual clothes) as they'd used for the *Please Please Me* LP cover, which ended up on the posthumous *1962-1966* and *1967-1970* compilations after the original *Get Back* LP failed to appear.

Okay, then: why are there so damned *many Get Back* recordings? Because they were being filmed so often—often in rehearsal in Twickenham Film Studios rather than a professional music recording studio, with all of the recordings from January 2–14 being made at Twickenham. (None of those, incidentally, were ever intended for record release; only one snippet of dialogue from those rehearsals was used on the *Let It Be* LP.) But if so much of this stuff was done at a film studio, why is the sound quality so good—almost as good as what you'd expect from genuine EMI outtakes? Because it was recorded with a mind to be used on the film soundtrack rather than record releases (and certainly rather than bootlegs!) on Nagra reel-to-reel, mono tape machines. This holds true even for most of the outtakes from their sessions at Apple Studios (and their January 30 rooftop concert), which were almost all sourced from the Nagra reels. While

not up to the standards of the equipment used at facilities such as Abbey Road, the sound on these is usually quite good, even if the balance and depth obviously are no match for stereo recordings done in a proper recording studio.

As a footnote, to make sure that as much of the sound was captured without interruption, two Nagra tape recorders were used, one for camera A and one for camera B. Each machine could only record for 16 minutes at a time, and having the "B" recorder running while the "A" recorder changed reels (and vice versa) ensured that nothing was lost in the changeovers. Hence a minor, but notable, source of angst and confusion for collectors of *Get Back* bootlegs, where the material is often identified as coming from "A-reels" and/or "B-reels," without much elaboration or explanation. Fortunately, one enterprising bootleg label issued an enormous *A/B Road* series combining the A-reels and B-reels so that *everything* recorded by one or another of the machines can be heard without interruption or overlap.

Finally getting to the actual contents of the tapes, be cautioned that scanning the raw song lists makes them look far more appealing than they really are. Who wouldn't get excited seeing literally hundreds of cover songs (many of them not available on any other Beatles recording, legitimate or otherwise); multiple alternate versions of many *Let It Be* and *Abbey Road* songs; a good number of original compositions that the Beatles would only release as solo artists, or would never release in any guise; and even reworkings of quite a few originals they'd already recorded, from "Love Me Do" all the way up to *The White Album*, not to mention some pre-"Love Me Do" compositions?

But it's *not* like suddenly opening the door to a bunch of unreleased Beatles albums of full, enjoyable performances, like suddenly getting all of their BBC broadcasts at once might be, roughly speaking. For a great many of these "songs" are not complete, polished performances, but brief and incomplete—usually incompletely performed, not incompletely recorded—versions that raggedly sputter out after a minute or two, or fail to even really get started, "lasting" for less than ten seconds. Some of them are shapeless jams and improvisations (often following a stock blues progression) that, even when they have vocals, are so disorganized that it's impossible to even give the songs titles. Most of the never-recorded "originals" are in fact just ideas or off-the-cuff doodlings, not proper full compositions. On both the originals and the covers (even some the Beatles had previously released), the band often forgets the words or even how the song goes. Between the music is plenty of dead air and dialogue that's often so faint as to be nearly inaudible. The tapes themselves are frequently interrupted by electronic beeps and announcements generated by the film crew. The frequent wah-wah effects and use of guitar fed through a Leslie speaker (giving the instrument an organ-like tone), while interesting in and of themselves, become tiresome when not placed in a long-playing album context, where the Beatles had always been sure to vary their textures with great eclecticism. And many of the relatively together performances are seemingly endless run-throughs of the same songs with similar arrangements, sometimes not so much perfected as wrestled to the mat.

For the uneven, and sometimes downright poor, quality of these performances, the Beatles have been pilloried far more than they deserve. It must be remembered that these *were* rehearsals, in large part. Many if not most bands would sound subpar if recorded incessantly in these conditions. That's the very nature of rehearsals and working up new material, with false starts, half-assed jamming on half-remembered oldies to fill up the time and get comfortable, laborious ironing out of troublesome passages, and, yes, some arguments from time to time. Undoubtedly the conditions at Twickenham—where the Beatles were rehearsing in a physically cold, large, and austere location, in daytime hours far earlier than the night-owl shifts they'd become accustomed to booking at EMI—didn't help.

In a sense, however, the Beatles brought it on themselves by arranging (and paying) for the cameras to be running for hours on end in the first place. Even in early 1969, when rock bootlegs were unknown, they were taking the risk of recording all the warts for posterity if the reels leaked out, as they eventually did. One can't help being reminded of Richard Nixon's own custom of taping so much of what should have been under-wraps conversations, sealing his eventual doom when the tapes were unearthed during the Watergate scandal. There, of course, an entire presidency was being brought down, while here it was just a band's almost unknowing breakup that was being documented—though many would argue that the end of the Beatles was a far more momentous occasion than the downfall of any presidency.

Still, the eventual mountain of bootlegs that resulted from the sessions was criticized, with some justification, as over-documentation. In *All Together Now: The First Complete Beatles Discography 1961–1975*, for example, Harry Castleman and Walter J. Podrazik argued that it "could be considered the philosophy of bootlegging taken to its extreme. We are able to follow almost every step in the process of artistic creation. But in the end, it defeats the main purpose of recorded music by putting working versions on the same par as finished products. It's as if you were to read all an author's rough notes before you read the finished novel." Even many specialist collectors would agree with this to varying degrees. Bootleggers have recognized this, designing some sets—whether one or two discs, or 16—that selectively zero in on some of the more palatable, complete musical performances to make the product more listenable, sometimes infinitely more so. And there *were* some good alternate versions of *Let It Be* songs recorded, particularly after they moved from Twickenham to Apple Studios and got down to more serious musical business, with the recruitment of Billy Preston as session keyboardist doing a great deal to both bolster the arrangements and lighten the atmosphere.

All that said, if you do have the stamina to trudge through most or all of the circulating *Get Back* sessions, they're rarely anything less than fascinating from a purely historical point of view. Among the most important aspects they illustrate of the band at this stage of their career, other than the oft-noted mounting differences and tensions that were threatening to break them up, were:

• The emergence of George Harrison as a more prolific songwriter than he'd been at any time in the past. Only two of the songs he was working on at this point ("I Me Mine" and "For You Blue") found a place on the *Let It Be* LP, but he was also presenting some material that would find a belated home on his debut *All Things Must Pass* album in 1970, as well as an early version of "Something." Sadly, this development was greeted by some indifference on the part of the two primary Beatles songwriters, who didn't seem to take George's contributions as seriously as their own, sometimes to the point of talking or even playing entirely different songs while Harrison was presenting the tunes to them for consideration. Paul McCartney gets more of the blame for this subjugation than John Lennon, probably

due to the famous scene in the *Let It Be* film where Paul and George argue about how to do a guitar part. Analysis of the tapes, however, proves that Lennon was at least as indifferent to Harrison's newly minted tunes—quite possibly more so, in fact, than the more diplomatic McCartney, who often made at least token efforts to work on George's material.

• The collaborative creative process of the group, still at work in some fashion, even if it was a bit like smoldering ashes rather than a full-on blaze at this point. Though John and Paul are now usually considered to have been working virtually separately by 1969, in fact they were helping each other out in polishing each other's songs. Paul, again, has borne the brunt of criticism for his bossiness. But on the evidence here it seems that he more than John was the one who got things moving in this regard, somewhat in the manner of an on-floor studio producer.

• The seeds of *Abbey Road*, an album usually thought of as being an entirely different, entirely subsequently conceived project. In fact, however, no fewer than 12 of the 17 songs on *Abbey Road* were played in some form on the tapes that have been heard. This in turn defeats another misconception about the *Get Back/Let It Be* project: that it represented a low point in the Beatles' songwriting, particularly John Lennon's. The problem was not so much the songwriting, however, as the way in which the songs were being selected, shaped, and arranged—something they did much better for *Abbey Road,* even though much of the raw material was already in development here.

• The seeds of the Beatles' solo careers, not just in how they were growing apart from each other creatively, but in numerous songs. As noted above, these sessions included several songs from George's *All Things Must Pass*—itself a warning sign, as it became more apparent that there was not enough room for Harrison's quality songs on Beatles albums unless John and Paul were prepared to give their junior partner more leeway. But there were also a number of compositions that eventually found their way onto John and Paul's early solo albums, at this point being presumably at least considered for full-on Beatles group arrangements.

• And, most of all: the simply vast scope of material performed by the group in what was, for all the hours and hours of tape, still a fairly small window of time. In addition to the original songs they were whipping up, the band covered, though often haphazardly, a simply amazing catalog of oldies, from the expected Chuck Berry and Buddy Holly numbers to wholly unexpected items from the likes of Guy Mitchell, George Formby, Bob Dylan, the Band, the Beach Boys, Randy Newman, and even old Quarrymen-era Lennon-McCartney originals. It's as close as we'll get to a trawl through the Beatles' musical subconscious, though, like many a psychiatric patient, they probably wished it weren't out there for all the world to pick apart.

Along the way, a lot of dialogue was also captured for the permanent record. While some of it's quite revealing, it's not only often hard to hear, but also sometimes not that interesting or easy to follow, the group often being incommunicative or talking in the kind of shorthand code that evolves among people who've known each other extremely well for many years. It might be better digested as a lengthy transcript than via audiotape. Some of the dialogue was indeed reprinted in the book that originally accompanied the initial UK edition of the *Let It Be* album, and in the *Let It Be . . . Naked* rejigging of the

stereo

Apple
EMI ELECTROLA

THE BEATLES

GET
BACK

with Let It Be
and 11 other songs

Though a bootleg, this LP accurately approximates what the Get
Back *LP would have looked like and how it would have sounded
had it been released in the spring of 1969 as originally planned.*

Let It Be material in 2003. But it's doubtful that the full blow-by-blow exchanges will see print, such is their length and frequent rambling disconnectedness. Fortunately, much of it's summarized in *Get Back: The Unauthorized Chronicle of the Beatles' Let It Be Disaster,* shedding some though not total light upon the influence of Yoko's presence upon the group dynamic, the wide disparity of the individual Beatles' enthusiasms and preferences for live concerts, and, of particular interest, the fact that George was actually having more problems communicating with John than he was with Paul. The cameras couldn't have caught everything that was being said, however, and were sometimes in fact told to stop running at times when the discussions became especially fraught and personal.

The Beatles also perhaps got more than they bargained for when they came to the realization, after the month was finally over, that someone had to go through the hundreds of hours of tape and film and make some sort of presentable album out of it (with a possible accompanying movie or TV special). The long, dragged-out process of dealing with that is another story in itself. But the group, like most partnerships in the process of dissolving, couldn't really see what was happening to themselves until the smoke had cleared. For the time being, they muddled along day by day, with the *Get Back* tapes eventually providing a sort of audio diary of a point in their lives that the participants probably never would fully comprehend, such was its tangle of uncertain goals.

As a final note, there is no uniform agreement on the dates and sequences in which this material was recorded. However, the numbering system devised by Doug Sulpy's books to sequence and date the immense number of *Get Back* performances is now considered standard among serious Beatles scholars, so much so that it's replicated on bootleg track listings. As Sulpy has studied the issue more than anyone, his system served as the reference for the entries below, although there are differences between some of Sulpy's dates and the ones listed on *Get Back* outtakes used on *Anthology 3.*

● January 2

Rehearsal Tapes
Let It Be *sessions*
Twickenham Film Studios, London

Don't Let Me Down (15 versions)
All Things Must Pass (two versions)
I Dig a Pony
Let It Down (two versions)
Brown-Eyed Handsome Man
A Case of the Blues
I'm Just a Child of Nature
Revolution
I Shall Be Released
Sun King (five versions)
Mailman, Bring Me No More Blues
Speak to Me
I've Got a Feeling (20 versions)
The Mighty Quinn (Quinn the Eskimo)
Well . . . Alright (two versions)
Two of Us (nine versions)

Other songs, titles uncertain:
Everybody Got Song
The Teacher Was a-Lookin'
We're Goin' Home
It's Good to See the Folks Back Home

Miscellaneous:
Instrumental improvisations/jams (four)
Vocal numbers, titles impossible to even guess (three)

The *Get Back* sessions got off to a relatively low-key start on January 2, tensions running lower than they would in just a few days. Perhaps that's because at this point, these really were rehearsals for an upcoming show, not serious recordings. That didn't mean, however, that there wasn't much scrubbing out of the kinks to be done, which would take its toll soon enough as Paul McCartney in particular became more exacting and fussy as to what the songs should sound like.

Most of the work on this date went into three songs that would indeed be performed in complete versions in the *Let It Be* film: "Don't Let Me Down," "I've Got a Feeling," and "Two of Us." All of these are pretty close to their final form, yet quite a bit more raggedly arranged and performed at this point. "Don't Let Me Down" in particular is kind of scrambled: as John Lennon sings it in its first run-throughs, most of the parts are present, but there's little shape to how they're assembled. In particular, at a few intervals John tacks on a line with a slightly more complex yet less gritty, more drifting melody that doesn't resolve satisfactorily. Eventually he enlists Paul's help in ordering the verses and choruses, Paul also decisively advising his partner to discard that recurring sweet, brief, detouring bit. It's an example of how even at this relatively late date—when John and Paul were often assumed to be writing totally separately—they did still help each other out, if more on a structural level than via full-on collaboration on the actual content.

The group made quicker progress on "I've Got a Feeling," one of the last genuine Lennon-McCartney contributions inasmuch as it joins distinctly different components from each composer. Most of the song is Paul's, but John takes the tune he'd worked up on his late-1968 home recording "Everybody Had a Hard Year" and slides it into a variant verse near the end. On John's very first pass at the tune, before Paul's arrived at the rehearsal, he sings and plays—perhaps for the very last time—a minute or so of the song (with haphazard second guitar from George) in its more wistful early "Everybody Had a Hard Year" form. He also sings a bit of the Paul-dominated part of the tune, however, indicating that the pair had already worked on combining the fragments into a whole.

Paul's already worked out "Two of Us," but the very first pass is interesting as he takes the vocal all by himself, without any harmonies from John. Clearly the rest of the band hasn't heard the tune much or at all, as at this point Paul's still calling out the chords to guide them at points—something that he in particular would do at various other learn-as-we-go rehearsals over the next few weeks. John joins in on the very next available performance, however, and Paul toys with the idea of speeding up the rhythm drastically for the second bridge, though it's clearly awkward and the notion's soon dropped. The song really doesn't sound all that different from its final incarnation, though it's perhaps a little less folky and funkier here, with references to boxer Henry Cooper

Songs Performed by the Beatles on Tapes Circulating from the *Get Back* Sessions

To be used eventually, in some form, on the *Let It Be* album:

"Two of Us"
"I Dig a Pony"
"Across the Universe"
"I Me Mine"
"Dig It"
"Let It Be"
"Maggie Mae"
"I've Got a Feeling"
"One After 909"
"The Long and Winding Road"
"For You Blue"
"Get Back"

Early versions of songs to be included on *Abbey Road*:

"Something"
"Maxwell's Silver Hammer"
"Oh! Darling"
"Octopus's Garden"
"I Want You (She's So Heavy)"
"Sun King"
"Mean Mr. Mustard"
"Polythene Pam"
"She Came In through the Bathroom Window"
"Golden Slumbers"
"Carry That Weight"
"Her Majesty"

Versions of songs to be used on 1969–1970 Beatles non-LP B-sides:

"Don't Let Me Down"
"Old Brown Shoe"
"You Know My Name (Look Up the Number)"

Early version of songs later used on John Lennon solo releases:

"Give Me Some Truth" (on *Imagine*)

Early versions of songs later used on Paul McCartney solo releases:

"Another Day" (on 1971 single)
"The Back Seat of My Car" (on *Ram*)
"Every Night" (on *McCartney*)

"Hot as Sun" (on *McCartney*)
"Junk" (on *McCartney*)
"Teddy Boy" (on *McCartney*; previously unreleased Beatles version from January 1969 issued on *Anthology 3*)

Early versions of songs later used on George Harrison solo albums:

"All Things Must Pass" (on *All Things Must Pass*)
"Hear Me Lord" (on *All Things Must Pass*)
"Isn't It a Pity" (on *All Things Must Pass*)
"Let It Down" (on *All Things Must Pass*)

Versions of original songs that had already been used on Beatles recordings:

"All Together Now" (*Yellow Submarine*)
"Back in the U.S.S.R." (*The White Album*)
"Dear Prudence" (*The White Album*)
"Every Little Thing" (*Beatles for Sale*)
"From Me to You" (1963 single A-side)
"Hello Goodbye" (1967 single A-side)
"Help!" (*Help!*)
"Hey Jude" (1968 single A-side)
"I'll Get You" (1963 single B-side)
"I'm So Tired" (*The White Album*)
"The Inner Light" (1968 single B-side)
"Lady Madonna" (1968 single A-side)
"Lovely Rita" (*Sgt. Pepper's Lonely Hearts Club Band*)
"Martha My Dear" (*The White Album*)
"Norwegian Wood (This Bird Has Flown)" (*Rubber Soul*)
"Ob-La-Di, Ob-La-Da" (*The White Album*)
"Please Please Me" (*Please Please Me*)
"Revolution" (1968 single B-side)
"Run for Your Life" (*Rubber Soul*)
"She Said, She Said" (*Revolver*)
"She's a Woman" (1964 single B-side)
"Strawberry Fields Forever" (1967 single, half of double A-side)
"When I'm Sixty-Four" (*Sgt. Pepper's Lonely Hearts Club Band*)
"You Can't Do That" (*A Hard Day's Night*)

Original songs never used on official Beatles group or solo albums, with probable principal/sole composers noted:
(titles taken from those assigned to the recordings in *Get Back: The Unauthorized Chronicle of the Beatles' Let It Be Disaster* and other Doug Sulpy books)

"All I Want Is You" (a different song than "I Dig a Pony") (John)
"Also" (Paul)

"Annie" (John)

"As Clear as a Bell" (Paul)

"Because I Know You Love Me So" (John and Paul)

"Blossom Dearie They Call Me" (John)

"Boogie Woogie" (John)

"Bring Your Own Band" (Paul)

"A Case of the Blues" (John)

"Catswalk" (Paul; the same song covered in 1967 by Chris Barber)

"Commonwealth" (John and Paul)

"Crazy Feet" (Paul)

"Cuddle Up" (Paul)

"The Day I Went Back to School" (Paul)

"Do the Bunny Hop" (John)

"Don't Start Running" (John)

"Enoch Powell" (Paul)

"Everybody Got Song" (John)

"Fast Train to San Francisco" (group jam)

"Get Off" (John and Paul)

"Get on the Phone" (John and Paul)

"Get Your Rocks Off" (George)

"Greasepaint on Your Face" (Paul)

"Hey, Hey Georgie" (George)

"How Do You Tell Someone?" (George)

"I Fancy Me Chances" (John and Paul)

"I Left My Home in the World" (Paul)

"I Lost My Little Girl" (John and Paul)

"I Told You Before" (group jam)

"I Will Always Look for You" (Paul)

"If You Need Me" (Paul)

"I'll Wait Till Tomorrow" (John and Paul)

"I'm Going to Knock Him Down Dead" (John)

"I'm Gonna Pay for His Ride" (Paul)

"I'm Just a Child of Nature" (John; later reworked into "Jealous Guy," for John's *Imagine* album)

"Is It Discovered" (George)

"Is That a Chicken Joke?" (group jam)

"It Blew Again" (John)

"It Was So Blue" (Paul)

"It's Good to See the Folks Back Home" (Paul)

"Jazz Piano Song" (Paul and Ringo)

"Just Fun" (John and Paul)

"Life Is What You Make It" (group jam)

"Little Piece of Leather" (John)

"Lowdown Blues Machine" (Paul)

"Madman" (John)

"Mr. Epstein Said It Was White Gold" (Paul)

"My Imagination" (Paul)

"My Rock and Roll Finger Is Bleeding" (John)

"My Words Are in My Heart" (Paul)

"Negro in Reserve" (John and Paul)

"Oh Baby I Love You" (Paul)

"Oh How I Love the 12-Bar Blues" (John)

"Oh Julie, Julia" (Paul)

"On a Sunny Island" (John and Paul)

"Over and Over Again" (Paul)

"The Palace of the King of the Birds" (Paul)

"Penina" (Paul; the same song covered in 1969 by Carlos Mendes)

"Picasso" (Ringo)

"Pillow for Your Head" (Paul)

"Quit Your Messing Around" (John)

"Ramblin' Woman" (George)

"The River Rhine" (Paul)

"Rocker" (group jam)

"San Ferry Ann" (Paul)

"Shakin' in the Sixties" (John)

"She Gets Heavy" (John)

"Song of Love" (Paul)

"Sorry I Left You Bleeding" (John)

"Sorry Miss Molly" (Paul)

"Step Inside Love" (Paul; the same song covered for a 1968 hit single by Cilla Black)

"Suicide" (Paul)

"Suzy's Parlour" (John)

"Taking a Trip to Carolina" (Ringo)

"Tales of Frankie Rabbit" (John and Paul)

"Talking Blues" (Paul)

"The Teacher Was a-Lookin'" (group jam)

"Tell All the Folks Back Home" (Paul)

"There You Are, Eddie" (Paul)

"They Call Me Fuzz Face" (Paul)

"Thinking of Linking" (John and Paul)

"Through a London Window" (Paul)

"Too Bad about Sorrows" (John and Paul)

"Torchy, the Battery Boy" (Paul)

"Watching Rainbows" (John)

"Water, Water" (Paul)

"Well, If You're Ready" (Paul)

"Well It's Eight O'Clock" (John)

"Well, Well, Well" (Paul; not the same as the song on John's *Plastic Ono Band*)

"We're Goin' Home" (group jam)

"William Smith Boogie" (group jam)

"Window, Window" (George)

"Woman" (Paul; the same song covered for a 1966 hit single by Peter & Gordon)

"Woman Where You Been So Long" (group jam)

"Won't You Please Say Goodbye" (John and Paul)

"You Are Definitely Inclined Towards It" (John)

"You Got Me Going" (Paul)

"You Gotta Give Back" (group jam)

"You Wear Your Women Out" (Paul)

"You Won't Get Me That Way" (Paul)

"Your Name Is Ted" (group jam)

Covers performed on past official Beatles releases:

"Act Naturally" (*Help!*)

"Bad Boy" (US 1965 LP *Beatles VI*)

"Devil in Her Heart" (*With the Beatles*)

"Dizzy Miss Lizzie" (*Help!*)

"Money (That's What I Want)" (*With the Beatles*)

"A Taste of Honey" (*Please Please Me*)

"Till There Was You" (*With the Beatles*)

"Twist and Shout" (*Please Please Me*)

Covers performed by the Beatles on the BBC, studio outtakes, or non-official live recordings:

"Besame Mucho"

"Carol"

"The Hippy Hippy Shake"

"I Got to Find My Baby"

"I'm Talking About You"

"Johnny B. Goode"

"Lucille"

"A Shot of Rhythm and Blues"

"Shout"

"Soldier of Love"

"Some Other Guy"

"Sure to Fall (In Love with You)"

"Sweet Little Sixteen"

"That'll Be the Day"

"That's All Right (Mama)"

"Three Cool Cats"

"Where Have You Been"

"Words of Love"

"You Really Got a Hold on Me"

Covers never heard on official Beatles albums, BBC Beatles sessions, or other Beatles recordings, with sources/original versions noted:

"Ach Du Lieber Augustin" (traditional German folk song)

"Adagio for Strings" (Samuel Barber orchestral composition)

"Agent Double-O-Soul" (Edwin Starr)

"All Along the Watchtower" (Bob Dylan)

"All Shook Up" (Elvis Presley)

"Almost Grown" (Chuck Berry)

"Around and Around" (Chuck Berry)

"Baa, Baa, Black Sheep" (traditional children's song)

"Baby, Come Back" (the Equals)

"Baby, Let's Play House" (Elvis Presley)

"The Ballad of Bonnie and Clyde" (Georgie Fame)

"Balls to Your Partner" (a "traditional Liverpool drinking rhyme," according to
   Get Back: The Unauthorized Chronicle of the Beatles' Let It Be Disaster)

"Bear Cat Mama" (Jimmie Davis)

"Be-Bop-A-Lula" (Gene Vincent)

"Black Dog Blues" (Blind Blake; probably learned from Koerner, Ray &
   Glover's cover on the 1964 album *Lots More Blues, Rags, & Hollers*)

"Blowin' in the Wind" (Bob Dylan)

"Blue Suede Shoes" (Carl Perkins)

"Blue Yodel No. 1 (T for Texas)" (Jimmie Rodgers)

"Bo Diddley" (Bo Diddley)

"Bring It On Home to Me" (Sam Cooke)

"Brown-Eyed Handsome Man" (Chuck Berry)

"Build Me Up, Buttercup" (the Foundations)

"Bye Bye Love" (the Everly Brothers)

"Cannonball" (Duane Eddy)

"Catch a Falling Star" (Perry Como)

"Cathy's Clown" (the Everly Brothers)

"Chopsticks" (Euphemia Allen piano composition)

"C'mon Everybody" (Eddie Cochran)

"C'mon Marianne" (the Four Seasons)

"Cocaine Blues" (Johnny Cash)

"Crackin' Up" (Bo Diddley)

"Crying, Waiting, Hoping" (Buddy Holly)

"Danny Boy" (traditional folk song)

"Daydream" (the Lovin' Spoonful)

" 'Deed I Do" (1920s pop tune)

"Diggin' My Potatoes" (Lonnie Donegan)

"Do Not Forsake Me Oh My Darling" (Tex Ritter)

"Domino" (1950s French pop tune, possibly learned from covers
   by Doris Day and/or Andy Williams)

"Don't Be Cruel" (Elvis Presley)

"Don't Let the Sun Catch You Crying" (Ray Charles)

"Early in the Morning" (Buddy Holly)

"F.B.I." (the Shadows)

"Five Feet High and Rising" (Johnny Cash)

"First Call" (traditional horse race bugle call)

"Flushed from the Bathroom of Your Heart" (Johnny Cash)

"The Fool" (Sanford Clark)

"Fools Like Me" (Jerry Lee Lewis)

"Forty Days" (Ronnie Hawkins)

"Frère Jacques" (traditional children's song)

"Friendship" (Cole Porter)

"Gilly Gilly Ossenfeffer Katzenellen Bogen by the Sea"
   (the Four Lads)

"Going Up the Country" (Canned Heat)

"Gone, Gone, Gone" (Carl Perkins)

"Good Rockin' Tonight" (Elvis Presley)

"Great Balls of Fire" (Jerry Lee Lewis)

"Green Onions" (Booker T. & the MG's)

"Hallelujah, I Love Her So" (Eddie Cochran)

"Happiness Runs" (Donovan)

"Hare Krishna Mantra" (Hindu chant)

"Hava Nagilah" (traditional Jewish song)

"Hello, Dolly!" (Louis Armstrong—though a camp version *was* done by
   the Beatles during the sessions for their 1964 Christmas disc)

"Hello Mudduh, Hello Fadduh! (A Letter from Camp)"
   (Allan Sherman)

"Hey Good Lookin'" (Hank Williams)

"Hey Liley, Liley Lo" (the Vipers Skiffle Group)

"Hey Little Girl (In the High School Sweater)" (Dee Clark)

"Hi Heel Sneakers" (Tommy Tucker)

"High School Confidential" (Jerry Lee Lewis)

"Hitch Hike" (Marvin Gaye)

"Honey Hush" (the Johnny Burnette Trio)

"Honky Tonk" (Bill Doggett)

"House of the Rising Sun" (the Animals)

"How Do You Think I Feel" (Elvis Presley)

"(I Can't Get No) Satisfaction" (the Rolling Stones)

"I Got Stung" (Elvis Presley)

"I Shall Be Released" (Bob Dylan/the Band)

"I Threw It All Away" (Bob Dylan)

"I Walk the Line" (Johnny Cash)

"I Want You" (Bob Dylan)

"I'm a Man" (Bo Diddley)

"I'm a Tiger" (Lulu)

"I'm Beginning to See the Light" (Duke Ellington)

"I'm Movin' On" (Ray Charles)

"I'm Ready" (Fats Domino)

"In the Middle of an Island" (Tony Bennett)

"It Ain't Me Babe" (Bob Dylan)

"It's Only Make Believe" (Conway Twitty)

"I've Been Good to You" (the Miracles)

"Jenny, Jenny" (Little Richard)

"Kansas City" (Wilbert Harrison; this is a different variation of
   "Kansas City/ Hey! Hey! Hey! Hey!" originally performed by
   Little Richard, which the Beatles covered on *Beatles for Sale*)

"Knee Deep in the Blues" (Guy Mitchell/Marty Robbins)

"Lady Jane" (the Rolling Stones)

"Lawdy Miss Clawdy" (Elvis Presley)

"Leaning on a Lamp Post" (George Formby)

"Let's Dance" (Chris Montez)

"Let's Twist Again" (Chubby Checker)

"Like a Rolling Stone" (Bob Dylan)

"Little Demon" (Screamin' Jay Hawkins)

"Little Queenie" (Chuck Berry)

"Little Yellow Pills" (Jackie Lomax)

"Lonely Sea" (the Beach Boys)

"Loop De Loop" (Johnny Thunder)

"Lost John" (Lonnie Donegan)

"Lotta Lovin'" (Gene Vincent)

"Love Is a Swingin' Thing" (the Shirelles)

"Love Story" (Randy Newman)

"MacArthur Park" (Little Richard)

"Mack the Knife" (Bobby Darin)

"Mailman, Bring Me No More Blues" (Buddy Holly)

"Malagueña" (traditional Spanish song)

"Mama, You Been on My Mind" (Bob Dylan)

"Maureen" (cited by George as a Bob Dylan song, although no other
   version exists by any artist)

"Maybe Baby" (Buddy Holly)

"Maybellene" (Chuck Berry)

"Michael Row the Boat" (Lonnie Donegan)

"Midnight Special" (Lonnie Donegan)

"The Mighty Quinn (Quinn the Eskimo)" (Bob Dylan)

"Milk Cow Blues" (Eddie Cochran)

"Miss Ann" (Little Richard)

"Move It" (the Shadows)

"Mr. Bassman" (Johnny Cymbal)

"My Baby Left Me" (Elvis Presley)

"My Back Pages" (Bob Dylan)

"Nashville Cats" (the Lovin' Spoonful)

"New Orleans" (Gary U.S. Bonds)

"Not Fade Away" (Buddy Holly)

"On a Clear Day You Can See Forever" (from a mid-'60s stage musical)

"On the Road Again" (Canned Heat)

"One Way Out" (Elmore James)

"Otis Sleep On" (Arthur Conley)

"Papa's Got a Brand New Bag" (James Brown)

"Party" (Elvis Presley)

"The Peanut Vendor" (Louis Armstrong)

"Peggy Sue Got Married" (Buddy Holly)

"Piece of My Heart" (Big Brother & the Holding Company)

"Please Mrs. Henry" (Bob Dylan)

"Positively 4th Street" (Bob Dylan)

"A Pretty Girl Is Like a Melody" (Irving Berlin)

"Queen of the Hop" (Bobby Darin)

"A Quick One, While He's Away" (the Who)

"Rainy Day Women #'s 12 & 35" (Bob Dylan)

"Ramrod" (Duane Eddy)

"Right String, Wrong Yo-Yo" (Carl Perkins)

"Rip It Up" (Little Richard)

"Rock and Roll Music" (Chuck Berry)

"Rock Island Line" (Lonnie Donegan)

"Rock-A-Bye Baby" (children's lullaby)

"Rockin' Pneumonia and the Boogie Woogie Flu" (Huey "Piano" Smith)

"Rule Brittania" (traditional song)

"Sabre Dance" (Love Sculpture)

"St. Louis Blues" (W.C. Handy)

"San Francisco Bay Blues" (Jesse Fuller)

"Save the Last Dance for Me" (the Drifters)

"School Day" (Chuck Berry)

"Send Me Some Loving" (Little Richard)

"Shake, Rattle and Roll" (Bill Haley/Elvis Presley)

"Shazam" (Duane Eddy)

"Short Fat Fannie" (Larry Williams)

"Singing the Blues" (Guy Mitchell)

"Slippin' and Slidin'" (Little Richard)

"Somethin' Else" (Eddie Cochran)

"S.O.S." (Edwin Starr)

"Speak to Me" (Jackie Lomax)

"Stand By Me" (Ben E. King)

"Sticks and Stones" (Ray Charles)

"Stuck Inside of Mobile with the Memphis Blues Again" (Bob Dylan)

"Take These Chains from My Heart" (Ray Charles)

"Take This Hammer" (Lonnie Donegan)

"Tea For Two Cha-Cha" (Tommy Dorsey)

"Tennessee" (Carl Perkins)

"Theme from 'The Beatles Cartoons'"
   (theme from the Beatles' cartoons!)

"Third Man Theme" (Anton Karas)

"Thirty Days" (Chuck Berry)

"To Kingdom Come" (the Band)

"Tracks of My Tears" (the Miracles)

"True Love" (Elvis Presley)

"Turkey in the Straw" (traditional folk song)

"Twenty Flight Rock" (Eddie Cochran)

"Twelfth Street Rag" (pop standard)

"Vacation Time" (Chuck Berry)

"The Walk" (Jimmy McCracklin)

"Watch Your Step" (Bobby Parker)

"The Weight" (the Band)

"Well . . . All Right" (Buddy Holly)

"What Am I Living For" (Chuck Willis)

"What Do You Want to Make Those Eyes at Me For?"
(Emile Ford & the Checkmates)
"What the World Needs Now Is Love" (Jackie DeShannon)
"What'd I Say" (Ray Charles)
"What's the Use of Getting Sober (When You're Gonna Get
Drunk Again)" (Louis Jordan)
"When Irish Eyes Are Smiling" (pop standard)
"When the Saints Go Marching In" (traditional folk song)
"When You're Drunk You Think of Me" (thought to be traditional folk song)
"Whispering" (pop standard)
"Whole Lotta Shakin' Goin' On" (Jerry Lee Lewis)
"You Are My Sunshine" (pop standard)
"You Can't Catch Me" (Chuck Berry)
"You Win Again" (Jerry Lee Lewis)
"Your True Love" (Carl Perkins)
"You're So Good to Me" (the Beach Boys)
"(You're So Square) Baby I Don't Care" (Elvis Presley)
"You've Got Me Thinking" (Jackie Lomax)

Songs principally or solely performed by Billy Preston:

"Everything's Alright" (later recorded for Preston's 1969 album
That's the Way God Planned It)
"I Want to Thank You" (later recorded for Preston's 1969 album
That's the Way God Planned It)
"Love Is the Thing to Me"
"Together in Love"
"Unless He Has a Song"
"Use What You Got" (later recorded for Preston's 1970 album
Encouraging Words)
"You've Been Acting Strange" (later recorded for Preston's 1970
album *Encouraging Words*)

Plus:

Dozens of untitled instrumentals, jams, and scraps of
unidentifiable songs!

inserted in one version, and a scatted "choom-choom-choom" into the end of the bridge in another. But Paul would drive the band through dozens more rehearsals and recording takes to get the song as perfect as he wanted it—a trait that, while inarguably key to refining the Beatles' music, would cause more and more frayed nerves among his band mates as the month wore on.

For all the other songs played at this session, there was virtually nothing that cohered into an actual whole, which could be said of most of the songs they played in some fashion this month that did not end up on *Let It Be*. The most interesting is certainly George Harrison's two-minute version of "Let It Down" (with minimal, unaccomplished second guitar from John), as that song would never find a place on a Beatles record, though George would use it on 1970's *All Things Must Pass*. Although George's vocals are unfortunately faintly miked, it's a beautiful song, sensitively performed here and largely written to completion even at this early stage.

Also heard on this day were brief passes at another Harrisong that didn't make it onto a Beatles record, "All Things Must Pass," though there would be more coherent, lengthier attempts at routinizing the song later in the month. Both "Let It Down" and "All Things Must Pass" had a light yet brooding, introspective grace, suggesting George might have been heavily influenced at this point by the Band, having spent time with them during his trip to the US in late 1968. As a further testament to the Band and Bob Dylan's influences, George sings lead, though again too faintly miked, on the drumless version of Dylan's "I Shall Be Released" (covered on the Band's debut LP). The whole band makes a shambles of Dylan's "Mighty Quinn," however, which dissolves after about a minute.

It wasn't too apparent on this day, and it certainly doesn't seem to have yet become a point of contention, but a seed of discontent about to flower within the band is apparent in hindsight. Whether due to his reported heroin use at the time or not, John Lennon was going through a dry spell as a songwriter. He had just one truly strong, new composition to offer the band, "Don't Let Me Down"; the less impressive "I Dig a Pony" was tentatively rehearsed once on this date, too. The excavation of "I'm Just a Child of Nature," here retitled "On

the Road to Marrakesh," from the spring 1968 *White Album* demos indicates that John may have been plundering his rejects for anything suitable to offer for recording. In this brief, flimsy version, he changes the location from Rishikesh to Marrakesh, perhaps wishing to further distance himself from any reference to their time with the Maharishi. A halfhearted, barely recognizable pass at a tune he'd taped at home in late 1968, "A Case of the Blues," is also here, and John would also return this month to "Across the Universe," recorded by the band in early 1968 but still unreleased.

Harrison, by contrast, was not only writing more than he ever had, but writing more than Lennon was at this point. Yet neither "Let It Down" nor "All Things Must Pass" would make it onto a Beatles record, despite their quality. It must have been hard for George to keep sitting on such songs while John (and Paul) got to put most of their tunes on disc without much of a wait, and the problem would fester throughout the rest of the Beatles' existence.

Although a number of other titles (and "untitles," as you might call the untitled brief improvs filling up space between the familiar tunes) were recorded on January 2, they read better than they look. "Revolution" is just an eight-second riff from that classic, and "Speak to Me" is a rickety Harrison-sung cover of a song from Jackie Lomax's recent Apple debut LP (which George had produced). The versions of "Sun King" lack any vocals, merely circulating its laconic opening guitar riffs; sometimes they segue into versions of "Don't Let Me Down," revealing a similarity between the two tunes that might otherwise never be detected. The covers of Chuck Berry's "Brown-Eyed Handsome Man" and Buddy Holly's "Well . . . All Right" are brief choppy jams, and the riffs in the untitled songs are neither familiar nor memorable, though at a couple of points a progression very similar to one heard near the end of the verses of "Something" ekes out.

So went the Beatles' first day of rehearsals for *Get Back*, the circulating material totaling two and a half hours and filling up two compact discs. Yet, hard as it may be to believe, most of the days on which they played music during this month would yield twice as many hours of recordings—and sometimes even more.

● **January 3**

Rehearsal Tapes
Let It Be *sessions*
Twickenham Film Studios, London

The Long and Winding Road
Oh! Darling (two versions)
Maxwell's Silver Hammer (eleven versions)
Adagio for Strings (two versions)
Tea for Two Cha-Cha (two versions)
Chopsticks
Torchy, the Battery Boy
Whole Lotta Shakin' Goin' On
Let It Be
Taking a Trip to Carolina (two versions)
Please Mrs. Henry
Picasso
Hey Jude
All Things Must Pass (37 versions)
Don't Let Me Down (ten versions)
Crackin' Up (two versions)
All Shook Up
Your True Love
Blue Suede Shoes
Three Cool Cats
Blowin' in the Wind
Lucille
I'm So Tired
Ob-La-Di, Ob-La-Da (three versions)
Third Man Theme
Sun King (four versions)
I've Got a Feeling (six versions)
Going Up the Country
On the Road Again
One After 909 (three versions)
A Pretty Girl Is Like a Melody
Thinking of Linking
Bring It On Home to Me
Hitch Hike
You Can't Do That
The Hippy Hippy Shake
All Along the Watchtower
Short Fat Fannie
Midnight Special
Two of Us (six versions)
When You're Drunk You Think of Me
What's the Use of Getting Sober (When You're Gonna Get Drunk Again)
What Do You Want to Make Those Eyes at Me For?
Money (That's What I Want)
Give Me Some Truth
The Weight
I'm a Tiger
Back in the U.S.S.R.
Every Little Thing

Piece of My Heart (two versions)
Sabre Dance
I've Been Good to You

Other songs, title uncertain:
Ramblin' Woman
Is It Discovered
Your Name Is Ted
Get on the Phone
My Words Are in My Heart
Negro in Reserve
Because I Know You Love Me So
I'll Wait Till Tomorrow
Won't You Please Say Goodbye
Over and Over Again

Miscellaneous:
Instrumental improvisations/jams (five)
Vocal numbers, titles impossible to even guess (seven)

The rehearsals at Twickenham became more of a grind on the second day, as the foursome began to labor intensely over a few specific numbers. Along the way, they pinwheeled off a sprawl of cover versions and half-baked improvs. It must have been an exhausting undertaking for a band unaccustomed, at least by the end of the '60s, to such intensive rehearsals of so much at once. It's also an exhausting listening experience, though not without some rewards.

It took a while for John to show up this morning, and the early part of this session featured just Paul on piano, previewing his works-in-progress, "The Long and Winding Road," "Oh! Darling," "Let It Be," and "Maxwell's Silver Hammer." His more loungeish all-around-entertainer face also surfaces on renditions of the classical-flavored "Adagio for Strings" and "Tea for Two Cha-Cha"—not bad for what they are, though hardly Beatlesque. Ringo, unusually, takes the chance to run through a couple snatches of a pleasantly bland, country-ish number he'd penned himself, "Taking a Trip to Carolina." Another Starr original, the generic boogie "Picasso," is even less impressive. (As an aside, it's seldom been reported that Ringo could play piano, but obviously he could do so, if only simply, as he's heard [and, in the *Let It Be* film, seen] at the instrument occasionally during the *Get Back* sessions.) In these warm-up exercises of sorts, another highlight, if only relatively speaking, is George's acoustic amble through the light-heartedly Dylanesque "Ramblin' Woman," which bears some passing resemblance to the obscure early Dylan tune "Mama, You Been on My Mind" (which George would also perform in January).

Even after John shows up, it takes a while for the circulation to really flow, as the band messes around on a bunch of oldies. As would be the usual case throughout the month of January, these oldies are kind of simultaneously turgid and half-serious, and likely far more lethargic and sloppier than the versions the band might have done back in 1962 and 1963. The Coasters' "Three Cool Cats," for instance, is not so much a darkly comic number here as it is a lament. For what it's worth, one of the jams sandwiched in this sludgy sequence, titled "Your Name Is Ted," is one of the few fairly interesting and listenable of the many such items in the *Get Back* tapes, with a tense, spiky, bluesy chord sequence, though it apparently never developed into anything more.

Unexpectedly, the band detoured into an off-the-wall reprise of a *White Album* song, "I'm So Tired," that's one of the highlights of the whole unreleased *Get Back* vault. It's not even that tight a version, but it would be remarkable if only because Paul, not John, takes lead vocals, and proves he could have done quite a good job with it, though he isn't keeping a straight face through the whole tune (throwing in the line "Lay off the booze boy!" at one point). There's a ragged-but-right feel to the arrangement, with swelling background harmonies at one juncture, and exceptionally scratchy guitar near the end. For all its brevity, it makes one lament that the band never got the chance to fool around in this manner with familiar late-'60s tunes like this onstage. In contrast, the hyper-charge through "Ob-La-Di, Ob-La-Da" isn't nearly as satisfying.

A bit more semi-memorable semi-comedy arrives with a fairly disciplined cover of the jaunty "Third Man Theme" and one of the weirdest not-quite-songs performed by the Beatles during the whole *Get Back* project, "Negro in Reserve." Using a Bo Diddley-goes-cowboy vamp as the backdrop, it's a pretty charming piece of nonsense—"There's a hole in the heart case" and "I've got a hole in my head, and his name is Ted" may not be deathless wit, but they're funnier than most of the lines they put on their Christmas records. Then, however, it's finally time to get down to brass tacks with rehearsals of some of the songs they were obviously considering for their upcoming performance/album, starting with "Don't Let Me Down." In contrast to the previous day, the song's pretty much there structurally, and while these takes aren't nearly as disciplined as the classic single, there's an engaging, loosey-goosey quality to the performances, with McCartney in particular taking a more devil-may-care approach to some of his vocal harmonies. On the very first pass of the day, John offers an interesting variation by inserting a bit from "Happiness Is a Warm Gun," to be met with a particularly creepy falling-off-a-building solo vocalization of the chorus by Paul.

Amongst some fairly serious work on "I've Got a Feeling" (complete with a scarily screamed bridge by McCartney at one point) and "Two of Us" (which has a more pronounced, quicker galloping beat at this stage), the group offered numerous glimpses of favorite oldies and embryonic originals ranging from entertaining to tedious. For the first time on the available tapes, the group dredges up the early Lennon-McCartney original "One After 909," here done with more of a funky busk than the zippier, more familiar arrangement worked up later in the month. Perhaps it was only first launched into as a way of killing time between the serious numbers, but if so, it seems to have quickly caught on as a suitable tune to work on for inclusion in their upcoming show. Around the same time they're reviving "One After 909" they're also revisiting what seem to be some other early Lennon-McCartney numbers—"Won't You Please Say Goodbye," "Thinking of Linking," "I'll Wait Till Tomorrow"—which usually have a doleful, country-ish feel (and unmemorable melodies). They do make it through a virtually complete version of one called "Because I Know You Love Me So," which sounds rather like early Carl Perkins at his most rural.

On the bits and pieces of oldies jammed upon, it's George Harrison, a little surprisingly, who comes off best, taking lead vocals on genuinely spirited, fairly together covers of Marvin Gaye's "Hitch Hike" and Larry Williams's "Short Fat Fannie." What a shame, though, that his singing is undermiked—as it is, for some reason, on many of the *Get Back* outtakes. The folk classic "Midnight Special" isn't bad either,

though John and Paul have trouble remembering all the lyrics—alas, a problem afflicting many of the "covers" recorded by the movie cameras this month. John's still toying with the instrumental riffs of "Sun King," but offers a work-in-progress of more substantial promise with "Give Me Some Truth," which would be revived for further consideration four days later.

If there was any one time at which a cloud began to hover over the January sessions, however, it might have come with the extended rehearsals of "All Things Must Pass"—several dozen of them on this day alone. For whatever reason, this fine, quasi-spiritual George Harrison composition seemed to resist a suitable arrangement and performance. It's often said that John and Paul didn't take George's compositions seriously—certainly not with the seriousness they applied to their own material—and that the failure of "All Things Must Pass" to find a place on a Beatles record was due to the comparatively low regard they held for Harrison's work. While the lighter priority given to George's songs is not in dispute, it doesn't seem quite reasonable to lay the entire blame at John and Paul's feet for the group's struggles with "All Things Must Pass" in particular. They're certainly putting a lot of time into the tune here. Paul puts some work into coming up with high vocal harmonies to support George's lead. John adds some tentative swirling organ, perhaps accommodating George's stated desire to give it a Band-like feel. Still, the group has a hard time lifting it out of dirge-like territory. The band would revisit the song later in the month (and George would even do a solo demo of it at Abbey Road in February), but it might just be that it wasn't meant to be a Beatles song, not reaching its true potential until a lusher and better recording (co-produced by Phil Spector and Harrison) was done for George's *All Things Must Pass* album in 1970.

If their failure to come to grips with "All Things Must Pass" was grinding them down, the mood was probably not improved by the repeated slogs through "Maxwell's Silver Hammer" at day's end. Though thought of as one of the more fun (if cutesy) numbers in the Beatles catalog, the group likely tired of the tune quickly when they first worked on it. John and George would subsequently admit they didn't care much for the song in the first place, though their memories might have been permanently tainted by the drudgery of Paul leading them through numerous rehearsals in which he didn't even have the words worked out for the most part. At this stage, the arrangement was much more of a straightforward, if jaunty, guitar-oriented rock bash, Paul calling/singing out the chords at points to guide them along (as can be seen in one sequence in the *Let It Be* film). Despite all the work put into it in January 1969, it wouldn't make the *Let It Be* album, and it would take a substantial (and much superior) rearrangement before it would resurface on the *Abbey Road* LP.

While it's rarely been noted, a possible reason for the bad feelings that quickly arose in the *Get Back* sessions is the quite abrupt, somewhat radical change in the group's working method. Usually, they had learned and recorded new songs in the studio quite quickly, even if they'd spent a great deal more time on overdubs upon the basic tracks in the past two or three years. As McCartney explained in *Paul McCartney: Many Years from Now*, "Normally John and I would go in the studio, sit down with the guys and say, 'Right, what are we going to do?' . . . We'd show it to the band over the course of twenty minutes, possibly half an hour. . . . Ringo would stand around with a pair of drumsticks, which he might tap on a seat or a screen or a packing case. John and I would sit with our two guitars. George would bring his guitar and see what chords we were doing and figure out what he could do. George Martin would sit down with us and then we would separate, go to each instrument and come out ready to fight. And we just did it, and within the next hour, we would have done it. We would have decided how we were going to play this song." Rigorous non-EMI rehearsals had rarely if ever been undertaken since Beatlemania set in; as Harrison told radio reporter Larry Kane in September 1964, "Paul and John write a song, bring it into the studio, and usually nine times out of ten Ringo and I haven't heard of the song before." Now, unused to live rehearsals for some years, it was taking hours and even days to decide how to play, the tempers fraying with increasing regularity.

● **January 6**

Rehearsal Tapes
Let It Be sessions
Twickenham Film Studios, London

Oh! Darling
C'mon Marianne
I've Got a Feeling (three versions)
High School Confidential
Hear Me Lord (eight versions)
For You Blue (two versions)
All Things Must Pass (nine versions)
Carry That Weight (four versions)
Octopus's Garden
The Palace of the King of the Birds
Across the Universe (two versions)
I Want You
Don't Let Me Down (28 versions)
One After 909 (three versions)
That's All Right (Mama)
Thirty Days
Leaning on a Lamppost
Annie
I'm Talking About You
Tracks of My Tears
Dizzy Miss Lizzie
Money (That's What I Want)
Fools Like Me
Sure to Fall (In Love with You)
Right String, Wrong Yo-Yo
Send Me Some Loving
Two of Us (20 versions)
Frère Jacques
It Ain't Me Babe
When the Saints Go Marching In
Loop De Loop
Let's Dance
She Came In through the Bathroom Window (seven versions)

Other songs, titles uncertain:
You Wear Your Women Out
My Imagination

I'm Gonna Pay for His Ride
They Call Me Fuzz Face
Maureen

Miscellaneous:
Instrumental improvisations/jams (14)
Vocal numbers, titles impossible to even guess (three)

Only a few days into the sessions, these rehearsals were becoming an exasperating mishmash of oldies, barely-worth mentioning jams, tentative presentations/tryouts of songs-in-development, and serious attempts at honing the more fully formed compositions. These were interspersed, all the while, with chatter and bickering about where they should be channeling all this effort. Whatever their gripes, everyone stuck it out: there are an astounding five CDs' worth of recordings from this day alone.

The songs receiving the most attention were "Don't Let Me Down" and "Two of Us." "Don't Let Me Down" in particular is tinkered with; some Latin-influenced beats are briefly considered and Paul works up some responsive harmonies for the bridge. While these harmonies are nice to hear as a variation from the familiar final arrangement, they clutter up a song that doesn't need more help, and are ultimately superfluous. "Two of Us" at this point remained a harder-charging rock song than it would become by its final, far more plaintive, folkier incarnation. This particular series of rehearsals of that number, however, was marred by the famous sequence in which McCartney and Harrison argued about how to play a certain guitar passage, George ending up grumbling, "I'll play whatever you want me to play, or I won't play at all if you don't want me to play. Whatever it is that'll please you, I'll do it." Caught for posterity in the *Let It Be* film, it's likely been blown up a little out of proportion, as it's just one of numerous internal conflicts undergone by the band in this period, and those conflicts weren't solely between McCartney and Harrison. It was, nevertheless, emblematic of both the nature of some of their disagreements and their growing unwillingness to sweep them under the rug.

Of most interest on the tapes that have emerged from this date, however, are the newer songs that were coming up for consideration, which would find various places on *Abbey Road*, *Let It Be*, and *All Things Must Pass*. The others don't seem terribly interested in George's performances of his just-written "Hear Me Lord," which he describes as a gospel song. First demonstrated acoustically, then with wah-wah guitar, it's a lovely, somber number. While George was likely hurt at the others' lack of enthusiasm, there might have been another factor that the Beatles weren't even consciously ready to acknowledge yet: that the good yet somewhat dirge-like, highly spiritual compositions he was increasingly leaning toward were simply not highly suited to the group's style. As with "All Things Must Pass," it wouldn't be until George recorded "Hear Me Lord" on his own, for the *All Things Must Pass* album, that it truly found its appropriate setting.

Elsewhere on the January 6 tapes, the day's first version of "Carry That Weight" has a particularly churchy organ base, with a completely different, rather good (if obviously incomplete) funky bridge that wasn't used at all in the final *Abbey Road* arrangement. Ringo offers a very rudimentary verse of "Octopus's Garden" on staccato piano; George plays an embryonic "For You Blue," much more a standard blues tune at this point, and virtually lacking in any lyrics whatsoever. John, perhaps tacitly acknowledging he hasn't been too prolific of late, gingerly revives "Across the Universe," the still-unreleased composition the Beatles had already recorded in early 1968; the day's second attempt, though a bit fumbling, isn't bad at all, though overuse of the wah-wah guitar crops up again here.

Perhaps in realization that they could use a fast out-and-out rocker for their upcoming live performance, "One After 909" is given some more attention, though it has a more relaxed shuffle beat here, as well as a perhaps inappropriately prominent wah-wah guitar. "She Came In through the Bathroom Window," rehearsed at some length at the day's conclusion, has a funkier tone than the *Abbey Road* arrangement, though it suffers from a more mundane tempo, less robust vocal harmonies, and—yes, again—wah-wah guitar. And "All Things Must Pass" is well on its way to rivaling "Not Guilty" as the George Harrison song the Beatles recorded the most without releasing while active, though the multiple versions here don't pull it out of sluggishness.

Although the bulk of the day's improvs/jams were, as par for the course, generic vamps not even worth analyzing, a few were rather interesting, at least relative to most of what the Beatles did in this vein at these sessions. The lengthy instrumental "The Palace of the King of the Birds," recorded years later by Paul for an unreleased children's album titled *Rupert the Bear,* has a particularly elegiac McCartney organ. Combined with its stately tempo and flowing, bluesy guitar lines, it sounds about as close as the Beatles came to progressive rock jamming—highly uncharacteristic territory for the group to be wandering into, but interesting precisely for that reason. Paul remains on the organ for another long, but harder-rocking and bluesier instrumental that follows soon afterward, eventually hitting (as all rock bands must at some point in their lives) on the requisite "Louie Louie" riff. McCartney sings with commendable raunch on the ordinary (if intriguingly titled) blues jam "You Wear Your Women Out," and whether consciously or unconsciously, he approaches something like his take on Yoko Ono primal scream territory on part of "My Imagination."

The most fully developed piece for which no certain title is known is "Maureen," sung by George with wah-wah guitar. Though fragmented and most likely incomplete in this presentation, it's a tender, tuneful number, with the kind of humility and bittersweet melody Harrison excelled at devising on much of his *All Things Must Pass* material. Here George claims that Bob Dylan (with whom he had met in late 1968 in the US) wrote the song, though there are no known Dylan performances of the composition. It's also unveiled as a possible single for Ringo, appropriately enough as the drummer was married at the time to a woman named Maureen—with whom, about five years later, George would have an affair, around the time both Harrison and Starr's first marriages were ending. Is it just possible that George already had some romantic feelings for Maureen back in 1969 that this song expressed, the author taking care to disguise his intentions by attributing its authorship to Dylan?

The oldies reprised by the Beatles on January 6 were not among their better such endeavors at the *Get Back* sessions, but an exception can be found in "Sure to Fall." It's no match for the best of their BBC performances of the song five years earlier, but it's virtually complete, and has a far more languorous country feel, overlaid with fluttering wah-wah guitar.

● January 7

Rehearsal Tapes
Let It Be *sessions*
Twickenham Film Studios, London

The Long and Winding Road (two versions)
Golden Slumbers
Carry That Weight
The Palace of the King of the Birds (two versions)
Lady Madonna
She Came In through the Bathroom Window (four versions)
Lowdown Blues Machine
What'd I Say (two versions)
Shout
Get Back (four versions)
My Back Pages
I've Got a Feeling (14 versions)
Stuck Inside of Mobile with the Memphis Blues Again
I Shall Be Released
To Kingdom Come
For You Blue (two versions)
Bo Diddley
What the World Needs Now Is Love
First Call
Maxwell's Silver Hammer (18 versions)
Oh! Darling (two versions)
Rule Brittania
Norwegian Wood (This Bird Has Flown)
Speak to Me
When I'm Sixty-Four
A Shot of Rhythm and Blues
(You're So Square) Baby I Don't Care
Across the Universe (12 versions)
Give Me Some Truth (three versions)
A Case of the Blues (two versions)
Cuddle Up
From Me to You
Rock and Roll Music
Lucille
Lotta Lovin' (two versions)
Gone, Gone, Gone
I Dig a Pony
One After 909 (five versions)
Don't Let Me Down (12 versions)
Devil in Her Heart
Thirty Days
Revolution
Be-Bop-A-Lula
Somethin' Else
School Day
F.B.I.

Other songs, titles uncertain:
Mr. Epstein Said It Was White Gold

Woman Where You Been So Long
Oh Julie, Julia

Miscellaneous:

Instrumental improvisations/jams (17)
Vocal numbers, titles impossible to even guess (one)

Haphazardly structured days would be the rule rather than the exception during the January 1969 sessions. As usual, January 7 drifted between intense rehearsals of specific numbers, peeks at newly emerging songs, and largely desultory covers and off-the-top-of-me-head filler. It was perhaps most notable for the first appearances of "Get Back," the kind of classic uptempo single the whole enterprise sorely needed to revive flagging energies. At this point, however, "Get Back" is also sorely in need of coherent lyrics, and isn't much more structured than the dozens of jams the group was undertaking to fill in the dead spaces on these cold Twickenham rehearsals. Much of the skeleton of the verse is there, however, and the chorus is virtually a done deal, though it seemed to take the group a few days to realize what a gem they had and to start working on it in earnest.

Much of the day was spent working on "I've Got a Feeling" and "Don't Let Me Down," two songs that had emerged as obvious strong contenders for the upcoming concert (and would indeed be performed on January 30 on the Apple rooftop performance seen in *Let it Be*). As with many of the songs rehearsed ad infinitum during January, however, the sense is not so much of a song evolving substantially, but of a band grinding it down to perfection via rote repetition. More contentiously, the group also spent a lot of time working on a song that *didn't*

One of hundreds, if not thousands, of collections of January 1969 Get Back material, with pictures of the group taken at their last photo session on August 22, 1969.

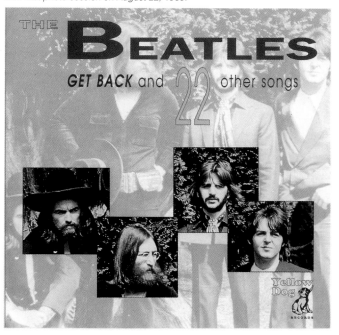

make it into the *Let It Be* concert or album, "Maxwell's Silver Hammer." They really weren't spending notably more time on this than the other numbers they were rehearsing most diligently, but perhaps because of John and George's distaste for the tune, it's the one that's usually fingered as the outstanding example of a song that was over-rehearsed to the point of exhaustion.

Taken in bite sizes, however, it's interesting to hear that it differed substantially in structure from the *Abbey Road* version, with a happy-go-lucky wordless intro/recurring refrain—whistled by several Beatles at once—that wouldn't survive the final cut. "That's lovely, fellas," Paul comments encouragingly during an early tryout of those whistles, sounding as if he's suppressing giggles during the next few lines. At least *he* was having some fun—in another early version, he breaks into unexpected double-time—even if the others weren't as gleeful at the prospect of devoting so much time to sanding off the edges. As McCartney's on piano here, George takes over the bass, and it would also be necessary for John to play bass at other points in January when Paul was on keyboards, due to the group's insistence on doing everything live, sans overdubs. He also toys with a showbizzy, curtain-closing ending wholly in keeping with the song's obvious homage to the British music hall tradition, as much as it might have been making Lennon and Harrison cringe inside.

Though John's evidently serious about getting "Across the Universe" re-performed or re-recorded, he's not doing his case any favors by his inability to remember all the words. Some are eventually retrieved, but the fact is that these attempts—complete with ambitious if unpolished McCartney harmonies, and at various points dusted with ghostly Harrison organ or gentle wah-wah guitar—lack the engaging cosmic lightness of the mysteriously discarded February 1968 studio track. Parts of a couple of renditions were used in the *Let It Be* film, and in his early-'70s *Rolling Stone* interview, John inaccurately and unfairly criticized Paul's indifference to the tune as follows: "Like in the movie, when I got to do 'Across the Universe' Paul yawns and plays boogie." Actually Paul doesn't yawn until the film cuts to them rehearsing "I Dig a Pony" immediately afterward, but the larger point is that John wasn't doing much to put life into the tune himself, and was sometimes himself guilty of sleepwalking through songs other than his own at Twickenham.

Perhaps getting lulled into a daze by both the woozy ambience of "Across the Universe" and their unsatisfactory progress, they suddenly break into a pretty fair, tight rendition of "Rock and Roll Music"—which, of course, they'd put on *Beatles for Sale* and performed live as recently as two and a half years back—with George's wah-wah intact. Getting into a rock 'n' roll mood, they soon revisit "One After 909," which continues to emerge as a stronger contender for the upcoming concert. The final version of the day, though sloppy, isn't far removed from the ultimate one on *Let It Be* (save the notable absence of Billy Preston's electric piano). More interesting is a 40-second take in which they slow the tune down by half into a funkier, bluesier pace, an approach left unpursued (if indeed it was even seriously considered at all).

And still, among the generally messy proceedings, new material kept gushing forth, some songs waiting months to get their due, others abandoned virtually at the starting line. "Golden Slumbers" makes its first appearance here, in what sounds like a deliberately strained McCartney solo piano/vocal performance. While the tempo of "She Came In through the Bathroom Window" is still too sluggish, it remains something of a mystery as to why it wasn't given heavier consideration for the rooftop performance, as unlike much of the material they were wading through, the song is strong, relatively hard-rocking, and virtually complete. "Give Me Some Truth" gets its final, brief airings, the last of them lasting about a minute, and yet seems to have been abandoned at this point despite its obvious promise, as was the more rudimentary "A Case of the Blues." It could be that John Lennon simply lacked the discipline at this particular juncture in his life to finish off songs that were clearly better than, say, "Dig It," which the Beatles *would* spend a good amount of time working up a few weeks later.

Among the day's off-the-cuff oldies covers, aside from "Rock and Roll Music," the clear highlight is Carl Perkins's stark rockabilly outing "Gone, Gone, Gone." In contrast to most such exercises during this month, the performance is brisk, mostly complete, and sung (by John Lennon) with conviction. Even the wah-wah solo works. A brief go at "Lucille" has similar energy, but it winds down by about its halfway point, and isn't even the best version of the song from the January 1969 sessions, let alone nearly as good as the ferocious takes the Beatles laid down of the same tune back in 1963 on the BBC. At one point they launch into "What'd I Say" like they really mean it, with an aggressive hunger lacking in almost every other oldies cover on the *Get Back* tapes. But they abandon the song after just 15 seconds or so—a symptom, sadly, of their overall lack of follow-through on so much of their "back to the roots" endeavors during these rehearsals.

Wrapping up the day's ephemera are two of the better jams from the *Get Back* vault, the bluesy "Woman Where You Been So Long" and the "Lucille"-like "Oh Julie, Julia" (with a decent McCartney vocal), though neither of these are properly developed "songs" by any stretch of the imagination. "To Kingdom Come" and Bob Dylan's "I Shall Be Released," which had both been featured on the Band's recent debut album, are both loosely covered here, where they're largely performed by George. They're not noteworthy renditions, except inasmuch as they further testify to the Band's substantial influence on Harrison, which would carry all the way forward to his *All Things Must Pass* album.

● January 8

Rehearsal Tapes
Let It Be *sessions*
Twickenham Film Studios, London

I Me Mine (41 versions)
I've Got a Feeling (two versions)
Honey Hush
Stand By Me
Hare Krishna Mantra (two versions)
Two of Us
You Got Me Going
Twist and Shout
Don't Let Me Down (two versions)
St. Louis Blues
One After 909
Too Bad about Sorrows
Just Fun
She Said, She Said

She Came In through the Bathroom Window (five versions)
One Way Out
MacArthur Park
All Things Must Pass (11 versions)
Mean Mr. Mustard
Fools Like Me
You Win Again
Right String, Wrong Yo-Yo
Boogie Woogie
Baa, Baa, Black Sheep
Mr. Bassman
Maxwell's Silver Hammer (13 versions)
How Do You Think I Feel
The Ballad of Bonnie and Clyde
Hello Mudduh, Hello Fadduh! (A Letter from Camp)
I Me Mine
F.B.I.
Oh! Darling
Let It Be (three versions)
The Fool
Domino
The Long and Winding Road (six versions)
Adagio for Strings
True Love
Shout
Sweet Little Sixteen
Malagueña
Almost Grown
What Am I Living For
Rock and Roll Music
To Kingdom Come

Other songs, titles uncertain:

Get Your Rocks Off
Well, If You're Ready
Life Is What You Make It
I'm Going to Knock Him Down Dead
Tell All the Folks Back Home

Miscellaneous:

Instrumental improvisations/jams (eight)
Vocal numbers, titles impossible to even guess (five)

A day of mixed results for the group. On the one hand, they have some of their strongest new material in pretty good shape, and also make some progress on a few other songs. On the other, they get bogged down with a couple of numbers that aren't meeting with wholehearted enthusiasm from everyone, as well as indecision about where to hold the upcoming show for which they're supposedly rehearsing.

Early in the day, the lads run through "Two of Us," "Don't Let Me Down," "I've Got a Feeling," and "One After 909" just once apiece. While not as polished as the official tracks (to wit, the self-mockingly Elvis Presleyoid McCartney vocals in the bridge of "Two of Us"), these also have a certain loose enthusiasm that the more familiar versions don't, possibly because they hadn't been over-rehearsed at this point. John lets go with a blood-curdling scream at the beginning of "Don't

Let Me Down," matched by Paul's joyous "Good morning!" shout at the end of the bridge of "I've Got a Feeling" and train-simulating "choo choo" yelps in "One After 909." For just a few minutes, the Beatles seem to be having as good a time as they (or at least Paul) had thought they would when the project was conceived.

The momentum flags, however, when they resume their repeated struggles with "All Things Must Pass." While it's true the group doesn't seem as happy to be doing this as, say, "One After 909," the fault lies not solely with John and Paul's condescension toward George's songwriting, but also George's inability to come up with an arrangement that gets the most out of his band mates' assets. Eventually, with John adding hammered piano notes, they squeeze out a reasonable complete take, though the harmonies have a somewhat off-putting, moaning quality. "She Came In through the Bathroom Window" still pounds along with an inappropriately sluggish tempo. But more grating are the revisitations of "Maxwell's Silver Hammer" (whistled sections and all), particularly as Paul still doesn't have all the words worked out, sing-mumbling his way through many of them. At one point a vocal harmony is sung behind Paul in unrelenting monotone—whether out of laziness, boredom, or spite, it's hard to say.

Still, the quartet makes a lot of headway on "I Me Mine," written by George just the night before, and first played as a lilting acoustic lament. By the end of the day, it has a respectable full-band arrangement complete with shifting tempos. At this early stage, it also has an interesting flamenco-like instrumental passage that was ultimately discarded when the song was tightened up for release. The point's been repeatedly made that Harrison's songs weren't taken with righteous seriousness by Lennon and McCartney, but they certainly *did* seem to be putting a lot of time, if not their highest level of sincerity, into both "I Me Mine" and "All Things Must Pass." "The Long and Winding Road" and "Let It Be" are also emerging as standout numbers worthy of intense concentration, though for now they're fairly basic run-throughs on which only McCartney's voice and piano seem sure of themselves, Paul focusing on communicating the basics of the tune to the others. "Mean Mr. Mustard" surfaces for the first time (though John had done a demo in May 1968), and isn't much different in structure than the *Abbey Road* version, though the arrangement is skeletal, and Mr. Mustard's sister is still named Shirley, not Pam.

Perhaps because the group was getting more intent on seriously polishing their new material, the oldies covers and incidental jams from this date were uninteresting even by the generally poor standards they brought to such things in January 1969. Many of them are very slight fragments, often played absentmindedly during discussions of more important songs or options for their upcoming show. "Stand By Me," largely sung by Paul with a country-ish tinge, would be done better in a couple of weeks; "Fools Like Me" and "You Win Again," neither too energetic, testify to their affection for Jerry Lee Lewis; and the idea of a rock 'n' roll version of "Hare Krishna Mantra" is much more interesting than the mundane reality. "Too Bad about Sorrows" and "Just Fun" hold some interest as very early Lennon-McCartney numbers, but the "versions" here last less than 15 seconds, though they're enough to let us know that they're probably uninteresting country-ish tunes. It's after "Too Bad about Sorrows," though, that John mumbles, "Queen says no to pot-smoking FBI member"—the sole crumb of audio from any of the January 1969 rehearsals at Twickenham to be used on the official *Let It Be* LP, where it can be heard before "For You Blue."

● January 9

Rehearsal Tapes

Let It Be sessions
Twickenham Film Studios, London

Another Day

The Palace of the King of the Birds (two versions)

Let It Be (16 versions)

The Long and Winding Road (five versions)

Her Majesty

Golden Slumbers

Carry That Weight

Oh! Darling

For You Blue (15 versions)

Two of Us (eight versions)

Baa, Baa, Black Sheep

Don't Let Me Down

Suzy's Parlour

I've Got a Feeling (five versions)

One After 909 (four versions)

Norwegian Wood (This Bird Has Flown)

She Came In through the Bathroom Window (seven versions)

Be-Bop-A-Lula

Get Back (six versions)

Penina

Across the Universe (12 versions)

Teddy Boy

Junk

Move It

Good Rockin' Tonight

Tennessee

House of the Rising Sun

Honey Hush

Hitch Hike

All Together Now

I Threw It All Away

Mama, You Been on My Mind

That'll Be the Day

Jenny, Jenny

Slippin' and Slidin'

Other songs, titles uncertain:

Shakin' in the Sixties

Commonwealth

Enoch Powell

Get Off (three versions)

Quit Your Messing Around

Ramblin' Woman

Miscellaneous:

Instrumental improvisations/jams (nine)

Vocal numbers, titles impossible to even guess (two)

January 9 was a rather all-over-the-map day of rehearsals, spread between refining songs that had already been worked over a lot, others that were emerging as the strongest new items, airings of less developed compositions, and quite a few oldies covers. If nothing else, it's a testament to the sheer bulk of material the group had to work with at this point, even if John Lennon was coming up pretty short in bona fide, hot-out-of-the-oven goodies. Again, the point needs to be made that the group's main problem wasn't that they didn't have enough good material to work with, but deciding what to actually do with it. The songs heard on this day, after all, included three that would in some way or another eventually become chart-topping singles. It's one of the more rewarding January days in terms of listening, though as usual it's quite exhausting, filling up five CDs.

On a number of days during January 1969, Paul McCartney was the first to arrive, and while waiting for the full group to assemble, he'd fill the time with solo piano performances. In a way, that was indicative of the far greater enthusiasm he brought to this project than the others. John certainly never arrived early to work on songs on his own, though George sometimes did to play new compositions on his acoustic guitar, and even Ringo occasionally worked on his own tunes on piano. From a fan's perspective several decades later, it's fortunate this happened, as we sometimes get to hear Paul in particular in a solo setting. The earliest section of the circulating January 9 tapes was especially rich in this regard, almost amounting to a solo piano/vocal performance of highlights from McCartney's contributions to *Let It Be* and *Abbey Road*. Alone or with the Beatles, he'd already played most of the songs in the previous week, but it marked the first time out for "Her Majesty," here played on piano in a rather "Maxwell's Silver Hammer" music hall style. He also unveiled a bridge-less version of "Another Day," never to be released by the Beatles, though he'd make it his first solo single in 1971. Considering that he'd already performed it with the Beatles earlier in the sessions, the brief excerpts of his haunting instrumental "The Palace of the King of the Birds" seem to signify that it wasn't just another time-filling improvisation, but an actual song that Paul had plans to genuinely develop, though it never did find its way onto an official release.

Early on in the day, a few of the songs that were obvious leading contenders for inclusion in the upcoming concert/film documentary were rehearsed several times each: "I've Got a Feeling," "One After 909," and "Two of Us," the last of which still has a considerably zestier, harder-rocking feel than the folkier arrangement ultimately used. If you're not a diehard Beatles fan and are actually trying to listen to all of the available January 1969 tapes in sequence, this is probably the point at which you give up forcing yourself to sit through these variations, since they're really not all that different from each other. There's a lot of minute tinkering going on, and the occasional moment of comic inspiration, as when John substitutes the lyric "Everybody got a facelift" in "I've Got a Feeling." Alas, it's not the end of the line for any of these numbers; all of them would be rehearsed many, many more times before the month was out.

As for what might be called one of the more "secondary" candidates, although a seed of "For You Blue" had been played three days before, it's much farther along now, though on its first run-throughs it has a rootsier, far more acoustic feel than it would take on by the final arrangement. Oddly, it gets turned into a chunky rocker, though in a couple of weeks it would revert to its far earthier, down-home, bluesier roots. "She Came In through the Bathroom Window" is subjected to some particularly sardonic joking, John at one time taking the lead vo-

cal over from Paul with some screamed near Cockneyisms. McCartney doesn't seem to mind, playing along with some good-hearted rejoinders; on other takes of the song, Lennon improvises some more silly responses, à la "Get a job, cop!" In turn, Paul slows it to a barroom pace and makes up his own variations: "I said my name was Dan LaRue [at that time a well-known British female impersonator], and when she said I've got the answer, I said but who the hell are you?" More silliness finds its way into "Across the Universe," which at a couple points gets busked in a vaudevillian double-time skiffle wholly at odds with the original reflective mood of the song. Some have been tempted to read actual disdainful boredom with the songs (and, in the case of Lennon and McCartney, with each other) into such obviously non-serious attempts at these tunes. That might have something to do with it, but more likely it's just the guys blowing off steam and introducing some levity into the proceedings, if only as a means of making it easier to get through several hours a day of such intensive musical work.

However, the fellows are clearly getting more serious about a couple of the best new Paul-penned tunes. "Get Back" is a downright vicious rocker at this point, with the cowboy gallop rhythm yet to be introduced. The main sticking point is the lyrics, which are hardly there at all except for some basic ideas; the characters don't even have their names yet, and are here referred to as Teresa and Joe, rather than Loretta and JoJo. Here lies one of the most notorious of all bootlegged Beatles performances, as Paul starts to make up words about Puerto Ricans and Pakistanis. When these tapes got into fairly wide circulation among collectors many years later, Paul was suddenly defending himself against speculations that the lyrics were racist, advising minorities (as the Pakistanis were in Britain) to get back to where they once belonged. This was, sadly, a genuine sentiment among some of the British public at the time, and voiced by Parliament member Enoch Powell, who felt that there were too many non-whites taking jobs in England.

Such accusations against Paul were fairly ridiculous. The Beatles, and certainly McCartney, had never been racist in their own public and private activities, and had actively championed black American music in particular, often touring and socializing with African-American performers. To boot, just a couple of weeks later, they would take on an African-American keyboardist, Billy Preston, as a virtually unofficial fifth member on the homestretch of the *Get Back* sessions, with Preston himself playing the electric keyboard solo on "Get Back" itself. (As if that wasn't enough, in his solo years Paul would record with leading American soul and pop stars Stevie Wonder and Michael Jackson.) The lyrics were meant ironically, and eventually discarded when the Beatles rightfully deduced that the public might not realize they weren't seriously advocating the deportation of Pakistanis ("Don't dig no Pakistanis taking all the people's jobs") or Puerto Ricans ("Don't need no Puerto Ricans living in the USA"). Of course, the lyrics eventually got out to much of the public via these unreleased tapes anyway.

In a considerably less frivolous mood, this was the first day on which the Beatles really gave their full energies to "Let It Be." George and John's backup vocal harmonies are more a part of the arrangement at this juncture, though the lyrics are unfinished, Paul making up some gap-pluggers that obviously aren't going to stay in place (i.e., "Read the *Record Mirror*, 'Let It Be'"). Though the strength of the composition is likely suppressing any objections among his colleagues, the surviving tapes are some of the strongest evidence available of McCartney's assertive qualities as an arranger of his own material, as he forcefully (but

An ambitious CD series that presented the Get Back sessions in a day-by-day format, though a yet more thorough series of bootlegs was subsequently produced.

diplomatically) calls out suggestions, advice, and instructions. Here's where the group's determination for a "live" sound again creates a disadvantage, however. As Paul's on piano, John takes over bass, and he's not only no match for McCartney's brilliance on that instrument, he's plodding and inadequate.

A few new-to-the-*Get-Back*-sessions McCartney tunes were heard about midway through the proceedings. "Penina" has little more than a power ballad chorus (and not a very good one, truth be told), though it holds mild interest as the only Beatles version of this song, "covered" in a barely-more-developed state by Carlos Mendes on an obscure 1969 single. "Junk," first played by Paul as one of the May 1968 Esher demos, is a barely recognizable 16-second sound bite here, sung in pidgin French, no less. There's also a 15-second bossa nova burst of "Teddy Boy," a McCartney tune that, unlike "Junk" and "Penina," the Beatles *would* return to later that month.

Some of the jams without official titles are, as those things go, much more interesting than most such things the Beatles wandered into over the course of the month. "Commonwealth" is a generic 1950s-styled rock 'n' roll tune, but interesting as it touches on some of the same jibes at Enoch Powell's "send them back to where they once belonged" stance that informed "Get Back." Though it's sung by Paul in a quasi-Elvis manner, John adds a lot of spice with his responsive shouts of "Yes!" in a sarcastic old man voice. "Get Off" is nothing more than a 12-bar blues jam, but entertaining for the dozens of names Paul and John call off the tops of their heads, ranging from well-known celebrities to friends from their Quarrymen days. (There's also John's priceless twisting of a line from "Why Don't We Do It in the Road," here rendered as "Why don't you put it on the toast?")

More cookie-cutter blues-rock is offered by "Suzy's Parlour," distinguished by John's deliberately ridiculous nasal vocals and a rat-a-tat staccato chorus. Even if you don't collect bootlegs, you might well have heard this tune, as it's included in the *Let It Be* movie. For that reason it was copyrighted, though it was mistitled "Suzy Parker"; most bootlegs, these days at any rate, use the more appropriate "Suzy's Parlour" title. Lennon sounds like he's nearing the end of his rope on "Shakin' in the Sixties," a hyper three-chorder with an inscrutable reference to Beatles publisher Dick James. On the half-minute "Quit Your Messing Around," John dispenses with subtlety altogether, announcing "I'd like to do a number just on the electric," followed by blasts of noisy guitar chords so overloaded they'd make the Velvet Underground scream in agony.

Though the group didn't drift as heavily into oldies retreads on this date as they did on many days in January, there are some such ventures that are above average as these things went. "Good Rockin' Tonight," which they'd learned from Elvis Presley's mid-'50s cover, has lots of energy but not many accurate memories of the lyrics, and "Tennessee," a fairly obscure early Carl Perkins tune, gets a vicious mock-hillbilly vocal treatment by John. "Honey Hush" is definitely one of the best early rockabilly covers from the *Get Back* sessions, almost in a glued-together-enough state that it might be enjoyed by even non-obsessive Beatles collectors. "House of the Rising Sun" is *not* that together, but it's certainly amusing, the group taking it at a downright funereal trudge that doesn't so much draw out its pathos as pound it into submission. John and Paul both take the piss out of the song's tragic lament with some of the most demented, distorted screaming summoned on a Beatles tape.

In a much gentler state of mind, George plays acoustic guitar and croons a solo version of Bob Dylan's "I Threw It All Away," which presumably he'd learned from Dylan himself (or a tape given to him by Dylan), since it was a few months away from getting released on Dylan's *Nashville Skyline*. This is followed by a similar take on Dylan's "Mama, You Been on My Mind," and while George's vocal is lamentably undermiked on both tapes, they're quite fetching performances. "Ramblin' Woman," presumably a Harrison original that never got to the stage of getting copyrighted, is very much in a similar style, and further testifies to the huge influence the late-'60s work of Dylan and the Band was casting over George as 1969 began. Despite the too-faint vocals, these are among the very most enjoyable *Get Back* outtakes, making one wish there were more, and better recorded, such unplugged Harrison performances available. And there are, actually, on a superb 15-song set of demos he did just after the Beatles broke up (see entry on page 281)—though these do not include any of the aforementioned three tunes.

In all, it was a fairly productive day for the group, albeit in the haphazard fashion that had become the modus operandi for the *Get Back* project. The tentative house of cards they were building would collapse, however, on the following day, threatening not just the performance/album/film documentary, but the survival of the Beatles themselves.

● January 10

Rehearsal Tapes
Let It Be *sessions*
Twickenham Film Studios, London

The Long and Winding Road (three versions)

Let It Be

Don't Let Me Down (two versions)

Maxwell's Silver Hammer (four versions)

I've Got a Feeling (four versions)

Get Back (22 versions)

She's a Woman

Hi Heel Sneakers (two versions)

Long Tall Sally

Theme from "The Beatles Cartoons"

Catch a Falling Star

Two of Us (six versions)

I'm Talking About You

A Quick One, While He's Away (four versions)

Till There Was You

C'mon Everybody

Mack the Knife

Don't Be Cruel

The Peanut Vendor

It's Only Make Believe

Adagio for Strings

Martha My Dear

Sun King

Dear Prudence

Other songs, titles uncertain:

On a Sunny Island

Through a London Window

Miscellaneous:

Instrumental improvisations/jams (16)

Vocal numbers, titles impossible to even guess (one)

Discontent that had been simmering all week—if not for months and years—finally boiled over on January 10, with George quitting the group. Before that happened, funnily enough, the Beatles had put in a fairly productive (by the peculiar standards of January 1969) morning. Weirder still, they continued to work for quite a while in George's absence, though "work" is a loose term for the improvisations and half-hearted rehearsals that filled up most of the afternoon.

As filming/recording began, Paul was playing, alone on piano, most of the songs the group had been working on hardest over the past week. Unfortunately he can only be heard way in the background in this segment, which is largely obscured by dialogue. Still, it's of note for the opportunity to hear him doing, in addition to the keyboard-oriented songs you would expect, other tunes like "I've Got a Feeling" and, especially, a hard-hammered "Get Back" on piano, rather than in the familiar guitar-oriented arrangements.

"Get Back" itself continues to evolve and get serious attention by the group as a whole, the earliest versions from this day including a bass-drums-vocal one and an early indication that Tucson, Arizona, will be the setting, though Paul admits he doesn't have many of the words. It's still an almost angry rocker with a searing, distorted guitar opening in this early stage and a straightforward hard-rock beat. Interestingly, John takes lead vocals at one point, lending his own slashing edge to the tune and indicating that perhaps he was seriously (if briefly) considered as the lead singer, even though this was mostly or wholly McCartney's

composition. They're still toying with references to Pakistanis in the lyrics, too, as well as some wah-wah effects in the guitar soloing. Ringo comes up with a most impressive fill to punctuate the end of a chorus (which would still be heard, in modified form, after the false ending on the eventual hit single). It's clear the Beatles dig the tune, as they're playing with a heart and fire missing from many of their *Get Back* sessions; they're just not entirely sure how to structure the song yet, on several levels.

After quite a few tryouts of "Get Back" (punctuated by a fair reading of the classic blues-rocker "Hi Heel Sneakers"), the group moved on to "Two of Us." That song was still in a harder-rocking state, with a beat that has such a brisk gallop that one wonders whether it influenced the band to eventually put a gallop beat into "Get Back." Considering the doldrums the guys had often lapsed into over the last few days, the mood for the morning as a whole seems pretty upbeat. It was shattered, however, by the abrupt departure of George Harrison after lunch. As previously noted, while historians have tended to emphasize the spats between Paul and George—and George would, in a February 23, 1971, High Court affidavit, cite Paul's criticism of his guitar playing as the deciding factor in his exit—it seems as though the argument that finally caused Harrison to walk out was between George and *John*. It's not wholly clear what the argument was, but certainly John can be heard making light of George's new songs in several instances on the early January tapes. It's also been speculated that George was fed up with John's inability to communicate openly with the group (and the frequent need to communicate with John via Yoko).

The remaining three Beatles' reaction at this point is most interesting. Perhaps out of shock, perhaps out of incomprehension, or perhaps on the assumption that George's resignation (like Ringo's during *The White Album*) is just a temporary huff, they continue to rehearse and jam as a three-piece. John, for one, seems more annoyed than brokenhearted, leading the others through a few distraught, distortion-heavy bits of the Who's "A Quick One, While He's Away" (which Lennon would have seen done in concert quite recently, as the Who had performed it just a month before as part of *The Rolling Stones Rock and Roll Circus*). At one point he calls out nonchalantly, "Okay, George, take it!"

This quickly leads into some of the most bizarre performances not only of this strange month, but of the Beatles' entire career. The band ambles into some shapeless, anguished, bluesy jams, the wordless lead vocals supplied not by John, Paul, or Ringo, but by Yoko, who shrieks as atonally as she does on most of her other recordings (with and without Lennon) of the late '60s. Some critics have seen this as the fulfillment, albeit temporary and perhaps unconsciously, of something that Yoko (and perhaps John) had been plotting and desiring all along: the absorption of Yoko Ono into the group as an actual Beatle. Whatever the motivation, these improvisations are some of the harshest, least listenable "tracks" that "the Beatles" ever recorded, though they do exert the same kind of fascination that makes it hard to avert your eyes from a gruesome car wreck.

Even when the band gets back to proper "songs," there's an almost violent undertone, as if it's only through musical aggression that they can express the anger they found it so hard to articulate in verbal, direct conversation. "I've Got a Feeling" and a must-be-heard-to-be-believed "Don't Let Me Down" are particularly nasty, John at times abandoning any notion of conventional vocal notes for gargled screams and cutting sarcasm. Even "Maxwell's Silver Hammer" gets run through the thresher, Lennon taking the vocal with a glottal Germanic accent akin to Peter Sellers's Dr. Strangelove, followed by a falsetto that would have done Monty Python's dowdy housewife characters proud. Even the detours into oldies covers seemed like vain attempts to distract themselves from the ghastly situation they now had on their hands, and predictably make for quite ghastly listening, especially when they maul Conway Twitty's melodramatic "It's Only Make Believe." As if to deliberately pick the song the most removed from the ugly realities at hand, John even leads the trio into the kind of mock-Latin-lounge send-up he'd often done on his home tapes with "On a Sunny Island," briefly quoting the Rascals' idyllic "Groovin'"—which the Beatles were definitely *not* doing on this particular day. The McCartney-sung "Through a London Window" likewise has a disquieting paste-a-crooked-smile-on-the-situation tone.

Serious attempts at continuing to work on, well, whatever it was the Beatles were doing (which of course hadn't really been decided) clearly couldn't continue. Much of the rest of the day was taken up by discussion among the group and the film crew, though Paul, perhaps seeking refuge, returned to the piano to again doodle away in the background. Yoko, seemingly oblivious to the gravity of the day's events, begins to vocally improvise while Paul's pounding out (of all things) "Martha My Dear" *and* while John's in the middle of an uncharacteristically serious conversation with Michael Lindsay-Hogg. (Incredibly, John was at this point advocating replacing George with Eric Clapton, one of George's best friends, if Harrison didn't come back within a few days.) As Yoko moan-calls John's name, Lennon—whether out of irony or genuine annoyance—plays the henpecked husband with an ear-splitting shout in response: "WHAAAAT!?!?" That very moment could be the absolute low point of the whole *Get Back* madness.

A few more brief jams led by Yoko's screams help wrap the day up, Paul handling drums and John guitar. Leave it to Ringo (who has little to say, incidentally, throughout the January tapes) to find some gallows humor in the situation, as he takes over the mike and declares in a mock-sports-announcer voice, "Yeah, rock it to me baby! That's what I like! You may think this is a full orchestra, but if you look closely, you can see there's only two people playing and one person singing. I know it sounds like Benny Goodman, but don't worry, it's the big sound of 1969! You bet your life! Oh, sock it to me, sock it to me!" As lightly as they were whistling in the dark, however, the Beatles had to be distressed over George's absence, and hoping that they'd manage to patch things up over the weekend.

● January 13

Rehearsal Tapes
Let It Be *sessions*
Twickenham Film Studios, London

Ob-La-Di, Ob-La-Da (two versions)
Otis Sleep On
Baby, Come Back
Build Me Up, Buttercup (three versions)
I Dig a Pony (two versions)
Get Back (15 versions)
On the Road Again

Miscellaneous:

Instrumental improvisations/jams (eight)

A weekend meeting of the Beatles at Ringo's house had not only failed to resolve their problems, but had perhaps made things even worse, George leaving early without agreeing to rejoin the band. Perhaps not knowing what else to do, or maybe hoping for some miracle, the other Beatles nevertheless assembled at Twickenham the following Monday, film crew on hand as usual. Not only did George not show up, however, but John wasn't even there for much of the day. The majority of the tapes in circulation from this day, then, are given over to (admittedly interesting) conversation, not music. Even some of the "songs" are just casual a cappella snatches and, in the case of "Ob-La-Di, Ob-La-Da" and "Otis Sleep On," conversation and singing along to a record by soul singer Arthur Conley.

Amazingly, considering the circumstances, the Beatles-minus-one *did* manage to get some modestly productive work done after John finally arrived. In particular, Lennon and McCartney had some time to work on some of the gaps and glitches in "Get Back." In one particularly interesting snippet of dialogue between the pair, we can hear Paul decisively opting to have the song take place in Tucson, Arizona, almost biting down on the word "Tucson" for emphasis. If nothing else, it's further proof that the Lennon-McCartney songwriting partnership, contrary to what's often been written, wasn't exactly dead in early January 1969, though it might have been more along the lines of helping each other refine structures and plug in phrases than full collaboration. The threesome manage a pretty full sound on "Get Back" despite the absence of their lead guitarist, and it's tempting to ponder whether playing a George-less version might have given John some incentive to work up lead guitar lines on his own (as he did, playing them in the final arrangement).

In some of the most revealing dialogue tapes of the *Get Back* sessions, the Beatles were captured discussing their problems, though rather gingerly and obliquely. Observed Paul flippantly, "It's gonna be such an incredible sort of comical thing like in 50 years' time, you know . . . they broke up 'cause Yoko sat on an amp"—evidently little suspecting that just that sort of speculation would happen, long before 50 years had passed. (Certainly everyone seemed more reluctant to discuss the negative impact Yoko was having on intermember communication when John was actually in the room.) Though it seemed little could be accomplished until George was persuaded to return, there would be one more day of sessions at Twickenham before the whole project changed direction.

● January 14

Rehearsal Tapes
Let It Be *sessions*
Twickenham Film Studios, London

Martha My Dear
San Francisco Bay Blues
The Day I Went Back to School
Lady Jane (two versions)
Talking Blues
Jazz Piano Song

Woman (three versions)

Cocaine Blues

Flushed from the Bathroom of Your Heart

On a Clear Day You Can See Forever

The Back Seat of My Car (two versions)

Hello, Dolly!

Mean Mr. Mustard (two versions)

Madman (three versions)

Watching Rainbows (two versions)

Take This Hammer

Johnny B. Goode (two versions)

Get Back

You Know My Name (Look Up the Number)

Oh! Darling (two versions)

Ob-La-Di, Ob-La-Da

Other songs, titles uncertain:

Oh Baby I Love You

Song of Love (two versions)

As Clear as a Bell

You Are Definitely Inclined Towards It

Don't Start Running

Miscellaneous:

Instrumental improvisations/jams (15)

In an advanced state of denial, the Beatles had somehow managed to keep rehearsing and filming without George Harrison. By the time of this final day of activity at Twickenham, however, they clearly couldn't delude themselves any longer. Whether rehearsing new material, introducing new songs, or retreating to old favorites, they were hitting a brick wall, and you can feel their spirit palpably sagging on these tapes, though they did contain some interesting peeps at songs-in-the-works.

When Paul McCartney can't summon the energy to hold court at the piano with his usual verve, you know the Beatles were *really* in trouble. That seems to be the case on the solo piano session that takes up the first part of the January 14 tapes, much of which has a going-through-the-motions, morning-after feel. As interesting as it might sound in theory to hear Paul cover the Rolling Stones' "Lady Jane," his interpretation is so nonchalant as to be almost meaningless. By the time of the incredibly fey "Song of Love" sung in a Tiny Tim–like voice, it seems like the most enthusiastic Beatle might finally be losing interest in the proceedings.

Yet in the midst of this near-nonsense are some performances that, dare we say, verge on the worthwhile. This is the only place where you can hear any of the Beatles (let alone the whole group) do "Woman," the song Paul had given to Peter & Gordon for a 1966 single, though the performances are rather perfunctory. "The Day I Went Back to School" is more fully developed than most of the seemingly off-the-cuff *Get Back* "originals," with phrasing that seems a little similar to, if not influenced by, John Lennon's "Give Me Some Truth" (which, of course, the Beatles had tentatively tried a few times earlier in the month). A boogie-woogie piano duet between Paul and Ringo, though generic, is lively, and as it was used for a scene in the *Let It Be* film, it was even copyrighted by Apple (under the title "Jazz Piano Song"). Most impressively, there's a luminous, heavily Brian Wilson–influenced ballad,

"The Back Seat of My Car," though the vocals aren't recorded as well as they could be. Certainly Paul isn't projecting with his assertive clarity, perhaps because he knows the song needs more work. Had the Beatles somehow remained together for one more album past *Abbey Road*, one imagines it might have been a contender for a full-group arrangement, though in the end it ended up being exhumed for McCartney's second solo album, 1971's *Ram*.

Much of the material on tapes from this date, like others made in George's absence, was taken up by dialogue among the Beatles and Michael Lindsay-Hogg. Even their more tedious banter always had moments of humor and insight, but by now the group had trouble making amusing jokes, let alone effectively discussing issues of real importance to the survival of the group. Eventually, however, John, Paul, and Ringo made an attempt at rehearsal that was principally interesting for the presence of a couple of Lennon originals that never progressed to genuine contenders for serious work. "Madman" sounds a little like a cross between "Hey Bulldog" and "Mean Mr. Mustard," but not as focused as either of those vitriolic tunes. "Watching Rainbows" is even less memorable, anchored by an uninteresting, chunky, two-chord riff and uninspired lyrics (one, about sitting in a garden, recycled from "I Am the Walrus"), some of them sung in the rapid-fire delivery characteristic of some of John's songs of the time (à la "Give Me Some Truth" and "Polythene Pam"). In the midst of this throwaway, however, John sings "Shoot me" several times—an idea that was, in turn, recycled for use half a year later in "Come Together."

Perhaps sensing that there isn't much to work with here, the group drifts into a tedious instrumental jam, and then back into oldies. The folk-blues standard "Take This Hammer" (which the group would reprise a few more times in January) isn't bad, but after a couple plods through "Johnny B. Goode," the session seems to disintegrate. Paul's the only Beatle left by the time he sings "Oh! Darling" with ridiculously over-echoed vocals, and by the time he inserts passages of Elvis Presley–style dramatic spoken narration, it's obvious he's not seeing much point in continuing with this charade. Shortly afterward, the session wraps up, the *Get Back* project not to be continued for a week, and then in an entirely different venue and mindset.

● January 21

Studio Outtakes

Let It Be *sessions*
Apple Studios, London

Window, Window

Somethin' Else

Daydream

You Are My Sunshine

Whispering

I'm Beginning to See the Light

I Dig a Pony (21 versions)

I've Got a Feeling (four versions)

Every Night

Watch Your Step

New Orleans

Madman

The Fool
Run for Your Life
My Baby Left Me
That's Alright (Mama)
Hallelujah, I Love Her So
Milk Cow Blues
I'm a Man
Little Queenie
When Irish Eyes Are Smiling
Queen of the Hop
Five Feet High and Rising
In the Middle of an Island
Gilly Gilly Ossenfeffer Katzenellen Bogen by the Sea
Good Rockin' Tonight
Forty Days
Too Bad about Sorrows
I'm Ready
Papa's Got a Brand New Bag
Shout
You've Got Me Thinking
Don't Let Me Down (two versions)
Let's Dance
Get Back
For You Blue
*She Came In through the Bathroom Window (five versions)
Madman

Other songs, titles uncertain:

My Rock and Roll Finger Is Bleeding
Do the Bunny Hop
Blossom Dearie They Call Me (two versions)
Oh How I Love the 12-Bar Blues
All I Want Is You
William Smith Boogie
San Ferry Ann
You Gotta Give Back
Well, Well, Well
Is That a Chicken Joke?

Miscellaneous:

Instrumental improvisations/jams (seven)
Vocal numbers, titles impossible to even guess (four)

one version appears on Anthology 3

On January 15, the four Beatles met again to discuss their precarious situation, with George Harrison—perhaps for the first time—in a position to set the terms. George agreed to rejoin the group if the rehearsals were moved from Twickenham to the new studio in the basement of their Apple headquarters in central London, and if the idea of a live concert—which no one could agree on where to hold or whether to hold at all—was dropped. It's also likely he made it clear to John and Paul that he expected to be treated with more respect, as both a musician and person. It should be added, incidentally, that George wasn't necessarily without blame for the Beatles' woes; he'd been consistently, vocally negative about the planned upcoming live show, in whatever form it might take, virtually since setting foot in

Twickenham. If he was really opposed to playing live at all, it could be argued that he should have made that clear to the others before the whole project got underway. Then again, such poor communication was lamentably fairly typical among all of the Beatles by the beginning of 1969.

The new ground rules didn't rule out, however, the possibility that a live concert could be staged for the film cameras (which is, in essence, pretty much what happened). Nor did it put a halt to the incessant presence of those cameras, which had originally been on hand to make a documentary that would precede the showing of the concert film. Now the film project would not consist of both a documentary and a concert, but would be a movie-of-the-making-of-an-album, perhaps with a live segment (for cameras, not a conventional concert audience) as well. So there was still considerable confusion, after all this negotiation, about exactly what the Beatles were doing—recording an album, rehearsing for a show, making a film, or doing all those at once.

At least recordings could commence for an official studio release, since some of the music would be taped not just on the cameras' sound recorders, but on official studio equipment. Even this didn't go as smoothly as expected, since the studio (built by their friend and supposed electronics genius "Magic Alex") was so amateurishly constructed that there was another day of delays while Apple arranged to borrow real equipment from Abbey Road. While the Beatles would film/rehearse/record at Apple for the rest of the month, and were often taped on recording studio equipment, it must be pointed out that most of the circulating tapes from these ten days or so are taken from the cameras' sound recorders, not Apple/EMI studio tapes. The quality is usually still pretty good, but not as good as it would have been on any studio tapes that were rolling—though a few studio tapes were used on official records and a few have also leaked out on bootlegs.

The Apple sessions got off to an inauspicious start on January 21, not just because of the delay while equipment was installed. Whether it's because they're tentative about regrouping after the blow-up at Twickenham, or because they're still not entirely sure of what all this activity is leading to, the Beatles' early recordings on this day seem rusty and halting. Eventually they rouse themselves to work on some of the songs they'd made progress on at Twickenham, "I Dig a Pony" getting by far the most attention. Combined with slides back into lackluster snippets of oldies and improvisations, it makes for one of the duller days of their January 1969 recordings.

The most interesting items, in fact, come not from their work on the more familiar *Let It Be* material, but from some of the more unusual originals that never got into the official Beatles canon. Paul's "Every Night" would eventually find a place on his debut, *McCartney*, though here it's a murkily recorded tune that's barely more developed than their numerous untitled jams. Paul later revealed that he'd had the first two lines for a few years before adding more lyrics on a 1969 Greek holiday. George Harrison's "Window, Window" isn't even really recognizable, and would take more shape a few days later and, more than a year later, as a solo demo (though he never would release a version). The early days of the Lennon-McCartney catalog are revisited in a minute-long version of "Too Bad about Sorrows," which reveals itself as a hokey, sub-Elvis doo wop–type ballad.

Despite the similarity of the title lyric to one used in "I Dig a Pony," John's "All I Want Is You" is an entirely different tune that has little more than energy and desperately half-shouted, half-moaned vocals going for it—though possibly its ultra-simple, ultra-passionate lyrics form a germ of another similar, repetitive phrase he'd use to anchor "I Want You (She's So Heavy)." John hasn't given up on "Madman," either, though he isn't helping his case by just repeating one verse over and over. The words of this verse are certainly zany enough to make one wish he'd done a little more follow-through: "Well don't you know that there's a madman coming, gonna do you no harm/he's wearing pink pajamas and he lives on a farm/he's got to get somewhere and see that he can be on his own." What/who exactly could John have been thinking of here? Could he even have been singing about himself?

The oldies covers from January 21 are worse than usual, yielding little of note other than documenting some of their conscious and subconscious favorites. To be cruel, they don't do "Hallelujah, I Love Her So" too much better than they had back in 1960 on their just-post-Quarrymen tapes. Admittedly it's a cheap thrill to hear John take the lead vocal on a bump-and-grind version of Bo Diddley's classic "I'm a Man," though such straight macho blues covers were never the Beatles' forte. No fewer than four mid-'50s Presley covers, too, make clear their affection for Elvis in his Sun days. But contemporary reality intrudes at the end of "Good Rockin' Tonight," where Paul reads from an article in the British press about the Beatles' current struggles, infamously attributed to "drugs, divorce, and a slipping image."

Still, the day wasn't entirely unproductive. Even when the playing's on the sloppy side, some enthusiasm (or, perhaps, relief at the Beatles somehow remaining intact) shines through. John livens up a shaky pass at "I Dig a Pony" with some witty improvisations, at one point digging a "skylight" (a noun not found in the official version), at another exclaiming, "You can do anything that you want to in this whole darn world, because all I want is you!" He also tosses in a quote from Little Richard's "Tutti Frutti" in "Don't Let Me Down," and an ad-lib from the "I Dig a Pony" takes, introducing the song as "'I Dig a Pigmy' by Charles Hawtrey and the Deaf Aids: phase one, in which Doris gets her oats," that would famously open the official *Let It Be* album. And in 1996, one of the takes of "She Came In through the Bathroom Window" was officially issued on *Anthology 3*. It's not, however, the best version of the song from the January sessions; it's still too sluggish, though interesting for the use of wah-wah guitar and their newly acquired Fender Rhodes piano (played by John). (Though given a January 22 date in the *Anthology 3* liner notes, this take is actually from a day earlier, according to scholars of the *Get Back* tapes.)

Note, by the way, that from this day forward, the tapes sometimes include the Beatles listening to playbacks of previous takes and talking/singing over them. Occasionally that's of marginal interest because you'll hear some comments about what they've recorded, though standard music fans will find the whole idea of listening to tapes of guys listening to tapes weird, if not downright disturbing.

● **January 22**

Studio Outtakes

Let It Be *sessions*
Apple Studios, London

I Shall Be Released (two versions)
Let It Down

Don't Let Me Down (18 versions)
*I've Got a Feeling (29 versions)
Some Other Guy
Johnny B. Goode
*I Dig a Pony (24 versions)
Going Up the Country
The Long and Winding Road (three versions)
A Taste of Honey
Oh! Darling
I'm Ready
Rocker
Save the Last Dance for Me
Carol

Miscellaneous:

Instrumental improvisations/jams (12)
Vocal numbers, titles impossible to even guess (two)
            one version appears on Anthology 3

Having gotten some of the bugs out of their system on their first day back on the job, the Beatles—as demonstrated by the relatively short list of songs they even attempted on this day—applied themselves to their material more seriously than at any prior time in January. Perhaps it was because they knew that time was finally starting to run out on whatever they'd do with the sessions, since Ringo was committed to begin filming his part of *The Magic Christian* in February. Or maybe they'd finally gotten used to the strange situation, to some degree.

Whatever the reason, most of their work was on songs that did actually make the *Let It Be* album. So relatively well did the session go, in fact, that a few of the takes were actually used in the first version of the album that was mixed for release in the spring. Another reason for the improved atmosphere was the addition of keyboardist Billy Preston, in town playing with Ray Charles and roped in by George Harrison. Preston doesn't appear on all of the day's recordings, but his presence does more than just help alleviate the tensions that had built up between the Beatles. It also fills out the sound, allowing the other four to concentrate more on other instruments—both vital considerations in view of their determination to play and record live, with no overdubs.

The elevated spirits are evident in the jovial asides and ad-libs (particularly from John Lennon) that pepper most of the songs. It's a little odd that they'd insert these kinds of things in takes that were presumably being recorded in consideration for official release, where performances with such irreverent alterations are usually not even in the running. It may be, however, that the Beatles were deliberately being informal, feeling that a certain looseness would be in keeping with the whole "live and spontaneous" ethos driving the *Get Back* enterprise. Most such takes were unused, of course, but at least we now have them to compare and contrast as interesting variations from the live (or pseudo-live) ones that did get issued on *Let It Be*.

While the arrangements on the songs done on January 22 aren't much different from the familiar official versions, you do get a whole lotta fun in the not-quite-100-percent-serious passages, though admittedly not everyone will be joyous at the prospect of wading through four CDs to hear them. So in "Don't Let Me Down," you hear the likes of John yelp-screaming the bridge, scatting in falsetto, or harmonizing with Paul in a low frog voice. In "I Dig a Pony," John can not only "indicate everything you see," as he exultantly adds, "If you want to, it's alright by me." In one "I've Got a Feeling," Paul scats distractedly before John sings his "Everybody had a hard year" section in a far lower voice than usual; in yet another, John sings that part with a gutter-growl rougher than Tom Waits'; in another, Paul speaks rather than sings the bridge; in another, he speeds up the bridge by almost half; in yet another, Paul has not merely "a" feeling, but "another" feeling. Then there's the part where they repeat the three-chord transition at the end of the verse for minutes on end, over and over, at times inserting ridiculous Roadrunner-type "beep beeps"—a segment whose tape looplike repetition would drive most listeners up the wall but didn't keep the Beatles from repeating the exercise yet again a few days later.

A few of the better ragged-but-right takes were selected by Glyn Johns (who would end up being credited as one of *Let It Be*'s three producers) for his first attempt at assembling a *Get Back* album a few months later. While the one picked of "Don't Let Me Down" isn't as good as the single, it has its own attributes, particularly the Ringo Starr cymbal crash after the intro and John's shout of "Hit it, Bill!" right before Preston's electric piano solo. The one selected of "I've Got a Feeling" can be heard on *Anthology 3*, and is fun for call-and-response exchanges about keeping on your toes between Paul and John, though it actually breaks down before the finish with a quizzical, sawed-off riff, Lennon bashfully admitting, "I cocked it up trying to get loud . . . not bad, though." Glyn Johns also took a version of "I Dig a Pony" for the first *Get Back* iteration, though the one heard on *Anthology 3* is a yet different take from this date, complete with the wailed "All I want is you" refrains at the start and finish that were sadly edited out of the track on the *Let It Be* album. Many years later in *MOJO*, Paul seemed quite pleased with this particular version, on which he felt that "John and I sing like angels."

A couple of oldies from the session were also included by Johns on the first version of the *Get Back* LP, puzzlingly so, as they're far from the best covers the Beatles did in January. The one arbitrarily titled "Rocker" (though it's shown up as different titles on bootleg) is a Chuck Berry–like jam off Fats Domino's "I'm Ready" with a whiplash guitar riff, segueing into a lugubrious version of the Drifters' classic early soul hit "Save the Last Dance for Me." With their revived focus, the Beatles actually didn't even do many oldies covers at all on January 22, and what few there were aren't worth noting. "A Taste of Honey" does start off with quite promising ghostly reverb, but breaks down almost immediately.

● January 23

Studio Outtakes

Let It Be *sessions*
Apple Studios, London

Octopus's Garden
Two of Us (two versions)
I've Got a Feeling (three versions)
Get Back (43 versions)
Words of Love
Twenty Flight Rock

Oh! Darling (three versions)
Let It Be (two versions)
Mean Mr. Mustard
Let's Twist Again
The Long and Winding Road (two versions)
Everything's Alright
I Want to Thank You
You've Been Acting Strange
Use What You Got
Happiness Runs
Shazam
I Dig a Pony
I'll Get You
Help!
Please Please Me

Other songs, titles uncertain:
Hey, Hey Georgie
If You Need Me
Love Is the Thing to Me
Together in Love
It Blew Again

Miscellaneous:
Instrumental improvisations/jams (12)

Judging by the amount of work that went into "Get Back" on this date, it seems the Beatles might have determined that it was a leading contender for the title track of the next album and a likely single. Certainly its chunky hard rock lent itself well to whatever the *Get Back* project would end up being, since it would obviously be an exciting number to perform live (or in a simulated live situation), as well as one that could be effectively recorded live as a full-band arrangement. Billy Preston was now virtually a temporary fifth member of the group, and his skittering electric keyboard work did much to give the song its final definition.

The takes of "Get Back" make up the majority of the circulating January 23 tapes. It's apparent from the first performances that they haven't settled on a rhythm, and that John Lennon hasn't developed a cogent guitar solo, though he's flirting with the obbligato patterns that he'd use in the final arrangement. They take some big steps up the ladder with the emergence of the coda, with its reference to high-heeled shoes (likely a play on Tommy Tucker's "Hi Heel Sneakers," which the Beatles played several times in January), and the contributions of Preston (who, incidentally, picked up the songs commendably quickly considering that he, unlike the other four, hadn't been rehearsing them ad infinitum throughout the month). Low, almost bass-like lead vocals an octave lower than the familiar ones are also dabbled with, though fortunately the idea didn't take, if it was even serious in the first place. And the references to Pakistanis have been dropped, Paul revealing in some between-take chatter that "it started off as a protest song, but it'll work, actually, just as these two [verses] . . . I like the *word* 'Pakistanis' [chuckles], but I think it works okay with just the two verses." Immediately afterward, in the same conversation, John advises giving one of his solos to Billy Preston. The impression's that he's doing this to make it simpler for him to get his own guitar part down ("Because I'm only going to be able to work one [solo] out"), but whatever the

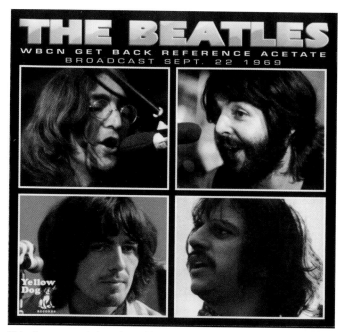

This album presented versions of Get Back *material that producer Glyn Johns had assembled on an acetate from a tape of an early broadcast (complete with DJ announcements) on a Boston radio station, September 22, 1969.*

motivation, the alternation of guitar and keyboard solos gave the arrangement a great boost of imagination and variety.

Enough solid progress was made on the tune, in fact, that one take was selected by Glyn Johns on the first acetate of rough mixes he assembled of the *Get Back* material (known as *Kum Back*), which in poorer fidelity became the very first widely circulated Beatles bootleg LP. Though less polished than the hit single, it's substantially the same in structure, the tricky tempos, lyrics, and John's piercing guitar solos having been virtually fully worked out—a remarkable achievement considering how far from the goal line they were as the day began.

Though the day was dominated by "Get Back," both new material and oldies were intermittently played as well. "Oh! Darling" got about 20 minutes of work, allowing us at various points to hear Paul sing the bridge an octave lower than usual, ending with a Presley-like vocal shudder. Some interesting guitar licks that didn't make the *Abbey Road* arrangement surface here too, like bursts of slashing offbeat chords in the bridge. Some circular arpeggio guitar lines make their way into these attempts as well, an idea that would be retained for the *Abbey Road* revamp. There's a (very) quickly abandoned spiky, speedy hard-rock tryout of "Two of Us," and Ringo's further along on "Octopus's Garden" (which he plays on piano), though it still has a dull, unvarying three-chord melody.

As on the previous day, not many oldies were attempted. As nifty as 1969 versions of "Help!" and "Please Please Me" might look on paper, these particular renditions (like virtually all of the vintage originals the group revisited in January) are disappointingly fragmentary and satirically tossed off. Each lasts less than a minute, with "Help!" given a slow, offbeat shuffle treatment and artless low-register lead vocal (complemented by bark-yelping McCartney backup vocals), and "Please Please Me" a twisted atonal melody that bears no relation to the original

save the use of the words of the first line. Better is the cover of Eddie Cochran's "Twenty Flight Rock," which is fairly lively despite Paul's inability to remember all the lyrics—a devastating irony, considering that McCartney played the song to Lennon when they first met on July 6, 1957, John being particularly impressed that Paul knew all the words!

A surprisingly coarse side of the group is revealed here and there between the serious takes. During some noodling around, a few voices break into atonal screams, John (of all people) declaring, "I'd like to do a piece by Yoko Ono" before launching into some Ono-like mad-bird squalls. John, making fun of Yoko? Maybe he wasn't quite as sensitive about critical blasts against her idiosyncratic talents as is usually assumed. Or it could be an outgrowth of an avant-garde, searingly feedback-laden untitled improvisation from slightly earlier on the day's tapes, Yoko eventually joining in on vocals as she had about a week before, though the results this time around aren't quite as grating (if only because the tapes aren't nearly as long).

In a different kind of irreverence, John dispenses with Donovan's "Happiness Runs" (which he had certainly heard during the visit to Rishikesh) with a rushed, ten-second flush-this-down-the-toilet busk. Then there's McCartney (of all people) calling Glyn Johns "fuckface" (!) when the engineer/producer accidentally interrupts the beginning of a take, Paul using a tone that's likely more in jest than malice, though it's hard to tell for sure. In the unlikely event any of the Beatles ever made it through the 100 or so hours of bootlegged *Get Back* tapes, little gems such as these might have made them regret their decision to get everything on tape or film. Or maybe not—all of them, even McCartney, were tired of their wholesome image by 1969, though it's doubtful they wanted *all* such laundry available for all the world to see and hear.

● **January 24**

Studio Outtakes
Let It Be *sessions*
Apple Studios, London

Get Back (21 versions)
(I Can't Get No) Satisfaction
What'd I Say (two versions)
Don't Let Me Down
Ob-La-Di, Ob-La-Da
Soldier of Love (two versions)
Cathy's Clown
Where Have You Been (two versions)
Love Is a Swingin' Thing (two versions)
She Said Yeah
I'm Just a Child of Nature
*Two of Us (21 versions)
You're So Good to Me
She Came In through the Bathroom Window
**Teddy Boy (six versions)
Ach Du Lieber Augustin
Maggie Mae (two versions)
I Fancy Me Chances
Polythene Pam
The Long and Winding Road

Window, Window (two versions)

Her Majesty

Every Night

Hot as Sun

Catswalk

Hello Goodbye

Diggin' My Potatoes

Hey Liley, Liley Lo

Rock Island Line

Tiger Rag

Michael Row Your Boat Ashore

Rock-A-Bye Baby

Singing the Blues

Knee Deep in the Blues

Dig It (four versions)

Little Demon

Maybellene

You Can't Catch Me

Brown-Eyed Handsome Man

Short Fat Fannie

Green Onions

Bad Boy

Sweet Little Sixteen

Around and Around

School Day

Stand By Me

Lady Madonna

Lovely Rita

Lonely Sea

Ramrod

Other songs, titles uncertain:

Balls to Your Partner

There You Are, Eddie (three versions)

Pillow for Your Head (two versions)

Miscellaneous:

Instrumental improvisations/jams (six)

Vocal numbers, titles impossible to even guess (one)

one version appears on Anthology 3

**part of one version appears on* Anthology 3

Much material was recorded on this date, but it lacked the focus of the previous day's work, possibly because Billy Preston wasn't present for much of the time. More work was done (by far) on "Two of Us" and (to a lesser extent) "Get Back" than any of the other new songs that were foremost in the group's plans. That left plenty of time for oldies busks, one-time-only passes at other songs they'd release in 1969 and 1970, and introductions of yet more new compositions. As it turned out, all that fooling around didn't go to waste: one of the impromptu busks actually made it onto the *Let It Be* album, one of the jams developed into another *Let It Be* cut, one of the ad-libs during those jams was used on *Let It Be,* and other takes were used on early (rejected and unreleased) versions of the *Get Back* LP.

The most progress was made on "Two of Us," which is here taking on the acoustic, country-tinged, folk-rock feel and hoofbeat rhythm familiar from the *Let It Be* arrangement. It also has its distinctive ringing acoustic guitar opening, as heard in the take officially issued on *Anthology 3*. It's actually not the best alternate take of "Two of Us," fouling up in the beginning of the second bridge and suffering from some feedback. It might have been chosen for the aside Paul utters to John ("Take it, Phil") at the end of the first bridge—a reference to Phil Everly, the song's close harmonies being especially reminiscent of the Everly Brothers. A different take from this day was selected by Glyn Johns for an early version of the *Get Back* LP, and it's superior on several counts. Not only does it boast a more effectively plaintive interpretation, but it also features false starts and a spoken ending by Paul ("And so we leave the little town of London, England") that, more than almost any other take they recorded, preserves the spontaneous roughness they were apparently trying to capture with the *Get Back* album, at least as it was originally conceived.

The most interesting "Get Back" variation from January 24 has exceptionally wobbly slide guitar à la "For You Blue," as does a subsequent version of "Two of Us." Played by John, whose understanding of the instrument is fractured to say the least, the slide guitar gets positively woozy on "Her Majesty." Here that ditty is sung by Paul in falsetto and lasts a good two and a half minutes, though it's just the single verse heard in the brief *Abbey Road* finale played over and over. John's memorable slide guitar part on "For You Blue" is usually thought of as a one-off use of that effect, but indications are he was toying with it a bit more extensively, though his colleague George Harrison would put the slide to far more creative, accomplished use in the early '70s.

Paul, as he said at the end of one take, introduced his "Teddy Boy" (which he'd actually started writing at Rishikesh the previous year) as another song for consideration, though a snatch had surfaced a couple of weeks before at Twickenham. Perhaps he chose this moment to put it forth as it lent itself to the same acoustic guitar–dominated treatment they'd worked up for "Two of Us," and it even gets the same sort of hoofbeat, though that might be because Ringo (like the rest of the band) is playing the song at the same time he's learning it. The merits of "Teddy Boy" are questioned by many Beatles fans and, one would guess, the Beatles themselves, since it almost but didn't quite make it onto the *Let It Be* album. Certainly it's a lightweight outing in the company of most of the new material they're working on, with a round-and-round structure verging on the vertigo-inducing. John Lennon evidently thought so, breaking into a sarcastic square dance call during one of the instrumental breaks.

Nevertheless, and conceding that as played here it might go round-and-round at a length that wears out its welcome, "Teddy Boy" does have archetypically McCartneyesque charms. There's a cunningly catchy, folky melody, winsome high vocals, and a witty if cutesy observational portrait of a British character type (this being a "Teddy Boy," the rough '50s British equivalent to an American hood or juvenile delinquent, though at heart he's more a mama's boy than a Teddy Boy). And while it wouldn't be worked on in the studio much this week, it was a serious contender for placement on the *Get Back* album, as a nearly six-minute version from this day was mixed on the first acetate Glyn Johns prepared of *Get Back* material. In fact, as this was thus part of the *Kum Back* bootleg, hundreds of thousands of Beatles fans heard this back in 1970 before *Let It Be* came out. The three-minute, 15-second version on *Anthology 3,* however, was edited together from this take and a subsequent one on January 28, to the consternation of purists who would rather have had one unedited take than a quarter-century-after-the-fact reconstruction. Paul did get to release another version of the song relatively soon after the *Get Back* sessions take, however, on his 1970 debut, *McCartney,* where the composition was solely credited to "McCartney," as it likewise is on *Anthology 3.*

Admitted Paul in a 1996 quote used in Keith Badman's *The Beatles After the Break-Up: 1970-2000:* "We've now put together a version, an edit of one of the takes of us trying it, which sounds interesting. You can hear on it that the band wasn't very interested in it. I don't know why. Maybe I hadn't finished it enough or something. Maybe it was just tension coming in. The bit I'd like to keep actually was John sort of making fun of it. He starts towards the end of it, going, 'Grab your partners, do-si-do,' so we've kept that on. And while it was, in some way, indicative of friction, it was good-humored friction." Johns echoed Paul's sentiments when interviewed for the BBC radio series "The Record Producers": "I loved it, and I was hoping they'd finish it and do it, because I thought it was really good. But my version does go on a bit, and they're just going round and round, trying to get the chord sequence right, I suppose, and the best bit is where John Lennon gets bored—he obviously doesn't want to play it any more, and starts doing his interjections."

A few more previews of *McCartney* (which of course had yet to be conceived) were also heard, as he again went through "Every Night." Played on acoustic guitar, it's pretty, like so much of Paul's work, but lacks much substance (and wouldn't get a whole lot more, even on *McCartney*). Another *McCartney* tune, the easygoing, Hawaiian-flavored "Hot as Sun," was actually written by Paul about ten years before this 1969 performance. Though cut as an instrumental for *McCartney,* here Paul scats some nonsense exotica sounds, adding the brief spoken semi-travelogue, "Welcome to the South Sea Islands, where the sound of a wave landing on the sand brings joy to the air." "Pillow for Your Head" sounds like the embryo of something that would fit in snugly with the cozily domestic ambience of *McCartney,* though it's never resurfaced.

Seemingly in a mood to give vent to his most lightweight, innocuous, folky side, Paul also plays "There You Are, Eddie," never released by him or the Beatles, although it's in a relatively advanced state, including both verse and bridge. Somewhat reminiscent of some of Donovan's cutesier compositions, it's another pleasant-on-the-surface but slight number, seemingly addressed (shades of "Martha My Dear") to a lovably misbehaved dog. It's been speculated that it might be a veiled reflection of his mixed feelings for the band mates with whom he was having trouble getting along, but the truth might be far more mundane. For as Hunter Davies revealed in the 1985 edition of his authorized biography of the Beatles, "I remember one tune he played for me in Portugal [in December 1968], which he had written on the lavatory (he rarely went there without his guitar), which was called 'There You Go Eddie.' Just a short verse, and I don't think he ever completed it. He had discovered that my first Christian name is Edward, something I've always kept quiet."

John also had a trifling ditty to play, though it turned out to be something the band would take more seriously. The several versions of the ultra-basic jam "Dig It" from this date actually bear little resemblance to the familiar *Let It Be* one, other than a generally improvised bluesy structure. The drunk-sounding slide guitar that had apparently caught John's momentary fancy features heavily, making the whole thing sound like a physically warped talking blues record. Though

the tune, bare as it was, would change a lot over the next few days, the idea remained the same: a rudimentary blues-rock bash, John (with some enthusiastic help from Paul) shouting phrases that came into his head, the only consistently used lyric being "dig it" itself. It was from one of these early takes, too, that the famous ad-lib connecting "Dig It" and "Let It Be" on the *Let It Be* album originated: "That was 'Can You Dig It' by Georgie Wood, and now we'd like to do, 'Hark the Angels Come.'"

John revives "I'm Just a Child of Nature," and the band actually makes it through most of the song fairly coherently, though Lennon doesn't sound wholly enthusiastic about the vocal. It's too bad they didn't follow through with this, as it's a better (and certainly more complete) song than some of the others John was offering for consideration from his scant bag of freshly minted tunes. Oddly, "Polythene Pam," which he'd demoed back in 1968, is given its one and only *Get Back* airing. It's a spirited Lennon performance (though everyone else seems unsure of what to play), yet somehow it was put on the back burner. There are also some piano tinkles quite close to the melody line of "Oh My Love"—a song John had demoed in late 1968, but would not (unless this counts) play whatsoever at the *Get Back* sessions. George's compositions were barely dealt with at all on January 24, although he did play part of yet another pretty Dylan-influenced original, "Window, Window," which he never released on an official album (though he did a full demo version in 1970).

Some of the oldies done on this day were well above average by the *Get Back* sessions' slim standards, but they also epitomize the frustration of listening to the Beatles' January 1969 covers. With just a little more work, at least a couple of them could have been genuinely good tracks, but the guys are just not bothering to give them even roughly complete interpretations. Take "Soldier of Love," for instance, which of course the group had done a great version of on the BBC in 1963. The first and longer version here starts off like it means business, with a slower but attractively funky gait and committed John Lennon lead vocal. It soon becomes obvious, however, that he's forgotten many of the words (a recurring problem with John throughout his career and in January 1969 specifically, even on some of his own songs). They also manage to play parts of more than half a dozen Chuck Berry classics without doing a distinguished job on any of them, though "Almost Grown" has a little more enthusiastic sparkle than the rest.

An even greater lost opportunity was their take on Guy Mitchell's mid-'50s hit "Singing the Blues," one of the very few oldies covers from the whole *Get Back* sessions which is in many respects an actual excellent performance. Paul's assured vocal here is simply magnificent, they manage to sing and play the tune pretty much the whole way through, and the band's arrangement is down-home funky. But John's slide guitar is predictably erratic, the recording quality is subpar even by the standards of the cameras' sound equipment, and the film crew chooses this of all takes to butt in with voiced-over announcements of roll/slate numbers. Had they just decided to do one or more takes with the same arrangement but dedicated themselves to eliminating the distractions and imperfections, it would probably stand as the best oldies cover of the entire *Get Back* shebang. As it is, it's one of the few that you can listen to (more or less) for actual pleasure, not just historical insight.

The acoustic nature of much of the material performed at this session seems to have gotten them in the mood to do a few more relics from their Quarrymen days. "Maggie Mae" goes back to their deepest

Liverpool pre-rock roots, and one of the versions they did on this day was chosen to end side one of the *Let It Be* LP, though it was actually just one of a few similar rundowns of the tune performed at this session. Of the other such tracks, "I Fancy Me Chances" is notable as an early Lennon-McCartney tune, though as rendered here it's little more than a speedy, basic folk-skiffle busk.

● January 25

Studio Outtakes

Let It Be *sessions*
Apple Studios, London

Another Day
Two of Us (seven versions)
Act Naturally
Nashville Cats
I've Got a Feeling
On the Road Again
I Lost My Little Girl
Bye Bye Love
*For You Blue (28 versions)
Take This Hammer
*Let It Be (18 versions)
Please Please Me
Mean Mr. Mustard
Tracks of My Tears
Piece of My Heart
Little Yellow Pills
Early in the Morning
Window, Window
I'm Talking About You
Martha My Dear
Love Story
Cannonball
Shazam
Isn't It a Pity

Other songs, titles uncertain:

Sorry I Left You Bleeding
Crazy Feet
Well It's Eight O'Clock
Fast Train to San Francisco

Miscellaneous:

Instrumental improvisations/jams (ten)
Vocal numbers, titles impossible to even guess (three)

one version appears on Anthology 3

It could have been because of Billy Preston's absence, but none of the three songs on which the Beatles concentrated on this date ("Two of Us," "For You Blue," and "Let It Be") were numbers destined for the live rooftop concert. Since "Two of Us" had pretty much been whipped into shape the day before, it's not clear why the group felt the need to keep

going over it, though they'd take this over-and-over-again approach to a bunch of tunes during the next few days. Whether out of boredom with the repetition, joy at being able to record in a studio in more casual circumstances than usual, or some combination of the two, these "Two of Us" takes—some of them quite lengthy, with sections repeated many times over—were stuffed with entertaining variations and ad-libs. John in particular adopted all manner of funny accents, including a quite credible, quite hilarious, grainy Bob Dylan imitation in which you can feel the phlegm rising from his throat. John and Paul both come up with rib-tickling exaggerations/approximations of Scottish, Jamaican, French, and German accents, as well as inserting deliberate off-keyisms, siren-like noises, "beep beep"s, and the like. These are by no stretch of the imagination the *best* "Two of Us" outtakes, but there are few variations from the *Get Back* sessions—or from the Beatles' entire career, for that matter—that are as goofily entertaining. More subtly, they make the point that for all the grief generated in January 1969, the Beatles, and John and Paul in particular, were still able to have a whale of a good time on occasion.

George Harrison had justifiably felt that the Beatles didn't give as much attention to his compositions as they did to Lennon-McCartney's efforts. But with "For You Blue," as with a few of his other songs in January, they do put in quite a bit of time, pretty much getting it into releasable shape by day's end. It sounds as if here they might consciously be thinking of getting a *studio* track in the can, rather than rehearsing a number for a show that might, coincidentally, result in an acceptable studio recording. For on the first versions, the execution from both composer and band mates is rather tentative and awkward. Soon enough, however, they come up with a workable full-band arrangement, one of which (complete with a false start, followed by rattling ice cubes and cry of "Quiet, please!") was chosen by Glyn Johns for the unreleased *Get Back* LP. An earlier, somewhat more hesitant take was selected for *Anthology 3*.

Maybe the group were already thinking they could use Billy Preston to play on "Let It Be," since the versions here—with Paul on piano and John taking over bass—are not always 100 percent serious. Specifically, *John* is not always 100 percent serious, putting in some basso profundo vocals, at one time gulping "Boof, boof, boof" in supposed harmony. Elsewhere, a beautiful practice run through high wordless harmonies is rudely interrupted by an Ono-esque Lennon scream. It could be, too, that he's unhappy at having to handle the unfamiliar bass, which he paws at with a clumsy, uncertain thump (and wrong notes aplenty). One of the final attempts from this session, with a few McCartney ad-lib sing-speaks of the title phrase at the end, was used on *Anthology 3*. Though historically instructive to the general Beatles fan, it's another instance in which it's hardly the best alternate available; some of the final lyrics are missing (or slightly different), there's no organ, and the guitar solo's mediocre.

With so much time taken up by three tunes (and listening to some playbacks of work done over the past few days), there was relatively little in the way of songs-in-progress and oldies covers, though they fit in a little such material between the main courses. Paul sings and plays a brief snatch of "Please Please Me" on piano in a silly lounge lizard fashion, and manages a brief snatch of "Another Day" on acoustic guitar. A drumless "Mean Mr. Mustard" still finds John veering off into an unfinished bridge that wouldn't even be started on the *Abbey Road* version. George's "Window, Window" is, weirdly, largely sung by Paul, whose silly, jolly-sailor tone indicates he might not have thought much of the song. Harrison's "Isn't It a Pity," eventually a standout on *All Things Must Pass,* is heard for the first time, though it's hard to make out anything but some chord sequences. "I Lost My Little Girl" is, according to Paul McCartney's recollection, the first song he ever wrote. It's odd, then, that John takes the vocal here, complete with improvised-sounding outrageousness about how "the police had taken her away due to her inconvenience, something to do about interstate nude." Lasting almost ten minutes, musically it's like many of the undistinguished *Get Back* blues-rock jams, though with a two-chord vamp that recalls their friend Donovan's "Season of the Witch." The late-'60s heavy rock feel is such, in fact, that it seems unlikely that the song was performed like this back in the late '50s.

One particular Lennon-McCartney exchange during the "Let It Be" rehearsals, incidentally, is as scathing as any spoken dialogue picked up during the whole month. The Beatles break into a brief cover of Chuck Berry's "I'm Talking About You," which Paul interrupts in his best teacher okay-kids-I-know-this-is-a-lot-of-fun-but-we-have-to-get-back-to-the-lesson-now voice: "Come on now, come on now, come on now, come now. Back to the drudgery!" Upon which John replies with an acid bite: "It's you that's making it like this! It's you that's bloody making it like this!" Even if it was intended in half-jest, it's an impossible-to-avoid signpost that all was not so harmonious as work on the rehearsal/recording sessions intensified.

● January 26

Studio Outtakes

Let It Be *sessions*
Apple Studios, London

Isn't It a Pity
Window, Window
Let It Down (two versions)
Octopus's Garden (eight versions)
Little Piece of Leather
Two of Us
I Dig a Pony
Let It Be (28 versions)
High School Confidential
Great Balls of Fire
Don't Let the Sun Catch You Crying
Suicide
Do Not Forsake Me Oh My Darling
You Really Got a Hold on Me (two versions)
Like a Rolling Stone
Twist and Shout
Dig It
**Rip It Up
**Shake, Rattle and Roll
Kansas City
Miss Ann
Lawdy Miss Clawdy
**Blue Suede Shoes
Tracks of My Tears

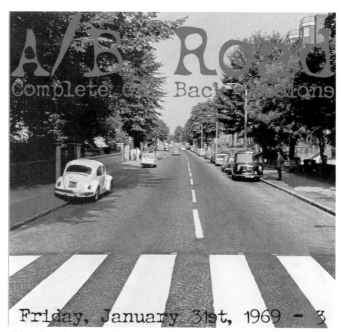

At long last: the very last installment of the marathon January 1969 Get Back sessions.

Agent Double-O-Soul
S.O.S.
Rockin' Pneumonia and the Boogie Woogie Flu
I'm Movin' On
Little Yellow Pills
*The Long and Winding Road (16 versions)

Other songs, titles uncertain:
It Was So Blue
I Left My Home in the World
I Told You Before

Miscellaneous:
Instrumental improvisations/jams (six)
Vocal numbers, titles impossible to even guess (three)

> *one version appears on Anthology 3
> **appears as part of edited-together medley on Anthology 3

"Let It Be" and "The Long and Winding Road" had been given rather light attention during the early *Get Back* sessions, but by now it might have become apparent that these were major songs demanding serious studio treatment. The Beatles spent most of their time on January 26 perfecting these tunes, ending up with releasable versions of each, though neither would make it onto the *Let It Be* album in these exact forms.

With Billy Preston on hand, the Beatles were now able to craft an arrangement for "Let It Be" using both piano and organ. After getting some rusty (and, sometimes, ridiculously exaggerated) Lennon falsetto harmonies out of their system early on, they get down to work on complete takes, where the churchy organ tone really enhances the song's strong gospel bent. (In fact, it's notably "churchier" in tone in some of the earlier takes.) The lyrics are still unfinished, and even in one of the later versions, Paul sings, "You will be a good girl" (presumably to his young stepdaughter-to-be, Heather, who was with him in the studio for this session) instead of "Shine until tomorrow." The day's final complete take, however, was pretty good, with a hip, slow, one-two-three-four count-in and an organ that remained more gospel-like in the mix than the one heard in the hit single version. It's not as good as the hit single, mind you (not least because the second and third verse still have identical lyrics), and the band is still playing together right from the start, instead of leading off with McCartney's solo piano. But it's nearly up to release standards, with some nice falsetto by Paul in the coda, and was in fact included on Glyn Johns's first acetate of *Get Back* mixes.

The day ended with about an hour and a half of work on "The Long and Winding Road," and while this miraculously produced a good take, the ramp leading up to it was about as grisly an exercise as any from the *Get Back* sessions—quite a feat, considering how many fraught passages there were in this stormy month. John was again stuck on bass, and his ghost-of-Stu-Sutcliffe-quality playing is so horrific that one's tempted to wonder whether he'd ever seen the instrument before, let alone played it. More shockingly, the guitar work on most of the takes is abominable. There are so many missed notes and clumsy interjections, in fact, that one also wonders if it's even George Harrison on most of these versions, so clueless is the execution. Could George have stepped out for an hour or so (perhaps because Paul was preoccupied with teaching electric pianist Billy Preston the tune), his place taken by a roadie, or even Heather?

Although it almost sounds like a competition to see who can play worse, Paul somehow remains unruffled. As they go over and over the tune, he introduces interesting variations, occasionally singing in winding falsetto bearing a muted Little Richard influence and scatting during the instrumental break. Better yet is a brief snatch done cha-cha style (seen in part in the *Let It Be* movie); weirder yet, he briefly produces a singing-through-a-snorkel-like underwater effect. Amazingly, everyone eventually comes together for a very good take, the roving atonal guitar eliminated, and John's bass, while still highly flawed, at least unobtrusive. This was the take chosen for inclusion in *Anthology 3*, and of course it's missing the heavy violin and choral vocal overdubs applied by Phil Spector (on this same take) for *Let It Be*. Those overdubs, as is well known, might have been the straw that broke McCartney's back in his decision to quit the Beatles, as he not only disliked the Spector-produced version, but claimed he wasn't given a chance to approve it. Even leaving aside the damage those overdubs caused to the Beatles' career, however, the "undubbed" "The Long and Winding Road" is vastly preferable from every angle. By wiping out the hugely objectionable, diabetically syrupy strings and choir, it allows us to hear the song in an au naturel setting that sounds positively humble in contrast.

Again, while certain songs had A-1 priority on this date, that didn't eliminate time for a bunch of oldies covers, as well as some compositions that weren't quite on the A-list at the moment. The second-class-citizen status often granted George's compositions might have been at the back, or even forefront, of his mind as he joined Ringo at the piano at the beginning of the session, introducing some new chords into "Octopus's Garden," which at this stage was a pretty musically dull composition. George seems to be going out of his way to help a songwriter whose

efforts had gotten far less support within the Beatles than his had, and magnanimously did not take any part of the songwriting credit when "Octopus's Garden" emerged in a yet different form on *Abbey Road*. (Part of this sequence, incidentally, is seen in the *Let It Be* film.) Right before working with Ringo, Harrison went through some of his own neglected songs on solo acoustic guitar, presenting a sweet version of "Isn't It a Pity" that's far more listenable than his one from the day before (though his vocals are still far too low) and fragments of "Window, Window" and "Let It Down." He also reveals that "Isn't a Pity" was about three years old at this point, but had been cursorily rejected by John Lennon.

Paul's "Suicide" lasts less than a minute, but it's a much more fully realized composition than most of the tossed-off *Get Back* snatches, with a jaunty tune, rolling piano, and delivery that would be very much suited for a pre-rock cabaret musical. Paul would later record and use a very small excerpt on his solo *McCartney* LP. As an aside, it's unusual that Paul, with such a wholesome and chipper public image, authored not one but two Beatles outtakes prominently highlighting the word "suicide" in the lyrics, the other outtake being 1965's "That Means a Lot."

Paul, also unusually for such an obscure tune, commented on its origins extensively in *Paul McCartney: Many Years from Now*, revealing that he'd written it as a teenager. "It was murder!" he exclaimed. "Horrible song! But you had to go through all those styles to discover your own. I only had one verse, so I cobbled together another." Years later, he added, he sent a demo to Frank Sinatra, who called him at Abbey Road asking for a song, but "apparently he thought it was an almighty piss-take . . . I think he couldn't grasp it was tongue in cheek. It was only supposed to be a play on the word 'suicide,' not the actual physical suicide. If a girl lets a guy trample all over her, she's committing some sort of suicide. I think he sent the demo back. Looking back on it I'm quite relieved he did, actually, it wasn't a good song, it was just a teenage thought."

The jams on the tune usually titled "I Told You Before" on bootlegs (totaling more than 25 minutes in all) aren't too compelling, but are nonetheless far more interesting than most of the "songs" made up on the spot during *Get Back*. George Harrison (who sings a few basic lines at times) and Billy Preston seem like the main motors behind this repetitive, bluesy, hard-rock workout, based around a reasonably but not terribly catchy descending riff, very slightly similar in tone to the long instrumental section that ends the Rolling Stones' "Can't You Hear Me Knockin'." It's not just a one-off, blow-off-steam exercise, either, as the band returned to it a few times over the following days, perhaps thinking something could be done with it, although nothing of substance was. It might be one small glimpse into a different direction the Beatles might have pursued more ardently had they stayed together longer; after all, both John and George put some long jams on their early solo albums, all of which were less listenable than this tune. It's too bad, however, that Heather sings/noise-makes for a while during the jam.

A jam that *was* used for "Let It Be" was a less-than-a-minute slice of "Dig It," as flimsy a tune as the Beatles ever officially released. Relatively few *Let It Be* owners are aware that it was actually excerpted from a marathon 12-minute version, much of which featured young Heather on overbearingly loud, untrained, and frankly massively annoying wordless vocals. The tune/riff, such as it was, of "Dig It" had changed substantially from the versions of a couple of days before, now falling close to the chorus of Bob Dylan's "Like a Rolling Stone"—which, the session tapes reveal, was very roughly covered (with John on unhinged lead vocals) just a couple minutes before the "Dig It" jam commenced.

At least in terms of yielding something useful for the *Get Back* project, this session did cough up a few oldies covers that eventually found their way onto record and film. Little Richard's "Rip It Up," Bill Haley/Joe Turner's "Shake, Rattle and Roll," and Carl Perkins/Elvis Presley's "Blue Suede Shoes" were all done in fairly tight, energetic fashion, with both piano and organ in the mix, though, in common with most of the *Get Back* sessions, the rhythm is a little too laidback and complacent. It's a testament to how generally lousy the *Get Back* oldies were, however, that these still-ragged performances were among the best of the whole batch, with edited portions finding release on a medley constructed for *Anthology 3*. The Beatles also do a (by their January 1969 standards) fair, if sloppy and snail-like, version of "You Really Got a Hold on Me" that's nonetheless far less exciting than their great 1963 recording of the same tune on *With the Beatles;* part of this performance is seen in the *Let It Be* film.

As for the most interesting leftovers, it's interesting to note that "Kansas City" is not the Little Richard adaptation ("Kansas City/Hey! Hey! Hey!") the group recorded for *Beatles for Sale.* Rather, it's the more famous variation made into a No. 1 hit by Wilbert Harrison in 1959, proving that the group *did* actually know both versions. Elsewhere, "Great Balls of Fire" would be a pretty good track if Paul (who sings it admirably) could have just remembered the whole song; he recalls yet less of another Jerry Lee Lewis classic, "High School Confidential."

● January 27

Studio Outtakes
Let It Be *sessions*
Apple Studios, London

Strawberry Fields Forever
Old Brown Shoe (two versions)
Baby, Let's Play House
*Oh! Darling (four versions)
Let It Be (12 versions)
The Long and Winding Road (six versions)
Little Demon
Save the Last Dance for Me
Hi Heel Sneakers
Get Back (32 versions)
Don't Let Me Down (five versions)
Hava Nagilah
I've Got a Feeling (nine versions)
You Are My Sunshine
Bring It On Home to Me
Take These Chains from My Heart
The Walk

Other songs, titles uncertain:
I Told You Before

Water, Water
You Won't Get Me That Way

Miscellaneous:
Instrumental improvisations/jams (eight)
one edited version appears on Anthology 3

The *Get Back* sessions reached the peak of their industriousness on January 27 and January 28, from which almost 15 total hours of tape circulates. As the Beatles still hadn't decided whether to do a live performance of any sort, it could be they were trying to fit in as much rehearsal/recording time as possible, for whatever purpose it might be used, in the few days they had left before Ringo would start filming *The Magic Christian.* While "Get Back" got far more attention than any other song on January 27, they also fit in a few takes of several other of the more prominent numbers they'd worked up during the month, slotting in a little time for jamming.

"Get Back" really got run through the mill at this session, so much so that it might have been a day like this that George Martin had in mind when he griped in *The Beatles Anthology,* "We would start a track and it wasn't quite right, and we would do it again . . . and again . . . and then I'd get to take 19: 'Well, John, the bass wasn't as good as it was on take 17, but the voice was pretty good, so let's go on again.' Take 43: 'Well, yes . . .' So you go on forever, because it was never perfect—and it got very tedious."

Listening to the 30-odd versions of "Get Back" here more or less in a row *does* push the borders of sanity, but you *can* hear some interesting approaches considered, or at least some entertaining spins introduced by the band to alleviate boredom. The very first take, for instance, takes off at an almost unbelievably fast pace, as if the galloping horse they're riding has broken loose from its reins, the Beatles just about managing to hold on for dear life. Perversely, they briefly tinker with slowing the tempo, John crying out during the break, "Hit me, Jo, I can feel it comin'!" Another version slows it down so much it's like listening to a 33 rpm record played at 16 rpm, McCartney compounding the strangeness by singing a quasi-spiritual ("Water, Water") while Lennon sings the standard "Get Back" lyrics. Mock-Japanese words are sung on one take, and another has Paul singing in pidgin German, John enthusiastically shouting "Raus!" in the background, no doubt flashing back all the way to their Hamburg days. Other memorable (at least within this context) ad-libs include John sing-chiding, "This is how you play" after a breakdown, and Paul deviating from the script to sing, "JoJo took his cap and filled it up with water." The most memorable ad-lib of all— John's "Sweet Loretta Fart, she thought she was a cleaner, but she was a frying pan"—was immortalized on the official *Let It Be* album, as part of the chatter preceding the version of "Get Back" used on that LP.

Nonetheless, some progress is being made. The group's refining the coda after the song's false ending, where Paul sometimes emits some forced laughs and grunts to drive the tune home; other passes at the coda are dominated by one repeated bee-stinging guitar note, or a jagged, bent, two-note phrase. The take that followed the "frying pan" bit, in fact, was thought good enough by Glyn Johns to be used on the unissued *Get Back* LP he compiled. The bulk of it was edited together with a coda from one of the takes on January 28 for the official single release, so the dozens of "Get Back" takes did pay off after all.

The group also put in a fair amount of work on "Let It Be" without making many significant changes. They experiment mildly with a quicker tempo for a while, and engage in some solely instrumental passages, perhaps in search of some inspiring new additional jimmies to sprinkle on top. Paul ad-libs an odd, spoken "Yes she does" at the end of one line, chuckling at his frivolity a couple of seconds later; near the end of that take both he and John launch into slightly, deliberately ridiculous falsetto. There's not much to add to "The Long and Winding Road" either, though one strange take is of interest for highlighting John briefly on intentionally Goonish lead vocals. Likewise, it's the humorous variations, not the increasingly similar-to-each-other typical run-throughs, that supply the most entertainment on "Don't Let Me Down": a cackle here, a breaking voice there, a "Little Willie, yeah!" shout to Billy Preston before his solo, a take where Paul uses operatic lead vocals at the beginning, and so on. Paul gets in a sharp ad-lib of his own with "I've Got a Feeling," sing-uttering, "I've got a blister, right between my toes. Oh yeah!"

Only one truly new Beatles composition was introduced on this date, but it was an interesting one: George Harrison's "Old Brown Shoe." Its first version, though sung and performed with just piano accompaniment, demonstrates that the song was pretty close to its final form already. Thirty-five minutes or so of rehearsals added organ and full band support, and it would get more dedicated work the following day. "Oh! Darling" was only worked upon briefly, but one nearly seven-minute version's of note not just for featuring Billy Preston on electric piano, but also for adding some fun call-and-response banter between Paul and John, especially in the bridge. An edited version is heard on *Anthology 3,* including John's declaration at a brief pause in the tune, "Just heard that Yoko's divorce has just gone through."

There's little between-proper-song noodling worth a mention, in keeping with the more serious work ethic the band seemed to bring to the session. The piano-dominated, drumless rendition of "Strawberry Fields Forever," while hardly a full-boned arrangement, is interesting as we hear Paul, not John, on lead vocals, though his singing is sometimes barely audible. In the instrumental improvisations, we can hear that Paul's still toying around with riffs from "The Palace of the King of the Birds." Too, the riffs from "I Told You Before" (done at one point just on piano, at another by the full band with a more Latin tinge than their first attempts on January 26) are still on the band members' minds, though nothing more would come of these tunes. Billy Preston's influence seems to peak on these heavier improvisations in particular, with these versions of "I Told You Before" and an additional (and less distinctive) untitled instrumental outing putting his forceful soul-rock organ playing to the fore.

Few oldies were played on this date, yet one, a brief stroll through Jimmy McCracklin's 1958 hit "The Walk," actually made it onto the initial acetate LP Johns assembled from the *Get Back* sessions (and was mistakenly titled "Can He Walk" on the *Kum Back* bootleg derived from that acetate). Though the Beatles don't perform the song in its entirety—they only do the chorus, really, and don't even replicate that faithfully—it's pretty good for what it is, with a solid walking beat and earthy, good-humored McCartney lead vocal, particularly when he inserts animal-like "arrr" growls not present in the original. Paul also seems to have a lot of fun singing a morsel of Ray Charles' "Take These Chains from My Heart" in a deliberately stentorian Paul Robeson–ish voice, as if he's making some inside joke whose context is unclear to us mere listeners.

● January 28

Studio Outtakes

Let It Be *sessions*
Apple Studios, London

Shazam
The Long and Winding Road
I've Got a Feeling (17 versions)
Rainy Day Women #12 & 35
The Inner Light
Blue Yodel No. 1 (T for Texas)
Tea for Two Cha-Cha
Dig It
I'm Just a Child of Nature (two versions)
I Dig a Pony (12 versions)
Get Back (seven versions)
Love Me Do
*Teddy Boy (two versions)
Don't Let Me Down (four versions)
One After 909 (four versions)
Old Brown Shoe (eight versions)
I Want You (She's So Heavy) (four versions)
Sticks and Stones
Something (five versions)
Bo Diddley
Two of Us (five versions)
All Things Must Pass (four versions)
Positively 4th Street (two versions)

Other songs, titles uncertain:

The River Rhine
I Will Always Look for You
Unless He Has a Song
How Do You Tell Someone?
Greasepaint on Your Face

Miscellaneous:

Instrumental improvisations/jams (two)
 *part of one version appears on Anthology 3

January 28 could have been the most hectic day of the *Get Back* sessions, at least as far as recordings went. Many of the songs that ended up on the *Let It Be* album were done over and over; some of the weaker contenders got some of their final chances, and, unbelievably, more new compositions continued to bubble up, including a future No. 1 single whose potential even the composer didn't seem to recognize at the time.

After a routine bluesy, jazzy tongue-in-cheek number ("The River Rhine") that reflects Paul's occasional nightclub singer inclinations, the Beatles plus Billy Preston carry the loose bluesiness over to their first tries at "I've Got a Feeling." You can picture George Martin holding his head in agony when, as they'd done on January 22, they play the three-chord transition at the end of the verse over . . . and over . . . and over, for 15 whole minutes. What they're after doesn't seem entirely clear even to themselves. More frustrating about sequences such as these, particularly if you're managing to listen to the *Get Back* sessions in order, is that it often seems as though the more they work on a song, the farther they get away from what they had in the first place. Not just with "I've Got a Feeling," but with the other songs they'd done to death by this point, and for which they seem to have already worked out satisfactory arrangements.

If you can manage to sit through all this, you can spot some moderately ear-catching variations here and there, like the time Paul diffidently sing-speaks the bridge, the attempt to integrate typically sloppy slide guitar into the song, and the "everybody had a sock shoe" lyric that graces one take. There are also versions where John takes over Paul's lead vocal part (with a little backup vocal support from Preston), to unimpressive effect, mock-sobbing on the line about missing a train on one version. Such role-switching wasn't being seriously considered; it was necessary as Paul had to leave for a while. Certainly these couldn't have been intended as studio takes; they were probably extra rehearsal takes to cover the possibility of a concert on Apple's rooftop in a couple of days' time, even though the band (and most particularly George Harrison) hadn't yet committed to it. In the last Paul-less take, possibly tired of the song, they offer a double-time, monotonous version that virtually strips it of any semblance of a tune. To vary the monotony, John somehow even manages to put some lyrics (such as they are) from "Dig It" to the tune of "I've Got a Feeling" for a while.

For the other *Let It Be* songs extensively rehearsed/recorded/filmed on this day, the same holds true, with just about enough variations of note to keep you from mentally tuning out as they grind the tunes into dust. There's a nice McCartney scat vocal on part of one of the versions of "I Dig a Pony," silly operatic scatting on the first try of "Don't Let Me Down," a "Two of Us" whose instrumental tag suddenly goes into the lyrics from the "Hello Goodbye" coda, a sloppy "One After 909" with fun call-and-response vocals (some in gibberish) between John and Paul in the bridge, and another raw "One After 909" with different, partly mumbled, improvised-sounding lyrics (something about a woman underneath a tree). At least they got the official version of "Don't Let Me Down" (first used as the B-side of "Get Back") on tape, though extra vocal overdubs were later added. The extended coda on one of the attempts at "Get Back" also proved of enduring use, as it was edited with a take from the previous day for the classic, official single version. And if you're looking for something different from the same-old in that regard, some "Get Back" takes have Preston on organ, not electric piano.

Maybe it was thought too late to get Harrison's "Old Brown Shoe" into either the album or concert, but a lot of work goes into it here. By the time they're finished, it's not far off the arrangement used a few months later when it was re-recorded for an official B-side, though the guitar work's pretty jagged. Near the end of those takes, apropos of nothing, it seems like some of the assembled start fooling around on an electronic keyboard, with which everyone seems fascinated ("Too much, man!" Billy Preston exclaims). Some might assume these are the first Beatles recordings on which the sound of the Moog synthesizer is heard—an instrument that George used on his 1969 solo album *Electronic Sounds,* and which would become a notable, if subtle, addition to the group's arsenal of effects on *Abbey Road.*

However, as Berkeley, California, vintage keyboard restorer/expert Matt Cunitz clarifies, "It is a stylophone. An organ without proper keys, it is instead played with a stylus (pen), ergo: stylophone! A popular toy in England at that time." As further verification, he adds, you "can hear the sound of the stylus taping or scraping against the key plate. The glissandos are not continuous. You can hear them jumping

half steps, and a pitch bend/frequency knob or ribbon controller, à la [the Moog on] 'Maxwell's Silver Hammer,' doesn't work that way. Also, you can hear someone say, 'Write your name in sound'—obviously with the stylus." The stylophone has been used on a few rock recordings, most notably David Bowie's 1969 hit recording "Space Oddity." But if there's any evidence the Beatles toyed with it again, it's not on any circulating tapes.

Most fascinating of all, however, are the first-ever versions of George's "Something," at this point bearing a somewhat heavier rock-oriented tempo. The recording quality is sadly subpar for the earlier takes, with some distracting spoken voices and generally faint lead Harrison vocals. Too, the song's clearly unfinished, not only missing some words, but also lacking a graceful transition from the bridge back to the verse. He even appeals to John and Paul for help to fill in the missing gaps: "What could it be, Paul?" Suggests John, apparently in earnest: "Just say what comes into your head each time. Attracts me like a 'cauliflower.' Until you get the word!" (George, chuckling, tries "Attracts me like a pomegranate.") Elaborates George, "I've been through this one like, for about, six months! I mean, just that line. I couldn't think of anything." Stuck for a bridge, he resorts to the nonsense, dummy place card lines "What do you know, Mr. Show? I don't know, I don't know." He also demonstrates, via a cappella scatting, the same bridge's familiar dramatic, stair-descending melody.

Most of the tune's there, however, and George seems to be getting genuine encouragement from Lennon and McCartney, who try out some backup harmonies, Paul praising one lyric as "a lovely image." In all, it's one of the most fascinating documents of a classic-in-the-making not just from the *Get Back* sessions, but from the whole of the Beatles' career. And it's one of the relatively few times on the January 1969 tapes that we hear John, Paul, *and* George all working together as a team and, to all appearances, very much enjoying the camaraderie.

"Something" doesn't seem to be recognized as an instant classic demanding inclusion on the forthcoming album, however, perhaps in acknowledgment of how much more work it needs. In fact, more work on this day and the next went into beating a dead horse, in a sense, with yet more attempts to work out some sort of adequate arrangement of another Harrison composition, "All Things Must Pass." It had been 20 days since the Beatles had last played it (at least as documented by the circulating tapes); maybe George felt that the organ of Billy Preston, who had a deep background in gospel as well as rock and soul, could bring an appropriately spiritual sheen to the song. But it's still not jelling all that well, despite the interesting experimentation of having Paul, John, and George trade off on lead vocals in the opening verse. John's harmony vocals are quite poor, especially on his grunted low notes, and it seems like he's not treating the song (or George's feelings, if Harrison was intent on somehow trying to salvage it) with the sensitivity it deserves. Elsewhere, George seems to be the guiding force behind "How Do You Tell Someone?", a promising if obviously incomplete mid-tempo rocker with a jovial bittersweetness, but there's no evidence it underwent any further development.

John has a new song of his own to unveil, and if at first it seems like nothing more than a jam, it would grow into the longest track on *Abbey Road.* The very first version here of "I Want You (She's So Heavy)," in fact, is instrumental, and little more than a primitive, nagging, bluesy guitar riff. That riff does contain most of the guitar patterns played on the verses of the final *Abbey Road* arrangement, and one wonders if the song actually grew out of this jam, which like so many from January 1969 seemed to offer little promise for further development. By the very next try, however, John has a lyric. The lyric, admittedly, isn't much, and wouldn't even get more complicated by *Abbey Road* time. But the tune's actually evolving, Preston adding some jazzy responsive piano rolls and even some of his own vocals of whatever little lyric exists. Just a few minutes before these two versions, Preston's jazzy piano features prominently on an untitled bluesy improvisation that's better than the average such item on January 1969 *Get Back* tapes. It's enough to make one wonder whether Preston's presence in the studio was an unheralded catalyst for getting "I Want You (She's So Heavy)" off the ground.

By the end of the day, it's obvious the song's become something more than just another improvised time-killer in the band's eyes, as they jam on it for more than 20 minutes at the end of the session. As a listening experience, those lengthy workouts can be repetitive. But it's obvious the band has found a groove they like, a violin-like slide guitar adding some textural interest, and the scathing starkness of the whole approach foreshadows Lennon's work in the near future with the Plastic Ono Band.

John and Paul each had a composition they didn't seem willing to abandon, despite past failures to push the material past quality control. Paul gives "Teddy Boy" another whirl, and though he breaks out into disquieting combination giggle-sobs at one point, part of the longer version from this day was edited with another (from January 24) to construct the track heard on *Anthology 3*. John rolls out, for perhaps the last time in the company of other Beatles, "I'm Just a Child of Nature" (which he's now definitely calling "On the Road to Marrakesh," as a pre-song comment makes clear). He seems to lack the will, however, to get the band to coalesce into a complete, coherent performance of the composition.

There wasn't the time or desire to play many oldies at this session, but a couple of very unexpected revisitations of previously released Beatles originals deserve mention. A low-key, half-minute version of George's 1968 B-side "The Inner Light" unusually (and probably uniquely) has John on lead vocals. There's also a version of "Love Me Do," perhaps recorded for consideration should the Beatles have decided to put some oldies onto whatever official LP might have resulted from the *Get Back* sessions. As is so dishearteningly typical of January 1969 song titles that look so cool on paper, however, the actual recording is a disappointingly low-energy, not-wholly-serious rendition, with a slow, funky, bluesy feel quite different from their 1962 debut single. In its own way, it signified the futility of the whole back-to-our-origins goal of the *Get Back* project. With rare exceptions like their revival of "One After 909," the forces that had driven the Beatles to play music together in the first place just couldn't be recreated with the same excitement the second time around.

● January 29

Studio Outtakes

Let It Be *sessions*
Apple Studios, London

Singing the Blues (five versions)
Rule Brittania

I Walk the Line
I Dig a Pony
I've Got a Feeling
Don't Let Me Down
Get Back
One After 909 (three versions)
She Came In through the Bathroom Window (three versions)
Two of Us (three versions)
Let It Be
The Long and Winding Road (two versions)
For You Blue (three versions)
Something (two versions)
All Things Must Pass (four versions)
Let It Down (four versions)
I Want You (She's So Heavy) (two versions)
Sexy Sadie
Old Brown Shoe
Dig It
Besame Mucho
Three Cool Cats
Sorry Miss Molly
I Got to Find My Baby
Some Other Guy
Honky Tonk
Vacation Time
Cannonball
Not Fade Away
Hey Little Girl (In the High School Sweater)
Bo Diddley
Maybe Baby
Peggy Sue Got Married
Thinking of Linking
Crying, Waiting, Hoping
*Mailman, Bring Me No More Blues
Teddy Boy
Bring Your Own Band
Lotta Lovin'

Other songs, titles uncertain:
Also
She Gets Heavy

edited version appears on Anthology 3

With the Beatles finally deciding at some point during this session to give a concert for the cameras on the Apple rooftop the next day, they eased off a bit on the intensity, perhaps hoping to ensure they approached the material with freshness when it really mattered. They go through each of the five songs they'll play in the live sequence (minus Billy Preston, who's not there at the start) just once apiece. There's a casualness to the approach, as if they're consciously conserving their energy, but that doesn't mean these takes are without their entertaining aspects. Flashing back to the Little Eva song they covered on the BBC back in early 1963, John sings "Keep your hands off my baby" during "Don't Let Me Down," Paul bluesily scats the title of "Get Back" in an extended coda, and "One After 909" turns into an almost country-rock amble. They also do a few less-hard-rocking finished pieces that are earmarked for in-studio filming the day after the concert, Paul engaging in some scatting during the instrumental break of the first version of "The Long and Winding Road," followed by some peculiarly strained, high singing. At the end of the tune, he's still calling out a *C*-minor key change. Could the other Beatles really not have known where to go at this point, after having virtually done it to death just three days before?

Possibly fishing for a George Harrison song to fit into the movie, the band then goes through some of his numbers, though none of these renditions would be featured in the film (though footage of a few performances of Harrison compositions from earlier in the month did make the *Let It Be* movie). Unfortunately, "Something" is not ready, "All Things Must Pass" and "Let It Down" still sound kind of torpid, and although they manage a somewhat complete group version of "Let It Down," it still seems like a tentative rehearsal. "I Want You (She's So Heavy)" isn't ready either, but a five-minute-plus jam on the tune reflects their growing enthusiasm for the song. It still has a brittle, bluesy tone, with Billy Preston unexpectedly adding some improvised lyrics (including "I had a dream!") for a while.

Their obligations fulfilled, the group devoted most of the last part of the day to oldies covers. There's a "last day of school" atmosphere to this part of the tapes, as if the Beatles, with the end of the interminable *Get Back* project finally in sight, are finally relaxing and playing for the fun of it, rather than because they're supposed to be coming up with something entertaining. The relief seems tangible in a seven-minute version of "Dig It" that kicks off this segment, during which John launches into a roll call of the more notable songs they've perfected over the past four grueling weeks, as if he's reeling off the list of diploma recipients on graduation day. That list is revealing inasmuch as it might offer a rough hint of the songs the Beatles were planning to assemble for whatever album emerged from the sessions, including not just most of the songs that did end up on the *Let It Be* LP, but also some that didn't: "Maxwell's Silver Hammer," "All Things Must Pass," "She Came In through the Bathroom Window," and "Teddy Boy." It's also interesting to hear that John's still referring to one of the songs as "All I Want Is You," though it would be retitled "I Dig a Pony."

Despite some haphazard playing, "Besame Mucho" (seen in the *Let It Be* film) is certainly one of the very best oldies covers they managed in January. Paul lets loose with terrific mock–Ricky Ricardo vocals, and the Spanish-tinged guitar work is both inspired (a rarity among *Get Back* session covers!) and quite different from the arrangement heard on the several existing tapes of the Beatles doing the song in 1962. In another flashback to the Decca audition, there's another dolorously slow version of "Three Cool Cats." John doesn't sound at all pleased, however, when Paul calls out for another rehearsal of "One After 909," mumbling, "Fuck you . . . we know this, don't we . . . it's like a waste of time . . . it's just another gig. . . ."

But better spirits prevail during much of the oldies section, the band seizing on the Bo Diddley beat for a while. The version of Buddy Holly's "Not Fade Away" isn't bad, with some more-enthusiastic-than-usual guitar riffing (and another faintly recorded George Harrison vocal), making one wish a more complete version had been attempted. A slow-but-steady Holly's "Maybe Baby" (with John on lead vocal) is virtually complete and one of the best covers from the *Get Back* sessions, even if the singing isn't captured with much clarity on the tape. While Holly's "Crying, Waiting, Hoping" was (no surprise) done far better by the group in 1963 on the BBC, this slightly slowed-down

version is okay, the love the band feels for the song overcoming the imperfect execution. The band also learned "Mailman, Bring Me No More Blues" from Holly's recording, but while a version with multiple edits (heavily criticized by some Beatles fanatics) made it onto *Anthology 3*, it's a fairly uninspired blues song, played and sung at a sleepwalk pace. As there were better oldies covers in the *Get Back* sessions, one imagines this mediocre one was chosen not because of the quality of the performance, but because it was (unlike the vast majority of such covers) relatively complete and well recorded.

The good feelings may well have dampened, however, when Paul inexplicably chose this time to reintroduce "Teddy Boy" for rehearsal. The musicians manage a somewhat fuller, rock-oriented arrangement with some two-note guitar slides, but it still plods along and it's likely the group never returned to it after this. John in particular seems like he's had enough by the time they return to "Two of Us," where he starts to sing with a guttural sarcasm. With some high-pitched banter at the end that straddles the line between the Lennonesque and Monty Pythonesque, it's finally time to pack up and prepare for the big event.

● January 30

Live Performance

Let It Be *sessions*
Apple Rooftop, London

---

*Get Back (five versions)
I Want You (She's So Heavy)
**Don't Let Me Down (two versions)
****I've Got a Feeling
One After 909
Danny Boy
***I Dig a Pony (two versions)
God Save the Queen
A Pretty Girl Is Like a Melody

> *one version appears on Anthology 3
> **edit combining both versions appears on Let It Be . . . Naked
> ***edited version appears on Let It Be
> ****edit combining version from Let It Be *LP* and second version
> appears on Let It Be . . . Naked

Against the odds (at least considering how disappointingly the *Get Back* project had gone in general over the last month), the Beatles (plus Billy Preston) assembled on the Apple rooftop to give a live performance that was genuinely exciting, committed, and fun. That in itself would have made the endeavor worthwhile, but it was also productive in terms of what the group needed for both the film and album. One take apiece of the five primary songs would be edited together to provide a suitably thrilling climax for the *Let It Be* movie (which included *two* takes of "Get Back"), three of the takes were judged good enough to use on the actual *Let It Be* album, and, decades later, three of the others were good enough to use on official Beatles archival releases.

In contrast with every other day of the January 1969 sessions documented here, much of the material recorded on January 30 is familiar to the average Beatles listener. Versions of "I've Got a Feeling," "One After 909," and "I Dig a Pony" all appeared on the original *Let It Be* LP, though

The complete tape of the famous January 30, 1969, concert on the rooftop of Apple headquarters has been bootlegged on numerous occasions.

unfortunately the beginning and closing refrains (featuring the song's original title, "All I Want Is You") were edited out of "I Dig a Pony." It's not so well known, however, that four of the five main songs were done (and recorded) twice to ensure that good performances were available for the film, with the fifth tune, "Get Back," done no fewer than *three* times (the other two "versions" in circulation are a poorly recorded rehearsal and a brief false start). Few would dispute that the film and LP picked the best available takes, particularly in the case of "I Dig a Pony," where the unused "version" quickly broke down. But the entire concert, complete with multiple versions and between-song fooling around, is also in circulation if you want it.

While listening to a concert tape with so many multiple versions makes for a somewhat jumpy, distracted experience, there are some rewards if you're up for it. The third version of "Get Back" has some speed-rapped lyrics about Loretta from McCartney, who sounds positively giddy with delight at finally being able to perform live again (albeit on a city rooftop where few people could see and hear them well). The unused version of "I've Got a Feeling" has some nice extra picked guitar work in the "Everybody Had a Hard Year" section and surplus grunts and shouts from Paul near the end, though you can also hear some slight feedback. The live renditions of "Don't Let Me Down" are excellent, but afflicted with Lennon lyrical flubs; the version assembled for *Let It Be . . . Naked* fixes this by editing together parts of both performances, though hearing John fumbling through his vocal mistakes has a goofy appeal of its own. The final version of "Get Back" was retrieved for *Anthology 3,* probably more because it was the last song the Beatles ever performed live than because it was one of the best performances of the concert. Paul's improvised digs in the coda at the police who'd come onto the rooftop to stop the show make it eminently worthy of preservation, however. ("I Want You (She's So Heavy)," "God Save the Queen," "Danny Boy," and "A

Pretty Girl Is Like a Melody," incidentally, are not proper performances, but brief off-the-cuff, casually tossed-off, fooling-around pieces to fill up time between the real takes.)

If you're one of those rare hardy souls who have actually managed to make it through all of the January 1969 tapes in sequence, what's striking is how much tighter and more refined these performances *do* sound in comparison to much of the previous ones, even though the arrangements of the songs are barely different. In that sense, all that endless, grueling, sometimes apparently pointless over-and-over rehearsal really *did* pay off, albeit with the possible unfortunate side effect of making the Beatles increasingly tired of each other on the whole. The Beatles do know these songs inside out (well, John's messing up of his own "Don't Let Me Down" lyrics excepted), and it shows, giving us our only real glimpse of just how good the Beatles could have been in concert had they decided to return to the road in the late '60s. Warts and all, a tape of the complete, as-is rooftop concert would have made a far better bonus disc to the *Let It Be . . . Naked* release than the fairly senseless 22-minute collage of January 1969 sound bites that was actually used.

● January 31

Studio Outtakes
Let It Be *sessions*
Apple Studios, London

Two of Us (seven versions)
Hey Good Lookin'
Take This Hammer
Lost John
Five Feet High and Rising
Bear Cat Mama
Black Dog Blues
Right String, Wrong Yo-Yo
Run for Your Life
Step Inside Love (two versions)
Friendship
Turkey in the Straw
Tales of Frankie Rabbit
'Deed I Do
I Got Stung
Let It Be (22 versions)
*The Long and Winding Road (19 versions)
Lady Madonna
I Want You (She's So Heavy)
Build Me Up, Buttercup
Party
Twelfth Street Rag
Oh! Darling (two versions)

Miscellaneous:
Instrumental improvisations/jams (one)
Vocal numbers, titles impossible to even guess (two)
            one version appears on Anthology 3

Most fans logically think of the *Let It Be* rooftop sequence as the finale to the Beatles' exhaustive music-making in January 1969. However, there was yet one more day of recording/filming to do, primarily so that live-in-the-studio versions of a few more songs could be included in the movie. All three of these were tunes that were quieter than the more raucous numbers performed on the rooftop, and the between-take chatter gives the impression that, Paul McCartney aside, the Beatles were eager to finally wrap the damn thing up. This didn't stop them from doing their job well, not only shooting satisfactory film sequences for each song, but also producing the *Let It Be* LP version of "Two of Us," and the take of "Let It Be" that (with different overdubs) supplied the base for the mixes used on both the single and album of that name.

The "Two of Us" take was obtained fairly quickly, leaving just a little time for the group to get in one final whirl of oldies and tomfoolery. These are typically undistinguished, highlighted, if that's even the right word, by a mighty silly version of "Step Inside Love," the song that had been given to Cilla Black only a year or so before. Singing in pidgin romance language, Paul comments midway, "I'll be alright in a cabaret act when I get older"—a jibe that the crueler critics of his solo work might find all too appropriate. And who knows what John and Paul were thinking when they sang a bland skiffle cover of Cole Porter's "Friendship," where Lennon sardonically intones, "If you're ever in the shit, grab my tit"? As further evidence that he might not exactly be thrilled to be there, John adds halfway through the next, similar tune ("Tales of Frankie Rabbit"), "Presenting the Beatles: half dead, and half alive."

The numerous versions of "The Long and Winding Road" done on this day are not much different (and no better than) the one from January 26 heard on *Anthology 3*. Sadly, John's bass and George's guitar are still often of a shockingly low standard on these takes. You have to think it was no small relief to Lennon that he wouldn't have to play stand-in bass for McCartney when the Beatles' newfound insistence on playing sans overdubs was dropped after the *Get Back* project; he demonstrates no more aptitude for the instrument than the legendarily inept Stuart Sutcliffe. George seems to have no real idea of what to play as far as single guitar notes, though he's just about adequate when chording along. Billy Preston at least seems to have his heart in the song, and some of these takes have more prominent electric piano and Leslie-amped guitar parts than the ones from earlier in the month, including on the performance seen in the film (and issued on the *Let It Be . . . Naked* CD). Oddly, Paul still seems undecided as to how to word one key line of the lyric, flitting between "You'll never know" and "You've always known"—a small but key difference, considering they convey wholly opposite meanings. As it happens, the take chosen for *Let It Be . . . Naked* uses "You've always known," so both variations eventually made it into official release.

The recording of "Let It Be" was quite involved, and did end up nailing a take for the ages, though the painstaking process might have worn on some nerves. The very earliest version from this day, amusingly, is a lighthearted skiffle busk with John on lead vocals, singing an entirely different tune than the "Let It Be" melody and urging, perhaps only partly in jest, "For goodness sake, let it be." Truth be told, Lennon sometimes sounds like he's reaching the end of his rope on these "Let It Be" takes, breaking into Tiny Tim–like squeals of "I got you babe!" on one, and (far more nastily) intoning in another, "And in my hour of darkness, she is standing left in front of me, squeaking turds of whisky over me." (Paul, as is his wont during these outbursts, keeps singing

as though nothing's happened.) In the beginning of the number announced as "take 25," some shaky-leaf backup falsetto harmonizing is followed with this wholly apt spoken falsetto observation: "What the shit in hell is goin' on here?" After the very next complete pass, however, John declares, "I think that was rather grand—I'd take one home with me." This version, like several that the Beatles recorded, has the unexpected lyric change that refers to "Brother Malcolm" (perhaps inspired by road manager Mal Evans) rather than "Mother Mary," as well as changing the "times of trouble" to "times of heartache."

If John or any of the other Beatles were getting fatigued by the numerous retakes, however, Paul wasn't about to let go before he was wholly satisfied, instructing Glyn Johns that he wants to "do one more just to cover ourselves." "We've got so many of the bastards!" gripes John. Actually, they do a few more; maybe Paul was set on getting the lyrics the way he wanted them. And sho' nuff, the next-to-last version is the one that (with overdubs) graced the hit single and (with overdubs, and in a significantly different, inferior mix) the *Let It Be* LP. The very last version (much of which is seen in the edit of two takes used for the *Let It Be* film sequence) introduced yet another lyric variation, substituting "There will be no sorrow" for "There will be an answer" in the last verse, though this was wisely passed over for the official release. That version, too, is the very last song recorded on the mammoth cache of music that circulates from the *Get Back* sessions. If you do manage to listen to all of those recordings in order, you'll feel like a marathon runner breaking the tape when this final take of "Let It Be" concludes, though there will be no medal awaiting you at the finish line.

The shambolic jam on "Lady Madonna" was actually mixed by Glyn Johns, but wisely never placed even on any of the unreleased versions of the *Get Back* LP he assembled, though it does contain Paul's wittily substituted lyric, "Lord and Lady Docker, in your private yacht, all the people wonder why you have such a lot!" Paul takes the vocal on the day's sole dig through "I Want You (She's So Heavy)," proving he could have done quite a good job with the singing if given the opportunity. The tune's getting closer to its more complex *Abbey Road* form in this five-minute version as well, though it's still lacking the "She's So Heavy" chorus. And, possibly with a mind to getting in just a little more work before the four Beatles scattered, there are a few versions of "Oh! Darling." Though the last of these is less than a minute, it's an intriguing glimpse of a wholly alternate arrangement with a far faster, funkier tempo, rather like Booker T. & the MG's might have done it, Paul improvising the lyrics "Bossa nova, bossa no, that's a no-no, that's a no-no!" That in turn leads to the very last untitled jam on the *Get Back* tapes, which likewise sounds a little Booker T.-ish, with a dynamic riff reminiscent of one of the hooks from Ike & Tina Turner's classic 1961 hit "It's Gonna Work Out Fine."

But while the *Get Back* project was ready to go in the can, it wouldn't work out entirely fine. Midway through the "Let It Be" takes, there's a telling moment when Michael Lindsay-Hogg runs down what sounds like a list of songs he's hoping to show performances of in the movie, asking if he might be able to film the group doing "Teddy Boy" and "All Things Must Pass." Responds Paul, "'Teddy Boy' is actually . . . that's as far as it's gonna get. I thought maybe we can come back after a week or something. . . ." One can just see the other Beatles wincing at the prospect of resuming the drudgery with just a week's rest. Not only would they not return to film "Teddy Boy" (or anything else), but "Teddy Boy" would never make it onto a Beatles album, or be attempted again in the studio until

Paul did his own version for his 1970 *McCartney* LP. Then Lindsay-Hogg asks, "How about 'All Things Must Pass'?" Dead silence for a moment. It's George who breaks the dead air, replying with do-we-have-to-do-this reluctance, "You see, I don't think . . . do we have to film them all? Every one of them?" Tension about how to finish these songs, and how to finish the album in general, was clearly still afoot. Uncertainty over how to finish the album off dragged on for over a year, and the way in which it was finally completed—after several failed mixes and reschedulings (see entry on page 282)—would help seal the Beatles' split for good.

● Circa February

Demo Acetate
7 Cavendish Avenue, London

Goodbye

One of the few Paul McCartney solo home tapes from the 1960s that has ever circulated is his demo of "Goodbye," soon covered for a hit on Apple Records by Mary Hopkin (where the song was credited to Lennon-McCartney, though it was almost certainly Paul's work alone).

George and his wife, Patti, in March 1969.

It's one of Paul's prissier Beatles-era songs, to be frank, and this demo is one of his prissiest Beatles-era performances, as he sing-croons near the top of his high range, accompanied only by his acoustic guitar. Then again, it *was* a song that he intended all along to be covered by a high-pitched female singer, and not one that he tried to place with the Beatles. For what it is, it's a pleasant, lightweight acoustic ditty, somewhat in the style of "Blackbird," though "Blackbird" sounds almost dark and heavy in comparison. This version also deviates from the more familiar Hopkin hit in its coda, where the tempo drastically slows and Paul elongates his vocal phrasing. And fortunately for collectors, it was pressed onto a Dick James publishing acetate, a copy of which was auctioned off in 1981, from which point it was just a few years until the track appeared on bootleg.

● February 25

Studio Outtakes
Abbey Road, London

*Old Brown Shoe (take 2)
*All Things Must Pass (take 2)
*Something (take 1)
All Things Must Pass (take 2, alternate mix)
Something (acetate mix)
　　　appears on Anthology 3

Perhaps emboldened by both growing frustration and confidence, George Harrison recorded solo demos of several songs from his bulging catalog at EMI on his 26th birthday. One wonders if the Beatles were even aware of this session; no individual Beatle had ever booked time at EMI to record on his own, without any of the others present. Maybe George was feeling like it was the only way to get some of his songs onto tape the way he wanted them. Maybe he was even thinking of starting to build the foundations of a solo album, though more than a year would pass before he seriously started working on one.

George handled all of the singing and instruments (guitar and piano) on these three songs, all of which have something of a stripped-down, unplugged feel, though the tracks don't suffer for that in the least. Takes of all three numbers were used on *Anthology 3,* and while each of them had actually been recorded the previous month by the full-band Beatles in the *Get Back* rehearsals, Harrison was probably getting closer to the vibe he wanted here, particularly on "All Things Must Pass," with its shimmering vibrato guitar. "Something" is the loveliest performance of the three, the song having moved much further to completion in the month or so since the Beatles first rehearsed it. Here it contains an extra, significant bonus in the form of an additional verse, roughly following the outline of the instrumental break in the official Beatles version. This verse is not too sophisticated or impressive either musically or lyrically, however, and it was appropriately decided not to include it when the group recorded the song for *Abbey Road.* "Old Brown Shoe" had been done quite a bit by the Beatles during the final days of the *Get Back* sessions, and its piano-pounding arrangement here is pretty similar. In fact, it's pretty similar to the version that soon showed up on the B-side of "The Ballad of John and Yoko," though there it was significantly boosted by the other Beatles' backup playing and singing.

For the diehards, bootlegs offer a different mix of "Something" from this session (taken from scratchy acetate) that adds a piano overdub and takes out some descending scat vocals from the end of the bridge. Not realizing what he had, George gave an acetate of "Something" to Joe Cocker, who recorded it in March; by the time Cocker's cover came out in November, however, the Beatles had fortunately determined to do it on their own, and released it in September on the *Abbey Road* album. Also on bootleg is a different mix of "All Things Must Pass" with a second vocal that was axed for the *Anthology 3* version, as well as a slightly longer version of the *Anthology 3* take of "Old Brown Shoe," with a mild piano flourish at the end.

● March 25-31

Private Tapes
Amsterdam Hilton Hotel, Amsterdam

Hava Nagilah
I Want You (She's So Heavy)
Jerusalem
Don't Let Me Down
Those Were the Days

During the last week of March, John and Yoko spent part of their honeymoon doing a "Bed-In" for peace at the Amsterdam Hilton Hotel. The idea was to get a lot of media coverage, which they did, submitting to numerous radio and TV interviews. During a radio interview with songwriter Akiva Nof (later a member of the Israeli Parliament) of Voice of Israel, John obliged listeners with a super-brief a cappella snatch of "Hava Nagilah"—probably the most familiar Hebrew-language song around the globe—before adding a far more interesting, gutsy (if primitively recorded), minute-long version of "I Want You (She's So Heavy)," sung with acoustic guitar, John signing off by singing, "Hello Israel." At least John was in no danger of forgetting the lyrics, there being so few to begin with; as he admits here, "I must admit to not knowing any songs all the way through, even my own!" Almost abashedly, he reveals at the end, "That's from the Beatles' new album"—though one wonders if he meant *Get Back* (the song having been started at the January 1969 sessions) or *Abbey Road*, which hadn't yet properly gotten off the ground. Lennon, Ono, and Nof also sang together briefly on one of Nof's own songs, "Jerusalem," with the kind of minor-key melody associated with much Hebrew-language music, John again playing guitar.

In a separate interview for a Dutch radio program, John summoned 40 or so seconds of a very raw "Don't Let Me Down" with acoustic guitar—of which, typically, he can't remember anything other than the chorus. He then segues into an amusing, unplugged "Those Were the Days" in which he seems determined to wail in as irreverently off-key a voice as he can manage.

● April 26

Studio Outtakes
Abbey Road *sessions*
Studio Two, Abbey Road, London

Oh! Darling (take 26, mono)
*Octopus's Garden (take 2)
 appears on Anthology 3

Although this marked the end of a three-month gap in unreleased material performed by the group as a whole, the Beatles *had* done some sporadic recording in Abbey Road in the meantime. Pieces for the *Abbey Road* album itself were slowly starting to get assembled, though it was likely the band hadn't yet made the decision to record an entirely different album than *Get Back*. This date, in fact, produced two studio outtakes of songs that had been heard during the January sessions. This mono version of "Oh! Darling" is in a much more polished form than it took in the *Get Back* days; in fact, it's the exact same take as heard on the *Abbey Road* album, minus a few overdubs. Paul McCartney's vocal is entirely different, and certainly milder and less forceful. He'd scream himself raw over the course of several overdubs in July to get the sawdust in his voice that he wanted, and it's another testament to his perfectionism that he kept on going and going to get what he heard in his head, when most other musicians would have been perfectly happy with what they already had.

While "Octopus's Garden" had also been heard in January, it was in a far less developed state at that point than "Oh! Darling." Three months

John and Yoko on March 26, 1969, at their Amsterdam Bed-In, during which several informal, lo-fi acoustic Lennon songs were recorded.

later, it's come a long way: it has a real melody with Beatlesque chord changes, instead of being another of Ringo's humdrum, country-tinged barroom piano boogies. But while take 2 might be closer to *Abbey Road* than *Get Back,* it's still a long way off its ultimate mark, with less disciplined George Harrison guitar lines, no backing harmonies or sound effects, and Ringo singing the same verse and bridge three times over. This is the take heard on *Anthology 3,* with a Starr spoken bit ("Well, that was superb") at the end that was airlifted from the conclusion of take 8.

● April 29

Studio Outtake

Abbey Road sessions
Studio Three, Abbey Road, London

Octopus's Garden (take 32, mono)

While a lot of "alternates" of *Abbey Road* songs exist, it will come as a disappointment to the average listener to find that many of those aren't all that different from the official versions, other than for the absence of some overdubs. Here's one, using the same basic track as the *Abbey Road* cut, but missing backing vocals, sound effects, and some touch-up, additional Starr singing. At least it does allow you to hear the guitar solo minus the underwater background vocals, if you're a fan of George's work and want to more clearly hear what's he doing.

● April 30

Studio Outtake

Let It Be sessions
Studio Three, Abbey Road, London

Let It Be

Most of the tracks selected for the various possible versions of the *Get Back* LP that Glyn Johns prepared for consideration were the actual January performances. However, "Let It Be" got some additional work on April 30, with George adding and subtracting some of his guitar work, substituting an entirely new (and better) solo. This is the version heard on the *Get Back* albums Johns assembled in both May 1969 and January 1970, both of which have been bootlegged (see sidebar, "Let It Be . . . Released," chapter 10, page 282).

● May 26–June 2

Private Tapes

Hotel Reine-Elizabeth, Montreal

Radio Peace
Get It Together
Happiness Is a Warm Gun
Because
Oh Yoko!

Give Peace a Chance
Good Old Air Canada

As they had in Amsterdam two months before, John and Yoko spent the last week of May doing a Bed-In for peace, this time in Montreal. Again interviews were given for radio, TV, and film cameras, with some interesting (if mediocre-fidelity) music making its way into the proceedings at times. "Radio Peace" (sometimes thought to have been recorded in Amsterdam, not Montreal) is just a 15-second jingle in which John and Yoko sing, "This is radio peace" a few times to a bland, two-chord melody and John's acoustic guitar accompaniment. "Good Old Air Canada" is another exceptionally brief "song," ad-libbed by John (again on acoustic guitar) in celebration of being allowed to enter the country; it can be seen and heard in the documentary of the couple's visit, *John & Yoko's Year of Peace.* Of greater interest is "Get It Together," again sung by John and Yoko to acoustic guitar, which has a chord progression rather like "Dear Prudence," though the melody is different (and not too imaginative). While it sounds like an ad-libbed ode to unity, with a passing mention of Timothy Leary, it does include the phrase "come together"—which, of course, would be the title of a much more substantial song that John was soon to write.

The other songs all found release on Beatles or Lennon solo records, though these are the first glimpses of a couple of them. "Because," soon to be recorded for *Abbey Road,* is plucked on acoustic guitar with a chunky rhythm that didn't make it into the Beatles' far more delicate arrangement, though unfortunately all but about a half-minute is obscured by dialogue. "Happiness Is a Warm Gun," lasting only about 40 seconds, is actually just John going through the early part of the tune on acoustic

John Lennon in 1969: still a Beatle, but working increasingly on his own and with Yoko, as heard on numerous unreleased private tapes recorded that year.

guitar, almost wordlessly except for a few hums and a delightfully lewd spoken interjection: "Mama, you're so beautiful this morning. I'd like to grab your weed!" (These performances of "Because" and "Happiness Is a Warm Gun" can be both seen and heard in the video documentary *John and Yoko: The Bed-In*.) And the 25-second "Give Peace a Chance," which was not part of the rehearsals or recording of the Plastic Ono Band single of the same name (see entry below), has just a few lines of John singing and playing acoustic guitar on his own, ending with typical Lennon spoken wordplay: "Last chance to give peace a chance, folks! Give chance a peace. Give peace a chance."

"Oh Yoko!", one of the highlights of John's *Imagine* album (and indeed of his whole solo career), here gets an enthusiastic acoustic guitar busk with Yoko on background harmonies. In the context of these Bed-In bits, it's also refreshingly lengthy and relatively complete, running four and a half minutes. There are a few different lyrics unheard in the studio version, and brief turns into rudimentary bridges consisting of little besides the lyric "I want you baby"—maybe John was making an in-joke reference to his "I Want You (She's So Heavy)" song, rather than seriously intending this to be part of the finished tune. Certainly an ad-libbed Little Richard quote he throws in ("A wop bop a loo bop, a wop bam boom!" from "Tutti Frutti") couldn't have been envisioned as a serious permanent addition, though it adds to the fun. This is likely the song that John referred to when he told *New Musical Express* in May 1969, "I think I'm going to make a pop record with Yoko. I've got this other song we were singing last night and I think it'll be quite a laugh for her to do a pop record. It's one I've written myself, and it's about Yoko. But I'll just change the word Yoko to John, and she can sing it about me."

Yoko's pop single didn't appear, but this tape does show that the song (unlike some others Lennon was working on from late 1968 through mid-1969) was relatively finished, making one wonder why it wasn't included on his first solo album, *Plastic Ono Band*. Perhaps it was felt too romantic and upbeat for a record largely devoted to excoriating catharsis. As for why the Beatles never recorded it, if only in retrospect, we can see that with this and other songs such as "Oh My Love," John was beginning to write material that was probably just too personal and specific to his relationship with Yoko to be comfortably integrated into a group context.

● May 31

Private Tapes/Studio Outtakes
"Give Peace a Chance" Plastic Ono Band single session
Hotel Reine-Elizabeth, Montreal

Give Peace a Chance (solo rehearsal)
*Give Peace a Chance (group rehearsal)
Give Peace a Chance (edited take from single)
    *appears on the John Lennon Anthology box set

Here the line starts to blur not only between private tapes and studio outtakes, but between John's career as a Beatle and a solo artist. Although tapes of recordings from this location were used to construct a commercially released hit single, they weren't done in a professional recording studio. The single, too, was the first Beatle solo release that was

not some tangential side project, but an endeavor truly intended for the commercial pop market, even if the composition was dutifully credited to Lennon-McCartney (though John later said that Yoko should have been credited as co-author). That's why one of the rehearsals was eventually commercially released on a John Lennon archival compilation, not a Beatles one.

The solo rehearsal that's circulated is about what you'd guess a solo version of the song would sound like (although you can hear a few voices trying to sing along and add encouragement in the background), and it's missing all the references to other people in John and Yoko's hotel room. The group rehearsal (released on the John Lennon *Anthology* box) is much more convivial and enthusiastic, with a less rigid tempo than the familiar hit arrangement, at least until John suggests clapping on the offbeat. There's also a minute-and-a-half version that's actually just a different, shorter edit of the take used for the single, though it's great to hear the obvious happiness in John's voice as he kicks off the tune with his "Ah-one, two, ah-one-two-three-four!"

● June 1

Studio Outtake
"Give Peace a Chance" Plastic Ono Band single session
Les Studios Andre Perry, Montreal

Give Peace a Chance (rough mix)

A rough mix of a song recorded in a hotel room? Yep—some vocal harmonies, percussion, and tape delay were added in a Montreal studio. The "rough mix" you'll see on bootlegs is actually from the soundtrack of the promo film for the single, and isn't much different except for the addition of some words of encouragement from John to his assembled backup singers at the start.

● Circa Spring

Private Tapes

The Maharishi Song
I Want You
Woman Is Nigger of the World

It's thought that these tapes, with John on grating (perhaps fretless) slide guitar and vocals (and some vocal assistance from Yoko), were probably done around spring 1969, though the exact date is unknown. "The Maharishi Song" may not be pleasant listening, but as have-to-be-heard-to-be-believed unreleased Beatles/Lennon–related tapes go, they're aren't many stranger ones floating around. Here, even more than "Sexy Sadie," John vents his rage at the Maharishi and his whole disillusionment with their 1968 visit to Rishikesh with artless bluntness. The tune's not much, and in fact it's pretty tuneless, bar some oblique, bluesy slides.

John's talking-bluesish rant, however, is something to behold, the choice excerpts including: "There were one or two attractive women there, but mainly looked like, you know, schoolteachers or something, and the whole damn camp was spying on the ones in the bathing suits. And they're supposed to be meditatin'! . . . me, I took it for real. I wrote 600 songs about how I feel. I felt like dying, and crying, and committing suicide, but I felt creative, and I thought, what the hell's this got to do with what that silly little man's talking about. But he did charm me in a way, because he was funny, sort of cuddly, like a sort of, you know, little daddy with a beard." Lennon goes on to accuse the guru of spreading rumors through his right-hand man and committing sexual indiscretions with a favored woman student. "He looked holy," John sings, Yoko (who wasn't in Rishikesh) rejoining, "But he was a sex maniac." John: "I couldn't see that, but he certainly wasn't . . ." Yoko: "Holy." John: "In the true sense of the word!" Obviously John was having a hard time letting go of his bitterness for quite some time, despite the world's perception that he'd pretty much swept the whole Indian episode under the rug after returning to England.

"I Want You" is not the *Abbey Road* song of the almost similar title, but an entirely different one, sung by John and Yoko and again featuring his, um, unique brand of slide guitar that sounds as if the neck has been unrecognizably warped out of its original shape. It's another semi-improvised number with a nearly tuneless blues melody, and like "The Maharishi Song" is perversely fascinating, in all senses of that phrase. For the lyrics are about as horny as any the couple ever put on tape, John moaning, "Put it on, lift it up, stick 'em out; I want to see you standing, I want you on your back, I want you on the floor and I want you on the rack!" Better still: "Yoko, you better lose some weight and get in them old pants!"

"I Want You" was not a commercially releasable composition by any stretch of the imagination (except, maybe, on Lennon and Ono's avant-garde LPs), but "Woman Is the Nigger of the World" became a single for the pair in 1972. Because of its radically political nature, it's usually assumed that it must have been written around the same time as the other songs on their *Sometime in New York City* album, which was full of such stuff. In fact, however, this rough, minute-long 1969 sketch demonstrates it was written at least three years before that release; in the *Playboy* interview shortly before his death, John said the title originated from "something Yoko said in 1968 in an interview." Though the structure's roughly similar, it has a far more mordant tune than what John and Yoko eventually recorded for commercial release, as well as more of that skin-crawling slide guitar. Like most of the private tapes of John and Yoko from this period, it's of marginal aesthetic value, at least in terms of conventional listenability. Whatever you think of the music, however, it's interesting that there's more unreleased Lennon-Ono material from the spring of 1969 than there is unreleased group-performed Beatles music from the same time span. It was one of many indications that John's focus was drifting from the band to his own work, whether with Yoko or alone.

● July 1

Studio Outtake
Abbey Road *sessions*
Studio Two, Abbey Road, London

You Never Give Me Your Money (take 30, mono)

As "same basic take sans overdubs outtakes" from *Abbey Road* go, this is the most interesting, featuring a much longer instrumental tag at the end. This, like some moments here and there throughout their 1969 work, gives us a glimpse of a heavier, more improvisational direction the band might have explored more deeply had they lasted at least a little longer. Not that it was a bad idea to shorten the tag, as some jarring piano starts to intrude on the lead guitar, taking the group away from the tune toward a basic uptempo blues-rock jam. It's better than most such things from the January 1969 sessions, but not much, ending with a fanfare of hammered piano and a thick guitar chord.

These aren't the only deviations from the official track by any means, as there's a different (not *real* different) lead vocal, and Paul sings the second verse on his own, rather than as part of a bunch of voices. All those luscious vocal harmony overdubs are missing, in fact, allowing you to hear Paul wail away wordlessly on his own in the instrumental break, with a "Woo!" near the end of the last verse so far upfront in the mix that it summons up the ghost of Little Richard. You can hear the guitar on the fade more prominently as well, particularly as the lyrics about kids going to heaven haven't been added. As a whole, though, it's not preferable to the far more polished *Abbey Road* production by any means, and illustrative (by what's missing) of just how much fine detail work was piled onto the album's root tracks.

● July 2

Studio Outtakes
Abbey Road *sessions*
Studio Two, Abbey Road, London

Her Majesty (take 3, unedited)
Golden Slumbers (take 1, take 13)
Carry That Weight (take 1, take 13)

With a good six weeks or so of concentrated work on *Abbey Road* now underway, some outtakes started to pile up in earnest. Still, in a return to the way of doing things that was more characteristic of the *Sgt. Pepper* era than the *Get Back* sessions, most of the ones that escaped into circulation were really variations in the elements used, rather than wholly different takes. Such was the case of take 13 of the "Golden Slumbers/Carry That Weight" part of the album's medley, though it's missing the orchestral overdubs, and has a mostly different McCartney vocal track (where you can really hear the strain during the "Carry That Weight" part). It's a shock, too, to hear the song come to a dead end on a piano chord, where we're so used to hearing it segue right into "The End." Too bad that whenever it's been bootlegged, there's been bad varispeed (from a damaged part of the tape) at the start of the first "Golden Slumbers" chorus. Take 1 of "Golden Slumbers"/"Carry That Weight" is heard in the scene where it's played back for Paul, George, Ringo, and George Martin on the bonus disc of the *Anthology* DVD series, though part of it's obscured by conversation (highlighted by Harrison's puzzled remark, "What album is this?"). It's similar to take 13, though from what we can hear, it has a pretty undefined ending, culminating in a ramshackle breakdown.

The very idea of an alternate "mix" or "edit" of "Her Majesty" will strike many as preposterous, since the song only lasted 23 seconds in the first place. As is by now well known among serious Beatles fans, however, the last chord got chopped off when it was initially planned for use in the medley on side two (where it would have been slotted between "Mean Mr. Mustard" and "Polythene Pam"). The "uncut" version, which ends not with a low guitar note but a full guitar chord, lasts an entire second longer, and has been bootlegged for all of us to enjoy.

● July 9

Studio Outtake
Abbey Road *sessions*
Studio Two, Abbey Road, London

*Maxwell's Silver Hammer (take 5)
   appears on Anthology 3

Though John and George were probably hardly thrilled at the prospect, "Maxwell's Silver Hammer" was exhumed for a thorough and far improved rearrangement at this session. While this is a wholly different take than the *Abbey Road* version (and is now available on *Anthology 3*), it's both pretty similar and not as good, lacking the trademark anvil, synthesizer, and background vocal harmonies. Paul's singing (to be fair, intended only as a guide vocal) isn't as spot-on either. He obviously hasn't finished (or has forgotten part of) the third verse, improvising some ridiculous nonsense syllables and breaking his stride with a chuckle, as well as scat-singing during the instrumental break and final section. There's also a superfluous opening drum roll by Ringo to kick off a brief, introductory instrumental section (replicating the instrumental transitions between the choruses and verses) lopped off the official track. Though academically interesting and notably different from the familiar version, this outtake just sounds kind of klutzy in comparison.

● July 10

Studio Outtake
Abbey Road *sessions*
Studio Two, Abbey Road, London

Maxwell's Silver Hammer (RS13)

This uses the same basic track as the *Abbey Road* version, but it still has that opening Ringo roll and instrumental intro, and its (for 1969) innovative Moog synthesizer overdubs are still almost a month in the future. Listen closely, too, and you'll hear Paul sing a "Whoo!" near the end that didn't make the final mix.

● July 11

Studio Outtake
Abbey Road *sessions*
Studio Two, Abbey Road, London

Something (take 37)

Work on the *Abbey Road* version of "Something" had actually been underway for a few months, the basic track getting embellished by several overdubs. Take 37 was the number given to the one that added George Harrison's lead vocal to the mix, though the strings that would sweeten the arrangement had yet to be added. As a consequence, you can hear George's lead guitar more clearly in parts—including, unfortunately for George, a bit at the end of the last verse where he doesn't so much play the last note of a phrase as stab at it. He'd later redo and improve the vocal and guitar solo, though what's heard here isn't much different than what you hear in the hit single—an indication of the perfectionism he was bringing to his songs by the end of the 1960s, perhaps subtly influenced by the same inclinations in his band mate Paul McCartney (who later overdubbed some vocal harmonies on the track himself).

All this would make this outtake of some interest to collectors, though not to many more general listeners. But what really makes it about the most interesting of all *Abbey Road* outtakes is the unclassifiably strange two-and-a-half-minute instrumental coda after the final note of what most of us know as "Something" fades. Melodically unrelated to the vocal part of the song, it's a downer of a jam that comes out of nowhere, plodding along at a tempo between a waltz and a dirge, built around a nagging, ominous, four-note piano riff wholly at odds with the blissful glow of the three minutes that have preceded it. The bass sometimes throbs like a giant rubber ironing board, George throws in some laconic, bluesy guitar licks, and the whole thing's barely any more cheerful than a march to the guillotine. It's been largely unnoted, however, that the piano riff would be resurrected by John for his *Plastic Ono Band* track "Remember," where a virtually identical piano figure both opens the song and reappears near the end of the verses.

An LP of Abbey Road *outtakes/alternates, wittily boasting an inner label featuring not the trademark Apple Records logo, but an apple on the verge of being eaten to the core.*

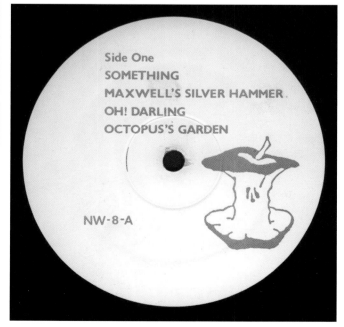

Side One
SOMETHING
MAXWELL'S SILVER HAMMER
OH! DARLING
OCTOPUS'S GARDEN

NW-8-A

What purpose the band had in recording this fadeout is unknown. It would have wholly undermined the romantic mood of "Something" had it been retained as the track's ending. Perhaps it's reading too much into the band's collective unconscious, but when this author hears it, it sounds like nothing less than a mournful requiem for the group itself. Much of *Abbey Road* had yet to be recorded, and the official breakup wouldn't happen for almost a year. But on this joyless jam, they seem intent on supplying the soundtrack for their slow, inevitable march to their own funeral.

● July 17–22

Studio Outtake
Abbey Road *sessions*
Studio Three, Abbey Road, London

Oh! Darling (vocal overdub)

For several sessions running, Paul McCartney kept recording and re-recording his "Oh! Darling" vocal, hoping to get it rough and right. It's not known exactly when this particular ten-minute tape was made, but it must have been at some point between July 17 and July 22. It's been derided as infuriatingly silly and self-indulgent, as Paul spends much of the time not singing "Oh! Darling," but testing his mike as he and/or the studio technicians mess with the tape delay effect. It's a fair point, but also consider this: most of the *Abbey Road* outtakes/alternates really aren't too much different from what ended up on the album. Here at least we have something *really* different from what ended up on the LP. Also, McCartney—unlike Lennon—rarely committed self-indulgent silliness to tape, at least on tape that's been found. Here's a chance to hear him act the fool, putting on funny (as in strange, not ha-ha) voices, spout nonsense, and even sing a bit in his mock–Elvis Presley style.

Of course, Paul's a better singer, for the most part, than he is a wit or party animal. And when he does get to his actual overdub of the "Oh! Darling" vocal, it's mostly excellent, even in a cappella isolation—though not, apparently, the one he wanted to use. The tape cuts off before the song's end, though not before he gets a chance to throw in an ad-lib ("Oh that's right, darling!") not heard in the finished track.

● July 21

Studio Outtake
Abbey Road *sessions*
Studio Three, Abbey Road, London

*Come Together (take 1)
    *appears on Anthology 3

The first take of "Come Together" (issued on *Anthology 3*) isn't nearly up to the polished standards of the hit single—John acknowledged in his 1980 *Playboy* interview that "the thing was created in the studio"—but that's not the point of digging up first takes. For a first take, this is actually pretty good, with a few spontaneous Lennon interjections that didn't survive to the final arrangement. Unfortunately, his

vocal is pretty rough at points, both in phrasing and texture. By the time he breaks down in occasional laughter, it's obvious this take won't be used, the group breaking into a double-time chorus. But you can hear him more clearly utter his immortal "Shoot me" asides, which first surfaced in the unreleased *Get Back* sessions number "Watching Rainbows." Not that much more clearly, though—the "me" of "Shoot me" is often mumbled or omitted entirely, as it would be in the official version. There are a few different lyrical references here as well, especially the who-knows-why one to Eartha Kitt near the end.

● July 24

Studio Outtakes
Abbey Road *sessions*
Studio Two, Abbey Road, London

*Come and Get It (take 1)
*Ain't She Sweet
    *appears on Anthology 3

One of the very finest of Beatles outtakes, though one now easily available on *Anthology 3*, is actually a one-man show, with composer Paul McCartney handling all the vocals and instruments. Intended not for *Abbey Road* but as a demo for Apple group Badfinger, this immensely catchy, lyrically enigmatic mid-tempo pop-rocker was very close to the version Badfinger issued on their hit single cover. This was, in fact, deliberately so, as Paul not only produced the Badfinger recording, but instructed them to replicate the demo as closely as possible. When "Come and Get It" was first heard on the radio, in fact, not a few listeners actually mistook it for a McCartney-penned Beatles track. While the Badfinger hit is understandably more polished than Paul's recording (which only took an hour), it's good to hear the composer himself handle the vocals, as no one sings McCartney like McCartney. Almost 20 years later, Paul came clean in Mark Lewisohn's *The Beatles Recording Sessions*, admitting, "I said to Badfinger, 'Look, lads, don't vary, this is good, just copy this down to the letter. It's perhaps a little bit undignified for you, a little bit lacking in integrity to have to copy someone's work that rigidly, but this is the hit sound. Do it like this and we're all right, we've got a hit. No one will know anyway. And if they do say anything, say, "Yes, Paul did the arrangement, big deal, it's not unheard of."'"

Once the actual Beatles group session got started, John Lennon took them all the way back to the very first vocal number they'd recorded in a proper studio. "Ain't She Sweet," which they'd recorded with John singing lead at the 1961 Tony Sheridan sessions, was even a Top 20 US hit single for them in 1964. Here, as they virtually always did on their 1969 oldies covers, they slowed the tempo *way* down. But the playing was, at least relatively speaking, far tighter than it had been on virtually all of the oldies covers from the *Get Back* sessions, even if John had an occasional frog in his throat and didn't quite remember all the lyrics. Nevertheless, it was a disciplined enough effort to gain a spot on the *Anthology 3* compilation, and is worth hearing if only for sentimental reasons, the group revisiting their ancient past when they were just weeks away from doing their final recording as a foursome. Ironically, it's also the final genuine unreleased performance—as opposed to an alternate mix—to have been recorded by the band as a foursome that has made it into circulation.

● July 30

Studio Outtake
Abbey Road *sessions*
Studio Three, Abbey Road, London

Huge Melody

There's no actual "song" called "Huge Melody." This, as well as "The Long One," was the name given to a test edit/rough mix of the long medley ("You Never Give Me Your Money"/"Sun King"/"Mean Mr. Mustard"/"Polythene Pam"/"She Came In through the Bathroom Window"/"Golden Slumbers"/"Carry That Weight"/"The End") that would take up most of side two of *Abbey Road*. While hearing it on bootleg would strike many as unnecessarily redundant with the actual album, there *are* some real differences, albeit of a somewhat academic nature. "You Never Give Me Your Money," in particular, has some different, quite sunny vocal harmonies in the upbeat second section, and an extra line of children going to heaven near the end. It crossfades to "Sun King"—not with cricket, bird, and bell noises, but with an angelic organ that was mixed out of the final medley altogether. "Polythene Pam" has a few extra spoken bits from John during the guitar solo, and "Golden Slumbers/"Carry That Weight" has a different McCartney vocal during the "Golden Slumbers" part, though it's still missing some overdubs, in particular the orchestral ones. "The End" is not only shorter and missing some guitar overdubs, but lacks any vocals whatsoever, which makes it sound more like an unfinished backing track than a complete song. Most noticeably of all, "Her Majesty" was still stuck between "Mean Mr. Mustard" and "Polythene Pam."

You'd never put this side-by-side with the completed *Abbey Road* medley as a comparable listening experience. But it does give us a worthy look at a jigsaw puzzle that's still missing a few pieces, and thus some insight into the complex creative process necessary to pull such a complicated notion off.

● August 4

Studio Outtakes
Abbey Road *sessions*
Studio Two, Abbey Road, London

*Because (take 16, vocals only)
Because (take 16, backing track only, fragment)
    *appears on Anthology 3

One of the less essential items unearthed for the *Anthology* project was a version of "Because" that isolates the vocal tracks only, though you can hear a little bit of the backing track leaking through. Still, it did have more involved three-part harmonies than any other Beatles recording. So it's nice, though not mind-blowing, to hear those voices by themselves in appreciation of just how fine John, Paul, and George were at combining their voices. If you're really hardcore, you can hear about half of the record's *instrumental* track, sans vocal, in one of the final scenes of the *Anthology* DVD, though it's nearly buried under interview material.

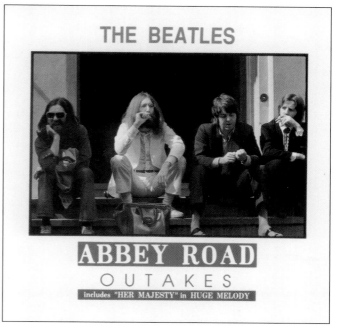

A cool photo of the Beatles in the same outfits they wore on the Abbey Road *cover adorns this sleeve, though the tell-tale misspelling of "Outakes" [sic] lets us know it's not the work of a conventional record label.*

There is, by the way, another cut on *Anthology 3* that might be considered an outtake, but the version of "The End" that concludes that package is really a remix (and not a very thoughtfully executed one). Although they would technically be in existence until April 1970, the group would never record as a quartet after August 1969, and there's a very sharp drop-off in the amount of unreleased Beatles material available—whether recorded under the Beatles name or individually—from this point until the group disbanded.

● Circa Late August– Early September

Private Tapes
Tittenhurst, Ascot

*Cold Turkey
Cold Turkey (with guitar/vocal overdub)
Cold Turkey (with Yoko Ono vocal overdub)
    *appears on John Lennon's Acoustic

Barely any time had passed since the final time the Beatles worked together in the studio (on August 20, finishing *Abbey Road*) when John set to work on what would become the Plastic Ono Band's second single, "Cold Turkey." If the stark blues-rock of "Cold Turkey" seemed minimalist compared to most of what the Beatles had done, these demos were barer still, John accompanying himself on weedy-sounding acoustic guitar. All of them feature the same base performance, one of them adding some guitar and harmonizing vocal overdubs, the other adding some characteristically volatile singing from Yoko Ono. While the studio single of "Cold Turkey" had a far more conventional, punchy (if still spare), electric rock arrangement, these demos have a brittle power on their own terms. That's particularly the case when John, in the most audible instance of Yoko's influence on his vocal style yet, puts leaf-shaking effects on his singing (and, sometimes, even his guitar playing), aurally simulating the tremors of heroin withdrawal that "Cold Turkey" was so harrowingly documenting.

Though the most basic of these demos was issued on John Lennon's *Acoustic* compilation, it's safe to assume that most fans will find the take with the guitar/vocal overdub most to their liking. While Yoko's contributions were likely something John wanted to incorporate into the song, they also undoubtedly made the song less conventionally listenable and commercial. The date of the recording is not known, but a reasonable guess would place it between the end of *Abbey Road* and September 13 (when he performed, and recorded, the song live in Toronto). A 2003 *Rolling Stone* article reported that the song had been offered to the Beatles during the *Abbey Road* sessions, but it seems much more likely that John didn't start writing it until after those sessions had wrapped up, particularly as the heroin withdrawal that inspired the tune is usually pegged as having taken place no earlier than mid-August.

If these were the demos John played the other Beatles when he was pitching the song as a single, it's hardly a surprise that they passed on the idea. It would have been an infinitely less commercial A-side, however the Beatles arranged it, than any other they'd issued, as demonstrated by its disappointing chart performance. It made No. 14 in the UK and only No. 30 in the US, in part because it was banned by some stations for its controversial lyrics, according to Lennon. Though it no doubt would have done better if it had been issued under the Beatles' name, it's unlikely to have made No. 1 in such a case, as John once claimed. But this might not have been their only reservation. Like some other songs he'd been writing (especially ones on which Yoko's influence was strongest), the lyrics were so reflective of John's inner anguish that the band might have been reluctant to mold them into statements ostensibly representing the group as a whole, or even felt wholly unable to do so.

The group's rejection of "Cold Turkey" would be just one more factor in John's decision, albeit announced, to leave the Beatles that fall. It's intriguing to consider, however, what might have happened had the others said yes to Lennon. Would *that* have been the final Beatles single of the 1960s—a very strange bookend for the most successful singles band of the decade? Or would disputes over how to record it and whether/how to release it have made matters even tenser than they were?

● September 28

Studio Outtake

"Cold Turkey" Plastic Ono Band single session
Trident Studios, London

Cold Turkey (rough mix)

This rough mix of "Cold Turkey," John Lennon's first true studio recording as a solo artist, has seldom been bootlegged—so seldom, in fact, that this writer hasn't heard it. It's known, however, to have a different lead vocal, as well as some electric piano not heard on the released version.

● November 6

Studio Outtake

Sentimental Journey Ringo Starr LP sessions
Wessex Sound Studios, London

Stormy Weather

Most of the discussion of the reasons for the Beatles' split focuses on John, Paul, and George. But Ringo was making some moves of his own to establish a solo career apart from the other three in both film and music, though it's doubtful he wanted to stop playing with the others. In late October, he began work on his debut solo LP, *Sentimental Journey*—the first full-length solo Beatles recording, believe it or not, that wasn't a film score or avant-garde project. Generally poorly received by critics and even Beatles/Ringo fans, it's hard to believe that many harbor a deep interest in outtakes from this endeavor, in which Ringo sang moldy, schlocky, pre-rock standards. But there is one—just one—circulating unreleased studio outtake from the sessions, a jazzy arrangement of "Stormy Weather" produced by George

In 1969, Ringo Starr—his absence, and the death of the Beatles as a group, symbolically indicated by the empty drum chair on this grab bag of outtakes—made his first solo recordings, though these attracted far less attention than John Lennon's.

Paul Is Dead—the Album

Most uncharacteristically, virtually nothing was heard from Paul McCartney in the last four months of 1969. He began working on his solo debut *McCartney* just before Christmas, but if he put anything on tape between *Abbey Road* and the holidays, there's no evidence of it. He was rarely even appearing in public, instead retreating to his Scottish farm with his new family. But he was still in the media as much as ever, thanks to the lightning spread of the infamous "Paul Is Dead" rumor, which tested the outer limits of Beatles fandom.

If you want to test the outer limits of Beatles *bootleg* fandom, there's no better evidence than the eight-CD bootleg *MissHimMiss-HimMissHim* (titled after a supposed "clue" uttered just before "Black-bird" on *The White Album*). You read that right: *eight* CDs, all of the material connected in some way to the "Paul Is Dead" hysteria. While this book is deliberately not covering bootlegged Beatles-related material not featuring actual music by the musicians, an exception must be made in this one case, if only as a testament to just how extreme and fanatical Beatles bootleg culture can become at its margins.

Most of *MissHimMissHimMissHim* is devoted to radio and TV reports of the hysterical speculation surrounding Paul's demise, complete with "clues" ranging from the intriguing to the truly ridiculous, as well as both dignified and furious denials from the Beatles and their associates. It doesn't get any stranger-than-fiction than the audio track from the syndicated exploitation TV special *Paul McCartney: The Complete Story, Told for the First and Last Time*, originally aired around Thanksgiving 1969. Here witnesses for both the "defense" ("Paul's *not* dead!") and the "prosecution" ("Paul *is*, or *might*, be dead") participated in a mock trial to determine the truth, presided over by famed defense attorney F. Lee Bailey. (And why hasn't *this* shown up on video?)

Unbelievably, the eight-CD set MissHimMissHimMiss-Him *was entirely devoted to media reports and exploitation discs spawned by the "Paul Is Dead" rumor.*

While some of the "witnesses" were clearly making a mountain out of a molehill, somehow Paul's close friend Peter Asher (late of Peter & Gordon) and Allen Klein got dragged into the "trial." Asked whether the rumor had increased the Beatles' publicity, an exasperated but eloquent Asher retorted, "Well, only because you people have taken it seriously enough to do all this incredible nonsense for an hour about something that really is just, you know, not true and, in Paul's own words, is bloody stupid . . . it's only news because people are stupid enough to want to believe it!" Klein's segment is intriguing as well, since, contrary to his uncouth public image, he comes across as quite intelligent, articulate, and reasonable. "They're not Jayne Mansfield," he points out. "They don't have to stoop to this type of publicity in order to financially reward themselves." The interviews on these discs with the Beatles' own denials of the rumor, nonchalantly dismissed with incredulous disbelief that anyone even had time to cook it up, should serve as proof not only that Paul never died, but that the Beatles themselves had no intention of creating such a myth.

There's not much music on *MissHimMissHimMissHim,* other than a disc dominated by "Paul Is Dead" exploitation novelty songs from the late '60s and early '70s, including "Saint Paul" (by Terry Knight, better known as the manager of Grand Funk Railroad), "Billy Shears and the Pallbearers," and "Brother Paul." And the post-1970 "Paul Is Dead" retrospective radio specials taking up some of the latter CDs are truly cretinous in their sensationalistic excavation of "clues" so absurd that they say far more about radio programmers' low estimation of their audience's intelligence than about any false hints the Beatles might have planted. The mere existence of this package, however, says much about the insane devotion of the lunatic fringe of Beatlemania, dedicated not only to propagating one of the most famous tall tales in history, but also to collecting holy relics of its imprint upon popular culture.

Martin. It might be damning with faint praise, but for what it's worth, it's about as good as anything on the official record, Ringo's wavering yet ingratiating vocal backed by a tight but staid ensemble that can't help but bring to mind well-rehearsed pit orchestras from TV variety shows of the day.

● November 26

Studio Outtakes
The White Album *sessions*
Studio Two, Abbey Road, London

What's the New Mary Jane (RS5)
What's the New Mary Jane (RS4/RS5)

White Album outtakes, from late 1969? Well, John hadn't given up on getting "What's the New Mary Jane" out somehow, even if it meant putting it on a Plastic Ono Band single. So he did some remixing on his own, though it didn't come out as a single after all, or in any form until *Anthology 3*. These two mixes—one (RS4) lasting nearly seven minutes, the other (a combination of RS4 and RS5) just two and a half minutes—manage, if anything, to make the track even more chaotically cacophonous than the 1968 mixes. The first adds some more vocals by John, Yoko, and some unidentified pals; the other, one of the most tortuous items the Beatles were ever involved with, actually has two mixes playing at once. If the idea behind making the two-and-a-half-minute mix (which, in any case, starts in the middle of the song) was to create a track short enough to place on a single, it was totally undercut by sound juxtaposition that made it about as uncommercial a proposition as any 45 on the market.

It was the last time John would try to rescue a song that remains among the most unpopular Beatles tunes ever recorded. "I had the distinct feeling that Yoko was really behind the making of that track, and that John was finishing it up just to keep her happy," wrote Geoff Emerick, who worked on the production of this session with Lennon, in *Here, There and Everywhere: My Life Recording the Music of the Beatles*. "She was taking the whole thing quite seriously—in fact, everything seemed to be a matter of grave importance to her—but John kept grinning at me conspiratorially as we were working on it."

● Circa Late Fall

The Beatles' Seventh Christmas Record
Tittenhurst, Ascot; 7 Cavendish Avenue, London;
3 Savile Row; London; Surrey

The Beatles' seventh and final Christmas disc was in several respects similar to the one they'd done in 1968. Kenny Everett produced/assembled it from parts recorded by the four members individually, all of them taping their contributions at their respective homes (except for George, who did his at Apple headquarters). Like the 1968 holiday record, it thus emphasized their impending separation more than it did their unity as a group. Yet now the fragmentation was even more obvious, and the sounds, while interesting in some respects, were even

more chaotic, reflecting the disorganization of both Apple and the Beatles as the group's very existence become less and less certain.

John and Yoko seemed to be the only participants who put more than a couple of minutes' thought into the project, and take up far more space on the nearly eight-minute track than Paul, Ringo, or George. Unsurprisingly, their bits are somewhat close to the experimental tapes John had done in the last three or so years, both on his own and with Yoko, though they're a little more humorous and listener-friendly. The surrealistic whimsy of their dialogue isn't all that inspired or imaginative, but the quasi-musical passages—especially when they duet to a horror-movie-like Mellotron waltz backing, John emitting sardonic Santa Claus laughs as Yoko titters in the background—do have a creepy attraction, as if they're not sure whether to give the fans a dose of wacky holiday cheer or scare them off.

In this context, Paul seems reluctant to touch the more experimental portion with a ten-foot pole, instead offering a brief, pleasant, lyrically simplistic ditty on acoustic guitar with Merry Christmas wishes. Ringo is more willing to ham it up, offering a rare performance on vocals and acoustic guitar, though it's little more than one chord and little more than a few lyrics offering stock pleasantries (unrelated, curiously, in any way to Christmas). He also gets in a plug for his new film, via a segment where his "Merry Christmas" greetings are sped up and slowed down until he's saying "Magic Christian." Most disappointing of all are George's "contributions," which last a mere six seconds; if he hadn't identified himself as George Harrison, some fans might have wondered if he was on the record at all.

Due as much (or more) to Everett's hurly-burly editing as the content within the individual tapes, *The Beatles' Seventh Christmas Record* does entertainingly, if haphazardly, mirror the crazy mixed-bag ethos of both its times and the Beatles' late-'60s milieu in particular. By this time, however, the Christmas discs had gotten about as far away from their original premise—the four lads from Liverpool thanking their fans for being so good to them—as possible. You could also say that musically by late 1969 the group had evolved about as far away from their 1963 style as possible, and certainly changed more than anyone could have imagined back when they made their first Christmas record. In that way, too, *The Beatles' Seventh Christmas Record* is a document of just how much the group had changed in six years, as well as how unlikely it would be that the band could continue into the 1970s.

● December 4

Studio Outtakes
Studio Two, Abbey Road, London

Item 1
Item 2 (fragment)

Having already released three avant-garde albums, John and Yoko recorded material intended for a fourth on this evening at Abbey Road. In the BBC television documentary *24 Hours*, which followed Lennon and Ono around for a few days in early December, fragments of the tracks titled "Item 1" and "Item 2" are seen and heard being recorded and played back in the studio. An acetate with about four minutes of "Item 1" has been bootlegged, and while it's unheard by this writer, based on what's shown in the *24 Hours* documentary, it must have been a lot more fun to make than hear. John, Yoko, and friends and EMI staff (several wearing rubber noses, John included) laugh with and at each other hysterically, as though nitrous oxide has filled the room. The little seen of "Item 2," in contrast, has a few of the assembled crowd striding up to the mike to whisper a phrase.

As Geoff Emerick remembered in *Here, There and Everywhere*, the session actually grew out of an idea to record a modern version of the children's record "The Laughing Policeman," overdubbing the strange laughter of engineer John Smith (who'd worked on some of the *White Album* sessions). When the time came, however, "they had decided that instead of recording 'The Laughing Policeman,' we were all to put on red rubber noses (probably the same ones Mal Evans had given out at the 'A Day in the Life' orchestral session two years previously), line up at a microphone, and whisper the first thing that came into our heads. Lennon had arranged for cases of booze to be brought in, and we soon all got out of our minds, making total fools of ourselves."

"The next thing that's sort of in the can is the next John and Yoko freak album," John told *Rolling Stone* in December 1969. "One side of it is laughing and the other side is whispering—so far, anyway . . . We started whispering the piece that Yoko had done. You whisper to one person and they have to pass it on to the next person and by the time it gets back, it's gobbledegook. They filmed us doing it." But Yoko and John must have been well aware that far from being an avant-garde concept, this "piece" was pretty much the same as the children's game usually known as "Telephone" in the US, and popular under different names in numerous countries throughout the world.

The album on which this might have appeared never came out, and in fact John and Yoko never did put out another avant-garde record, though they did much recording (both together and separately) for the remainder of Lennon's life. Another section of the *24 Hours* movie, incidentally, shows them sitting together at a Mellotron in their home, producing soothing instrumental tones that are quite a bit more edifying than "Item 1" or "Item 2." A whole album of that would have probably made for a better record than any of their 1968–1969 experimental LPs, had they been so inclined.

On a side note, John, Yoko, and George performed as part of the Plastic Ono Band at the Lyceum in London on December 15, 1969, with two of the songs getting released in 1972 on John and Yoko's *Sometime in New York City* album. Technically speaking, those are group-related recordings that didn't come out while the Beatles were active, but they won't be covered here, as they were commonly available on a standard solo LP by one of the members shortly after the breakup.

● December 8

Studio Outtake
Studio Two, Abbey Road, London

Octopus's Garden (take 10)

The lines between the Beatles' career as a group and solo artists continued to blur with this strange recording, made for a British TV tribute to George Martin, *With a Little Help from My Friends*. The "Octopus's Garden" track from *Abbey Road* was reworked so it could be mimed,

solo, by Ringo on the program. Not only did Ringo record a new lead vocal, but the backing track was also largely re-recorded (not by the Beatles, but by musicians of unknown identity), though the drums and rhythm guitar from the Beatles' version were kept, as well as some vocals and sound effects. Is it any surprise that this artificial-sounding "remake" was not as good as the original?

● December 18

Private Tape
Ronnie Hawkins's Farm, Mississauga, Canada

Give Peace a Chance
Dear Prudence
Sun King
Blues Improvisation
Mind Games

Most of this nearly ten-minute tape, recorded while John and Yoko were on another of their peace campaigns in Canada, has Yoko delivering a spoken Japanese message, for reasons unclear (perhaps it was intended as a radio broadcast). It's of some musical value, however, for the inclusion of the pair singing a snatch of "Give Peace a Chance," backed by John's acoustic guitar, John merrily declaring "Moshi-moshi" (or "Hello," roughly, in Japanese) at times. You can also hear John strumming acoustic guitar behind Yoko's voice throughout much of the tape, including vocal-less tours through "Dear Prudence," "Sun King," and a basic blues progression. In much more of a surprise, you can also hear him going through an instrumental sequence that would evolve into "Mind Games"—another sign that he was already working on some material that wouldn't emerge until some ways into his solo career, with "Mind Games" becoming a hit Lennon single in late 1973. John and Yoko would continue their international travels into the New Year, which Lennon apparently considered more important than resuming work with the Beatles, as the couple were vacationing in Denmark when the other three assembled for the final Beatles recording sessions in the first week of January 1970.

1969 Noncirculating Recordings, Known and Rumored

● January

Rehearsals & Studio Outtakes
Let It Be sessions
Twickenham Film Studios & Apple Studios, London

As scary as the very notion of the mere existence of more January 1969 outtakes might be to even contemplate, it's certain there are even more lying around than the 100 or so hours that have already circulated. It's known that Glyn Johns, working separately from the film crew's Nagra sound equipment, recorded the group (probably in mono) while they were rehearsing at Twickenham January 7–10 (and maybe January 13 too). Not only might he have caught some performances that the film crew missed, but even if his recordings largely duplicated what the cameras caught, they'd likely have better fidelity. In his book *Let It Be*, Steve Matteo reports that they've been lost or recorded over, though Johns might have made some acetates from the tapes.

It's also known that some of the camera rolls used to record and film the band have never turned up, or at least that the music they recorded has never circulated. This includes, frustratingly, a roll that was taping just as George quit the band on January 10, almost raising suspicions that this was deliberately hidden or destroyed if it contained particularly damning arguments that the Beatles or their intimates did not want preserved for posterity. It's probable that there isn't much or anything of huge value on the missing tapes—almost certainly, they're just more versions of some of the numbers the Beatles were rehearsing over and over, oldies covers, nondescript jams, and so on. Still, there could be some additional revelatory dialogue giving us insight into how well or poorly the Beatles were getting along, and you never knew what unpredictable cover tune they might launch into next, though you could usually depend on it not being performed too well.

The Beatles were recording at Apple for the last ten days or so of January, and although it's unlikely the EMI studio tapes rolling during that period caught much material that wasn't captured by the Nagra recorders, undoubtedly they got some. Even if they do largely duplicate each other, the EMI tapes would be of great value solely for preserving the performances in appreciably better sound than the less sophisticated Nagra equipment would have been able to capture. And there is one performance—cited in *The Beatles Recording Sessions* as having been recorded on January 26—that has never shown up on any

Numerous shots from the Beatles' final photo session on August 22, 1969, have shown up on the covers of bootlegs such as this one.

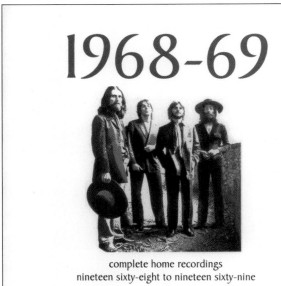

1968-69

complete home recordings
nineteen sixty-eight to nineteen sixty-nine

bootleg. This was a three-minute solo demo, with just voice and guitar, of George Harrison's "Isn't It a Pity," which as a seven-minute track would become one of the highlights of *All Things Must Pass*"(and, as the B-side of "My Sweet Lord," pick up quite a bit of AM radio airplay on its own). This is almost certainly *not* the same recording or performance of the song on January 26 that, as taped by the film crew, has shown up on bootlegs. Mark Lewisohn describes the demo as lasting three minutes and three seconds, but the bootlegged version is less than two minutes, and seems far more informally performed than it likely would have been had George been making a studio demo. That might explain why George didn't include it in his February 25 session of solo demos at Abbey Road, assuming a demo of a similar nature had already been made for the tune. It *doesn't* explain why it wasn't chosen for *Anthology 3*, where it would have made for a nice never-before-heard addition (and a more interesting one than some of the tracks that *were* selected for that compilation).

As a footnote, international headlines were made on January 10, 2003, with the announcement that police had found more than 500 unreleased Beatles tapes from January 1969. While the more sensationalistic accounts played this up to almost give the impression that they contained dozens if not hundreds of hours of material that had never before been heard, in fact it's likely that most or all of these tapes are ones that had already been bootlegged for years. That doesn't mean they wouldn't be worthwhile to hear, as they presumably would boast better sound quality, and might contain at least some material that's never escaped. The possibility that they hold a treasure vault of never-circulated stuff, however, is probably slim to none.

● February 22–August 20

Studio Outtakes
Abbey Road sessions
Abbey Road, London

Abbey Road's painstakingly layered production did not lend itself to the creation of many outtakes that were wholly or largely different from the tracks that ended up on the LP. Going back to the album's baby steps, it's known that George Harrison did two takes each of "Old Brown Shoe" and "All Things Must Pass" when he recorded solo demos on February 25. Only one take each of those songs was used on *Anthology 3*, and the others might be different and worth hearing, if only because the sparse nature of these demos' production could have lent themselves to rougher and more spontaneous performances.

"Something," another of the songs that George demoed, was first recorded on April 16 and then redone from scratch starting two weeks later. But this first attempt probably isn't as exciting as it might sound, since it was a backing track with no vocals. The remake initially ran nearly eight minutes, by virtue of its repetitive instrumental coda; the circulating bootleg take is two minutes shorter, so that final part exists somewhere, though it's probably just more of the same downbeat instrumental jam.

At the same July 24 session that produced the outtake of "Ain't She Sweet" heard on *Anthology 3*, the group also jammed on Gene Vincent's '50s rocker "Who Slapped John?" and "Be-Bop-A-Lula." Mark Lewisohn's *The Beatles Recording Sessions* notes that the sound on these "was also good and precise," so it can be assumed that these, like "Ain't She Sweet," sound rather like way-above-average oldies covers from the *Get Back* sessions. *The Recording Sessions* also notes that all seven takes of "The End" had different types of drum solos.

A four-and-a-half-minute version of "I Want You (She's So Heavy)" purporting to be a February 1969 outtake with Paul McCartney on vocals has shown up on a few bootlegs, but its authenticity is in dispute. Some experts dismiss it as a fraud; others are convinced it's legitimate. It's *possible* it's genuine, but to this writer it doesn't *quite* sound like that's Paul singing—or like any of the other Beatles are singing, for that matter.

● April 14

Studio Outtakes
"The Ballad of John and Yoko" single session
Studio Three, Abbey Road, London

John and Paul were the only Beatles to play on "The Ballad of John and Yoko," and there are ten takes of basic rhythm tracks (with John on acoustic guitar and vocal, and Paul on drums) that weren't used. While they must be far less fleshed-out than the final version (on take 10, which added a bunch of overdubs), they carry historical weight, as they're probably some of the final tapes of Lennon and McCartney working closely together, alone. Interestingly, the only two writers to have heard these had different impressions of the vibe between John and Paul on this session, done at a time when the business and personal pressures tearing them asunder were really starting to take their toll. Mark Lewisohn's *The Beatles Recording Sessions* reports that their "great talent, humor, musical understanding and togetherness shone through from start to finish."

In the January 24, 1994, *New Yorker,* however, Mark Hertsgaard (who was able to listen to the tapes, with Lewisohn present, a few years after Lewisohn did his research) begs to differ: "As we sit listening, Lewisohn murmurs to me, 'Great musical kinship on this. They were coming apart in every other way, but they could still bury that under the music.' Well, yes, but just barely, it seems to me. Lennon and McCartney may not be chewing each other's heads off—in fact, they seem to be trying very hard to get along—but there is a forced, polite quality to their joking, and none of the enthusiastic electricity heard during earlier Beatles sessions (or during John's [*Plastic Ono Band*] sessions eighteen months later, for that matter). Making a record has become a job—a job that John and Paul do extremely well, but a job nevertheless. They are coming apart, and they know it."

● Circa Summer

Studio Outtake

The August 1969 issue of *Beatles Monthly* reported that the next Plastic Ono Band release would be "a long and heavy instrumental single" titled "Rock Peace," to be issued at the end of August. Whether "Rock Peace" was a title for another song that later appeared under a different guise is unknown, but in any case, no Lennon-related track called "Rock Peace" came out on a single or anything else.

1970

All Things Must Pass Away

The Year in Review

The Beatles did very little recording as a group (and none with John Lennon's involvement) in 1970 before breaking up on April 10 when Paul announced that he was leaving the band. With the benefit of several decades of subsequent research, it's now widely known that the conflicts leading to the split had been serious since at least January 1969, and had been seriously escalating ever since the start of the sessions for *The White Album*. It's also now common knowledge that before Paul's exit, each of the other three members had unofficially quit (Ringo during *The White Album*, George during the *Get Back* sessions, and John right after *Abbey Road*), though this did not leak to the media at the time. The Beatles' actual breakup was still a profound shock to their fans, most of whom had no idea just how deep and irreparable the disagreements among the four (and particularly between McCartney and the other three) had become.

There is just one Beatles unreleased track from 1970 that eventually made its way into circulation, and even that has been officially issued on *Anthology 3*. Ironically, however, unreleased Beatles music might have been more in the public eye right after Paul's departure in the spring of 1970 than ever—before or since. For it was then, 16 months after the *Get Back* sessions, that the whole mess of what to do with the 100-plus hours

of recordings and film was finally resolved, with the release of the *Let It Be* LP and movie. It was also then, owing to the interminable delays holding up the album's appearance, that Beatles bootlegs finally started to get manufactured in a big way; if the group wasn't going to release the stuff promptly, their most enthusiastic fans were going to find a way to issue and hear at least some of it. For the band's indecision about what to put on the album and how to mix it led to several different unreleased versions of the LP getting produced, some of which were bootlegged. That long and complicated story is told in a sidebar a little later in this chapter. For now, suffice it to say that the officially packaged *Let It Be* album was a messy, compromised production that didn't wholly please anyone. It's necessary to hear those preliminary versions—which were, generally, far more faithful to the *Get Back* project's original intention to present the group in a live, back-to-the-roots setting—to gain a full appreciation of just how tangled *Let It Be*'s genesis was, and just how much the album's concept and actual music changed between its inception and belated release.

In the fallout from the group's implosion, however, there was some interesting, and sometimes even excellent, unreleased 1970 solo material that's come to light, even if this has been pretty much exclusively from

279

MoMac's Hidden Tracks
The McCartney Recording Sessions: Volume 2

There's not much unreleased Paul McCartney material in circulation from the immediate aftermath of the Beatles' split in 1970, though there's a little on this collection of outtakes.

George Harrison and John Lennon. As noted in this book's introduction, it's not the mission of this volume to examine the Beatles' unreleased post-split solo work, which would take another humongous study of its own. However, this chapter *will* cover post-breakup unreleased recordings by John, Paul, George, and Ringo through the end of 1970, for several reasons. One is that they contain numerous compositions that were undoubtedly written, or starting to be written, while the group was still together; in some cases, there are even Beatles or Beatles-era recordings of the songs. Another is that they give us some insight as to why the members came to feel as though they needed to express themselves on record outside of a Beatles, or even group, context.

In addition, it shouldn't be overlooked that there's some very fine music contained on these early unreleased solo outings. George's spring 1970 unplugged-type *All Things Must Pass* demos in particular are not only a vital, largely unheard link between his Beatles days and his first proper solo album, but delightful listening on their own terms, and comprise about as likable (and listenable) a bootleg as has ever been made, by the Beatles or anyone. While not quite as fab in either musical or historical terms, Harrison's *All Things Must Pass* outtakes, as well as the numerous outtakes John produced during the making of *Plastic Ono Band* and the home tapes he made in its aftermath, are also fascinating (and at times inspirational) listening. The near-absence of any Paul McCartney unreleased tapes whatsoever from this period is lamentable, and perhaps says something about the relative diligence with which he's guarded his early recordings, at least in comparison with John and George.

The considerable merits of some of the early solo work of the individual Beatles (particularly George's, which would never have been given the space it deserved on a group release) still couldn't compensate for the permanent loss of the greatest musical group of the 20th century. The solo Beatles never reached the musical heights they'd scaled as a team, and Harrison and Lennon, in fact, would never do any solo work as good as what they crafted in the immediate aftermath of the Beatles' split in the early '70s. Paul McCartney's decision to sue the other three Beatles for a dissolution of their partnership on the last day of 1970 put to rest any serious prospect of the band reuniting, sealing a body of work that—for all its enormous and enduring popularity—continues to be excavated, examined, and, yes (in terms of unreleased material), bootlegged just as avidly in the 21st century as it was when the members first went their separate ways.

● January 3

Studio Outtake

Let It Be *sessions*
Studio Two, Abbey Road, London

---

*I Me Mine (take 16)

   *appears on Anthology 3

The last true Beatles recording sessions took place on January 3 and January 4, 1970, without John Lennon, who was on vacation with Yoko Ono in Denmark. Some overdubbing was done on "Let It Be" on January 4. The previous day, "I Me Mine" was recorded as it would be seen in the *Let It Be* film, and thus needed to be included on the accompanying album. "I Me Mine" had been rehearsed and taped by the film cameras' recorders in January 1969. But unlike the overdubbing on "Let It Be," which worked off a base studio take on January 31, 1969, "I Me Mine" would be recorded on this January 1970 date without incorporating any previously taped elements.

Take 16, which appears on *Anthology 3*, is actually the same one heard on *Let It Be*, even though it's much shorter, lasting only about a minute and a half. Phil Spector subsequently artificially lengthened it by almost a minute by repeating a bridge and verse, also overdubbing brass and strings. The *Anthology 3* version hence has a less cluttered sound that's truer to the *Get Back* ethic, though by January 1970 the Beatles probably weren't worried about simulating a live performance, and more concerned with just getting the cleanup work on the album over with. *Let It Be . . . Naked* adds yet another variation, dispensing with the Spector overdubs but edited to match the length and structure of the tune as it had originally appeared on the *Let It Be* LP.

The sardonic George Harrison comment heard at the beginning of the *Anthology 3* version, obliquely referring to John's absence, was actually from take 15, and edited onto the beginning of the track. And if you want a yet more niggling variation, one bootlegged version adds scraps of guitar fiddling at the beginning and end, as well as a count-in at the start.

● February 11

Live Performance
For television program Top of the Pops
Television Centre, London

Instant Karma! (We All Shine On) (take 3)
Instant Karma! (We All Shine On) (take 4)

Well, not *exactly* a live performance. However, John did put live vocals onto a mono mix of the official studio backing track of "Instant Karma!" for these two takes, recorded not in the studio, but in front of cameras for the BBC television program *Top of the Pops*. The vocals are different from those heard on the single, noticeable especially when he seems to somehow forget the first line of the chorus on take 3, singing something like "Well we all have on." The vocals are even different from take to take, as a testimony to either John's spontaneity or his noted tendency to forget lyrics. Take 3 is incomplete, cutting off about a minute and a half before the end of the song; take 4 was issued on the 1992 home video *The John Lennon Video Collection*. As a strange footnote, Yoko's seen occasionally singing on take 4, but she's certainly not heard on the audio track, as if someone at the BBC has decided not to place a working mike in front of her.

Unlike "Cold Turkey," "Instant Karma!" *could* have been a viable Beatles single, both in terms of its commercial appeal and lending itself to a group arrangement. Yet when John decided to put it out as a solo 45, with heavily reverbed production (by Phil Spector) unlike that heard on any Beatles track, it couldn't help but fuel increasing speculation among observant fans and media that the group might not continue for much longer.

● March 8–October

Studio Outtakes
"It Don't Come Easy" Ringo Starr single sessions
Trident Studios, London

It Don't Come Easy (rough mono mix #1)
It Don't Come Easy (rough mono mix #2)
It Don't Come Easy (rough stereo mix, George Harrison guide vocal)

Ringo Starr managed to start work in February 1970 on what would become a genuinely catchy hit single, but recording wasn't finished until October and somehow the track wasn't released until April 1971 (though Ringo could have really used a smash to quickly establish himself as a viable solo artist). As producer, guitarist, and uncredited co-songwriter, George Harrison was a big help in polishing off the recording, which was remade from scratch starting on March 8 after a few previous attempts on February 18 and 19. A couple of rough mixes have shown up that are missing brass and vocal parts, one of them missing a Gary Wright piano overdub as well. Far more interesting is a different mix with a fairly enthusiastic, committed guide vocal by George. He proves he could have made it into a viable hit single for himself if he'd wanted, though his singing is understandably not as refined as it probably would have been had he released it under his own name.

● March 15

Live Performance
For television program Frost on Sunday
Talk of the Town, London

Sentimental Journey

The last circulating unreleased performance by any of the Beatles before their official split is decidedly anti-climactic: Ringo Starr putting a live vocal on top of a mono mix of the title cut of his debut album *Sentimental Journey*. This was done at the Talk of the Town nightclub in London for broadcast a couple of weeks later on the British TV program *Frost on Sunday*. With its devotion to covers of corny, pre-rock pop standards, the *Sentimental Journey* album was never going to be a big hit, even among Beatles fans. In any case, it was soon wholly overshadowed by the news on April 10 that Paul McCartney was leaving the Beatles—a decision instigated, at least in part, by the way the January 1969 *Get Back* sessions had been packaged for release (at long last) on the *Let It Be* album, which finally came out in May.

● Late May

Studio Outtakes
George Harrison's All Things Must Pass *demos*
London

Run of the Mill
Art of Dying
Everybody, Nobody
Wah-Wah
Window, Window
Beautiful Girl
*Beware of Darkness

Let It Be . . . Released

When *Let It Be* was finally released on May 8, 1970, it was the culmination of about 15 months of confusion of what to do with the mammoth vault of material the Beatles had recorded in January 1969. Although three tracks ("Get Back," "Don't Let Me Down," and "Let It Be," the last issued as a 45 in March 1970) had already been put out officially on singles, the album's release had been pushed back about a year from the original target date. The title had even changed, from *Get Back* to *Let It Be*. Most confusingly of all, several different versions of the album had already been assembled, and one of them had even widely circulated as a bootleg. What's more, several different versions of the album continue to circulate on bootleg (and, starting in 2003, official Apple releases) today, crossing up even some veteran Beatles collectors in their attempt to identify what's what. The crossfire of small details conspiring to create this logjam is extensive enough to fill a mini-book, but here's a rundown of the main issues to keep in mind.

It can be said that the very first versions of *Get Back* were actually compiled before the sessions were even finished. On the night of January 24, 1969, as he later recalled in *The Record Producers*, Glyn Johns "mixed a bunch of stuff that they didn't even know I'd recorded, half the time. I just whacked the recorder on for a lot of stuff that they did, and gave them an acetate the following morning of what I'd done, as a rough idea of what an album could be like . . . that became an obsession with me." On January 26, however, "they came back and said they didn't like it, and that was the end of that" (although Paul at least can be heard expressing some enthusiasm for them on bootleg tapes from the day).

Actually, however, Johns continued to play back rough mixes to the Beatles over the next few days. He did an LP-length acetate on the night of January 30, after the rooftop concert, that contained most of the songs (though not the same takes) used on *Let It Be*, as well as a couple of numbers that didn't make the eventual cut ("Teddy Boy" and "The Walk"). He also did a second one-sided acetate with a different version of "I've Got a Feeling," "Dig It," and a bunch of oldies covers. Like all of the acetates discussed in this sidebar, these are *not* the same mixes as the ones heard on other bootleg recordings of the same performances that were recorded on the film sound cameras; these are made from studio tapes, with a correspondingly fuller sound.

Both of Johns's acetates were bootlegged, though the LP-length one is by far the more widely circulated. While rougher than *Let It Be*—complete with abruptly edited between-song chatter and false starts—this actually does have an appeal of its own, the group sounding a little more spontaneous, raw, and human than they did on the more cleaned-up ultimate versions. If nothing else, it's also a truer reflection of the original intention of the album to capture the Beatles in a live setting, with no overdubs or corrections of flubs.

Judging from a comment McCartney made on January 31, 1969, the Beatles, or he at least, might have been considering doing some more recording and filming for the *Get Back* project in February. They rarely recorded as a group at all over the next two months, however, perhaps due to several unforeseen circumstances: Ringo was busy filming *The Magic Christian*, George Harrison had his tonsils taken out in February and was busted for pot possession in March, Paul and John

each got married in March, Johns was going on his honeymoon and traveling to the US to work with Steve Miller, Billy Preston needed to return to the US for a short tour of Texas, and management, publishing, and Apple business disputes were heating up.

It may also be that the Beatles were uncertain of what to do with the tapes, or whether to make an album out of them at all, even though Apple had already jumped the gun and announced that 12 tracks had been completed at the end of January, with just four more songs needing to get finished before an April 1969 release. In Steve Matteo's *Let It Be*, this was disputed by Alan Parsons (who'd worked as an engineer on the sessions), who remarked, "I'm not really sure that they thought they had anything else other than a soundtrack for the film. I think probably they came away thinking that they hadn't made a record and it was just going to get put on the shelf."

Nonetheless, according to Johns, around early March, Lennon and McCartney "pointed to a big pile of tapes in the corner, and said, 'Remember that idea you had about putting together an album? Well, there are the tapes. Go ahead and do it.'" This Johns did, though the first acetate of his mixes from this round has only circulated on an obscure vinyl bootleg with one channel missing. By the end of May, he'd prepared yet another acetate that actually mostly used the same takes as the one he'd done back at the end of January, adding versions of "Maggie Mae," "Dig It," "One After 909," and a medley of "Rocker" and "Save the Last Dance for Me." It also used the more polished "Let It Be" that would provide the basis of the official single release. This has also been widely bootlegged, and is probably the best representation of the album as it would have been packaged had it come out before *Abbey Road*. Truth be told, it's not too much different from the ultimate official *Let It Be* release, though of course the track lineup is slightly different, "The Long and Winding Road" is still in its string-less state, and the mixes have been criticized by some aficionados as not being all that lively (and the track sequencing not that inspired).

At this point, the album seemed on track for an early summer 1969 release. The famous cover photo (of the Beatles replicating the pose and location of the picture on their *Please Please Me* sleeve, later used on the compilation *The Beatles 1967-70*) had been taken on May 13, and a title had been chosen (*Get Back, Don't Let Me Down, and 12 Other Songs*, in a parody of the full title of their first album, *Please Please Me with Love Me Do and 12 Other Songs*). John Lennon, describing it as "like an unfinished rehearsal for the show that we never did," told *NME* that the record would come out in July.

It didn't, of course, and here's where the waters start to get real murky, as it's hard to say with any certainty why it kept getting pushed back. One cause was a wish to make it coincide with the release of the film they'd made in January, the completion of which kept getting delayed. Another may be that the Beatles were simply dissatisfied with the record, or the mix, or just didn't feel that it met their usual LP standards, in which case some criticism might be deflected if it were marketed as a soundtrack-cum-live-album.

Another cause might have been that work on their last true studio LP, *Abbey Road*, was starting in earnest, and they wanted that much more coherent, polished record to be their next album, knowing it would likely be of considerably superior quality. As *Abbey Road* got finished in August 1969, they were now faced with the unattractive option of releasing both albums at once. That, nonetheless, might have been less absurd than what actually happened: as discussed in the 1969 chapter, *Let It Be* was **recorded before** *Abbey Road* (except for a bit of 1970 recording) but **released after** *Abbey Road*.

As an even more absurd premise, the word was put out that there might be an entirely different, additional album compiled from the January sessions consisting simply of oldies covers. The sad fact is, however, not only was there no entire album of quality January 1969 oldies covers, there probably wasn't even one releasable oldies cover in the whole batch. (Leaving aside the absence of a single suitable cover, there were—at most—half a dozen such cuts that were highly enjoyable performances per se, such as "Besame Mucho," "The Walk," and the best versions of "Singing the Blues" and "Rock and Roll Music.")

Around the time *Abbey Road* came out in September 1969, things got even weirder. John quit the Beatles, though he was persuaded by Paul and manager Allen Klein not to announce this to the public, for fear of jeopardizing a new Beatles recording contract that had just been negotiated with EMI. The film release, and hence the album release, kept getting pushed back yet further. Most intriguing of all, a tape of the very first acetate Johns had prepared back on January 30, 1969, somehow slipped out to a few radio stations, who broadcast it in full—quite a coup, given that just two of the songs had been released (on the "Get Back"/"Don't Let Me Down" single, and even then in different versions). The acetate Johns had done in early May slipped out for radio broadcast as well. There was even a track-by-track description of the *Get Back* album, seemingly taken from one of the acetates Johns had prepared in May, in the September 20, 1969, issue of *Rolling Stone.*

Remarkably, a tape of one of the actual radio broadcasts itself (September 22, WBCN-FM in Boston) of the January 30 acetate has been bootlegged, complete with DJ patter by Steve Segal. An entertaining document of just how thrilling this illicit acquisition was to risk-taking radio stations of the time, it's also, in a way, revealing of just how uncertain the media was about Apple's plans for *Let It Be* and why it was surfacing at almost the exact same time as *Abbey Road.* As Segal enthuses, "Listen while you can, because if the past is any indication as to the future . . . we will be in some way stopped from playing this album by the record company itself after the next couple of days . . . it won't be out till Christmas . . . this is all of side two, from the Beatles' *next* next album, called *Get Back* . . . if you're taping this off the radio, someone's going to come to your house and say, 'Listen, I'm sorry, you can't play that album in your house' . . . in fact, if you tape that, you might be the first person on your block to get a telegram from Apple, saying, 'Don't play the record in your house . . . you can't even have it. In fact, flush it down your toilet!'"

Even more remarkably, the tape WBCN used for broadcasting the acetate soon made its way around to other radio stations, as well as onto bootleg cassette. Finally, around the time 1969 turned to 1970, much of the tape was bootlegged onto vinyl on the *Kum Back* LP, the first popular Beatles bootleg, and in fact one of the first widely sold rock bootlegs ever. As a product, *Kum Back* was shoddy. The sound quality was substandard and obviously several generations removed from the source. The speed at which the tracks played was off. It was packaged in a flimsy, blank white sleeve. The inner label, perhaps deliberately or perhaps because of some honest wrong guesses, gave a bunch of incorrect song titles: "Don't Keep Me Waiting" (for "The Long and Winding

Road"), "Sweet & Lovely" (aka "For You Blue"), "Who Knows" (aka "I Dig a Pony"), "Tojo [sic] Was a Loner" (aka "Get Back"), "On Your Way Home" (aka "Two of Us"), "Teddy Don't Worry" (aka "Teddy Boy"), and "Can He Walk" (aka "The Walk"). Still, it was a genuine thrill for Beatles fans, for the very first time, to be able to hear tapes that had not been released and songs that were not yet available in any form. It also likely gave Apple an increased sense of urgency in getting an official version of the album out in some form, seeing as how bootleggers were both racking up substantial sales and airing material that the Beatles had never approved to hundreds of thousands (if not millions) of listeners.

As another complication, the film was now being produced as a theatrical release, rather than a television show. That meant more delays, and it also meant that the Beatles felt they needed to make new, acceptably presentable studio recordings of a couple of the tracks. In early January 1970, without John, they recorded George's "I Me Mine" from scratch, and gave "Let It Be" yet more overdubs. Johns prepared yet another version of the album, mildly differing from the one he'd done in late May, chiefly in that it added the new recording of "I Me Mine," remixed the February 1968 recording of "Across the Universe" (included as it was to be seen played by the Beatles in the film), and used a version of "For You Blue" with a new vocal overdub (as well as dropping "Teddy Boy"). This too went unreleased and, of course, has also been bootlegged should you want to do a comparison. Were it not for the impending film, one wonders if any album would have come out, so rapidly were the Beatles heading toward a split in early 1970.

That split was ensured by John and George's decision to have Phil Spector work on the tapes. "It was not satisfactory to any of them," claimed Spector, presumably of the latest Johns-assembled version, in *Rolling Stone.* "They did not want it out as it was. So John said, 'Let Phil do it,' and I said, 'Fine.' Then I said, 'Would anybody like to get involved in it, work on it with me?' 'No.' They didn't care." This part of the story, at least, is fairly well known, with Spector not only doing remixes, but also adding strings and choral vocals to a few tracks. In the cases of "I Me Mine" and (to a lesser degree) "Across the Universe," these weren't too controversial, even if many Beatles fans felt with the passage of time that "Across the Universe" was better left untouched in its original 1968 incarnation. Not so with "The Long and Winding Road," where Paul's ballad was drenched with violins and a choir.

It's never been completely established whether McCartney (then busy wrapping up his first solo album) was completely unaware of Spector's overdubs to the song. An April 14, 1970, telegram from Paul to Allen Klein reprinted in *The Beatles Anthology* states, "In future no one will be allowed to add to or subtract from a recording of one of my songs without my permission," implying the mix was done without his approval. In the *Evening Standard,* he added, "I was sent a remixed version of my song 'The Long and Winding Road,' with harps, horns, an orchestra and women's choir added. No one had asked me what I thought. I couldn't believe it. I would never have female voices on a Beatles record." (Although there actually *had* been female voices on Beatles records on occasion, most recently at the January 1970 overdubs for the "Let It Be" single, which included harmonies by Linda McCartney; Mary Hopkin also recalled singing on this session.)

Ringo, however, told *Melody Maker,* "He heard it. I spoke to him on the phone and said, 'Did you like it?' and he said, 'Yeah, it's okay.' He didn't put it down. And then suddenly he didn't want it to go out . . . two weeks after that, he wanted to cancel it." For his part, George

LET IT END

A brutally irreverent satire of the Let It Be *cover on one of innumerable bootleg LPs drawn from the* Get Back *sessions. Its title aptly sums up the viewpoint more cynical fans hold toward the whole* Get Back/Let It Be *mess.*

Martin told the same paper, "John insisted that it was going to be a natural album, a live album, and he didn't want any of the faking, any of the *Pepper* stuff, any production. . . . When the record came out, I got a hell of a shock. I knew nothing about it, and neither did Paul. All the lush, un-Beatle-like orchestrations with harps and choirs in the background—it was so contrary to what John asked for in the first place."

Yet this is what came out, and history generally accepts the overdub of "The Long and Winding Road" as one of the last straws that finally led Paul to throw in the towel and quit the group on April 10, 1970. As an additional mitigating factor, the other Beatles had also asked him to push back the release of his *McCartney* album from April 17 to June 4 so that it wouldn't conflict with *Let It Be,* which had been penciled in for April 24. Paul not only refused, but threw Ringo out of his house when the drummer came by to deliver the news. *Let It Be*'s release was pushed back one final time, to May 8, to accommodate McCartney.

It still remains somewhat puzzling as to just why the group couldn't decide on a version of the album to release, and why it took so long to get the damn thing out. While not quite up to the usual excellence and consistency of a Beatles LP, there was a lot of fine music; the performances were good, and if they weren't perfect, as repeatedly noted, that was part of the "live album" idea in the first place. *Let It Be*'s year-plus delay continues to confuse fans to this day, many (perhaps most) of whom still think *Let It Be* was recorded after *Abbey Road.* In particular, it seems mystifying that Paul McCartney would want to sit on an obviously classic hit single, "Let It Be," for more than a year. Maybe he thought it could be used as the follow-up single to "Get Back" ("The Ballad of John and Yoko" swooping into that slot instead); maybe he really was never satisfied with the recording until the January 1970 overdubs; maybe he really did intend to "give it away" to Aretha Franklin, who recorded it in 1969 after getting his acetate (though the Beatles thought better of it and ordered Atlantic not to release it until the group's official single version came out in March 1970).

All things considered, perhaps they really should have just put out the version Glyn Johns assembled in late May 1969. Or perhaps they should have buckled down and finished off both the album (maybe adding some properly recorded oldies covers) and film for a spring 1969 release, roughly in accordance with the original plan. However messy the results would have been, they couldn't have been messier than what actually took place. Ultimately, however, there was probably just too much chaos in the Beatles' camp, too many lingering bad feelings about the sessions, and too much ambivalence about the worth of what they had done to bring the customary focus they had usually brought to such tasks before 1969.

Almost 35 years later, the surviving Beatles, and Paul McCartney in particular, did try to go back in time and get *Let It Be* right. In late 2003, the *Let It Be . . . Naked* CD gave the album a substantial overhaul, even as it used many of the same takes as the bedrock. The idea came to Paul while he considered plans to put the *Let It Be* film on DVD (which, as of this writing in early 2006, has still not occurred). "The more I thought about it I realized that the music in the film is unadorned, or naked, as I was calling it," he explained to *MOJO.* "I had been listening to the original mixes without any of the overdubs, thinking, 'Wow! These are almost scary, it's so bare.' I really liked it. I've always had a secret lingering love for those tapes. So, thinking if we were to do the DVD, then the soundtrack could be from the original tapes." The album was then mixed from scratch to put it more in line with the "live" sound that had originally been the intention, as well as resequenced. "Maggie Mae" and "Dig It" were dropped; a different take of "The Long and Winding Road" was used; "Don't Let Me Down" and "I've Got a Feeling" were both edited together from two January 30 rooftop performances; "Let It Be" was edited together from two January 31 performances *plus* some of the overdubs it was given in early 1970; all the between-song chatter was discarded; some of the fades were slightly shorter; and, most pointedly, none of Phil Spector's orchestral or vocal overdubs were used.

This was not, however, *Let It Be* or *Get Back* in its purest form. The Pro Tools computer software program, decades away from development in 1969, was used to remove some noises, "fly in" bits from other takes, and even fix some mistakes (most notably John's clumsy bass work on "The Long and Winding Road"). Certainly *Let It Be . . . Naked* gave the music a loud, fresh clarity, and overall it's a superior listen to *Let It Be,* with an earthier, live-sounding feel (and the vital subtraction of the strings and choir from "The Long and Winding Road"). The praise was not unanimous, however, and reading intense Beatlemaniacs' appraisals is rather like flipping through the stereo-vs.-mono debates over different Beatles mixes. Some listeners hail the brilliance of *Let It Be . . . Naked*'s reconstruction with wild-eyed fervor; others dismiss it as not only overhyped, but inferior to the versions heard on the original LP. At times, too, the remixing got a little carried away, particularly in boosting Ringo's drumming so far up front in "For You Blue" that it became more of a distraction than an enhancement. And the use of Pro Tools ran counter to the group's original intention to present the group in as live and natural a setting as possible, though one of the CD's three mixers, Allan Rouse, contended in *MOJO* that the band "didn't have the time and resources to complete the album as we did. [Begging the question, it must be interjected, as to whether the 15 months between the recording of most of *Get Back* in January 1969 and the release of *Let It Be* in May 1970 was not sufficient time for the band to complete the album.] If Pro Tools had been around in 1969 they would have used it. It's a brilliant editing tool, but that's all. Sonically, everything is still analogue."

Finally, the 22-minute "Fly on the Wall" bonus disc, consisting of admittedly interesting bits and pieces of both musical performances and dialogue from the *Get Back* sessions, was seen by almost all knowledgeable fans as a lost opportunity. Much preferable would have been a full disc of actual unreleased January 1969 tracks drawn from alternate versions of songs used on *Let It Be* and *Abbey Road,* unissued attempts at originals never released by the Beatles while they were an active unit, and the many oldies covers they attempted. Or, failing that, a straight issue of the complete tape of the actual rooftop concert. As it is, the main achievement of the "Fly on the Wall" disc, quite ironically considering its Apple-authorized compilation, was probably to spark interest in buying the actual *Get Back* bootlegs.

Ultimately, *Let It Be . . . Naked* is a worthwhile release, and in many ways an improvement on the original. It's not so much the definitive version, however, as it is yet one more version of this troubled album. The fact is, at this late date, no one can assemble the definitive version of *Get Back*–slash–*Let It Be.* That opportunity slipped away in the many months of indecision that nearly sank the project altogether in 1969 and 1970.

Let It Down
Tell Me What Has Happened to You
Hear Me Lord
Nowhere to Go
Cosmic Empire
Mother Divine
I Don't Want to Do It
If Not for You

appears on 2001 expanded edition of All Things Must Pass

George had been making noises about doing a solo album as far back as January 1969, when tapes caught him discussing the possibility during the *Get Back* sessions. His frustration seemed at least as much to do with the limited opportunity for getting the songs recorded at all as it did with whether he should be doing them with the Beatles. On the second day of the sessions, he seemed generally content about continuing to work within the framework of the group, declaring, "There's so much material for us to get out, and there's no one better to get it out with than us, for me, really." Yet just four days later, he was complaining that he had about 20 tunes ready to go, but knew that they wouldn't be well received if he brought them up in the studio for consideration. As he told *Crawdaddy* years later, Lennon and McCartney "had such a lot of tunes, and they automatically thought that theirs should be the priority, so I'd always have to wait through ten of their songs before they'd even listen to one of mine. It was silly. It was very selfish, actually."

George's backlog was getting too fat to record with the Beatles even if they'd consented to give him equal space on the band's LPs. As he divulged to *New Musical Express* shortly before the split, "I've also thought of doing an album of my own, mainly just to get rid of all the songs I've got stacked up. At the rate of two or three on each Beatles album, I'm not even going to get the ones I've [already] done out for three or four years." At one point in 1969, he even estimated that he'd written 40 songs

*One of several collections of unreleased
George Harrison solo material from 1970.*

that had yet to make their way onto record. While that might have been an exaggeration, even if there was only half that, clearly there was no way they'd fit onto Beatles albums within a year or two.

Inasmuch as there were any good things to come out of the Beatles' breakup, the best was that George was finally free to record—in the way he wished—all of the songs he had accumulated, some of which (such as "The Art of Dying" and "Isn't It a Pity") had been written as far back as 1966. The split might have even been the kick in the pants he needed to overcome any reticence and finally buckle down to the task. John, Paul, and even Ringo had already released solo records for the pop market; George had yet to do so, though he'd done the Wonderwall soundtrack and the avant-garde Electronic Sounds LP.

It was probably around late May 1970 that George laid down some spare demos for what would become the *All Things Must Pass* album. Fifteen of these have escaped into circulation, in stellar sound quality, none of them featuring drums, and all of them featuring nothing but George on guitar and vocals (except "Wah-Wah," where he's accompanied by an unknown bass player). Though he plays electric guitar on three cuts ("Hear Me Lord," "Nowhere to Go," and "Wah-Wah"), otherwise he plays acoustic. The result is something like hearing Harrison unplugged, at the very moment he's taking the plunge into the solo spotlight for the first time. There's a bit of tentative nervousness at the occasion, but that's more than overcome by a sense of joy and freedom at finally being let loose to express himself, free from the constrictions of Beatledom. Most importantly, the music itself is lovely, with the combination of humility, spiritualism, and deft melodicism that would characterize the *All Things Must Pass* album. Here, however, it's related in a gentler, folkier manner than it would be on *All Things Must Pass,* where co-producers George Harrison and Phil Spector constructed much more elaborate arrangements.

Seven of the songs ("Run of the Mill," "Art of Dying," "Wah-Wah," "Beware of Darkness," "Let It Down," "Hear Me Lord," and the Bob Dylan–penned "If Not for You") would be re-recorded for *All Things Must Pass.* It's a delight to hear them in their stripped-down state, complete with a bit of pre-song fumbling around. "Art of Dying" in particular has a more mournful, subdued air than the hard-rocking LP version. From a more academic standpoint, it's clear that, despite Harrison's stack of unrecorded compositions, he was obviously still in the midst of writing new material. "This one . . . is the last one I wrote the other day, and it's . . . a few words are needed yet," he reveals before playing "Beware of Darkness," which has a sly line—"Beware of ABKCO," ABKCO being new manager Allen Klein's company—that wouldn't get into the *All Things Must Pass* version. Though no doubt intended as a harmless in-joke, it carried more weight than George realized at the time; a few years later, he'd be joining John and Ringo in struggling to get out from under Klein's clutches. With a wicked humor even George might have appreciated, *Beware of ABKCO!* was the exact title given to the first bootleg of these demos. It's no longer an in-joke for a select group of collectors, either, as it's the sole recording from this batch to have been officially issued (as a bonus track on the 2001 expanded edition of *All Things Must Pass*).

Parts of one of the less developed tunes, "Everybody, Nobody," would become absorbed into "The Ballad of Sir Frankie Crisp (Let It Roll)," though here you can hear George's low, monkish enunciation of Crisp's name (a little) more clearly than you can in the similar passage on the *All Things Must Pass* track. As for why a couple of standout numbers from *All Things Must Pass* that are known to have been written by January 1969 ("Isn't a Pity" and "All Things Must Pass") are absent, perhaps that's because George had already done solo demos of each for EMI in the first two months of 1969.

Most interesting of all is the inclusion of seven Harrison originals that didn't make it onto *All Things Must Pass* in any form. Again, this indicates that he was probably not merely recording everything that had built up in his songbook, but still in the process of writing material and cherry-picking the best numbers. None of the seven songs here that didn't make the cut would have been highlights on *All Things Must Pass*, but neither would any of them have disgraced that record. "Window, Window" had been performed in fragmentary fashion back in the *Get Back* sessions, and it's a nice lilting, troubadourish ballad, introduced by George as "a bit silly"; his throat-clearing coughs after the first couple of lines probably guarantee that it won't appear on any officially sanctioned archive release in the near future. "Beautiful Girl," like so many of Harrison's songs from the time, has a bittersweet melody that avoids the dirge-like flavor to which he was occasionally prone, though it seems it's not yet finished, as he wordlessly scats his way through where the bridges should fall (and gets rid of some leftover phlegm from his coughing fit along the way). It might not, in fact, have been finished for some time, as Harrison didn't release a version until his 1976 album *Thirty-Three & 1/3*. "Tell Me What Has Happened to You," which alternates an ominously ascending riff with a more conventionally folky part, could be the least impressive song, and likewise doesn't seem nearly finished; maybe it, unlike "Beautiful Girl," was abandoned before that could happen.

"Nowhere to Go," which had been part of the low-fidelity, two-song tape George had previously done with Bob Dylan, might be the best of the never-officially-recorded songs in the batch. The chord progression is intricate, jazzy, and melancholy, and Harrison, as was sometimes his wont, alleviated the surface despair of the lyrics with vocals of fragile sensitivity that somehow make the mood more uplifting than despondent. There's certainly a sour allusion to his March 1969 bust for pot possession when he sings, "I get tired of policemen on the prowl, look-

ing in my bowel, every time somebody's getting high." And how about this for disillusionment with Beatlemania: "I get tired of being Beatle Jeff, talking to the deaf, every time some whistle's getting blown."

Just a few weeks before (on May 1), incidentally, Harrison cut quite a few studio tracks with Dylan, then working on his *New Morning* album in New York. Though these have sometimes been misleadingly billed as a Dylan-Harrison session, George was really just a sideman, with Dylan handling all the lead vocals, even on a dreary cover of the Beatles' "Yesterday." And in truth, the 20 or so unreleased tracks that have leaked out from this studio date are a grave disappointment, despite the excellent fidelity. As most of the time's spent going through rock 'n' roll oldies (though you would have thought George would have had his fill of that in the *Get Back* sessions!) and songs that Dylan had already recorded in the '60s, it seems more like a pleasant jam session between friends than a genuine attempt to record something creative. Dylan takes virtually all the lead vocals, and while George's guitar work is competent, it's oddly colorless and restrained. The lackluster feel of the whole enterprise leaves the impression that they were just playing together for moral support, George probably still feeling uncertain about his future in the wake of the Beatles' split, Dylan being in the midst of a fairly fallow songwriting period.

George's lighter, more humorously upbeat side comes through well on the buoyant, jaunty "Cosmic Empire," which apparently he envisioned as being "full of chorus voices," as he says before a false start, though the song doesn't seem quite complete. His propensity for mixing allusions to holy spirits and lovely women surface with "Mother Divine," a stately mid-tempo number that nonetheless is a little too heavily dependent on repetitions of its chorus. A good song's there with some more work; why it wasn't applied remains a mystery. The touchingly nostalgic, previously unrecorded Bob Dylan song "I Don't Wanna Do It" has a very attractive alternation of bittersweet verses with more cheerful, driving bridges. On the tape, George seems to think it will find a place on the album, as he expects that "we'll do this one tomorrow." Whether they did it tomorrow or not, it didn't

Beware of ABKCO! presented 15 George Harrison demos for All Things Must Pass, *only one of which has been officially released.*

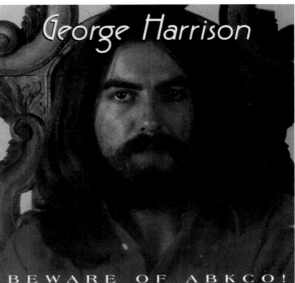

George Harrison
BEWARE OF ABKCO!

1. Run Of The Mill *(Acoustic version)*
2. Art Of Dying *(Acoustic version)*
3. Everybody, Nobody *(Acoustic version)*
4. Wah-Wah *(On Electric Guitar)*
5. Window, Window *(Acoustic version)*
6. Beautiful Girl *(Acoustic version)*
7. Beware of Darkness *(Acoustic version)*
8. Let It Down *(Acoustic version)*
9. Tell Me What Has Happened To You *(Acoustic version)*
10. Hear Me Lord *(On Electric Guitar)*
11. Nowhere To Go *(On Electric Guitar)*
12. Cosmic Empire *(Acoustic version)*
13. Mother Divine *(Acoustic version)*
14. I Don't Wanna Do It *(Acoustic version)*
15. If Not For You *(Acoustic version)*

(All songs composed by George Harrison except #14 & #15 by Bob Dylan)

"Strawberry Records" is an independent record label.
"Strawberry" products are developed by Yellow Dog.

℗ 1994 Strawberry Records

5 400000 166617

STR 001

STRAWBERRY RECORDS

George Harrison BEWARE OF ABKCO!

make *All Things Must Pass,* though it was recorded much later for, of all things, the 1985 soundtrack to *Porky's Revenge.*

There was yet still more to come as far as an overflow of Harrison songs that didn't make *All Things Must Pass,* a good half-dozen emerging on outtakes after the sessions got started for real. So prolific was he at this point that one wonders if yet more demos were recorded before production got underway. It's also been speculated that these tapes are not actual solo, unaccompanied performances, but ones on which other musicians were following George beyond the reach of microphones. As off-the-wall as that might seem, there's some credibility to that notion, as there's not only a bass on "Wah-Wah," but also some piano that can be occasionally heard between takes. There's even some speculation that the bootlegged tapes just pick out George's part from a multi-track, and that full-band versions of all these performances might exist. In a way, it would be a shame if that were the case, since so much of the charm of these demos is conjured by our mind's-eye picture of George singing and playing on his own. But however it was recorded, the material projects an intimacy that's rare in recorded music, and perhaps unmatched by any other Beatles-related recording. The obvious abundance of quality surplus material also makes one wish George had decided to make the third disc of the *All Things Must Pass* triple-LP set standard songs instead of disposable jams, as he clearly had enough to fill out two more album sides without resorting to throwaways.

● **May 26**

Studio Outtakes

George Harrison's All Things Must Pass *sessions*
London

Dehra Dhun
*I Live for You
I Live for You (without backup vocals)
Going Down to Golders Green
Om Hare Om (Gopala Krishna)

     appears on 2001 expanded edition of All Things Must Pass

---

Much or all of the first day of the *All Things Must Pass* sessions, oddly, was devoted to songs that actually didn't make the album. Nor, with one exception, do they sound like songs that *should* have been included. Combined with the rather casual performances and sparse arrangements, it leads one to suspect that this was somewhat of a warm-up, the intention being for George to get comfortable and acclimate himself to working in the studio as a solo artist, rather than start serious work on the album's core tracks.

A snatch of "Dehra Dhun" was actually performed by George on the grounds of his house (in the company of Paul and Ringo) in a scene in the *Anthology* video, where he recalled writing it in India in 1968. That sounds accurate, particularly as the Indian town of Dehra Dhun is near Rishikesh, where the Beatles were studying with the Maharishi. (He also introduces it as one of a number of songs he penned in India "which I've never recorded to this day," perhaps forgetting about this May 1970 outtake.) There's no evidence that George ever proposed it for consideration as a Beatles recording, and it's not one of his stronger late-'60s works, with a repetitious chorus bearing influences of Indian prayer-chants, though the easygoing sections between the choruses aren't bad. The Indian influence gets stronger on "Om Hare Om (Gopala Krishna)," which likewise has a lyric reminiscent of a repetitious prayer-chant. It's an attractive enough tune, however (even if it goes on a little too long), and the low-key arrangement nicely blends flowing organ, slide guitar, and what sound like congas.

"Going Down to Golders Green," in contrast, is a pretty dispensable shades-of-early-Sun-Records rocker, with a tune that loosely follows Elvis Presley's mid-'50s single "Baby Let's Play House." George's Carl Perkins–like rockabilly chops are in good shape, however, and it's certainly tighter, more enthusiastically performed, and more enjoyable overall than most of the *Get Back* session throwaways. Golders Green, incidentally, is a fairly nondescript London neighborhood; it's not known why George would write a song about going down there in his limousine as if it's an occasion on par with going down to Memphis or some such mecca of hipdom. It's probably just a flash of Harrison's subtle, underrated humor; it's doubtful a song with a lyric like "At night I don't go out much, I stay at home for peace, I try to make the most out of my 99-year lease" could have really been intended as a serious statement.

"I Live for You" is the real standout of the songs that have circulated from this date. Like some other compositions on *All Things Must Pass* (such as "Behind That Locked Door"), it has an overlooked country music influence, largely by virtue of the steel guitar (presumably by Pete Drake, who played the instrument on several official *All Things Must Pass* cuts). There's also a late-'60s Bob Dylan influence in its laconic, romantic country-rock, though this is more tuneful than most of what Dylan was coming up with in the style, and dusted with George's inimitably devout-but-dignified tone. Fortunately, its quality was recognized 30 years later, when it was added to the expanded edition of *All Things Must Pass* as a bonus track, with backup vocals not present on the similar bootlegged version.

Asked by Chris Carter why "I Live for You" wasn't released the first time around in a February 15, 2001, interview promoting the 30th anniversary reissue of *All Things Must Pass,* George explained, "I think originally, it didn't sound like we'd got it. You know, on some of those songs we recorded them and then listened to them back and said, 'Naw, I don't like it, we haven't done it right.' . . . Nobody had a feel for it except for the pedal steel guitar player and the rhythm guitarist. And so I didn't want to use it. I didn't think we got it and I think at the time I was thinking, 'The song's a bit fruity anyway. We've got enough songs, we leave it off.' So I just went back and fixed it up, because people like to have bonus tracks."

At this point, we reach the stage where—in contrast to the meticulous documentation of the sessions undertaken by the Beatles as a group—the exact dates of solo Beatles recording sessions have not been determined, or at least widely circulated in general publications. It's known that all the tracks above were done on the first day of the sessions, May 26, but dates have not been pinned down for when other recordings were made for the album. Thus all of the *All Things Must Pass* outtakes noted in the following entry (as well as ones by John Lennon detailed later in this chapter) are lumped into the time frame in which one specific album is known to have been recorded, rather than separated into individual dates.

● May 26–November

Studio Outtakes

George Harrison's All Things Must Pass *sessions*
Abbey Road, Trident Studios, Apple Studios, London

My Sweet Lord (stereo rough mix)

Wah-Wah (stereo rough mix)

Wah-Wah (mono rough mix)

What Is Life (mono rough mix)

What Is Life (three stereo rough mixes)

*What Is Life (instrumental backing track)

If Not for You (mono rough mix)

Behind That Locked Door (two mono rough mixes)

Let It Down (mono rough mix)

Let It Down (four stereo rough mixes)

*Let It Down (alternate version)

Run of the Mill (three stereo rough mixes)

Beware of Darkness (four stereo rough mixes)

Apple Scruffs (takes 1–18)

Apple Scruffs (three rough mixes)

Ballad of Sir Frankie Crisp (mono rough mix)

Awaiting on You All (mono rough mix)

Awaiting on You All (three stereo rough mixes)

All Things Must Pass (false start)

All Things Must Pass (mono rough mix)

Art of Dying (take 9)

Art of Dying (mono rough mix)

Art of Dying (three stereo rough mixes)

Isn't It a Pity (Version Two) (mono rough mix)

Hear Me Lord (two rough mixes)

Plug Me In (mono rough mix)

Down to the River

Whenever (aka I'll Still Love You)

Get Back

Pete Drake and His Amazing Talking Guitar

appears on 2001 expanded edition of All Things Must Pass

The Making of All Things Must Pass *contained no fewer than three CDs of outtakes from the* All Things Must Pass *sessions, though most of these were alternate mixes/versions.*

A few songs that didn't make the album in any form are available too, though these are pretty marginal items.

While some of the rough mix variations are so subtle as to barely be worth noting, a few *do* offer substantial differences, and this entry will concentrate upon those. The one available rough mix of "My Sweet Lord" is missing backing vocals and lead guitar, and while that alone means it's not as good as the No. 1 hit version, it does put the essential sweetness of the song in greater relief. Both takes of "Wah-Wah" are without vocals, the mono one being the more interesting, as it has a train-whistle-like guitar mimicking the sound of the backup singing of the title phrase. The "What Is Life" takes differ only in balance and number of overdubs, though all of the stereo rough mixes are virtually instrumental (and the rough mono mix is totally instrumental), if you really want to focus on the dynamics of the backing track. (A yet different mix, this one stereo and wholly instrumental save for some faint vocal leakage, appears as a bonus track on the expanded 2001 edition of *All Things Must Pass*.) One of the rough mixes of "Behind That Locked Door" has a guide vocal where George doesn't seem wholly certain of the final lyrics; at least, he's not clearly enunciating some of them.

"Let It Down" is one of the few songs where the alternate mixes really do differ substantially. Each one runs more than two minutes longer than the official version, though it's just a longer repetitious fadeout; George did have a tendency to tag those on in his early solo career, and the decision to trim this one was appropriate. The earlier mixes of these, however (including an instrumental one), reveal how much more of a hard-rock song it was without the many overdubs, particularly emphasizing some viciously slashing, bluesy guitar chords. As good as the final Spectorized track was, these are highly worthwhile variations that bring a tougher cast to the tune. Certainly at each stage, it's far more full-bodied than the Beatles' tentative attempts at the song back in the January 1969 *Get Back* sessions.

They might not add up to anything as excessive as the *Get Back* outtakes or even alternate "A Day in the Life" mixes, but *All Things Must Pass* sure did produce a boatload of bootlegged alternate mixes, as well as a few outtakes. In fact, as much material as the official triple-disc *All Things Must Pass* contained, the unreleased music from those sessions that have been bootlegged adds up to considerably *more* than three LPs on their own (especially if you throw in the 15 demos done just before the sessions started). Like the aforementioned Beatles items, these aren't for the Johnny-come-lately fan; there are just too many multiple versions and too many similarities to the familiar released mixes. For the more specialized listener, however, they're quite a boon, particularly as the finished *All Things Must Pass* album was so densely (though purposefully) layered and arranged. This bounty of rough mixes allows us to hear the songs in somewhat more stripped-down states, in some cases enabling us to hear certain parts more clearly, and in a few cases to hear instrumentation without any vocals at all.

There's a yet different outtake of "Let It Down" on the expanded 2001 edition of *All Things Must Pass* that's a real puzzle, as the acoustic rhythm guitar and vocal is obviously from the same track as the version heard on the demos he did around late May 1970. However, this recording, while still drumless, has additional instrumentation—particularly a bluesy lead guitar—not present at all on the bootlegged demo. Whether these parts were overdubbed later in the *All Things Must Pass* sessions (or perhaps even later than that), or whether this might even be a recording from the May 1970 demo session on which more parts were taped besides the rhythm guitar and vocal, is undetermined.

The most interesting rough mix of "Run of the Mill" is not only missing some overdubs, allowing greater focus on the song's acoustic guitar base, but also has a guide vocal. In common with most guide vocals it's less assured and accomplished than the final one. You'll really notice the vocal on the mix with the piano and organ overdub, however, where an occasionally off-key George wordlessly mimics where he wants the horn part to be placed. The most basic of the rough mixes of "Beware of Darkness" has another Harrison guide vocal, and a largely serviceable one, though his phrasing gets a little stumbling and slurred.

"Apple Scruffs," uniquely among the circulating *All Things Must Pass* outtakes, is represented by actual takes (as opposed to alternate mixes), about half of the 18 ending in breakdowns. None of them are actually too different from the final version, other than yielding the chance to hear this effectively good-natured Dylanesque song done with nothing more than a single voice, acoustic guitar, and harmonica. George is not so much changing the arrangement during these as fine-tuning how much and how loudly some of the elements should be played. He introduces a tapping beat, and between take 13 and take 14 unwinds a bit by playing some instrumental licks from Bob Dylan's "Mama, You've Been on My Mind" (which he had performed back in the *Get Back* sessions). Just-ex-Beatles-roadie Mal Evans supplies a harder tapped beat starting with take 16, and take 18 is the one chosen to get overdubs of backing vocals and slide guitar. And if you want three rough mixes of *that,* those are out there too.

The sole circulating rough mix of "Ballad of Sir Frankie Crisp (Let It Roll)" is an instrumental backing track, as are the multiple rough mixes of "Awaiting on You All," the earliest of which allows you to really hear the piercing slide guitar work. Things get more interesting with the alternate take (not just a rough mix) of "Art of Dying." The arrangement's much more bare-bones, highlighting piano, drums, and acoustic guitar, lending the song a more sorrowful tone than it would boast when James Bond–strength horns and furious electric guitars were used (and effectively so) on the album take. Too, George's vocal is not the same as the one on the official version (though it's not much different).

Finally, the rough mixes of "Hear Me Lord," which brought the song-oriented part of the original *All Things Must Pass* to a conclusion, are of considerable interest as they run more than a minute and a half longer than the LP version. Again, this is just an extended repetitive fade that didn't need to be there (albeit with some good, spiky guitar work), though one of the mixes offers the additional bonus of yet another guide vocal that was ultimately replaced, complete with a few spoken instructions. "Bridge!" calls out George right before, yes, a bridge, and "End at the next one!" before the track comes to a cold close with a long, gothic organ chord—one nice touch not heard on the final album.

Three outtakes of songs not represented on *All Things Must Pass* in any shape have also circulated. "Down to the River" is a silly, light-hearted, good-time-riverboatin' country-blues tune, complete with Dixieland brass and not entirely successful Harrison yodeling. "Whenever" (originally copyrighted in 1972 as "When Every Song Is Sung" and sometimes titled "I'll Still Love You" on bootlegs) is more substantial, with a Harrisonesque dolorous, winding, yet memorable descending melody and a sad, jazz-tinged horn. He certainly does a better job with it than Ringo Starr did on the 1976 LP *Ringo's Rotogravure* (though George had previously tried to record it with Ronnie Spector, Cilla Black, and Leon and Mary Russell). Unfortunately, the take that's escaped seems to be missing the first part, and George doesn't seem to have filled in some of the lyrics, giving the impression this might be a work-in-progress demo of sorts.

Weirdest of all is a version of "Get Back" (its first part apparently cut off), with horns and a diffident, perhaps deliberately careless vocal by George. Not only does he sometimes unpredictably leap into near-falsetto range, he also improvises some incoherent new lyrics, as well as imploring an unknown pianist to "Take it, JoJo!" before the instrumental break, and asking Mal (Evans, one assumes) to "Get a mop and another glass of orange juice." The last thing George probably wanted to do on his solo debut was cover a recent Lennon-McCartney song that he'd done ad infinitum during the *Get Back* sessions, and this must have been a between-takes jam. It's also been speculated that it was recorded during sessions for the Harrison-produced *Doris Troy* album, during which a cover of "Get Back" was recorded (for a B-side), though with a different backing track. Another outtake, titled "Pete Drake and

George on September 17, 1970, shortly before the All Things Must Pass *sessions ended.*

His Amazing Talking Guitar," is tacked onto some Harrison bootlegs. But though it was done during the *All Things Must Pass* sessions, and though George can be heard talking to Drake on the track, it's not really a Harrison performance; it's just Drake amusingly demonstrating, using the tunes of "Danny Boy" and Paul Simon's "Bridge Over Troubled Water," how he can make his steel guitar simulate human singing.

Due to their inclusion of multiple versions and mixes that don't vary much from the LP cuts, it's doubtful that many or any of the wealth of *All Things Must Pass* outtakes will find official release. For those who want to gain a full appreciation of George Harrison's accomplishment with this monumental album, however, they're a fascinating insight into the perfectionism he (and co-producer Phil Spector) brought to the project. It's not often noted, but the material also suggests that John Lennon, Paul McCartney, and George Martin not only underestimated Harrison's songwriting talent, but also his production skills. As much as all Beatles fans lament the passing of the group in 1970, it's impossible not to rejoice in George's great triumph, surpassing the expectations of even his most devout fans—and, perhaps, even surpassing his own.

● June 26

Studio Outtake
Ringo Starr's Beaucoups of Blues *sessions*
Music City Recorders, Nashville

The Wishing Book

Ringo was not just the first Beatle to do a solo album for the pop market, he was also the first Beatle to do *two* solo albums for the pop market. Quantity does not equal quality, however, and like *Sentimental Journey*, *Beaucoups of Blues* was a rather uninspired dive into a non-rock genre. At least Ringo was more suited toward singing Nashville country than pop standards, but that didn't make for a memorable album, let alone a commercial one.

Although there must be a limited demand for such things, one outtake from the sessions, "The Wishing Book," did surface in 1992 among some acetates from the collection of Mal Evans that were being auctioned. It's low-key, inoffensive, wistful, and ordinary Nashville country-pop, and could have fit in *Beaucoups of Blues* without a hitch. Maybe it's the song's abnormally short length—just a minute and 16 seconds—that made it seem dispensable.

● June 26–28

Studio Outtakes
Ringo Starr's Beaucoups of Blues *sessions*
Music City Recorders, Nashville

Fastest Growing Heartache in the West (two versions)

A couple of poor-quality rehearsal versions of the *Beaucoups of Blues* track "Fastest Growing Heartache in the West" have appeared on hard-to-find bootlegs—so hard to find, in fact, that this author has never found them. Also appearing on a limited-edition bootleg from the same source is an acoustic-guitar-and-vocal rehearsal of another track from the album, "Waiting," but Ringo doesn't appear on it.

● June 27

Studio Outtake
Ringo Starr's Beaucoups of Blues *sessions*
Music City Recorders, Nashville

---

*Nashville Jam
Nashville Jam (different edit/mix)
   *appears on the 1995 CD reissue of Beaucoups of Blues

The 1995 CD reissue of *Beaucoups of Blues* added two bonus tracks: the non-LP B-side "Coochy-Coochy" and the routine, title-descriptive, six-and-a-half-minute instrumental "Nashville Jam." For the record, a different edit and mix of "Nashville Jam" has been bootlegged that, while lasting just over three minutes, has some sections not on the official CD.

● Circa Summer

Private Tapes/Studio Outtake
Demos for John Lennon's Plastic Ono Band; Plastic Ono Band *sessions*
Los Angeles

Love
Mother
**My Mummy's Dead (two versions)
***I Found Out (two versions)
**God (four versions)
When a Boy Meets a Girl (two versions)
*Well, Well, Well
Look at Me
   *appears on John Lennon's Acoustic
   ** one version appears on John Lennon's Acoustic
   ***edit of one version appears on John Lennon Anthology box set

---

Curiously, though John Lennon was the first Beatle to release recordings for the pop market on his own (with the "Give Peace a Chance," "Cold Turkey," and "Instant Karma!" singles), he was the *last* to start work on a full-length solo album. In part that was because he and Yoko spent several months of the spring and summer of 1970 undergoing primal therapy with Arthur Janov in Los Angeles. It's thought that these demos, comprised largely of songs that were re-recorded for *Plastic Ono Band* later in the year, were recorded in the summer while John was still in California. Not all of the songs from *Plastic Ono Band* are here, and one song that *is* here, "When a Boy Meets a Girl," wouldn't show up on *Plastic Ono Band* or anywhere else. Since several of the songs are performed two or more times, however, you have about an album's worth of music here that gives a good indication of where John was at before heading into the studio, though these are all solo performances, not band ones.

About half of these takes feature John singing and playing an electrified acoustic guitar, which gives the instrument an odd, shaky timbre.

"Love" and "Mother" in particular are almost overloaded with a tremolo effect, though it actually suitably matches the fragile state of Lennon's psyche at the time, without overwhelming or drawing attention away from his vocals. Maybe the slightly imperfect fidelity on these will block their release on an authorized compilation, but "Love" is a very nice performance, with a certain shimmer that was lost in the somewhat more polished official arrangement (which added piano). "Mother" is nothing to be ashamed of, though John was probably conscious of wanting to deliver a more refined vocal when it came time to do it in the studio, and the absence of band accompaniment might make it sound more plaintive and sweeter than Lennon ultimately intended.

One of the takes of "My Mummy's Dead" was actually used as the final track of *Plastic Ono Band,* though it's been bootlegged in its natural state, rather than the slightly processed one it was given for the LP (hence its classification as a "studio outtake" in this entry, though it wasn't done in an actual studio). It's not all that notable a song (though it was an effective album-closer within the *Plastic Ono Band* context), and a very brief one, lasting all of 48 seconds. The second version, issued in 2004 on the *Acoustic* compilation, only lengthens it to a minute and 16 seconds, and doesn't add too much other than some sticky-fingered instrumental guitar work at the end. The electric-acoustic guitar on "I Found Out" gets really sludgy and grungy, though effectively so, like a slightly avant-garde cousin of Bo Diddley's early innovations in amplified distortion. The merits of this solo arrangement were acknowledged when the longer of the two was included, with very slight edits, on the Lennon *Anthology* box in 1997. There's also a slightly shorter, still-unreleased take of equal value with even dirtier guitar, though it lacks the introduction found on the *Anthology* one. Both versions have a wobbly offbeat missing from the *Plastic Ono Band* track, which has a far more standard rock 'n' roll feel.

"God," offered here in no less than four versions, is quite a bit different from the *Plastic Ono Band* arrangement in all cases. Whereas the official recording features a heavy, ponderous tempo and gospel-tinged piano, all of these demos are on acoustic guitar, strummed with a much folkier lilt. Had anyone any doubt that the Beatles era was truly coming to an end, John confirmed it by including the group in the list of things in which he didn't believe. These acoustic versions have a lightheartedness missing from the *Plastic Ono Band* cut, John proclaiming with a chuckle, "Hallelujah, eureka brother, I got the news, it came to me in the night, yeah!" like an old-time preacher near the end of one run-through. It's a lightheartedness somewhat at odds with the thrust of the song's renunciatory tone, but a refreshingly different twist all the same.

Moving to a different key for another try, John actually laughs after a muffled first line and makes fried toast out of his throat when he tries for some high notes. He goes back to the wobbly electric-acoustic guitar tone for the other two passes at the tune, finding a far more comfortable key for his range and dramatically slowing the tempo (not to mention adding a cliff-hanging pause after announcing his disbelief in Beatles) near the end of the longest of these, which lasts nearly four minutes. The version selected for *Acoustic,* however, is probably the best, beginning as it does with another mock-preaching message, delivered in a Martin Luther King "I have a dream" tone. Note how, on what appears to be the earliest attempt, John hasn't quite come up with the full list of things he doesn't believe in yet, mumbling his way through lines in this section he hasn't determined. Also note how, when he includes Bob Dylan in the list on the subsequent versions, he sings "I don't believe in Dylan,"

not "I don't believe in Zimmerman" (Zimmerman being Bob Dylan's real last name), as he does on *Plastic Ono Band.*

The version of "Well, Well, Well" on *Acoustic* sounds like the same performance that has been bootlegged, but processed so that the acoustic guitar has a much more distorted electro-acoustic feel. At just a minute and 17 seconds, it's much shorter than the *Plastic Ono Band* track, which runs nearly six minutes. The official version, it has to be conceded, is much more effective, with its biting blues-rock guitar and heartbeat bass, but this is an effective folk-blues sketch all the same. And, finally, there are two acoustic-guitar-and-voice versions of a song that *didn't* make it onto *Plastic Ono Band* (or anything else), "When a Boy Meets a Girl." Though it has a fair tune and a nice, gentle, folky air, it might have been scrapped for several reasons. For one, its sunny tone would have fit far better into the *Imagine* album. For another, John hasn't finished the lyrics, or at least isn't clearly singing a lot of them. And for another, part of the melody is quite similar to the tune of the main hook of Ruby & the Romantics' 1963 No. 1 girl group hit "Our Day Will Come." Remember how much trouble George Harrison got into for the similarities between his No. 1 hit "My Sweet Lord" and a 1963 No. 1 girl group hit, "He's So Fine"?

The grouping of "Look at Me" with this batch of demos is uncertain. This is one *Plastic Ono Band* song whose composition is known to have dated from the Beatles era, John telling *Rolling Stone* it was written around the time of *The White Album.* Probably for that reason, this demo has sometimes been identified as a 1968 recording on bootlegs, though most experts agree that's not the case. It's certainly not a studio recording, either, with the same kind of cheapish fidelity heard on the aforementioned summer 1970 recordings. As it seems to have been wholly composed by this point, the guess here is that it was probably done around the same time as the other summer 1970 demos. It's actually much the same as the *Plastic Ono Band* version, right down to the "Julia"-styled guitar picking, though the official version naturally has much better sound quality.

If *Plastic Ono Band* was one of the rawest, nerves-exposed albums of all time, then these demos are yet closer to the bone, despite—or, to some degree, maybe even because of—their bare arrangements and basic (though highly listenable) fidelity. For that reason, they're essential to major fans of that record. At the same time, they're conspicuously lacking in the sort of hummable hooks John had spun out so prolifically throughout his career in the Beatles. This didn't exactly doom *Plastic Ono Band* to cult status, but it ensured that the record would not be nearly as big a seller as *All Things Must Pass,* or even *McCartney.*

● September 26–October 27

Studio Outtakes

John Lennon's Plastic Ono Band *sessions*
Abbey Road, London

Mother (rough mix)
*Mother (two alternate takes)
**Hold On (alternate take)
I Found Out (two rough mixes)
**Working Class Hero (alternate take)

**Isolation (alternate take)

Remember (rough mix)

**Remember (alternate take)

**Love (alternate take)

Well, Well, Well (rough mix)

Look at Me (two rough mixes)

**Look at Me (alternate take)

**God (alternate take)

**Long Lost John

That's All Right (Mama)

Glad All Over

Honey Don't

Don't Be Cruel

Hound Dog

Unknown

Matchbox

Jam

*one alternate take appears on John Lennon's Anthology *box set*

**appears on John Lennon's Anthology *box set*

Enough alternate takes from the *Plastic Ono Band* sessions have been unearthed to make an alternate *Plastic Ono Band* album of their own. Alternates of no less than eight of the 11 songs, in fact, appear on disc one of the four-disc Lennon *Anthology* box. And as pre–*Plastic Ono Band* demos of some of the other songs appear on *Acoustic,* including the three ("I Found Out," "Well, Well, Well," and "My Mummy's Dead") unrepresented by alternates on *Anthology,* an entire alternate *Plastic Ono Band* album could be said to have already been commercially issued, even if you'll have to part with quite a bit of bread to get all the material.

John Lennon looks a little like Groucho Marx on this collection of Plastic Ono Band *outtakes.*

Going through the outtakes in the same order as the songs appeared on the LP, the *Anthology* version of "Mother" is quite different from the official one. Guitar, not the piano, anchors the arrangement, and the pace is a bit faster, though the vocal is similarly anguished. "That was more like it," declares John at the end, though it must not have been enough to his satisfaction to use. The take available only on bootleg is considerably closer to the released track, particularly as piano has been substituted for guitar as the prominent instrument, though there are no tolling bells opening either outtake (as there were on the record). The *Anthology* "Hold On" outtake is actually quite different from the *Plastic Ono Band* version, with a spry rockabilly gait, but unfortunately only lasts about 45 seconds.

No outtakes of "I Found Out" have surfaced, though very interesting demos had been done earlier, as noted in the previous entry. A couple of rough mixes are out and about, however, the more interesting of which has a fadeout lasting about 20 seconds longer than the *Plastic Ono Band* version, giving us a chance to hear John sing much more of his detour into Carl Perkins's "Gone, Gone, Gone," as well as some congas that were eliminated from the final track. Also dig the spoken intro, where John's advice to "just play how you feel, 'cause it is Carl Wolf" gives a clear indication of the sound (a mixture of Carl Perkins and Howlin' Wolf) he wants. Too, the heavy echo on his spoken voice spells out just how drenched in reverb the album's production was.

The "Working Class Hero" on *Anthology* isn't much different from the *Plastic Ono Band* track, also using just John and acoustic guitar, though there's some chatter in which he asks Yoko to "A&R" the cut. You wouldn't think there was much of a way to lighten this most vitriolic of Lennon songs, but as he does on most *Plastic Ono Band* outtakes and demos, he manages to do so here, breaking into a gutsy snatch of "Well, Well, Well" at the end. The *Anthology* outtake of "Isolation" isn't much of a variation either, but does offer some interesting chatter between John, Ringo (who confesses responsibility for missing his cue), Yoko, Phil Spector, and Klaus Voormann after a take breaks down at the beginning. Again, John's mood ("That was very good, wasn't it? Remember those bits, we'll keep 'em!") is much more lighthearted than many would expect, given the heavy, probing tone of the album's material and vocalization.

The alternate take of "Remember" yet again captures a more humorous side of Lennon than he allowed to seep into the LP, with giggly, improvised asides as the band struggles with the beat ("So if you ever change your mind . . . or the rhythm" he snigger-sings). The musicians really *were* having trouble finding the right tempo, as a ludicrously hyper-quick snippet at the beginning makes clear. But rather than getting upset with the struggle, John's actually having fun with it, even if he does confess at the end, "That was silly." The bootlegged rough mix is by no means inconsequential, lasting almost four minutes longer than the *Plastic Ono Band* version, as well as using a Jew's harp that was dropped from the final track. The extra minutes comprise an amusing if superfluous tag, with some repetitious jamming, manic laughter, and murky, silly made-up-on-the-spot Lennon sing-speak (highlighted by his announcements that "avant-garde is French for bullshit"—this from the same guy who'd done three avant-garde LPs with Yoko just a year or two before—and "Yoko's grown a beard and John's lost another baby, and both of them are going to live in the Isle of Wight"). Has anyone ever noticed how the dour, four-note piano phrase that anchors this jam—also heard at the very beginning of, and at other points within, the official mix—is very much like the piano riff the Beatles jammed off of in the long fadeout on their unreleased version of "Something" (see July 11, 1969, entry)?

The *Anthology* version of "Love" is a very worthwhile counterpart to the official track. The one on *Plastic Ono Band* is not exactly overproduced, but the "unplugged" outtake, with acoustic guitar accompaniment (whereas the LP version has both piano and acoustic guitar), is sparse in comparison. (The versions of both "Love" and "Working Class Hero" on *Acoustic,* incidentally, are slightly edited versions of the takes used on *Anthology.*) The rough mix of "Well, Well, Well" doesn't contain substantial variations, but the *Anthology* alternate take of "Look at Me" is another matter, with a strummed rather than picked acoustic guitar (which is done in the style of *The White Album*'s "Julia" on the official track)—not much of a change, admittedly, but enough to make it notably different. The two rough mixes will sound much the same to most ears, though one does have some trivial chatter at the beginning. Wrapping up the trunk of *Plastic Ono Band* outtakes, the *Anthology* take of "God" has, in keeping with most of the material discussed here, a lighter touch than the official version, where again a forcefully struck piano is pretty much substituted for a folky acoustic guitar. (There's also an outtake of the brief album closer, "My Mummy's Dead," discussed in the prior entry dealing with summer 1970 demos, as it was recorded at that time.)

And there are yet more outtakes, though these are wholly different in character than the songs that made the LP. "Long Lost John" (issued on *Anthology*) is a throwback to his skiffle days, and had been a No. 2 UK hit (as "Lost John") for Lonnie Donegan in 1956; the Beatles had done a brief, lethargic version on the last day of their *Get Back* sessions on January 31, 1969. John and his backing crew bring more uptempo energy to the tune here, though it's still not all that remarkable an interpretation. Clearly the song meant a lot to Lennon, however, as he sang a bit of it on the fade of "I'm Losing You" on his final album in 1980, *Double Fantasy.*

On a track that *hasn't* been released, John leads the band through an 11-minute medley of early rock 'n' roll classics, including Elvis Presley's "That's All Right (Mama)," "Hound Dog," and "Don't Be Cruel," and Carl Perkins's "Honey Don't," "Glad All Over," and "Matchbox," several of which of course had been recorded by the Beatles for EMI or the BBC. These aren't deathless renditions, and certainly not nearly as good as the best ones that the Beatles did from this batch. But they're reasonably spirited, broken up by a brief passage in which John goes into a doo wop pastiche with indecipherably mumbled lyrics (titled "Unknown" on most bootlegs), ending with some disheveled, quasi-rockabilly jamming. The main function of both "Long Lost John" and the medley were, most likely, to supply some light relief in sessions devoted to material that was quite gut-wrenching. It's worth noting, though, that John and his band (and George, for that matter, in his occasional ventures into similar fare during the *All Things Must Pass* sessions) play with considerably greater tightness, enthusiasm, and conviction than the Beatles usually did when they tackled these sorts of oldies during the *Get Back* sessions.

The *Plastic Ono Band* outtakes, demos, and rough mixes are consistently interesting and quite often considerably entertaining. Ultimately, however, they don't carry the soul-busting gravity of the more deliberately sober official album, in which John seemed to be consciously both exorcising some lifelong demons and repudiating his Beatles past. They certainly aren't nearly as different from the album to which they

correspond, or as historically interesting in shedding a new light upon his work from the era, in the way that George Harrison's *All Things Must Pass* demos are. What they *do* indicate, however, is that John was actually in a much happier, fun-loving mood during *Plastic Ono Band*'s creation than anyone would assume from listening to the final product. That's confirmed by Mark Hertsgaard's article "Letting It Be" in the January 24, 1994, *New Yorker,* for which he and Mark Lewisohn got to listen to some unreleased *Plastic Ono Band* session tape, and which describes some cheerful dialogue amongst John, Ringo, and unexpected guest George Harrison after the end of take four of "Remember." "You listen to this album and you think he's almost suicidal," Lewisohn told Hertsgaard as they were listening. "But actually on the tapes you hear John laugh a lot during these takes. It's been really nice for me to find out how happy these sessions were."

John was also, interestingly, declining to use some relatively happy, romantic songs for *Plastic Ono Band* that had already been composed and recorded in some unreleased form, such as "Oh My Love," "Oh Yoko!," and "I'm Just a Child of Nature" (all of which appeared on 1971's *Imagine,* the last as the rewritten "Jealous Guy"). It's true he was also sitting on an aggressive number, "Give Me Some Truth" (heard in embryo by the Beatles during the *Get Back* sessions), which would have fit well into *Plastic Ono Band*'s oft-angry, scathing vibe. It's also true that "Oh My Love" might have been a little too close in mood and tune to "Look at Me" for both songs to comfortably sit within the same LP. Still, one wonders if John was deliberately tailoring the song selection to fit the bleaker worldview he apparently wanted to project on *Plastic Ono Band.* In several comments he made after the Beatles' breakup, he made a point of saying how constricted he often felt by the group's image, and how he relished the freedom to now be as hard-nosed, confrontational, and soul-baring as he wished. Could it just be, however, that, for *Plastic Ono Band* at least, he actually intentionally suppressed his funnier, happier side to make himself appear angrier and more serious than he really was?

● Circa Early October

Studio Outtake
Ringo Starr's "It Don't Come Easy" single session
Trident Studios, London

Happy Birthday, John

For John's 30th birthday on October 9, 1970, several fellow musicians recorded musical greetings of sorts for him to commemorate the occasion. One was this 75-second blast from Ringo, accompanied by Stephen Stills, Billy Preston, Klaus Voormann, and others. There seems a good chance it was done in early October shortly before the actual birthday date, as it's known Ringo finished his "It Don't Come Easy" single that month. It's a fun, brash bash, but virtually tuneless, sounding like a "Johnny B. Goode" (complete with "Johnny B. Goode"–styled break) that uses only two of its chords. George's "It's Johnny's Birthday" (from the "jam" disc of *All Things Must Pass*), by the way, was also recorded for this purpose, as was Janis Joplin's "Happy Birthday, John (Happy Trails)," sung seriocomically to the tune of "Happy Trails" and eventually issued officially on the 1993 *Janis* box set.

● Circa Late 1970

Private Tape
Tittenhurst Park, Ascot

*Make Love Not War

I'm the Greatest (two versions)

How? (four versions)

I'm Just a Child of Nature (two versions)

Oh Yoko! (three versions)

Sally and Billy (two versions)

Rock & Roll People

Help!

Instrumental

Happy Christmas (two versions)

People Get Ready

Can't Believe You Wanna Leave

Mailman, Bring Me No More Blues

*I Promise

You Know How Hard It Is

I'll Make You Happy (two versions)

partial version appears on John Lennon's Anthology *box set*

The cover of Compositions *not only contains more than an hour of material John taped at home in late 1970, but also shows the house (in Tittenhurst Park, Ascot) where it was recorded.*

John wasn't long done with *Plastic Ono Band* at the time he recorded these solo piano-vocal performances, usually described as a composing tape and lasting a little more than an hour; estimates and reports of the dates it was recorded vary between November and December. As he stops and starts some tunes, and did not finish or officially record all of them, there's no universal agreement among authorities in these matters as to how many takes he did of each song, or what all of the songs are titled. For the sake of convenience, this entry will follow the track listing of the most common bootleg (*Compositions*) on which all of this material appears, with the exception of "Can't Believe You Wanna Leave." That song is titled "My Heart Is in Your Hands" on the boot, but it was later determined that it's a cover of an actual song called "Can't Believe You Wanna Leave," originally recorded by Lloyd Price.

Though it's undeniably of considerable historical interest, as actual listening goes, it's a little disappointing. Not only does the use of the same piano on all of these make for a certain monotony in the arrangements; the poorly tuned piano itself seems to have seen better days, as does John's sometimes halting, clumsy playing. His voice isn't in top (by his very high standards) shape, and the fidelity, while quite acceptable, isn't so great. It may be harsh to so critically judge a recording that was certainly not intended for public scrutiny, and probably only meant as a reference of sorts as John cast about for what to do next after *Plastic Ono Band* was in the can. All that said, it's rather sluggishly performed, and when you add in the similarity in the tempos, it gives you a depressing, rainy-day feeling when heard all at once.

It's not quite accurate to view these as demos of sorts for John's 1971 album *Imagine*, as only three of those songs are routined here. John seems to have a good idea of what he wants to do with one of that record's better songs, the pensive "How?", although it would benefit immensely from orchestration in its *Imagine* incarnation. One of the versions segues out of a brief, under-half-minute cover of the Impres-

sions' classic soul anthem "People Get Ready"; another uses a lilting piano rhythm much like that heard in the hit single "Imagine," which one guesses wasn't yet written, as it's hard to imagine such a strong waiting-in-the-wings composition wouldn't have been taped here.

"I'm Just a Child of Nature," however, still has surprisingly long to go before it mutates into "Jealous Guy," and in fact John makes a false start with a first line that refers to Rishikesh, even though he'd changed the word to Marrakesh in versions played at the Beatles' January 1969 *Get Back* sessions. (As a side note, despite John's famous disillusioned bitterness over how the Rishikesh jaunt had ended, he certainly seemed to carry the experience around with him for a long time; even in 1980 he was still referring to it in song, as proved by the home-recorded "The Rishi Kesh Song" [sic] included in the Lennon *Anthology* box.) "Oh Yoko!" is not a song meant to be played as a piano ballad, and these run-throughs are actually considerably less lively than the acoustic guitar busk he'd done back in the late spring of 1969 at the Montreal Bed-In. It's almost as if he were getting further away from, not closer to, the spirit of the song, though fortunately he found his way back to it by the time the *Imagine* track was recorded.

Some of the other songs offer glimpses of numbers that wouldn't emerge on disc for about three years. "Make Love Not War," first heard as an instrumental sequence noodled by John on guitar behind a spoken Yoko Ono message a year earlier (see entry for December 18, 1969), would evolve into his 1973 hit single "Mind Games." That was after a nearly wholesale revamp of the lyrics, starting, of course, with the title itself; maybe John, always restlessly moving on to the next phase, had had enough of peace activism by the time he finally released the tune. Or, as he claimed in his 1980 *Playboy* interview, "It was originally called 'Make Love Not War,' but that was such a cliché that you couldn't say it anymore, so I wrote it obscurely, but it's all the same story. How many times can you say the same thing over and over? When this came out, in the early '70s, everybody was starting to say the '60s was a joke, it didn't mean anything, those love-and-peaceniks were idiots." The bridge here goes into a different, more subdued melodic direction in its second half as well, topped off with some boogie piano figures. The 1973 reworking, however, *did* repeat, almost verbatim, the first line of "Make Love Not War" in its fadeout, though you've got to crank the volume *way* up to make it out.

"I'm the Greatest," of course, was a highlight of Ringo Starr's chart-topping 1973 *Ringo* album, though John obviously had it in his reserve pile for quite some time before that. As he explained in his *Playboy* interview, "I couldn't sing it, but it was perfect for Ringo. He could say 'I'm the greatest' and people wouldn't get upset. Whereas if I said 'I'm the greatest,' they'd all take it *so* seriously." "Rock & Roll People" eventually saw the light of day, in a 1973 version, on the posthumous Lennon collection *Menlove Ave.* As the material on this particular home tape goes, it's not bad, with a more lively feel than most of its surroundings, and a more animated rock 'n' roll piano style.

John chose to revisit "Help!" at this point for unknown reasons, and it's actually a pretty dreary interpretation, conclusively proving the song's much better heard as a fast guitar rock arrangement (as the Beatles did it) than a slow, drawn-out piano one. As "Help!" was written in 1965, this recording's sometimes mistakenly identified as dating from the mid-'60s, but it in fact definitely originates from this set of tapes. John might have been genuinely interested in reworking it as a slow arrangement at this late date because of his dissatisfaction with the Beatles' original, telling *Rolling Stone* around this time, "I don't like the recording that much; we did it too fast, trying to be commercial. . . . I might do 'I Want to Hold Your Hand' and 'Help!' again, because I like them." When Yoko offers a suggestion during a pause, however, John lets her know who's in charge of the music: "I don't care how you want to sing it, dear, I'm singing it meself at the moment."

If the way this tape was sequenced on the *Compositions* bootleg actually corresponds to the order in which it was done in real time, the session seemed to go downhill after "Help!", with the exception of three approximately five-minute versions of "How?" "Sally and Billy" is a lighthearted, jaunty, insubstantial hokey love story, as if John is overcompensating for submerging that side of himself on the *Plastic Ono Band* LP; ironically, for just a few moments, the melody strays fleetingly close to Paul McCartney's "Teddy Boy." An untitled instrumental doesn't contain seeds of any familiar John Lennon song, or much of any tune at all. The two "Happy Christmas" musical messages (sung by both John and Yoko) might have been trying to approximate the zany fun of the Beatles' Christmas records, but they sound strained in comparison, especially as much of the charm of those 1966–1969 Beatles fan club discs was in their editing together of tapes from many sources, rather than sticking to just one performance.

Tiring, perhaps, of the effort involved in trying to devise new original material in such a concentrated dose, John ultimately retreats into some oldies covers. When he launches into Lloyd Price's "Can't Believe You Wanna Leave"—whose melody bears a resemblance to the bridge of "Don't Let Me Down"—his energy level seems to rise and his mood brightens almost instantly. Obviously in a '50s mood, he then goes into "Mailman, Bring Me No More Blues," which the Beatles had done in the *Get Back* sessions (modeling their version on Buddy Holly's recording).

John doesn't seem to be fully on board with this rendition, however, bleating his way through some of the vocals. "I Promise" is in the same '50s R&B ballad style, but zigzags in and out of the bridge to "Make Love Not War." The Lennon *Anthology* box set does include parts of both "Make Love Not War" and "I Promise" from this tape, by the way, and also labels them as 1973 recordings, though the sound of the piano itself makes it obvious they come from these late-1970 performances.

Finishing the tape off, "You Know How Hard It Is" is a minor-keyed rocker that seems to have some promise, with a riff that strongly recalls the Zombies' classic "She's Not There," but the lyrics seem uncharacteristically puerile for Lennon. "I'll Make You Happy," though nominally a different song, sounds like an extension of the same tune, and the lyrics don't get much better, though the second take of "I'll Make You Happy" has a strange blend of sulking moodiness and determination to make things better. Yoko sings along faintly in the background during this version, not fitting in at all well with what John's trying to achieve.

No doubt inadvertently, this set of tapes is cumulatively more dreary than inspirational. Though the following opinion is admittedly from an author who's far more interested in the work of the Beatles than the individual members' solo careers, it also seems bereft of several of the essential elements—optimistic energy, the exchange and blending of ideas among different but immensely talented composers and instrumentalists, a drive to see ideas through to completion—that made the Beatles so great.

● Circa Late 1970

Private Tapes

1882
Dear Friend

As readers will have no doubt noticed by now, virtually no Paul McCartney unreleased solo material has circulated from between the end of the Beatles' *Abbey Road* album and the end of 1970. If you were reading this book as your primary reference guide to the Beatles' career, in fact, you might deduce that Paul really *was* dead by late 1969, as was so widely rumored at the time. Of course, he wasn't inactive during this period by any means, releasing a full-length solo debut album (*McCartney*) in April 1970, and playing a major part in the ruckus over the release of *Let It Be.* For whatever reason, however, close to nothing has circulated from this time in the way of unofficial recordings.

That's unfortunate, even though *McCartney* was (with the exception of "Maybe I'm Amazed") disappointingly slight. Much of that album was (in a step quite unusual for a major artist of the time) home-recorded, however, and you'd think there must be some outtakes from that time, as first time studio home-recorders always have to experiment and discard material as they're getting used to the process. If there were any such outtakes from *McCartney* from that period (and many others of Paul's pre-1995 career, for that matter), it seemed he would have had a good chance to air them when he hosted the "Oobu Joobu" radio series in 1995. He did not, however, in keeping with his image of someone quite coy about revealing his innermost self. Or it may be that he was simply more careful not to let any of his unreleased 1969–1970 material out to other hands than John, George, or even Ringo were.

The recording dates of these two solo piano-vocal demos are unknown, though educated guesses put them in late 1970, shortly before the sessions for Paul's second album (1971's *Ram*) began (though some feel the two tracks were done after 1970). "1882" is a fair, though hardly great, number featuring a characteristically haunting McCartneyesque tune with some wordless vocalizing that seems to be trying to imitate a gnarly guitar riff. Paul would never release the song, though it was performed in concert during early Wings tours. "Dear Friend," saved for Wings' critically lambasted 1972 album *Wild Life,* is another minor-keyed song that, while boasting an obvious level of craftsmanship far above the average pop singer-songwriter, is similarly far below the level of most of the songs he'd been writing not too long before that for the Beatles. To be harsh, considering that he'd unveiled most of his *Abbey Road* material during the January 1969 *Get Back* sessions, it seemed that Paul had managed to write little truly outstanding material over the entire past two years.

There are, incidentally, a number of *Ram* outtakes that have circulated. But the author's opted not to include them here, since the *Ram* sessions ran from November 1970 to March 1971, and it hasn't been determined which might have been recorded before this book's end-of-1970 cutoff date. For the record, these include the jaggedly forceful, if melodically barren, rocker "Rode All Night," which rambles on for nearly nine minutes; the shades-of-Beach Boys-gone-exotica instrumental "Sunshine Sometime"; the slow, lightweight, nearly instrumental "When the Wind Is Blowing"; another instrumental track for the country-influenced "Hey Diddle"; and three vocal mixes plus one instrumental backing track of the inoffensive but inconsequential *Ram* outtake "A Love for You." There are also rough mixes of instrumental tracks for two songs that did make *Ram,* "The Back Seat of My Car" and "Long Haired Lady."

● December

Private Tape
New York City

Acoustic Guitar Improvisation

During the filming of John and Yoko's avant-garde movie *Fly,* John recorded this little-bootlegged guitar instrumental. The author hasn't heard it, but it's described as a "rockabilly styled 12-bar" in Chip Madinger and Mark Easter's *Eight Arms to Hold You: The Solo Beatles Compendium.*

1970 Noncirculating Recordings, Known and Rumored

● January

Private Tapes
Aalborg, Denmark

While John and Yoko were vacationing in Denmark, they spent time with her ex-husband Tony Cox, his new wife, and the daughter Yoko had with Cox, Kyoko. Tapes from this visit were auctioned in 2002 and 2003, some of them featuring John devising childlike songs with Kyoko. This is probably pretty unentertaining listening, but according to the MastroNet auction catalog, one tape does include a part where "John suddenly rattles off a song consisting of a nonsensical list of words, 'Boys and bees and chimneys and trees and cheese and wax and cigarettes, oh!' The rhythmic beat of John's voice calls to mind his memorable singing and chanting on 'Give Peace a Chance.'"

A 2002 report in *Record Collector* gave more details: "They feature Lennon telling stories to the girl, and vamping blues, folk and funk guitar riffs as she improvises songs and nursery rhymes. Along the way, he debuts his *Imagine* tune, 'Oh Yoko!' (retitled in honor of Kyoko) [actually another home tape of the tune predates this; see entry on page 266], runs down the riffs to Beatles tunes such as 'Sun King' and 'I Got a Feeling,' and even accompanies Kyoko as she breaks into an unlikely rendition of Frank Zappa's 'Jelly Roll Gum Drop.' John, Yoko and Kyoko join forces for a brief romp through 'Yellow Submarine,' while Lennon reveals a previously undocumented talent for penning children's ditties, including a touching fragment addressed to his own son, Julian."

● February 8–11

Private Tapes

There are videotape recordings of John and Yoko by Yoko's ex-husband Tony Cox, sold to US collectors 30 years later, including John playing the old Sam Cooke hit "Bring It on Home to Me" and "Across the Great Water" (which would evolve into the *Plastic Ono Band* cut "Remember") on piano.

● February 18–19

Studio Outtakes
"It Don't Come Easy" Ringo Starr single sessions
Studio Two, Abbey Road, London

Under the working title "You Gotta Pay Your Dues," the first couple of sessions for "It Don't Come Easy " were done at EMI, with Ringo on drums and vocals, George on guitar, Klaus Voormann on bass, and Stephen Stills on piano. It was decided to remake the song entirely starting on March 8; in fact, it had been decided to remake the song entirely on February 19, when the 20 takes from the first session were set aside and ten others laid down. So it's likely there are not one but at least two arrangements among these outtakes that differ from the familiar hit single.

● May 26

Studio Outtakes
George Harrison's All Things Must Pass *sessions*
London

And in the End . . . December 31, 1970

The official date on which the Beatles broke up was April 10, 1970, when Paul McCartney announced (albeit in a press release in promotional copies of his solo album) that he was leaving the group. There nevertheless continued to be speculation throughout the rest of the year that the rift was temporary and that the band might manage to somehow patch up differences and record again, though probably under much-altered circumstances. But even the most optimistic Beatles fans had to concede that any prospect of reconciliation was virtually nixed when Paul filed a lawsuit on December 31, 1970, against John, George, Ringo, and Apple seeking to dissolve the group's partnership.

Even without the business disagreements, however, could the Beatles realistically have continued any longer than they did? As this chapter makes clear, in the final eight months of 1970, each member was not only recording prolifically on his own, but also exploring musical directions that would not have been compatible with a more or less egalitarian band setup. John, Paul, and George were already working on songs that wouldn't even be released for years, in some cases. John had experienced a taste of uncompromising musicmaking that would have been utterly impossible within the Beatles. Paul was getting so involved in family life that he wasn't making many social rounds at all, let alone interacting with many other musicians. Most dramatically, George, at the very end of 1970, was just starting to experience his first bout of superstardom as a solo artist, with both *All Things Must Pass* and the "My Sweet Lord" single rushing toward the No. 1 spot. Why would he be in any hurry to regroup with the Beatles, especially now that he'd been the surprise winner in the first round of their solo efforts? And even if they reunited, didn't the divergent stylistic paths they were already pursuing on their own make it unlikely they could ever again mesh as magnificently as they had in the 1960s?

Each of the Beatles built up large discographies as individual artists, and indeed piled up quite a few unreleased recordings along the way. Nothing they did separately, however, could match the magic of what they did as a unit, or even the artistic high points of their best early solo releases. It's partly for that reason that fascination with the music they did together continues unabated. And it's a major reason that hunger for even their unreleased work—and, likely, efforts to excavate and issue even more of it, legitimately or otherwise—will continue to grow and grow.

Timeline of Major Events Leading to the Beatles' Breakup

August 29, 1966: Last official public concert in Candlestick Park, San Francisco.

August 27, 1967: Death of manager Brian Epstein.

December 26, 1967: British television premiere of *Magical Mystery Tour* becomes first major Beatles project to meet with failure.

March–April 1968: Group trip to India to study with the Maharishi ends with separate, premature returns to England.

May 1968: John Lennon starts serious, public romance with Yoko Ono.

August 22, 1968: Ringo Starr quits the Beatles for about ten days during sessions for *The White Album*.

In 1970, for the first time since 1963, no Beatles fan club Christmas disc was released. Instead, an LP of all the 1963–1969 Christmas discs was compiled, its cover featuring shots of "the boys"—now men, and no longer working as a unit—in various phases of their storied career.

December 10–11, 1968: John performs without the Beatles, fronting a band with Eric Clapton, Keith Richards, and Mitch Mitchell for the *Rolling Stones Rock and Roll Circus* film.

January 10, 1969: George Harrison quits the Beatles for five days during the *Get Back* sessions.

January 27, 1969: John and Yoko meet manager Allen Klein; a week later, Klein and Paul McCartney's soon-to-be brother-in-law and father-in-law, John Eastman and Lee Eastman, are hired by Apple to help sort out the company's affairs.

March 12, 1969: Paul marries Linda Eastman.

March 20, 1969: John marries Yoko Ono.

May 8, 1969: John, George, and Ringo sign management contracts with Klein; Paul never does.

May 19, 1969: The Beatles lose their bid to control Northern Songs, publisher of most of their original compositions.

July 4, 1969: John (as leader of ad hoc Plastic Ono Band) releases "Give Peace a Chance" single.

August 20, 1969: Final Beatles recording session in which all four members are in attendance.

September 13, 1969: John fronts Plastic Ono Band in concert in Toronto.

September 20, 1969: John announces he's leaving the Beatles, but is persuaded by the others and Klein not to make the decision public.

October 20, 1969: Plastic Ono Band releases single of "Cold Turkey," after John's suggestion that it be recorded for a Beatles single was rejected.

January 4, 1970: Final Beatles group recording session, without John.

February 6, 1970: John's "Instant Karma!" single released.

March 27, 1970: Ringo's *Sentimental Journey* album released.

April 1, 1970: Final Beatles recording session, with *Let It Be* overdubs overseen by producer Phil Spector.

April 10, 1970: Paul officially quits the Beatles.

April 17, 1970: Paul's *McCartney* album released.

November 27, 1970: George's *All Things Must Pass* album released.

December 11, 1970: John's *Plastic Ono Band* album released.

December 31, 1970: Paul sues John, George, Ringo, and Apple to dissolve the Beatles' partnership.

It's known that at least one version other than "Dehra Dhun" of the one that's circulated was taped on May 26. Also on May 26, there was at least one take laid down of "Sour Milk Sea," the George Harrison composition that Jackie Lomax had recorded on a Harrison-produced 1968 Apple single, and which the Beatles themselves had done back in 1968 on their *White Album* demos. (It would be interesting to see how George might have updated his interpretation.) It's also been rumored that George did a version of "Woman Don't You Cry for Me," which he re-recorded for his 1976 *Thirty-Three & 1/3* album, during the *All Things Must Pass* sessions. Plus, it's known that a version of "What Is Life" was recorded without the descending riff that was so crucial to making it a hit, though it hasn't yet surfaced. For the diehards, it's also known that an alternative mix was done of "Johnny's Birthday," one of the cuts from the bonus jam disc.

● June 28

Studio Outtakes

Ringo Starr's Beaucoups of Blues *sessions*
Music City Records, Nashville

And for the even harder diehards, there are rumored to be way-longer versions of the two jams from the last day of Ringo's *Beaucoups of Blues* sessions: a 20-minute "Nashville Jam" and a "Coochy-Coochy" lasting 28 (!) minutes. Plus—acetates of outtakes and alternate versions from *Beaucoups of Blues* were auctioned by Sotheby's in 1992 on two 12-inch discs, with many of the tracks, according to *The Beatles After the Break-Up 1970-2000,* containing "additional sounds and various count-ins."

● September 26–October 27

Studio Outtakes

From John Lennon's Plastic Ono Band
Abbey Road, London

An alternate take of "Working Class Hero" with a spoken introduction has been reported to exist.

PART 2

The Unreleased
and Rare Beatles on Film:
A Selective Guide

Introduction

From around the time "She Loves You" was released in August 1963 until the end of their career, the Beatles were constantly chased not only by fans, but also by the media. There's a great deal of footage of the group on film, whether in live concert, television broadcasts, or promotional clips. And that's not even counting their five feature films (the animated *Yellow Submarine* counts; they did appear live briefly at the end, remember?), press conferences, news reports of comings and goings around the world, home movies, and segments in which they were interviewed collectively or individually.

It would be impossible to document all of the instances in which one Beatle or more appeared on film without filling up another entire book, even if such a volume were confined to footage that is not currently commercially available. This chapter will concentrate, then, on the very best and most interesting such clips that are not in commercial circulation, or are in such limited commercial circulation that they might easily be missed. It will also focus on live (as opposed to lip-synced) footage of the band performing music; they mimed to records on several broadcasts between 1963–1966, but it's this author's opinion that such performances are rarely too enlightening or enjoyable, and certainly not nearly as exciting as genuinely live performances.

As with the Beatles' music, it would be foolish to assert that the unreleased and rare film footage of the group is as good, or better, than what's easily obtainable (or, these days, rented). It's also true that parts of virtually all of the best Beatles movie clips can be seen in their *Anthology* DVD/home video series, and those might be enough for some. For those who want more, however, there's not only a *lot* more, but also a lot of stuff that's genuinely excellent and historically valuable. Certainly the full-length preservations of their first US concert in Washington, DC in 1964, a Paris show in 1965, and two Tokyo sets in 1966 are essential documents of different phases of their concert career. Several of their 1963–1965 television performances are among their best live work ever caught on camera. And while there's not much footage of the group playing live after 1966, their 1965–1969 promotional films, though sometimes corny, did help innovate the music video form, with the group managing to play live for the cameras on some occasions after their retirement from touring in August 1966.

A great deal of pleasure from appreciating the Beatles can only come from seeing as well as hearing them. Their recordings, as great as they were, couldn't fully capture their wit, charm, humor, and charisma, or the full extent of their musicianship. Although some of their hard-to-find film bits have rough image and (as is often true of their unreleased music) audio quality, there's much sheer delight to be had by viewing the best of them, and usually fascinating obscure trivia to be found even in the least of them.

The Beatles' first appearance on BBC television, April 13, 1963.

1962

● Circa February
(possibly February 20)

Unknown (possibly Floral Hall, Southport)

A 30-second Super 8mm silent color clip (actually comprised of two segments) of the Beatles playing onstage in the early '60s was discovered in the 1970s by the son of the person making the film, and became widely known to the public when it was auctioned at Sotheby's in 1996. Initially it was reported to date from February 1961, but the kind of intense scrutinizing this sort of thing generates among Beatleologists quickly cast doubts. Because the Beatles are in leather clothes (which they didn't get until their second Hamburg residency in April–June 1961), because Paul is playing a Hofner bass (which he didn't get until said Hamburg residency), and because a blow-up revealed Valentine's Day decorations, it's now believed the segment actually dates from around Valentine's Day in February 1962. Parts of the film can be seen on the Pete Best documentary DVD *Best of the Beatles,* and a 28-second clip from this source was broadcast on the US *Extra* program, though some analysts believe that *Extra* broadcast was actually a six-second excerpt, artificially edited to appear to last half a minute long. It *is* obvious that it's not at the Cavern Club.

However, there's not much value to the film, other than a purely historical one. There's no sound (though some think they're doing "Kansas City/Hey! Hey! Hey! Hey!"), it's very brief (however long it really lasts), and Pete Best can't be seen at all. It's thought that the two segments are taken from two different songs, as Paul's seen singing in one and George in the other, John apparently not taking vocals when the camera was turned toward the stage. As an endnote, this is not just quite possibly the oldest surviving film of the group of any sort, but also the first color photography of any sort to capture the band after they'd adopted the name Beatles.

By the way, it's been reported that there's a silent, three-minute 8mm color film of the Beatles performing at the Top Ten Club in Hamburg during their residency there between April and June 1961. It's never been shown in public, however, and if it is at the Top Ten, its archival value might be slightly diminished by the reported failure of the camera to capture Pete Best in any of the frames.

● August 22

Cavern Club, Liverpool

Some Other Guy

The Beatles were not professionally filmed until August 22, 1962, when Granada TV took footage of them performing at the Cavern Club. The resulting electrifying clip of them singing "Some Other Guy" fortunately escaped destruction and has been screened often; it can be seen in the *Anthology* video series. (The audio portion has been frequently bootlegged as well; see entry on page 32). But exactly what images you

see, and what sound you hear, depends very much on where you see it. For the Beatles were actually filmed not only doing "Some Other Guy" with sound, but also for a further four minutes or so of silent footage, for cutaway shots that could be inserted into the clip for variety. Bootleggers, kind souls that they are, have assembled all of the footage together for our appraisal, sometimes adding sound from early unreleased Beatles recordings as the backdrop.

There's not much of astonishing value in those supplementary images, though many of them give you a chance to see close-ups of individual Beatles and angles shot from the side and back of the stage (as well as a few additional glimpses of the Cavern audience). It's also evident that they're not singing "Some Other Guy" in all of these shots, some of which have George (who did *not* sing on "Some Other Guy") and Paul, or John and George, singing into the same mike; some who've studied the matter think they might be playing "Kansas City/Hey! Hey! Hey! Hey!" or "Money (That's What I Want)" at times. It does make for a change from the usual edits of the clip, which (as is only proper) emphasize standard shots from the audience's point of view in which the full band can be seen. If nothing else, a few shots of a smiling Ringo make it clear that although he's only been in the band a few days, he's already having a good time—and likely smiling a lot more than Pete Best ever did onstage. These are the only pre-fame moving images of the Ringo lineup, and as the solitary document of their Cavern days it carries considerable historical import and (particularly considering the dark, shadowy tone of the film) haunting ambience.

1963

● August 27–30

BBC documentary The Mersey Sound
Little Theater, Southport; various locations, Manchester and Liverpool

Twist and Shout
She Loves You

Although the Beatles almost immediately began appearing on British television pretty regularly after they were filmed in the Cavern in August 1962, no other sound clips of the band survive predating August 1963. No one realized the historical (and simple entertainment) value of pop music footage in general, let alone Beatles footage in particular, and the film was lost, destroyed, or even erased and reused as a cost-cutting measure.

The first live sound footage of the Beatles after their ascent to popularity is contained within the half-hour BBC documentary *The Mersey Sound.* Even if it splits "Twist and Shout" into fragments (though "She Loves You" is thankfully complete and uninterrupted), and even if it was actually shot in an empty theater (overdubbed and intercut with audience screams and reactions), it really is at least being performed live. And it's truly the first such footage to capture the group as they initially became known to Britain and then the world, singing and bobbing their hearts out (and shaking their heads) in their collarless suits. It's this clip of "She Loves You," by the way—and not their far more renowned February 1964 *Ed Sullivan Show* appearances—that was the first widely noticed screening of a Beatles performance in the United States, when it was used on *The Jack Paar Program* on January 3, 1964.

A good amount of interview material (often excerpted for other documentaries) with each Beatle was included as well, and these were probably the first such conversations to demonstrate to the British masses that these were intelligent, clever, and surprisingly reflective young men, not the noodlebrains that many people thought pop stars were. As for the most intriguing musical comment, it's interesting to hear Paul speculating that he and John will, in the far-off future, "write songs as we have been doing as a sort of sideline now, we'd probably develop that a bit more, we hope." Most of us can now grin knowingly and say, "And didn't they!", but in 1963 no one envisioned rock music becoming a long-lasting cultural force. Pragmatic Paul was probably thinking ahead to the time (which, thankfully, never came) when the hysteria would subside, the Beatles would fall out of fashion, and they'd need to concentrate on songwriting, rather than performing, to maintain their foothold in the entertainment business. John's there to prick his bubble, though; when Paul dismisses their early-'60s leather stage outfits as something people were starting to laugh at, John mutters in protest offscreen, "They didn't laugh at 'em in Liverpool...."

The Beatles, incidentally, are only featured in part of this documentary, which really does take an overall view of the Merseybeat explosion, not just Beatlemania in particular. Though dated, it's a satisfactorily thoughtful piece that's pretty forward-looking for 1963 considering rock music was rarely considered a worthy subject for serious journalism. As for the other groups featured in performance, Group One (their real name) are pretty lame. But the Undertakers cut memorably macabre figures in their onstage undertaker suits, complete with huge top hats and fronted by a young, yelping Jackie Lomax—the same Jackie Lomax who would record for Apple in the late '60s, where he'd be produced by George Harrison and cover a Harrison song never released by the Beatles, "Sour Milk Sea."

● October 30

Swedish television program Drop In
Narren-teatern, Stockholm, Sweden

She Loves You
Twist and Shout
I Saw Her Standing There
Long Tall Sally

Even those who've swallowed the oft-posed (and incorrect) judgment that the Beatles weren't a good live band are almost always won over to the other way of thinking after seeing this amazing clip. While not nearly as celebrated as, say, their *Ed Sullivan* shows or rooftop *Get Back* concert, it's a contender for the most exciting live Beatles performance on film ever—it's really that good. Never was the group (or, perhaps, *any* group) so visibly happy to be playing the music they loved, the already ebullient playing gaining an added spontaneous edge when they were asked, impromptu, to play a couple more songs than planned. Those two songs, "I Saw Her Standing There" and "Long Tall Sally," are included in *Anthology,* and the boys rock out about as hard as they ever

did in front of the cameras while the upstaged, poker-faced Swedish house band sullenly claps along in the background.

The entire clip circulates in excellent quality, and if the initial songs ("She Loves You" and "Twist and Shout") aren't quite as amazing as the final pair, they're great as well, the newly converted Swedish Beatlemaniac audience clapping along with the latter number. Even George looks unabashedly happy. Paul, of course, never had problems letting viewers know what a good time he was having, and his head-shaking delight here is positively contagious—as well as being perhaps *the* most crucial factor to whipping up audience enthusiasm as Beatlemania took root.

● November 4

The Royal Variety Performance
Prince of Wales Theatre, London

From Me to You
She Loves You
Till There Was You
Twist and Shout

The Royal Variety Performance, done before an audience including Princess Margaret and the Queen Mother, was—in combination with the group's appearance on *Sunday Night at the London Palladium* the month before—the television spot most responsible for making Britain Beatles-mad. Most of it, happily, was used in *Anthology,* but one of the four songs, "She Loves You," is not included in that package. This was done, one would think, to avoid redundancy with other *Anthology* footage of them playing the song, rather than any problem with this specific performance, which is quite exciting, though Paul seems a bit rushed and breathless when he announces it. While this is far from the only clip that demonstrates this point, was there ever another band where two singers—in this case Paul and George—harmonized so well, and joyfully, into a single microphone?

● November 20

The Beatles Come to Town *newsreel*
ABC Cinema, Manchester

She Loves You
Twist and Shout
From Me to You (instrumental reprise)

The first color sound film of the Beatles performing live was in this six-and-a-half-minute Pathé newsreel. While it's been excerpted in numerous places (including *Anthology*), it's cool to see the whole thing uninterrupted, even though this version of "Twist and Shout" lasts only a little more than a minute, and "From Me to You" is only heard as an instrumental tag as the curtains are closing. This was, too, the first footage to really capture the pandemonium of Beatlemania. The previous surviving live 1963 clips had been done either in an empty theater or for somewhat controlled television broadcast audiences; here, the wildly screaming audience is starting to overwhelm the music.

● December 2

UK television program The Morecambe and Wise Show
Elstree Studio Centre, Borehamwood

All My Loving
This Boy
I Want to Hold Your Hand
Moonlight Bay

The last part of this clip, in which the Beatles take part in a fairly (by variety show standards) humorous sketch with host comedians Eric Morecambe and Ernie Wise and don straw hats to sing the standard "Moonlight Bay," is included on *Anthology*. The three songs they sang before this on this episode of *The Morecambe and Wise Show*, however, were not. The group might not be as exuberant here as they are in the best of their early clips, and John's voice cracks during the bridge of "This Boy." But because they're playing both sides of their brand-new single, as well as the best song off their just-released *With the Beatles* LP, the performances have a freshness, and one imagines the boys were delighted to be playing these tunes live to a television audience for the first time.

There *is* one naughty bit from the end of the comedy sketch that does *not* appear in *Anthology*. Asked for a joke, John Lennon steps forward and gleefully starts, "There was two old men sitting in a dirty deckchair . . ." Unfortunately, he doesn't get any further than that.

● December 7

UK television special It's the Beatles
Empire Theatre, Liverpool

I Want to Hold Your Hand
Money (That's What I Want)
Twist and Shout
From Me to You (instrumental reprise)
Third Man Theme

How sad that, although the first concert the Beatles gave in their hometown as British superstars was made into the TV special *It's the Beatles*, only about ten minutes of footage survives. And though the image and sound quality are very good, even these few minutes are afflicted with missing snippets of film and small audio glitches. The performance itself is confident and powerful, and notable if for no other reason than that it contains the only live version of "Money (That's What I Want)" on film. Quite good it is, too, especially when Paul and George converge on the microphone for their harmonies, though they uncharacteristically sing a wrong line shortly before the instrumental break of "Twist and Shout." Overall, however, the Beatles were unhappy with how the show was filmed, complaining in the press about both the sound balance and the camerawork.

Still, what remains demonstrates that their act had certainly gotten polished by this time, and it seems the only really spontaneous deviation from the program might have occurred during the peculiar instrumental reprise of "From Me to You" at the end. Here the lads go into exaggerated dance steps, and look as though they're waiting for a cue from the camera crew to stop playing, easing into a few notes of "Third Man Theme" just as the screen finally starts to fade out. The entire audio portion of the concert *is* available (see entry on page 76), but in much worse fidelity than is heard on this footage.

Earlier on this date, incidentally, the group appeared on the BBC television rate-a-record program *Juke Box Jury*, but no one's been able to find the film, if it even survives in any form. Wrapping up 1963 Beatles film rarities, it can also be noted that no copy of their October 13 *Sunday Night at the London Palladium* broadcast—which marked the official start of Beatlemania in Britain—has been found either, though the audio portion has circulated (see entry on page 71).

And as for the strangest bit of non-musical Beatles film that's made its way onto unofficial DVDs, look for the part of their October 4 *Ready, Steady, Go!* TV appearance in which British star Helen Shapiro, singing her throaty "Look Who It Is," turns John, Ringo, and George to the camera one by one for them to make silly and self-mocking faces. That episode of *Ready, Steady, Go!* (in which they mime a few songs, and which has largely been issued on official video) also shows Paul judging a mime contest. In a stranger-than-fiction twist, winner Melanie Coe would in 1967 become the real-life inspiration for "She's Leaving Home" after she ran away from home herself, McCartney writing the song after reading a newspaper article about the event.

1964

● February 11

Washington Coliseum, Washington, DC

Roll Over Beethoven
From Me to You
I Saw Her Standing There
This Boy
All My Loving
I Wanna Be Your Man
Please Please Me
Till There Was You
She Loves You
I Want to Hold Your Hand
Twist and Shout
Long Tall Sally

Ask most people to name the Beatles' first American concert, and they'd probably say it was their February 12 appearance (at which they actually gave two shows) at Carnegie Hall in New York. However, it actually took place the day before in Washington, DC, at the Washington Coliseum, though the group had already played before a nationwide television audience on *The Ed Sullivan Show* on February 9. So big a phenomenon were the Beatles already in the United States—though they'd been virtually unknown in the country only about six weeks before—that the performance was filmed by CBS television on black-and-white video, with Brian Epstein's permission. On March 14 and 15, the film CBS made

The Beatles appeared on Ready, Steady, Go! *in October 1963 with Helen Shapiro and Dusty Springfield—one of their most amusing television spots.*

from what they shot—together with separate footage from Beach Boys and Lesley Gore concerts—was shown in movie theaters as a closed-circuit broadcast. (The Beach Boys and Gore did *not* play on the Coliseum bill, though it's sometimes been mistakenly reported that they did, due to all three acts' appearance in the same telecast.)

Excerpts from the film have shown up in numerous video compilations, including *The Beatles Anthology*. What's more, in 2003, Passport released a DVD entitled *The Beatles in Washington D.C., February 11, 1964*. So what makes this qualify as an entry in an overview of unissued Beatles footage?

Plenty, actually. For as happens way too often when historically important films are repackaged for video and DVD release, that disc neither contains the whole concert, nor can it help breaking what doesn't need to be fixed, by adding audio interview snippets over some of the between-song passages. Yes, it does add a few clips from press conferences and promo ads for the event. But really, an event as momentous as this should be experienced start to finish, without unnecessary editing and overdubs. It's fortunate that the original film does exist, not only because it's the straight historical record, but also because it might just be the most exciting on-screen, genuinely live Beatlemania of all.

There are things to be said against the video of this concert. The image quality is dark, grainy, and flickery; the audio imperfect, particularly in the instrumental balance; and the camera angles few and basic. The stage setup was surprisingly primitive in some respects, with

vocal microphone failures and rudimentary amplification that barely stood a fighting chance against eight thousand hysterical fans. But guess what? It doesn't really matter. For here are the early Beatles at their on-stage best. They're more visibly delighted, indeed almost overwhelmed, by the crowd's enthusiasm here than at any time before or since. Despite the seeming overnight success of their invasion of America, it had in reality been a long hard climb to the top, taking about seven years of diligent work and numerous excruciating setbacks, and also a year or so where they'd made virtually no inroads into the US market despite their mushrooming British superstardom. This was the payoff, and though the group would get fed up with touring before screaming teenagers within a couple of years, at the Washington Coliseum they were if anything having an even greater time than their admirers. They said as much in a few comments directly after the concert (as quoted in Bruce Spizer's *The Beatles Are Coming!*), Paul calling the gig their "most exciting yet," and Ringo adding, "Some of them even threw jelly babies in bags and they hurt like hailstones, but they could have ripped me apart and I couldn't have cared less. What an audience! I could have played all night!"

The first thing most viewers notice about the concert is how almost shockingly amateur the conditions are considering this is a show in a large facility for the biggest entertainment phenomenon going. As the Beatles were playing in a boxing ring, they needed to rotate their instruments every few minutes, so that each section of the audience had at least one chance to see the group head-on. Despite their status as kings

The Beatles' first US concert, Washington, DC, February 11, 1964—the best concert-length film of early Beatlemania.

of the hill, there wasn't a big crew of roadies on hand to do the heavy lifting; they had to do some of the lugging of mikes around themselves, Ringo tugging his drums around the circle on a large, revolving platform all on his own at times. ("The man told us to keep movin' round, y'see, so . . . we're keepin' movin' " states McCartney, almost apologetically and begrudgingly, into the mike at one point.) If there was a sound check done before the band came on, it's certainly not evident. For when the boys finally launched into "Roll Over Beethoven" after a few tense minutes of tuning up and getting everything in place, George Harrison's lead vocal could hardly be heard due to an apparent malfunctioning microphone, though he coolly moved over a few steps to a better one near the end of the first verse without breaking a sweat or missing a beat.

In spite of the handicaps, the Beatles played with tremendous energy. If that meant that many of the songs got sped up a tad—and, in the cases of "Please Please Me" and "Till There Was You" more than a tad—they certainly didn't let it affect their playing or their vocals, which are amazingly spot-on, even in the complex three-part harmonies of "This Boy" (itself a challenge in this environment, where ballads couldn't combat the audience noise with as much volume as the rockers). Here, too, is the only place where you get to hear an entire 12-song set from their first American visit, as opposed to the piecemeal extracts doled out over the course of their three *Ed Sullivan* programs. And what a set it is, including all four of their first British chart-topping singles, three of which were riding high on the American hit parade at the moment; "All My Loving," the best of the non-45 originals from *Meet the Beatles,* then resting at No. 1 on the LP charts; "I Saw Her Standing There," the B-side of "I Want to Hold Your Hand" and a big hit under its own steam; another ballad with "Till There Was You," which like "This Boy" helped enormously in varying the pace; and the all-out rockers of "Roll Over

Beethoven," "I Wanna Be Your Man," and "Twist and Shout." Too, you get to hear all four of the Beatles on lead vocals, not just Lennon and McCartney, with Ringo Starr taking his turn for "I Wanna Be Your Man," though his bum mike unfortunately made his singing all but inaudible.

Entertaining in their own right are the constant cutaways to the reactions of the crowd, from the proud moms escorting their teenage daughters to one 13-year-old-looking boy in a mock Beatles collarless suit, grinning ear to ear, delightedly sporting what might have been the first American Beatle haircut ever caught on film. Also amusing is the band's own between-song patter, with their onstage personas already set: McCartney Mr. Smooth as the master of ceremonies, Lennon threatening to lapse into comic bad taste with his mock-spastic clapping. Paul does get off a line worthy of Lennon when introducing "Please Please Me," though: "This song was released in America, it didn't do anything. It was released later again, and . . . well, it's doing something, you know?" (Even Lennon laughed hard at that.)

While they were playing the songs they rarely looked more animated, Ringo shaking his head like mad behind the drums, Paul bouncing up and down with joy, and even the less habitually ebullient John and George unable to contain their smiles or jiggling dance steps. Some highlights: the way the audience spontaneously erupts into screams when Lennon hits the anguished high note at the end of "This Boy"; McCartney yelping to kick off the instrumental break to "All My Loving," he and Harrison quick-stepping back to the mikes at just the right moment to resume the vocal; the nearly-out-of-tune instrumental intro to "I Want to Hold Your Hand," negated by the almost raw grittiness with which they lean into the riffs; Paul taking care to acknowledge the Isley Brothers in his spoken preface for "Twist and Shout"; and Paul and George singing some of their backup lines in the wrong order during the same tune. Alas, in the original film you don't get to hear or see the last half of "Twist and Shout" or anything from the finale, "Long Tall Sally." (The appearance of "Long Tall Sally" on the electronic press kit for the *Anthology* project in 1995, however, helped lead to confirmation that the entire concert videotape, complete with the full "Twist and Shout," does exist at Apple.)

Do you really miss a lot of the original film—even besides the missing half of "Twist and Shout" and entirety of "Long Tall Sally"—if you opt for Passport's *The Beatles in Washington D.C., February 11, 1964* DVD? Not really—only "Twist and Shout," "This Boy," and "All My Loving" are missing, though all of those are great songs and performances. And if you want the entire film as originally telecast on closed-circuit TV, it's on the not-wholly-kosher-looking DVD compilation *Beatles Around the World,* complete with the original overexcited theatrical trailer. That trailer, incidentally, is most amusing for a simulated conversation between a teenage boy and his date, part of whose hilariously dated hipster lingo follows:

Boy: "Like, wow, the Beatles! Aren't they the swingin', livin' end! You dig, chick?"
Girl: "I dig, Chuck!"
Boy: "That's one scene I gotta make!"
Girl: "Me too, Chuck!"
Boy: "Great! We'll make it together! . . . Chick, you got the date! I'll borrow wheels, and we'll go girl go!"
Girl: "Crazy!"

However, you can tell *Beatles Around the World* is a "gray market" release, in spite of it sneaking into some wholly above-board retail outlets, by the absence of chapter markers for each individual song (which are usually standard in commercial concert DVDs), as well as somewhat iffy transfer quality. The original film—sound and image cleaned up as much as current technology allows, with the missing one-and-a-half songs from the end added, if available—is another to add to the list of Beatles videos that should be released in their entirety, the way they were meant to be seen.

● February 16

US television program The Ed Sullivan Show *(rehearsal, not broadcast)*
Deauville Hotel, Miami Beach

She Loves You
This Boy
All My Loving
I Saw Her Standing There
From Me to You
I Want to Hold Your Hand

The Beatles' three 1964 *Ed Sullivan Show* appearances—taped on February 7 (in New York) and February 16 (in Miami)—were not only superb performances, but monumental milestones of popular culture. All of their 1964 clips, as well as their August 1965 *Ed Sullivan* spot, have been officially released on the two-DVD set *The Four Historic*

Ed Sullivan Shows Featuring the Beatles. This also includes the entire episodes, multiple fellow guests and commercials intact, should you want to experience or revisit them as they were originally broadcast. It's an essential video document for any committed Beatles fan.

It's not so well known, however, that yet more *Ed Sullivan* footage exists that was never broadcast. Prior to the live broadcast from Miami on the evening of February 16, the Beatles did a dress rehearsal of the same six numbers used in the final show. So these clips, naturally, are similar to what you see in the February 16 *Ed Sullivan* episode, except that the sound and image are worse. But it's hardly a waste of time—the sound and image are still decent, the performances are just as spirited as the broadcast version, and there are some amusing technical foul-ups. Even considering that network television was far less slick in 1964 than it is today, it's still surprising to see a mike set up at such a low height that John (to his visible chagrin) almost has to squat to sing into it during "She Loves You." The problem is not satisfactorily fixed during the dress rehearsal, and what's worse, Paul's vocal mike gives out entirely for the first part of "I Saw Her Standing There," leaving John's harmony as the sole singing to be heard. John's mike, too, remains considerably louder than Paul's for the rest of the show.

Perhaps knowing it was a dress rehearsal, John seems to be taking more liberties than usual during the between-song patter, slurring, "Shut up while he's talkin'!" when Paul's preamble to "I Want to Hold Your Hand" is interrupted by screams. Then comes the usual Lennon

The Beatles being filmed by network television for a February 1964 appearance on The Ed Sullivan Show.

cripple imitations (conspicuously not attempted in the live set that was broadcast later that day), as McCartney urges the audience to clap their hands and stamp their feet. Paul even shoots John a (scripted?) dirty look at one point, adding a disapproving shake of the head to the audience. But the Beatles still look like they're enjoying themselves mightily through all the snafus, and none of their clowning changes Ed Sullivan's glowing assessment of the foursome as "four of the nicest youngsters we've ever had on our stage" at the set's finish.

● February 27

Studio Two, Abbey Road, London

There's little footage of the Beatles recording in the studio, and nothing predating 1967 other than these five minutes of silent clips. (No, the scene of the group recording "You're Going to Lose That Girl" in *Help!* was not at EMI, or a real recording session, though ironically enough, it was filmed at Twickenham Film Studios—where the Beatles *would* be filmed and recorded rehearsing during the *Get Back* sessions/*Let It Be* movie in early January 1969.) The original idea was to use these studio clips for promoting *A Hard Day's Night,* with studio recordings as the soundtrack. As it turned out, however, its ultimate use was more long-term, as brief bits have been excerpted in several documentaries. The Beatles are playing "And I Love Her" during at least part of this footage—Paul can clearly be seen singing some of the lyrics—leading some bootleggers to craftily sync up the footage to the studio recording, so that it sometimes almost appears as though the Beatles are actually recording the track.

Because of both the absence of sound and the stringing together of numerous shots lasting just a few seconds or so, these clips' entertainment value is limited. But they do give you a sense of some of the lighthearted fun the boys had in the studio during their early days—John pulling a cripple face at the camera, Paul and Ringo playing a game of patty-cake that slips into fake boxing, Ringo playing the piano until the instrument's cover almost closes on him. And by 21st-century standards a shocking amount of cigarette smoking is going on (by George Martin as well as the Beatles), and the equipment looks positively antiquated, though it was pretty modern for 1964. You also realize how relatively stark and bare the studio's decor was, which by 1968 or so the group would be itching to escape, at least to the point of complaining about it vocally to the EMI staff.

● March 30

Pete Best on US television program I've Got a Secret
New York City

Strictly speaking, this entry is cheating a bit, as Pete Best had been out of the Beatles for about a year and a half by the time he filmed this segment for the US TV program *I've Got a Secret.* This is a must-see, however, both since there's so little footage of Best from the '60s, and because you'd never believe it really happened if it weren't preserved on film. *I've Got a Secret* was something of a lesser-known cousin of

the show *What's My Line,* the premise being a "secret" that a panel had to discover by asking questions of an unidentified mystery man or woman. This episode's mystery man was Pete Best—who, it should be remembered, was not well known in March 1964 as the drummer replaced by Ringo Starr, particularly in America.

It was sometimes written that Best did little to exploit his ex-Beatles status considering what he could have done, and generally that's true. Obviously, however, he did break down on at least this one occasion, and one can't help cringing in embarrassment on his behalf as the panelists (including 1945 Miss America Bess Myerson) and host Garry Moore crack bad jokes about Beatles haircuts. They do quickly guess Best's secret—that he used to be a Beatle—and though Pete puts on a brave, shit-eating grin, you can't help thinking that he's not only crying inside, but is inwardly wishing he was anywhere else *but* playing it up for laughs and money on national television.

What's most interesting about the clip, however, is Best's painful shyness and utter lack of charisma or confidence—*this* is the guy some have claimed to be the most popular Beatle in the early '60s? It reinforces conviction that the Beatles never made a better move than replacing him with the far more likable, media-friendly Ringo Starr. Too, Pete doesn't do his credibility any favors when he claims he left the Beatles because he wanted to start a group of his own, rather than admitting he was kicked out.

The clip can be seen as part of an obscure but commercially available DVD compilation of Beatles-related footage, *Fun with the Fab Four.* A little more vintage live Best can be seen in *Best of the Beatles,* which uses footage taken from a March 1, 1964, BBC television interview with him and his mother, Mona. Tellingly, however, it's his Mom who does much of the talking—could you imagine any of the other four Beatles letting a parent be the spokesperson during such an interview sequence?

● April 26

NME Pollwinners' Concert
Empire Pool, Wembley

She Loves You
You Can't Do That
Twist and Shout
Long Tall Sally
Can't Buy Me Love

Perhaps because this was their first live appearance in two months (owing to the filming of *A Hard Day's Night*), the Beatles played with considerable fresh vigor at this event, sponsored by the British music weekly *NME.* If five songs seems like a short set, it was actually longer than anyone else's, as the show had to cram a host of award-winners onto a single program. The sound balance and equipment weren't ideal either, the group spending much time during the first few songs trying to get a vocal mike to stay in place. It was the first time they'd ever done "You Can't Do That" before a live audience (unless you count miming to the record in an unused scene during the filming of *A Hard Day's Night*'s concert sequence), and John doesn't have it down pat, leading to one of the funniest scenes of any Beatlemania-era filmed show: John's premature screaming in anticipation of launching into the instrumental break, while the other Beatles, as is proper, go into the bridge that Lennon seems to have forgotten about. Then when the instrumental break comes, George tries to recreate the backup vocal chants from the record—which *Paul* seems to have forgotten about, leaving Harrison to give up. Then there's John going into the wrong verse of "She Loves You" at one point (and *how* many times had he already sung that tune?).

But as was observed in several entries for Beatles live recordings in this book's main section, something that made them different from most acts was their unfettered reaction to such mishaps. Many other bands would have allowed themselves to become distracted and upset; the Beatles plow on regardless, and if they're unnerved, they don't let it show. In fact, their intensity heats up during the last few songs, with all of them (not just Paul) bouncing madly during "Long Tall Sally." This is probably the most ferocious version of "Can't Buy Me Love" they summoned in concert (seen in part during *Anthology*), and even though they must have done "Twist and Shout" too many times to count before this show, this is one of the most animated performances of that song they ever did before the cameras. In sum: a great clip, for all its imperfections, capped by the Beatles receiving their trophy awards from a pre–James Bond Roger Moore.

Speaking of *A Hard Day's Night*—which the Beatles had finished filming just a couple of days before—don't expect any outtakes from the movie to come to light. For when director Richard Lester went to Twickenham Film Studios in June 1970 to try and obtain some copies of outtakes from *A Hard Day's Night* and *Help!* for himself, he discovered that all of them had been discarded, as United Artists—no doubt never envisioning how much of a commercial gold mine such extras would become in the DVD era—got rid of outtakes after five years as a matter of policy. At least that unused clip of "You Can't Do That" (first shown on *The Ed Sullivan Show* back on April 17, 1964) from the film's classic mimed concert scene was eventually released on the home video documentary *The Making of a Hard Day's Night*.

● April 28

UK television special Around the Beatles
Wembley Studios, Wembley

Twist and Shout
Roll Over Beethoven
I Wanna Be Your Man
Long Tall Sally
Love Me Do/Please Please Me/From Me to You/She Loves You/
   I Want to Hold Your Hand/Can't Buy Me Love (medley)
Shout

Yes, the Beatles were playing music during only part of this 55-minute television special, and they were miming to pre-recorded tracks, not playing live. The other half is devoted mostly to second-division British Invasion acts, as well as a corny, seven-minute satire of Shakespeare's *A Midsummer Night's Dream* in which the group—in full costume—played Pyramus (Paul), Thisbe (John), Moonshine (George), and Lion

The soundtrack of the 1964 NME *Pollwinners' Concert* is on this CD, though it makes more sense to watch the actual film if you can.

(Ringo). For all its contrivance, however, it's a ripping good time, and a program that still hasn't been seen in its entirety by many devoted Beatles fans. The Beatles themselves were certainly pleased with the result, Paul and Ringo citing it to *Let It Be* director Michael Lindsay-Hogg as their favorite television appearance.

In its favor, the extended sequence in which the Beatles mime is about as good as lip-synced segments get. That's principally because they're not miming to the records, but to a pre-recorded soundtrack of different studio versions (itself bootlegged, in pristine fidelity minus the screams of the studio audience; see entry on page 93). They also took advantage of this to record and mime to a couple of tracks they hadn't done in the studio, one being an awkward medley of all six singles they'd recorded to date. The other, however, is a far more exciting cover of the Isley Brothers' "Shout" that worked especially well before the cameras, as each of the four Beatles switched off on lead vocals. Beyond all this, the Beatles play, or mime if you will, with great enthusiasm, even if some of the lip-syncing and editing doesn't always match the images precisely to the music (and occasionally makes it clumsily obvious the performance isn't live). George especially never looked happier before a camera than he does while singing "Roll Over Beethoven" here.

The supporting acts on the bill—Cilla Black, Millie Small, Long John Baldry, P.J. Proby, the Vernons Girls, and Sounds Incorporated—may be no one's idea of the cream of the British Invasion. Yet they're perversely quite a gas to see here, if for no other reason that much less film footage has been screened of them (at least in the US) than of the more famous British Invasion acts. Some of those segments are a lot more entertaining than you'd expect, whether it's Cilla Black crooning her best single (and biggest US hit) "You're My World" and getting down, relatively speaking, with "Heat Wave"; Millie Small doing her sole big hit, "My Boy Lollipop"; New York DJ and self-proclaimed "Fifth Beatle" Murray the K doing a special introduction; and Long John Baldry pawing at his suit as if it's an oversized dog collar. The audience simply goes wild throughout, the adroit camera work (in a huge TV studio lined with catwalks) adding to the frenetic pace, though of course the kids really raise the roof when the Beatles come onstage. As carefully manufactured a setup as this well-directed television special might have been, it's impossible not to get caught up in its excitement, even if it was of a calculatedly innocent sort that the Beatles were on the verge of outgrowing. It was broadcast on American television by ABC on November 15, 1964, but has not been easy to view in its entirety since—at least until its inclusion on the DVD *Beatles Around the World*, whose authorized nature has been questioned, but which is certainly commercially available.

● June 5

Dutch television program The Beatles in Nederland
Cafe-Restaurant Treslong, Hillegom, The Netherlands

She Loves You
All My Loving
Twist and Shout
Roll Over Beethoven
Long Tall Sally
Can't Buy Me Love

Although mimed to records, this is about as interesting as such artificial constructs get, for several reasons. First, this is one of the concerts the Beatles gave while Jimmy Nicol was temporarily filling in for an ill Ringo Starr, and remains by far the best-quality footage of that short-lived lineup. Second, the group's vocal mikes were left open, so these versions do actually differ slightly from the record, adding a somewhat fattened, echoed effect resulting from them singing along with the official tracks. (George might have wished for a second that he hadn't done so, as he sings the wrong line right before the instrumental break of "Roll Over Beethoven"!) Third, the 11-minute interview segment is above average considering what banal questions the Beatles were usually asked in 1964 (though there are some of those here), with several queries (some from the studio audience) actually probing into their *music*. And fourth, the finale is really wild, the audience spontaneously rushing the stage and surrounding the group—well, John, Paul, and George, at least.

Starting with the interview portion (in which John introduces himself as "John Leopard"), the most interesting question (translated into English from the Dutch one posed by a teenager in the audience) asks what their favorite other British groups are. They quickly and astutely cite the Searchers and the Rolling Stones—which, more than 40 years later, many rock critics would agree *were* the best other British bands to have emerged before the summer of 1964 (remember that the Animals, Kinks, Yardbirds, Manfred Mann, and other contenders had just started to make records). Jimmy Nicol looks ill at ease (though not as ill at ease as Pete Best on *I've Got a Secret*!), understandably so as he'd only gotten the call to join the group a couple of days earlier. Jimmy also misses his cue to come in on time when the soundtrack rolls on the first number in the Beatles' set, "She Loves You."

The audience starts to get more and more raucous as the program continues, throwing small objects onstage, sidling up to dance near the stage and, finally, nearly mobbing the band during the "Can't Buy Me Love" finale. Concerned for their safety (as are road managers Mal Evans and Neil Aspinall and publicist Derek Taylor, who can be seen trying to keep the fans from getting too close), John, Paul, and George abandon their positions. But Jimmy Nicol keeps pounding along on his drum riser—a surreal climax to a memorable program, of which only a little is seen in *Anthology*. Again, the Beatles' collective cool defuses what could have been an uncomfortable situation—their road managers seem a lot more worried than they are, and in fact, John, Paul, and George (who even puts on a silly hat thrown from the crowd) seem more mightily amused than threatened by the audience participation.

● June 6

The Beatles in Nederland
Veilinghal Op Hoop Van Zegen, Blekker, The Netherlands

I Saw Her Standing There

As brief as this Dutch newsreel clip (circulating in three variant forms) is, it's notable for one very important reason—it's the *only* truly live footage that has surfaced of the Jimmy Nicol lineup. You couldn't really expect someone called to duty at a moment's notice to be doing much better, but he really isn't fitting in nearly as well as Ringo. Not only is he playing too hard and busily, he's trying too hard, hunched over the kit and flailing away without Ringo's (or the other Beatles') sense of cool. (The audience, though, is going absolutely bananas, even by Beatlemania measures.) While it's likewise understandable, he didn't cut a terribly colorful figure, either, when the Beatles were interviewed during his short stint, barely uttering a couple of sentences during a filmed press conference in Sydney on June 11.

● June 17

Australian television program The Beatles Sing for Shell
Festival Hall, Melbourne, Australia

I Saw Her Standing There
You Can't Do That
All My Loving
She Loves You
Till There Was You (fragment)
Roll Over Beethoven (fragment)
Can't Buy Me Love
Twist and Shout
Long Tall Sally

Just a couple days after Ringo rejoined the band, the Beatles filmed this concert for Australian television, sponsored by Shell. (As young men in their early twenties during a more naive era, it's doubtful that the Beatles thought much or at all about the repercussions of doing a concert sponsored by Shell, a huge oil company often condemned by environmentalists and political activists over the next few decades.) Though only brief fragments of "Till There Was You" and "Roll Over Beethoven" survive in the circulating tape, all of the other seven songs are seen in full.

Despite the missing bits, this is one of the best-sounding (though imperfectly balanced) and best-looking of filmed Beatles concerts, the group playing with an enthusiasm that might have been just a bit more perked up than usual, due to their delight and relief at having Ringo back in the band. It's certainly a better version of "You Can't Do That" than the one at the *NME* concert, especially when John shakes his head and screams right before the instrumental break (remembering to do so at the correct point this time!). George playfully pokes at Paul's face after McCartney scratches his nose during "Twist and Shout," neither of them missing a vocal or instrumental note. And for more purely (if politically incorrect) comic relief, this has (before "Can't Buy Me Love") about the most extended close-up of John's "spastic" routine on film, complete with a little dance at the end.

Certainly the most exhilarating moment comes right before the finale ("Long Tall Sally"), where Paul exclaims, "It's very nice for all of us to have back with us now, Ringo!" Whereupon the drummer stands and raises his fist and drumsticks like a heavyweight champion returning to the ring. Better yet is the bit at the end of "Long Tall Sally" itself, where a guy who seems determined to look and dress as much like John Lennon as possible runs onstage to shake John's hand. Rather than getting flustered, John laughs and keeps on playing as the police escort him off—another instance of the group keeping a level head during an intrusion that would have thrown most bands off balance.

● October 3

US television program Shindig
Granville Theatre, London

Kansas City/Hey! Hey! Hey! Hey!
I'm a Loser
Boys

A brief but nice segment recorded in London for the American program *Shindig*. It's not, refreshingly, mimed to the records, though it's been deduced that the Beatles weren't playing live either, instead lip-syncing to a pre-recorded soundtrack that they must have done especially for the occasion. Still, you can tell it's *not* the record just by the extended instrumental intro to "Kansas City/Hey! Hey! Hey! Hey!", the bluesy, not-like-the-record guitar solo in "Boys," and the different harmonica part in the instrumental break of "I'm a Loser." John's both playing guitar and (via aid of a neck rack) harmonica on that song, à la Bob Dylan, as he would when filmed doing the song in Paris in June 1965.

Before leaving 1964, incidentally, it can be noted that an approximately 20-minute black-and-white film of their August 23, 1964, Hollywood Bowl show does exist. But both sound *and* camerawork are so subpar that it can't be recommended as an entertaining, watchable experience, despite its historic value.

1965

● April 11

NME Pollwinners' Concert
Empire Pool, Wembley

I Feel Fine
She's a Woman
Baby's in Black
Ticket to Ride
Long Tall Sally

Just as they had in 1964, the Beatles played the *NME* Pollwinners' Concert after a relatively long layoff—it had been almost three months since their last live show and they had been busy since then recording and filming *Help!* And once again, despite some occasional rough spots, the group gave an excellent performance, though perhaps not quite as jazzed up as the one from 1964. Actually, it's remarkably smooth considering the three-month gap and the usual audience noise; the only screw-up is a small one, when John sings some wrong words at the very end of "I Feel Fine." This was the first live outing for "Ticket to Ride," and this version has some of the best shots you'll see of John and Paul harmonizing on the same mike. "Long Tall Sally" isn't played as frenetically as it had been at the 1964 event, but George throws in some nice raw variations in his guitar solos. The Beatles look a little different, too, as this was the first concert at which they wore the new military-style jackets they used at other 1965 gigs (most famously their Shea Stadium show); they'd gotten the idea for these while they were in the Bahamas to film scenes for *Help!* and Paul borrowed a soldier's clothes. Parts of "I Feel Fine" and "She's a Woman" can be seen in *Anthology*, though as usual the whole set's well worth seeing.

The author's emphasized this point a few times, but it's worth reiterating: though some critics have panned the Beatles as an unexciting live band, this is one of numerous clips that prove just the opposite. For the Beatles put on by far the best show of the many acts on the two hours of film that have circulated from this concert—and those acts included virtually all of their stiffest competition from Britain, among them the Rolling Stones, the Animals, the Kinks, Them, Donovan, Dusty Springfield, the Searchers, and the Moody Blues. (By the way, two hours of film also circulate from the similar all-star-studded 1964 *NME* concert, the other acts including the Stones, Searchers, Hollies, Manfred Mann, Gerry & the Pacemakers, Billy J. Kramer, and the Merseybeats.) Overlooked forerunners of sorts to the rock festivals of the late '60s and beyond, these concerts really should be issued officially in their entirety. It's just a tragedy that the Beatles were *not* filmed (at their request) when they did the *NME* concert for the last time on May 1, 1966—their final official British show ever.

● June 20

French television program Les Beatles
Palais des Sports, France

Twist and Shout

She's a Woman

I'm a Loser

Can't Buy Me Love

Baby's in Black

I Wanna Be Your Man

A Hard Day's Night

Everybody's Trying to Be My Baby

Rock and Roll Music

I Feel Fine

Ticket to Ride

Long Tall Sally

Along with their February 1964 Washington Coliseum gig and a pair of mid-1966 shows in Tokyo, this is—believe it or not—one of only four films of a complete (or virtually complete) actual live Beatles concert. Unfortunately, the circulating film, though perfectly watchable and boasting decent sound, is dark and wavy. It would be of note, however, for nothing else than including the only clips of live versions of "I'm a Loser" and "Everybody's Trying to Be My Baby." Apple cannily realized this, cherry-picking portions of those two songs (and nothing else from the concert) for the *Anthology* DVD/video, where (in common with several other performance clips used throughout the documentary) they were cleaned up considerably. "A Hard Day's Night," sung with fire by John, is another highlight, as—oddly enough—there's no other decent live version on film.

In general, the Beatles weren't as frenetic onstage in 1965 as they were in the first couple of years of Beatlemania. But as this film and others prove, they were still, basically, the best group around—both in the studio *and* in front of an audience. The playing and singing are usually mighty fine, and if the Beatles were getting bored of touring by this point, they don't show it. Look at how gleefully John and Paul dance around and share a mike during "I Wanna Be Your Man." Even George, by reputation the Beatle who got fed up with touring the most and the earliest, grins like he's having a whale of a time during his featured vocal, "Everybody's Trying to Be My Baby." If the Parisian audience supposedly gave the Beatles a cool reception during the band's first trip there in early 1964, they've certainly come around, chanting, clapping, and even (during "Can't Buy Me Love") singing along with a zest just short of abandon. And it certainly couldn't be put down to the group's halting attempts to announce some of the songs in French.

When this concert was broadcast on French TV, incidentally, the songs were resequenced and "I Feel Fine" was omitted. Fortunately, the program circulates in its original order, "I Feel Fine" included.

● August 1

UK television program Blackpool Night Out
ABC Theatre, Blackpool

I Feel Fine

I'm Down

Act Naturally

Ticket to Ride

Yesterday

Help!

Other than their January 30, 1969, rooftop concert, this was the last truly great, wholly live Beatles performance to be captured on film. It's often lazily asserted that the group's live work deteriorated almost from the time Beatlemania set in, but really, that's only audible and visible in their 1966 concert clips and recordings. They're still at the top of their game here, as they would be, in fact, for their final *Ed Sullivan* appearance on August 14, 1965 (which has been officially issued as part of the two-DVD set *The Four Historic Ed Sullivan Shows Featuring the Beatles*). This was tacitly acknowledged by Apple, who put recordings of four of the six songs (all except "I'm Down" and "Act Naturally") on the *Anthology 2* CD and used footage from every song except "I Feel Fine" in the *Anthology* video.

That means this particular clip might not be as thrilling for collectors as many of the others listed in this chapter, at least judged by the thrill of seeing something for the first time. On its own terms, however, it's a great sequence. It's the best version of "Act Naturally" the group did before the cameras (Paul particularly shining on backup vocals), boosted by Ringo's witty intro, "And now we'd like to do something we don't often do, give someone a chance to sing who doesn't often sing, and here he is all out of key and nervous, singing 'Act Naturally,' Ringo!" (Ringo would do the same schtick, almost verbatim, in his intro to "Act Naturally" a couple weeks later on *The Ed Sullivan Show*.) "I'm Down" is their best live version of that rocker ever, John sliding up and down the organ with his elbows. "Ticket to Ride," like their version from the *NME* concert in April, illustrates how well John and Paul could harmonize live, even if George flubs a bit of his guitar solo at the end of the bridge. Too bad John has to fake his way through words he forgets during "Help!", though as compensation you have him introducing the classic as "Our latest record, or our latest electronic noise, depending on whose side you're on."

It must have been an odd moment for the group when they premiered "Yesterday" here, as it was the first time they'd ceded the solo spotlight to one member in such a public forum. Paul sang it alone, on acoustic guitar, with (most likely) pre-recorded string backup, John and George leaving the stage, though Ringo, oddly, remained seated at the drums. George and John seem unperturbed, however, Harrison introducing him as follows: "And so for Paul McCartney of Liverpool, opportunity knocks!" Upon returning to the stage, John offers flowers to Paul, adding, "Thank you, Ringo, that was wonderful!" Joker John, however, takes the flowers back, leaving Paul holding cut stems—though Paul's stagey, amused reaction gives the impression the joke was worked out beforehand.

This particular performance, incidentally, had some personal meaning for Paul that remains unknown to most fans. An ex-girlfriend of his, Iris Caldwell (sister of Rory Storm, in whose band Ringo had drummed before joining the Beatles), had broken up with Paul in 1963. When Paul tried to call her, his mother told him Iris would not come to the phone because Paul had no feelings. The week of this broadcast, he called up Caldwell's mother to tell her (as reported in Steve Turner's *A Hard Day's Write: The Stories Behind Every Beatles' Song*), "You know that you said that I had no feelings? Watch the telly on Sunday and then tell me that I've got no feelings."

The Beatles, by the way, also did a spot of similar length for the *Blackpool Night Out* program in July 1964. But while the audio portion has been bootlegged (see entry on page 102), the film itself has not turned up.

● August 15

Television special The Beatles at Shea Stadium
Shea Stadium, New York City

Twist and Shout
I Feel Fine
Dizzy Miss Lizzy
Ticket to Ride
Can't Buy Me Love
Baby's in Black
A Hard Day's Night
Act Naturally
Help!
I'm Down

The Beatles' 1965 concert at Shea Stadium was undoubtedly a major event in their careers, as it was not only the biggest show they ever did, but the biggest *anyone* had ever done up to that point. The 50-minute TV documentary of the concert was a worthy cinematic record of the evening, including not only color footage of much of the Beatles' set, but also pre-show scenes and interviews with them and Brian Epstein. Despite its quality it can't be considered one of the very best Beatles films, for the simple reason that the music soundtrack isn't wholly live—though that information wasn't widely known for decades, and still isn't that widely known today.

The Beatles at Shea Stadium is not wholly devoted to the concert itself, nor does it include their entire set. After the clip of "I'm Down" near the beginning of the film, in fact, no onstage footage of the group is shown for about 20 minutes. This part of the movie instead takes in scenes of the growing hysteria as the fans gather and the band travels to the stadium by helicopter, the frenzy continuing to build as the quartet prepares backstage. Highlight, albeit a manufactured one: an MC's voice exults, "They'll be out in a few moments . . . they can't wait to make this their greatest appearance!" The onscreen image tells a different story: Ringo, slouching in the dressing room with a cigarette, looking as if he's about to fall asleep from boredom. There are also glimpses of opening acts King Curtis, Brenda Holloway, and the Brian Epstein–managed Sounds Incorporated (who also appeared in *Around the Beatles,* and some of whose members would play on the Beatles' "Good Morning, Good Morning") that actually hold some interest for serious all-around music fans. For footage of those artists isn't exactly plentiful, though the soul of Curtis and Holloway comes across far better than Sound Incorporated's segment, which somehow manages to be painfully lame and ludicrously raucous at the same time.

There is a *lot* of onstage footage of the Beatles, which does include most of their set (which, remember, was only about a half-hour long anyway). Their launch into "Twist and Shout" reminds us just how difficult it was to play in these circumstances, with relatively puny equipment and tens of thousands of people screaming their heads off. The instruments are notably out of tune, though the vocals are amazingly spot-on. And so it goes throughout the rest of the show—unavoid-

ably ragged, but performed with contagious exuberance. More than in any other of their 1965 live clips, the Beatles to a man are obviously getting an enormous charge out of the surroundings, which must have produced an adrenaline rush experienced by few professional entertainers. (Though that probably doesn't explain why John incorrectly introduces "Baby's in Black" as a track off the *Beatles VI* album.) Enhancing our own adrenaline rush, even 40 years later, are the intercuts to the audience. It's perhaps the wildest (and certainly the loudest) Beatlemania ever caught on film, complete with fainting girls getting carried away by policemen, who are also kept occupied chasing down interlopers who've managed to make it onto the baseball field. Observed George of the madness in a 1996 *Billboard* interview, "You can see in the film of Shea that there's a bit of us just playing to ourselves, because we were not quite sure if anybody can even *see* us, let alone hear us."

And there are few more thrilling Beatles concert sequences than the "I'm Down" finale, seen in two differently edited versions. While a sweat-soaked Paul screams his heart out in ecstasy, a demented John goes berserk with his elbow slides on the organ, he and George unable

The Beatles' legendary 1965 Shea Stadium concert was filmed and broadcast on British and American TV, but can now only be seen in its entirety on bootlegs such as this one.

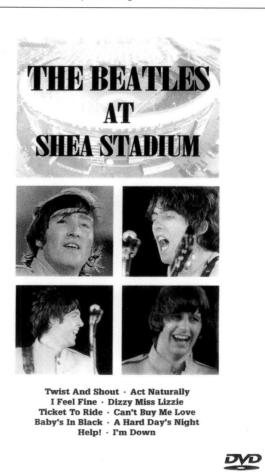

to contain their laughter on their backup vocals, especially when John deliberately sings a line a full octave lower than usual. "If you look at the film footage you can see how we reacted to the place," said Ringo in the 1990s in the *Anthology* book. "It was very big and very strange. I feel that on that show John cracked up. He went mad; not mentally ill, but he just got crazy. He was playing the piano with his elbows and it was really strange." Commented Lennon himself in a 1965 quote reproduced in *Anthology,* "I didn't really know what to do, because I felt naked without a guitar, so I was doing all Jerry Lee [Lewis]—I was jumping about and I only played about two bars of it."

Of the interview material (some of which is heard in voiceover), the most revealing is actually a passage from Brian Epstein in which he comments most astutely on the reasons for the Beatles' universal appeal. "I'm very much a Beatle fan," he proudly confesses. "In fact, I've always realized this, that I've always been, right since I've known them. I've felt, probably, everything that any Beatles fan"—here he chuckles, perhaps realizing that he's getting a little *too* revealing about his homosexuality, which was very much a secret to the public at the time—"*male* Beatles fan has ever felt. All the various things I've liked, I think, is what the fans have liked . . . the marvelous quality [of] the Beatles both in their music and in their general manner is that they in fact do original things, and new things, as they go along. Their songs are always new and different, and so are their performances, in sort of different, small, subtle ways." Although these observations are uniformly accepted today, back then few adults could see that the group's unparalleled thirst for change and artistic evolution was a key to their astronomical popularity and influence. While Epstein has sometimes been criticized for failing to appreciate the full dimension of the Beatles' aesthetic sensibilities, this comment seems proof enough that such accusations hold no merit.

Many viewers watching the film today marvel that the Beatles were able to play as well as they did. Part of the reason they sound as relatively good as they do here, however, is that what you're hearing was not precisely what they played that night. It was decided that the music wasn't up to scratch for what would be a widely screened film, shown twice on the BBC in 1966 and then in January 1967 by ABC in the States. So on January 5, 1966, at CTS Studios in London, Paul overdubbed new bass parts on "Dizzy Miss Lizzy," "Can't Buy Me Love," "Baby's in Black," and "I'm Down"; John overdubbed a new organ track on "I'm Down"; and totally new versions of "I Feel Fine" and "Help!" were done. For "Twist and Shout," tape made at the Hollywood Bowl in 1965 was used, and for "Act Naturally," the actual record was overdubbed. The only number heard in the film not to be doctored was "A Hard Day's Night," which was largely obscured by interview voiceovers anyway. "She's a Woman" and "Everybody's Trying to Be My Baby," which the Beatles did play at Shea, aren't in the film at all (though the audio of the latter song appears on the *Anthology 2* CD).

According to Beatles personal assistant Tony Bramwell's memoir, *Magical Mystery Tours: My Life with the Beatles* (co-written with Rosemary Kingsland), he and Brian Epstein determined the overdubbing was needed after screening the movie. Bramwell also remembered that he and George Martin arranged the overdubbing at CTS Studios, Martin deliberately not informing EMI lest they try to put a stop to it. As to why "Twist and Shout" wasn't given overdubs, according to Bramwell's account, John was "fed up" with the time all the painstaking post-synchronization was taking, and left early to go to a party instead!

Despite the audio trickery, *The Beatles at Shea Stadium* remains an exciting, even essential document of the group at one of the most famous concerts of the 20th century. It's been theorized that Apple has remastered the whole film for possible DVD release, and that the company might also have the movie with the original undubbed soundtrack, though the footage with the original sound (which would make an excellent bonus DVD feature) might not be used if it's made commercially available. Which, as of this writing in early 2006, it's not—leaving, once again, bootleggers to meet the demand for a product that inexplicably remains off the shelves.

● November 1–2

UK TV special The Music of Lennon and McCartney
Granada TV Centre, Manchester

There's no live Beatles music in this 45-minute program, although the boys are seen miming "Day Tripper" and "We Can Work It Out," and Paul (who does a lip-synced verse of "Yesterday" on his own) and John do a few awkwardly contrived introductions and announcements. Why

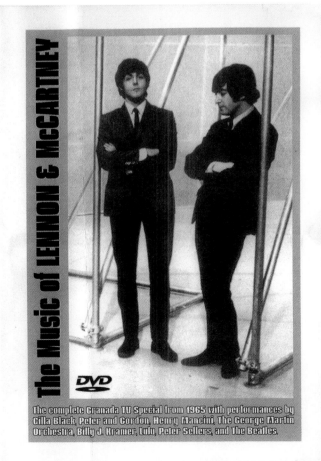

An unauthorized DVD release of the British TV special The Music of Lennon & McCartney, *filmed in November 1965.*

list it here, then? Well, for the sheer bizarre fascination of seeing a parade of artists, both well-suited and ill-equipped, tackle a series of Lennon and McCartney compositions in a program that seems designed to demonstrate how many ways they can be interpreted. Though all of the presentations are hokey to some degree (complete with period Swinging London dancers), a few come off reasonably well. Peter & Gordon's "A World Without Love," Billy J. Kramer's "Bad to Me," and Cilla Black's "It's for You," after all, had actually been expressly given to those artists to record. American soul-pop singer Esther Phillips's "And I Love Him" was one of the relatively few covers the Beatles themselves enthusiastically endorsed. And Lulu's raunchy, sassy "I Saw Him Standing There" is a real highlight, especially as she never officially released a version of the song on record.

On the other hand, you have to put up with Antonio Vargas doing "She Loves You" as a Spanish flamenco, Fritz Spiegl's Ensemble's classical medley of "She Loves You"/"I'll Get You," Henry Mancini's piano rendition of "If I Fell," Marianne Faithfull's surprisingly disappointing "Yesterday," and Dick Rivers's so-dumb-it's-fun French interpretation of "Things We Said Today." George Martin's here too, leading an orchestra through bland versions of "This Boy" and "I Feel Fine." As needed comic relief, however, there's Peter Sellers's "A Hard Day's Night," spoken (not sung) with Shakespearean drama—a genuinely funny, can-you-believe-this-actually-happened performance. (And, believe it or not, the record Sellers made of this "A Hard Day's Night" recitation went all the way up to No. 14 in the British charts in early 1966.)

John and Paul don't seem terribly enamored of the project during their segments, where they go through the motions of delivering corny scripted dialogue, though it's a hoot to hear excerpts (from discs) of their songs being mauled by Anthony Newley, singing chipmunks, and Japanese, Italian, Swedish, and French artists. Paul later confirmed, in fact, that they did the show partly as a favor to producer Johnny Hamp, who'd put them on television back when their recording career had just started. John, for his part, expressed regret that Peggy Lee, Ella Fitzgerald, and Keely Smith were unavailable for the program. While it's not known whether this went through their minds then, it wouldn't be a surprise if it were at just around this time that they determined it wasn't necessary, at least as a group, to put on smiley faces and go through the paces on variety shows anymore. And for the remainder of their career, they didn't—although each one of them would appear, individually, on such variety shows during their solo careers, Paul and Ringo even hosting variety specials of their own.

● November 23

Promo films for:

We Can Work It Out (three versions)
Day Tripper (two versions)
Help! (one version)
Ticket to Ride (one version)
I Feel Fine (two versions)
Twickenham Film Studios, London

As one indication of the Beatles' desire to stop doing the variety show go-round, as well as a symptom of their growing, unprecedented power within the business, they determined in late 1965 to stop promoting singles with television appearances. Instead, they would send *film* of them playing the singles (or cavorting to the music on those singles) for network television stations to broadcast. Not many, if any, other acts could have gotten away with this in the mid-'60s. But such was the Beatles' popularity that television decision-makers knew the promo films would be about as hot ratings spikers as live spots anyway.

The group *did* actually make a couple of other appearances that were transmitted live, one to mime to "Paperback Writer" on *Top of the Pops* on June 16, 1966, the other to perform (with assistance from some pre-recorded backing tracks) "All You Need Is Love" for worldwide broadcast on June 25, 1967. Too, the promo for "Hey Jude," though not broadcast live, was at least performed live (with the assistance of pre-recorded backing tracks) before an audience. In large part, however, the Beatles were through with promoting their recordings in the conventional manner. This first batch was done principally to push their upcoming double-sided chart-topper ("We Can Work It Out"/"Day Tripper"), the group taking the opportunity to film similar clips for their three previous singles while they were at it.

Though it's always fun to see the Beatles together in almost any context, these first outings into music videos of sorts (all in black and

The cover of this DVD compilation of rare 1965 clips shows the Beatles filming a batch of promos for several singles at once in Twickenham Film Studios that November.

The Beatles' Promo Films

From the end of 1965 through 1970, most of the A-sides from Beatles singles—and, sometimes, their B-sides—were promoted with short films produced especially for television. This saved the group the considerable effort of having to travel (even if it was just to a London studio) to plug their records, which would have been a bothersome interruption at a time when their work in the studio was becoming particularly intense and time-consuming. The reasoning, roughly speaking, was that if the Beatles weren't going to tour they'd send out the promo films to tour instead, with the advantage of being able to have them shown nationally in the UK and US, as well as in different parts of the world.

Many critics have hailed these promos as pioneering efforts that not only helped create the whole concept of music video, but elevated it to an art form. This author, however, takes a somewhat dissenting position. It's certainly better to have some footage of the Beatles performing these songs (or, in the promos where they don't even play instruments, some sort of footage of the group from the era to accompany those songs) than none at all. That doesn't mean, however, that many of the videos aren't full of contrivances that aren't corny or dated in some way, such as obviously mimed performances, colorful but not particularly meaningful costumes and decorations, or close-ups of the band members striking poses not particularly or at all related to the record. It can also be pointed out that these kinds of videos were by no means unknown before 1965. Many artists from France, the UK, and sometimes even the US had filmed similarly structured (though far cheesier) Scopitones for video jukeboxes in the early '60s, and brief promo clips for other artists had been filmed for television or cinemas even prior to that. To be even more of a killjoy, it can also be pointed out that pioneering music videos is not necessarily a feat to be enormously proud of, given the low (and often puerile) standard of many such items in the last few decades, especially after the rise of MTV.

Still, the Beatles did put some creativity into some of their clips, particularly the psychedelic-surrealistic ones for "Strawberry Fields Forever"/"Penny Lane." These too are dated in a way, but at the time, they were pretty far out, and also important vehicles for announcing to the world at large that the group had ditched (permanently, as it turned out) their cheerful moptop image. The clips for "Hey Jude" and "Revolution" were hugely enjoyable quasi-live performances (though only the vocals were truly "live"), and even the sillier or more mundane spots ("Hello, Goodbye," "Lady Madonna") preserve for the ages just how the Beatles looked and dressed at a specific time in their trajectory.

Every A-side (or half of a double-A-side, in some cases) from "I Feel Fine" to "Let It Be" is represented by at least one promo clip, with the odd exception of the 1966 double-A-sided "Yellow Submarine"/"Eleanor Rigby." Several B-sides—"Rain," "Revolution," "Don't Let Me Down"—were also accorded the honor. While a two-DVD set of every single promo film, all multiple versions included, would not make for the most exciting Beatles archival video release, it would certainly be a pleasant and valuable one. As with so many other such Beatles video projects, however, there hasn't been such a compilation, despite an obvious market for it. And as with so many other such Beatles video projects, that's left a gap for bootleggers to exploit, with numerous bootleg DVD releases conveniently assembling copies of most or all of them into a single package, though it would be far better to have an anthology that mastered the films from the best available sources.

white) weren't all that auspicious, unless you find the mere idea of a group self-consciously making fun of the whole miming process groundbreaking. That's what they do throughout most of the proceedings, not making a pretense of trying to exactly match their singing and playing to the soundtrack. "We Can Work It Out" and "Day Tripper" are fairly straightforward clips of the group playing their instruments on a sparse studio set with vaguely pop art decorations. A dash of surrealism (by 1965 pop group standards at any rate), however, makes its way into one of the versions of "Day Tripper," where Ringo (standing with George in a railroad car) waves his drumsticks without a kit in sight, at some point wielding a saw to cut through some of the obviously fake scenery. A third version of "Day Tripper" was done on this date, incidentally, but it has not yet circulated among collectors.

Things get even more nonchalantly silly on one version of "I Feel Fine," performed amid exercise equipment and on which Ringo doesn't even drum (though he pedals a stationary bike diligently). Nor does he bring his drums to the "Help!" clip, on which the four sit behind each other on a board as if they're a crew team, Ringo holding an umbrella for no apparent reason—until some fake snow falls at the end of the clip, in a low-budget foreshadowing of the non sequitur imagery that was to become standard in the MTV era. There is, by the way, another "Help!" clip sometimes billed as a promo film. But this is just the sequence from the movie *Help!* in which they play the song, though without the darts thrown at the screen in the full-length feature (hence its frequent designation as, we kid you not, the "dartless" version).

Truly weird (and not just "look how weird we are"), however, is the second version of "I Feel Fine," in which the four don't make any attempts to play or sing whatsoever, instead stuffing their faces with greasy fish and chips, seemingly oblivious to any promo obligations (even faked ones). Image-conscious Brian Epstein did not want this version (done while the Beatles were supposed to be on break) distributed, but it's easily available on bootleg DVD/video anyway. In a way, it could be said to show a more human side of the band than most of what they filmed—though many fans prefer to see them in their publicly charismatic poses, not mundanely stuffing their faces like everyday people do.

1966

● May 19, 1966

Promo films for:

Paperback Writer (four versions)

Rain (three versions)

Studio One, Abbey Road, London

The Beatles were filmed in the recording studio for these black-and-white clips promoting the "Paperback Writer"/"Rain" single, doing multiple versions of each. Which version you might have seen back in 1966 depended on where you were living and what television station you were watching, and it would be difficult if not impossible to track down where each individual version was used. These did serve the purpose, however, of offering television outlets a choice. In addition, one version each of "Paperback Writer" and "Rain" was done (on the following day; see May 20, 1966, entry) in color, though the rest were in black and white.

These are straightforward lip-synced performance clips, with miming that's more conscientious than on the batch of promos they'd done in November 1965. There isn't, however, anything too exciting or innovative, though at the time they did serve as kind of a subtle announcement that the group was becoming more casual about their image, no longer dressing in uniform fashion and donning odd (by the standards of the era), various-shaped sunglasses. As far as unusual features to pick out, you'll notice that Paul has an ugly front chipped tooth, the result of a recent moped accident, though it would be fixed by the time the group went on tour in June. And you'll have to freeze-frame to catch this one, but note the photo transparencies Paul's holding near the beginning

of the color version; the image is from the sessions for the infamous "butcher cover" for the US album *Yesterday . . . and Today.*

These clips (as well as the ones for the same songs shot elsewhere the following day) were directed by Michael Lindsay-Hogg, who would work with the Beatles for more promos in 1968 and, most famously, direct *Let It Be.* When the color versions were shown on *The Ed Sullivan Show,* the Beatles also sent a brief spoken introduction that survives, Ringo apologizing for not being there in person, as "everybody's busy these days with the washing and the cooking."

Though the color sequences in particular are seen as fairly innovative music video precursors, Lindsay-Hogg revealed in a 2000 interview with Bill DeYoung (posted on www.billdeyoung.com) that there had been plans for something more ambitious: "When we did 'Paperback Writer,' I'd wanted to have a kind of story video, like Paul playing a writer or something in his little garret," he remembered. "But Brian Epstein didn't want that. He said story videos had no future and that the audience wanted to see them play."

● May 20, 1966

Promo films for:

Paperback Writer

Rain

Chiswick House, London

The Beatles on Top of the Pops *on June 16, 1966: a film clip that remains unfound.*

The Beatles filmed one additional version each of "Paperback Writer" and "Rain," both in color, in the park-like grounds of Chiswick House. These are more ambitious than the previous day's clips at EMI; instead of just being straight shots of the band performing, they make use of a beautiful English natural setting that allows the band to strike various poses without their instruments. It's still pretty artificial, but the Beatles carry it off with dignity, and the color's beautiful. The color wasn't fully appreciated, however, until gloriously restored, slightly edited versions were used in *Anthology,* with "Rain" incorporating some previously unseen outtake shots. They're more proof that an official DVD compilation of promos with extras could be assembled that would wipe out the underground market for them, should those with the power ever decide to take the plunge. Film of the group's live appearance (albeit lip-synced to the record) to play "Paperback Writer" and "Rain" on *Top of the Pops* on June 16, 1966, by the way, has never been found.

● June 24

German television special Die Beatles
Circus-Krone-Bau, Munich

Rock and Roll Music
She's a Woman (fragment)
Baby's in Black
I Feel Fine
Yesterday
Nowhere Man
I'm Down

Though the two shows the Beatles filmed a week later in Tokyo (see entries below) are much more widely known, this is another good-looking document of their 1966 world tour. It's in black and white (whereas the Japanese gigs were filmed in color), but otherwise it's well shot and circulates in very good condition. Unfortunately, as this is just the second show of a tour that the Beatles probably weren't all that thrilled to be on in the first place, it's also erratically and sometimes sloppily performed. The performances preserved by the Tokyo films (particularly the first) have been critically mauled for those exact reasons, though in this Munich clip's favor, the group looks like they're having a better time here than in Japan.

In all, however, this film's not terrible, and some of the problems can be attributed to the substandard sound balance, with John's vocal notably undermiked on the opening "Rock and Roll Music." It's the first (and one of the only three, actually) of the full-band, live, string-less arrangements of "Yesterday" (introduced by George, incorrectly, as a song from *Beatles for Sale*) to survive on film. "Nowhere Man," despite more problems with the vocal sound balance, isn't bad at all, with some fine harmonies that are lamentably clouded at points by a poor sound mix; in fact, it was deemed good enough to include in *Anthology.* They make a mess, though—if amusingly so—of "I'm Down," where Paul totally screws up both the words and the order of the verses. John actually cues him with some of the opening lines right before the song starts—whereupon McCartney goes into the *second* verse, not the first. And considering how often the Beatles sang "I Feel Fine," was it really that hard to coordinate the lead and backup vocals so that they were singing the same lyrics?

Only a few seconds of "She's a Woman" are heard, by the way, and a few other songs played at the concert ("If I Needed Someone," "Paperback Writer," "Day Tripper," and "I Wanna Be Your Man") aren't heard at all; there's also a noticeable, sloppy edit that cuts out most of

The Beatles performing at the Circus, Krone-Bau in Munich on June 24, 1966, one of the first shows of their world tour that year. Much of the evening show on this date was broadcast on German television.

the last part of "I'm Down." It's doubtful the whole filmed concert will surface, as word is that the uncut version no longer exists. When this material is bootlegged, it's often packaged with footage from the same German TV program of support acts Cliff Bennett & the Rebel Rousers, the Rattles (a German band), and Peter & Gordon. If you're into Beatles-related rarities, Peter & Gordon's wholly live version (with horns) of the single Paul McCartney wrote for them, "Woman," is the standout, though Gordon Waller gives up playing guitar partway through the number and fusses with his suit as though he's in a sauna.

● June 30

For Japanese television special The Beatles Recital,
From Nippon Budokan Hall, Tokyo
Nippon Budokan Hall, Tokyo

Rock and Roll Music
She's a Woman
If I Needed Someone
Day Tripper
Baby's in Black
I Feel Fine
Yesterday
I Wanna Be Your Man
Nowhere Man
Paperback Writer
I'm Down

The biggest act in the world plays the most prestigious venue in Japan, filmed in color for television—and somehow, they can't manage to supply the Beatles with microphones that will stay in place. That's only one of the problems afflicting this concert, often used as Exhibit A in proof of how the group's onstage playing and enthusiasm had deteriorated by 1966. It's not as bad as you might have been led to believe by some accounts, but it's probably the worst of the major live Beatles films, though ironically it's one of the best in terms of image quality, audio fidelity, and camerawork. It's not common knowledge on this side of the pond, but it was actually released officially by Apple in Japan on home video and laserdisc as *Beatles Concert at Budokan 1966,* though it's never come out elsewhere.

The failure of their vocal mikes to stay in place *is* a problem and maybe one that was rattling the Beatles on this occasion, though they usually dealt with such setbacks in stride. Still, their slow slides away from the Beatles' mouths during much of the show starts to get comical after a while, the singers sometimes nearly colliding when two of them share a single mike while they're attempting to angle themselves in position. Paul, to his credit, puts up with it amazingly well, repeatedly taking a hand off his bass to slap the mike back into place (especially during "Paperback Writer"), never becoming visibly annoyed. But it had to become a distraction after a while, and is perhaps partly to account for the group's troubles in sticking to a steady tempo throughout much of the set.

A bigger flaw, however, is the palpable lack of enthusiasm on all of their parts, except the ever-dependable, showman-like McCartney. Ringo looks incredibly bored and indifferent; it's hard to believe it's the same guy who, only about two and a half years earlier, was grinning,

shaking his head, and pummeling like a boxer at their first US concert in Washington Coliseum. John and George don't *look* bummed out, but much of their singing has a strangely weary, lugubrious quality, as if they've just been roused out of bed. It's especially evident on some of the harmonies, which have a moaning, almost sickly flavor, as if the lads haven't gotten over jet lag. George's guitar also often has an anemic, got-up-off-the-wrong-side-of-bed tone, and barely seems to be sticking to any set pattern at all on the dissonant solo for "I Wanna Be Your Man." And though this has, believe it or not, the first footage of the Beatles performing a George Harrison composition in concert, George does a frankly awful, wavering, off-key job with "If I Needed Someone," where it sometimes seems his mind's not on the song at all.

There are also more mundane bugs like wrong notes and shaky harmonies. "Day Tripper" is downright lousy—something you can say of very few filmed versions of any Beatles song—and they're really out of time with each other on "Paperback Writer," although (due in part to the presence of 3,000 police) there's much less deafening screaming from the audience than at most Beatles concerts. There are some truly abysmal harmonies from John and George on "Paperback Writer," in which you can see Harrison stop playing and wave frantically at the crowd at one point, as he does several times in the Tokyo movies. In the *Anthology* video, George admitted such gestures were made in part to generate screams that would cover their flubs. Paul, more diplomatic as ever, noted that the harmonies of "Paperback Writer" and "Nowhere Man" were simply hard to reproduce in concert. True, the intricate three-part harmonies on "This Boy" had given them no trouble in 1964. But now the Beatles were using yet additional harmony overdubs in the studio that added up to more than three parts.

As Neil Aspinall summarized in the *Anthology* book, "For the first time in a long while the audience could hear. There was no loud screaming, which came as a surprise: the band suddenly realized they were out of tune and they had to get their act together." And the show they filmed at the same venue the following day (see next entry) was indeed better, though still hardly one for the ages.

● July 1

For Japanese TV special The Beatles Recital,
From Nippon Budokan Hall, Tokyo
Nippon Budokan Hall, Tokyo

Rock and Roll Music
She's a Woman
If I Needed Someone
Day Tripper
Baby's in Black
I Feel Fine
Yesterday
I Wanna Be Your Man
Nowhere Man
Paperback Writer
I'm Down

The film of the Beatles' June 30 Tokyo concert was not satisfactory, owing both to the roving microphone problems and the group's own instrumental and vocal inadequacies. So this gig at the same venue was filmed the next day, and while some of the same sluggishness and lack of tightness remained, it was an appreciably better effort. The pesky microphones had been fixed, for one thing. But overall, it almost seems as though the Beatles were finally shaking off some sort of jet lag. If they're not nearly as bubbly as they had been in earlier years, they at least seem reasonably happy to be there, and not like prisoners forced to perform for their captors. The two shows, incidentally, can easily be differentiated from each other by the color of their suits, which are dark in the June 30 film and light in the July 1 film—indeed, they're often labeled as "dark suits" and "light suits" versions on bootleg copies.

For all its shortcomings, this film would be valuable for including the best of the few available live versions of "Day Tripper" (done *much* better than they had managed a day earlier), "Paperback Writer," and "Yesterday." John, too, seems to be getting closer to actually starting "I Feel Fine" with something simulating the feedback heard on the record, though the tone his guitar emits has a flutter unlike the sound on the studio version. George never did seem to get a grip on "If I Needed Someone," however, and his lead vocal is still crummy, especially near the end of the second bridge where it sounds like he almost can't be bothered to finish the line (not that he seems to mind,

The two Beatles concerts filmed in Tokyo by Japanese TV have been packaged together in their entirety, but only on unauthorized video releases.

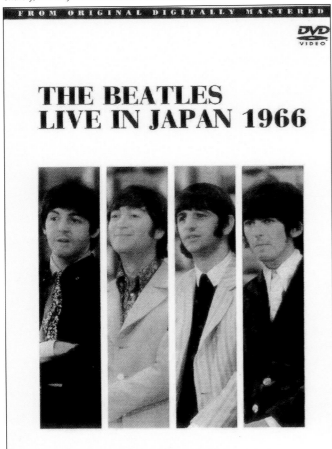

sporting a wide grin as he ducks away from the mike at that very moment). As "If I Needed Someone" was the only Harrison original the Beatles did live, you'd think George would have some vested interest in doing a good job. But then, George was the Beatle most eager to stop touring, and judging from the evidence on the screen, he just didn't care at this point.

Why Apple chose to release the considerably inferior June 30 show on home/video laserdisc for its Japan-only *Beatles Concert at Budokan* while bypassing the July 1 concert altogether is another one of those mini-mysteries that only those overseeing the group's catalog could answer. As is the question of why both shows aren't combined together on an official DVD release, though it may be that Paul, Ringo, and the estates of George and John are still somewhat embarrassed by its flaws after all these years.

Hard as it is to believe, unless you count their rooftop concert on January 30, 1969 (which was actually seen by few human beings), there would be no more film of a high standard documenting the Beatles in front of a concert audience. There's some newsreel and home movie footage of parts of subsequent shows on their 1966 world tour, including their last concert at Candlestick Park in San Francisco on August 29. But the most interesting Beatles film clips from the last half of 1966 would show the group talking, not performing—whether it was John Lennon trying to explain (at an August 11 press conference in Chicago) his remark about the Beatles being more popular than Jesus; their lengthy press conference on August 24 in Los Angeles, the final such event that the Beatles did as a touring band of which film circulates; or the December 20, 1966, interviews with each Beatle on the doorstep of Abbey Road, where they were becoming immersed in recording *Sgt. Pepper.* In keeping with their retreat into the studio, when the Beatles next appeared on film in a musical context, there would be no attempt to even mimic a conventional performance situation.

1967

● January 30–31

Promo film for:

Strawberry Fields Forever
Knole Park, Sevenoaks

Probably the most creative, and popular, of the Beatles' promo films were the ones they did for "Strawberry Fields Forever" and "Penny Lane" in early 1967. This was as much for the way the group looked as the imagery and the music, since it was really the first time they were widely seen in their psychedelic guise worldwide, complete with moustaches and colorful (and for the time, outlandish) clothes. Of course "Strawberry Fields Forever" itself was a very unexpected evolution of the band's music, and was here complemented by a surreal (again, by 1967 standards at least) parade of disconnected scenes.

Shot in beautiful Knole Park in Sevenoaks, Kent, the Beatles are shown walking backwards and running in slow motion in a patch that's largely bare except for some kettledrums, a dead oak tree, and

JUNE 25, 1967 ● *A Selective Guide* **323**

a cobwebbed piano (over which they pour paint near the end). Some nighttime shots added an eerie overlay, and the bit where Paul jumps backwards into the tree, though gimmicky, is at least in keeping with the "nothing is real" ethos of the lyrics. Overseeing the clip was Swedish television director Peter Goldmann, recommended by their old friend Klaus Voormann. Goldmann would later recall that the Fabs' finery was not artificially exaggerated specially for the filming, noting that of the seven changes of clothes, all came from their own wardrobes except four red coats bought specially for the production.

It was while filming in Sevenoaks, as is well known by Beatles folklorists, that John Lennon came upon the poster in an antiques store that would provide the inspiration (and, indeed, many of the actual words) for "Being for the Benefit of Mr. Kite." Although much of the clip appears in *Anthology,* the complete version circulates on many unauthorized videos/DVDs.

● February 5 and 7

Promo film for:

Penny Lane
Angel Lane, London, and Knole Park, Sevenoaks

Also directed by Peter Goldmann, the promo clip for "Penny Lane" wasn't quite as weird or memorable as the one for "Strawberry Fields Forever," but did likewise use unusual psychedelic and non-linear imagery. There are more of the standard close-up shots of individual Beatles here, and while John's seen strolling down a public street it's not Penny Lane, but Angel Lane in London (though shots of the real Penny Lane, without any of the band members, were inserted). It's not devoid of abstract scenes, however, the highlight being when the red-coated four (in a return to Knole Park) ride horses to have tea on a table with a white cloth and candles in the middle of an otherwise deserted field. Butlers in powdered wigs (played by roadie Mal Evans and personal assistant Tony Bramwell, who was by now involved in production of the group's promo videos) "serve" them guitars, whereupon John capsizes the mini-banquet—not much to do with "Penny Lane" but a good touch nonetheless. Of the horses ridden by the Beatles, incidentally, all are white except George's, which is black. So why didn't this give rise to "George Is Dead" rumors, as did the scene in *Magical Mystery Tour* where Paul wore a black carnation?

While the "Penny Lane"/"Strawberry Fields Forever" single was a No. 1 hit in the US, it's often forgotten that not all their fans took an instant liking to the band's new image. A segment of *American Bandstand* survives in which Dick Clark screens both promo clips for his teenage audience, passing around the mike afterward to solicit comments on what they've just seen. Some kids are baffled or even disappointed, grousing, "They looked older and it ruins their image . . . they're ugly . . . it reminded me of Hollywood about a hundred years ago . . . their moustaches are weird . . . they're as bad as the Monkees . . . they just looked different than they used to . . . they looked like somebody's grandfather!" The hipper fans, however, dig it fine, one boy asserting, "They have the right to look any way they want!" At any rate, with the Beatles becoming if anything even more popular by the end of the decade, most of the naysayers likely got used to the new look very quickly.

● February 10

Promo film for:

A Day in the Life
Studio One, Abbey Road, London

On the day dramatic orchestration was overdubbed onto "A Day in the Life," seven cameras were on hand to film the session. The clip that resulted included no live music, instead matching excerpts to the classic *Sgt. Pepper* studio recording of the song. The rapid-fire editing of super-brief scenes—mostly from the studio, although a few outdoor images of London life were also inserted—combined with a handheld, blurry quality to create a fairly convincing, suitably psychedelic effect.

Even if the conceit of creating quasi-psychedelia from such shots isn't your cup of tea, the segment's valuable for providing a genuine glimpse of the Beatles at work in the studio during *Sgt. Pepper*. Admittedly, their "work" on this date did not involve playing instruments but roving around Studio One, communicating with the musicians and schmoozing with friends they'd invited to the session, including Donovan, Mick Jagger, Keith Richards, Marianne Faithfull, George's wife Patti, members of the Fool (who did psychedelic design work for Apple that was notoriously excessive), and Mike Nesmith of the Monkees. Looking even odder than the psychedelic-era Beatles on this one occasion were the orchestra musicians, wearing fake noses and other novelty-shop props to get into the spirit of the piece. Yet somehow, the image that sticks with this viewer the most is not the flower-power haze, but the three-second bit in which a distraught, gate-crashing, ordinary fan (who looks a little like, but certainly is not, Lulu) is roughly ejected from the premises by Neil Aspinall. The Beatles might have been holding a psychedelic party, but it was a pretty exclusive one.

The idea was apparently to use this clip as part of a *Sgt. Pepper* television special that never materialized. It's been suggested that the BBC "banned" the clip because of what they deemed to be too-controversial drug references in the lyrics, as they had done for BBC radio airplay. But it's arguable whether the clip would have been screened on its own in the first place, as it was made for an album track, not a single. It seems more likely that it was shelved because the television special fizzled out. Or maybe, with the *Magical Mystery Tour* idea starting to germinate a few months later, the Beatles—always hungry to look into the future instead of wallowing in the recent past—preferred to move on to that television special rather than work on a *Sgt. Pepper* program.

For many years, this was a wholly "lost" clip, its very existence known to few. It's hardly a secret now, though: most (though not quite all) of it is included in *Anthology.*

● June 25

Television program Our World
Studio One, Abbey Road, London

All You Need Is Love

Although strictly speaking this wasn't an official promo clip, what better promotion could the "All You Need Is Love" single have than being broadcast by satellite to hundreds of millions of people? (And promotion, in a larger sense, for something much bigger than a hit single, George Harrison calling it "a subtle bit of PR for God" in the *Anthology* book.) Rebroadcast many times since the summer of 1967, and included in several documentaries, it's the best footage of the Beatles in the psychedelic period. For one thing, much (though not all) of what they're singing and playing is actually live, albeit with orchestral accompaniment and the help of some pre-recorded backing tracks. For another, it captures Flower Power at its zenith, with enough irreverence to avoid pomposity, what with the sandwich boards of lyrics, the florid clothing and decor, and celebrity guests in the form of Mick Jagger, Marianne Faithfull, Donovan, Keith Moon, Graham Nash, and Eric Clapton. (It's rarely been noted, incidentally, that Jagger was sentenced to jail, though he was quickly bailed out, for trumped-up charges of drug possession just five days later. If he was in a good enough mood to take part and clap along in such a happy-go-lucky TV shoot just five days earlier, one would guess that he was not at all expecting to serve time, and that the viciousness of the verdict must have been a tremendous, surprising shock to him.)

Most of the clip, including the entire performance of the song, is included (in a mostly colorized version; the original was in black and white) in *Anthology*. A little bit more of the preamble (also broadcast live), in which the Beatles, George Martin, and engineer Geoff Emerick can be seen preparing for the performance, is available on the full version (with voice-over intro by announcer Steve Race). And as small a bonus as that portion is, it's worth it just for the bit where John Lennon, warming up for his vocal, sings the chorus of "She Loves You" only to have his voice break wildly—though it's never been revealed whether that was for intentional comic effect or out of genuine nervousness.

● November 10

Promo films for:

Hello Goodbye (three versions)
Saville Theatre, London

The least striking and most conventional of the promo films for 1967 Beatles singles are these clips for "Hello Goodbye," shot at the Saville Theatre (which had been leased by Brian Epstein to present shows shortly before his death) and directed by Paul McCartney. These are straight mimed performances, the main attraction being the only chance to see the Beatles performing in their *Sgt. Pepper* uniforms. This dominates the most widely seen version (screened on *The Ed Sullivan Show* a couple of weeks later), though there are also funny insertions of the group wearing their 1963 collarless suits and waving cheekily at the camera. The Hawaiian-dressed dancers at the end are a nice touch, matching the actual musical flavor of that coda.

A sequence featuring the Beatles recording "All You Need Is Love" was broadcast live by satellite to hundreds of millions of viewers around the world on June 25, 1967.

A second version of the Beatles in "street" clothes (which were still more fashionably psychedelic than what almost anyone else was wearing in late 1967) was also done, and yet a third version combines shots from the other two clips with different footage. The third version is actually the best, as it gives you a chance to see the Beatles in all the guises they donned for this promo shoot: the *Sgt. Pepper* uniforms, the "everyday" clothes, and the 1963 Beatlemania suits, plus the bonuses of John wildly dancing the Charleston and the Hawaiian-style dancers at the finale. The version in *Anthology,* if you're curious, is mostly drawn from the most common one with the *Sgt. Pepper* costumes, though material from all three clips was edited together in the coda.

For a relatively uncomplicated production, the promos caused their fair share of headaches for the Beatles in Britain, where a Musicians Union ban on miming prevented them from being broadcast. Because no one could be seen playing the viola in the "Hello Goodbye" promo, George Martin even prepared a special viola-less mix for the soundtrack to create the impression that the song was being performed live, but the miming was still so apparent that this version wasn't aired either. When *Top of the Pops* aired a promo on December 7, it was cobbled together from still photographs and scenes of the group editing *Magical Mystery Tour* footage. Yet another version exists that doesn't circulate, constructed by *Magical Mystery Tour* editor Roy Benson from footage taken during the making of that movie.

Magical Mystery Tour itself could be said to contain several music videos that could have been considered promo films if they were isolated from the rest of the program, particularly the sequence for "I Am the Walrus." Considering that more than ten hours of footage were shot for *Magical Mystery Tour,* and that some outtakes from the production showed up in *Anthology,* there's no doubt surplus material that might make for good DVD extras. This is yet another Beatles project with a sizable, captive audience that is, however, unavailable in the US as of this writing. Some silent footage from the *Magical Mystery Tour* filming, shot by Mal Evans, has shown up on fairly obscure, commercially available videos, but these essentially amount to home movies, and not very interesting ones.

1968

● February 11, 1968

Promo films for:

Lady Madonna (two versions)
Hey Bulldog
Studio Three, Abbey Road, London

Maybe it was because they were in a hurry to wrap things up before their already delayed trip to study TM with the Maharishi in India, but the "Lady Madonna" promo clips were considerably less ambitious than their 1967 ones. The soundtrack of the single was simply matched to images of the Beatles recording at the studio. It's been suggested that this may have been done, at least in part, to get around the problems of the miming ban that had prevented the "Hello Goodbye"

clips from being broadcast in the UK. While the end result isn't that creative, at least it gives you shots of the Beatles working together in the studio and, to all indications, getting along famously. This could have been the very last such session of their career in that regards, as tensions would enter the picture almost from the start of *The White Album,* largely due to the omnipresence of Yoko Ono. (John, incidentally, recalled the "Hey Bulldog" session as the first attended by Ono in his early-'70s *Rolling Stone* interview, though she's not visible in any of the shots in this film.)

It wasn't noticed (or at least commented upon) at the time, but "Lady Madonna" was actually *not* the song the Beatles were recording in this footage. That track was actually "Hey Bulldog," which ended up not even as the B-side, but as part of the *Yellow Submarine* soundtrack. The head of Apple's film division, Denis O'Dell, told *MOJO* that he'd "spent a few days coming up with ideas for 'Lady Madonna', [but] when the Beatles wanted to get on with recording 'Hey Bulldog,' all that went out the window!" Cannily enough, when *Yellow Submarine* was reissued for theatrical release in 1999, Apple took some of the original footage to construct yet a third promo film, this time synced to "Hey Bulldog," and distributed it as publicity for the *Yellow Submarine* movie relaunch.

● Circa Early March

RAI 1 Italian television footage
Rishikesh, India

When the Saints Go Marching In
You Are My Sunshine
Jingle Bells
She'll Be Comin' Around the Mountain
Happiness Runs
Instrumental
Blowin' in the Wind
Hare Krishna Mantra
O Sole Mio
It's Now or Never
Catch the Wind

This might not exactly be a performance clip, but the Beatles *are* seen playing music in this film of them walking to and hanging out by the river with the Maharishi, taken by Italian television. Nor is it exactly a group performance, as Ringo's missing. Assuming it was taken after his departure from Rishikesh, that means it's certain this was filmed in the first half of March, as it was broadcast on March 15. And nor, to further dampen your hopes, is the music particularly interesting. It's more like dropping in on an acoustic campfire sing-along with the Beatles, their wives/girlfriend, and their friends, prominently including Donovan, Mike Love of the Beach Boys, and Mia Farrow. No Beatles originals are performed, perhaps consciously so; John, Paul, and George were writing prolifically in India, but might not have wanted any of their efforts aired before they'd had a chance to release them on record. What's more, much of the sound is obscured by Italian narration.

As for the music, it's pleasant if bland, and has often been bootlegged (see entry on page 194). Its greatest value is in offering a glimpse of what life might have been like in Rishikesh for the group, and, more subtly, how acoustic folky music might have been coming to the fore as an influence on their songwriting while they were there. Each of them would subsequently express some dissatisfaction with how their stay turned out, John Lennon sometimes angrily so, and sometimes in song. Based on what we see here, however, they seem genuinely relaxed and enjoying their respite from the world—albeit a respite that did not preclude the presence of European television crews to document how they were getting away from it all.

● June 11

Promo clip for Apple Records, titled Apple

Blackbird
Helter Skelter
Studio Two, Abbey Road, London

These brief excerpts are actually part of a larger, ten-minute promotional clip not for the Beatles per se, but for the newly launched Apple Corps. In keeping with the generally hectic way Apple was run, *Apple* the film is a pretty scrambled, non-linear affair, giving the impression (no doubt inadvertently) that lots was going on at the company, but that nobody was really in control or giving it a focus. A tougher side of Paul than usual is seen in a meeting (with John also present) with publisher Dick James. It's impossible to tell what they're arguing about, but there's no doubting that McCartney's not one to bow down any longer to those administering the Beatles' affairs when he concludes testily, "So, Dick, that's it. You go away, and you come back with something which you know won't start this argument again."

In the midst of the footage of business meetings, London, and various Apple enterprises (including its electronics division, explained in uncertain, halting English by "Magic Alex" Mardas, who looks more like a mad scientist than a corporate employee) were some actual scenes of Paul McCartney playing acoustic guitar at a *White Album* session. These are quite nice, if very brief, snatches of "Blackbird" and, in an embryonic folk-blues state, a sweetly sung "Helter Skelter." Many takes of "Blackbird," as well as less serious ones of "Helter Skelter" and a few other songs (all done by Paul solo), have been bootlegged from this session in outstanding fidelity (see entry on page 202). The woman seen for a few seconds sitting near Paul's feet, incidentally, is Francie Schwartz, with whom he had a short fling around the time he was breaking up with Jane Asher.

There's a little more music in the clip, too, in the form of new Apple artist Mary Hopkin singing the Bee Gees' "In the Morning" in Paul's backyard, with cameos not just by Paul, but by his sheepdog Martha, of "Martha My Dear" fame. For those who want more of the same, Paul also appears alongside Mary in the studio in a Hopkin promo video for her 1969 single "Goodbye" (a Lennon-McCartney cover), as well as in a promo video for another Lennon-McCartney cover single, Cilla Black's "Step Inside Love" (where he's seen playing guitar at a Black recording session, George Martin also making an appearance). And should you want a more comprehensible document of what the Beatles were trying to achieve with Apple, it's discussed (along with several other topics) in a ten-minute interview they gave Larry Kane in New York on May 14, 1968. It's now available as part of a DVD with Kane's book

Lennon Revealed, the footage marking the last time John and Paul were interviewed together on film.

Incidentally, at a brief filmed press conference in Minneapolis on August 21, 1965, the Beatles had been asked if they would ever start their own record company. Responded John, "We'd never start our own label. It's too much trouble." As things turned out, he was half wrong, and half right. . . .

● July 30

Documentary Music!
Studio Two, Abbey Road, London

Hey Jude

As part of this documentary (which covered all types of British music), the Beatles were shown working on "Hey Jude" in the studio. Refreshingly, it wasn't just silent footage shown to a mimed finished record or some such thing. These were actual scenes, with actual sound, of them polishing a classic-in-progress, with actual unreleased music (though only heard in fits and starts) on the soundtrack. Paul's characteristic ebullience here is to be expected, but it's also interesting to note John's all-out enthusiasm; he might have been critical, sometimes nastily so, of some of Paul's songs after the Beatles broke up, but he always had high praise for "Hey Jude." The vocals are obviously a little too self-consciously, humorously exaggerated in this footage for a finished take, and it would actually take a couple more days of recording before the group had the finished track. "I keep getting me trousers caught on the pedal," complains Ringo mildly at the end of one version. "Take 'em off!" quips John.

There's an indication all might not have been happy behind the scenes, however, as George Harrison is not participating in the recordings at this stage, instead sitting in the control room with George Martin and engineer Ken Scott. Paul, as is now famous among Beatle scholars, had rejected George's idea for using responsive guitar phrases in the song, and at least at this stage his role in the recording looks nearly nonexistent. There must be more footage that wasn't used, incidentally, as a few outtakes showed up (though without sound) in *Anthology.*

● September 4

Promo clips for:

Hey Jude (three versions)
Revolution (two versions)
By George! It's the David Frost Theme (three versions)
Twickenham Film Studios, London

"Hey Jude" might be the best known of all the Beatles' promo films—though, in common with many of the others, several versions were made, and which one you saw at the time (or, indeed, since) depended on where you lived and what television network you were watching. Regardless of which version you see, however, a big part of its charm is the very physical presence of a large studio audience, crowding close around the Beatles but not chasing or threatening them in any way. The many different kinds of people seen swaying, clapping, and singing along to the long fadeout in the clips—old and (admittedly, mostly) young and multi-racial—emphasized their universal appeal, and, more subtly, their general ethos of open-minded tolerance and promotion of peace and love between everyone. (In a sad note, a young man who can be seen standing behind Ringo in some shots would die the following week of cancer; he was the son of Apple film division chief Denis O'Dell.) Some critics have gone as far as to see the clips, brief as they are, as an affirmation of oneness between the Beatles and their audience, ironically coming at a time when they were starting to experience serious problems in getting along among their own four selves. Indeed, this was Ringo's first professional activity with the band in nearly two weeks, as he'd temporarily quit during a *White Album* session on August 23.

There aren't huge differences between the clips, though for the record, two versions are full takes (take one and two); another is an edit of part of take one with part of yet another take, take three; and the version seen on *Anthology* edits together parts of all three takes, including scenes from take three that were previously unavailable. (The *Anthology* version also doesn't cover the whole seven-minute length of the song, lasting just six minutes, with some overlaid interviews obscuring some of the audio.) And as with "All You Need Is Love," this isn't a wholly "live" performance, though it convincingly created the

A minimally packaged, to say the least, two-DVD compilation of most of the Beatles' promo clips, named after an unreleased song the group played during the January 1969 Get Back *sessions.*

THE BEATLES

WATCHING RAINBOWS

illusion of one. Only some of the vocal parts, and none of the instrumental ones, were live. A few brief skips through "By George! It's the David Frost Theme" (the second take of "Hey Jude" was to be screened on Frost's TV show in the UK and introduced by the host) *were* live, however. "Beautiful! Absolute poetry!" Frost sarcastically enthuses on the only one of these attempts at the loungeish instrumental to circulate on video (though the audio tracks of a couple others have been bootlegged; see entry on page 212).

Not as well known, but at least as impressive, were the two clips the group made of "Revolution" on the same day, though without an audience in attendance. True, it's disappointing, at least to purists like the author, that the instrumental backing track is the same as the record (if someone argues with you that it isn't, ask why you can hear Nicky Hopkins's electric piano part, even though no keyboard instrument is visible on screen). But the vocals *are* live, and what's more, they vary appreciably from the record, George and (particularly) Paul singing doo wop–like backup harmonies that aren't on the single at all. Dressed more informally than they'd ever been for any filmed music performance, the fellows look pretty elated to be playing live again as a ballsy rock band, even in this quasi-live setup.

Incidentally, there were almost certainly yet more takes of both songs filmed, though it's not yet known whether any have survived. Lindsay-Hogg told Bill DeYoung that there were "seven or eight" takes of "Hey Jude," and takes in which Paul and George tried different harmonies for "Revolution." It's too bad what they were doing *between* takes of "Hey Jude" wasn't filmed as well, since according to Lindsay-Hogg, the Beatles used that time to entertain the crowd with jams, including some Motown songs. As another piece of "Hey Jude" video trivia, the group had considered doing a 38-scene clip with a storyboard devised by *Magical Mystery Tour* editor Roy Benson, though the idea was dropped.

The "Revolution" clips are, with the benefit of hindsight, small tasters of how the Beatles might have sounded and looked had they decided to play actual concerts in the late '60s, dressing and acting as they pleased without the image-conscious constraints that had helped sour them on touring. Sadly, that never came to pass, but the day's filming might have whetted their appetite for doing so in some sort of situation. For just a few months later, they'd attempt to do a filmed live show with the same director who worked with them on the "Hey Jude" and "Revolution" promos, Michael Lindsay-Hogg. As Lindsay-Hogg remembered in Steve Matteo's *Let It Be* book, "They were jamming and having a good time and having a better time than they thought they were going to have. So they sort of thought maybe there is some way they can do something again in some sort of performance way." The attempt to do so eventually turned into the *Let It Be* movie—which, for all its significance as a historical document, was quite different from what they had originally envisioned.

● December 11–12

From The Rolling Stones Rock and Roll Circus
Stonebridge House, London

Yer Blues (two versions)
Whole Lotta Yoko

John Lennon led a band including Eric Clapton, Keith Richards, and Mitch Mitchell for his appearance in The Rolling Stones Rock and Roll Circus *on December 11, 1968.*

The first film footage of a Beatle playing in a band other than the Beatles was taken at *The Rolling Stones Rock and Roll Circus,* where John Lennon sang "Yer Blues" with a group including Eric Clapton on guitar, Keith Richards on bass, and Mitch Mitchell on drums. For a long time, very few fans of either the Beatles or the Stones had seen this production, but it did finally come out on home video in 1996. Credited to "The Dirty Mac," this includes one version of "Yer Blues," as well as "Whole Lotta Yoko," where the same band (with the addition of violinist Ivry Gitlis) backed Ono.

The 2004 DVD adds a second take of "Yer Blues" as part of its bonus footage, with a split screen utilizing four different camera angles, as well as brief outtakes of John and Mick Jagger bantering and singing a snatch of "Yer Blues" together a cappella. They're joshing around with each other, yet the bonhomie seems a little strained, as if the two titans can't come up with the kind of immortal summit meeting/sound bite for which the filmmakers might have hoped. (A similar but wittier exchange between the pair appears in the final cut of the film.) The official DVD performance will be enough for most Lennon/Beatles fans, but an Austrian television crew doing a documentary on John and Yoko was also on hand to film as well. Some footage has emerged from that production that primarily differs from the official take of "Yer Blues" in its greater emphasis on close-ups of Lennon. There's a strange moment at the end of one take where the song ends and John stares blankly at the camera, as if he's holding a pose until he hears the word "cut," or is indifferent to the reaction of the audience, or is fighting off nerves from his first wholly live public performance in more than two years.

The Rolling Stones Rock and Roll Circus was directed by Michael Lindsay-Hogg, who in just a few weeks would be directing *Let It Be.* In the many hours of dialogue from tapes made during the January 1969 *Let It Be* filming, Lindsay-Hogg sometimes comes off as a fey, wishy-washy figure. You've got to feel a little sorry for the guy, however, as it must not have been an easy task for him to be working on both of these troubled projects almost simultaneously. Not only did he have to deal with the monumental egos of the two biggest bands on earth one right after the other, but he also had to sit on the footage for what must have seemed an eternity while the groups bickered over what to do with it. *Let It Be* at least came out in the spring of 1970, but *The Rolling Stones Rock and Roll Circus* would have to wait a lot longer—about a quarter-century longer, in fact.

● Mid-December

From John Lennon and Yoko Ono's film Rape
Kenwood, Weybridge

Everybody Had a Hard Year

Most of the films John and Yoko made in the late '60s and early '70s appeal only to extremely hardcore Lennon/Ono fans and/or avant-garde movie aficionados. Nearly lost in the mounds of footage, however, is a genuinely musical scene with the roots of a genuine Beatles song. Following the credits of their film *Rape (Film No. 6)* (in which cameramen stalk a young woman despite her protests), there's a brief clip of John (on acoustic guitar) and Yoko singing "Everybody Had a Hard Year." Combined with another tune on which Paul McCartney was working, this plaintive, folky ditty would soon evolve into "I've Got a Feeling."

The audio has been bootlegged on its own (see entry on page 222), but it's more effective to see the black-clad pair, peculiarly dressed as benign witches of sorts, sitting in a desolate wintry garden. After picking out the tune for a bit, John segues into riffs from "Julia," after which the image and music fade. It's an extremely short but haunting scene, as if the embattled couple are taking refuge in each other after the blows of Yoko's miscarriage, John's drug bust, and the general media harassment hurled their way. He hasn't lost his humor, though, interrupting the song, for no reason whatsoever, to point a finger at the camera and utter, "Surprise, surprise"—the surprise presumably being the sudden appearance of John and Yoko after a Lennon/Ono film in which they didn't appear at all. Here's another surprise you might have missed: the clip was included on the official *Lennon Legend* DVD, which the unwary might have skipped on the assumption that it wouldn't contain Beatles-era rarities.

It's beyond the scope of this book to document the numerous experimental films on which John and Yoko collaborated in the late '60s and early '70s, of which *Rape* was just one. Still, this question must be posed: why hasn't there been a compilation of this work, not seen by many even in its day and rarely screened since, on DVD? As esoteric and (almost wholly) un-Beatles-related as it is, there must be some sort of market for it. And it's got to be more interesting than the four-DVD set of Mal Evans silent home movies of Paul McCartney that actually *were* officially issued in 2005. . . .

1969

● January 2–14

Let It Be *film outtakes*
Twickenham Studios, London

Don't Let Me Down
All Things Must Pass
Tennessee
Across the Universe
House of the Rising Sun
Commonwealth
Enoch Powell
Improvisation

And now for the question you might have been awaiting with an anxious mixture of anticipation and dread. As if the 80 or so CDs' worth of mostly unreleased music the Beatles' January 1969 *Get Back/Let It Be* sessions produced weren't enough, wouldn't there also be a lot of unreleased *film* lying in the can as well? And wouldn't that be, like those approximately 100 hours of music, almost as much a nightmare as a dream for Beatles collectors?

Well, yes and no. Certainly there *must* be quite a bit of unseen footage lying around, perhaps literally in a can, considering that cameras were filming the Beatles almost every day of the month. But there's almost certainly not 100 hours of film. When the Beatles were being *recorded* by the Nagra tape machines that were part of the film crew's equipment, they weren't necessarily always being *filmed* at the same time. It's been reported that at least 30 hours of footage were actually produced, which leaves more than 28 hours that haven't been released.

Naturally, some of those outtakes have circulated among collectors. But whereas it seems like most (and certainly the majority) of the unreleased audio outtakes that could have been taped have escaped onto bootlegs, a much lower percentage of the available film outtakes have escaped onto unauthorized videos and DVDs, adding up to a little less than two hours or so altogether. And what *has* surfaced is often missing sound, often of disappointingly poor black-and-white image quality, and often captures only fragments of performances, not complete versions. Too, as it's raw footage, the shots will often linger on one of the Beatles (or John and Yoko) for long periods without a break, instead of employing the cross-cutting to different members that most documentarians will use to ensure variety and watchability.

Conscientious bootleggers have done their best to make the material more viewable by syncing these scenes up to the unreleased audio recordings that they're obviously performing in these outtakes. But these are still, for the most part, often unpleasantly tedious to watch, much as some of the *Get Back* sessions audio bootlegs are pretty tough to enjoy on purely musical grounds. Nonetheless, like those audio outtakes, these scenes are at the very least historically instructive, with the odd flash of inspiration and here-and-there episodes that illuminate the interrelationships among the band and their associates at the time.

If there's any great revelation, however, it's that the *Let It Be* film, for all its flaws, is here revealed to have astutely selected what were probably the most entertaining moments of the *Get Back* project. The movie's sometimes cited for itself being tough to sit through, having inadvertently documented some of the Beatles' tensest as well as most lackadaisical hours for posterity. But if these outtakes are a general indication of what fell to the cutting-room floor, what was left out was a lot harder to watch than what was culled for the final product.

It's possible to construct, with total or near-total accuracy, a timeline of what pieces of this unreleased footage were done on what date. For the purposes of this book, however, it will make more sense to divide the outtakes into the general range of time at which they were done at a specific location, rather than choppily separate them into separate days. As it's not 100 percent confirmed whether the soundtracks on these unauthorized materials are always accurately synced up to the images, the author will not attempt to note how many versions of each song are on these outtakes, instead only listing the titles of each number that can be heard (though the majority of these are indeed only performed once in the circulating footage). Fortunately, there was at least *one* aspect of the *Get Back/Let It Be* mess that was pretty simple: with the exception of a few outdoors shots of the neighborhood surrounding Apple headquarters, filming was done at only three locations: Twickenham Studios (January 2–14), Apple Studios (January 23–29 and January 31), and the Apple rooftop (January 30). This first entry will discuss the footage that's circulated from Twickenham, briefly noting dates for those who like to keep track of such things.

About 20 minutes have been unearthed from the Twickenham sessions, most of which concentrates on shots of John and Yoko. What these illustrate, more graphically than any of the books discussing Yoko's effect on the group's recording sessions, is just how incessant a stony-faced presence she was at these events. That's particularly evident in the rehearsals of "All Things Must Pass" (from January 8), where she paces back and forth in a five-foot radius around Lennon, sometimes rubbing shoulders and whispering to him. Ostensibly he's rehearsing a song here, and the shots are both a testament to the close bond between the couple *and* how distracting she likely was to both John and the rest of the group as they struggled with their arrangements. It's not entirely grim; there are some genuine laughs and horseplay from John during some of the other songs, especially "House of the Rising Sun" (which, like "Commonwealth" and "Enoch Powell," was filmed on January 9). There's also a 25-second color clip of "Don't Let Me Down" whose date of origin is uncertain to this author, though it's obvious that it's set in Twickenham, and hence must have been shot between January 2 and January 14.

Remarkably, a three-minute color scene does capture a loud, angry jam by John, Paul, and Ringo with a black-clad, black-hatted Yoko on caterwauling, wordless vocals, just hours after Harrison temporarily left the band on January 10. This must have been one of the strangest, tensest passages, not just of the entire *Get Back* sessions but of the Beatles' whole career. If Yoko seems distraught about the group's crisis, she certainly doesn't show it. Indeed, she's smiling radiantly, fueling conspiracy theorists who view this segment as evidence of her not-so-subtle pleasure at being the center of attention for once within a Beatles performance and perhaps her delight at the prospect of a possible group breakup. Ringo's seen flailing as wildly and energetically on his drums as he ever was during the January 1969 filming. Paul, perhaps more out of grim "if you can't beat 'em, join 'em" resignation than anything else, contributes to the chaos by studiously, humorlessly massaging a speaker with his bass to coax some appropriate feedback out of the instrument.

It still boggles the mind to think the band was grinding this out, with cameras recording the action no less, just at the point when their very survival was more in doubt than it had been since they became a foursome. Shock and incomprehension at George's abrupt departure seems like the only possible explanation. As Ringo reflected in the *Anthology* book, "George had gone home. When we came back [from lunch] he still wasn't there, so we started jamming violently. Paul was playing his bass into the amp and John was off, and I was playing some weird drumming that I hadn't done before. I don't play like that as a rule. Our reaction was really, really interesting at the time. And Yoko jumped in, of course, she was there."

Not as heavy going, but still surprisingly tense and awkward, is a two-minute scene of Peter Sellers (who was soon to star with Ringo in *The Magic Christian*) dropping by to visit the George-less Beatles on January 14, their last day at Twickenham. For someone who had just been busted for marijuana (an offense which would cause him untold headaches in his multi-year quest for a green card when he moved to the US), John's pretty careless in his on-film banter, reminding Sellers, "Remember when I gave you that grass in Piccadilly?" Continues Lennon after Sellers walks off, "I know what it's like for showbiz people, they're under a great strain, and they need a little relaxation. It's a choice between that and exercise, you know? And drugs win hands down." And

then comes an exchange feeding speculation that John and Yoko were on heroin at the time, Ono offering, "Shooting is exercise." Agrees Lennon: "Shooting is exercise. Oh yeah."

● January 2–April

Promo film for:

The Ballad of John and Yoko
Various Locations

Chronological continuity in listings of Beatles promo films starts to get much tougher near the end of their career, as they were starting to piece together the clips from various sources, rather than doing them as a group in one or two days as they had in the past. "The Ballad of John and Yoko," of course, would not even be written until about two months or so after the *Get Back* sessions had finished, not recorded until April 14, and not released until May 30. But its earliest footage (with both the rehearsing Beatles and a knitting Yoko) was shot on January 2 in Twickenham, explaining its placement here, in the middle of the *Let It Be* coverage.

As a video, "The Ballad of John and Yoko" isn't nearly as creative as the song, just stringing together a bunch of brief scenes from John and Yoko's lives that had been caught on film in early 1969. There were fitful attempts to match the lyrics with the images: that's *the* Peter Brown picking up the phone, and, less subtly, John and Yoko by the river, as well as glimpses of their Amsterdam Bed-In and, in what might be the best shot, a reporter holding a mike up to a white bag in which they were snuggling. In this context, the shots of the Beatles rehearsing at Twickenham (not playing "The Ballad of John and Yoko," of course) were a little irrelevant and misplaced. John might have felt obligated to put in *some* Beatles content, however, if only to make it clear that it was a Beatles record, not a John Lennon one—albeit a record on which, it was soon revealed, George and Ringo did not play at all. Nor did, for that matter, the fellow seen chanting cross-legged near the Beatles on the Twickenham set who seems to be a Hare Krishna devotee—an acquaintance of George's, one would guess.

There's some confusion, incidentally, as to how many promos of "The Ballad of John and Yoko" were made. Mark Lewisohn's *The Complete Beatles Chronicle* reported that two "essentially similar" promos were made, but the only other one that's circulated is in black and white, has no Beatles footage, and contains scenes of John and Yoko in 1968 that aren't in the version described above. One thing's for certain: the clip detailed in this entry is the only one that's relatively widely available on the collector circuit.

● January 6 and January 30

Promo film for:

Don't Let Me Down
Twickenham Studios, London; Apple Rooftop, London

As troubled and protracted as the *Let It Be* film and album release was, the January 1969 sessions did yield some fairly immediate, useful results in the form of the chart-topping "Get Back"/"Don't Let Me Down" single. It's not always remembered that promo films were promptly prepared for both of those songs, and that the first footage from the project was actually viewed back in April 1969, when promo films were broadcast for each. What's more, each used some footage from the *Let It Be* filming that didn't make it into the final movie, so you need to get the promos if you're a Beatles January 1969 completist.

There was nothing too fancy about the promo of "Don't Let Me Down," which combined footage of their January 30 performances of the song in their Apple rooftop concert with scenes of them working on the number at Twickenham on January 6. Obviously the images don't perfectly correspond to the music (which was taken from the January 28 studio track issued on the official single), and it's certainly not as exciting as the wholly live rooftop version seen in the *Let It Be* film. But it does contain numerous shots that didn't make the movie (even in the rooftop portions), which, although taken from the same performance seen in the film, use some different camera angles.

● January 23–29

Let It Be *film outtakes*
Apple Studios, London

Get Back
I've Got a Feeling
Help!
Please Please Me
Improvisation
Two of Us
Bye Bye Love
Let It Be
For You Blue
Instrumental Blues Jam
I Told You Before
Dig It
The Long and Winding Road
Little Demon
I Want You
All Things Must Pass

When the filming/recording action for *Let It Be*/*Get Back* moved to Apple Studios on January 21 after George returned to the band, it's been reported that the atmosphere substantially improved almost immediately. That's borne out to some degree by about a half hour of outtake film footage from the January 23 sessions that are largely devoted to rehearsals of "Get Back," interrupted by a brief go at "I've Got a Feeling," followed by mock-desecrations of "Help!" and "Please Please Me." For much of the "Get Back" rehearsals, the Beatles and Billy Preston (in just his second day as a sideman) gather round in a rough circle, Yoko seated next to John of course. To all appearances, everyone seems to be getting along quite pleasantly, and working on the arrangement with productive amiability. For those of us who've slogged through so many dozens of hours of *Get Back* outtakes where the Beatles *weren't* getting along so well, or at least weren't too communicative with each other, it's frankly a great relief to come upon a bit where they seem so demonstra-

bly at ease with each other. John and George, who just a week or two before were almost at each other's throats, break out into wide, nearly ecstatic grins almost simultaneously during one take, flashing back (if almost fleetingly) to those Beatlemania days when such sparkly good vibes were routine, not rare.

Most likely, this is the kind of scene everyone envisioned and hoped for when the *Get Back* project was first planned, making it a bit of a surprise that the final *Let It Be* film didn't incorporate a shot or two of it. Glyn Johns, a co-producer of the *Let It Be* album, criticized the movie for not showing more such lighthearted moments in an interview for the BBC radio series *The Record Producers*: "The film . . . was atrocious," he contended. "I was there when it was being shot, and there was some amazing stuff—their humor got to me as much as the music, and I didn't stop laughing for six weeks. John Lennon only had to walk in a room and I'd just crack up. Their whole mood was wonderful, that was the thing, and there was all this nonsense going on at the time about the problems surrounding the group, and the press being at them. In fact, there they were, just doing it, having a wonderful time and being incredibly funny, and none of that's in the film." Johns might have been thinking of sequences such as their silly busk through "Help!" from the January 23 outtake footage, where a funny-faced Paul squawked backup vocals like a taciturn parrot. Also amusing is another scene from this date where, after Johns's voice accidentally interrupts the beginning of a take, Paul adopts a Teddy Boy pose to scold him, waving his finger and glowering: "Look, fuckface. Don't come in!" One imagines Glyn couldn't have been too disappointed at the failure of *that* scene to make the cut.

Johns is seen as well as heard in a few scenes of the group listening to playbacks in the control room. These make for kind of dull viewing, but they do capture a point at which the band seems to be deciding to make "Get Back" a single. Intriguingly, Lennon seems to suggest that it be done as a two-part 45, with a second, instrumental part of the tune being used as the B-side. Obviously that idea didn't hold, with "Don't Let Me Down" ending up as the flip side to "Get Back."

Also from January 23, there's footage of another Yoko-sung jam just as jarring and grating as the one she'd led on January 10 after George had quit. Whether the rest of the band were putting up with this interlude to appease John is unknown, particularly as there are no shots of anyone but Lennon and Ono during this sequence. John does seem to be mightily enjoying the clamor, though, delightedly pounding guitar strings with his hands, waving the instrument in front of a microphone and speaker to produce the obligatory feedback, and at one point even picking up what looks like a screwdriver to scrape up and down his fretboard.

Yoko, perhaps understandably bored by the endless rehearsals, finally does leave John's vicinity during the outtakes of "Two of Us" (from January 25, also including a few seconds of the Everly Brothers' "Bye Bye Love"), hanging a white sheet on a sound baffle to paint Japanese calligraphy. The footage of "Let It Be" from the same day mostly shows John sitting cross-legged on the floor, gamely trying to cope with his unfamiliar bass guitar. Yoko's back by his side, and at the beginning of one take, Lennon—knowing that he doesn't have to sing or play until after the intro—takes advantage of the brief downtime to smooch with Yoko. In another "Let It Be" take he takes more liberties, lying on the floor with crossed legs on raised knees, head in Yoko's lap. It's not the most efficient of positions for recording, but then he probably knew he wasn't going to be a bass virtuoso no matter how he played it.

As for other highlights or moments of insight from the Apple Studios film outtakes, there aren't many. But it's interesting to see a brief shot (from January 26) of Paul's young, soon-to-be-stepdaughter Heather sitting next to a good-natured John during the jam "I Told You Before" and commandeering his mike to warble into it tunelessly; maybe she'd seen part of a Yoko jam and assumed such improvisation was par for the course? Billy Preston is barely seen in these scenes at all, but looks delightedly animated (on January 28) to be going through the over-and-over repetitions of the tricky transition in "I've Got a Feeling." An excerpt of an exciting early, skeletal workout on "I Want You (She's So Heavy)" from the same day is probably the highlight of all the Apple Studios outtake footage, but sadly only lasts about half a minute. And a part of "All Things Must Pass" on January 29 gives a little ammunition to those who feel that John didn't put his full weight behind this Harrison song: John's seen smoking and talking to Yoko, but at no time does he have an instrument in his hands. John and Yoko are the focus of the camera in most of these outtakes, though there are 12 minutes of pretty unremarkable scenes of the group recording "For You Blue" that give George some screen time.

For the record, a few scenes of control room playbacks from January 25 and January 27 are interspersed with this footage. There are also scenes of brief versions of "Let It Be" and a bluesy jam (from January 26), "The Long and Winding Road" (a very brief clip from January 27, also including a snippet of the Screamin' Jay Hawkins oldie "Little Demon"), and "Dig It" (from January 28).

● January 30

Promo film for:

Get Back
Apple Rooftop, London

Like the performances of "Get Back" seen in the *Let It Be* movie, the promo film for the song was taken from footage of the rooftop concert. To detail the differences, it's necessary to get somewhat technical. The *Let It Be* "Get Back" features both the second and third versions they performed that day, while the promo edits together shots taken of all three versions. And as with the promo film of "Don't Let Me Down," the soundtrack of the "Get Back" promo uses the January 28 studio track issued on the single, not any of the January 30 live recordings. It's still an effective, exciting clip, especially as it opens—unlike either of the movie versions—with a long-distance shot of the roof from across the street, dramatically swooping down until the group comes into view.

● January 31

Promo film for:

Let It Be
Apple Studios, London

"Let It Be" wouldn't be released for more than a year after the basic track had been recorded, owing to the usual tangle of indecision and complication surrounding the whole *Let It Be* movie and LP. At least that meant, however, that when the time came to assemble a promo film for its March 1970 release, a presentable clip of the Beatles performing the song was in the can. No two of the Beatles were even able to appear in the same frame for their "Something" promo (see entry later in this chapter); with all the animosity sprouting every which way by early 1970, it's hard to fathom how they might have come together for, or even in any way collaborated upon, a brand-new promotional film.

A complete version of "Let It Be" is performed in the *Let It Be* movie itself. But the promo, in keeping with how *Let It Be* outtake footage was dispersed for numerous other projects, is *not* the same as the film sequence featuring the song; it largely uses footage of the take immediately preceding the similar one seen in the movie. Nor is what you hear on the soundtrack exactly the same as what they're playing, since the track underwent some subsequent overdubs. Still, it's shot, played, and sung (Paul cannily playing to the camera with his facial expressions) in a suitably stark, somber, and dignified manner, as befitting the tone of the classic song.

As a side note, "Let It Be," "Get Back," and "Don't Let Me Down" weren't the only clips from the *Let It Be* footage used as promo films. The full-length studio performance of "Two of Us" seen in the movie was shown (along with the "Let It Be" promo) on *The Ed Sullivan Show* on March 1, 1970, more than two months before the track was issued on the *Let It Be* album. Watching Sullivan's intro today, you can't help but feel sad as he gleefully exclaims, "Ladies and gentlemen, singing one of their newest songs—the Beatles!" Of course, it wasn't one of their newest songs, having been recorded and filmed more than a year before this broadcast. And by the time this "new" song came out, the Beatles wouldn't exist.

Before taking leave of the bountiful surplus *Let It Be* footage that's surfaced to date, it should also be noted that there's not only no doubt that much else lingers in the vaults, but also that some other minor yet tantalizing dribs and drabs have leaked out in official releases over the years. Some previously unseen (albeit brief) outtakes are available in *Anthology,* and while some of these are mostly there for background ambience, there are some quite worthwhile musical bits and dialogue as well, such as one in which the Beatles are seen working on "Get Back" with Billy Preston in the studio. Especially revealing is a sequence in which the group seems on the verge of deciding to do the rooftop concert, George characteristically still expressing some reluctance. Other brief outtakes surfaced in promotional materials for *Let It Be . . . Naked* (such as a sequence of "One After 909" with Preston in the studio, rather than on the rooftop) and the unreleased "director's cut" of *Anthology* (showing the Beatles chaotically discussing some recording issues with George Martin at Apple Studios). Some outtakes had even come out as early as 1984 in the documentary *Yoko Ono: Then and Now.*

It's also known that a much longer cut of *Let It Be* existed before it was first released. "We did a rough cut and screened it for them, the same day Neil Armstrong landed on the moon [July 20, 1969]," Michael Lindsay-Hogg told Bill DeYoung in 2000. "It was a much longer cut originally. There was an hour more. There was much more stuff of John and Yoko, and the other three didn't really think that was appropriate because they wanted to make it a 'nicer' movie. They didn't want to have

This is a new phase **BEATLES** video album...
essential is the content from the film, LET IT BE in that they performed
live for most of the tracks; in comes the warmth and freshness of a live
performance; as directed for film by Michael Lindsay-Hogg.

GET BACK

SESSION_____ BEATLES   PPDVD13-1

GET BACK   FOR YOU BLUE   DVD   NTSC: Color/B&W
                                     VIDEO   Region: All
DON'T LET ME DOWN DIG IT   Aspect Ratio: 1.33 : 1
                                            Running Time:
I'VE GOT A FEELING TWO OF US   Approx. 200 min.
                                   digital 2 DVD set, Not Rated
ONE AFTER 909   THE LONG AND WINDING ROAD SOUND
                                   STEREO
DIG A PONY   LET IT BE   PICTURE

GET BACK   I ME MINE   DVD
                  GET BACK   PERFECT PRODUCTIONS

Also includes over 60 minutes of unreleased footage from the GET BACK Sessions.

Additional Disc:

...Winter Of Discontent

A unique insight into the Beatles at work in rehearsal and in the recording studio during January 1969.
(See gatefold of booklet for further details.)

Designed by ATU Productions, Ltd. Photographs by Ethan Russell and Angus McBean

Quality for the 21st Century © 2005 Picture Perfect DVD Company. All rights reserved.
Artwork and Design © 2005 Across The Universe Productions, Ltd. All rights reserved.

A DVD compilation with "over 60 minutes of unreleased footage from the Get Back *sessions," with artwork and design by "Across the Universe Productions."*

a lot of the dirty laundry, so a lot of it was cut down. So then we ended up with an hour and a half." Along the same lines, as he observed in Roy Carr's *The Beatles at the Movies*, "There was material in that film which was the most accurate anywhere about the breakup, showing the kind of ennui they felt. But, because they were the stars as well as the producers, they didn't want that material to be scrutinized by the public. So it came out and part of what I wanted to tell suffered." For his part, John would charge, a little mean-spiritedly, in his early-'70s *Rolling Stone* interview that "the camera work was set up to show Paul and not to show anybody else . . . the people that cut it cut it as 'Paul is God' and we're just lyin' around there. That's what I felt. And I knew there were some shots of Yoko, and me, that had been just chopped out of the film for no other reason than the people were oriented towards Engelbert Humperdinck."

An authorized DVD of *Let It Be* has supposedly been in preparation since at least the time of the *Let It Be . . . Naked* album release in 2003. Even if it only included the outtakes that have appeared on authorized projects, those would add up to substantial extra features.

Given the large amount of unused footage that probably exists (John Lennon said there were 68 hours in April 1969, though other estimates have varied widely from that figure), the opportunity's there to put on a load of interesting-to-fascinating bonus material—at least as much, you'd think, as there is in the *Let It Be* movie itself. It's also known that the footage was remastered in 1992, which would make for a substantial upgrade over the original version that suffered from graininess after being blown up from 16mm to 35mm. As of this writing in early 2006, however, such a DVD has not appeared—another lost opportunity for the Beatles, and another prime opportunity for bootleggers in possession of these outtakes to exploit.

● Circa May 26–September 13

Promo film for Plastic Ono Band single:

Cold Turkey
Various Locations

Of all the promo films for John Lennon and Beatles releases in the late '60s and early '70s, "Cold Turkey" is the only one that approximates the avant-garde sensibilities John and Yoko were investing in their experimental movies of the period. Anxiety-provoking cuts between brief clips of their recent activities (particularly their Montreal Bed-In of late May and early June, and their appearance onstage in Toronto in September) are the backbone of this video collage of sorts. Adding to the tension are insertions of footage of street traffic, police brutality, and the sky, as well as overexposures, blurring, frame-speed manipulation, and wavering of the frame itself. It's not classic filmmaking, but it does mirror the stress 'n' sweat of the "Cold Turkey" track itself, reflecting something of the mania that presumably drove John to the heroin use (and withdrawal) so wrenchingly detailed in the song.

On December 21, 1969, John explained in an interview with CBC television, "When we were in Montreal, Jonas Mekas, who some people will know as the, like, daddy of underground films, was making these quick clips of us. We didn't know what he was making, now we can see it, you know? And then he sent it to us in England with a message which we never received, somebody opened the package saying 'Play this with "Give Peace a Chance," 'cause we were doing the 'Bed-In' in Montreal and he was filming that. But we were looking around for a bit of film to show with 'Cold Turkey,' you know, like a promo film for the pop shows in England. And so we just tried it, we put on his film with the record and just went, 'Bam, bam,' it just fitted so well, the timing and the length and everything."

Obviously the finished clip used at least some footage not taken in Montreal as well. While it was the Plastic Ono Band's second single, the "Cold Turkey" video used footage spanning at least from the Montreal Bed-In (which began on May 26) to the Toronto concert (on September 13), though there's no way of dating the scenes in which John and Yoko don't appear. Hence its placement in this chapter before the entry for the footage of "Give Peace a Chance." The "Cold Turkey" promo can be seen on the out-of-print early-'90s release *The John Lennon Video Collection*; the footage accompanying "Cold Turkey" on the more recent *Lennon Legend* DVD is not taken from the original promo film.

● May 31

Promo film for Plastic Ono Band single:

Give Peace a Chance
Hotel Reine-Elizabeth, Montreal

Although technically speaking "Give Peace a Chance" was given some overdubbing and studio tweaking the following day, the promo film for the single was about as genuine as such clips get, showing the song being recorded live in John and Yoko's hotel room at their Montreal Bed-In on May 31, 1969. It's thus one of the most powerful and moving of all Beatles-related promos, capturing a sense of the occasion and also the diversity of the participants, including Timothy Leary, Tommy Smothers, Petula Clark, and Hare Krishna followers. Odd bedfellows (in a literal sense!) to be sure, but an assembly that reinforced the ethos of the lyrics, uniting seemingly disparate personalities for the common cause of peace.

Petula Clark's presence at this event has rarely been explained, and it might surprise some historians that John and Yoko had time for someone from a much more standard showbiz milieu than they inhabited. She happened to be performing in Montreal at the time, however, and undergoing some troubles of her own, as some of the local audience wanted her to sing only in French and other customers wanted her to perform only in English. It might have been a minor hassle compared to the struggle for world peace, but nonetheless, as she reported in Andrea Kon's *'This Is My Song': A Biography of Petula Clark,* "Late one night, I decided that I would go and see him. It was open house; a very odd kind of atmosphere. Anyway, I went in and there they were. Just sitting in bed. There was nothing saucy going on. It was really a very nice thing. I sat on the edge of the bed and talked, more with him than with her, and we talked about lots of things. He told me that I should do what I liked and what I could and that it was too bad if people didn't understand. I guess I knew that—but I think it helped just being able to talk about it with someone who was completely out of my circle and perhaps hearing his views on it." Lennon also told Clark how Buddhism "had offered him so much inner peace. How he lived not from day to day but from minute to minute and how it teaches that if you give out energy, it comes back to you. Relatively, it wasn't a heavy conversation at all."

Edited versions of the "Give Peace a Chance" promo are seen in the home videos *The John Lennon Video Collection* and *John and Yoko: The Bed-In,* but the full six-minute version isn't available. As with "Cold Turkey," the "Give Peace a Chance" clip in *Lennon Legend* is *not* the original.

● Circa October

Promo film for:

Something
Tittenhurst, Ascot; Kinfauns, Esher; Brookfield, Elstead;
  Campbelltown, Scotland

The final film project on which all four Beatles knowingly collaborated was, ironically, one that at no time showed any two Beatles together. The promo for "Something" simply edited together romantic scenes of each of the Beatles and their wives, shot in the grounds of their respective homes (John and Yoko at Tittenhurst, George and Patti at Kinfauns, Ringo and Maureen at their new home in Brookfield, and Paul and Linda at their farm in Scotland). In a way, it's one of the corniest and least imaginative of all their promo films, devoted as it is to close-ups and shots of couples strolling and romping around their homes, proving how close and devoted they are to each other. At this particular time, however, it was logistically and perhaps temperamentally impossible to get them all together in one place, and maybe to get them to do anything that was too involved on the technical/creative end for a mere promo shoot. And "Something" *was* an out-and-out upbeat, devotional love song to a woman—something that, rather surprisingly, no Beatles A-side or B-side had been since "I Feel Fine"/"She's a Woman" back in late 1964.

Like the 1968 and 1969 Beatles Christmas records, the "Something" promo may have said more by what was missing than what was there—namely, the absence of any interaction between the members whatsoever. It could only be seen in retrospect, but in that sense, it emphasizes their separateness and split into individual personal/family interests as the 1960s came to a close. Most of the clip is included in *Anthology,* which is missing only the first few seconds.

1970

● February 11

Promo films for John Lennon solo single:

Instant Karma! (two versions)
BBC Television Centre, London

Taped specifically for the BBC television program *Top of the Pops,* most of the music on these two performances was supplied by a backing track, John Lennon's lead vocal being the only live element. As such things go, however, these clips are pretty dynamic. The first to be screened (on February 12) had some groovy dancers swinging behind a headphone-clad John and his band (Klaus Voormann on bass and Alan White on drums), while a blindfolded Yoko held up cards with slogans such as "Peace" and "Smile." There's a mike in front of Yoko, and she appears to be singing or speaking "Smile" into it when she holds up the relevant card, but whether by intentional design or not, her voice can't be heard on the soundtrack. The second version (broadcast on February 19) was similar, but can be easily differentiated from the first as Yoko's knitting in this one, B.P. Fallon (from Apple's staff) is miming the bass (although Voormann's still playing onstage too), and Mal Evans can be seen playing tambourine.

This marked the second time in a few months, the first being at the Plastic Ono Band's September 13 concert in Toronto, that John had been filmed playing with a band that didn't include any of the other Beatles. Though George Harrison had indeed played on the "Instant Karma!" single itself (and had, for that matter, been filmed in December 1969 playing onstage with Delaney & Bonnie for a Danish TV program), the *Top of the Pops* appearances had to be chalked up as more warning signs by those watching for clues that the group was on the verge of splitting. Never before, incidentally, had film cameras caught John with such short hair, as he and Yoko had gotten buzz cuts shortly after the New Year—another declaration, perhaps, of independence from the standard Beatles image.

The first version was included on *The John Lennon Video Collection*. The second is, unlike virtually everything else reviewed in this chapter, easily available commercially on the *Lennon Legend* DVD and described here for the sake of making it easier to identify the rarer first version. There was a yet different, third promo clip for the single, seen on *Top of the Pops* on February 5, 1970, which was not filmed in a studio as the other two were, but used non-performance footage. These included shots from an Apple business meeting and the Lennon/Ono film *Apotheosis 2*, as well as shots of "Magic Alex" Mardas, who was somehow still in good enough graces with John to appear in a film such as this a full year after he'd thoroughly screwed up construction of Apple Studios. This third version, however, remains out of circulation, if it even survives at all.

As a wrap-up to the limited amount of musical footage captured of Lennon in 1969 and 1970 before the Beatles split, it should be mentioned that he was the subject of a couple of quite interesting British television documentaries in December 1969. The more entertaining of these, the 30-minute *24 Hours,* was broadcast by the BBC on December 15. While the premise was presenting a typical day in John and Yoko's life, actually the filming took place over a few days during the first week of December. The pair are seen chatting with journalists, shooting *Apotheosis 2,* making avant-garde sounds both at home and in the studio (see entry on page 274), and lounging in bed, where John—in a scene that's chilling in retrospect—reads mail from someone who predicts he'll be the target of an assassination attempt (which Lennon dismisses nonchalantly). John was also chosen by anthropologist Desmond Morris as one of the three "men of the decade" for the ATV special *Man of the Decade* (along with John F. Kennedy and Ho Chi Minh). Interview footage for Lennon's 20-minute segment was shot on December 2, at the same time the BBC was doing *24 Hours.* (In a Warholian moment, *24 Hours* includes a scene of the BBC filming ATV filming its own documentary.) The ATV interview leaned toward more political and philosophical territory than *24 Hours'* more cinema verité approach, and the mere selection of John as one of the

John Lennon performing "Instant Karma!" on Top of the Pops, *February 12, 1970, with the enigmatic mute assistance of a blindfolded Yoko Ono.*

three most important men of the 1960s was itself something that must have seemed unimaginable just a few years before, even at the height of Beatlemania.

These television specials were just two of many events that were helping to reshape John's image as both the Beatle with the highest profile in the media and the most political Beatle, as well as helping to establish an identity for himself that was almost wholly separate from his position in the band. It's doubtful that the other Beatles were jealous, though one never knows—Paul McCartney, after all, was just as important to the brilliance of the Beatles music, but British television networks weren't selecting *him* as a man of the decade, or trailing him and his wife around for days on end. In fact, startlingly enough, there hadn't been *any* documentaries about the group that were as serious and thoughtful as these two were about Lennon in particular. But, only in hindsight, as usual, these documentaries can be viewed as further indication that John was—perhaps not wholly known even to himself—drifting into a solo career. They'd make a great two-for-one package on a commercial DVD. Of course, these rarely screened films

The Lost Lennon Films: 1969 *DVD combines the* 24 Hours *and* Man of the Decade *documentaries onto one disc.*

THE LOST LENNON FILMS

1969

still remain unavailable—which, naturally, means that bootleggers have taken the ball and run with it, putting these lost Lennon films together on unauthorized two-for-one DVD packages of their own.

John *was* still a Beatle when those documentaries were filmed, but one telling exchange in *24 Hours* (with *NME* reporter Alan Smith) indicates how fragile that status was by the final month of 1969. "How long do you think you can go on being a practicing Beatle?" Smith asks. John's response is not the hearty, upbeat affirmation for which many fans must have hoped: "It depends how I feel and how they feel . . . because sometimes we go through hell recording, and sometimes we don't. And sometimes it's not worth it. The problem now is . . . in the old days, when we needed an album, Paul and I got together to produce an album, or produce enough songs for it. Nowadays, there's four of us, three of us writing prolifically, and trying to fit it on one album. And it's not like we wrestle it in the studio trying to get a song on, we all do it the same way, you know. We take it in turns to record a track. But usually George lost out, you know, 'cause Paul and I are tougher. It's not worth . . . it gets to, we don't want to fight about it. Now half the tracks on *Abbey Road,* I'm not on something, half the tracks on the double album, and way back, it depends . . . sometimes only two people are on a track. But it's got to the situation, if we have the name Beatles on it, it sells, you know. And when we begin to think like that, there's something wrong. Then you begin to think, what are we selling?"

● March 15

Promo clip for Ringo Starr Sentimental Journey *LP track:*

Sentimental Journey
Talk of the Town, London

Ringo Starr's declarations of independence might have been a tiny ripple compared to John Lennon's shock waves. But he was making some moves of his own, this promo film for the title track of his debut LP, *Sentimental Journey,* among them, although there wasn't much that could be done to make the song more exciting (or less dull) than it was. Nonetheless the clip, directed by Apple's Neil Aspinall at the Talk of the Town nightclub, did about as much as it could to liven things up. The vocal was live (though the backing wasn't), Ringo was surrounded by large groups of white-clad men and women dancers, the stage was shadowed by huge American and British flags, and an equally large photo of Ringo's hometown Liverpool neighborhood served as the background. In the middle of all this semi-excess, Ringo crooned and lightly swayed like the lounge lizard that must have been crawling under his skin for years, just itching for a coming-out party such as this. Still, the end result is likable at best. Keep an eye on the platform that drops down at the end of the clip; those three backing singers are American soul vocalists Doris Troy (who'd had a big hit in 1963 with "Just One Look" and would soon release an album of her own on Apple), Madeline Bell (by then a top session singer on UK sessions and a member of British hitmaking group Blue Mink), and Marsha Hunt (best known as the mother of a daughter fathered by Mick Jagger in 1970, *before* he got married to Bianca).

The *Other* Anthology

This chapter has taken its share of shots at the official steward-ship of the Beatles' visual legacy, criticizing the commercial absence of numerous materials that are not only hugely enjoy-able and historically important, but also have a huge market. Let this be stated clearly, however: when Apple *did* decide to produce a lengthy, official overview of the group's career, it did an excellent job. If you want to see footage of the Beatles, either as an introduction or a summary of highlights, the best source remains Apple's five-DVD *Anthology* set (whose main feature lasts around ten hours, and whose fifth disc adds an hour and 20 minutes of relatively inessential bonus material). It's not only the best documentary on the band ever produced, but one of the most popular documentaries of *any* sort ever produced.

Sure, there are some nitpicking shortcomings that keep it from be-ing perfect. The absence of voices other than the Beatles, George Martin, Neil Aspinall, and Derek Taylor means that the viewpoints of important figures in the story such as Pete Best, Yoko Ono, and Allen Klein are under-represented, slightly unbalancing the overall perspective (and perhaps steering it away from one which might have been somewhat more unflat-tering). The end of the group is lightly summarized as a natural parting of ways, glossing over the tumultuous conflicts that tore the members apart (though, oddly, the companion *Anthology* book goes into their final days in considerably more, and considerably more honest, detail). A few surprisingly important details are omitted, such as the death of Stuart Sutcliffe. But the excerpts of vintage footage cover a huge range of sources, and are chosen and used with great intelligence; the 1990s interviews with the surviving Beatles are quite informative and entertaining; and the many parts are smoothly combined by the directors and producers into a coherent whole that covers almost all of the important bases.

Having read the last several hundred pages, however, you should not be surprised to learn that there is an entirely different version of *Anthology* that has circulated on the underground market. Billed as the "director's cut," with about as much material as the official version, it sold through you-know-where outlets for exorbitant prices (which came down, of course, when "knockoff" DVD-R copies were done to bootleg the bootleggers). The way it was advertised by its sellers couldn't help but pique the curiosity of even some casual Beatles fans—one sticker, for instance, describes it as the cut "presented to Paul, George, Ringo, & Yoko before they made changes and cuts! Contains 85% unreleased never before seen material!" So is it an actual alternate version of *Anthol-ogy* that contains as many revelations as you'd suspect (or at least might have been led to believe)?

Sadly, it does not, although it *is* a noticeably different early cut. Many of the variations are actually interview segments filmed in differ-ent locations in which—take note—the interviewees actually answer the same questions, and tell essentially the same stories. Sure, you can tell that some of the shots are in different settings than the corresponding ones in the final cut. But basically, the Beatles are telling similar tales, though in somewhat different words. The decision to use different takes, or retakes, seems to have been dictated more by cosmetics than content: perhaps the Beatles were not as concerned by what they were saying as making sure that they looked, and were filmed, in a different way

in accordance with their wishes. What about the vintage footage? Well, although it's edited differently, there's not a great deal that isn't in the official version, and very little that had barely been seen before at all.

As for controversial or particularly interesting obscure nuggets, there are surprisingly few of those, at least judged against one's ex-pectations after reading hype intimating that some embarrassing or too-frank material got the axe. For this viewer, the only especially note-worthy bits that were cut from the official *Anthology* are:

- **George owning up to being the main force behind Pete Best's ouster, though the details are not exactly fulsome:** "I was actually quite re-sponsible for stirring that Pete episode up, you know, getting the oth-ers to agree that, you know, we should have Ringo in the band." (He makes the same point in only slightly different wording, however, in the *Anthology* book.) Another excised Harrison interview snippet, discussing the audience's displeasure at Ringo's first Cavern Club gig, also puts a little (very little) dirt into his early moptop image: "We kind of ignored it, but after about an hour of that, or half an hour of that, it was just getting a bit tiring, and I shouted to the audience . . . 'Oh, fuck off!'" (This is amended to "bugger off" in the official ver-sion.) For which, after the show, George was rewarded with the black eye from a Cavern fan that was still visible when the Beatles were photographed at their "Love Me Do" recording session at EMI.
- **A surprisingly lengthy (two-minute) segment on the group's little-known (and only) shows in Spain, which took place on July 2 and July 3 of 1965.** The memories of playing bullrings are forcefully neg-ative. George: "It was okay, except we kept stepping in these turds."
- **George finally names the dentist (John Riley) who slipped LSD into his coffee, as well as John's and their wives', for their first acid trips.** Generally speaking, the Beatles' remarks about drugs, and occasional lapses into profane language, were shortened and softened for the official version.
- **An eight-minute sequence in which George Martin discusses and isolates tracks at the mixing console for "A Day in the Life."** Martin's talked about this recording, with similar commentary, for other books and films (particularly in the 1992 TV documentary *The Making of Sgt. Pepper*). Still, this is a nicely detailed, lengthy segment, and actually aired a few snippets of outtakes for the first time anywhere, albeit of the sort that would only interest obsessives. The official *Anthology* used different, much shorter interview material with Martin about the track that—though few have noticed—edited together segments previously used in the aforementioned *The Making of Sgt. Pepper* TV special.
- **The allegations that the Maharishi made a pass at one of the women at the camp where the Beatles were studying in Rishikesh.** Prompt-ing the departure of the two remaining members, John and George, these allegations are wholly ignored in the official *Anthology*. In the director's cut, they're not. However, this isn't as much of a bonus as it might appear, since most of the comments do appear in the very much on-the-record *Anthology* book, though it's interesting to hear George reveal that "Magic Alex" Mardas "was the one also who set about the nasty rumor about Maharishi."

- **A good number of comments about Yoko Ono's influence on the band—most of them negative.** But again, virtually all of these appear in the *Anthology* book, which almost anyone who digs up this director's cut would have already.
- **Two bonus "special features" discs that despite their impressive length—three hours and 20 minutes—deliver relatively little in the way of truly interesting stuff.** Though there's some interview material in which Paul McCartney, George Harrison, Ringo Starr, George Martin, Neil Aspinall, and George Martin discuss the *Anthology* project, they divulge little in the way of uncommon information. (Indeed, they sometimes give the impression that the Beatles and George Martin know less about vault rarities and group trivia than their most knowledgeable fans do.) Also on hand are the music videos for the singles recorded by the three surviving Beatles in the 1990s, "Free as a Bird" and "Real Love." Most dishearteningly, however, much of the space is occupied by commercials and promotional press kits related to the *Anthology* project, of interest only to the most completist fanatics and extremely hard going to watch all at once.

There are also some notable differences in how the overall documentary is structured. Each episode, for instance, starts with a frankly time-wasting introductory "series flashback" that recapitulates highlights seen in the previous installments. The quality of the archive footage, too, is notably inferior to what ended up in the final product, sometimes still including time-code bars on the screen. While the ending of the official *Anthology* was disappointing inasmuch as it basically didn't cover the post–*Abbey Road* months leading to the band's split, the director's cut goes it one worse, ending with their January 30, 1969, rooftop concert and not covering *Abbey Road* at all. In fact, the finished *Anthology* is substantially superior in every respect to the so-called "director's cut"—which was, it should be stressed, a preliminary early test version of sorts and not seriously considered as a possible alternative version for release. In that sense, it's quite instructive to film students, particularly those with

documentary ambitions. For Beatles fans, however, the "extras" are slimmer than one hopes or expects, and perhaps not worth the (usually) high price if you're selective in the rarities you purchase.

The *Anthology* was extraordinary commercially successful in both its video/DVD formats and spin-off three-volume, six-CD series of unreleased/rare recordings. It's therefore surprising that few other significant Beatles archive releases have been attempted for the DVD market (exceptions being *The Four Historic Ed Sullivan Shows Featuring the Beatles* and the DVD editions, with bonus material, of *A Hard Day's Night* and *Yellow Submarine*). For what it's worth, here's a list, ranked in order of importance, of Beatles material that isn't currently available on DVD, but *should* be issued:

- *Let It Be* (with the two hours or so of extras that could easily be tacked on as bonus footage)
- *Help!* (believe it or not, unavailable on DVD in the US as of this writing)
- *Magical Mystery Tour* (also unavailable on DVD in the US as of this writing)
- **Washington Coliseum concert, February 11, 1964** (the complete version, not the incomplete one issued on *The Beatles in Washington D.C., February 11, 1964*)
- *The Beatles at Shea Stadium* (TV special of August 15, 1965, concert)
- *Around the Beatles* (British TV special, April 28, 1964)
- *The Beatles Sing for Shell* (TV special of June 17, 1964, concert in Melbourne, Australia, if its missing fragments can be found)
- *Les Beatles* (TV special of June 20, 1965, concert in Paris)
- **Tokyo concerts from June 30, 1966, and July 1, 1966** (both combined onto one DVD)
- Compilation of all Beatles promotional films, 1965–1969
- **December 1969 John Lennon TV documentaries** *24 Hours* **and** *Man of the Decade* (combined onto one DVD)

● Circa Early April

Promo clip for Paul McCartney McCartney *LP track:*

Maybe I'm Amazed
Various Locations

The promo film for "Maybe I'm Amazed," like the *McCartney* album itself, was hardly a pull-out-the-stops production. In fact, there were no moving images in it at all. Instead, it presented a montage of still photos of Paul enjoying life with his family, with images of various combinations of him, his wife Linda, his stepdaughter Heather, and his and Linda's newborn girl, Mary. It's not a rare technique to use for a music video, but as it happened, none of the Beatles promo films had employed it. As it was first shown on *Top of the Pops* on April 19, just nine days after Paul announced he was leaving the Beatles, it's

reasonable to assume that it was probably finished shortly before this broadcast, and quite possibly finished before the Beatles officially split on April 10. As a solo artist, Paul was often derided for celebrating the very sort of joys of domesticity reflected in this clip—but had he consistently come up with songs as strong as "Maybe I'm Amazed," it would never have become an issue.

It's strange that "Maybe I'm Amazed" was never released on a single, though many critics cited it then and since as an obvious hit that never was (though a live version, recorded on Paul's 1976 US tour, made No. 10 in the American charts in 1977). The preparation of this promo clip hints that the prospect was at least considered, promo films for LP-only tracks still being uncommon at the time. Had the Beatles somehow managed to remain together in 1970, it might have been considered as a *Beatles* single. But that's an alternate-universe scenario that didn't happen, leaving "Maybe I'm Amazed" as not just Paul's first solo promo film, but also the last one issued by any of the Beatles in the period covered by this book.

PART 3

Here, There, but Not Everywhere

The only officially released album, issued in 1979, to include most of the versions of the songs Lennon and McCartney gave away is now itself a rarity.

The Songs the Beatles Gave Away

Introduction

There were quite a few songs that one or more of the Beatles wrote (and, in two instances, co-wrote) that the group did not record before splitting—but which *were* released by other artists. Hardliners may question, then, whether such material should be covered in a book ostensibly devoted to music that is both by the Beatles and was not released before the band broke up (or ever). These 25 compositions *are* worthy of attention, however, for several reasons. First, they form a significant adjunct to the group's main body of work. Second, they really aren't all that well known, even though many of them were fairly big hits, and they're certainly not nearly as well known as the Beatles' own records. And third, there's some good music on these discs—and even when it's not so good, at the very least the records provide interesting looks at some of the group's more secondary efforts, discarded as unsuitable or too weak for their own recording sessions.

There were several reasons why the Beatles "gave away" some of their compositions to other artists, especially in 1963 and 1964, when more than half of these donations were made. First, by the time the group's career really got moving in early 1963, John Lennon and Paul McCartney had built up a considerable backlog of tunes, which almost

without exception weren't nearly as strong as the ones they were now writing for their own new releases. A few of them had been among their best original material just a year before, as evidenced by the inclusion of "Hello Little Girl," "Love of the Loved," and "Like Dreamers Do" at their January 1962 Decca audition. Rather than consign them to the cupboard, however, John and Paul—very keen to develop their standing as songwriters as well as recording and performing artists—knew that some of these could be fobbed off on other groups and singers. That not only brought them some cash, but solidified their value (if only commercially) as composers within the record and publishing world. The same held true for a few songs they wrote after early 1963 that, they realized, were too weak or unsuitable for the Beatles to do, but might still make hits for other performers.

Second, Lennon-McCartney and Brian Epstein both saw that the surplus could be used to help other artists in the Epstein management stable, who were usually Liverpool friends as well. In fact, every Lennon-McCartney song given away in 1963 went to a fellow Epstein act, whether Billy J. Kramer & the Dakotas, Tommy Quickly, the Fourmost, or Cilla Black. Not coincidentally, Kramer, the Fourmost, and Black were all also produced by George Martin and signed to the Beatles' label, Parlophone. The first such composition given to a non-Epstein act, "World Without Love" (a Transatlantic No. 1 for Peter & Gordon), was still keeping it in the family, as Peter Asher was the brother of Paul's girlfriend, Jane.

There were a few exceptions, but as a general rule of thumb, the songs the Beatles gave away were more lightweight—at times, they were out-and-out wimpy—than any of the original compositions that were finding a place on the group's own releases. This enabled John and Paul to have their cake and eat it too, in a way, by getting royalties from these auxiliary hits without having such innocuous throwaways dilute the Beatles' official product. When asked about such gifts in their early years, the group would diplomatically reply that they simply felt that a few of the songs they'd written weren't suitable to do themselves and would be better handled by others.

After 1963, for whatever reason, most of the Lennon-McCartney giveaways were primarily or wholly penned by Paul. John seemed to lose interest in this sideline virtually entirely, perhaps finding the whole idea of crafting material for more pop-inclined acts too much of a sellout. After 1964, even Paul seldom offered an unrecorded tune to someone else. And on those occasions when he did, it was usually because it was obviously a style that was too alien for the Beatles, be it the showbiz variety television theme of Cilla Black's "Step Inside Love," the Black Dyke Mills Band's instrumental brass number "Thingumybob," or the jazz instrumental "Cat Call" (though the last of these had been part of the Beatles' onstage repertoire in their Cavern days). As George Harrison began to increase his extra-group activities, he too entered the fray with a giveaway (to Jackie Lomax) and an outside songwriting collaboration (for Cream with Eric Clapton) near the end of the 1960s, though he seemed to save most of his extras for his own *All Things Must Pass* solo debut in 1970.

There are few truly outstanding songs among the compositions the Beatles gave away. Only "Bad to Me," "World Without Love," "Woman," "Badge," and "Come and Get It" are at or close to the standards of the group's own records, and none of those would have counted among the band's most excellent tracks. Too, in almost every instance where there's an unreleased Beatles (or solo Beatle) recording of a song they gave away—be it a studio outtake, demo, BBC recording, or even some tossed-off home tape—the Beatles version is *way* superior and gutsier. Still, almost all of the issued recordings of their giveaways are at least modestly catchy and enjoyable, with just a couple outright stinkers. A CD compilation of all 25 of them would make for a great collection, but somehow it's never appeared, even though most of the recordings are controlled by EMI. Most of them did make it onto a fine 20-song 1979 LP compilation by EMI in the UK, *The Songs Lennon and McCartney Gave Away*. Yet even that was missing the five giveaways that came out on Apple (as well as Cream's "Badge"), and it's long been out of print. Bootleggers have tried to jump into the gap with pirate anthologies, but these don't do the job properly. For instance, even leaving aside its failure to master from the best original sources, the bootleg *Every Song the Beatles Gave Away* cuts off the first few seconds of a few tracks, and uses the Gerry & the Pacemakers version of "Hello Little Girl" instead of the one by the Fourmost (who were the first to release it, as well as having the hit with the song). Add this, then, to the long list of Beatles and Beatles-related projects that should be available officially, but aren't. In the meantime, here's a rundown on what you might be missing.

● I'll Be on My Way

Billy J. Kramer & the Dakotas
Recorded: March 21, 1963
Released: April 26, 1963 (Parlophone, UK)
Chart Position: None (B-side of "Do You Want to Know a Secret")

"I'll Be on My Way" was the very first Lennon-McCartney song to be covered that the Beatles themselves didn't record. Billy J. Kramer's cover has lost a little of its luster since the emergence—first on bootleg, then on the official *Live at the BBC*—of the Beatles' own, considerably better version, recorded for the BBC on April 4, 1963 (see entry in previous chapter). Still, it's a nice Buddy Hollyesque song, competently (though not excitingly) done by Kramer. He, the Beatles, and George Martin couldn't have thought *that* much of the song, as it was used as a B-side, albeit to Kramer's cover of another Lennon-McCartney song, "Do You Want to Know a Secret" (which reached No. 2 in the UK). Still, it generated just as much publishing income as a hit A-side, since "Do You Want to Know a Secret" was on the flip.

In the mid-'60s, by the way, some canny American bands realized there were a few Lennon-McCartney songs that had never become hits in the US that were ripe for cover. The Rockin' Ramrods, from Boston, were among the first, and did a quite good version of "I'll Be on My Way" on an obscure 45—better than Kramer's, and harder rocking than either Kramer's or the Beatles.'

● Bad to Me

Billy J. Kramer & the Dakotas
Recorded: June 27, 1963
Released: July 26, 1963 (Parlophone, UK)
Chart Positions: No. 1 UK; No. 9 US

"Bad to Me" was the best of the Beatles' 1963 giveaways, and the only such Lennon-McCartney gift besides "World Without Love" to make the Top Ten in the US. Its catchiness quotient is about on par with most of the original material the Beatles cut in early 1963, and whether the resemblance was intentional or not, it's a little like an uptempo counterpart to "Do You Want to Know a Secret." It's perhaps just a tad innocuous even by early 1963 Beatles standards, and that might explain why the Beatles never attempted it in the studio. (Plus, unlike most of the 1963 giveaways, "Bad to Me" was, according to Lennon, deliberately commissioned for Kramer by Epstein.) The Beatles' scratchy acetate demo (see entry on page 55) is certainly a nice performance, though Kramer's George Martin–produced recording had a proper full-band arrangement. Like a bunch of the early Beatles singles, Kramer's "Bad to Me" wasn't released in the US right away, and wasn't a hit there until mid-1964, a few months after the British Invasion had gotten underway.

● Tip of My Tongue

Tommy Quickly
Recorded: July 1963

Released: July 30, 1963 (Piccadilly, UK)

Chart Position: None

Soundly derided by most critics, "Tip of My Tongue" was also one of the least successful Lennon-McCartney discards, failing to even make the British charts. Of all the songs discussed in this section, this is one of the most peculiar, with a jaunty, herky-jerky structure; awkwardly phrased lyrics that jam too many words into the verse without a pause for breath; bizarre, pin-prick, high-pitched female backup vocals; and a showbiz finale of a coda where you can just see a variety show cast lining up to spread their arms at the front of the stage as the curtain prepares to drop. Even Paul was embarrassed about the song when he (briefly) discussed it in *Paul McCartney: Many Years from Now*. If a minority view can be offered here, the song really isn't that bad (or good); it *is* corny, but there's some embryonic Merseybeat catchiness as well. The Beatles did think enough of it to consider recording it in late 1962 at their "Please Please Me" single session, but apparently never got it on tape. It's best regarded, as is "Like Dreamers Do," as an example of Paul finding his feet as a composer. He's starting to probe unconventional chord progressions, but somewhat clumsily structuring them, as if he's tripping over his own tongue.

● Hello Little Girl

The Fourmost

Recorded: July 3, 1963

Released: August 30, 1963 (Parlophone, UK)

Chart Position: No. 9 UK

As discussed in part one, "Hello Little Girl" had been around since at least 1960, when the Beatles made a Buddy Holly–like home recording of the song. By the time they played it at their Decca audition on January 1, 1962, they'd made it much more Beatlesque, with counterpoint backup harmonies and a bridge that went in a much different melodic direction than the verse. It was still a pretty basic and modest, if promising, effort, and understandably the group had moved on from such material by the time they selected the numbers for the *Please Please Me* LP. The Fourmost's version is out-and-out pop Merseybeat and frankly less appetizing than the Beatles' Decca demo, with some screechy falsetto harmonies and an instrumental bridge with an unnecessary celeste (presumably producer George Martin's idea). They did add an upward key change for the final part of the song, and it certainly did well enough for them, reaching the British Top Ten (though neither it nor any other Fourmost single would so much as make the Top 100 in the US). "Hello Little Girl," incidentally, was also recorded by fellow Liverpool band Gerry & the Pacemakers (on July 17, 1963), but their cover—inferior to both the Beatles and Fourmost versions—was not released until 1991.

● Love of the Loved

Cilla Black

Recorded: August 28, 1963

Released: September 27, 1963 (Parlophone, UK)

Chart Position: No. 35 UK

Another discard that had been part of the Beatles' Decca audition, "Love of the Loved" became Cilla Black's debut single. Though she and producer George Martin certainly put a lot of energy into the tune, the result sounded somewhat like Ethel Merman gone Merseybeat, and the squawking horns now sound especially embarrassingly dated. Again, the Beatles' Decca rendition, as relatively primitive as it is, makes for a far better, more enjoyable and rock-oriented listen of this fairly decent, haunting tune. Black, interestingly, has remembered being disappointed with her own recording, telling *Record Collector* in a 1997 interview, "I walked into the studio expecting a pop group, not proper musicians. And there was a brass section which I wasn't keen on: it sounded too perfect. I wanted that rawness, that sound that the Beatles had playing in the Cavern." The relatively underwhelming chart performance of the single didn't keep Black from trying Lennon-McCartney leftovers a couple more times, but strangely, none of her interpretations ranked among her biggest UK hits. The best cover of "Love of the Loved," in fact, is found on an obscure 1966 single by the E-Types (a California band), who gave it a smooth, harmonized, mid-tempo rock arrangement.

● I'll Keep You Satisfied

Billy J. Kramer & the Dakotas

Recorded: October 14, 1963

Released: November 1, 1963 (Parlophone, UK)

Chart Positions: No. 4 UK; No. 30 US

Other than possibly Peter & Gordon, no act benefited as much from Lennon-McCartney extras as Billy J. Kramer, who probably wouldn't have gotten a single hit if John and Paul hadn't supplied material. "I'll Keep You Satisfied" was too bland and genteel to have made for even an adequate Beatles LP track. But as tuneful, mid-tempo Merseybeat goes, it wasn't bad, and made for another Kramer smash, though not quite as big a hit as his first two Lennon-McCartney–penned singles were.

● I'm in Love

The Fourmost

Recorded: Circa October-November 1963

Released: November 15, 1963 (Parlophone, UK)

Chart Position: No. 17 UK

Besides "Tip of My Tongue," this is the least known of the songs John and Paul gave away in 1963, though it did fairly well on the British charts. It's actually one of the better ones in the batch, with a nicely haunting, downward-spiraling Merseybeat melody and acceptably sub-Beatles vocal harmonies. In common with some of the other extra-Beatles Lennon-McCartney songs covered in 1963, however, it's got a strange and somewhat awkward structure, with sudden jerky tempo changes and a feeling that the finished tune has been pieced together from different, not wholly simpatico works-in-progress. It's also one of the rare instances in which

Cilla Black (pictured here with Brian Epstein) covered several Lennon-McCartney songs the Beatles never released.

the released cover version is better than the sole existing unreleased Beatles-related one, on which John sluggishly works on the song on piano by his lonesome (see entry on page 60). The song was also attempted in the studio by Billy J. Kramer on October 14, 1963, with Lennon in attendance, though his version (which was distinctly less impressive than the Fourmost's) wasn't released until 1991.

● World Without Love

Peter & Gordon
Recorded: January 21, 1964
Released: February 28, 1964 (Columbia, UK)
Chart Positions: No. 1 UK; No. 1 US

This author's vote for the best song the Beatles gave away goes to "World Without Love," which was also the most commercially successful such item, going to No. 1 in both the UK and US. Unlike the songs they'd doled out to others in 1963, this did not bear either the marks of an early, pre–"Please Please Me," finding-our-way effort, or something that had been passed over as being too dainty for the Beatles' own records. Certainly it would have made for one of the lighter 1963–1964 Beatles tracks if the group had decided to do it, but it wouldn't have stuck wildly out of place. Instead, it was simply a solid, immensely tuneful, tightly constructed composition that lent itself well to close harmonies. It was also the first Lennon-McCartney giveaway not to be produced by George Martin, which might have actually worked to its advantage. Martin's productions of non-Beatles Epstein-managed acts tended toward the saccharine. Peter & Gordon's "World Without Love," however, was given a fairly straightforward guitar rock arrangement and a prominent organ (especially in the solo), ably supporting the duo's strong Everly Brothers–cum–British Invasion harmonies.

On June 27, 1964, "World Without Love" became the first British Invasion single not by the Beatles to top the American charts. Though *Paul McCartney: Many Years from Now* reports the song was written when Paul was 16, Peter Asher confirmed in a 1995 *Goldmine* article that some additional work went into it shortly before the Peter & Gordon recording. "I'd heard it in passing," he remembered. "It didn't have a bridge. It wasn't until EMI had signed us up and wanted to make a record that I went back to Paul and said, 'Would you write a bridge for that song and may we do it on our first album?' and he said yes. Then I had to nag him a couple more times to actually write the bridge and then he did." Both John and Paul have recalled how John thought the opening line, in which the singer begs to be locked away, was silly, and maybe that hindered it from ever being considered for a Beatles session. After it became a Transatlantic No. 1, one wonders if they began to consider whether they'd never fully realized what they had.

● One & One Is Two

The Strangers with Mike Shannon
Recorded: March 20, 1964
Released: May 8, 1964 (Philips, UK)
Chart Position: None

While "World Without Love" might have been the best Lennon-McCartney song that was given away, the very next such composition to be released was one of the *worst* Lennon-McCartney songs to find a home outside of the Beatles. What's so surprising about "One & One Is Two" is its near absence of Beatlesque touches. Even the lesser Beatles rejects, like "Tip of My Tongue" and "Like Dreamers Do," had some of those. "One & One Is Two," by contrast, sounds like generic, by-numbers, grind-it-out Merseybeat with tepid R&B inflections. The Strangers bring decent energy to the song, but there's just not much that can be done with the material. It had in fact first been written with Billy J. Kramer in mind, and offered to the Fourmost. Its very placement with the Strangers with Mike Shannon, a hitless group about whom little is known, indicates that this was one of the very rare Lennon-McCartney songs that had a problem finding *any* takers. A piano-guitar Beatles demo of the song from early 1964 has circulated (see entry on page 86), and that's none too impressive either, though it does offer the benefit of hearing Paul himself sing the tune.

● Nobody I Know

Peter & Gordon
Recorded: April 1964
Released: May 29, 1964 (Columbia, UK)
Chart Positions: No. 10 UK; No. 12 US

Although several of Peter & Gordon's 1964 singles bear Lennon-McCartney songwriting credits, it's now reasonably well known that all of these were pretty much McCartney solo efforts. Such was the case with "Nobody I Know," which wasn't nearly as solid a tune as "World Without Love." Like some other Lennon-McCartney giveaways, there's a tra-la-la sing-along quality about it that rarely made it into the original material on Beatles records in such a concentrated syrupy dose. The bridge, too, doesn't transition back to the verse nearly as neatly as it does in most of the Beatles' songs, and the Beatles seldom employed jumps to higher keys for dramatic effect near the end of their tracks, as Peter & Gordon did here. For all that, it's another respectably catchy tune, well harmonized by Peter & Gordon, with prominent, folky acoustic guitar licks that (at least in retrospect) established the duo as folk-rock precursors of sorts. And it was a pretty big hit for the pair on both sides of the Atlantic, though not nearly as big as "World Without Love."

● Like Dreamers Do

The Applejacks
Recorded: Circa May 1964
Released: June 5, 1964 (Decca, UK)
Chart Position: No. 20 UK

The last of the three Lennon-McCartney originals from the Decca audition to find a home on a commercial release, "Like Dreamers Do" was covered by the Applejacks. A relatively obscure Birmingham band who unusually (for the mid-'60s) included a female bassist, they never made the Top 100 in the US. They'd had a Top Ten hit in the UK with "Tell Me When," however, so they weren't no-names, though the failure of the song to get placed with an Epstein act hints that it wasn't easy to find a taker for the tune. Despite being fairly successful in Britain (where it reached No. 20), the Applejacks' version of the song is considerably worse than the one on the Beatles' Decca tape. It had an overly bright, jaunty arrangement that—like several of the early Lennon-McCartney giveaway covers—took the slight but pleasant song, with its steep, staircase-climbing chord progressions, away from the rockier guitar base of the Beatles' arrangement. Ironically, the single was produced by Mike Smith—the same guy who'd produced (or at least taped) the Beatles' version at that Decca audition. One wonders if he recognized or remembered the song from that day, and whether he grimaced at having to make a single out of a composition played at the audition he'd so infamously rejected.

● From a Window

Billy J. Kramer & the Dakotas
Recorded: May 29, 1964
Released: July 17, 1964 (Parlophone, UK)
Chart Positions: No. 10 UK; No. 23 US

A slightly lesser cousin of "I'll Keep You Satisfied," "From a Window" had a similar blend of guitar and piano on this tuneful but hardly super-memorable slice of mild Merseybeat. It's distinguished from its predecessor by its rolling beat, the stuttering, emphatic way the bridge ends, and its unexpected branch into a rich, harmonized line at the finish heard nowhere else on the song. On the final word of that line, you can hear Paul singing high harmony, Kramer never being good at hitting high notes. This was the last Lennon-McCartney song given to Kramer, whose career, uncoincidentally, quickly sank afterward. In any case, with the arguable exception of "I Don't Want to See You Again," Lennon and McCartney would no longer be writing the kind of lightweight Merseybeat fare that Kramer was adapting.

● It's for You

Cilla Black
Recorded: July 2, 1964
Released: July 31, 1964 (Parlophone, UK)
Chart Positions:No. 7 UK; No. 79 US

The first song the Beatles had given to Cilla Black, "Love of the Loved," was something of a clean-out-the-closet throwaway. Indications are that the second Lennon-McCartney exclusive she nabbed, "It's for You," was taken more seriously, Paul recalling in *Paul McCartney: Many Years from Now* that it was written specifically for her. It was certainly a more mature work than "Love of the Loved," with subtly shifting, waltz-like tempos, unexpected jumps between keys, and an overlay of the melodically haunting quality that was so specific to much of McCartney's work. It was a dramatically effective tune, and as one with perhaps too much of an adult pop flavor to be suitable for a Beatles record, it made sense to give it to Black, who was already making moves into that sort of all-around-entertainment market. Perhaps, however, it was a little *too* complex to be a huge hit-parade success. It did well but not spec-

tacularly (peaking at No. 7) in the UK, and hardly charted at all in the US, where Black never did make a big breakthrough.

The Beatles seemed to take this composition more seriously than they did others they were crafting for other artists, to the point of helping with the promotion themselves. They had Black sing it on a guest spot on one of their BBC sessions, broadcast just days after the single's British release. Said Paul in *Many Years from Now,* "I remember when we first went over to America, plugging it to all the DJs, we used to talk to endlessly, 'Look, there's this girl singer in our stable and you should listen out for this song.'" Extraordinarily, at a press conference in Indianapolis on September 3, 1964, he went as far as to name "It's for You" as one of the best Lennon-McCartney compositions. For more rock-oriented listeners who don't care for George Martin's jazzy, orchestral production of Black's single, the best straight rock interpretation, with magnificent vocal harmonies, is found on an obscure mid-'60s single by the Texas band the Mods, reissued on CD at least once (on the compilation *Acid Visions: The Complete Collection, Vol. 3*).

● I Don't Want to See You Again

Peter & Gordon
Recorded: August 1964
Released: September 11, 1964 (Columbia, UK)
Chart Position: No. 16 US

One of the least-discussed Lennon-McCartney giveaways, "I Don't Want to See You Again" was, like the previous two such items Peter & Gordon had covered, really the work of Paul McCartney. While it's no gem, it's actually a bit of an underrated tune, with a nice dramatic, minor-keyed, folky melody and overall more downbeat feel than Paul usually adopted. That's especially to the fore in the opening few bars, where Peter & Gordon sing the title phrase with a couple of emphatic, declarative guitar chords, followed by a brief pause and tumble of drums. The sadness of the lyrics was accentuated, after the verse, by the introduction of orchestration, though the violins and cor anglais might have been too gushy, contributing to the fairly low estimation with which many British Invasion fans and critics regard the track. "I Don't Want to See You Again" was the first Lennon-McCartney charity case to become a hit in the US but not even chart in the UK.

● That Means a Lot

P.J. Proby
Recorded: April 7, 1965
Released: July 5, 1965 (Liberty, US)
Chart Position: No. 30 UK

Unlike every previous song Lennon and McCartney had given away, the Beatles had actually recorded "That Means a Lot" at EMI for consideration on one of their own releases. In fact, they put a good amount of effort into it, trying out several arrangements at different sessions before giving up on it (see relevant entries in the 1965 chapter). The best Beatles version of "That Means a Lot" came out on *Anthology 2,* and it's actually a fairly decent recording (and song), though not a great one. P.J. Proby's

The Beatles gave four songs away to Peter & Gordon in the mid-'60s, a connection fostered by Paul McCartney's romantic relationship with Peter Asher's sister, Jane.

interpretation is worse in every respect than the Beatles' fairly straightforward, mid-tempo, guitar rock rendition, from the overly melodramatic lead singing to the grandiose, slowed-down orchestral arrangement and backing vocals. Proby, an American who moved to England in the mid-'60s and found far more success in the UK than at home, was probably awarded the song as he'd been friendly with the group for a while, appearing on the *Around the Beatles* TV special in April 1964.

● Woman

Peter & Gordon
Recorded: December 1965
Released: January 10, 1966 (Capitol, US)
Chart Positions: No. 28 UK; No. 14 US

Though it was far from the most successful song the Beatles cast off, "Woman" is one of the better-known such tunes, mostly because of the circumstances under which it was released. Initially the songwriting credit was given to one "Bernard Webb"; US copies listed "A. Smith" as a co-composer. It soon emerged that the actual writer was Paul McCartney, who—like Peter & Gordon—wanted to see if a song he gave away would be a hit if it were credited to a pseudonym. And it was a hit, though not a very big one, doing much better business in the US than the UK. "People

come up to [Peter & Gordon] and say, 'Ah, we see you're just getting in on the Lennon-McCartney bandwagon,'" explained Paul at a Los Angeles press conference on August 24, 1966, during the Beatles' final tour. "That's why they did that one with our names not on it, 'Woman,' because everyone sort of thinks that's the reason they get hits. It's not true, really." And Peter & Gordon did have a number of hits not written by Lennon and McCartney—more than, say, Billy J. Kramer did—though their Lennon-McCartney covers are the ones that remain their most famous tracks.

The song itself, like the earlier "It's for You," had something of a more adult pop flavor than most of what Paul had written for the Beatles. Still, it's a fairly strong, yearning number with an upbeat sort of drama. It's certainly much more thoughtfully constructed in both the melodic and lyrical department than most of the original material the Beatles were not electing to record themselves. If it's hard to imagine as a Beatles recording, that's in part due to the densely orchestral, brassy production, which is much more fussily flamboyant than anything the Beatles did (even after they started to use strings and brass). If Paul and the Beatles were hoping the true identity of "Bernard Webb" would slip by unnoticed, however, they were sadly mistaken, the publishing credit for Northern Songs being an instant giveaway. As Gordon Waller admitted in *Record Collector*, "Unfortunately the first review said, 'This Bernard Webb has an amazing talent. Could even be Paul McCartney!' and a couple of weeks later it was out of the bag."

Apparently, Peter & Gordon and McCartney all regretted the track's overproduction, Peter Asher remarking in Kristofer Engelhardt's *Beatles Undercover*, "We ended up cutting the song twice for some reason and Paul and I weren't crazy about the way it ended up. We didn't like the Bob Leaper arrangement too much. We started cutting it; he was there for day one. Paul had some arrangement ideas, some of which our producer ignored, and I think that's why he didn't come back. Paul wanted the song to be much smaller, and what [producer] John Burgess did was take Paul's ideas, and then have Bob Leaper turn them into a very big orchestration which Paul wasn't crazy about. I think in retrospect Paul was right. We could have made a better record, it was a great song." Three years later, while doodling on the song on piano at a January 14, 1969, *Get Back* session, Paul agreed, claiming, "We did a much better one, very first time we ever did it. It was very dry, just little, with like about eight violins . . . it really sounded like a little string quartet, you know. But, I don't know, we were very fussy at the time, and didn't like it. And so it got turned into a mammoth ballad. It's a great song . . . we did a great version the first time we did it. Only Gordon couldn't get the high notes."

● Cat Call

The Chris Barber Band
Recorded: July 20, 1967
Released: October 20, 1967 (Marmalade, UK)
Chart Position: None

A real oddity, "Cat Call" was actually a retitled version of a very early Paul McCartney instrumental, "Catswalk," that the Beatles had done in their Cavern days. In fact, there are a couple of unreleased versions of the Beatles themselves doing "Catswalk" on a late-1962 rehearsal tape (see entry on page 36). Back then, it was a jazzy, slinky, haunting instrumental with the standard rock guitar-bass-drums lineup. When it was exhumed in 1967, however, it was thoroughly overhauled into a Dixieland-style traditional jazz number by the leading trad jazz outfit in the UK, the Chris Barber Band, who'd been recording since the late '40s. Several of the assembled guests—including Brian Auger, Jane Asher, Barber's wife Ottilie Patterson, ex–Pretty Things drummer Viv Prince, Barry Jenkins and Vic Briggs of the Animals, and McCartney himself (who also added keyboards)—added wordless vocals in the manner of fugitives hiding out in a Prohibition-era speakeasy. The rhythm slowed to a stripper-like bump-and-grind near the end, giving everyone a chance to weigh in with applause and whistles, like partygoers welcoming the nude girl stepping out of the cake.

As fun a record as it was in its modest way, it wasn't hit material. As a side note, the Plastic Ono Band's "Cold Turkey" is usually cited as the first record written by John Lennon or Paul McCartney for the pop market to bear a songwriting credit in which just one name (John's, in that case) was listed. Not so—"Cat Call" was the first, the single listing Paul McCartney as the sole composer. (Earlier in 1967, Paul's soundtrack for the 1967 movie *The Family Way* also bore songwriting credits for McCartney alone, but this is generally not considered a release for the pop market, although it did yield a single by George Martin & His Orchestra, "Love in the Open Air." And speaking of George Martin & His Orchestra, Martin's 1965 instrumental LP *Help!* included three Lennon-McCartney songs with titles not found in the Beatles' official catalog:

"Scrambled Egg," "That's a Nice Hat (Cap)," and "Auntie Gin's Theme." However, these are merely instrumental versions of "Yesterday," "It's Only Love," and "I've Just a Seen a Face" respectively, recorded when those songs still had early "working" titles that changed by the time the Beatles recorded them for their own *Help!* album.)

● Step Inside Love

Cilla Black
Recorded: February 28, 1968
Released: March 8, 1968 (Parlophone, UK)
Chart Position: No. 8 UK

Custom-written by Paul McCartney as a theme song for Cilla Black's late-'60s British television variety series, "Step Inside Love" had been written by November 21, 1967, when Black did a demo of the song with Paul helping out on acoustic guitar and vocals. (That demo was eventually issued on the 1997 Black compilation *1963–1973: The Abbey Road Decade*, and there is also a lo-fi, late-1967 McCartney solo demo of the song; see entry on page 183). The number served its purpose well—it was certainly above average for a late-'60s TV variety theme—but no one would call it one of Paul's more outstanding compositions. In its finished form it had something of a brassy bossa nova feel, and if you ever wondered what McCartney might have written had he decided to pen a Burt Bacharach–influenced tune for Dionne Warwick (whose "Anyone Who Had a Heart," incidentally, Black had covered for a No. 1 hit in the UK in 1964), here's your chance. Black's demo is in a way more appealing, featuring as it does only Paul's acoustic guitar (and, on the bridge, his hummed, wordless vocals). *1963-1973: The Abbey Road Decade*, incidentally, features an earlier, fully orchestrated take of the song (also recorded on November 21, 1967) with a more pronounced bossa nova feel. And if you *really* can't get enough of the tune, it also has Black's Italian-language version, "M'Innamoro."

In *Goldmine*, Black remembered, "The BBC kept sending me all these very big 'There's No Business Like Show Business' kind of songs, which wasn't me at all. And I got a phone call out of the blue [from Paul] and he said, 'I know what they're all doing at the BBC. They're sending you all these songs, Billy Cotton Band show-type songs, and that's not you. You're the kind of person that should invite yourself into their houses, start off quiet and build up,' and he was totally right." Black also recalled Paul finishing "the middle in the bathroom" when, after singing just the beginning and ending on the TV show, demand was sparked for a single. As colorful a story as this is, it seems incorrect, as the complete song was first recorded on November 21, 1967, more than a couple of months before the first episode of the series (which was broadcast live) was aired.

● Sour Milk Sea

Jackie Lomax
Recorded: June 24–26, 1968
Released: August 26, 1968 (Apple, UK)
Chart Position: No. 117 US

It's well known by now that George Harrison built up a considerable backlog of unrecorded compositions in the last few years of the 1960s, dating back to at least 1966. It's a little surprising, then, that he didn't try to get at least a few of them recorded by other artists, if only to serve as evidence that he had more to offer as a composer than he was given space to demonstrate on Beatles releases. The only instance in which he did give a song away for official release was for Jackie Lomax's "Sour Milk Sea," which he had demoed in May 1968 as part of the pre–*White Album* Beatles recordings done at his Esher home. The Beatles never attempted "Sour Milk Sea" in the studio, but the Lomax cover comes close in a sense to being a *White Album* recording, as all of the Beatles except John are playing on it. For that matter, two of the other musicians on the single had prominent guest roles on two major actual Beatles recordings, pianist Nicky Hopkins playing on the "Revolution" single and lead guitarist Eric Clapton on "While My Guitar Gently Weeps." The Beatles knew Lomax well, as he'd been in a fellow Liverpool group in their Cavern/Hamburg days, the Undertakers, and George worked with him especially closely after Jackie signed to Apple, producing Lomax's debut LP *Is This What You Want?* (which included the "Sour Milk Sea" single).

For all the effort involved, however, "Sour Milk Sea" isn't that great a song. It's a serviceable hard-rock number with a bluesy boogie feel, its tense chord ascensions slightly recalling the considerably superior Harrison *White Album* track "Savoy Truffle." The lyrics take, as George often did, a rather dour look at life's predicaments, coming off as a blend of encouragement and mild scolding. In his semi-autobiography *I Me Mine,* the composer revealed the song was "about meditation. I used 'Sour Milk Sea' as the idea of—if you're in the shit, don't go around moaning about it; do something about it."

Although it was one of the four singles simultaneously issued as Apple's first batch of releases in late August 1968, it didn't make the UK charts at all, and barely made the US listings, where it bubbled under the Top 100. That was still a better showing than one of the other four 45s from that group (see following entry).

As a bizarre side note to the whole Apple deal, late-'60s pop-rock star Tommy James said in an interview with Gary James on the classic bands.com website that "Lennon and McCartney were just starting Apple Publishing Co. before they started the label, and they approached me with some tunes that a couple of members of the Beatles had written for me. They came to my apartment. I wasn't home. However, my manager, who was in the same building, was there, and they came to him with the tapes. I didn't particularly care for the tunes and I never recorded them . . . I don't think they were ever recorded. I have them somewhere in my library of tapes." Why John and Paul would be eager to offer Tommy James—whose enjoyable but lightweight brand of music was far removed from what they were doing in 1968—otherwise unrecorded Beatles songs is unclear. There might be more foundation to the story than some would think, however, as the first serious rock music reference book, 1969's *Lillian Roxon's Rock Encyclopedia,* claimed that when James's "Mony Mony" "made number one on the English charts in the summer of 1968, George Harrison sent him some Beatles songs."

● Thingumybob

John Foster & Sons Ltd. Black Dyke Mills Band
Recorded: June 30, 1968

Released: August 26, 1968 (Apple, UK)
Chart Position: None

The most bizarre song the Beatles gave away, and one of the strangest (or at least most uncharacteristic) they had anything to do with as composers, was John Foster & Sons Ltd. Black Dyke Mills Band's instrumental "Thingumybob." Like "Step Inside Love," however, it arose directly as a result of Paul McCartney accepting the commission to write a TV theme, this one for the British comedy series *Thingumybob*. The Black Dyke Mills Band, a long-established brass band founded in the 1940s, cut the track in Bradford. Paul himself traveled up there to help with conducting and arranging, having first tried and failed to do it with different musicians in London. It's a spry, zippy tune that brings to mind an accomplished village brass band welcoming a dignitary onto the platform at some civic celebration. But a hit single it wasn't, even though it was released simultaneously with three other 45s in late August 1968 in the very first group of Apple releases. That might not have been as much of a help as it might seem, as aside from Jackie Lomax's "Sour Milk Sea" (see above entry), that batch also included the Beatles' "Hey Jude" and Mary Hopkin's "Those Were the Days." Both latter singles were international chart-toppers, and couldn't help but overshadow the other Apple 45s issued at the same time.

According to a comment by Peter Asher in *Goldmine,* Paul "always loved brass band music. It's a big thing in England. [All the mills and factories] in the north of England would traditionally each have amateur brass bands, assembled from the workers, and there would be a big competition. We'd been asked to do [the TV theme] and Paul said 'I want to do this with a brass band.' So we found out who the competition winners were at that time and it was the Black Dyke Mills Band. So we went up north and did it there with them. We all drove up together."

As peculiar footnotes to a peculiar single, the US "Thingumybob" single bore the songwriting credit "McCartney & Lennon," a reversal of the way the names had virtually always appeared since mid-1963. As further evidence that Paul's venture into the world of brass bands might not have been a mere passing fancy, when asked what kind of music he listened to at home by Bill Aylward in Indianapolis on September 3, 1964, Paul checked off rhythm and blues, country and western, Bach, modern jazz . . . and brass brands. Interjected Ringo, "Well, I'm not too struck on brass bands." "I was only joking," claimed Paul. "I know you were, Paul," sarcastically affirmed Ringo. But was he?

● Badge

Cream
Recorded: Late November 1968
Released: February 5, 1969 (Atco, US)
Chart Positions: No. 18 UK; No. 60 US

Despite its modest chart success as a single (partially attributable to Cream having broken up shortly before its release), "Badge" is certainly one of the most famous songs discussed in this chapter. You can argue that it shouldn't be considered a song that the Beatles "gave away" since it was not so much a surplus reject or specially commissioned extra-curricular activity as it was a compositional collaboration between one

Beatle and a fellow superstar. Still, George Harrison *was* in the Beatles when he wrote "Badge" with Eric Clapton, and the Beatles never recorded (or considered recording) it themselves. It's certainly one of Cream's best recordings, marrying their chunky rock power to a catchy pop melody, as well as a graceful yet enigmatic lyric. With such high-class results as this, one only wishes that Harrison and Clapton had written more together, though their ascendancy to superstardom as individuals in the early '70s would have probably made ongoing collaborations impractical.

As is now common knowledge, George played rhythm guitar on the track as well, though to avoid contractual hassles his contribution was credited to "L'Angelo Misterioso." Although he's not named in the songwriting credits, George also revealed in his 1977 *Crawdaddy* interview that Ringo contributed "that line about the swans living in the park," which would make "Badge" the sole composition recorded by an artist other than the Beatles that the drummer had a hand in writing in the 1960s. (By the way, George also wrote a verse for Donovan's "Hurdy Gurdy Man" that was not used in the 1968 hit version of the song, though subsequent Donovan live recordings of the tune included the missing lines.)

● Goodbye

Mary Hopkin
Recorded: March 1, 1969
Released: March 28, 1969 (Apple, UK)
Chart Positions: No. 2 UK; No. 13 US

Paul McCartney had taken a great interest in Mary Hopkin's career, signing her to Apple after a tip from Twiggy and producing her debut

The unavailability of a comprehensive collection of Beatles giveaways has led to the appearance of unauthorized anthologies such as this one.

LP, *Post Card* (which included her mega-smash 1968 hit single, "Those Were the Days"). He wrote her follow-up single to the LP, "Goodbye," which—while it was no "Those Were the Days"—did quite well, in fact becoming her only other big US hit. Paul had recorded a demo with just his voice and acoustic guitar (see entry on page 264), but here's a rare instance where the officially released interpretation is better than the existing unreleased recording by one or all of the Beatles. The bittersweet (if generally upbeat) music hall folk tune was simply a much better fit for a high-voiced female vocalist such as Hopkin. Plus the single—again produced by McCartney—had a far fuller, more effective arrangement.

In a 1995 interview with *Goldmine,* Hopkin admitted to having mixed feelings about "Goodbye," at a time when she would have preferred getting into more serious, folkier material (as she eventually did on the 1971 album *Earth Song, Ocean Song*). "A year went by [after she first recorded for Apple] before he wrote 'Goodbye,'" she reminisced. "And that was after I'd said, 'Look, how about another single?' But I understood. Obviously his priority was the Beatles, that's natural. He said he wrote 'Goodbye' in about ten minutes. I'm not sure how true that is! It probably is. . . . And Paul put a thigh-slap on there—on his own thigh, I might add! It's a good song for its kind, but whether it was suited to me, I don't know. It was so easy to do those songs. They were fun little pop songs. So it was very easy for me to say, 'Oh. Okay. Yes.' But as soon as I realized what was happening, I started putting the reins on, and putting my foot down about what material I was going to do. I trusted Paul's judgment, anyway. I would never condemn him for what he did, because he did what he felt was right for me. And I really enjoyed working with him."

As a sad footnote, John Lennon—who had presumably profited handsomely by several songs Paul had written for others but allowed to be credited to Lennon-McCartney, such as "Goodbye"—made a subtle putdown of Hopkin at an autumn 1969 meeting between him, Paul, and George Harrison at Apple. Complaining about some of Paul's more lightweight numbers, John asked him (as quoted in Anthony Fawcett's *John Lennon: One Day at a Time*), "Wouldn't it be better, because we didn't really dig them, yer know, for you to do the songs you dug, and 'Ob-La-Di, Ob-La-Da' and 'Maxwell['s Silver Hammer]' to be given to people who like music like that yer know, like Mary [Hopkin], or whoever it is needs a song?"

● Penina

Carlos Mendes
Recorded: Circa early 1969
Released: July 18, 1969 (Parlophone, Portugal)
Chart Position: None

Beating out even the Strangers with Mike Shannon's "One & One Is Two" as the most obscure, most insignificant song the Beatles ever gave away, "Penina" was released as a Portuguese-only single by the mysterious Carlos Mendes. Paul used some of these extra-Beatles compositions to try on styles that had no place within the group, and "Penina" was a surprisingly bland, repetitive, easy-listening number, the kind you might find a hack lounge singer improvising to fill out his sets. As blithe

The Songs The Beatles *Almost* Gave Away

In addition to the compositions the Beatles didn't put out but gave to other artists to record, the group also sometimes gave other acts advance crack at a song that ended up appearing on an official Beatles release as well. In most cases, this was usually done with the knowledge that the non-Beatles version would not appear *before* the Beatles' recording was available, though sometimes the different versions would be issued simultaneously (and, in a couple of cases, the cover versions would never gain release at all). Obviously, these songs had to have been offered to, and recorded by, the other performers before the Beatles' rendition was in the shops. In that sense, these compositions could be considered ones that the group did give away in a limited fashion, with the knowledge that the tunes would be recorded (though not necessarily released) by others before the world had heard the Beatles themselves do them. Such pseudo-giveaways include:

Kenny Lynch, "Misery." Lynch, who had a few lightweight soul-pop hits in the UK without making a dent in the US market, was one of the acts on the Beatles' first British tour in early 1963. His March 22, 1963, single "Misery" was the very first Lennon-McCartney cover, issued the same day as the *Please Please Me* LP, which included the Beatles' own version. Lynch's recording, complete with strings and weedy, reverbed guitar, was kind of wimpy and not very good, failing to chart in the UK. It's interesting, however, for its inclusion of a few minor lyric variations, indicating he might have gotten the song before the composition was 100 percent finalized. John and Paul had actually written "Misery" with the intention of having Helen Shapiro (at that time a very big British star, and the headliner on the Beatles' first national UK tour) record it, but her producer turned it down without her knowledge. As Paul admitted in *Paul McCartney: Many Years from Now*, "It was just a job, you could have called us hacks, hacking out a song for someone," though the Beatles ultimately thought enough of it to put it on their first album.

Duffy Power, "I Saw Her Standing There." Although Power's cover of this classic, offered to him specially by the group, didn't come out until about a month after the Beatles' track of the song was issued on *Please Please Me*, Duffy had first recorded it in February 1963, when the band was taking off nationally. The Beatles didn't like the recording (on which he was backed by the Graham Bond Quartet with future stars John McLaughlin on guitar and Jack Bruce on bass), feeling it was too jazzy. "I actually didn't like the song very much," he admitted to the author in a 1996 interview for the book *Unknown Legends of Rock 'n' Roll*. "But I did it, and I changed it. And Bond played like mad on it, because he wasn't used to it. He didn't know anything about limits. When you're doing a two-and-a-half-minute record, you've got to give it a structure. You can't just go mad all over it. People laugh when they think I actually changed the tune of a Lennon-McCartney song, [putting] all these blues notes here. And they said, 'Aw, no, that's not our song!' So we had to go back and do it again."

So a remake (which wasn't vastly different, frankly) was done a month later and issued on a 45, though it didn't chart. Power does an adequate soul-R&B interpretation, but it's nowhere near as good as the Beatles' immortal recording. Both the unissued original attempt and the officially issued remake are on the Power CD compilation *Leapers and Sleepers*. It should be added that while his take on "I Saw Her Standing There" wasn't great, the underrated Power made some excellent blues-folk-rock recordings in the 1960s and early '70s that are well worth checking out.

Billy J. Kramer, "Do You Want to Know a Secret." This really slips just under the wire, as it was recorded on March 21, 1963, just the day before the Beatles' version of "Do You Want to Know a Secret?" appeared on *Please Please Me*. Certainly, however, the song was supplied to Kramer as a deliberate strategy by the Beatles, Brian Epstein, and George Martin to get Billy J.'s career off the ground. Kramer had actually first attempted the song in the studio a week before, but equipment malfunctioned and just one take captured his vocals—a take later issued, by mistake, on the various-artists LP *The Mersey and the Beat*. Kramer had also been doing the song onstage before the March 21 session that yielded his debut single. Rather blandly arranged and sung, it was much inferior to the Beatles' *Please Please Me* track. But it did become the first commercially successful Lennon-McCartney cover, reaching No. 2 in the UK, though it would be the Beatles' own version that was the hit in the US (where it likewise reached No. 2) after Beatlemania broke in the States in early 1964.

Billy J. Kramer, "I Call Your Name." When the Beatles issued "I Call Your Name" on April 10, 1964, on the US LP *The Beatles' Second Album* (putting it on a British EP a couple months later), it marked the only time they waited more than a few weeks to release an original song someone else had already recorded. "I Call Your Name" had been recorded by Billy J. Kramer back on June 27, 1963, and thrown away as the B-side of his second single, "Bad to Me," a month later. For whatever reason—perhaps to help meet the insatiable demand for new product as Beatlemania gripped the world—the group recorded "I Call Your Name" on March 1, 1964. "I Call Your Name," much of which John had written years before the Beatles signed with EMI, might be one of the group's more secondary early songs. But it must be said that the Beatles' interpretation absolutely slaughters Kramer's far blander, more easygoing version in every way. The insistent pounding beat, the electric 12-string guitar, the unexpected ska-tempoed instrumental break, and above all John Lennon's typically searing vocal—all exhibited an artistry and passion, even on such a relatively innocuous tune, that the likes of Kramer couldn't touch.

The Rolling Stones, "I Wanna Be Your Man." Undoubtedly the most famous song the Beatles *kinda* gave away, "I Wanna Be Your Man" was recorded by the Rolling Stones for their second single. Actually released (on November 1, 1963) three weeks ahead of the appearance of the same song on *With the Beatles*, it became the Stones' first substantial British hit single, falling just short of the Top Ten. As fine as the Beatles' version is, here's one instance in which the cover is better, the Stones giving the song a vicious, pile-driving attack that was both more powerful than the Fab Four's and took a wholly different approach. Particularly outstanding was Brian Jones's slide guitar, whose wailing howl gave the tune a raunchy bluesiness missing in the Beatles' more straightforward rock 'n' roll arrangement.

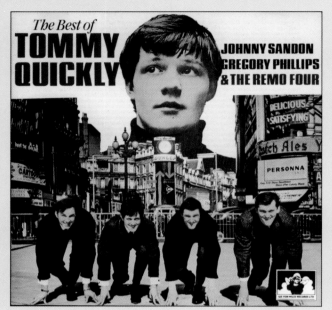

One of the most obscure artists to cover Lennon-McCartney material the Beatles never released was Tommy Quickly, whose '60s output is contained in full on this equally obscure CD compilation.

The story behind the Rolling Stones' acquisition of the song has been told in numerous books and varies a little according to the teller, but the basic premise is fairly consistent. Stones manager Andrew Loog Oldham (who had done some publicity for the Beatles early in their recording career), desperately seeking suitable material for the group's second 45, met John and Paul by chance on a London street. He convinced them to, on the spur of the moment, go with him to a Stones rehearsal. The pair finished writing "I Wanna Be Your Man" in minutes and generously allowed the Stones to record it, though the Beatles still found a place for it on their own LP. As much as the press sometimes liked to paint the two groups as rivals, in fact they were pretty friendly with each other, as different as they might have been stylistically, and "I Wanna Be Your Man" did a lot to help launch the Rolling Stones as a hit recording act.

As John remembered shortly before his death in his 1980 *Playboy* interview, "Paul just had this bit and we needed another verse or something. We sort of played it roughly to them and they said, 'Yeah, OK, that's our style.' So Paul and I just went off in the corner of the room and finished the song off while they were all still there talking. We came back and that's how Mick and Keith got inspired to write, because, 'Jesus, look at that. They just went in the corner and wrote it and came back!' Right in front of their eyes we did it. So we gave it to them. It was a throwaway. The only two versions of the song were Ringo and the Rolling Stones. That shows how much importance we put on it: We weren't going to give them anything *great*, right!?"

Tommy Quickly, "No Reply." Though it eventually became one of the stronger tracks on *Beatles for Sale*, "No Reply" was first targeted as a giveaway single to Tommy Quickly, who'd already cut a Lennon-

McCartney reject on his 1963 single "Tip of My Tongue." An August 7, 1964, release was even scheduled on Pye Records, but a Quickly cover never appeared, although it was apparently attempted in the studio. As bassist Don Andrew of Quickly's backing group the Remo Four remembered in Spencer Leigh's liner notes to the CD compilation *The Best of Tommy Quickly, Johnny Sandon, Gregory Phillips & the Remo Four,* "We recorded the backing first and we double-tracked the guitars, which was the first time we had done anything other than a straight one-off. We added extra percussion and Paul McCartney was playing tambourine. John Lennon was clinking Coke bottles together. It was a great rocking backing and all Tommy had to do was add the vocal. It was a combination of nerves and drink, but Tommy couldn't take it. He strained his lungs out but he couldn't sing in tune. [Producer] Tony Hatch was tearing his hair, and although he must have had some finished tracks, it was never released." Remo Four guitarist Colin Manley has recalled that the Beatles demo off which Quickly was working lacked a middle eight, though such a middle eight is already present on the June 3, 1964, outtake used on *Anthology 1* (see entry on page 95). As Quickly wasn't much of a singer, it's extremely doubtful that this version would have been nearly as good as the Beatles', particularly with the absence of that middle eight.

Cliff Bennett & the Rebel Rousers, "Got to Get You into My Life." A rather journeyman British blue-eyed-soul group, Cliff Bennett & the Rebel Rousers were fortunate enough to get slipped "Got to Get You into My Life" about six weeks in advance of its release. When Bennett and his band supported the Beatles on some German shows near the end of June 1966, as he remembered in *Beatles Undercover,* "Paul came into the dressing room and said, 'We've written a great song, John and I, and we think it would be ideal for you.' They actually demonstrated the song right there for us on acoustic guitar. Following a break in the tour, Paul came into the studio to help produce the song. Dave Paramor, our producer, just took a back seat. He let Paul come in and help with the arrangement and this and that. He was great because he was encouraging everybody; he was a great believer in our band. Paul played a little piano, the glissando, on the backing track and we finished at about midnight. We put the vocals on the following day." Bennett's single was released the exact same day as the Beatles' own version, which came out on the *Revolver* LP on August 5, 1966. It was a serviceable, competent cover sticking very close to the Beatles' arrangement (in fact, the aforementioned glissando was about the most notable difference), and managed to reach No. 6 in the UK. But it was no match for the Beatles' own version—the commercial viability of which was demonstrated when it made No. 7 in the US charts in 1976, a good six years after their split.

Mortimer, "Two of Us." In early 1969, the American group Mortimer recorded an entire Peter Asher–produced album for Apple that remains unreleased. When Paul McCartney visited a session, as Mortimer's Tom Smith remembered in Stefan Granados's *Those Were the Days: An Unofficial History of the Beatles Apple Organization 1967–2002,* "Paul noticed that we played a lot of acoustics and he said 'I've got a song I think you guys would be perfect for,' and played us 'Two of Us,' which was then still called 'On Our Way Home.' He played us an acetate of him and John playing it on acoustic guitars . . . they were joking together like the Everly Brothers saying, 'Take it Phil' and things like that. [If Smith's memory is accurate, this is likely the January 24,

1969, take of "Two of Us" that can be heard on *Anthology 3,* on which Paul can indeed be heard uttering that aside.] It was nice, but honestly I don't think any of us thought that it was a single. But the fact that Paul gave it to us and that Peter said 'let's go and try it,' we went and recorded it." The Beatles' "Two of Us" didn't come out until the release of the *Let It Be* LP about a year later, but Mortimer's version *never* came out. In fact, Mortimer was never able to put out anything on Apple, although according to Granados's book, the 11 songs they cut for the label comprised "an excellent collection of folk-influenced harmony rock."

Joe Cocker, "Something" and "She Came In through the Bathroom Window." It's hard to believe that George Harrison was so incognizant of the strength (and commercial appeal) of "Something" that Joe Cocker was allowed to record it around April 1969, a good five months before the Beatles' version appeared. (Even before that, Harrison had told George Martin's assistant Chris Thomas during the *White Album* sessions that he was giving "Something" to Jackie Lomax, a much lesser talent than either Harrison or Cocker.) What's more, Cocker has recalled George and Paul helping him record demos of both "Something" and "She Came In through the Bathroom Window" at Apple Studios at this time. The Beatles might have been eager to have Joe do more of the songs, as Cocker's cover of "With a Little Help from My Friends" had been particularly impressive, topping the UK charts in late 1968 in one of those rare occasions where an interpretation of a Lennon-McCartney song was wildly different from the Beatles' arrangement but of approximately equal artistic merit. Fortunately, Cocker's official version of "Something" didn't come out until his *Joe Cocker!* album in November 1969, by which time both *Abbey Road* and the "Something" single were high on the charts. *Joe Cocker!* also included his impressively slow, soulful reading of "She Came In through the Bathroom Window"—another track that he interpreted much differently than the Beatles had—which gave him a No. 30 US hit. George, incidentally, would almost give the second-biggest hit of his career away just a year later when Billy Preston's cover of "My Sweet Lord" appeared on a September 1970 single, more than two months before Harrison's immeasurably more successful 45 of the same tune was issued.

Aretha Franklin, "Let It Be." Some mystery still surrounds the circumstances under which Aretha Franklin recorded "Let It Be," but it seems likely that she did it sometime in 1969, perhaps as early as May—well before the Beatles released it on a March 1970 single. As Franklin's producer Jerry Wexler told it in *Beatles Undercover,* "They

sent me an acetate, I don't remember if it was Paul or the Beatles organization, with the suggestion that I do the song with Aretha. I loved it very much. I played it for Aretha and she didn't like it! As time went on, she decided that she did like it, so we cut it and had it in the can. I got a legal stop order from them [the Beatles] mandating that I could not put out the record. Once the [Beatles'] record was out, I could legally put it out. I could have legally put it out before the Beatles' version if I would have acted in time." Franklin's more gospel-flavored interpretation did come out (as part of her album *This Girl's in Love with You*) almost simultaneously with the Beatles' single, and possibly a couple of weeks before if that LP's reported February 21, 1970, release date is correct, though it's been speculated that this album wasn't out until the Beatles' "Let It Be" single was also available.

Trash, "Golden Slumbers"/"Carry That Weight." Although the Apple single of "Golden Slumbers"/"Carry That Weight" by Trash came out just after *Abbey Road* had been released, it had been recorded just before that LP was issued. How that came to pass is just one small reflection of how chaotic things were for both Apple and the Beatles at the time. As Fraser Watson remembered in an interview with the author in 2000, Apple/Beatles publicist Derek Taylor "sneaked in Neil Aspinall's office and stole his acetate, and gave it to us. He said, 'Take the most commercial song off that.' We went back home, recorded it in our tape recorder. We picked 'Golden Slumbers'/'Carry That Weight,' we thought it was quite catchy. George Harrison had some studio time that he wasn't using. Derek got us George Harrison's studio time, and George Martin gave us the scores for the string sessions for 'Golden Slumbers,' which we used ourselves. I played electric guitar, using George Harrison's Leslie [amp] cabinet, to get that kind of effect."

Continued Watson, "We had to get two Beatles to say yes to release it [on] Apple. And McCartney said, 'No, we're not releasing it.' The story was at that time that he was jealous, because Derek had gone behind his back, and because he thought it was a better version. But certainly the [Trash] version was different. It was heavier. Ronnie Leahy played some lovely organ in it. It was a good single, a commercial single, but a bit different from the Beatles. So Derek arranged for a couple of us to go down and see John Lennon, talked about the whole thing, and he said, 'I'll give you a decision.' About an hour later, we were sitting in the office, and Yoko came up and said, 'Yeah, John says that's fine.' And the whole place erupted." But Trash's version, which was their second single on Apple, got no further than No. 35 in the UK charts. Trash broke up soon afterward, and their cover of "Golden Slumbers" has never been reissued on CD.

an assertion as that might sound, the circumstances under which it was conceived turn out to be not far off that mark. In a 1994 issue of the Paul McCartney fan magazine *Club Sandwich,* the composer revealed, "I went to Portugal on holiday [in late 1968] and returned to the hotel one night slightly the worse for a few drinks. There was a band playing and I ended up on the drums. The hotel was called Penina, I made up a song with that name, someone made inquiries about it and I gave it to them. And, no, I shouldn't think I'd ever record it myself!"

Such was the obscurity of the single (on which Paul was credited as sole composer) that for many years, even Beatles collectors remained unaware of its existence. The Dutch group Jotta Herre cut it as well on a 1970 single, with a similar lack of commercial success. The Beatles did a minute-long version of "Penina" at the *Get Back* sessions on January 9, 1969, but in common with many of the tunes they briefly touched upon that month, it's a half-serious effort that's barely recognizable as a song.

● Come and Get It

Badfinger
Recorded: August 22 and August 26, 1969
Released: December 5, 1969 (Apple, UK)
Chart Positions: No. 4 UK; No. 7 US

After the fiasco that was "Penina," the history of Beatles '60s giveaways ended on a high note with "Come and Get It." With its instantly memorable, hummable, keyboard-based, mid-tempo tune and coyly enigmatic lyrics, it was not only a prototypical Paul McCartney song, but could have made a respectable Beatles LP track. It's now no secret that Paul first recorded it as a one-man demo of sorts at an actual Beatles session on July 24, 1969, the resulting outtake officially released on *Anthology 3* (see entry on page 270). It wasn't so much a Beatles outtake, however, as it was a two-pronged side project, fulfilling the dual purposes of supplying a theme song for *The Magic Christian* film (co-starring Ringo) and a hit single to get an Apple Records act (Badfinger) off the ground. As Badfinger's then-bassist Ron Griffiths remembered in Dan Matovina's *Without You: The Tragic Story of Badfinger,* Paul had been "surprised to read [in the British music paper *Disc & Music Echo*] that we felt neglected at Apple. He said, 'Look. I've been asked to do the score for this film, *The Magic Christian,* which I'm not particularly wanting to do. I'm quite prepared to let you have a song I've written as a single release.'"

Paul also produced the single, deliberately replicating the arrangement from his July 1969 demo as closely as possible. The Badfinger version *is* different, however, with vocal harmonies and fuller production, and according to Badfinger's Tom Evans (again as quoted in *Without You: The Tragic Story of Badfinger*), "Paul had told us that if he didn't think our version was as good as his original demo, he'd put it out himself. Of course that challenge really made us work hard in the studio." Fortunately, Badfinger soon established themselves with worthy group-penned material, quickly casting off accusations that they were nothing more than Beatles copyists. For more than a few listeners *did* mistakenly think they were listening to a Beatles track when "Come and Get It" was released in early 1970, the songwriting credit listing—as another sign of the times, with the Beatles breakup impending—Paul McCartney as the sole composer. And just a couple of weeks after the single entered the US Top Ten, the Beatles *did* break up, making "Come and Get It" the last of the hits the group's songwriters would give away.

● Ain't That Cute

Doris Troy
Recorded: October 1969
Released: February 13, 1970 (Apple, UK)
Chart Position: None

Best known for her sole American hit single, 1963's "Just One Look," Doris Troy was actually a superb soul singer, as well as a fine songwriter. By the late 1960s she, like several US soul artists, had moved to England, where she found more appreciation and work than she was able to muster on her home soil. She sang backup vocals on Billy Preston's initial Apple LP, 1969's *That's the Way God Planned It,* and was signed to Apple as a solo artist shortly afterward. She'd certainly met the Beatles before 1969, however, having appeared with them on an April 16, 1965 episode of *Ready Steady Goes Live!,* on which the Beatles were also featured. On that episode she also sang, along with members of the Beatles, Kinks, and Herman's Hermits, as a backup vocalist on Adam Faith's version of "I Need Your Loving," which concluded the program. George Harrison was a particular fan, the late Troy telling the author in a 1996 interview that when she sang on Preston's album, "George said he had everything I ever did. I couldn't believe that. Then he picked up his guitar and started playing 'Just One Look' and stuff like that, and I thought it was so hip."

George took a particular interest in Troy's Apple recordings, playing guitar on her 1970 *Doris Troy* LP and producing the A-side of her February 1970 Apple single, "Ain't That Cute." He also co-wrote that song with Troy, in a collaboration that was not just far less celebrated than his co-composition of "Badge" with Eric Clapton, but was so obscure that it's escaped many lists of the songs the Beatles gave away. It's frankly a pretty average soul-rock tune, with an ascending riff just before the chorus that faintly recalls a similar one in "Savoy Truffle," though perhaps some of George's worldview can be heard in the lyrics, which views social climbers with some sour cynicism. The punchy horns, fluid lead guitar work (which Peter Frampton has said was his), and assured Troy vocal couldn't compensate for the lack of memorable, catchy hooks. It missed both the US and UK charts entirely, bringing the era of Beatles songwriting giveaways to a quiet close.

John Lennon and Paul McCartney wrote numerous songs that were never recorded by the Beatles or anyone else, though most of these date from the years before the group began recording for EMI.

For No One: Beatles Compositions That Were Never Recorded

Introduction

For all the great wealth of songs the Beatles recorded (and, in a couple dozen of instances, gave away to others to record), there were a few more that have still never seen the light of day on an official release. Indeed, if you discount the numerous joking/tossed-off fragments of Quarrymen-era originals and improvisations/works-in-progress heard during the January 1969 *Get Back* sessions, there are a good many that were *never* recorded in a serious fashion on any official *or* unofficial release. Exactly how many there were will never be known, especially as John Lennon and Paul McCartney didn't preserve diligent records of all the songs they worked on together prior to 1962. Without many or any supporting audio documents, it's difficult to speculate on what most of these would have sounded like. But here we'll try to put together the pieces of what's known to have been written, even if that amounts to no more than a song title in some cases.

The vast majority of unrecorded Lennon-McCartney tunes were written in the first five years they knew each other, from their initial meeting in mid-1957 through the recording of the first Beatles single, "Love Me Do." For years, it was believed that there was an enormous back catalog of material from this period. Hunter Davies's 1968 authorized biography, *The Beatles,* was the main fuel to this fire, noting that "John and Paul wrote about a hundred songs together that first year [they were composing]. Only one was ever used later, 'Love Me Do.' A lot of them were thrown out years later by mistake by Jane Asher when she was cleaning out Paul's cupboards." The same volume later reported that "in those pre-1963 years they wrote hundreds of songs, most of them now forgotten or lost. Paul still has an exercise book full, but they don't show much. The words are of the simple 'Love Me Do,' 'You Know I Love You' pattern and the music consists of a few *do re*

355

mis. Only they could work out at the time how the tune was supposed to go. They've forgotten now." The few such works that surfaced, in part or in full, on their 1958 and 1960 tapes and the *Get Back* sessions confirm Davies's impressions.

Much later, Paul McCartney would reveal that these estimates were considerably exaggerated. "Most of what we called our 'first hundred' . . . was probably about five," he admitted in *Anthology*. "We would lie our faces off then to get anyone to notice us." Rather contradictorily, a little later in the same book, he states "Our legendary 'first one hundred' was probably in reality less than half that amount of songs." Whatever the exact number, it's undoubtedly much fewer than a few hundred or one hundred, and in any case, even the words to many of them are now beyond recovery.

If John, Paul, and George wrote more than a very few songs they never recorded in any fashion, or gave to other artists, after 1962, there's no evidence that they did so. There are a few home recordings they made of complete tunes bearing pop-rock structures that the Beatles never attempted in the studio, but even most of these—à la "Junk," "Sour Milk Sea," "Circles," and "I'm Just a Child of Nature"—would eventually find a home on solo releases or other artists' records. They, like many and probably most songwriters, likely seldom publicly aired or taped compositions they didn't think had a serious chance of being recorded by somebody. Most of the song titles long believed to have been written (and sometimes recorded) by the group over the years have turned out to be false rumors or outright fabrications, though there are just two or three instances where something was definitely written and no tape has ever surfaced. This chapter will divide this mysterious body of unheard Beatles originals into three categories: the pre-EMI contract years, spanning the first five years or so of the group's career, the slim body of such work they penned from 1962–1970, and the songs they've been falsely reported to have written (and, sometimes, recorded).

● The Pre-EMI Years
Lennon-McCartney Compositions (probably)

Technically speaking, a few of the pre-mid-1962 songs we're discussing here *have* been recorded, as part of the *Get Back* sessions or (in one case) for the bonus disc of the *Anthology* DVD series, or (in another case) for Paul McCartney's *Unplugged* album. None of those recordings could be considered attempts to tape complete or serious performances, however, though they'll be referred to here for the hints they give as to what the full compositions might have sounded like. Though in some instances the title has been confirmed as the correct one by Paul McCartney or a printed source, others are known only by the "best guess" titles assigned to them by bootleggers. It's also possible that had these songs eventually been released, some might have borne a "McCartney" or "Lennon" songwriting credit rather than listing both their names. For example, "Catswalk," which they performed in the early '60s (and even recorded on a late-1962 rehearsal tape), listed only "McCartney" when the Chris Barber Band covered it as "Cat Call" on a 1967 single. It can be reasonably assumed, however, that most or all of these are Lennon-McCartney collaborations.

"Because I Know You Love Me So": Heard on the tapes of the group at Twickenham Studios on January 3, 1969, this good-natured, harmo-

nized number is generally assumed to be a pre-EMI-era composition, though its title is unknown for certain. It's actually one of the more developed early Lennon-McCartney songs revisited during the *Get Back* sessions, with a pronounced country feel, like some of the lesser, most country-oriented tracks laid down by artists at Sun Records in the mid-'50s.

"I Fancy Me Chances": The *Get Back* session recording of an early Lennon-McCartney original that's most illustrative of their skiffle roots, though this half-minute busk is mighty repetitive. It's performed right after "Maggie Mae" during their January 24, 1969, session, heightening the similarity between the songs, intentional or otherwise.

"I Lost My Little Girl": Paul's first composition, using just three chords (*G*, *G7*, and *C*), written at the age of 14 just after his mother's death. It was this song that, after Paul played it to John, made them decide to write original material together. A quite lengthy, if repetitive, version was done on January 25, 1969, and while it's not a bad bluesy jam (at least by the standards of the *Get Back* sessions), one wonders if it really had that shape when Paul first showed it to John. Paul finally put a slightly more developed brief version (the songwriting credit given solely to "McCartney") on his *Unplugged* album in 1991, though he'd certainly added at least a little to the song in the meantime, as there were now lyrics self-consciously referring to the tune as the first one he ever wrote.

"I'll Wait Until Tomorrow": Performed just minutes after "Because I Know You Love Me So" on January 3, 1969, and another tune where the title's not known for sure, though it sounds like another early Lennon-McCartney effort. There's only an informal minute or so of performance on the tape, but it's another country-influenced number, though in some respects it sounds much like an early (if generic) Elvis Presley ballad as well.

"Just Fun": One of the more upbeat snatches of Quarrymen-era material to peek out of the *Get Back* sessions, with a not-quite half-minute strummed on January 8, 1969. It sounds like an innocuous folky tune, and a bit like the skiffle number that Michael McKean and Christopher Guest sing a cappella during *Spinal Tap*, though it's not self-consciously satirical. Paul sang a verse when he was interviewed by John Lennon's half-sister Julia Baird on British radio in 1986, and in *Paul McCartney: Many Years from Now* he recited a few lines, including the rhyme "There's no blue moon that I can see, there's never been in history," which he and John judged as "horrible. When we heard that rhyme we just went off that song in a big way. We were never really able to fix it either."

"Keep Looking That Way": One of the Lennon-McCartney numbers mentioned by Paul in a letter he wrote to a journalist plugging the Beatles in 1960, reprinted in Hunter Davies's authorized biography.

"Looking Glass": An instrumental, also mentioned in Paul's 1960 PR letter. After playing another instrumental from those days, "Hot as Sun" (later included on his 1970 *McCartney* LP), on January 24, 1969, during the *Get Back* sessions, Paul can be heard asking, "How did 'Looking Glass' go?" Although the Beatles released very few instrumentals on their records, original instrumentals were a reasonably sizable part of their early repertoire. A couple others (including "Catswalk") are mentioned in Paul's 1960 letter, and, lest we forget, the very first original Beatles composition to be recorded in a proper studio was an instrumental, "Cry for a Shadow" (at their Hamburg sessions for Polydor in June 1961). Perhaps these songs were felt necessary due to the popularity of instrumental rock in the early '60s and of the UK instrumental combo the Shadows, the biggest British group before the Beatles.

According to a list given to Cavern Club DJ Bob Wooler by a fan who regularly attended Wooler-MC'd Beatles shows there in the early '60s, the group did another instrumental as part of their repertoire called "Beatles Bop." This might, however, be a generic name for a different instrumental listed elsewhere in this chapter, like "Catswalk" or even "Looking Glass."

"Pinwheel Twist": Possibly the latest of the songs in this section to have been written, as it was a pun on Joey Dee & the Starliters' huge late-1961 hit, "Peppermint Twist." In Spencer Leigh's *Let's Go Down the Cavern: The Story of Liverpool's Merseybeat*, Billy Kinsley of the Liverpool group the Merseybeats remembered, "Pete Best sang 'The Pinwheel Twist.' Pete got off his kit, Paul went on drums, George played Paul's left-handed bass right-handed, and Pete sang." Added Pete Best in the same book, "Paul wrote the song and asked me to do it. He coupled it with Joey Dee's hit 'The Peppermint Twist.' I used to get up and do the twist on stage and Paul played my drums. It was a little novelty act and it went down well with the fans."

The Beatles and Brian Epstein must have thought something of this number, as it's one of the seven Lennon-McCartney compositions on the list of 33 songs that Epstein suggested George Martin listen to at their June 1962 EMI audition. On that list, however, it's grouped with the songs Paul was supposed to sing, indicating that he, not Pete, might have sung it onstage. That notion's reinforced by Mark Lewisohn's *The Complete Beatles Chronicle*, which lists McCartney as the Beatle who sang it in performance. Yet page 69 of that same book shows a picture of the group at the Cavern on April 5, 1962, with Pete at the vocal mike and Paul on drums, captioned: "Paul takes to the drums while Pete Best moves centre-stage for a performance of Lennon-McCartney's unreleased 'Pinwheel Twist.'" It's far down the list of Beatles mysteries, but it's thus still unclear who sang the tune, though at a guess it's possible that photo is of Best doing "*Peppermint* Twist," not "*Pinwheel* Twist." Whatever the case, it probably wasn't much of a song, as the Beatles never taped it and as it was likely heavily derivative of "Peppermint Twist."

"That's My Woman": Listed as a Lennon-McCartney song performed by the group live in the late '50s. Nothing else is known, not even the lead singer.

"Thinking of Linking": A little more is known about this tune than most of the songs in this batch, although (like the others) it's still not easy to get a firm handle on what it might have actually sounded like when the Beatles were performing it. Paul thought enough of it to mention it in his 1960 PR letter, yet told Mark Lewisohn in a late-'80s interview for *The Beatles Recording Sessions*, "'Thinking of Linking' was terrible! I thought it up in the pictures, someone in a film mentioned it [imitates an actor in a film] 'We're thinking of linking' and I came out of there thinking 'That should be a song. Thinking of linking, people are gonna get married, gotta write that!' . . . Pretty corny stuff!" A 25-second "song" identified

as "Thinking of Linking" by bootleggers was done on January 3, 1969, at Twickenham Studios, but it collapses almost immediately after launching with a typically 1950s chord progression. John Lennon ad-libs lyrics about thinking of linking during a January 29, 1969, cover of Buddy Holly's "Peggy Sue Got Married," indicating that the song, in its original form, might have been Buddy Holly–like, understandable as Holly was a huge influence on Lennon-McCartney's early compositions.

At long last, on June 23, 1994, the surviving three Beatles performed a verse from "Thinking of Linking" a couple of times for the cameras, the footage getting included in the bonus disc of the *Anthology* DVD. Here it's revealed to be a *very* Buddy Holly–like song and quite a bit, indeed, like "Peggy Sue Got Married." It seems possible, even probable, that the song was no longer being performed by the Beatles by the time Ringo joined in August 1962, but he joins in this semi-jam amiably enough. Here Paul says there's no second verse, and also changes the story he'd told Lewisohn slightly, describing the song as inspired by "a commercial in the cinema for Link Furniture, called 'Thinking of Linking.'" "I hadn't heard that song in 40 years—nobody could've!" McCartney exclaimed in *Record Collector*. "If George had not remembered it, it would just have gone, because I'd forgotten it completely."

"Too Bad about Sorrows": Remembered by Paul as the first song he and John wrote together, "Too Bad about Sorrows" was given an absolutely shambolic brief "performance" on January 8, 1969. A much more (at least in comparison) fully formed minute-long rendition followed a couple weeks later on January 21. Paul's operatic Elvis Presley vocals on this corny, late-'50s doo wop–styled ballad seem far more like a deliberate self-parody than an accurate approximation of how it might have actually been performed originally.

"Winston's Walk": The last of the three instrumentals mentioned in Paul's letter to a journalist named "Mr. Low" in 1960.

"Won't You Please Say Goodbye": Yet another doleful country lament of uncertain title, though slower and more dolorous than the other such early originals the Beatles did almost all at once on January 3, 1969, at Twickenham Studios.

"Years Roll Along": Another song mentioned in Paul's 1960 "Mr. Low" letter about which little is known, though Paul quoted a lyric ("It might have been winter when you told me") in *Paul McCartney: Many Years from Now.*

Indications are, then, that of the unused early Lennon-McCartney backlog, nothing was of such exceptional merit that it deserved exhumation once the Beatles' recording career was underway. Indeed, if the bits that were later informally recorded are any indication, the songs were not only extremely derivative, but often lacking in the melodious, uplifting, imaginative qualities that were such strong hallmarks of the original material the group recorded for EMI. These years weren't a total waste of time in terms of yielding future actual Beatles songs; early versions of "Love Me Do," "I'll Follow the Sun," "I Call Your Name," "One After 909," "Ask Me Why," and "When I'm Sixty-Four" are all known to have been written during this period. As for the ones that never gained commercial release, however, their primary use was as tools for John and Paul to teach themselves the art of composing, getting all their crummy songs out of the way in the process.

As odd footnotes, it's been claimed by a pair of singers the Beatles backed in the early '60s that John and Paul helped them out with a couple of tunes. Johnny Gentle says that John helped him out with the middle eight of "I've Just Fallen for Someone" while the Beatles were backing him on a brief Scottish tour in May 1960. As Darren Young, Gentle recorded the song (with the orchestra of famous film composer John Barry) on the B-side of an obscure April 1962 single. Tony Sheridan has said he co-wrote a song with Paul, "Tell Me if You Can," in 1961 or 1962, though neither he nor anyone else has released a version.

Oddest of all, Stuart Sutcliffe apparently wrote a few songs shortly before his death. Judging from the titles that have been reported— "Ooh, Ooh, Ooh," "Yea Cos Your [sic] a Sure Fire Bet to Win My Lips," and "Everybody's Ever Got Somebody Caring"—Stu had an awkward way with words at this phase, and as the Beatles were barely even doing any Lennon-McCartney songs onstage at this point, it seems doubtful they ever performed (or considered performing) Sutcliffe's efforts. A reproduction from his sketchbook of handwritten lyrics to another title, "Peace of Mind," is included in Alan Clayson and Pauline Sutcliffe's book *Backbeat: Stuart Sutcliffe, The Lost Beatle,* which also prints lyrics from "Everybody's Ever Got Somebody Caring." As to how good these tunes might have been—well, Sutcliffe, by almost all accounts, was a woefully inept bass guitarist. Is there any reason to believe he would have been a decent songwriter?

● The EMI Years

Although you'd think that John, Paul, and George might have written at least a few songs at some point during 1962–1970 that have never circulated on any tape, virtually no such animals have been reported. Only a few were done at EMI, including "Etcetera," "Shirley's Wild Accordion," and the jam "Anything," all of which are discussed as non-circulating studio outtakes in part one of this book.

There is, however, one George Harrison song that was described in some detail in print and has rarely been discussed since, perhaps because the source was so well known and obvious that many fans missed it when combing through obscure materials for clues. Hunter Davies's authorized biography reports George working on an untitled composition for Marianne Faithfull, probably sometime in 1967 when most of Davies's research was done. Wrote Davies, "She'd asked him to write one for her to sing, something like 'Within You, Without You.' He wasn't sure how it was going to turn out. He had the song in his head, but the words were becoming jokier and jokier. He thought they might end up too silly and he'd have to dump them. 'I'd got, "You can't love me with your artichoke heart," which is not bad.' He sang and played the song on his Hammond organ. 'But I'm not sure about continuing the joke—"You can't listen with your cauliflower ear" or "Don't be an apricot fool." I don't know. I'll just see how it turns out.'"

Probably it didn't turn out to his satisfaction, as it's never been heard from again. Ironically, one of the few other Beatles compositions never recorded by the group or anyone else, Paul McCartney's "Etcetera," was also written with Faithfull in mind. But as it turned out, Marianne never did any previously unrecorded Beatle-penned songs. It wasn't the last time George made strained references to fresh produce in a work-in-progress song lyric, however, trying out the line

Both Paul McCartney and George Harrison wrote songs intended for Marianne Faithfull that were never released by her, the Beatles, or anyone.

"Attracts me like a pomegranate" during an early version of "Something" at the *Get Back* sessions on January 28, 1969.

● Beatles Songs That Never Existed

While it's hardly a phenomenon on the scale of the "Paul Is Dead" rumors, over the years there have been numerous false reports of Beatles originals that were supposedly written or even recorded during the 1960s. Most of the ones discussed here were listed in the bootlegs section of the 1975 book *All Together Now: The First Complete Beatles Discography 1961–1975* by Harry Castleman and Walter J. Podrazik (who, to be fair, were only passing on titles that had been previously reported in an assortment of media sources). Since then, they've been widely discussed in the collecting community, and even now the titles often show up on published lists of Beatles rarities. None of them exist, even on non-circulating tapes, although quite a few persistent completists continue to insist that they're really out there.

"Always and Only": In July 1964, the *Beatles Book* magazine reported that Paul McCartney had written a song of this title while on vacation in late May and recorded it after coming back to England. But no Beatles EMI track exists of the composition, which wasn't copyrighted either. It's been speculated this song was really "It's for You," the Lennon-

In With the Outfakes

Due to both honest misconception and unscrupulous intention, numerous songs performed by artists other than the Beatles have been passed off as "Beatles outtakes" on bootlegs. Sometimes even a threadbare resemblance will be enough. The mid-'60s Fourmost recording "I Love You Too" (from the soundtrack of *Ferry Cross the Mersey*) has been fobbed off as an unreleased Beatles cut, for instance, merely because of some lightly Beatlesque harmonies and a lead vocal that's slightly reminiscent of Paul McCartney in the bridge. A version of "Oh My Love" (first released on John Lennon's *Imagine*) alleged to be the Beatles turned out to be an early-'70s cover by the Wackers, issued quite legitimately on a prominent record label as part of their Elektra album *Hot Wacks*. There are, however, just a few commonly mislabeled Beatles outtakes worthy of note, both because they're rather cool musically and because of the (admittedly faint) possibility that one of them just might be the Beatles.

"Have You Heard the Word": Variously rumored to have been from the Beatles' last recording session, or one or some of the Beatles playing with some or all of the Bee Gees, this came out on an obscure UK single on the independent Beacon label in 1970, credited to "the Fut." And it does get close to the late-'60s Beatles sound, with its mid-tempo piano-guitar chug, tinnily distorted Lennonesque vocal, pseudo-McCartney bass, cheekily enigmatic lyrics, and unexpected leap into a contrastingly peppy, uptempo bridge. It's on the slight and rambling side compositionally, and the vocal harmonies don't seem to be taking themselves at all seriously, but it does sound like a Lennon song they might have done to amuse themselves during some studio downtime in 1968 or 1969. Most intriguing of all, the track stumbles to a close very much in the way that many actual Beatles outtakes did, the lead vocalist wittily improvising some new lyrics, the singing and instruments stopping in disorganization at different points, and a Lennon-like spoken voice asking, "So you've heard the word then?" A slightly Harrison-like voice responds: "I've heard the word, yes."

As enjoyable as this is, it's *not* the Beatles, the full story coming out some years later, though at least part of the rumor did get it right. Maurice Gibb of the Bee Gees *did* participate in this August 6, 1969, session, which was largely the work of Tin Tin, an Australian duo he was managing and producing. Gibb, Tin Tin (Steve Kipner and Steve Groves), and Billy Lawrie (brother of Lulu, to whom Maurice was married at the time) came up with "Have You Heard the Word," apparently well lubricated by a bottle of Jack Daniels. Gibb later claimed that both John Lennon and Paul McCartney showed up at the session as well to contribute to the semi-jam, although his memories aren't supported by anyone else known to have been in attendance. On September 27, 1974, Lennon himself told a caller on Los Angeles FM radio station KHJ that the song was not a Beatles cut, though he did admit, "It sounds like us. It's a good imitation."

The track did fool a bunch of people, and not just bootleg buyers; Yoko Ono copyrighted it as a John Lennon composition on September 20, 1985, though it had been copyrighted to Kipner and Groves in the US in 1974. When finally issued on CD as part of the Bee Gees covers compilation *Maybe Someone Is Digging Underground: The Songs of the Bee Gees* in 2004, it was credited to Kipner, Groves, and Lawrie, and it really is extremely doubtful that Lennon or McCartney had anything to do with the writing or recording of the track. Tin Tin had a Top 20 US hit in 1971 with "Toast and Marmalade for Tea," and Kipner later wrote hits for Olivia Newton-John, Cher, and Christina Aguilera. As to why the single was credited to "the Fut," supposedly the subject of "Have You Heard the Word" was a four-letter "word" that started with the letters "fu," but did not end with a "t". . . .

"The L.S. Bumble Bee": Though this was passed off as a Beatles outtake as early as the mid-'70s, and although it *is* a very funny (and early, considering its January 1967 release) semi-psychedelic spoof of LSD's much-vaunted magical properties, it's *not* a Beatles track. Nor were any of the Beatles involved in writing it. Nor does it even sound that much like the Beatles, particularly in the vocal department, despite a fairly catchy melody, high harmonies, and imaginative sound effects–laden production. Nor, finally, were the performers that obscure: Peter Cook and Dudley Moore, two of the most popular comedians in Britain, had issued the musical parody on a British single in January 1967. Rumor-mongers then spread it about that John Lennon was involved in the track in some way, if only as a songwriter, but it was certainly penned by Cook and Moore themselves.

In a letter dated December 15, 1981, Moore wrote, "Regarding 'The L.S. Bumble Bee,' Peter Cook and I recorded that song about the time when there was so much fuss about L.S.D., and when everybody thought that 'Lucy In The Sky With Diamonds' was a reference to drugs. The exciting alternative offered to the world was L.S.B.!, and I wrote the music to, in some ways, satirize the Beach Boys rather than the Beatles. But I'm grateful if some small part of the world thinks that it may have been them, rather than us!" (Interestingly, Moore himself did not seem to remember here that "The L.S. Bumble Bee" was written, recorded, and released *before* the Beatles had even recorded "Lucy in the Sky with Diamonds.")

So how did the whole myth get started? As David Kerekes points out in his chapter on Beatles outfakes in the book *Lovers Buggers & Thieves Vol. 1*, it probably originated when John made a brief appearance as a lavatory attendant on a December 26, 1966, episode of Cook and Moore's BBC television series *Not Only . . . But Also*. For on the same program, the duo also premiered their upcoming 45 as part of a sketch in which they (as lead singers of a group called "the Mothers") record their next single. But "The L.S. Bumble Bee" has continued to show up on many bootlegs in the past few decades, which actually isn't such a bad thing, as it's not only a good track, but also better than many of the lesser genuine Beatles outtakes with which it's packaged.

"Peace of Mind": One of the few mysteries of unreleased Beatles ephemera that remains unsolved, "Peace of Mind" was taken by many as a genuine 1967 group outtake when it was first bootlegged in the 1970s. Wrote Harry Castleman and Walter J. Podrazik in *All Together Now*, "'Peace of Mind' contains intriguing lyrics woven around very complicated beat changes. In spite of the very bad recording available, it still deserves close attention." The song *does* sound a little like something that the group

The British comedy team of Peter Cook and Dudley Moore, whose 1967 single "The L.S. Bumble Bee" has often been mistakenly identified as an unreleased Beatles track.

they sometimes favored in 1967, even if it seems exaggeratedly naive even by the psychedelic Beatles' own sometimes exaggeratedly naive standards. It sounds like something John Lennon could have written, just about, or more distantly, something George Harrison might have done (though *not* like a flight of fancy Paul McCartney would have taken). There's no percussion, and on the off-chance it *is* a Beatles outtake, it would seem that Ringo Starr had no role in the track.

In time, most experts who study Beatles outtakes came to the conclusion that it was *not* the group, sometimes dismissing the track as not only devoid of collectable value, but also aesthetically worthless. That's a little too harsh; as primitive as the recording is, it's got some period psychedelic charm. If this was indeed created by bootleggers intent on crafting a psychedelic Beatles imitation, there are far worse, less authentic such things crawling around on illegitimate releases. What's still unknown, however, is exactly *who* plays on the track, sometimes described—without unassailable backup evidence—as a tape that was literally found in the trash in Apple. If so, could it have been one of those demos the Beatles naively solicited in an open call to the public in 1968 and never listened to? Even more remotely, could it be a private tape the Beatles themselves made—perhaps one day in Rishikesh (accounting for the acoustic instrumentation and the absence of both drums and Ringo, who left India after only about ten days)? Had they gone to the trouble of composing a complete song such as this, however, it seems that it would have probably been copyrighted, which it wasn't. (And the lyrics are *not* the same as the ones in the Stuart Sutcliffe "song" "Peace of Mind" noted earlier in this chapter.) Unless some surprising proof is unearthed, it must be assumed that "Peace of Mind" is not the Beatles—though not beyond the shadow of a doubt.

might have cooked up around, say, the "Across the Universe" period (or on a privately taped recording while they were studying with the Maharishi at Rishikesh), with its heavily meditative, psychedelic feel, snatch of eerie backwards tapes at the beginning, folky guitar picking, and quasi-Eastern-Indian drones in both melody and instrumentation. It *is* very unusually constructed, the key rising every few lines, sounding almost like a 33 rpm disc gradually speeding up to 45 rpm. The three-part harmonies are very close and Beatlesque, and the lyrics ("A safety pin returns my smile, I nod a brief hello") are in keeping with the surrealistic imagery

McCartney tune given away to Cilla Black, though the phrase "always and only" doesn't appear in the lyrics.

"Colliding Circles"; "Pink Litmus Paper Shirt": Probably the most notorious of fake Beatles outtake titles, these were listed as *Revolver* outtakes in an article by Martin Lewis in *Disc* magazine in 1971. "Colliding Circles" was said to have a John Lennon lead vocal, with "Pink Litmus Paper Shirt" sung by George Harrison. Although the titles themselves were somewhat exaggerated psychedelicisms, they could have theoretically fit within what the Beatles were recording circa mid-1966. Probably coincidentally, one of the titles, "Colliding Circles," was indeed close to the title of a song from the group's May 1968 *White Album* demos that didn't get recorded at EMI, George Harrison's "Circles," though it seems unlikely anyone would have known this at the time.

In the late '90s, Lewis finally came clean and confessed it was all a hoax. By then, however, the titles had circulated for so long that they'd become part of Beatles mythology, and ironically he had a hard time convincing some fans that he'd made the whole thing up. As an in-joke homage to the apparently never-ending misconception, singer-songwriter-comedian Neil Innes used both titles in "Unfinished Words," a song on the 1996 Rutles "comeback" album, *Archaeology.*

"Not Unknown"; "India": Supposedly 1967 George Harrison songs, "Not Unknown" was probably "Not Known," which in turn was the working title for "Only a Northern Song." "India," according to John Winn's *Lifting Latches,* is "an unidentified *Wonderwall* soundtrack recording" (*Wonderwall* being the film George scored in late 1967 and early 1968). George was reported to have sung lead on another 1967 outtake, "Anything," but although there is a 1967 outtake by that name, it's a 22-minute instrumental dominated by Ringo Starr's drumming (see entry on page 187).

"Annie": Listed in *All Together Now* as a 1967 outtake with Paul on lead, little is known about this (or whether there's any reason to believe it was a Beatles outtake), though it's been rumored it was done by McCartney under the pseudonym Busker Sam Sellers.

"Lullabye for a Lazy Day": An April 1988 article in *Musician* on "The Lost Lennon Tapes" radio series described an unreleased recording as "the Beatles performing 'Lullabye for a Lazy Day,'" adding, "Official co-writer Paul McYou-Know-Who is unlikely to give clearance to allow the finished (but not incredible) song to be broadcast." This tape was not only *not* the Beatles, but *not* a Lennon-McCartney song, and not even titled "Lullabye for a Lazy Day." It's actually a demo of "Lullaby" by the fairly obscure British group Grapefruit. Written by Grapefruit's George Alexander, brother of the Easybeats' George Young and AC/DC's Malcolm and Angus Young, the composition appeared on the band's 1969 LP *Around Grapefruit. Musician* was at least right, though, that the song wasn't "incredible." As heard in its officially released LP version, it's fairly standard, sluggish late-'60s UK psych-pop, vaguely emulating the fruitier, more florid aspects of the *Sgt. Pepper* mindset, as were so many British records of that time. The only reason it was mistaken for a Lennon/Beatles tape/composition is that it was found among John's 300 hours of home tapes when "The Lost Lennon Tapes" was being researched. Yoko Ono or someone else, however, must have made a similar mistake a few years earlier, as the song was incorrectly copyrighted as a Lennon composition on September 20, 1985. A possible explanation for its presence on Lennon's tapes is that George Alexander had a publishing deal with Apple.

"I Should Like to Live Up a Tree": This supposedly Ringo-sung *Abbey Road* outtake seems to be a mangling of a reference in a March 29, 1969, *NME* story to a recently recorded song on the forthcoming Beatles LP "by Ringo titled 'In an Octopus's Garden (Or I Would Like to Live Up a Tree).'"

"Four Nights in Moscow"; **"When I Come to Town"**: Also rumored as *Abbey Road* outtakes, these were actually provisional titles for Ringo Starr's "Early 1970" (the B-side to his 1971 hit "It Don't Come Easy"), appearing on an October 3, 1970, Abbey Road session sheet.

SMILIN' EARS

THE BEATLES
THE DECCAGONE SESSIONS

SIDE 1
SEARCHIN'
LIKE DREAMERS DO
THREE KOOL KATS
HELLO LITTLE GIRL
HOW DO YOU DO IT
TRYING, WAITING, HOPING
BOUND BY LOVE
THERE'S NOTHING SHAKING

SIDE 2
LOVE OF THE LOVED
MEMPHIS
SEPTEMBER IN THE RAIN
SHIEK OF ARABY
REVOLUTION
SOME OTHER GUY
EVERYONE WANTS SOMEONE
I'M GONNA SIT RIGHT DOWN
SHOT OF RHYTM AND BLUES

All Rights Reserved
All Wrongs Reversed
7701

The Beatles on Bootleg

There's no getting around it—in almost all cases, the only way to hear Beatles music that has not been commercially released is on unauthorized recordings, or "bootlegs." As stated in the author's introduction, this book has deliberately concentrated on the unreleased *music* the group recorded, rather than on the LPs and CDs on which they've been distributed. It would be impossible to gain a complete picture of this mammoth vault of material, however, without at least a brief rundown of how it's reached public ears. A whole book could be written about Beatles bootlegs (and the collector culture that's sprouted around them), and this chapter is just an outline of their 35-year history, still going strong and unfolding even as you read this.

Somewhat apocryphally, the first Beatles bootleg might have been produced way back in 1962 or 1963, when Brian Epstein supposedly had some acetates pressed of one of the versions of "Some Other Guy" they did for Granada TV in August and September of 1962. (See more details on the actual recording in the entries on pages 32-35.) As it's been reported they were even sold in Epstein's NEMS record shops, this would—ironically—make the first Beatles bootleg an item that was, in a way, authorized by their own management. As few copies of the acetate have surfaced, however, this might be something of an urban legend.

Hard as it might be to believe today, when there must be literally millions of rock bootlegs floating around that were actually recorded in the 1960s, the manufacture and consumption of such bootlegs was virtually unknown in the 1960s themselves. No one had any real idea of how valuable and sought-after the material would become (and probably was at the time, frankly), and vinyl bootlegging of commercially unreleased recordings was still pretty much reserved for opera, classical, jazz, and soundtrack music.

All that changed at the end of the 1960s, when major bootleg releases appeared in quick succession by the artists most critics would consider to be the three most significant rock acts of the decade: the Beatles, the Rolling Stones, and Bob Dylan. Dylan's *The Great White Wonder* is generally considered the first rock bootleg to enjoy significant distribution, even if it was a hodgepodge of studio outtakes, home tapes, and other miscellany from throughout the 1960s; the Rolling Stones' *Liver Than You'll Ever Be,* from a November show on their 1969 American tour, was popular enough to spark the release of an official recording of a live LP from the same tour (*Get Yer Ya-Ya's Out*) the following year. In between these LPs came the first widely available Beatles bootlegs, consisting of outtakes from what was then known as the *Get Back* album.

Estimates of how many copies bootleg releases of the time (or any time) sold are understandably variable, and official figures non-existent. Still, the bootlegs of *Get Back* material, of which *Kum Back* was the most popular, undoubtedly sold remarkably well considering they weren't available in standard retail outlets (or most standard retail outlets, anyway). True, the 100,000 copies of one version (Lemon Records' *Get Back*) reported as sold in the New York and Los Angeles markets alone by *Entertainment World* in March 1970 was probably a wild overestimation. But taken together, the various bootlegs of *Get Back* material must have shifted tens of thousands of units at the least, particularly as underground head shops carrying unauthorized LPs (in addition to their usual stock of hip official albums and various counterculture paraphernalia) were becoming increasingly widespread. So, too, were underground FM rock radio stations, who were willing to give bootlegs considerable airplay. If an eight-year-old in the Philadelphia suburbs could buy *Kum Back,* as the author did in the spring of 1970, how difficult could finding it be?

Clinton Heylin's book *Bootleg: The Secret History of the Other Recording Industry* is recommended to those readers who want a general overview of how the rock bootleg industry as a whole took off from there. The specific effect of *Kum Back* and other *Get Back* bootlegs, however, was to launch Beatles bootleg culture in particular (and, possibly, to even help motivate the Beatles themselves to finally get their "official" version out to the public via the *Let It Be* LP and movie). As poor as the fidelity was on these early boots (as was discovered in subsequent years when far higher-quality tapes of the same material were bootlegged), listening to unheard, genuine new Beatles songs and recordings was an entirely new and thrilling experience in early 1970. Of course, it quickly became evident that this was a one-shot deal of sorts, as the Beatles soon broke up and there would never again be an opportunity to gain, in a sense, an advance preview of material they had yet to release. But *Kum Back* and similar bootlegs of *Get Back* outtakes couldn't help but stoke insatiable hunger for more unissued Beatles, even at a point when no one had any idea of just how huge a mountain of stuff remained to be unearthed from the vaults. As early as July 9, 1970, another Beatles bootleg (of vaguely described mid-'60s live material), *The Beatles "Live",* was given a full review in *Rolling Stone,* complete with a plea for Capitol/Apple to give concert recordings such as their Hollywood Bowl tapes official release.

Most of the early Beatles bootlegs that followed in the next few years were of relatively poor sound quality (at least, as with *Kum Back* and *The Beatles "Live",* relative to the fidelity in which much of the material was eventually found to exist), and almost always poorly packaged. Too, much of the best stuff remained locked up (or unknown to even have been recorded), including virtually all of their studio outtakes and most of their BBC tracks. Significant non–*Get Back* material nonetheless started to appear almost immediately, including the 1964 Hollywood Bowl concert, some taped-with-a-mike-next-to-the-radio-speaker BBC sessions, and yet more *Get Back* sessions that hadn't been included in the first round of bootlegs from that source. (Who knew then that about *100 hours* would eventually come to light?) Only a year or so after the Beatles broke up, in fact, there was major coverage of post–*Kum Back* bootlegs in the music press, and comments weighing in on the topic from the ex-Beatles themselves. *Melody Maker* put a "BEATLES ARE BOOTLEGGED AGAIN!" headline on its front page on May 15, 1971,

claiming that a tape of "about 30 unreleased songs" might soon find its way onto illicit vinyl.

The sleeves of these early bootleg LP releases were usually exceptionally cheaply designed, often with mimeographed papers literally pasted onto the front cover. (Often packaged in a plain white cover, *Kum Back* didn't have any "design" whatsoever.) Besides boasting blurry, crummy photos and childish graphics, there were usually virtually no details as to the origination of the tracks (which themselves were sometimes mistitled or amateurishly misspelled). Plus, often the sources of the material were, intentionally or unintentionally, wildly misidentified. Occasionally, tracks that weren't the Beatles were incorrectly marketed as Beatles recordings; even less ethically, some fake "rarities" were manufactured by manipulative channel separation or, at worst, overdubbing of new and decidedly non-Beatle (or even non-professional) instrumentation.

In addition, many of the releases mixed tracks from various eras without much rhyme or reason, as well as recycling material from other bootlegs, or at least mixing cuts that had already appeared on one or numerous previous boots with brand-new discoveries. As a result, Beatles fanatics determined to collect each and every unreleased item (or most of them) were forced to buy much of the same material many times over—a costly nuisance that continues to be one of the most irritating aspects of bootleg collecting to this day. And as an unfortunate consequence of getting burned by inferior product 30 or so years ago, many Beatles fans—again, to this very day—*still* mistakenly assume that most or all unreleased material by the group sounds lousy and isn't worth bothering with.

Yet as tinny as the fidelity on some of those early bootlegs was (you'd never put on the transistor-radio-quality *Yellow Matter Custard* collection of BBC airshots today when it's all available on modern bootlegs or official releases in excellent fidelity), at the time they did serve their purpose. First, listening to LPs like *Yellow Matter Custard*— which did, for all its substandard sonics, offer many songs the Beatles *never* did on their records—was the best you could get back then, and thus far better than nothing. Second, like the *Get Back* rehearsals that were slowly dribbling out, it alerted collectors, experts, and likely bootleggers that there could well be more untapped material from the same sources. The hunt was on, and more bits and pieces continued to ooze out throughout the rest of the 1970s. The rapid recycling of already-found material on different bootlegs, as well as the ongoing absorption of listeners from a younger generation into the ranks of Beatles fanatics, continued to ensure a large market for unauthorized product. The packaging and graphics even started to get steadily (if very slowly) better. But if someone had attempted to write a comprehensive book covering all circulating unreleased Beatles material in the late '70s, the resulting volume would have been much, much shorter than the doorstop you're currently holding in your hands.

If only in retrospect, there were some particularly major finds and events over the past 30 years that cumulatively led to this massive increase in the availability of previously unreleased Beatles material. Simultaneously, they also led to massive increases in our knowledge of just how much the group recorded behind the scenes and (finally) official, authorized releases of much of that music. Inevitably, this was accompanied by an explosion in the Beatles bootleg market itself, both in terms of the sheer number of different titles that have been produced, and the quite large amount of sales those records tallied. Some highlights include:

- **In 1976, Capitol/EMI became free to repackage the Beatles' music after the group's contract with the label (covering their back catalog and solo releases) had expired.** As far as unreleased material was concerned, their efforts were generally disappointing, as they concentrated on thematic repackages and a *Rarities* album of previously officially issued tracks and mixes that had been hard to find in the US. But they did also yield the 1977 LP *The Beatles at the Hollywood Bowl*, which was the first (and, for a long time, only) indication that authorized packages of previously unavailable Beatles recordings were at least theoretically possible. And, probably unintentionally, it made many fans hungry for more, and aware that other, unauthorized concert recordings from the Beatlemania era were to be had with just a little effort.

- **In 1977, the Decca audition tape—already described and referred to in several Beatles books but rarely heard—began to leak out, eventually filling up both sides of seven bootleg 45s.** (The final and 15th track, "Take Good Care of My Baby," also came out when all of the material was finally compiled onto one bootleg LP, 1979's *The Decca Tapes*.). Here was a sudden wealth of studio outtakes where the fidelity was almost on par with 1960s studio recordings, and the first such case (unless you count the poor-sounding, haphazardly assembled *Kum Back*) where the material could logically be grouped together to make a missing Beatles album of sorts. There was even a handsome sleeve and liner notes—rarities for *any* bootleg of the time, let alone ones by the Beatles.

- **In 1980, *The Beatles Broadcasts* presented 18 BBC performances from 1963–1964 in quality that was excellent by any standard and positively** stunning compared to the ones that had previously made the rounds. Not only was the sound vastly better, but there was a song that even dedicated fans never suspected the group had done, "Clarabella." You might have even suspected it of being an "outfake" when you first saw the sleeve, except there was no doubting it was Paul McCartney on vocals when the track played. Even the packaging was a big step up from most previous Beatles bootlegs (with recent exceptions such as the aforementioned *Decca Tapes*). You could tell it was unauthorized by the unconventional design, but was still pleasant to look at, had a bunch of good mid-'60s color photos of the band, boasted professional layout and typesetting, and might even fool conventional record buyers into thinking it was a legitimate release. And, naturally, it made buyers curious as to whether there might be more where it came from, which was delivered sooner than anyone expected, when . . .

- **In 1982, the BBC aired a special dedicated to the Beatles' radio sessions, mixing interviews with complete and partial versions (of variable quality) of many actual live-at-the-Beeb performances.** In a reversal of the way these things usually work, it was expanded in length when it was syndicated to the US the same year, with a few additional songs. Naturally, the entire special was soon bootlegged (complete with commercials), and this time you didn't even have to buy the bootleg to hear it and add it to your collection; all you had to do was tape it off the radio. Besides awakening interest among the general public for an official release of the material, it greatly expanded the knowledge of the Beatles' BBC work among specialist collectors. Unfortunately it would be a dozen years before much of it was granted authorized release. But even before the program was produced, top Beatles expert Mark Lewisohn had compiled a list of all the songs broadcast on their 50-plus BBC shows, much of which would soon come to light as well.

- **In the summer of 1983, while Abbey Road was temporarily closed to install more modern equipment, the studio offered a multimedia presentation to the public called *The Beatles at Abbey Road* that included some unreleased outtakes.** Unsurprisingly, a few of the fanatics in attendance managed to smuggle in tape recorders, and the extracts of outtakes they captured were soon bootlegged. Despite their low fidelity, these again jacked up interest in unissued Beatles studio material, if for no other reason than their confirmation that many such tracks probably existed. A terminally ill Abbey Road engineer, John Barrett, had already cataloged the group's EMI tapes the previous year, and it's strongly suspected that a considerable amount of the studio outtakes that escaped onto bootleg near the end of the 1980s were copied from the source during research for these projects.

- **In 1984, an actual single-disc Beatles outtakes album, *Sessions*, was prepared for EMI.** Its planned early 1985 release, however, was scrapped at a late hour. But by the end of that year, bootleg copies of the *Sessions* album, featuring what generally speaking were the very most interesting complete Beatles studio outtakes, were widely available, complete with extremely professional-looking artwork. For the first time since the *Kum Back* era, a Beatles bootleg was getting some mainstream media coverage, and if the album itself wasn't coming out, even some fans who didn't customarily buy unreleased music became determined to track it down.

The first album to include all of the Decca tapes, from 1979.

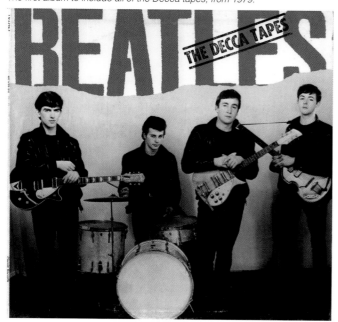

The inner label of the Not for Sale *bootleg LP, with four actual beetles [sic], was cheekily credited to NEMS Records, NEMS being the name of Brian Epstein's company.*

• Between late 1986 and late 1988, the 13-volume vinyl bootleg series *The Beatles at the Beeb* presented what most fans welcomed as an unimaginable wealth of tracks, in largely good-to-great fidelity. Even the previously booted material was often given substantial sonic upgrades, and the packaging set new standards for the bootleg industry as a whole, surpassing in some respects much official reissue product (including the sleeve that would have been on the nixed *Sessions*).

• In early 1988, "The Lost Lennon Tapes" radio series unleashed a mind-boggling quantity of John Lennon rarities. While most of these were from John's post-Beatles years, there were also some home tapes from the mid- to late '60s, including avant-garde experiments, works-in-composition, and, most amazingly, some of the May 1968 *White Album* demos recorded at George's house (all Lennon compositions, as you'd expect). The point's been made elsewhere in this book, but it's worth returning to: for all the grumbling most major stars do about being bootlegged, much of the material only escapes into circulation because *they* are directly responsible for putting it out there. And so it was with "The Lost Lennon Tapes," which anyone could tape off the radio. Could it have been a surprise to anyone involved with Lennon's estate or recording catalog that the series almost immediately spawned off dozens of bootlegs, including the first appearances of those *White Album* demos—which no one had even known existed, and which naturally made aficionados curious as to whether there were more?

• Though the CD format had been commercially introduced in 1982, it wasn't until the late '80s that it truly caught on as a medium that rivaled (and soon surpassed) vinyl LPs and cassettes in popularity.

Likewise, it wasn't until the late 1980s that CD bootlegs started to become common. While it wasn't an entirely logical development, the popularity of the CD format encouraged commercial labels to radically expand their reissue programs, partly in the hopes/assumptions that many collectors would replace their LPs with CDs. The same mentality, evidently, caught hold in the bootleg community—and, as a consequence, the sheer amount of music of any sort getting bootlegged substantially increased, the Beatles at the forefront as usual.

• Published in late 1988, Mark Lewisohn's classic book *The Beatles Recording Sessions* examined all of their EMI studio recordings in great detail. It wasn't just that it listed what was confirmed to exist; Lewisohn had actually *heard* almost everything he was writing about, and offered, for the first time, in-depth description of the *musical* content of the outtakes residing in EMI's vaults. Now, Beatles fans were *really* dying to hear this stuff, and they'd get the opportunity to hear a lot of it sooner than anyone predicted when . . .

• Also in 1988, the first installment in the *Ultra Rare Trax* series appeared. Eventually running six volumes, it happened to feature some of the more interesting outtakes discussed in *The Beatles Recording Sessions*, in excellent quality. While Mark Lewisohn was not involved in leaking these, they almost had the effect of acting as complements to the book, each reinforcing interest in the other.

• In 1991, the *Unsurpassed Demos* CD unearthed another major chunk of previously undocumented material by presenting no fewer than 22 May 1968 *White Album* home demos cut at George Harrison's home. The John Lennon songs in this batch had already made the rounds, but now Paul McCartney's and George's could be heard as well, making this one of the relatively few bootleg releases that could stand on its own as a quasi-lost Beatles album.

• In 1994, Apple/EMI at long last acknowledged the demand for "new" (i.e., previously unreleased) Beatles material with their two-CD *Live at the BBC* compilation. This was followed over the next couple of years by the three two-CD *Anthology* volumes of outtakes/live performances/demos and assorted rarities. By doing so, the Beatles were tacitly acknowledging the immense popularity of this material, rightfully cutting themselves in for some of the profits rather than leaving it all to the bootleggers. And they shrewdly used the *Anthology* CDs to cross-fertilize interest in two other hugely profitable projects: the *Anthology* TV documentary/home video/DVD series and the No. 1 best-selling *Anthology* book.

Yet, one wonders if it ever crossed their minds that, at the same time as they were rubbing out some bootleg profits, they were also inadvertently refueling demand for *more* Beatles bootlegs. If you wanted more BBC material than *Live at the BBC* offered, you could get a ten-CD box set of it. Like some of those video clips in the *Anthology* documentary? The entire concerts from which they were sourced were bootlegged on DVD. There were even bootlegged "alternate" *Anthology* CDs, compiling some of the most interesting stuff the official volumes had missed, and a "director's cut" (see sidebar, "The *Other* Anthology," part two, page 337) of the *Anthology* documentary with unused footage. Far from wiping the bootleggers out

THE BEATLES
ULTRA RARE TRAX
VOLUME 5 & 6

The Ultra Rare Trax *series not only presented never-before-heard studio out-takes, but also used relatively seldom-seen images of the band on the covers.*

(if that was even an intention), the *Anthology* projects in a way made those products more popular and sought-after than ever, merely by making many average fans aware that so much unreleased material existed in the first place.

• Doug Sulpy and Ray Schweighardt's 1997 book *Get Back: The Unauthorized Chronicle of the Beatles' Let It Be Disaster* was another milestone in raising awareness of the magnitude of the January 1969 *Get Back* tapes cache. For that matter, a good many more surfaced in the years after that volume was published, although it does cover the substantial majority of them. Many of the tapes documented in the book were already in circulation and exorbitant packages like the five-LP *The Beatles Black Album* (packaged with a wonderfully designed mock-up of the *White Album* poster featuring entirely different photos on one side and selected transcripts of *Get Back* sessions dialogue on the other) had been done as early as the mid-'80s. But now bootleggers prepared ever more elaborate and massive packages, culminating in the 83-CD (that's not a typo; *eighty-three-CD*) *A/B Road* set—possibly the largest single multi-volume series commemorating one body of musical work ever created, officially or unofficially.

By the beginning of the 21st century, the acquisition and exchange of unreleased music was taking on a new dimension as it began to circumvent commercially sold bootleggers (and, sometimes, even physical bootlegs themselves) entirely. Home compact disc burners enabled listeners to duplicate their records, and even create handpicked assortments of individual tracks from many different records, for as many of their friends as they wished. At the same time, the Internet was making it not just possible but commonplace for users to send, receive, and exchange "files" of music tracks. It had been easy for at least a quarter-century or so to copy and distribute songs via home cassettes, but now it was that much easier than ever, to the point where the computer industry had a huge impact on sales in the above-ground commercial recording industry. What's been less noted is that it's also had a huge impact on the bootleg industry, both in terms of making unreleased music far more widely and easily available than ever before, and in cutting heavily into the sales of bootleg CDs. It's now theoretically possible to assemble a complete collection of the circulating unreleased Beatles recordings without ever buying a bootleg—or, for that matter, ever putting a CD, LP, or tape into a stereo, if the hard disk or disks onto which the tracks are being placed have enough space.

Recently, the booming popularity of the DVD format has sparked the same kind of explosion in unauthorized videos that the CD format did with albums. Rare rock videos had been traded on the bootleg market since VCRs became household items. But at this writing, DVDs are the fastest-growing sector of the rock bootleg market, with a plethora of titles that was inconceivable just five years ago. The Beatles, naturally, have had much of their footage bootlegged on DVD, and all of their more prominent commercially unavailable film projects—including the Shea Stadium documentary, their 1966 Japanese TV shows, the *Around the Beatles* special, their promotional films, and much more—are obtainable in that format. As with audio-only bootlegs, labels were quick to expand from straightforward releases of specific performances into more ambitious imaginative compilations, such as a two-DVD anthology of *Let It Be* performances and outtakes, or a multi-volume set that assembles most of the rare Beatles short clips (and some of the long ones) in chronological order.

Every year or two, it seems, you'll read about renewed efforts by the Recording Industry Association of America (RIAA) and its UK equivalent, the British Phonographic Industry (BPI), to crack down on bootleggers in efforts to make their product unavailable. In spite of some high-profile busts, however, the music bootleg trade in unreleased music (as opposed to pirate and counterfeit reproduction of authorized releases, which is a related but quite different field) continues to do fairly big business—as it has for about 35 years, despite periodic crackdowns and raids throughout that period. The Beatles, who, according to the RIAA, are the all-time bestselling recording act, probably remain the all-time bestselling recording act in the bootleg world as well, stiff competition from Bob Dylan and the Rolling Stones notwithstanding. And the group's probably No. 1 in the competition for most individual bootleg titles as well—even by 1995, according to the book *Black Market Beatles*, there had been more than 1,600 Beatles bootlegs, and that number has surely increased greatly in the last decade.

So for all their relative obscurity to the mainstream music consumer, Beatles bootlegs have served, and continue to serve, an enormous audience with items that can't be found in the local chain store. Even if (for the sake of argument) there are "only" 2,000 Beatles bootlegs, which sold on the average just 1,000 copies each, that still adds up to two million copies sold. And the number's likely several million more than that, considering that the most popular Beatles bootlegs of the 1980s were reported (in Clinton Heylin's *Bootleg*) to have sold close to 20,000 copies. And even if all physical bootlegs were somehow seized and taken out of circulation, file-sharing and CD-Rs/DVD-Rs have ensured that there's no way of stuffing that genie back in the bottle. Unreleased Beatles material is going to circulate, among an expanding base of literally millions of listeners, for as long as people are around to listen.

Many Beatles bootlegs now boast cover art so professional that they could be mistaken for legitimate releases by inexperienced collectors.

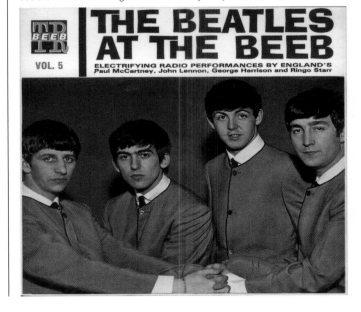

Some veteran collectors feel that sales of Beatles bootlegs and bootlegs in general are actually slacking off, and not just because of file-sharing and CD-Rs. They point out that many of the old-time Beatles fanatics already have most or all of what they want; some of the older collectors are, sad to say, literally dying off; and much of the younger generation isn't as familiar with, or interested in, a group that did, after all, disband more than 35 years ago. But the Beatles bootleg, as a physical product, hardly seems like an endangered species. As much as new technology has cut down on sales, it's also probably, at least in part, forced bootleggers to come up with more imaginative packaging. The days of tatty sleeves and nonexistent/horribly misinformed sleeve information are largely gone. Now there are slick covers with gorgeous rare photos that, in many instances, look better than actual commercial releases; liner notes that are, in some instances, more scholarly and informative than said major-label releases; and, often, a certain irreverent wit that you'll *never* find in major-label releases. There are even multimedia components to some releases, such as CD-ROMs of supplemental information and MP3s of interview excerpts. The one thing that hasn't changed (and probably never will), unfortunately, is the inordinate amount of duplication between different bootleg packages (now complicated by major-to-nonexistent "upgrades" claiming to offer better sound quality than previously available versions of the same recording). That forces completists to fork out many times more money than they would if the material were issued just once, in a logical order/grouping—though major label CD reissues are guilty of the same practice, to some extent.

And the hunger for unreleased Beatles product remains not just strong, but occasionally avid to the point of hysteria. Nothing illus-trated this better than a false alarm in the summer of 2004, when it was reported in worldwide headlines that a British tourist had found hours of unreleased Beatles songs in a suitcase he bought for $36 in an Australian flea market. As it turned out, all of the "unreleased songs" were merely copies of stuff that had already been bootlegged. A similar, brief media frenzy accompanied the January 2003 raid by British and Dutch police that netted 500 unreleased tapes from the *Get Back* sessions, which, too, had already been bootlegged. The late John Peel, the most respected radio DJ in Britain, embarrassed himself mightily not long before his 2004 death when he listened to three hours of Beatles tapes claimed by a 64-year-old woman to be "unreleased" and declared them "an exciting and almost dangerous find"—though these turned out to be cassettes of the already officially available *Anthology* series. Even the mere hint that one avant-garde Beatles track, 1967's "Carnival of Light," *might* come out sparked a flurry of excited news reports in 2002—all this for a recording that would probably be one of the least conventionally listenable tunes by the group should it ever be available (which, as of this writing, it isn't).

Some veteran collectors who *are* running out of unreleased Beatles music to acquire, however, are indeed wondering: is there any more, or have we finally reached the bottom of the well? Meanwhile, both veteran collectors and more general fans are also pondering a related question: will the Beatles themselves consent to allow more unreleased material to enter the official marketplace? The answers to those questions are highly uncertain and dependent to a large degree on the Beatles' (and their estates') own attitudes toward their unreleased catalog. Which brings us to our final chapter . . .

MAS LP TER

TITLE
OF
WORK

FILE UNDER:

TAPE
LIBRARY NO.

GN70075-1

COMPOSER & AUTHOR
THE BEATLES

CONDUCTOR

ORCHESTRA

	SEQUENCE OF TITLES, PARTS OR MOVEMENTS	ARTISTE(S) ETC.	L.P. MATRIX NO.	E.P. MATRIX NO.	STANDARD MATRIX NO.	STANDARD PLAYING TIME	L.P. OR E.P. RILLS	
1.	Come And Get It	The Beatles	GN 70075-1/A			1:40	1:40	1.
2.	Shake, Rattle, & Roll					2:05	3:48	2.
3.	Leave My Kitten Alone					2:45	6:36	3.
4.	I'm So Tired					2:16	8:55	4.
5.	Not Fade Away					2:52	11:48	5.
6.	I Me Mine					1:42	13:32	6.
7.	Third Man Theme					1:50	15:23	7.
8.	Bad To Me					1:25	16:52	8.
9.	Christmastime (Is Here Again)					6:33	23:45	9.
1.	Goodbye	The Beatles	GN 70075-1/B			2:06	2:06	1.
2.	Blue Suede Shoes					2:02	4:51	2.
3.	If You've Got Troubles					1:43	6:40	3.
4.	Negro In Reserve					:50	7:32	4.
5.	That Means A Lot					2:01	9:34	5.
6.	Get Back					3:00	12:35	6.
7.	One After 909					2:47	15:20	7.
8.	I Dig A Pony					3:49	19:18	8.
9.	Dialog					3:32	22:54	9.

BGH301

This mishmash of outtakes was packaged to simulate a classified document, in keeping with the Beatles and EMI's secretive plans for issuing the group's unreleased recordings.

The Last Word: The Official Legacy of the Unofficial Beatles

As the size of this book proves, the Beatles, Apple, and EMI have not attempted to release the vast majority of the group's unreleased recordings. The decisions guiding what they *have* allowed into release (as well as when they've decided to release it) have struck many Beatles fans as quixotic, or even downright peculiar. That could be said, it must be emphasized, of many major stars with a huge catalog. The world's been waiting for what seems like an eternity for a long-promised archival Neil Young box set; the Rolling Stones have never given sign of a serious effort to exhume their 1960s BBC sessions and outtakes; and Bob Dylan sat on arguably the most famous bootleg of all time for decades before *Live 1966: The "Royal Albert Hall" Concert* was finally issued in 1998. The Beatles finally got with the program to some extent in the mid-'90s, putting out eight CDs of what most listeners would acknowledge as their most significant vault holdings. Yet much continues to remain commercially unavailable. Predicting if and when more material might gain official release has been impossible to do with accuracy, with most hints from the corridors of power having led us down blind alleys.

In a way, the Beatles' ambivalent-at-best attitude toward their unofficial legacy might date all the way back to their breakup. Their last album, after all, wasn't even released while they were active, owing to disagreements over how or even if to put it out. Yet intriguingly, it's been speculated that John Lennon himself was the source, albeit probably unwittingly, for some of the first bootlegs of *Get Back* material. As John himself commented (as quoted in Roy Carr's *Beatles at the Movies*), "One of those versions [of the *Get Back* LP] that was put together when it was still *Get Back* was pretty damn good. It was the one that turned up as a bootleg and I got the blame. People reckon I was responsible for it. Maybe I was. Can't remember! They said it came from an acetate that I gave to someone who then went and broadcast it as being an advance pressing or something. If that's true, then I suppose I am responsible. But it's not as though I was pressing them up and selling them out the back door!"

The personal acrimony and financial chaos in which the Beatles were embroiled in the early '70s probably put any notions of how to plunder their archives way in the back of their minds, even as Beatles

MAS[LP]TER

TITLE OF WORK

FILE UNDER: II

TAPE LIBRARY No.		
COMPOSER & AUTHOR	THE BEATLES	
CONDUCTOR	CH ORCH	G. MARTIN
ORCHESTRA	LON. SYMPH.	
	70075-1/b 2c;2d;3	

SEQUENCE OF TITLES, PARTS OR MOVEMENTS	ARTISTE(S) ETC.	L.P. MATRIX No.	E.P. MATRIX No.	STANDARD MATRIX No.	STANDARD PLAYING TIME	L.P. OR E.P. RILLS	
1. Not Guilty	The Beatles	GN 70077-1/A			3:23	3:23	1.
2. Besame Mucho					2:37	6:07	2.
3. Catswalk					1:06	7:20	3.
4. Here We Go Again					1:21	8:48	4.
5. While My Guitar Gently Weeps					3:29	12:23	5.
6. Suicide					1:30	14:00	6.
7. Mailman, Bring Me No More Blues					1:55	16:00	7.
8. Spiritual Regeneration W.W.F.					2:16	18:22	8.
9. The Inner Light					2:35	21:03	9.
10. Shout!					2:02	23:11	10.
1. Im Looking Through You	The Beatles	GN 70077-1/B			2:58	2:58	1.
2. Strawberry Fields Forever							
a. Take #1/ Key of C/ Adagio					2:56		
b. Take #7/ Key of B/ Adagio					3:24		
c. Orchestral Take/ Key of C/ Andante					3:27		
d. Take #25/ Key of C/ Andante					3:23	16:12	2.
3. A Day In The Life					5:12	21:31	3.
4. I Want You (She's So Heavy)					1:04	22:37	4.

BGH301

bootlegs immediately began to proliferate. Too, as individuals, the Beatles were signed to EMI through 1976, and probably didn't want "new" Beatles releases taking the spotlight away from their efforts to establish solo careers. At times it seemed as if they wanted to sweep the whole issue under the rug; asked by *Melody Maker* in August 1970 whether there was "any recorded material still unreleased," an unidentified Apple "official spokesman" replied, "No. Even if there was it would never be issued." Still, there's evidence an archival release was considered as early as May 1971, when Apple told the same publication there were tentative plans to issue a *Live at the Hollywood Bowl* LP, as a "reply to the bootleg *Live at Shea Stadium* album currently circulating London in large quantities."

The Beatles themselves were certainly aware of the bootleg trade in the group's albums virtually from its start. An August 1971 letter from a *Melody Maker* reader complaining about the quality of the *Live at Shea* boot actually got a response the following week from John Lennon, who asked, "Why buy the bootleg in the first place? You must have read how bad they are before now. Anyway, the reason we haven't released the old stuff is because we haven't got round to remixing it yet." Rather than heeding his own advice, however, Lennon actually collected Beatles bootlegs such as *Live at Shea* quite voraciously. Material from a Shea Stadium bootleg was found in his personal tapes when research was done for "The Lost Lennon Tapes" radio series, and he wasn't just picking up two or three of the group's most famous boots, enthusing about their relatively obscure 1963 live Sweden recordings in a 1974 interview. In an interview done just a couple of days before his death with Andy Peebles of the BBC, Lennon went as far as to claim, "I buy all the pirate records and file them away. I don't play them, you know. I keep them. . . . Stuff from Sweden and things like that, where there was good live shows done." It seems possible Yoko Ono might have taken her late husband's liberal attitude toward unreleased material into consideration when administering John's estate. For quite a bit has gotten into circulation with her official blessing, whether via authorized CDs or as bootlegs from "The Lost Lennon Tapes" radio series.

The other Beatles were not so vocally enthusiastic (or vocal in general) about bootlegs, though Wings' 1972 hit single "Hi Hi Hi" refers to someone holding a bootleg in its very first line. In July 1971, Ringo told *Melody Maker*, "Bootlegs I hate, I may as well tell you that, because the product . . . is not a good representation of the artist. It's just some crumb who doesn't do anything making all the bread. I wouldn't mind a bootleg if it went to charity or somewhere but all those—are very negative people. They just pick up something by luck and shove it out and make all the bread, and it's not a good product and they're conning the kids."

Asked in the same interview whether there were "50 or less" unreleased Beatles tracks, Starr didn't go to the extent of denying (as Apple had the previous year) that there was nothing, but did seem to be unaware of just how much existed when he replied, "No, no, nowhere near that. I mean, once you've canceled out the Shea, and there were a few other tours that were recorded—the live stuff would do about three albums, I think—the actual tracks we did in studios, the songs and jams . . . I'd say there'd be 20 or 30 tracks at the most. . . . We put everything out because we always worked like a dog to get everything right. I mean, there are great rumors about there's enough material for another 25 years and all that, but you mustn't believe that rubbish."

In 1975, John espoused even more ignorance as to the group's studio outtakes, insisting there was nothing in the can. Even had they been diligently counting all their alternate takes and home recordings as "tracks," however, the Beatles might not have been keen to cooperate with EMI on liberating some of their vault tapes in the late '70s and early '80s at any rate. All of them (John included) had left EMI for different labels by 1980, and they couldn't have been too pleased at the generally half-baked thematic compilations repackaging some of their work that appeared in the meantime (à la *Rock 'n' Roll Music*, *Love Songs*, *Reel Music*, and *Rarities*).

The viability of a reasonably well done album of previously unavailable material was nonetheless demonstrated when the one such project to appear on EMI during these years, *The Beatles at the Hollywood Bowl*, went to No. 2 in 1977. Yet the group probably wasn't too over the moon that it came out, having objected to the tapes' release back in the mid-'60s, and one gathers it's *still* not something the surviving Beatles and their estates are keen to have available, as it hasn't appeared on CD. As for the other album of hitherto unissued live recordings to appear, *Live! At the Hamburg Star-Club in Hamburg, Germany; 1962,* it only came out against the Beatles' wishes and they were *still* challenging its legality in court in the late '90s. Too, the disappointing commercial performance of that set could have been viewed as validating their reluctance to let loose recordings with notably subpar fidelity. (In less celebrated activity, the Beatles also took action to prevent the Decca tapes from being legally distributed in the 1980s.) And while it might have seemed logical for a compilation of BBC performances to get issued after the syndicated radio special devoted to these aired in 1982—what better free promotion could there have been?—no moves were made to put such an anthology together.

In 1981, EMI publicist Brian Southall had claimed at the Liverpool Annual Mersey Beatle Extravaganza convention that apart from the outtake "Leave My Kitten Alone" and "the Christmas disc tapes, EMI has no other completed issuable material." Further straining credulity, he added, "It would seem that when a song had been recorded, one or another of the Beatles would take the tapes home, strictly against EMI's wishes, and would only return material they themselves wanted released." EMI had, nonetheless, been making some exploratory surveys into what studio outtakes they might be able to assemble as far back as spring 1976. The very enlistment of John Barrett to thoroughly catalog the group's tapes in the early '80s might be seen as a preparatory measure in the event that some could be released. Too, the use of some of those outtakes in the 1983 multimedia show *The Beatles at Abbey Road* could have served at least in part as a gauge of public interest.

At least they knew what to look for when they finally assembled an LP of outtakes, *Sessions*, in 1984, produced by the next best candidate to George Martin, Geoff Emerick (who'd been chief engineer on many Beatles sessions from *Revolver* onward). Its 13 tracks focused on the most completely realized studio recordings of songs the Beatles never released ("How Do You Do It," "Besame Mucho," "Leave My Kitten Alone," "If You've Got Trouble," "That Means a Lot," "Not Guilty," "What's the New Mary Jane," "Come and Get It") and the most radically different complete alternate versions of tunes they *did* release ("I'm Looking through You," the 1963 recording of "One After 909," "While My Guitar Gently Weeps"), adding a more-or-less complete *Get Back* outtake ("Mailman Bring Me No More Blues") and a snatch of their 1967 Christmas fan club recording ("Christmas Time (Is Here Again)") for good measure. Another alternate version, of "Ob-La-Di, Ob-La-Da," was targeted for the

The cover designs for the Sessions *bootlegs were so slick that some fans were fooled into thinking they were official releases.*

B-side of a single ("Leave My Kitten Alone" would have been on the flip). *Sessions* got as far as test pressings and a cover design before release plans were halted, possibly because there were still royalty disputes between the Beatles and EMI.

Hardcore fans were frustrated by the non-appearance of *Sessions*, though anyone with a little gumption could easily find it on bootleg. The failure of it and any BBC sessions to appear, however, might have been a blessing in disguise in the long run. The 13-volume bootleg series *The Beatles at the Beeb* unearthed many more performances than EMI probably would have realized existed had it tried to do a BBC compilation in 1982, as well as proving there were higher-fidelity versions of tapes that had aired in the radio series. And had *Sessions* been released in 1985, it probably would have been a disappointment to uninformed buyers and critics, many of whom would have found it meager and unworthy compared to what they might have been expecting. (Not to mention that it used some artificial loops to extend some of the tracks slightly, as well as excising parts of "Not Guilty.")

More crucially, without the support of the Beatles or an accompanying project to reinforce its promotion, *Sessions* would likely have underperformed commercially—which could well have made it that less likely that *any* additional similar projects would have been attempted by EMI. As with the BBC material, this also gave bootleggers a few more years to hunt down and distribute the alternate takes that appeared on the *Ultra Rare Trax* series. That proved there was a substantial market not just for the few outtakes of unreleased Beatles songs, but also for the different versions of songs they did release, even if they varied from the official tracks in subtle rather than drastic fashions. Plus some previously unknown material from *outside* of EMI began to emerge, such as their May 1968 *White Album* demos and 1960 home tapes, that gave EMI

more options to pursue should they decide to issue recordings not done in the studio—which, as everyone knows, they eventually did.

All of this might have been moot had not the surviving three Beatles and Yoko Ono gotten some business/financial issues cleared up, both among themselves and with EMI. That removed obstacles that could have prevented them from cooperating, finally, on a program that could exploit the Beatles' reserve of unissued material on a scale that no one probably thought possible back when *Sessions* was being assembled. They might have been starting to weigh such possibilities as early as December 1990, when Ringo admitted to *Musician,* "We always felt that what came out is what we wanted out. That was the musician in us. We weren't really interested in the avid fan who wants *anything.* I think we're moving more along those lines now, because some of the 'Take 2's would really be interesting."

The project that could serve as the vehicle for such material was *Anthology,* which spawned three two-CD sets of vault recordings, a massive film documentary (which itself aired some outtake snippets unavailable elsewhere, even on the *Anthology* albums), and a bestselling book. The endeavor wasn't as suddenly conceived as it might have appeared. Way back in 1970, Apple's Neil Aspinall had started work on a documentary of the group, then titled *The Long and Winding Road* (though it lasted a relatively short hour and 45 minutes in this incarnation). George Harrison even referred to it in a May interview that year, and Neil Innes of the Rutles had used it for reference in 1976 when helping to create the classic television spoof of the Beatles saga, *All You Need Is Cash.* But it took until 1992, and all the constellations to fall into the right place, before it could properly proceed.

Even before *Anthology* was unveiled, however, *Live at the BBC* became the Beatles' first major archive release since *Live at the Hollywood Bowl* when it hit the stores in December 1994. Although unrelated to the *Anthology* projects, in a way it was a test run for both their viability and the way the *Anthology* CDs would be assembled. As much as some fans would have liked it, EMI's *Live at the BBC* was not a complete, gargantuan-sized box set of all their known recordings for the network assembled in chronological order. Instead, it was a relatively pruned-down "best of" of sorts, rightfully concentrating on the songs they did on the BBC that had no studio counterparts on their official releases, as well as adding some of the more notable BBC versions of numbers that *did* find a place on their LPs, EPs, and singles. Some of the material would never have been found had bootlegs not done some of the legwork in advance.

Some of the experts and completists groused about the non-chronological sequencing, the artificial crossfades that obscured small parts of some endings, and how, at least in their opinion, the mastering made the sound on some of the tracks inferior to the versions heard on bootlegs. Since you're reading this book, you may well be one of the fans who wanted a bigger, less slickly edited compilation. And not all of those fans are the stereotypical obsessives who have nothing better to do than make A–B comparisons of noise reduction on bootleg and EMI versions of "I'll Be on My Way." Upon its release, Allan Kozinn hotly criticized the set in *The New York Times,* citing the best available bootleg box at that time (Great Dane's nine-CD *The Complete Beatles BBC Sessions*) as a far better alternative. "Will [Apple and EMI] realize that sitting on the material for years and then issuing a compilation that cannot compete with more comprehensive bootlegs is not a wise marketing strategy?"

he asked. "Will they decide that further archival issues are not worth pursuing? Or will they take stock of their priceless resources and put together the thoughtfully organized collection the Beatles' music deserves?"

Yet it has to be remembered that *Live at the BBC* was packaged not with expert enthusiasts such as Kozinn (or you and me) in mind, but for a general public that never buys nine-CD box sets by *anyone*, not even the Beatles. On those grounds, it was an unqualified commercial success, cruising to No. 3 in the charts and selling, as of this writing, four million units (according to the RIAA). While this opinion won't be welcomed by the hardcore collectors, *Live at the BBC* was an aesthetically successful release, too. It did present the vast majority of songs the group did for the BBC that never found a place on their records, with the exception of a few that largely failed to make the cut because of poor fidelity. Plus these two discs, due to the elimination of multiple versions and the selective presentation of highlights, were more listenable and enjoyable on their own terms than any of the many bootlegged discs of Beatles BBC sessions, whatever their size. If you wanted more (and were willing to part with two or three C-notes), you could always spring for the bootleg box, as recommended in no less a pillar of the establishment as *The New York Times*. And if the Beatles, Apple, and EMI had any doubts as to whether "further archival issues are not worth pursuing," they were set aside as they prepared to aggressively market the three *Anthology* volumes.

Even shortly before the *Anthology* CDs were produced, some high-rankers in the Beatles camp were insisting that nothing respectable could be chiseled out of what remained in EMI's vaults. In March 1993, George Martin claimed in *The Times* that, having "listened to all the tapes," everything left was "all junk. Couldn't possibly release it." Yet by the end of the year he was on board as producer of the *Anthology* CDs, promising *Record Collector* that "we're going to put in everything that I consider to be valid from every source, including the Beatles' own private collections, demos that they made, outtakes and alternate versions of songs." There were some practical concerns here at work, naturally; the surviving Beatles (and George Martin) were interviewed extensively for the *Anthology* documentary and weren't about to badmouth the accompanying CDs. Quite the contrary, it now behooved them—for the first time—to be talking up their unreleased material, though not to the point of acknowledging that it had been all those bootlegs that were largely responsible for creating this market in the first place.

There were also hints that the Beatles themselves were unaware of just how much of musical merit was in the vaults until they were reintroduced to it during the course of this project. In a 1995 interview with *Independent on Sunday*, Paul described it as "quite strange, but quite exciting as well. It's like being archaeologists. We're finding tracks that we didn't remember recording, that we didn't want, or thought, 'No, that's not too good.' Now, of course, after 30 years, they don't look too bad at all." Conceded George in a 1996 *Billboard* interview, "When we came across these other takes, it was like, 'Wow, what was *that*?' It was a surprise to us, too." Added Ringo in the *Anthology* DVD bonus disc, "The attitude it was like at the beginning [of working on a track] to seven takes later is just like a mile. You know, it's not like, 'Oh, we changed a note.' I mean, we changed the whole thing, working on it, working on it, changing it, changing it."

For all their commercial success, the merits of the *Anthology* CDs remain a topic of considerable debate a decade or so after their release. Beatles archaeologists again pounced on some of the liberties taken

with the editing and production. Some of the mixes were slammed as less than stellar (and, occasionally, less worthy than those heard on some bootlegged versions). Displeasure was vented over the shortening of some tracks (which, again, were sometimes available in longer versions on boots). Genuine outrage was sparked by some creative reconstruction that edited together different parts of different takes to construct brand new outtakes—or "outfakes," as the more sarcastic aficionados labeled them. Geoff Emerick, for all his fine work as a Beatles engineer in the 1960s, came under fire from some specialists for using the same edits and mixes on some of the tracks that he'd prepared for the ill-fated *Sessions* LP in 1984 rather than devising new ones. Plus some outtakes reported to be in the running never made it onto *Anthology* or any other official release, including a few—such as alternate versions of "Love You To," "Think for Yourself," and "Getting Better," the legendary 27-minute "Helter Skelter," and a full December 1962 Hamburg live performance of "Red Hot"—that have still never even been bootlegged.

For general fans who'd never bought a bootleg in their life (and many such listeners *did* buy the *Anthology* volumes), there was not so much outrage as some genuine puzzlement at hearing tracks that were both different than what they expected, and not nearly on the same artistic level, for the most part, as finished Beatles cuts on their proper albums. There were even anecdotal reports of attempted returns when listeners discovered that the versions of famous Beatles songs on the compilations were not the originals with which they were familiar, but different and usually notably less developed "alternate" takes. Disillusionment with the packages, whether for this or other reasons, might be reflected by the sharply declining sales of the second and third *Anthology* volumes.

But make no mistake about it: each volume *did* sell lots of copies. The first volume has shifted eight million units as of this writing, and while the four million chalked up by *Anthology Vol. 2* (and the three million by *Anthology Vol. 3*) might seem poor in comparison, that's still phenomenal for outtakes by a group that had been defunct for a quarter-century when they were first released. And like *Live at the BBC*, the music really was chosen and presented about as astutely as is possible for a release targeted toward the general public. Just as the *Beatles at the Beeb* bootlegs had done some of the advance scouting for *Live at the BBC*, Mark Lewisohn's *The Beatles Recording Sessions* could be said to have done much of the legwork for the *Anthology* CD series. Lewisohn is usually acknowledged as the top Beatles expert in the world, and the great majority of the most interesting outtakes and alternate versions that he cited in his book (including all of the ones that would have appeared on *Sessions* back in 1984, and numerous ones that had *never* been bootlegged) were on the *Anthology* volumes. Lewisohn even wrote the liner notes.

In addition, the tracks were drawn not just from EMI outtakes, but also from concerts, television/radio performances, the Decca audition, the Tony Sheridan recordings (the only ones to have seen previous official release), and home tapes—again, with much of the non-EMI material likely only being available or known about in the first place due to the past efforts of bootleggers. The cuts were also sequenced chronologically and to avoid multiple versions, making for about the best and smoothest listen given the wide disparity of styles, eras, and sources that had to be merged into some kind of mainstream product. For all the kvetching by the hard-nosed sticklers for detail, you'd find very few Beatles collectors—even ones with hundreds of bootlegs in their collection—who would consider trading in or giving away their *Anthology* volumes.

The *Anthology* project was a massive financial success, and not just in terms of the CDs. By the RIAA's count, the video series (which itself used many clips that had only been available on video bootlegs) has been responsible for sales of 13 million units. The *Anthology* coffee-table book, published after the documentary and CDs had been released, entered *The New York Times* bestseller list at No. 1 and has sold more than two million copies worldwide. All this doesn't even take into account *Anthology*'s ongoing stimulation of the Beatles' standard back catalog: in 1996 alone, the Beatles sold more albums than they did in any year in the 1960s.

It's no stretch to say that none of this would have been possible, at least to nearly the same extent, had not bootlegs cultivated such a strong, ongoing interest in the Beatles' unreleased material since 1970. No one disputes the Beatles have gotten ripped off to the tune of millions, perhaps billions, of dollars by bootleg records of that material, and no one would deny them their right to reclaim some of that pie for themselves. But the group might have made back that lost money with interest with the *Anthology* products, though it's impossible to calculate for certain (and it could be argued they haven't really "lost" money from bootleg sales at all, considering it's probable that the vast majority of Beatles bootleg collectors already own all of the group's official product). As for the record company putting it out, EMI spokesperson Brian Southall had termed bootlegs as a "damaging part . . . of Beatles culture" to the *L.A. Weekly* around the time *Sessions* was scrapped. But again, by making the *Anthology* CDs possible, those bootlegs could be viewed as paying back with interest whatever losses the label incurred.

It's probably just a coincidence, but the more decades removed the Beatles got from the end of their career, the more indications there were that their attitudes toward bootlegs and unreleased material, if not exactly gung-ho, were starting to at least soften. George might have been the least enthusiastic about revisiting the Beatlemania days, but it was he who let slip that he still had the tape of *White Album* demos done at his house in May 1968, some of which were used on *Anthology 3*. Asked about the *Ultra Rare Trax* bootlegs at a February 2, 1990, interview in Auburn Hills, Michigan, Paul responded, "If people are interested, it's fair enough. I mean, I don't get uptight about bootlegs. What are you going to do?" (In a 1997 *New York Times* article, Allan Kozinn quotes McCartney as telling him, "I have no problem with bootlegs, although every time I say that, my lawyer says, 'Oh yes you do.'") Ringo Starr sensibly told *Rolling Stone* in 1991, "These bootlegs came out and there were enormous sales. I want to put out Beatles bootlegs by the Beatles. You know, instead of someone else putting them out, we should do it. Because it's out there anyway."

But will the Beatles, Apple, and EMI ever engage in an archive series of sorts for the group's unreleased recordings, or even any more such *Anthology* releases? The decade or so that has elapsed since the last *Anthology* CDs does not give us much hope. The only appearance of "new" material, *Let It Be . . . Naked,* was in fact a rejigged release of *Let It Be* in which you had to have a timer handy to detect what material had been edited in and out of the old version. Even if the appearance of un-Spectorized mixes was to be welcomed to some degree, the bonus disc of 22 minutes of piecemeal excerpts from the vast body of *Get Back* sessions did not augur well for sensitive treatment of those outtakes for

possible authorized issue. As for more *Anthology*-type volumes, George didn't seem keen on the notion in his 1996 *Billboard* interview, exclaiming, "After I had joked that after 'Volume 3,' anything else should be called 'Scraping the Barrel,' George Martin said, 'Yeah, we'd have to put a government health warning on it!'"

Those who argued that fans were tired of the same old golden oldies endlessly recycled were soundly refuted by the astonishing success of 2000's *1,* a by-the-book collection of chart-topping Beatles singles that—despite its unforgivable omission of "Please Please Me"—not only topped the chart itself, but has to date sold an astronomical ten million copies. *The Capitol Albums Vols. 1 & 2* offered stereo and mono versions of the first eight Beatles LPs that Capitol issued in the US, but while these were a godsend for alternate mix hounds, there was nothing in the way of cuts that hadn't yet seen the official light of day. Even the revamp of *Yellow Submarine* into *Yellow Submarine Songtrack,* as much as it improved the listenability of the album itself, added no previously unreleased tracks. On the video end, a promised with-extras DVD edition of *Let It Be* has yet to see the light after several years of rumor, and *Magical Mystery Tour* and even *Help!* are currently unavailable on DVD in the US. Admittedly the Beatles have less control over video product than record releases, but there's been little in the way of concert footage issued either, except for *The Four Historic Ed Sullivan Shows Featuring the Beatles* and an incomplete presentation of their first American concert at the Washington Coliseum in February 1964.

The Beatles, Apple, and EMI are now in an unusual position regarding the clearance of additional unreleased material for official consumption. No other recording artist commands as much demand for such product, yet few recording artists have yielded so seldom to that demand. As frustrating as this might be to devoted fans, if only to play devil's advocate, the positions the Beatles might be considering in these decisions should be at least briefly noted and respected. From a cold, financial point of view, it's doubtful that subsequent packages of unreleased material will do nearly as well as the *Anthology* and *Live at the BBC* volumes, with diminishing returns the sooner the bottom of the barrel comes into view. From a moral point of view, as much as fanatics hunger to hear everything possible, few could reasonably argue against the Beatles having the ultimate right as to what they want added to their official catalog.

Paul McCartney has also expressed concern that if a flood of alternate takes comes out, fans might get confused as to which is the official version and which is the outtake. Although that might seem like an overly cautious concern to those well schooled in the Beatles' discography, unfortunately the expertise of general consumers in this respect can't be overestimated, as demonstrated by the confusion many expressed when the *Anthology* volumes contained alternate versions rather than the finished ones. There might also be a desire at work to keep the Beatles catalog fairly trim so that everything in their official canon is regarded as strong and special. They almost certainly wouldn't want to dilute its financial worth and aesthetic legacy with endless repackages and reissues with a few meager or marginally different outtakes, as RCA has done with Elvis Presley.

All that said, some other major artists with huge storehouses of hugely sought-after vault holdings have provided models of sorts worth considering. For decades, Bob Dylan collectors were infuriated by Columbia's indifference to issuing his most coveted outtakes and live concerts. But over the last 15 years, seven multi-disc volumes of such material have finally come out, titled "The Bootleg Series," no less. (Dylan also made some live 1962 recordings available on a CD that could only be bought at Starbucks, though many socially conscious fans fervently hope the Beatles don't go that particular route.) At the least selective end of the spectrum, the Grateful Dead have made many of their concert recordings available as part of a special *Dick's Picks* series, now up to an astonishing three dozen volumes. Frank Zappa even went to the extent of issuing some previously available bootlegs (complete with original cover art) legally, and his estate continues to assemble archive recordings from his vast body of unissued work. In all of these artists' cases, these officially blessed CDs are clearly marked in the packaging as special-interest, previously unavailable recordings, hopefully doing as much as can reasonably be expected to make it clear they don't duplicate what's long been out on well-known albums.

Another option is to make "special editions" of standard albums from the official canon. In the CD era, it's become increasingly common to take an original vintage album (classic or otherwise) and embellish the material in a number of ways. Stereo and mono versions are presented side by side; demos, outtakes, and live versions are added as bonus tracks; and, sometimes, all such variations are thrown together (with DVD components becoming increasingly popular as well). The Beatles' catalog has long been criticized for not offering both stereo and mono versions, and for how those tapes have been remastered. All of their principal albums could be repackaged/remastered to include both, adding on the best outtakes/supplementary material relevant to the album/era as well. In a more modest fashion, the individual Beatles have done some similar repackaging for some of their solo work, with Paul and George doing expanded anniversary editions of *Band on the Run* and *All Things Must Pass* respectively. Yet another avenue to letting outtakes trickle out with official blessings is to make them available as downloadable sound files via the Internet, though these would undoubtedly immediately be both bootlegged on physical CDs and exchanged between collectors through file-sharing.

If it sounds like a lot of work to retool the classic Beatles albums in this manner, it should be noted that bootleggers have been doing this for years, presumably to appreciable sales considering how many such packages continue to be constructed. Music industry associations (and some other pundits) have sometimes characterized buyers of such bootlegs (and buyers of bootlegs in general) as gullible dupes who are committing crimes of their own by denying performers their rightful financial reward. This overlooks the reality that the substantial majority of Beatles fans would *much* prefer options that would allow performing and songwriting royalties from their purchases of this sort to go to the group. They would also generally much prefer CDs of rare/unreleased material with sound taken from the best possible sources, with reliably professional mastering and packaging, and the lower price and much easier availability that official product would allow. It is only the absence of such product from the official shelves (or, now, online retailers) that drives them to consume bootlegs. That plus, it must be stressed, an obsessive passion for the music, the bootleg buying done out of a deep love for the Beatles' art, not out of a desire to rip the group off.

There are also a few possible titles of unreleased material that could hang together on their own, unattached to standard Beatles studio albums. All 27 known May 1968 *White Album* home demos, for instance, could make for a fine if unconventional album, hopefully benefiting from the kind of improved sound quality heard when a few were included on

Anthology 3, and perhaps bolstered by any additional tracks not previously known to exist from the same source. The 15-song January 1, 1962, Decca audition tape has been bootlegged to death, but that might be all the more reason for the damned thing to be made available in a legitimate package once and for all, maybe with extras like the six songs they did on the BBC with Pete Best in 1962 (low fidelity notwithstanding). While not the most musical projects they ever did, and also bootlegged to death, all of their 1963–1969 Christmas fan club discs should likewise finally be compiled onto one CD and given official blessing, with outtakes from those sessions (some of which have already circulated) added as well. If and when *The Beatles at the Hollywood Bowl* finally makes it to CD, that would be a good opportunity to do an expanded edition including all the tapes they made at the venue in 1964 and 1965.

It would also be possible to do a two-disc catch-all *Anthology 4* with the most interesting material the first three volumes missed, from the 1960 home-taped versions of "I'll Follow the Sun" and "One After 909" to some more *Get Back* outtakes. Other possibilities include a single disc or two-CD set of said *Get Back* outtakes, or a single or two-CD set of the most interesting radio performances not contained on *Live at the BBC*. But don't hold your breath for any such projects. None of them would likely sell as well as the first three *Anthology* volumes, *Live at the BBC*, or *Let It Be . . . Naked,* in part because, as even enthusiastic collectors would have to admit, the very best material of this nature was already plundered by those aforementioned releases.

As to whether the Beatles and their associates view what's left at EMI as worth issuing, the signs are not positive. In a March 2006 interview with this author for *Record Collector*, Geoff Emerick couldn't "think of anything that was of any value that was not put out." George Martin pooh-poohed the notion while preparing *Anthology*, commenting to the monthly CD newsletter *ICE* that after the series would be done "we can all go home, put the light out over our heads and say goodnight." As this very chapter was written, however, Martin seemed to once again change his mind as to whether anything else should be retrieved from the vaults. For it was reported in April 2006 that the producer was remastering previously unreleased Beatles recordings for use as background music in, of all things, a Cirque du Soleil show in Las Vegas.

However, it was soon confirmed that much of the music being assembled for the Cirque du Soleil production actually recombined elements of various recordings into wholly new tracks. One piece, for instance, was described by *Rolling Stone* as "'Girl' with a drone from 'Lucy in the Sky with Diamonds,' a drum roll from 'Being For the Benefit of Mr. Kite' under the chorus, and a guitar figure from 'And I Love Her.'" "Octopus's Garden," also according to *Rolling Stone*, flew in strings from "Good Night," drums from "Lovely Rita," and a break from "Polythene Pam"; "Within You Without You" took drums from "Tomorrow Never Knows," George Martin commenting in all apparent seriousness, "'Within You' is not the most memorable song, but it's much more interesting with that rhythm." Another Cirque du Soleil special actually added a newly written and recorded Martin score to the acoustic version of "While My Guitar Gently Weeps." Whatever one thinks of the artistic validity of such exercises, these are not unreleased Beatles recordings, but long-after-the-fact manipulations of tracks into entirely different creations. Such exploitation of the Beatles' vaults struck some as gauche, and certainly funneled the material through an outlet that was unaffordable to the average fan, though *Variety* revealed that Apple was planning to release an album of "completely new music" from the show.

As to what might be left that no one's ever bootlegged (or no one even knows about), that's a great unknown, though this book has done its best to speculate on what might be around. The EMI tapes having been thoroughly cataloged, the best hope lies in privately held recordings and acetates. While it seems very unlikely that much such material's been preserved, let alone that it will ever be made officially or unofficially available, isolated tracks and chunks do unexpectedly pop up, even if the trickle's grown ever slower in the past few years. Home composing tapes would seem to be the leading possible source for new revelations in this area, John Lennon having admitted at an August 22, 1966, press conference that all of them were already recording at home, and George Harrison having been the first of the group to install a home studio back in 1964. With the exception of the many Lennon home tapes (mostly from the post-Beatles era) Yoko Ono has made available, however, little such material has emerged—and had John not died so young, much of what Yoko's allowed out might still be buried. George's death in 2001 has not so far been followed by any similar projects, though his possession of the May 1968 *White Album* demos would lead one to think there might be more such goodies moldering. Paul did not use his 1995 "Oobu Joobu" radio series to air any Beatles-era home tapes, leading one to believe he either doesn't want them in circulation or that he might even have lost track of them in the ensuing years.

It's the author's guess that, given the vast historical significance of the EMI recordings (and many of the ones recorded elsewhere), they all *will* eventually be made officially available to the public. But only after the Beatles and everyone reading this are no longer around to enjoy them, only after they cease to be commercially exploitable to their descendants and the label that recorded them, and only after the entertainment industry and the way music is distributed and acquired for listening changes in ways that we can't foresee. At that time, perhaps they will be considered public property, accessible via museums or hi-tech private channels for study and enjoyment, much as we currently appreciate manuscripts

The Beatles' unreleased material: Not for Sale, *but hugely enjoyable and educational for millions of listeners for many generations to come.*

and drafts of great, centuries-old literary, visual, and musical works that were never available in their creators' lifetimes. The Beatles' music *is* that important. For as commercially unviable or aesthetically unsuitable for public hearing as most of the recordings and films covered in this book are officially considered, *all* of it is worthy of study—and, more satisfyingly, much of it is vastly entertaining and inspiring.

Bibliography

Babiuk, Andy. *Beatles Gear.* San Francisco: Backbeat Books, 2001.

Badman, Keith. *The Beatles After the Break-Up 1970-2000.* New York: Omnibus Press, 2000.

Badman, Keith. *The Beatles Off the Record.* New York: Omnibus Press, 2001.

Barrow, Tony. *John, Paul, George, Ringo & Me: The Real Beatles Story.* New York: Thunder's Mouth Press, 2006.

Beatles, The. *The Beatles Anthology.* San Francisco: Chronicle Books, 2000.

Berkenstadt, Jim and Belmo. *Black Market Beatles.* Burlington, Canada: Collector's Guide Publishing, 1995.

Best, Pete, and Patrick Doncaster. *Beatle! The Pete Best Story.* London: Plexus, 1985.

Best, Roag, with Pete Best and Rory Best. *The Beatles: The True Beginnings.* New York: Thomas Dunne, 2003.

Bilyeu, Melinda, Hector Cook, and Andrew Môn Hughes. *The Ultimate Biography of the Bee Gees: Tales of the Brothers Gibb.* New York: Omnibus Press, 2000.

Bramwell, Tony, with Rosemary Kingsland. *Magical Mystery Tours: My Life with the Beatles.* New York: Thomas Dunne, 2005.

Buskin, Richard. *Inside Tracks.* New York: Spike, 1999.

Carr, Roy. *Beatles at the Movies.* New York: HarperPerennial, 1996.

Castleman, Harry, and Walter J. Podrazik. *All Together Now: The First Complete Beatles Discography 1961–1975.* New York: Ballantine Books, 1975.

Clayson, Alan, and Pauline Sutcliffe. *Backbeat: Stuart Sutcliffe: The Lost Beatle.* London: Pan Books, 1994.

Davies, Hunter. *The Beatles,* 3rd ed. New York: McGraw-Hill, 1985.

Dean, Johnny, ed. *The Best of the Beatles Book.* London: Beat Publications Ltd., 2005.

DeCurtis, Anthony, and James Henke with Holly George-Warren, eds., original editor Jim Miller. *The Rolling Stone Illustrated History of Rock & Roll.* New York: Random House, 1992.

DiLello, Richard. *The Longest Cocktail Party.* New York: Playboy Press, 1972.

Doggett, Peter. *Let It Be/Abbey Road: The Beatles.* New York: Schirmer, 1998.

Emerick, Geoff, and Howard Massey. *Here, There and Everywhere: My Life Recording the Music of the Beatles.* New York: Gotham Books, 2006.

Engelhardt, Kristofer. *Beatles Undercover.* Burlington, Canada: Collector's Guide Publishing, 1998.

Everett, Walter. *The Beatles As Musicians: The Quarry Men through Rubber Soul.* New York: Oxford University Press, 2001.

Everett, Walter. *The Beatles As Musicians: Revolver through the Anthology.* New York: Oxford University Press, 1999.

Faithfull, Marianne, with David Dalton. *Faithfull: An Autobiography.* Boston: Little, Brown, 1994.

Fawcett, Anthony. *John Lennon: One Day at a Time.* New York: Grove Press, 1976.

Giuliano, Geoffrey, and Vrnda Devi. *The Lost Beatles Interviews.* New York: Cooper Square Press, 2002.

Gottfridsson, Hans Olof. *The Beatles—From Cavern to Star-Club.* Stockholm: Premium Publishing, 1997.

Granados, Stefan. *Those Were the Days: An Unofficial History of the Beatles Apple Organization 1967–2002.* London: Cherry Red, 2002.

Harrison, George. *I, Me, Mine.* New York: Simon & Schuster, 1981.

Heylin, Clinton. *Bootleg: The Secret History of the Other Recording Industry.* New York: St. Martin's Press, 1994.

Howlett, Kevin. *The Beatles at the BBC.* London: BBC Books, 1996.

Ingham, Chris. *The Rough Guide to the Beatles.* New York: Rough Guides, 2004.

Jones, Martin, ed. *Lovers, Buggers & Thieves, Vol. 1.* Manchester, England: Critical Vision, 2005.

Kane, Larry. *Lennon Revealed.* Philadelphia: Running Press, 2005.

Kane, Larry. *Ticket to Ride.* Philadelphia: Running Press, 2003.

Kon, Andrea. *'This Is My Song': A Biography of Petula Clark.* London: W.H. Allen & Co., 1983.

Leigh, Spencer. *Drummed Out! The Sacking of Pete Best.* Bordon, England: Northdown Publishing Ltd., 1998.

Leigh, Spencer. *Let's Go Down the Cavern: The Story of Liverpool's Merseybeat.* London: Vermilion, 1984.

Leitch, Donovan. *The Autobiography of Donovan: The Hurdy Gurdy Man.* New York: St. Martin's Press, 2005.

Leng, Simon. *While My Guitar Gently Weeps: The Music of George Harrison.* Hal Leonard, 2006.

Lennon, John, Yoko Ono, and Andy Peebles. *The Last Lennon Tapes.* New York: Dell, 1981.

Lewisohn, Mark. *The Beatles Recording Sessions.* New York: Harmony Books, 1988.

Lewisohn, Mark. *The Complete Beatles Chronicle.* New York: Harmony Books, 1992.

Lydon, Michael. *Rock Folk.* New York: The Dial Press, 1971.

Madinger, Chip, and Mark Easter. *Eight Arms to Hold You: The Solo Beatles Compendium.* Chesterfield, MO: 44.1 Productions, LP, 2000.

Martin, George. *With a Little Help from My Friends: The Making of Sgt. Pepper.* New York: Little, Brown & Co., 1994.

Matovina, Dan. *Without You: The Tragic Story of Badfinger.* San Mateo, CA: Frances Glover Books, 1997.

Matteo, Steve. *Let It Be.* New York: Continuum, 2004.

McCabe, Peter, and Robert D. Schonfeld. *Apple to the Core.* New York: Pocket Books, 1972.

McCartney, Mike. *The Macs—Mike McCartney's Family Album.* New York: Delilah Books, 1981.

McCoy, William, and Mitchell McGeary. *Every Little Thing: The Definitive Guide to Beatles Recording Variations, Rare Mixes & Other Musical Oddities, 1958–1986.* Ann Arbor, MI: Popular Culture, Ink., 1990.

Miles, Barry. *Paul McCartney: Many Years from Now.* New York: Henry Holt & Co., 1997.

Norman, Philip. *Shout! The Beatles in Their Generation.* New York: Fireside, 1981.

Paytress, Mark. *The Rolling Stones Off the Record.* New York: Omnibus Press, 2003.

Peel, Ian. *The Unknown Paul McCartney: McCartney and the Avant-Garde.* London: Reynold & Hearns Ltd., 2002.

Perkins, Carl, and David McGee. *Go, Cat, Go!* New York: Hyperion, 1996.

Pieper, Jörg, and Volker Path. *The Beatles Film & TV Chronicle 1961–1970.* Stockholm: Premium Publishing, 2005.

Roxon, Lillian. *Lillian Roxon's Rock Encyclopedia.* New York: Grosset & Dunlap, 1969.

Schaffner, Nicholas. *The Beatles Forever.* New York: McGraw-Hill, 1977.

Sheff, David, edited by G. Barry Golson. *The Playboy Interviews with John Lennon & Yoko Ono.* New York: Playboy Press, 1981.

Shepherd, Billy. *The True Story of the Beatles as Personally Told to Billy Shepherd.* New York: Bantam, 1964.

Spizer, Bruce. *The Beatles Are Coming! The Birth of Beatlemania in America.* New Orleans: 498 Productions, L.L.C., 2003.

Sulpy, Doug. *The 910's Guide to the Beatles' Outtakes, 2004 Edition.* Albrightsville, PA: The 910, 2004.

Sulpy, Doug, and Ray Schweighardt. *Get Back: The Unauthorized Chronicle of the Beatles' Let It Be Disaster.* New York: St. Martin's Press, 1997.

Tashian, Barry. *Ticket to Ride: The Extraordinary Diary of the Beatles' Last Tour.* Nashville: Dowling Press, 1997.

Trynka, Paul, ed. *The Beatles: 10 Years That Shook the World.* New York: Dorling Kindersley, 2004.

Turner, Steve. *A Hard Day's Write: The Stories Behind Every Beatles' Song.* New York: HarperPerennial, 1994.

Wenner, Jann. *Lennon Remembers.* New York: Popular Library, 1971.

Williams, Allan, and William Marshall. *The Man Who Gave the Beatles Away.* New York: Macmillan Publishing Co., 1975.

Winn, John. *Lifting Latches: The Beatles' Recorded Legacy Vol. 3: Inside the Beatles Vaults.* Sharon, VT: Multiplus Books, 2005.

Winn, John. *That Magic Feeling: The Beatles' Recorded Legacy Vol. 2: 1966–1970.* Sharon, VT: Multiplus Books, 2003.

Winn, John. *Way Beyond Compare: The Beatles' Recorded Legacy Vol. 1: 1957–1965.* Sharon, VT: Multiplus Books, 2003.

Acknowledgments

When I began work on *The Unreleased Beatles: Music and Film,* I knew that for all the hundreds of hours of material I had, there was much more to locate and research. What I didn't realize was just how *much* was out there to be corralled. To reference a Beatles song title, at times, it really did feel as though I were peeling a glass onion, each layer leading to yet more unsuspected sounds and connections that needed to be made. And to reference another Beatles classic, I couldn't hope to investigate all of it without a little help from my friends.

No friends were more helpful to this project than Jon Arnold and Sam Hammond, who went above and beyond the call of duty in aiding with research and computer assistance. For many months, and on many occasions, they quickly and generously came to the rescue when it looked as though all other alternatives were exhausted. Without all of the time and skill they selflessly donated, this book simply would not exist.

Also vital to filling out major areas of investigation were Keith Copas, Matt Cunitz, Stuart McLean, Pete Nash, Pat Thomas, Kevin Walsh, and Martin White. Thanks to all of you for the considerable time and effort invested in making this work possible.

Many others helped this project in numerous ways, whether providing leads to further avenues for research, helping to make necessary connections, or providing useful advice and encouragement.

Thanks to Gordon Anderson, Clay Banes, Andrew Croft, Erik Flannigan, Deb Fox, David Gans, George Gimarc, Finbar Hammond, Jonathan Hess, Pete Howard, Matt Hurwitz, Chris Ingham, Alan Korn, Stuart Kremsky, Kristan Lawson, Alan Lewis, Owen McFadden, Fred Mills, Peter Miniaci, Cheryl Pawelski, Ian Peel, Kay Ritchie, Janet Rosen, Diane Wallis, and Dave Zimmer. Agent Sheree Bykofsky and her assistant Janet Rosen (no relation to the Janet Rosen listed above) supplied professional and sympathetic representation. My parents, Sue and Elliot, were as usual fully supportive of my endeavors.

As they've done with several of my previous books, Backbeat Books put their resources behind a volume that probes into some of the most rewarding, esoteric corners of rock history. Thanks are due to Sales Coordinator Kevin Becketti (especially for helping to initiate this project), Editor Richard Johnston, Publisher Matt Kelsey, Publisher Dorothy Cox, Production Manager Gail Saari, Marketing Communications Manager Nina Lesowitz, Marketing & Sales Coordinator Steve Moore, Copyeditor Julie Herrod-Lumsden, Designer/Compositor Leigh McLellan, Cover Designer Rich Leeds, and Proofreader Tom Hassett. Thanks also to these boosters at Backbeat UK: Mark Brend, Tony Bacon, and Nigel Osborne.

Finally, a huge thanks to John Lennon, Paul McCartney, George Harrison, and Ringo Starr for making such an immortal body of great music together, both released and unreleased.

About the Author

Prior to *The Unreleased Beatles: Music and Film,* Richie Unterberger's most recent books were issued as a two-part history of 1960s folk-rock, *Turn! Turn! Turn!: The '60s Folk-Rock Revolution* (Backbeat, 2002) and *Eight Miles High: Folk-Rock's Flight from Haight-Ashbury to Woodstock* (Backbeat, 2003). His other books include *Unknown Legends of Rock 'n' Roll* (Backbeat, 1998), which profiles 60 underappreciated cult rock artists of all styles and eras, and *Urban Spacemen & Wayfaring Strangers: Overlooked Innovators & Eccentric Visionaries of '60s Rock* (Backbeat, 2000), containing in-depth surveys of 20 underrated greats of the era.

Unterberger is also author of *The Rough Guide to Music USA,* a guidebook to the evolution of regional popular music styles throughout America in the 20th century. He is a frequent contributor to the All Music Guide, *MOJO,* and *Record Collector,* and has written dozens of liner notes for CD reissues. He lives in the San Francisco Bay Area.

More information about Richie Unterberger, his books, and the music he documents can be found on his Web site at www.richie unterberger.com. E-mail can be sent to richie@richieunterberger.com.

Photo Credits

Index